Self-Concept Development and Education

Self-Concept Development and Education

Robert B. Burns MA, MEd, Phd, ABPsS

Deputy Chairman of the Post-Graduate
School of Education at the University of
Bradford

HOLT, RINEHART AND WINSTON
London · New York · Sydney · Toronto

Holt, Rinehart and Winston Ltd: 1 St Anne's Road,
Eastbourne, East Sussex BN21 3UN

To P, H and R

British Library Cataloguing in Publication Data

Burns, Robert
  Self-concept development and education.
  1. Self-perception 2. Educational psychology
  I. Title
  370.15   LB1083

ISBN 0–03–910354–4

Printed in Great Britain by Henry Ling Ltd., at the Dorset Press, Dorchester, Dorset

Last digit is print number: 9 8 7 6 5 4 3 2 1

Preface

This book is concerned with (1) the development of the self-concept during the first two decades of life, (2) the effects of the self-concept on behaviour, (3) the effects of teachers' self-concepts on the quality of teaching and learning and (4) the ways in which the self-concepts of pupil and teacher may be enhanced.

The focuses of the development and behavioural manifestations that are emphasized are the home and the school. We are not concerned simply with education in the narrow sense, i.e. formal institutionalized teaching and learning, but with educating the whole person, emotionally and socially as well as cognitively. In both home and school contexts there is the possibility of providing the wealth of conditions that nourish or starve the developing self-concept, for in each there are ample opportunities for parents, siblings, peers, teachers to demonstrate to the child that he has or has not an inherent value.

The construct of the self-concept is now considered to be a major outcome of education, childhood socialization, and child-rearing practices as well as influencing consequent responses to these influences. There is constant interplay between all these variables so that cause and effect are impossible to untangle. Improvement of an individual's self-concept is becoming valued as an outcome in its own right. But even if it were not so valued, the construct has potential scientific importance for interpreting behaviour and educational performance in pupils and teachers, and for its relationship to prejudice, delinquency, anxiety, teaching style, expectations and many other vital issues. Although a wide range of such relationships could be discussed in this book, a restricted number only have been chosen because they appear subjectively to be more important focal ones, and possess a reasonable body of substantive research findings to illuminate the issues.

Psychologists and educationalists are becoming more aware of the fact that an individual's self-concept, or his attitudes to and perception of himself, are intimately related to how he learns and behaves. Evidence suggests that low performance in school work, poor motivation, misbehaviour and academic disengagement—so characteristic of the underachiever, the early leaver, the disadvantaged and the delinquent—are due in part to negative self-attitudes and perceptions. Many students have difficulty in school not as a result of low intelligence or physical impairment, but because they have come to perceive themselves as unable to do academic work. Success in school, work, or life appears to depend as much on how a person feels about the qualities and attributes he possesses as on those qualities themselves. When a student says, 'I will never understand this material', he is saying more about himself than about the subject matter. It is likely that a student feeling like this will not cope, essentially because he believes he is not competent to succeed. While nothing succeeds like success, the expectation of failure reaps its poor harvest.

For personal happiness, adjustment and effective functioning, a favourable and positive self-concept is essential. Those children who have a negative self-concept tend to encounter difficulties in almost every area. They have a high level of anxiety, find difficulty in making friends, adjust less easily to school and tend to be hampered in school achievement. It is essential to acknowledge that highly important part played by parents in the early development of the self-concept before the significance of teachers' judgements come to bear. Teachers can reinforce the poor opinion a child already has of himself when he begins school, but they can also, in fact, help to reverse this opinion and to create in the child a more positive view of himself and his abilities.

Having a positive self-concept seems to depend, according to many writers (e.g. Diggory 1966; Felker 1974), on possessing well-grounded feelings of acceptance, competence and worth. For every human wants to be accepted or belong to a group, initially a family group. Such acceptance implies that others regard one as of worth and competent in some relevant behaviours. As a valued member of a group, a person derives a sense of worth. Behaviour has an end or purpose and the ability to achieve that end brings with it a sense of competence. For most pupils, school behaviour has its end in the mastery of subject matter; for most teachers, school behaviour has its end in the mastery of the science of controlling and teaching students to a required standard. Successful achievement of these aims will encourage the pupil or teacher to evaluate himself as competent, a very necessary element for a positive self-concept. The third element, that of worth (or its opposite, worthlessness) derives from the overall valuation the individual attaches to himself through his acceptance and competance.

These three basic elements of belonging, competence and worth are learned in a social environment through interaction with others. Parents, teachers and peers provide much of the feedback about the child that tells him he is wanted, accepted, coping and succeeding with necessary tasks, and generally of worth. This feedback may concern such areas as the child's physical development, his social competencies, his academic achievements and his emotional balance.

This book has a somewhat deeper implication than simply providing an array of knowledge about educating a positive self-concept and its relationship to parental and school variables. Education is a compulsory transmission of cultural experience and knowledge. Part of that transmission should be an understanding and acceptance of each individual's inherent value. This emphasis on the worth of the individual and on human relationships is not to be taken as a philosophy which argues for soft molly-coddling or radical deschooling to counter existing cognitive and control objectives in education. On the contrary, affective components of education have regularly been stressed by educators in the past. There is nothing new in this save that previous emphases have tended to be on negative affective aspects such as fear of punishment, failure and anxiety. Here we shall try to concentrate on the positive aspects of affective behaviour in the educational context. To emphasize affective aspects is not to relegate cognitive objectives to second place. The author has a high regard for 'fundamentals' not as an end in themselves but as a means to acquiring more education.

Cognitive and affective aspects of education are complementary. Individual experiences, expectancies, responses to instructional style and interpretation of educational context all complement the cognitive aspects of learning performance. Education is the educating of the total person not just his cognitive dimension.

The recognition of the individual and his intrinsic value, is part of an attempt to defend and strengthen democracy by facilitating individual growth and freedom, and by recognizing the basic rights of individuals. Those who through parental, educational and societal practices have developed a positive self-concept are more able to accept the worth of others, to defend others from shameless words and deeds, and to possess the inner strengths that tell them they are competent, creative, and worthy themselves. Thus they are unwilling to lie down in the face of tyranny.

This view of the role of self-concept development as a help in maintaining individual rights and people's democratic freedom is perhaps an unusual one. Yet the promotion of positive self-conception is a necessary complement to the technological computer and microchip era which could so easily lead to a lessening of the worth of the individual. Education development has a far more important responsibility than hitherto.

The scope of this book is broad and it has an extensive research base. But underlying all the themes, topics and research is a frame of reference which goes under a variety of names, such as humanist, phenomenological or perceptual. This perspective looks at behaviour from the point of view of the person who is doing the behaving. The self-concept falls within this ambit.

We sometimes find it difficult to understand the child because we are looking at him from our own perceptual framework. There is much needless conflict between adults and children resulting from their differences in perspective. There is the story of the village moron who, having found a lost donkey which his more 'intelligent' neighbours had been unable to locate, explained his success by saying that he had tried to think where he would go if he were a donkey! Clinicians have rarely seen a parent who deliberately sets out to destroy his child, but frequently they see parents who accomplish just that—parents who do vicious things in the firm conviction that they want the best for their child. People do their best to be adequate according to their perceptions, no matter how futile and misguided their behaviour may be to a person whose phenomenal field is more enlightened. They simply need to develop a more adequate perspective.

It is hoped that this book will be a useful source of research findings, ideas and discussion in courses concerned with the preparation of teachers, counsellors, social workers, educational psychologists and others who are interested in understanding a little more about the behaviour of children, and who will be able to apply such knowledge and ideas in their daily work.

R.B.B.

Acknowledgements

I am deeply indebted to the many students and colleagues who have made so many valuable comments during seminars and discussions. It is their gems that produce any sparkle in this book. I am solely a collator, trying to put together theories, ideas, research findings and insights into one volume which can be of benefit to a wide range of 'educators'.

My thanks go particularly to my wife for her patient support during the long dark winter of writing. The stalwart devotion of my three typists, namely my wife, Mrs W. Jackson and Mr A. Jackson, as they prepared a legible typescript from my handwritten draft, cannot be underestimated in its importance. Without their efforts this book would never have made the deadline.

Ilkley, West Yorkshire 1981

Contents

1

Introducing the Self-Concept

Look at the figure over the page. Which of these statements describes you? Look at them again and draw a circle (lightly in pencil so you can erase it afterwards) around each statement that expresses how you feel about yourself most of the time. Go on—do it now!

For each sentence circled indicate the relevant box on the right-hand side how you feel about being like that. How many of your circled statements please you? Most, I hope! When you look at your responses you are getting a picture of yourself—a small fraction of your self-concept.

This little exercise has no reliability or validity. It was made up purely to help you get started thinking about your self-concept so that this term does not seem to be too abstract a concept at the outset. You may now perhaps have a rudimentary understanding of what the term self-concept implies.

Now that you have completed the scale consider what you were doing. You probably noticed that you were providing (1) a description of yourself and (2), a crude indication of the degree to which each of the descriptive statements applying to you, in this rather restricted measuring instrument, generated emotional evaluations about yourself. These two elements form the two basic parts of the self-concept as it is conceived in this book, that is, an evaluated set of beliefs about the individual. The descriptive element is often termed the *self-picture*, or *self-image*. The evaluation is frequently referred to as *self-esteem, self-worth*, or *self-acceptance*. The self-concept is composed of all the beliefs and evaluations you have about yourself. These beliefs (self-images) and evaluations (self-esteem) actually determine not only who you are, but what you think you are, what you think you can do and what you think you can become.

SELF-CONCEPT AS A SET OF ATTITUDES TO THE SELF

This view of the self-concept as a compound of two elements, self-image and

	I like being like this	I am indifferent	I dislike being like this
I am happy			
I am a mess			
I am successful			
I am a slow learner			
I am clumsy			
I am a bore			
I am a loser			
I am conscientious			
I am a cheat			
I am an introvert			
I am a daydreamer			
I am an optimist			
I am reliable			
I am irritable			
I am a good friend			
I am moody			
I am sociable			
I am religious			
I am intelligent			
I am weak-willed			
I am rash			

Fig. 1 Self-Concept Scale.

self-evaluation places the self-concept within the ambit of attitude study. Most definitions emphasize that an attitude contains three essential ingredients:

(a)   a belief which may or may not be valid,
(b)   an emotional and evaluative connotation around that belief and
(c)   a consequent likelihood of responding (or behaving) in a particular way.

For example if

Belief   (a)   I believe members of a certain political party are traitors to the country then,

Evaluation   (b)   I am likely to evaluate members of that party in an extremely negative way since they engender strong emotive feelings. As a result,

Response   (c)   I will probably oppose their policies by voting against them in
or   any election, argue against their policies and generally reveal
Behaviour   intolerant and prejudiced responses to such members.

I have come to possess an attitude towards that political party.
    The basic components of an attitude are similarly revealed in self-attitudes so that the self-concept combines:

(a)   Self-image—what the person sees when he looks at himself;
(b)   affective intensity and evaluation—how strongly the person feels about these various facets; and whether the person has a favourable/unfavourable opinion of various facets of that image;
(c)   behavioural possibilities—what the person is likely to do in response to his evaluation of himself.

    Let us look at an aspect of the self-concept relating to the physical body in this way. (Later you will see how important body image is within the structure of the self-concept.)

Self-image   (a)   I might believe that I am overweight and since I regard having a pronounced midriff as not good for my health and not contributing to a desired athletic, muscular, body image, this creates emotional feelings and

Self-esteem   (b)   I may come to evaluate my physical appearance in a rather
or   negative way, and be more easily swayed into
Evaluation

Response   (c)   doing something about my weight such as dieting, or taking
or   exercise or, in the extreme, withdrawing from social interaction
Behaviour   so that I avoid the negative interpretations I may place on feedback from others about my corpulence.

    Other important areas of self-conceptualization are academic competency, and adequacy in social relationships. Can you now write out along the attitudinal structure above, the components of the belief, evaluation and response categories for the two following examples of vital areas of self-conceptualization?

(i)   I believe I am a bright student.
(ii) I believe I am an introvert.

A fuller consideration of these three components of self-attitudes would now seem appropriate.

The Belief Component

The belief knowledge or cognitive component of the self-concept represents a proposition about, or a description of, the individual irrespective of whether the knowledge is true or false, based on either objective evidence or subjective opinion. The belief component of the self-concept is the practically limitless number of ways in which each person perceives himself.

If we were asked to describe a person we know we might come up with a list of adjectives such as considerate, sociable, physically strong, conscientious. These terms are all general abstract ones not tied to any one specific incident or behaviour. They express generalized conclusions about the other person reflecting in part his consistent behaviour and in part our selective perception of him. We do the same thing when we define ourselves. We use words which are generalized descriptions reflecting the consistent and habitual way we have come to perceive ourselves.

Why not write down a list of descriptions and attributes relevant to yourself, about what you are, and how you see yourself? My list, when I tried this task, contained elements such as these: male, white, middle-aged, married, lecturer, house owner, car owner, psychologist, teacher, ambitious, not tall, bespectacled, enjoys classical music. There is little doubt your list would contain similar items and categories of beliefs and knowledge about yourself.

This sort of listing can continue *ad infinitum* as the list can conceivably contain all one's attributes, self-conceptualizations, role and status characteristics, possessions and goals. All these elements can be ranked in order of personal importance since some self-conceptions are more central than others to our sense of well-being, and these may change rank depending on context, experience or momentary feelings. With only 16 elements in a global self-concept, there are 20,923,000,000,000 possible ways of ordering them by importance!

President Lyndon Johnson once labelled himself as 'a free man, an American, a United States senator, a Democrat, a liberal, a conservative, a Texan, a taxpayer, a rancher and not as young as I used to be nor as old as I expect to be'. Such descriptions serve to distinguish the person as unique from all other persons.

The Evaluation Component

These qualities and attributes we ascribe to ourselves are rarely objective in the sense that our possession of them is also agreed to by others. Only in the case of actual age, sex, height, political group membership data etc., will objective data be present. Most data and descriptive attributes carry evaluative and personal interpretative overtones. In other words, the self-concept is a set of subjectively evaluated attributes and feelings. Even such 'objective' data as age and height referred to above are affected by gross subjective distortion in terms of their meanings and implications within the self-concept structure. To be aged 40 will be subjectively regarded by some as being in the prime of life and by others as the start of the decline into senility; likewise to be 5 feet 8 inches can be regarded as an acceptable and reasonable height by some men but as not being tall enough by others. Most attributes and qualities take on their meaning for an individual through the general evaluation of that quality or attribute in their particular society. Fatness is generally regarded undesirably and hence those who regard themselves as fat (subjectively, though they may not be so judged objectively) will tend to regard themselves as undesirable in general. There exists a human if rather unfortunate tendency for those who possess characteristics socially valued as undesirable to begin to perceive themselves as undesirable.

The continual bombardment of negative impressions conveyed from the social environment, even if not meant to be so, creates a difficulty for those who are physically unattractive, handicapped, socially inept, minority group members (or believe subjectively they are) to develop positive self-concepts. Even seemingly affectively neutral beliefs about one's own self carry implicit evaluative overtones. For instance, part of my self-concept includes the facts that I live at a certain address, and possess a certain model of car. Superficially there is no evaluation of affective component present, but implicitly, perhaps at a barely conscious level, there is. This arises because the possession of that address or car can be good or bad. For example, I live in X road (and that is good because it is a high-class district); I have a Z car (and that is good because it emphasizes my wealth and masculinity). Of course, these aspects might well have been evaluated negatively. Think about some of your self-descriptions. Are there any that convey no emotive, evaluative overtones whatsoever? To be male or female, white or coloured, a success or a failure, hard-working or lazy, a sportsman or a spectator, tall or short, or any other attribute, involves some loading with evaluative connotations derived from subjectively interpreted feedback from others and from comparison with objective standards and subjectively interpreted cultural, group and individual standards and values. The affective component of an attitude exists because the cognitive component arouses emotions and evaluations of varying intensity depending on context and cognitive content.

Consider some of the elements in your own list of beliefs and attributes. How does your standing in them in relation to societal, group norms and your own values affect your behaviour; do your conceptions of yourself influence your behaviour? Without knowing anything about any of you, I can, with some confidence, answer the question and say on your behalf, 'Yes, quite considerably.'

This evaluative loading of the self-concept is learned, and since it is learned it can alter in direction and weighting as other learning experiences are encountered. For example a person may have a concept of himself as a bright student deriving from his performance in school examinations and the feedback he receives from teacher and peers. This brings pleasure and satisfaction, since being a bright student has positive connotations within society and at home where the achievement motive and success have been positively reinforced. However, this positive self-evaluation may fluctuate as increasingly harder work brings poorer examination results, or as significant others in the peer group begin to evaluate other behaviours, e.g. athletics, as more important. Again as time passes the bright student might find in adulthood that academic success is not the sole criterion of happiness or getting on in life, so that a lowering of the weighting will occur though it will still remain positive. So self-evaluation is not fixed; it relates to each particular context. The evaluative significance of most concepts is taken from the surrounding culture, in that many evaluations have become normative. Dull, fat, immature all have negative evaluations for instance, while clever, athletic, dependable possess positive overtones. Not only are the evaluative overtones learned from the culture, but by self-observation and by feedback from social interaction such evaluative concepts come to be applied to the individual by the individual himself.

The terms 'self-image' and 'self-picture' have frequently appeared in the literature with the implication that they are synonymous with the term 'self-concept'. The writer prefers to avoid these two terms as they give a rather static and neutral appearance to what it has been argued is a dynamic, evaluative and considerably emotive concept. They fail to convey the attitudinal content of the self-concept. So the self-image or self-picture is only one of two elements of the self-concept; the other component is the evaluation which the individual attributes to particular descriptions. Most writers employ 'self-esteem' to designate this self-evaluation component. By self-esteem, Coopersmith (1967) refers to 'the evaluation that the individual makes and customarily maintains with regard to himself; it expresses an attitude of approval or disapproval and indicates the extent to which the individual believes himself to be capable, significant, successful and worthy. In short, self-esteem is a personal judgement of worthiness that is expressed in the attitudes the individual holds' (p. 4). Rosenberg (1965) defines self-esteem in a similar vein as 'a positive or negative attitude towards a particular object, namely, the Self' (p. 30). Self-esteem seems to imply that the individual feels he is a person of worth, respecting himself for what he is and the extent to which he feels positively about himself, and not condemning himself for what he is not. Low self-esteem suggests self-rejection, self-derogation and negative self-evaluation.

Self-esteem in terms of self-evaluation refers to the making of a conscious judgement regarding one's significance and importance. Anything related to the person, it has been argued, is liable for such evaluations on the basis of criteria and standards involving one or many consensual goals (e.g. wealth or prestige), levels of achievement, moral precepts and norms of behaviour.

Three principal points appear pertinent in self-evaluation. First, the comparison of one's self-image with the ideal self-image or the kind of person one would wish to be. This sort of comparison has been a dominant theme in numerous approaches to psychotherapy (e.g. Horney 1950; Rogers 1959) whereby congruence of these two selves is an important indicator of mental health. Even James's (1890) classic view of self-esteem (see p. 16) as the ratio between actual accomplishments and aspirations is a statement of this major point in self-evaluation, the actualization of ideals.

Those who are fortunate enough to live up to their standards and realize their aspirations develop a strong sense of self-esteem. Those who do not measure up to their own ideals are likely to possess low self-esteem.

The second point involves the internalization of society's judgement. This assumes that self-evaluation is determined by the individual's beliefs as to how others evaluate him. This view of self-esteem was initially promoted by Cooley (1912) and Mead (1934).

The third and final point involves the individual evaluating himself as a relative success or relative failure in doing what his identity entails. It involves not that what one does is good in itself but that one is good at what one does. The pattern that emerges is of individuals fitting into society as best they can. If roles are played properly then collective purposes are served and individual esteem satisfied. Society provides the opportunities for developing self-esteem, but to ensure this at an individual level it can only be achieved by adjustment to what is provided.

Hence to measure self-esteem it is best to regard it as self-evaluation, with a phenomenological orientation implied. The evaluation is subjective, whether involving one's own assessment of performance or one's interpretation of others' assessment of oneself, both in relation to self-appointed ideals and culturally learned standards.

Osgood's investigation (Osgood, Suci and Tannenbaum 1957) into connotative meaning showed the consistent appearance of evaluation as the major dimension. Hence if we assume self-images are central features of the individual's psychological self-meaning, it is not unreasonable to accept the pervasive nature of evaluation of such pictures since evaluation is a basic and normal approach to any psychological object.

Another factorial approach that demonstrates the attitudinal organization of the self-concept stems from the recent work on the factorial structure of motivation by Cattell and Child (1975). They demonstrate the consistent appearance of what they call the 'self-sentiment'. This pervading self-sentiment they describe as a 'collection of attitudes all of which have to do with that self-concept which the human level of intelligent abstraction makes possible and which we all possess' (p. 97). Their analysis suggests that this dynamic self-concept is composed of attitudes concerned with the preservation of the physical self, self-control and the need for self-esteem. This objective finding of a consistent and ubiquitous motivational and attitudinal structure is additional support for viewing the self-concept as an attitude with all its evaluative and predisposing behavioural implications. Thus, from a variety of independent sources the view promoted in this book that the self-concept is best regarded as a dynamic complex of attitudes held towards themselves by each person is given consistent support.

A positive self-concept can thus be equated with positive self-evaluation, self-respect, self-esteem, self-acceptance; a negative self-concept becomes synonymous with negative self-evaluation, self-hatred, inferiority and a lack of feelings of personal worthiness and self-acceptance. Each of these terms carries connotations of the others and have been used interchangeably by various writers (e.g. Wylie 1961; Coopers   , with high self-appraisal and self-esteem generally accept the   those who attribute negative values to themselves have little self-esteem, self-respect or self-acceptance. The terms 'self-concept', 'self-attitudes' and 'self-esteem' will be regarded henceforth as synonymous in this book. They are all evaluated beliefs about the person which can range along a positive-negative continuum.

Two major writers on the self-concept have produced extended definitions of the construct which accord with the view being conveyed in this chapter. Rogers (1951) states that the self-concept,

> is composed of such elements as the perceptions of one's characteristics and abilities; the percepts and concepts of the self in relation to others and to the environment; the value qualities which are perceived as associated with experiences and objects; and the goals and ideas which are perceived as having positive or negative valence. It is then the organized picture, existing in aware-ness either as figure or ground, of the self and the self-in-relationship, together with the positive and negative values which are associated with those qualities and relationships as they are perceived as existing in the past, present, or future. (p. 138)

Similarly, Staines (1954) provides a definition which places the self-concept into the realm of attitude study. He states that it is,

> a conscious system of percepts, concepts, and evaluations of the individual as he appears to the individual. It includes a cognition of the evaluative responses made by the individual to perceived and conceived aspects of himself; an under-standing of the picture that others are presumed to hold of him which is the notion of the person as he would like to be and the way in which he ought to behave. (p. 87)

When the term self-concept is used in this book it implies the plurality of self-attitudes even though it is stated in the singular.

The Behavioural Tendency Component

It is a well-documented fact that individuals do not necessarily behave in a way that is consistent with their evaluated beliefs (e.g. La Piere 1934). Evidence suggests that quite frequently social constraints (social acceptability of behaviour, overriding moral values, or 'fear of the consequences etc.) prevent or modify the direct behavioural expression of an attitude. So the behavioural expression of a specific self-attitude may not always be made. The adolescent schoolboy who, from a variety of sources and causes, has come to regard himself as a 'hard man' may not feel able to demonstrate this behaviour towards his male teachers. Equally a student teacher who regards herself as humane, caring and anti-authoritarian, may have to behave in a different way to become congruent with the rules and ethos of a particular school she is attached to.

Attitudes are emotionally formed beliefs directed towards or against something or someone. Self-attitudes only differ from attitudes to other things in that they are reflexive, with the individual being the object of his own attitude. Because of this inward direction, the emotions and evaluations aroused by the belief component of the attitude are very strong. It is possible to avoid, rationalize, project and use a wide variety of defences to devalue the attitudes of others to oneself. For instance, if you do not approve of the cut of my new suit I can always retort that you have no taste, or that you possess no knowledge of current trends in male dress to offer any valid criticism. But with attitudes to the self, how can one walk away from these with a simple verbal manipulation? Like the person who changes his job, or emigrates, or takes a long holiday to get away from things, you always take yourself with you, there is no getting away from yourself. Escapism is a myth, you are still yourself and how can you fail to recognize yourself?

IMPORTANCE OF SELF-CONCEPT

The self-concept is forged out of the influences exerted on the individual from outside, particularly from people who are significant others. These people influence what the individual interprets himself as. Every contact focuses on him as though he were the centre of attention and indicates his degree of competence and worthiness; but from the moment the self-concept is born it too becomes active in shaping the interpretation of experience. The self-concept appears to have a three-fold role, maintaining consistency, determining how experiences are interpreted, and providing a set of expectancies.

Self-Concept as a Maintainer of Inner Consistency

A number of researchers in personality have dealt with the first factor—the idea that human beings operate in ways which maintain an inner consistency. If individuals have ideas, feelings or perceptions which are out of harmony or in opposition to one another, a psychologically uncomfortable situation is produced. This psychologically uncomfortable position has been labelled 'dissonance' (Festinger 1957). An important aspect of dissonance is that there is a strong motivation to be comfortable, and, as dissonance makes an individual feel uncomfortable, he is likely to take any sort of action that will allow him to feel comfortable again.

One of the first writers to connect this type of reasoning with self-concept was Lecky (1945). It was Lecky's argument that an individual is a unified system with the problem of maintaining harmony between himself and his environment. In order to maintain this type of harmony (it is interesting that the opposite of harmony is dissonance), the individual may refuse to see things in the environment, accept as valid things which other people tell him about himself or he may strive to change things about himself or others.

What an individual thinks about himself is a vital part of internal consistency. Therefore, the individual will act in ways which he thinks are consistent with how he sees himself. If he feels he cannot do a task and that he is 'thick', then he is likely to act and behave in such a way as to come out looking 'thick'.

A few years ago I was dealing with a girl who scored above average on standardized intelligence tests. This indicated that she had the ability to master the school tasks required, but she was not doing well in basic subjects at school. In a counselling session, the girl said that she could not do the work because she was 'not clever enough'. In the conversation, remarks were made about the fact that she was clever enough to do the work, and the standardized test scores were used as evidence. The next term when I tested her IQ it had dropped to below average. While many have questioned the validity of such tests, I was firmly convinced from my experiences with the girl that she *needed* to score low on the IQ tests so that she could achieve an inner consistency. Higher scores were inconsistent with her view of herself as being not clever enough. She had been told that she had done well on a test which showed that she was able to do the work, and a lack of harmony between this view and other evidence resulted. This was so out of harmony with the view she held that it tended to make her feel uncomfortable. The girl brought things back into harmony by doing poorly on the next IQ test. It is interesting that she did not change her view of herself but acted in a way consistent with that view. It was the view that determined her behaviour, not the behaviour that determined her view.

The use of the term self-concept in the singular is somewhat misleading. We each possess a plethora of self-concepts, some relating to our general behaviour, others to specific areas of endeavour e.g., sport, academic performance. Look at this amorphous blob of jelly.

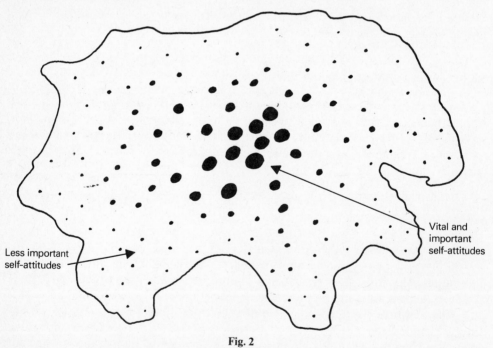

Less important self-attitudes

Vital and important self-attitudes

Fig. 2

This figure is a representation of your self-concept. It is like a single globule of frog spawn, unified, permanent and firm, held together by dynamic life forces yet flexible and resilient enough to be moulded into slightly different shapes by environmental forces. Rather than the one dot in the frog spawn, the self-concept jelly contains many thousands of self-attitudes forming a meaningful, integrated system. Some self-attitudes are more important behaviours than others and so appear larger and more centrally positioned. Other self-attitudes are less important and take up peripheral positions. Any new experience is interpreted in the light of relevant beliefs and attitudes accumulated within the 'frog spawn'. If the new experience is consistent with existing self-conceptions then it can be incorporated and assimilated enabling the jelly blob to grow a little larger. If, on the other hand, the experience is in no way consistent with the existing self-perceptions then the outer skin of the blob acts as an impermeable screen to prevent an alien body invading the host. An experience that is only slightly incongruent can be assimilated if the potentially relevant self-perceptions can accommodate to it. In many ways this description is almost Piagetian and the self-concept may be thought of as a complex but inter-related set of schemas.

A discrepant experience can be made potentially capable of being assimilated through defence mechanisms too, such as rationalization. Such mechanisms help to maintain a consistent self-concept even in the face of objective evidence to the contrary. For example, a typical 10 year-old lad is involved in stealing some cigarettes. He defends his concept of himself as 'not a bad kid' by arguing that it was one of the other members of the group that actually took the cigarettes, that he was forced into the situation, and it was a valuable experience since smoking one of the stolen cigarettes made him sick, so he vows he will never smoke again. This maintenance of the self-concept appears to be a prime motivator in all normal behaviour. Of course, the reasons may seem irrational and behaviour even bizarre to others, but we must always remember that we need to be inside the skin of the other person to comprehend the environment fully from his point of view and understand his reasons for behaving as he does. This empathic approach is part of the phenomenological rationale which will be discussed in more detail later.

Secord and Backman (1974) have suggested several stabilizing procedures we use to defend and maintain self-esteem.

(a) We tend to devalue the person who criticizes us; we may say that his opinion is not worth listening to in the first place.
(b) We choose, as far as we can, other like individuals with whom to interact.
(c) We reject the criticism as unjustified.
(d) Finally, we can accept the criticism as valid.

Not all the separate aspects of the global self are equally relevant, or important, and they may change their relevance and importance from one context to another. The self-concept of being 'the youngest brother, smaller and weaker than the older ones' may only be important within the family. Among the peer group such an evaluation is unlikely to apply. This 'context relevant' quality of many self-conceptions helps to explain the paradox of inconsistency. Many theorists promote the view that the organism strives for consistency in self-conception and the voluminous literature on cognitive dissonance suggests the same tendency. The resolution of the paradox that a person may have a number of conflicting self-concepts lies in the fact that the dissonance only exists when both conflicting elements are simultaneously present or relevant and the person is aware of this conflict. The tough, autocratic realist teaching in the innercity comprehensive may well be a gentle sentimentalist at home. Since the teacher may well be able to leave school behind him once out of the gates these two dissonant conceptions create no dissonance for him. Only if both become salient simultaneously (as when he takes his family to the school sports day) is dissonance likely to be aroused as he fulfils both the role of teacher and parent. Inconsistency between self-concepts would appear to be normal in view of the wide range of roles and diverse contexts each of us is involved in every day. But at the same time there is a tendency to reduce inconsistency where it arises.

The differentiation of self-concepts across situations is valuable for it helps to ensure that a negative self-attitude in one aspect may not be easily generalized. A man may see himself as a husband but not differentiate between the numerous roles involved there as father, wage-earner, painter, electrician, toy mender, gardener, car driver, etc. When such a person is criticized in one of these aspects, the inability to differentiate means that the criticism is of the totality; whereas a man who can differentiate may not be particularly bothered if his inept gardening is criticized since it is separate from his other activities as a husand.

The rationale of dissonance theory (Festinger 1957) is that inconsistent cognitions are intolerable and individuals will adopt strategies to eliminate such discrepancies, e.g. rationalizing so that someone whose negative opinion about us conflicts with our own opinion is judged as an incompetent assessor or one whose opinion matters little. Discrepancies between different self-conceptions though will often give rise to stress since they may be the result of realistic appraisals in different contexts. Additionally the functional value of some of the self-conceptions may be of a very low order, for whether inconsistency occurs or not depends on the ability to differentiate between particular self-images, and on their importance. James (1890) with his ingenious formula pointed the way on this choice of what one sets out to be:

$$\text{self-esteem} = \frac{\text{success}}{\text{pretensions}}$$

It is fairly simple to demonstrate that the individual can maintain, or enhance, his self-esteem by reducing the denominator or increasing the numerator. It is the subjective assessment of success in relation to what he wants to be that counts. As James (1890) so wisely understood, 'our self feeling in this world depends entirely on what we back ourselves to be or do' (p. 64). Certain roles, attributes, etc., are not selected as important, hence evaluation on these aspects is irrelevant on most occasions. The selection of certain standards by which success may be subjectively attained is open to all individuals over many facets of life, and this wide choice pushes the evaluation in a position direction. But the freedom to select the issues and the standards they are judged from is not without limitation, since certain facts cannot be evaded. Students with consistently low marks are less likely to consider themselves good students than those with higher averages; a poor man cannot consider himself wealthy; a short man cannot consider himself tall; not as long as they are in contact with reality, at any rate. Again, self-values might have been chosen before there had been any opportunity to test them adequately. It might only become apparent later that the individual did not have enough of the necessary qualities or expertise. Many 'star' pupils from small primary schools have found this to their cost on moving to a large secondary school.

Finally, since man is a social animal and lives in society, he cannot avoid the social and cultural roles, values and norms stemming from this environment. He finds himself judged by the criteria of his society and relevant subgroups, not merely those criteria of his own making. If he seeks his own approval and that of the group's he must excel in terms of their values. Certainly it is possible to enhance the self-concept by renouncing society's values and ultimately by abandoning society, but even subgroups outside 'normal' society have certain values and standards of their own, e.g. hippy groups. Self-values cannot easily be manipulated to suit the individual's psychological convenience, but the selection of self-values does have wide latitude because of the huge range of alternatives available and the private nature of self-values.

Interpersonal selectivity is highly limited in childhood. Most communications about oneself at that period of life come from parents with whom one is stuck for better or for worse. If they love him, he is given at the outset a decisive basis for thinking well of himself; if he perceives disparagement and rejection, then it is difficult for the child to avoid the conclusion that he is unworthy. With no options there can be no selectivity.

The work of Hovland, Lumsdaine and Sheffield (1949) like that of Sherif and Sherif (1956), clearly demonstrates that the attitudes that are easiest to change or form are those that are least structured. Sherif and Cantril (1947) have shown that attitudes, once formed, tend to maintain themselves. It is precisely in childhood that the self-concept is most unformed and unstructured. Hence, with parents holding the monopoly of interpersonal communications while the child is emerging into self-consciousness with nothing to base a self-estimate on, their attitudes have powerful significance.

There are important limits on the selectivity of values and standards on which self-attitudes come to be based. Several of these limits obtain in childhood when interpersonal communications are most decisive in developing self-attitudes. So that despite the theoretical assumption that the individual could lower his pretensions to achieve more self-esteem, living within a particular culture pattern in which evaluations against objective standards are frequently made has real limitations. This makes it easy to see why some people do possess negative self-attitudes despite individual preference to 'accentuate the positive'.

Self-Concept as an Interpretation of Experience

A second reason why the self-concept is a powerful determinant of behaviour is that it shapes the way in which individual experiences interpret things that happen to us. Every experience is given a meaning by the individual. Exactly the same thing can happen to two people, but one will interpret it one way, and the second will interpret it another. If a young man offers his seat on a bus to a lady, she might interpret it as a kindly act, an insult about her age and ability, or even as an improper advance and call a policeman! Each of these interpretations is dramatically influenced by the view that the woman has of herself.

Just as there is a strong tendency to act in ways which will show that one's behaviour and one's view of oneself are consistent, there is a strong tendency to interpret experiences in ways which are consistent with individual views. This factor makes it extremely difficult to change a self-concept that is formed and operating.

We often think in a naive way that the only thing we need to do to provide those children currently suffering from a negative self-concept with a more positive one is to give them more positive reinforcement. So we lavishly praise them, or give them some position in class or school that should show them that we feel they are competent. But there is no guarantee that the child will interpret such actions in the way they were meant. He could well interpret them negatively, saying to himself, 'I must be dim, or else the teacher wouldn't keep trying to tell me I'm not,' or 'since I am thick why is she making me form captain this term? She's got it in for me—just trying to show me up in front of the rest so they can all see how stupid I am.'

There is no action that a teacher can take that a child with a negative self-concept cannot interpret in a negative way. No matter how positively others might interpret the action or how positively the teacher might mean the action, the child can still interpret it in a negative way. This makes the self-concept and the forming of a positive self-view extremely important. The self-concept is like an inner filter— every perception that enters the individual must go through the filter. As each perception passes through the filter, it is given meaning, and the meaning given is determined largely by the view the individual has of himself. If it is a negative view every experience is stamped with a frown. If it is a positive view, each new experience is stamped with a smile.

Self-Concept as a Set of Expectations

The self-concept operates to determine what individuals do in situations, and it operates to determine how individuals interpret what other persons do in situations. The third part of the self-concept's power and influence is that it also determines what individuals expect to happen. This set of expectancies has been identified by some researchers as the central facet of the self-concept. According to McCandless, the self-concept is 'a set of expectancies, plus evaluations of the areas or behaviours with reference to which these expectancies are held' (McCandless 1967).

Children who are anxious about school frequently say something like, 'I just know I am going to make a fool of myself,' or, 'I just know that I am going to fail that test.' While some of these statements are attempts to elicit encouragement, some of them reflect a set of real expectancies. The child views himself in a certain way, and this determines how he is going to develop his expectations, and consequently how he will perform or behave.

People who view themselves as worthless expect others to treat them in a manner consistent with this expectation. Children who have suffered severe maternal deprivation feel worthless and the failure to develop close, affectionate bonds with a mother or a substitute mother results in the child avoiding social contacts as much as possible since these too may lead to rejection. The way the self-concept controls expectancies and behaviour leads to a self-fulfilling prophecy. We will examine this in detail in Chapter 9.

Every individual carries with him a similar set of expectancies which determine how he is going to act. If he expects good experiences, he acts in ways which bring them about. If he expects bad experiences, he acts in ways which make these expectations come true and then says to himself, 'See, I was right.' Children who perceive themselves as being unlikeable expect people not to like them and then act either in ways consistent with this or interpret everything so that if fits with this expectancy.

THE SELF-CONCEPT IN PSYCHOLOGICAL THEORY

Four major theoretical approaches which permeate research and thinking about the self-concept are:

(a)   the pioneer work of James,
(b)   symbolic interactionism, particularly by Cooley and Mead,
(c)   the work of Erikson on identity,
(d)   phenomenology, particularly by Rogers.

While many other theorists have discussed the self-concept (often in idiosyncratic ways) it is the four approaches above which provide the most stimulating notions of self theory.

(a) William James's Pioneer Work

William James was the first psychologist to elaborate on the self-concept. James considered the global self as simultaneously Me and I. They were discriminated aspects of the same entity, a discrimination between pure experience (I), and the contents of that experience (Me). This difference is quite apparent in the linguistic sense and it probably appears to be emphasizing the obvious to state that we all recognize that humans have the characteristic of consciousness and this permits our awareness of environmental elements one of which is ourselves. However obvious this distinction may seem, it does pose difficulties at a psychological level since the self-reflexive act involved in identifying the Me, at the same time indissolubly links and integrates the knower and the known. Each cannot exist without the other; the self is simultaneously Me and I.

It is impossible to imagine either consciousness in an abstract form without any content, or content existing apart from the consciousness that permits awareness of it. Experience must involve experience of something. James was aware of this criticism and noted that while language allows us to categorize in terms of knower and the known, they are only discriminated aspects of the singularity of experience, a global self which is no less than the person himself. James is presenting, therefore, a model of a possible structure of the global self and it must be regarded as just that and not reality.

For James, the self-as-known, or Me, is in the widest sense everything that a man can call his. He detected four components to this objective self which he classed in descending order of importance. These four are the spiritual self, the material self, the social self and the bodily self.

James's Law. One thing about a complex society is that we can choose between several goals. We can set our own goals, each one related to different components of the self, and evaluate our success at them. This leads us to James's 'law'. It all depends on what you see yourself as. James elaborated on the determinant of the level of a person's self-evaluation. He argued that it is the position a person wishes to hold in the world—contingent on his success or failure—that determines self-esteem. Though we want to maximize all of our various selves, limited talent and time prevent this so each of us has to choose particular selves on which to stake our salvation. Having chosen, our level of self-regard can be reduced only by deficiencies (or raised only by achievements) which are relevant to our 'pretensions'.

For example, if a person 'backs' himself to be a first-rate tennis player but is relegated to the reserve team then he will have to do one of three things: a) rationalize his below par performances, b) lower his expectations, or c) do something else in which greater success is more possible. Expectations are self-imposed and refer to our personal levels of aspirations, for what is success for one can be failure for another.

The major difficulty with this formulation is that it is assumed that being the best will automatically result in high self-esteem. However, there are some skills and jobs which society does not rate very highly, so to consider oneself as the most competent dustman or café waitress is unlikely to lead to high self-esteem.

However, James did produce a rich and comprehensive formulation of the Self as Known which included descriptive categories, evaluation and feeling, a view that anticipated future conceptions. He had detected the integrative aspects of the self-concept.

(b) Symbolic Interactionists

The study of the self-concept moved temporarily away from mainstream psychology during the first few decades of this century into a more sociological field, in which Mead and Cooley became the major theorists. They were symbolic interactionists, who produced a new perspective on the individual–society relationship.

Symbolic interactionism involves three basic premises. First, humans respond to the environment on the basis of the meanings that elements of the environment have for them as individuals. Second, such meanings are a product of social interaction, and third, these societal/cultural meanings are modified through individual interpretation within the ambit of this shared interaction. Self and others form an inseparable unit since society, constructed out of the sum of the behaviours of the humans composing that society, places social limits on individual behaviour. While it is possible to separate self and society analytically, the interactionist assumption is that a full understanding of one demands a full understanding of the other, in terms of a mutually dependent relationship. Cooley and Mead provided the basic ideas.

C. H. Cooley. Cooley's original view was that individuals are prior to society, but later modified his beliefs and laid a heavier emphasis on society to the extent that 'self and society are twin born . . . and the notion of a separate and independent ego is an illusion' (1912, p. 5). Individual acts and social pressures modify each other. A further shift in emphasis was to come later when Mead argued that self actually arises from social conditions.

It can be demonstrated experimentally that a major perspective of the self-concept is the 'other self', or how you think others think of you. The contents of the 'self as others see you' and the self as you believe you are, have been shown repeatedly (e.g. Sheerer 1949; Burns 1975) to be very similar. It was Cooley who first pointed out the importance of subjectively interpreted feedback from others as a main source of data about the self. In 1912, Cooley introduced the theory of the 'looking-glass self', reasoning that one's self-concept is significantly influenced by what the individual believes others think of him. The looking-glass reflects the imagined evaluations of others about one.

> Each to each a looking glass,
> reflects the other that doth pass
> (Cooley, 1912, p. 152)

There must be few people who have never once been acutely conscious of their existence and appearance, in essence an extremely heightened sense of self. A person who faces an 'audience' of any sort, or who has to interact with others may fidget, feel tense, have 'butterflies in the tummy' and perspire. This is more concern with 'what are they thinking of me?', than with the real concerns of the interaction. This concentration with how one is evaluated can have quite a serious effect on the performance of such groups as teachers, actors, interviewers and the like.

This looking-glass self arises out of symbolic interaction between an individual and his various primary groups. Such a group characterized by face-to-face association, relative permanence and a high degree of intimacy between a small number of members produces an integration of individuality and group. The face-to-face relationships within the group serve to produce feedback for the individual to evaluate and relate to his own person. Hence the self-concept is formed by a trial-and-error process by which values, attitudes, roles and identities are learned.

G. H. Mead. Mead, in agreement with Cooley's conception of the 'looking-glass self', suggested that the self was essentially a social process within the individual involving two analytically distinguishable phases—first identified by James—the 'I' and the 'Me'. Mead further proposed that through the learning of a culture (an elaborate set of symbols shared by the members of society) man is able to predict other men's behaviour as well as the predictions other men make of one's own behaviour. Not only are objects, actions and characteristics defined (given some shared meaning and value), but the individual himself is also so defined. Accordingly, Mead felt that the definition of oneself as a specific role-player in a given relationship was accomplished by recognizing and sharing the meanings and values others have of you. This Mead called the 'Me'. That is, Mead saw the 'Me' as representing the incorporated 'other' within the individual.

Mead's 'I' was the perception of oneself as reflected by the shared meanings and values of 'others'. He suggested that the incorporated attitudes (meanings and values) of others constituted the organized 'me'; that the way one perceived the 'me' constituted the 'I' and that both combined constituted the nature of self.

But the 'I Me' dichotomy specified by Mead was different in one major way from James's initial formulation. Mead's 'I' was the impulsive tendency, the unorganized, undisciplined, undifferentiated activity of the individual (almost a parallel to the Freudian *id*). Every behaviour commences as an 'I'. but develops and ends as a 'Me' as it comes under the influence of societal constraints. 'I' provides the propulsion; 'Me' provides direction.

Mead (1934) explained the child's development of a reciprocal, interpersonal perspective by playing alone, first directly imitating others and subsequently taking roles of both participants in the imagined interaction, as the rules of play (or more correctly, the game) are understood. The role-playing allows him to experience, or at least approximate, the type of response which his own action elicits in others. Without such a repertoire of shared attitudes, feelings and acts, communication with others is severely restricted. A young child may play (in the sense of taking the role of significant others) but until he grasps the rules which make a game a game—until he can govern his conduct in the light of the 'referee's perspective', or in Mead's terminology, the 'generalized other'—the child is only playing and not 'gaming'. A child's play involves learning the general pattern of social relations in society. Through this, a fundamental communality of attitudes is ensured without suppressing the possibility of uniqueness in individuals. These longitudinal changes in the form and function of play correspond to the growth sequence of images, thoughts and language, and the formation of self-concept is well under way. Social sanctions, demands, rationales and models are gradually translated into personal values, and incorporated in the self-concept.

In this way the individual comes to respond to himself and develop self-attitudes consistent with those expressed by others in his world. He values himself as they value him; he demeans himself to the extent that they reject, ignore or demean him. The result is the conclusion Cooley had already reached in a very similar theory, that the individual will see himself as having the characteristics and values that others attribute to him.

To Mead, like Donne, 'no man is an island' and psychology shows repeated acceptance of the fact that society gives shape and meaning to individual self-conceptualization.

(c) Erikson on Identity

Erikson used the concept of identity in his writings rather than self, and provided an extension of Freudian theory emphasizing ego development in the cultural context. He demonstrated (1965) how cultures elaborate an identity, out of a biologically given basis, which is appropriate to the culture in question and manageable by the individual. Erikson indicated that identity comes from 'achievement that has meaning in the culture' (p. 228). Identity arises from a gradual integration of all identifications, therefore, it is important for children to come into contact with adults with whom they can identify. Erikson described eight stages of identity growth, and detailed the particular conflicts which are characteristic of different stages and the qualities that emerge on resolving these conflicts. Identity is a particular problem in adolescence and Erikson paid considerable attention to the crisis and diffusion of identity at that stage. He defined identity as a 'subjective sense of an invigorating sameness and continuity' (1968, p. 19), yet he was somewhat reluctant to provide a tight definition of identity which was not just the sum of roles assumed by the person but also included emerging configurations of identifications and capacities, a function of direct experience of self and the world, and perceptions of the reactions of others to self. It was psychosocial in that it also involves an individual's relationships with his cultural context.

This process of identity formation is similar to the Cooley–Mead formulation concerning the role of the generalized other. But Erikson saw these processes as for the most part unconscious. He criticized terms such as self-conceptualization, self-image and self-esteem, which provide a static view of what he considered an evolving process, 'for identity is never established as an achievement in the form of a personality armour, or of anything static and unchangeable' (1968, p. 24). Identity formation, like the ideas of Rogers on self-actualization, is a continuing process of progressive differentiations and crystallizations which expand self-awareness and self-exploration. A sudden awareness of the inadequacy of existing identity as life advances generates initial confusion followed by exploration of new identities and new ways of being. Erikson claims that an optimal sense of identity means knowing where one is going and having inner assuredness. The specific contents of experience are less important in furnishing the person with an identity than the capacity of the person to recognize continuity—separate experiences belonging to the same being.

(d) Phenomenological Approaches to the Self-Concept

The phenomenological approach in psychology (sometimes called a perceptual or humanistic approach) is a perspective which attempts to understand man through the impressions of the subject and not through the eyes of an observer. It seeks to understand how the individual views himself; how his needs, feelings, values, beliefs and unique perception of his environment influence him to behave as he does. Behaviour is a function of the personal meanings attached to an individual's perception of past and contemporaneous experiences. We cannot change events but we can change our perceptions and interpretations of them. Therapy does just this; it does not 'remove' a problem but enables the client to perceive himself in a new way and cope in more effectively.

Perception and the Phenomenal Field

Perception is the central concept in phenomenology and refers to the processes of selecting, organizing, and interpreting material into a coherent construction of the psychological environment. This environment has variously been termed the perceptual field, the psychological field, the phenomenal field or life space. But terminology apart, we are concerned with personal meanings that exist for any person at any instant and which determine his behaviour. Behaviour for a phenomenologist can only be understood from the point of view of the behaving individual. Reality exists not in the event itself but in the unique perception of the event. Perceptions are selective and are often quite erroneous as a result of the distortions engendered by motives, goals, attitudes, and defence mechanisms (Bruner and Goodman 1947). The old adage 'seeing is believing' is perhaps closer to the truth when reversed as 'Believing is seeing'.

A tenet of both cognitive psychology and phenomenology, then, is that behaviour is the result of the individual's perception of the situation, as it appears to him at the moment. Perception is other than what is physically out there. Yet what is perceived is 'reality' to the perceiver, the only reality by which he can guide his behaviour. The phenomenological approach to behaviour, into which the self-concept has become cemented, interprets behaviour in terms of the phenomenal field of the subject, and not in terms of analytical categories imposed by an observer. That is to say that behaviour can best be understood as growing out of the individual.

It makes a great deal of difference to how you perceive school if you see yourself as a successful or unsuccessful teacher, headmaster, pupil or parent. Depending on the pupil's self-concept an examination can be viewed as a challenge or something to avoid, and the front row of the classroom can be perceived as under the eye of the teacher or the best place for hearing and seeing him. This selective perception also enhances existing perceptions and makes them more difficult to change. The pupil who considers himself bad at handicraft work is likely to avoid such courses or by developing high levels of anxiety when doing such a course produce inadequate work on tasks he believes himself incapable of doing anyway. All this validates his initial hypothesis about himself. It would seem that the very act of initiating a negative perception almost ensures that subsequent behaviour will produce evidence to support the perception. This has been called the 'boomerang effect' a self-fulfilling prophecy. Happily this prophecy works equally well with positive self-attitudes, so that supportive evidence tends to augment and nourish favourable self-concepts. Evidence reveals that it is possible to make subjects report perceptions contrary to the evidence of their senses. (Asch 1955; Crutchfield 1955).

Carl Rogers. Phenomenology, with the perceived self-concept as its core, was appropriated by Rogers to underpin his developing client-centred approach to psychotherapy. He was able to describe therapeutic change in terms of a perceptual frame of reference. The present state and formulation of self-concept theory owes much of Rogers's work, and developed out of his experiences with clinical cases.

The self is a concept developed by reflexive thought out of the raw material of the stimulus imput. Around the concepts gather evaluative and affective attitudes so that each one becomes good or bad. These evaluative items are internalized from the culture and from others, as well as from self. Rogers's self-concept (1951) may be thought of as an 'organized configuration of perceptions of the self . . . It is composed of such element as the perceptions of one's characteristics and abilities; the percepts and concepts of self in relation to others and to the environment; the value qualities which are perceived as associated with experiences and objects; and goals and ideals which are perceived as having positive or negative valence' (p. 136).

The central points of Rogers's theory (1951, 1959) are:

1. The theory of the self, as part of the general personality theory, is phenomenological. The essence of phenomenology is that 'man lives essentially in his own personal and subjective world' (1959, p. 191).
2. The self-concept becomes differentiated as part of the actualizing tendency, from the environment, through transactions with the environment—particularly the social environment. The process by which this occurs is not detailed by Rogers, but is presumably along the lines described by Cooley and Mead.
3. The self-concept is the organization of self-perceptions. It is the self-concept, rather than any 'real' self, which is of significance in personality and behaviour. As Snygg and Combs (1949, p. 123) noted the existence of a 'real' self is a philosophical question, since it cannot be observed directly.
4. The self-concept becomes the most significant determinant of response to the environment. It governs the perceptions of meanings attributed to the environment.
5. Whether learned or inherent, a need for positive regard from others (acceptance, respect, warmth) develops or emerges with the self-concept. While Rogers leans towards attributing this need to learning, it seems appropriate to include it as an element of self-actualization.
6. A need for positive self-regard, or self-esteem, according to Rogers, likewise is learned through internalization or introjection of being positively regarded by others. But alternatively, it may be considered an aspect of self-actualization.
7. When positive self-regard depends on evaluations by others, discrepancies may develop between the experiences of the organism and the needs of the self-concept for positive self-regard. There is thus incongruence between the self and experience, or in other words psychological maladjustment. Maladjustment is the result of attempting to preserve the existing self-concept from the threat of experiences which are inconsistent with it, leading to selective perception and distortion, or denial of experience by incorrectly interpreting those experiences.
8. The organism is an integrated whole, to which he attributes, like the organismic theorists, one dynamic drive—that of self-actualization—a basic tendency to 'actualise, maintain and enhance the experiencing organism' (1951, p. 487).
9. The development of self-concept is not just the slow accretion of experiences, conditionings and imposed definitions by others. The self-concept is a configuration. Alteration of one aspect can completely alter the nature of the whole. Thus, Rogers is using the term 'self-concept' to refer to the way a person

sees himself. As he goes on to develop his theory, however, his use of the concept also incorporates the second sense—a process controlling and integrating behaviour. But in Rogers's theory the self-concept is not an executive or doer. There is no need for positing such a role. The organism is by nature continually active, seeking its goal of actualization, and the self-concept as part of the organism is also seeking actualization through its constant activity. The self-concept thus influences the direction of activity, rather than initiating it and directing it entirely. In this way, Rogers avoids the problem of reification and the ambiguousness of the concept of the 'I' or the ego as an executive. In this way the self as known and the self as knower are fused. Behaviour is 'the goal directed attempt of the organism to satisfy its needs as experienced in the field as perceived' (1951, p. 491).

10.   In his formulation of the concept of the ideal self, Rogers says that as a result of therapy the perception of the ideal self becomes more realistic, and the self becomes more congruent with the ideal. This suggests that personality disturbance is characterized by an unrealistic self-ideal, and/or incongruence between the self-concept and the self-ideal. This formulation has been the basis of some research by the client-centred school (e.g. Butler and Haigh 1954). Rogers's theory does not emphasize conflict between the self-concept and the self-ideal as a source of disturbance, but stresses the conflict between the self-concept and organismic experiences as its source. This is in contrast to some other theories in which the self-ideal is a central concept and an important factor in psychological adjustment or maladjustment (e.g. Horney 1950). He presented the theory to the public in 1951 formulated out of a series of nineteen propositions. The first seven refer to the organism and the phenomenological character of the environment, the eighth introduces the concept of self, while the rest form an essay on self psychology.

There is a major problem with Rogers's phenomenological approach to the self-concept, which comes with the use of defensive processes to cope with a state of incongruity between the organism's experience and the existing self-concept. Rogers regards behaviour as an attempt to maintain consistency of the self-concept. Hence in response to a state of incongruence i.e. a threat presented by recognition of experiences that are in conflict with the self-concept, the individual will employ one of two defensive processes. *Distortion* is used to alter the meaning of the experience; *denial* removes the existence of the experience. Rogers emphasizes the former, since if denial leaves an experience completely unsymbolized how can a phenomenological approach ever deal with such a process? Distortion is in the direction of making the experience consistent with self. Meaning is given to events, not in and of themselves, but by individuals with past experiences concerned about the maintenance of their self-concepts. Rogers used client-centred therapy as a technique to modify self-conceptualization, thereby balancing experience and self-concept, and producing a state of psychological adjustment.

Maladjustment develops if experiences are blocked or distorted and are prevented from being adequately assimilated into the self-concept. Thus, Rogers views maladjustment as a state of incongruence, the most serious source of incongruence being between self and organism. This can arise when a person's concept of self is heavily dependent on values and definitions from others that have been internalized. So, incongruence would occur where an individual's self-concept heavily stressed love and concern for others, and that person found himself in a situation where as a result of frustration he felt strongly aggressive. These feelings might then be blocked as his self-concept could not assimilate the idea that he could hate. Incongruence between self and organism would result. Rogers gives as an example a rejecting mother who cannot admit to herself her feelings of aggression towards her child. She therefore perceives his behaviour as bad and deserving punishment. She can then be aggressive towards him without disturbing her self-concept of 'good and loving mother' because he is seen as worthy of punishment. The origins of such incongruence between self-concept and organismic feelings often lie early in life. Parental affection and 'positive regard' are often conditional on a child disowning his true feelings. If he really does want to smack Mummy then he is a 'bad boy', a person of no merit. Rogers argues that it is important in bringing up children not to demand that they disown or distort their own feelings as a condition of their worth and acceptance, even though they may be required to inhibit the actual expression of their feelings. Rogers urges instead that parents should indicate to the child that although they understand his feelings he is not allowed to act on them because of the damage or distress such behaviour would cause, rather than express disapproval at the possession of the feelings themselves. The child should thus be encouraged to inhibit the expression of certain feelings rather than disown them. This is a considerable help in avoiding later maladjustment.

Rogers views man's nature as essentially positive, moving towards maturity, socialization and self-actualization. He contends that Freud has presented us with a picture of man who at heart is irrational, unsocialized and destructive of self and others. Rogers accepts that a person may at times function like this, but at such times he is neurotic and not functioning as a full human being. When man is functioning freely, he is open to experience and free to act in a positive, trustworthy and constructive manner. 'One of the most refreshing and invigorating parts of my experience is to work with such individuals and to discover the strongly positive directional tendencies which exist in them, as in all of us at the deepest levels.' (Rogers 1961, p. 27.)

Generally then, the phenomenological approach has been part of a significant effort by some psychologists to come to terms with human experience, by seeking to take behaviour as it is. It has two potential major limitations, though; it may exclude certain critical variables from investigation, and it can lead to unscientific speculation.

A POSSIBLE STRUCTURE FOR THE SELF-CONCEPT

This chapter on the theory and structure of the self-concept shows us that while many have used the self-concept as a major element in their theories of human behaviour there is considerable confusion over the definitions of the wide range of self-referent constructs which some writers use interchangeably, and which others consider as discriminating between subtle aspects of self-conception. In an attempt to clarify the situation the following structure is proposed (Fig. 3) as a summary.

We can best envisage the self-concept as a hierarchical structure. At the top is the

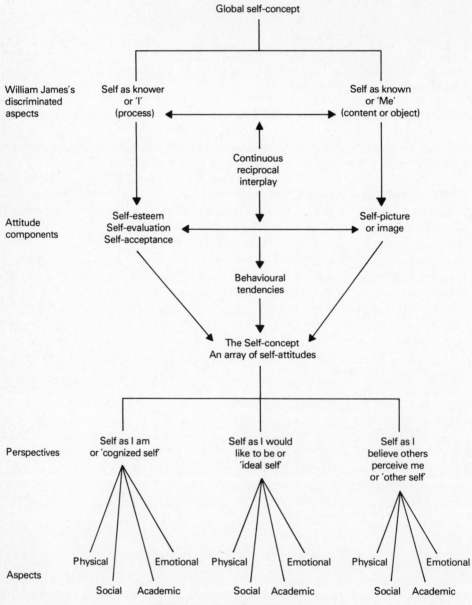

Fig. 3   Structure of the self-concept.

global self-concept which is the total of all the possible ways an individual conceives of himself. It is the 'stream of consciousness' of William James, that sense of continuity and singularity of the individual. It is composed of the two elements first differentiated by James the 'I' and the 'Me'. But it must be remembered that these two discriminated aspects are a semantic model and psychologically are so reciprocally interactive that the distinction is false. The Me can only exist through the process of knowing, and the process only has content because the human organism can reflect on self. One cannot exist without the other. Likewise the self-image and the self-evaluation the products of reflexive thought and its processes are conceptually distinguishable but psychologically interlocked. The image and the esteem dispose the individual to behave in a particular way so that the global self-concept can be regarded as a set of attitudes to the self. But these attitudes can be taken from a number of perspectives.

The perspectives, which can be separated, are composed of the following:

1. The cognized self-concept, or the individual's perception of his abilities, status and roles. It is his concept of the person he thinks he is.
2. The other or social self. This is how the individual believes others see and evaluate him.
3. The ideal self. This is the kind of person the individual hopes to be or would like to be.

Most workers (e.g. Strang 1957; Staines 1954) have employed these perspectives in their work. Strang's social self was renamed by Staines as the other self, a self derived from the reflected appraisals of significant others (following Mead and Cooley). It is a major source of data about the person. Impressions and inferences from statements, actions, subtle gestures of others towards the individual gradually establish a self-concept as the person believes he is seen by others on all aspects of the cognized self. As will be seen when we look at developmental aspects of the self-concept, the other self and cognized self must contain similarity of content. In contrast, various degrees of discrepancy are usually measurable between the content of the ideal and cognized selves.

The ideal self is a set of interpretations about the individual when he is revealing his most personal wants and aspirations, part what he wishes to do or be and part what he ought to do or be. It may not be in touch with reality at all. Horney (1950) has shown that it may be so far away from our cognized self that its unhappy possessor is dragged down with depression through its unattainability. She indicates that to abandon a striving to attain an unrealistic ideal self is 'one of the great reliefs of therapy' (p. 136). Murray (1953) describes the idealized picture of the self as a set of ambitions leading to a goal conceived by the person as himself as his highest hope. For Erikson (1956), the ego is a set of 'to be strived for but for ever not quite attainable ideal goals for the self' (p. 76). According to Allport (1961) the ideal self-concept defines one's goals for the future. 'Every mature personality may be said to travel towards a port of destination, selected in advance, or to several related ports in succession, their ideal always serving to hold the course in view' (p. 285). Combs and

Soper (1957) regard this ideal self as the kind of person the individual would like or hope to be, 'the aggregate of those characteristics of Self which the person feels are necessary to attain adequacy (sometimes unfortunately perfection)' (p. 140). It would seem that for many self-concept theorists the ideal self is an important aspect, and through reinforced social learning, a person accepts the cultural ideal or norm with respect to a specified characteristic or behaviour as his own personal idea. It is always there, so much part of the person, yet often leading dangerously to varying degrees of condemnation when attempts to meet its demands fail.

There are considerable problems of definition and use over the construct of the self-concept. In this book the term self-concept refers to all aspects of the individual's view of his or her self. The term self-concept comprises the notion of self-image (the individual's description of the self), as well as that of self-esteem (the individual's evaluation of the self). The term identity is taken to have essentially the same meaning as self-concept, but it will be used only in areas where it is common, i.e. in the consideration of sex-role identity and in discussion of Erikson's views of adolescence. The problems of defining the self-concept and its related terms have had their influences in the measurement of the self-concept; there have been almost as many measuring devices as there have been self-concept studies. Investigators have used numerous approaches in their attempts to measure the self-concept; Wylie (1961, 1974) cites several hundred that have been employed since 1959. There has also been a marked tendency for researchers to devise instruments of their own rather than to use other researchers' instruments. As a result it is very difficult to collate and integrate the existing self-concept research. Furthermore, since little is known regarding the psychometric characteristics—reliability, validity, or normative data—of such instruments, the meaning and usefulness of studies using them are limited.

A plethora of self-concept measures have arisen because clearly there is no superior measure in existence, hence it is tempting to create one's own. However, this profusion means that it is difficult to decide what measure to use, and the continued casual generation of new scales, before extant scales have been adequately validated, is irresponsible.

The failure of experimenters to consider whether all these various scales and techniques are measuring the same thing makes the generalizability of results doubtful and explains some of the discrepancies. What it all means is that self-concept as measured by test X may not be the same as self-concept measured by test Y.

PROBLEMS IN MEASURING THE SELF-CONCEPT

Do you remember filling in the short and rather artificial self-concept scale at the start of this book (p. 2)? Here it is again below (Fig. 4). It illustrates many of the problems involved. Complete it again here without looking back at your previous responses. Now consider this scale critically and how you responded to it:

	I like being like this	I am indifferent	I dislike being like this
I am happy			
I am a mess			
I am successful			
I am a slow learner			
I am clumsy			
I am a bore			
I am a loser			
I am conscientious			
I am a cheat			
I am an introvert			
I am a daydreamer			
I am an optimist			
I am reliable			
I am irritable			
I am a good friend			
I am moody			
I am sociable			
I am religious			
I am intelligent			
I am weak-willed			
I am rash			

Fig. 4   Self-Concept Scale.

(a)   Does it cover adequately the range of any individual's possible self-concept elements?
(b)   How were the items selected?
(c)   Is the meaning of each adjective clear to you?
(d)   Is the meaning you have ascribed to each trait likely to be held by other readers?
(e)   Is the scale measuring the self-concept? I have claimed it does—is that sufficient? How do I know it measures what I say it does? i.e. is the scale valid?
(f)   Did you answer honestly or give answers that were socially desirable or which defended the 'you' you do not wish to acknowledge.
(g)   Did you reproduce your responses from the previous occasion fairly faithfully or were there considerable discrepancies? i.e. is the scale reliable?

These questions make us face up to many of the important problems involved in measuring the self-concept (of course these questions are equally valid when raised with many other psychological constructs e.g. introversion, or anxiety).

Self-concept measuring instruments tend to be essentially of a self-report type, e.g. rating scales. Questionnaires and such carefully designed techniques provide the best way of assessing the self-concept, especially for group administration.

Combs, Soper and Courson (1963) argue that most of the studies purporting to explore the self-concept are not studies of self-concept at all; they are studies of the self-report. The fact that many studies of self-concept rely on a self-report does not provide justification for using the terms synonymously. Combs and Soper (1957) note that self-concept as measured is what an individual is willing to say about himself. Although the difference in terminology may appear to be minor, Combs and his colleagues (1963) argue that the concepts are different and cannot be used interchangeably. They say:

The 'self-concept' as it is generally defined is the organization of all that seems to the individual to be 'I' or 'me'. It is what an individual believes about himself; the totality of his ways of seeing himself. On the other hand, the 'self-report' is a description of self, reported to an outsider. It represents what the individual says he is. To be sure, what an individual says of himself will be affected by his self-concept. The relationship, however, is not a one-to-one relationship. The self-report will rarely, if ever, be identical with the self-concept. The self-report is essentially an introspection and is no more acceptable as direct evidence of causation in modern phenomenological psychology than in earlier, more traditional, schools of thought.

How closely the self-report approximates to the subject's 'real' self-concept will, presumably, depend on at least the following factors:

1.   the clarity of the individual's awareness;
2.   the availability of adequate symbols for expression;
3.   the willingness of the individual to cooperate;
4.   the social expectancy;
5.   the individuals feeling of personal adequacy;
6.   his feeling of freedom from threat.

Parker (1966) following this line of reasoning, states: 'if these factors do, in fact interfere with the reliability of the self-report, self-concept study with such instruments will produce questionable results.' (p. 698)

On the other hand, many researchers believe that studies of the self-concept have to depend on a procedure in which the subject is asked to give information about himself because phenomenological theory necessarily demands a conscious process. Generally, this process involves a verbal or written response to one of the instruments described later. The use of such a process rests on the assumption that the subject's response is determined by his conscious awareness of his world. This assumption, however, is untested, and it would be naïve to take for granted that a subject's response is so determined because he gives a response that is influenced by other factors. For example, it might be conditioned by the subject revealing only what he wishes to reveal. The problems of self-concept measurement and surveys of specific measuring instruments are provided in more detail in Burns (1979) and Wylie (1974).

SUMMARY

The self-concept is the sum total of the views that a person has of himself and consists of beliefs, evaluations, and behavioural tendencies. This implies that the self-concept can be considered to be a plethora of attitudes towards the self which are unique to each individual.

The self-concept is important in explaining behaviour because it maintains consistency of behaviour, determines the interpretation of experience, and provides a set of expectancies. James, Cooley and Mead stand out as early influences in this area in the development of theory about the self-concept.

James discriminated between two global aspects of the self:

(a) I or self as knower/process/doer;
(b) Me or self as known which can include a variety of sub-selves, e.g. physical, social, other, ideal, etc.

Cooley and Mead emphasized the origin of the self-concept through social interaction. Erikson promotes a developmental theory of identity formation.

The basic premises of the phenomenological approach as developed by Rogers are that:

(a) behaviour is the product of one's perceptions;
(b) these perceptions are phenomenological rather than 'real';
(c) perceptions have to be related to the existing organization of the field, the pivotal point of which is the self-concept;
(d) the self-concept is both a percept and a concept round which gather values introjected from the cultural pattern;
(e) behaviour is then regulated by the self-concept;

(f) the self-concept is relatively consistent through time and place, and produces relatively consistent behaviour patterns;
(g) defence strategies are used to prevent incongruities occurring between experience and the cognized self-concept;
(h) there is one basic drive, that of self-actualization.

Self-concept development is fraught with problems due to

(a) the lack of agreement over definitions of the self-concept;
(b) inadequate research techniques that are hard to validate;
(c) the weakness of self-report techniques that require the subject to respond truthfully and willingly.

Further Reading

Burns, R. B. (1979) *The Self Concept: Theory, Measurement, Development and Behaviour,* London: Longman.

Gordon, C. and Gergen, J. K. (eds.) (1968) *The Self in Social Interaction*, vol. 1, New York: Wiley.

Hall, C. S. and Lindzey, G. (1970) *Theories of Personality* (2nd edn). New York: Wiley.

Pervin, L. A. (1970) *Personality*. New York: Wiley.

Wylie, R. (1974) *The Self-Concept*, vol. 1, Lincoln: University of Nebraska Press.

Wylie, R. (1979) *The Self-Concept*, vol. 2, Lincoln: University of Nebraska Press.

2

Some Developmental Features

INTRODUCTION

This chapter and the following chapters concentrate on the development and sources of self-concept from infancy through to, and including, adolescence. If those engaged in the education and care of children wish to understand children, help some maintain and enhance positive views of themselves, and help others to change their views then it is necessary to look at the factors influencing self-concept development as the sources and principles are effective right through childhood. Teachers, parents and other caretakers may also come to understand their own self-concepts better and what influences affected theirs. The material in these chapters cannot be exhaustive but will delineate the major forces and social interactions that influence self-concept development.

The self-concept is learned; it is not innate. It is derived from the myriad of sensory inputs impinging on our nervous system. Sounds, smells, sights and tactual feelings all come from our surrounding environment; we are constantly receiving a wide range of sensory data. Even as you read this book you are the recipient of visual input, tactile input from your seating position, auditory input from noises around and outside, etc. Though the physicist might be able to define objectively the stimuli—say, in terms of wavelengths—these raw sensory data mean something slightly different to each person and are therefore unique. The statements you read in your morning paper may have particular meanings for you. The sound of a radio in the background may be heard as a pleasant pop tune or as a meaningless and distracting cacophony. Your position may be comfortable or uncomfortable. Have a look at yourself in a mirror. Do you see yourself as taller than you really are? Or fatter? Have you ever heard your own voice on a tape recorder? It was probably a rather disillusioning experience. The way you hear your voice normally is from inside your mouth and throat while other people hear what actually comes out. So you can perhaps realize that there is really no way in which others can share exactly what you see, hear or feel. Your perception of the sense data is uniquely yours. This is perhaps more apparent in the misinterpretation of verbal communication which can lead to argument because one party did not interpret what was said in the way the other party meant it to be. Raw sensory data are filtered and interpreted by the receiver to make them meaningful to him in terms of his unique past experience, expectations and existing beliefs about his environment and himself. It is only as the individual absorbs sensory information about himself, interprets it and attaches personal meanings that he can be said to possess a self-concept.

As meanings become attached to the sensory input, the individual is progressively defining further who and what he is. In turn previous meanings help to define and give meaning to new inputs and the whole process becomes a self-validating prophecy.

This phenomenological perspective of the perceiving organism is particularly helpful when dealing with children or counselling others. We must always attempt to see things from their perspective. We must have empathy. A good children's photographer is usually able to catch the world through the eye of a child, and for a young child this may mean perceiving the world through a moving forest of adult legs or continually raising their eyes to see adult facial responses (provided adult tummies do not protrude too far and hide them!) Try lying on the floor in a crawling position or sitting on the floor in a crowd of standing adults. You will soon come to appreciate the perspective of the young child. The feeling of what it is like to be a small child in a large adult world has been depicted vividly by Young (1966) in the book *Life Among the Giants*.

There are many diffuse theories about the developmental aspects of the self-concept. It is diffuse because the literature tends to focus on what are believed to be core issues at particular life stages: e.g. the emergence of a sense of self as a separate person in infancy; the development of gender identity in the young child; and the possible diffusion of a sense of identity in adolescence. It becomes difficult to see threads that hold the structure together, not only because of these core issues, but also because the content of the self-concept varies with age (p. 43). There is no doubt though that two essential themes permeate self-concept development at all ages, the role of feedback about self and the role of significant others. These themes will arise repeatedly through the book.

NEONATAL CAPACITIES AS A BASIS FOR SELF-AWARENESS

When the neonate changes his address from womb to world he brings with him a capacity for interpreting sensory information, responding to environmental feedback, and even initiating interaction with others, far greater than early psychologists believed. The blooming, buzzing confusion of the infant's world, as William James believed it was, is far from accurate. Visual capacities permit the neonate to interact with its social and physical environment very soon after birth (Haith 1966; Greenman 1963; Fantz 1963; Haith, Bergman and Moore 1977; Cohen 1978). This ability to detect patterns, faces and colours is the beginning of social responsiveness through which self-definition is developed.

On superficial examination, the neonate appears to possess little to begin the long, complex development towards adulthood beyond a set of rudimentary reflexes, many of which do not immediately seem very useful. The baby sleeps and wakes at irregular intervals, and when awake is usually either drowsy or feeding. Periods of alert activity are few and far between, and those motor movements that occur seem to be fairly uncoordinated and purposeless most of the time. Strong stimuli of noise or pain produce gross reactions of the whole body, and crying occurs frequently.

An initial impression from looking at an infant is probably of a primitive and naïve organism, highly dependent on environmental influences to produce learning and organization. But research is now showing us that the infant is more highly developed and more able to interact with his environment early on than we ever suspected (Bower 1974). For example it was believed that inevitably the newborn infant 'sees' very little, that the visual world is chaotic, confusing and overwhelming, and that it takes a long time for the infant to 'learn to see'.

The first signs that this generalized assumption might be wrong came, not surprisingly, from the work of a number of animal researchers. (Sperry 1956; Hubel and Weisel 1962). Working with human infants, Fantz (1961) found preferences for human faces rather than simple patterns. Carpenter (1974) has shown that three-week-old infants can tell their mother's face from a stranger's face. Visual ability appears well developed soon after birth.

Newborn infants are not passive, unresponsive creatures who spend most of their time sleeping. New experimental techniques reveal that they interact quite markedly with their environment, after starting interaction with other humans by movement of the limbs and eyes.

Rheingold (1969) argues that the infant is not only an active partner in the mother–child interaction but in fact the prime mover through the social signals he gives by smiling and crying. The parent indeed adapts to the child as the latter teaches the parents how caretaking operations ought to be performed to satisfy him. It is these first social contacts that markedly influence the child's social and emotional development, particularly his self-concept.

All infants tend to seek closeness to particular people, especially the mother who tends to their needs. This tendency from which security is obtained is termed attachment, the security apparently stemming not only from the food-provision basis of mothering but from the contact, comfort and acceptance an infant obtains.

Hence the perceptual abilities and the social interaction required for self-concept development are present in a rudimentary form soon after birth. The infant, therefore, is not an empty organism but one who is well prepared in a variety of ways for development into an adult, and for self-awareness.

ERIKSON'S BASIS TO EARLY SELF-CONCEPT DEVELOPMENT

(a) The Development of Basic Trust

Erikson (1963) locates the foundation of all later personality development in the first phase of his developmental stage theory (birth to 18 months). The infant needs to acquire a sense of trust and overcome a sense of mistrust, as a basis for positive self-feeling. A sense of basic trust enables the child to move on to new experiences, to later phases and to other developmental tasks; basic mistrust will hamper his development, since he will not move on to other activities willingly or easily. A trusting environment enables the infant to feel he is accepted and loved, a firm basis for future interaction with others and for developing positive feelings about oneself.

The sense of trust is not something that develops independently of other manifestations of growth. It is not that the infant learns how to use his body for purposeful movement, learns to recognize people and objects around him, and also develops a sense of trust. Rather, the concept 'sense of trust' is a short-cut expression intended to convey the characteristic flavour of all the child's satisfying experiences at this early age. Or, to say it another way, this psychological formulation serves to condense, summarize, and synthesize the most important underlying changes that give meaning to the infant's concrete and diversified experience.

Trust can exist only in relation to something. Consequently, a sense of trust cannot develop until the infant is old enough to be aware of objects and persons and to have some feeling that he is a separate individual.

(b) The Development of Autonomy

From 18 months to three to four years of age, Erikson (1963) in the second phase of his developmental theory, sees the child recognize his own individuality and himself as agent, as the child becomes conscious of his own actions. But performance is not always perfect; failure and perhaps criticism accrue, hence the possibilities of low self-esteem developing if support and encouragement are not given. During this period, the child's world changes very rapidly. There is a dramatic maturation, which results in the accomplishment of the simple, but necessary, physical skills like walking.

The principal developmental goal of this period is the acquisition of a sense of autonomy. That is, the child must move on from a position of being dependent on the adult world for everything to a stage where he sees himself as an independent entity, capable of carrying out at least some activities on his own. As an infant he was dependent on the adult world for every mouthful of nourishment, for being picked up and moved about, or put down to sleep, for being given toys and rattles which he could not reach himself. Now he must learn to do many of these things unaided.

However, the adult world sets limits upon these independent activities. The child can explore the house, but must not touch the fire; he can play in the garden, but must not go out on to the road. Of course, he cannot know what these limits are until he runs up against them. Here we have the possibility of conflict. The child's striving for autonomy expresses itself in experiment and self-assertion, which from time to time brings him into conflict with his parents. Such conflict may result in the emergence of feelings of doubt about his capacity, and about his own autonomy. Autonomy and doubt are the two antithetical solutions Erikson sees to the typical problem of early childhood, and again the solution chosen is going to affect all departments of a child's later development.

The child's need at this period is for sympathetic support and encouragement in his exploration of the world, so that his emerging autonomy will be fostered, and so that the necessary conflicts with adult restrictions do not thrust him into shame and self-doubt, and he develops self-control without loss of self-esteem.

In terms of actual behaviour, we see this development in the child's determination to do things on his own, and in the indignant repudiation of attempts to feed him, to hold his hand when he's walking somewhere, to dress him, to open the door for him. The plea of this period is, 'Me do it'. Self-reliance and self-adequacy are important pillars of the self-concept at this age.

The matter of mutual regulation between parent and child (for fathers have now entered the picture to an extent that was rare in the earlier stage) now faces its severest task. The task is indeed one to challenge the most resourceful and the most calm adult. Firmness is necessary, for the child must be protected against the potential anarchy of his as yet untrained sense of discrimination. Yet the adult must back him up in his wish to 'stand on his own feet', lest he be overcome with shame that he has exposed himself foolishly and by doubt in his self-worth. Perhaps the most constructive rule a parent can follow is to forbid only what 'really matters' and, in such forbidding, to be clear and consistent.

Shame and doubt are emotions that many primitive peoples and some of the less sophisticated individuals in our own society use in training children. Shaming exploits the child's sense of being small. Used to excess it misses its objective and may result in open shamelessness, or, at least, in the child's secret determination to do as he pleases when not observed. Such defiance is a normal, even healthy response to demands that a child consider himself, his body, his needs, or his wishes evil and dirty and that he regard those who pass judgement as infallible. Young delinquents and others who are oblivious to the opinion of society may be produced by this means.

Those who would guide the growing child wisely, then, will avoid shaming him and avoid causing him to doubt that he is a person of worth. They will be firm and tolerant with him so that he can rejoice in being a person of independence and can grant independence to others. As to detail procedures, it is impossible to prescribe, not only because we do not know and because every situation is different but also because the kind and degree of autonomy that parents are able to grant their small children depends on feelings about themselves that they derive from society. Just as the child's sense of trust is a reflection of the mother's sturdy and realistic faith, so the child's sense of autonomy is a reflection of the parent's personal dignity.

It is not only in early childhood, however, that this attitude toward growing children must be maintained. The period of life in which they first come into being is the most crucial, it is true. But threats to their maintenance occur throughout life.

Not only parents, then, but everybody who has significant contact wth children and young people must respect their desire for self-assertion, help them hold it within bounds, and avoid treating them in ways that arouse shame or doubt. We shall look at research on child-rearing practices and their effects on self-concept in more detail in Chapter 4. So childhood, particularly the early stages, when basic tasks are learned, is a very important period for self-concept formation. It is for many a make-or-break time.

So for Erikson the pre-school child needs to develop a basic trust in his environment particularly in his parents, and a sense of autonomy within a structured consistent framework of rules. Both of these developments enhance positive self-esteem as the child feels warmly accepted that parents care, and that he knows he is competent in a range of tasks. A sense of worth emanates from this reflected glow of parental and self-approval.

For the very young child just developing a sense of personal agency, ability to cope with the world in a purely physical sense is an important component of self-esteem. White's concept of competence or Erikson's feelings of autonomy correspond with self-esteem at this level. The child who is more eager to assume control of himself as manifested in attempts to feed or dress himself and who is more eager to strike out and explore his environment, might be attributed with greater self-esteem. This is the child who is actively seeking to discover the limits of his capacities. He is not cognitively aware of himself; very likely he is incapable of introspection; but he is aware of his ability to control his own movements, as well as those of others through cries, vocalizations, and signalling across distances. Since appropriateness of exploratory behaviour may be related to the pattern of the infant's attachment to his mother (Bowlby 1969; Ainsworth et al. 1971) there may be a basis for implicating the mother's reactions to her child in an explanation of the strength of a child's developing self-esteem. A measure of self-esteem at this level might therefore involve differences in willingness to explore the environment and assume care for the self. The degree to which the child feels capable of controlling events in his life may be related to the strength of his sense of self, but this hypothesis needs testing with the pre-school child.

(c) Initiative versus Guilt: Erikson's Third Stage

This period commences around four years of age and concerns the child learning what kind of a person he can become and defining the limits of what is permissible. His learning starts to become vigorous and intrusive with curiosity dominating his explorations. This leads him away from limitations of infancy to the dawning of greater possibilities. All this is encouraged by his ability to move around freely, developing language for questioning and early conceptual understanding, and an expanded social environment. The manner in which parents deal with this exploratory curiosity is critical for later development. The danger according to Erikson is that a child may develop guilt over his curiosity and goals; this may blunt his sense of initiative. An immature harsh, self-derogatory conscience must be avoided at all costs if positive self-esteem is to continue developing.

(d) Industry versus Inferiority: Erikson's Fourth Stage

In the fourth stage, which encompasses the school years and corresponds to the latency period in psychoanalysis, a child is concerned with doing things, alone and with others. At Erikson observes '. . . before the child, psychologically already a rudimentary parent, can become a biological parent, he must begin to be a worker and potential provider' (1963, p. 258). Thus, during the latency period a child learns to seek recognition and praise by producing things; by adjusting himself to the impersonal laws of tools and craftsmanship, a child develops a sense of industry, a capacity for productive and self-expressive work.

In all cultures children at this age are taught the roles of adulthood and the techniques of economic survival in an organized and didactic fashion. In the modern industrial state, however, these tutorial practices have become inappropriate. The goals of modern technology and considerably removed from the necessities for survival and are thus diffuse and ill-defined. Adult roles have also become ill-defined. The education process is no longer tied to the concrete goals of individual economic survival; education has become an end in itself, a self-contained enterprise divorced from social reality.

Erikson does not comment on the sort of parent–child relationship necessary to promote a sense of industry. He is, however, clear about the consequences of failure at this stage. If a child fails to develop a sense of industry, he will have feelings of inadequacy concerning his tool-using skills, sense of craftsmanship, and status among his co-workers. He may lose confidence in his ability to take part in the working world. Thus one's self-image as a competent, productive, and capable worker is closely tied to the outcome of the school years.

The child in school is brought into contact with a wider world of adults. He sees how much more they know than he does, how many more things they can do than he can: he sees, in short, that he is a child, and this may bring about undue feelings of inferiority. By this, we do not mean that to avoid the difficulty the child must see himself as knowing as much, or being able to do as much, as adults; this would simply be delusion. What we mean is that the child's perception of his incompleteness and present inferiority should not lead him to a defeatist attitude in which he feels that there is just too much to do, too much to learn; that there is no point in trying, and that he might just as well relax. To overcome these fears of inferiority, the child needs to develop a sense of industry, a determination to succeed with what he is doing, and experiment with everything from physical skills to school work and symbolic thought.

One of the struggles which humans face throughout life is between competence and incompetence. This struggle is intensified in school for youngsters by the fact that the child appears somewhat incompetent, because daily he is faced with new learning tasks. Much learning goes on in childhood. Almost by definition, the child is incompetent in those tasks which have not yet been learned. Actually, the struggle throughout life is not so much between being competent as opposed to being incompetent but in perceiving oneself in a positive way in spite of the incompetencies which may be present.

The child must begin the task of looking at incompetencies as learning tasks rather than as personal defects or personal fate. 'You can't do it now but you *will* be able to do it', should be the almost constant reaction of the parent and teacher to the child's incompetencies.

Luckily by late adolescence (and perhaps even more so in adulthood) we have a greater range of choice in our behaviour and activity, choosing events and situations we can cope with, avoiding those where we would be shown up with the minimum loss of self-esteem. But in childhood most tasks and behaviours are obligatory being vital to physical, social and intellectual development; they cannot be opted out of no matter how inept at them one might feel one is. The child has to reveal, often very publicly, his incompetencies.

Erikson's fifth stage, that of identity formation, will be considered in Chapter 6 on adolescence.

WHEN DOES THE SELF-CONCEPT BECOME EXPLICIT?

To attempt a study of how a self-concept first becomes explicit, Bannister and Agnew (1976) had adults write essays on the first memories of self-consciousness in their childhoods. Such material is not very valid or reliable as evidence due to memory failure, retrospective distortion, defence mechanisms and so on, but some interesting reports were produced which provide a glimmer of the sort of experiences that might effect a firmer self-definition. The instructions were: 'Think about how you became aware of yourself as an individual when you were a child. Write an account of any experience or experiences (events, situations, ideas) which significantly contributed to your developing a feeling of being a separate individual, a 'self', during your childhood' (p. 116).

Bannister and Agnew (op. cit.) summarize two basic themes in their research on development of the self-concept in young children: First, when the person comes to be defined in terms of being different from others rather than being particularly unique. Secondly, when reflexivity is achieved so that the child is able to consider the way he is perceived by others and defined by others.

Possessions—the meaning of *mine*. 'Perhaps the first time I remembered that I had a vague feeling of self was when playing with one of the children and we exchanged toys. On returning home, the distinction between my toys and the toys belonging to others was pointed out, and it became obvious that life was not so simple as it had appeared. There was a difference between what others had and what I had, and there was therefore a distinction between them and me.' (p. 118).

Realization of how one appears to others. One man describes being mocked by his father because he could not correctly wire up a radio he had been given for Christmas. 'It was from incidents like this I learned I was a stupid and ignorant person.' (pp. 121–22). In this last example, the child adopted the evaluation of himself as seen by a significant other, an excellent example of Cooley's looking-glass self!

EARLY LANGUAGE AS AN AID TO SELF-CONCEPT DEVELOPMENT

The concept of the self-concept receives further elaboration and refinement as pre-school children achieve mastery of language. An indicator of the child's growing sense of being a separate individual from others is the acquisition of the pronouns 'I', 'me', 'you', 'it' and 'them'. As we shall see, understanding these words is more difficult than learning the meaning of such words as cup or bed. Indeed, the proper use of personal pronouns may call for some ability to take the perspective others take toward the self, because inversion is required. The child must understand that when others use 'you', this refers to what the child calls 'me'; the child is not 'you' to himself, nor is he 'I' when someone else speaks. Many parents have witnessed this confusion in two-year-olds. For example one of my own children, Richard, when that age was visiting some distant relatives who he did not know and a game developed to teach him who was who. This involved pointing at a person when that person was named e.g. 'point to Uncle Brian', Richard soon learned the various relatives' names but then someone asked him, 'point to yourself, point to Richard'. He was very hesitant, then started pointing randomly. Suddenly it dawned; he had sorted out the semantic problem partially—'you are Richard' he claimed triumphantly pointing to himself. Many children use their own name rather than 'I' at this stage, e.g. 'Susan want cup' rather than 'I want the cup'. Children reversing 'I' and 'you' tend to reverse 'mine' and 'your' also. Clark (1976) suggests that the 'I–you' distinction is one of shifting reference, which requires the child to work out a rule for using them. 'I' refers to who ever is using it. Clark suggests that children may adopt one or two hypotheses to work out this problem of reference: (1) 'I' implies an adult who is speaking with a child while 'you' implies the child; or (2) 'I' means whoever is speaking and 'you' means whoever is spoken to. The child who adopts the first hypothesis has overlooked the shifting reference rule.

Some children employ the incorrect hypothesis and then abandon it after several months; other children use the second hypothesis directly. We do not know why some children have more trouble than others in understanding the shifting reference. It may be as in the case of Gallup's (1977) apes, correct use rests on some rudimentary ability to regard one's self as an object—to take the perspective of others towards one's self and to understand that you can be a 'you' to others in the same way that the others are 'you' to your self. This line of thought suggests that children use a social mirror to achieve the required perspective, and that something about their early social experience facilitates the necessary inferences. We do not know what social experiences are most helpful in achieving this result, but we do know that the correct distinctions are usually mastered within the first two and a half years of life.

Increasing use and accuracy of pronouns reflects the child's increasing ability to conceive of himself as an individual with feelings, needs and attributes. But the pronouns are only one indicator that a differentiation has been made between self and others. Their absence, however, must not be taken as implying that differentiation has not been established. Cooley (1912), for example, reported that although his oldest son was slow in using pronouns he engaged in acts which displayed a differentiation between self and other. Children also learn early on that their name stands for them. It is rather interesting that the reaction of a child to his name is a valid and reliable indication of his self-concept (Boshier 1968). If the child likes his name, he tends to like himself; if he dislikes his name, he tends to dislike himself. It is impossible at this point to say whether that attitude towards the name comes first or whether the child in fact learns to dislike himself and then attaches these self-attitudes to the verbal symbol which stands for him. He hears his name repeated over and over by others who accompany it with appropriate gestures, actions, and words which come to indicate their feelings for and beliefs about him. By association and conditioning such indications tagged to his name and being become as much an identifying and categorizing mark of him as his name. He begins to think of himself along lines similar to the conceptions others have of him. Thus the genesis of true self-conceptualization may come for many infants when they grasp the fact that they have a name. This suggests a naming or labelling hypothesis for self-development. The child's knowledge of himself depends on a separation of self from others. Central to the creation of self as social object is an identification of that object which will be called self, and this identification involves naming. But once an object is named and identified, a line of action can be taken towards it.

Allport (1961) supports this conclusion. Although he presents no data, he suggests that the child gradually sees himself as a distinct and recurrent point of reference, by hearing his name repeatedly. The name acquires significance usually in the second year of life. With it comes awareness of independent status in the social group. For some three-year-olds, names must be printed and 'tagged-on' clothes and pegs before they (name and self) exist. Uncertainty over one's personal name is also revealed in a desire to have the name publicly announced. Such announcements ensure that the child will be reacted to in at least one consistent fashion across encounters (e.g. by the name). Wolfenstein's (1968) discussions of name-games in early childhood amplify this conclusion over identity–uncertainty for three-year-olds. Wolfenstein studied such games as name-switching, name-reversals, name-calling and name-loss. She notes that frequently a child who is called by a different name becomes disturbed. Such children, it would be predicted, have yet to be committed fully to their own personal identity. Loss of name makes the child a non-person, his essential self as a distinct person has been denied.

The ability to acknowledge feelings verbally as one's own is also proof of the child possessing a rudimentary self-concept, for instance, as when the child says 'I'm happy today' or 'I'm in a bad mood'. Parents can help children to define themselves by using language simply and precisely, and encouraging verbalization.

Body language (non-verbal communication) also conveys information to others about self and reflects what others think of one. A study of body language, e.g. Argyle (1967) reveals that there are codes and signs which speak louder than words. We may speak with our mouths, but as Abercrombie (1968) cogently notes we communicate with the whole body. For example, a frown, a nod, a smile, a wipe of the forehead or an aggressive movement of the arm are all examples of non-verbal communication which convey as powerfully as language one's attitudes to oneself and to others. Some might say body language is more potent, since while it is relatively easy to lie verbally (even for tactful purposes) it is almost impossible to distort the non-verbal communications emitted. These latter messages are conveyed with stark reality and truthfulness; feelings and attitudes to self and others cannot be distorted in this form of communication which we use all the time, often without realizing it.

THE ROLE OF COGNITIVE DEVELOPMENT

One aspect of self-concept development, previously neglected, concerns possible strutural changes in the type of constructs used to describe oneself. Both Piaget (Inhelder and Piaget 1958) and Werner (1961) have argued that an individual's cognitions about the physical world undergo important qualitative changes between childhood and adolescence. Werner's 'orthogenetic principle' states that, whenever development occurs, it proceeds from a state of relative globality and lack of differentiation to a state of increasing differentiation, articulation and hierarchic integration. Werner's principle suggests that as an individual matures, his thoughts about the physical world undergo a shift from a concrete to an abstract mode of representation.

The orthogenetic principle, although not specifically concerned with orthogenetic changes in social cognition, can be fruitfully extended to the area of the development of person perception. An individual's developing ability to think abstractly allows him to differentiate between another person's appearance or behaviour and his underlying dispositional qualities.

Such an approach may also be advantageously applied to the development of other aspects of social cognition such as self-conceptualizations. As a general statement about development, the orthogenetic principle suggests that an individual's increasing ability to think abstractly, not only results in greater use of psychological and abstract constructs to describe others, but, also, a correspondingly greater use of these types of constructs to describe the self. In addition, social psychologists consider the knowledge that an individual acquires about himself and about others to be the result of interaction. (Mead 1934)

The concrete–abstract change is not a simple linear one, however, since additional findings suggest that curvilinear changes occur in the use of categories that could be either concrete or abstract. These changes primarily involve the use of concrete descriptions by adolescents rather than the use of abstract descriptions by children. For example, many adolescents referred to concrete characteristics such as their sex and name when describing themselves, suggesting that this type of information has an important phenomenological meaning even to individuals who characteristically define themselves in more abstract terms. Alternatively, few young children described themselves in abstract terms with the exception of the many twelve-year-olds who referred to themselves as 'a person' or 'a human', abstract ideas which may reflect the initial appearance of advanced cognitive skills.

The pre-adolescent self-concept seems rather shallow and undifferentiated. Adolescents, however, describe themselves in terms of their beliefs and personality characteristics, qualities which are more essential and intrinsic to the self which produce a picture of the self that is sharp and unique.

Self-concept development is not an additive process. Adolescents do not simply add more complex and abstract ideas about themselves to their earlier, childish, concrete conceptions. Compared to children, adolescents see themselves quite differently; earlier notions either drop out or are integrated into a more complex picture.

Self-conceptualizations appear to undergo a developmental transformation, perhaps based on the developing ability of the individual to draw inferences and form hypotheses about underlying characteristics. It is not uncommon, for example, for a young child to say that he likes to play baseball, football, hockey and so on. An adolescent rarely responds in this way. A much more common response would be for him to say 'I am an athlete' or 'I like sport'. Adolescents seem to infer from their own behaviours the existence of underlying abilities, motives and a personality style. As Inhelder and Piaget (1958) point out, adolescent thinking is a 'second order system' in that the adolescent does not solve problems in terms of concrete data but uses those concrete facts to form hypotheses about an underlying reality. What appears to be the self for the child is only the set of elements from which the adolescent infers a set of personal beliefs and psychic style and uniquely characterize himself.

COMPONENTS OF SELF-DEFINITION

Little has been done to discern at the point of school entry what are the main contributors to the self-concept. Gilbert and Finell (1978) investigated the contributors to a differentiated self-concept in 69 kindergarten children. Seven scales measuring areas thought to be important to self-concept formation at age five were applied. A factor analysis revealed a major factor accounting for 70 per cent of the common variance which was defined by body awareness. The two other self-awareness measures were loaded on this factor also—affective awareness (awareness of emotional states) and make-believe tendency (ability to differentiate between reality and fantasy). This gives strong support for the theory that body image, effective awareness and tendency to make-believe mutually contribute to the self-concept of the school starter, with body image being the major element. The other two elements suggest that, at this age, the child is able to recognize changes in his emotional, internal states which aid self-identity and make-believe play facilitates a symbolization of himself in a range of roles and feelings that permit a differentiation between self and others.

Dixon and Street (1975) investigated the ability of children, between six and sixteen, to distinguish between self and not-self. Each child was presented with a list of 42 items covering body parts, personal identifying characteristics, objects, possessions and psychological processes. The mean number of items consistently identified as a self varied from a mean of 18.60 items for six-year-old boys to 33.20 for the sixteen-year-old girls. Overall age differences were significant ($r < 0.001$). Girls identified more items as self at every age ($r < 0.001$). There was no significant relationship between age and sex.

The frequency of self-identification shows the following order: body parts, identifying personal characteristics, psychological processes, others, and objects. The order varies slightly from males and females. There is little increase from one age to another in the first three categories. The last two categories, significant others and self-related objects or possessions, seem to account for most of the age-related increase, with females again showing slightly more self-identification. Despite this relatively greater increase, however, the first three categories clearly make up the major self-definition at all ages with both sexes. An analysis of specific items may provide some clues as to why certain items are more frequently included in one's self-definition.

Feeling proud and doing good things vied for first place at all ages, and both sexes, for inclusions in one's self-image. Feeling ashamed, angry or afraid and doing bad things, were less admissible but more often admitted than not. The only other psychological process which showed any contrast at all were wishing compared to dreaming and doing something on purpose rather than without thinking. Body parts and personal identifying characteristics were second most frequently identified with self but there were no marked contrasts either within or between these categories. Significant others are not a significant part of the self of six- to eight-year-olds but become somewhat more identified with self thereafter.

The general direction of self in this age group appears to be one of self-extension after the self–other differentiation of infancy and early childhood. The data suggest that the 6 year-olds, especially the boys, may have been in a stage of transition since they seemed more concerned with discriminating between things than perceiving similarities. The areas of greater extension—identification with related others, one's possessions and related objects—is reminiscent of William James's conception of the material 'me', that a person becomes whatever he can call his. The age-related change appears to involve a reconceptualization of self and not-self relations and is no doubt related to the child's growing conceptual ability, as well as his growing network of relationships.

Along with a fairly regular increase in self-extension with age, is the small but consistently greater frequency of self-extension in girls than boys. At least two factors may plausibly fit the data. Girls of the same age are generally more mature than boys physically, in social orientation, cognitive skills and interests. In this connection Dixon and Street (op. cit.) noted that the percentage of items identified as self by boys corresponds more closely to those of girls two years younger than girls of the same age. Another factor, an acquiescence response set, is also reported by Tyler (1965) to be more frequent in girls. Although the questions were worded to avoid an agreement response set, it is possible that the mere requirement to affirm or deny elicits the set to some degree and, hence, could elevate the girls' scores.

CHANGES IN CONTENT BY AGE

Livesley and Bromley (1973) tried to document the changes in children's self-concept by having 320 subjects from seven to fourteen years of age write a description entitled 'Myself'. These responses were analysed and put into thirty categories. A number of variables were considered in connection with these. Categories showing a decrease in proportion with increasing age were:

1.   Appearance
2.   General information and identity
3.   Friendships and playmates
4.   Family and kinships
5.   Possessions

Categories showing an increase with increasing age were:

1.   General personality attributes
2.   Specific behavioural consistencies
3.   Orientation
4.   Interests and hobbies
5.   Beliefs attitudes and values
6.   Attitudes towards self
7.   Relations with the opposite sex
8.   Comparisons with others
9.   Collateral facts and ideas

The types of information that were given less frequently with age are the more objective categories. As the subjects get older they tend to stress personal attributes, values and attitudes. This agrees with a similar study by Jersild (1951), which showed that younger children tended to describe themselves by external character-istics and physical attributes whereas older students mention inner resources and the quality of relationships with others.

Both studies showed the increased ability of subjects to give abstract and sophisti-cated information about themselves as they get older. The young subjects are reported to be egotistical in their self-descriptions while the older students are much more aware of others and seem to have the ability to see themselves of a more detached manner. Piaget postulated that this is due to an increase in cognitive ability and the ability to see the world from another's perspective. This may also explain the observance that older students often report negative characteristics about themselves while younger students rarely do.

The categories of expressive behaviour and evaluations showed an increase and then a decrease with age. The most frequently used category was preferences.

Young students tended to write shorter reports on others than on themselves while older students tended to write longer reports on others. This again illustrates the Piagetian concept of decentration. The observation that descriptions of others get longer as the age of the subject increases suggests that the individual has gained understanding of other people's roles, attitudes and abilities. With the younger students, preferences and aversions, while frequently used to describe self, were rarely used to describe others. This shows the importance of affective factors in defining oneself but, at the same time, these factors are of a personal nature. One is unlikely to experience another's likes and dislikes.

During middle childhood, changes in description of others, like self-description, tend to show an increase in abstract thinking. However, the written reports are still poorly organized. Only with adolescence do the reports become more structured, consistent and coherent. Adolescents use the categories of motivation and arousal and orientation to describe themselves but only rarely are these used to describe others. These types of statements show subjective thinking about oneself and are experienced privately; they are particularly difficult to infer in others and this may explain the differences in use.

Adolescents show by their responses, that they are concerned with others' impressions of themselves as well as their effect on others. They also show an increase in their responses in the category of beliefs, attitudes and values. This may suggest an increasing desire to become part of the social structure by identifying with cultural values. Adolescents are also reported to be involved in the struggle between maintaining their identity as individuals and still being part of the peer group. These observations again illustrate the loss of egocentrism and an increasing ability to become more concerned with others as they get older.

Livesley and Bromley (op. cit.) also looked for the effect of other variables of the categories of responses. The sex of the subject had few effects showing only a significant difference in three categories. Girls referred to their interests and hobbies less frequently than boys, and girls responded more frequently to the categories of relations with the opposite sex and family and kinship. In these studies, the differences were attributed to the varying rates of maturation between boys and girls. However, the differences may be due to society's expectations or simply to sex differences.

The intelligence of the subjects was another variable considered in this experiment. They found that students who were judged to have a lower intelligence tended to give responses that were more concrete and more superficial. This agrees with the theories of Piaget which infer that cognitive development and the ability to decentrate are a function of the environment and the innate capabilities of the individual. Thus, the older, but less intelligent, subject would compare with the younger but more intelligent subject.

Subjects in this study by Livesley and Bromley were also asked to write a description of another person. These descriptions were compared with the self-descriptions. The following examples serve to illustrate the concreteness of typical descriptions written by seven-year-old children in Livesley and Bromley's study. A boy aged seven describes himself:

> I am seven and I have brown hair and my hobby is stamp collecting. I am good at football and I am quite good at sums and my favourite game is football and I love school and I like reading books and my favourite car is an Austin.

Hobbies are usually highly valued at this age and ego-involved activities form a central part of their personal identity. The emphasis on aptitudes and abilities suggests that competence and excellence are important values for the schoolchild too, and probably involve implicit comparisons with others as he attempts to define his self-concept in the context of school activities.

During middle childhood, developments in self-description lead to increased abstractness and sophistication of content. Psychological qualities of all kinds are referred to and the child begins to show some understanding of his personal motivation and arousal. Descriptions are not, however, better articulated or better organized. The description usually consists of a list of qualities without any attempt to relate and organize them.

Adolescence brings further changes in the contents of self-description and increases in references to beliefs, values, attitudes and relations with others. These presumably, reflect the adolescents attempt to understand himself and achieve a stable, enduring sense of identity incorporating basic values.

The older subject's self-descriptions were better organized than those of younger subjects and attempts were made to structure the information and to make it consistent and coherent. A girl aged 12.10 describes herself in Livesley and Bromley:

> I have a fairly quick temper and it doesn't take much to rouse me. I can be a
> little bit sympathetic to the people I like but to the poor people I dislike my
> temper can be shown quite easily. I'm not thoroughly honest. I can tell a white
> lie here and there when it's necessary but I'm trying my hardest to redeem
> myself, as after experience I've found it's not worth it.

It is interesting to note the social awareness of adolescents as revealed by their self-impressions. They are concerned with how other people see them and what other people think about them and they are often concerned with the effects they have on others. Most adolescents appear to be aware that they are moody and irritable and they wish to minimize the effect that this has on other people, although many seem to feel that these are feelings they cannot control.

Adolescents are also concerned with being different from other people, yet most are ambivalent about this. They are likely to be thought of as 'modern', 'with it', 'one of the crowd', but at the same time they do not want their identity to become lost and submerged with that of their peers. Often they attempt to be different from the rest, usually in rather simple ways, like wearing different clothes or behaving in an odd manner, and they are quite pleased when other people react strongly to it. While wanting to be thought different from the rest, most adolescents also take account of group stability and cohesion. Many adolescents, especially the girls, mention their dislike of group arguments and disagreements, and state that they are always trying to stop them.

Montemayor and Eisen (1977) investigated self-concept development from childhood to adolescence using a cognitive perspective, and provide similar evidence of change. They hypothesized that young children primarily conceive of and describe themselves in terms of their physical appearance and possessions, while adolescents conceive of themselves more abstractly and describe themselves in more psychological and interpersonal terms, a reflection of the adolescent's greater use of various constructs to describe himself.

The responses of 262 American children and adolescents aged between nine and seventeen to the question 'Who am I?' were analysed by a 30 category scoring system. Between childhood and adolescence there was a significant increase in self-conceptualizations categorized as follows: occupational role; existential, individuating; ideological and belief references; the sense of self-determination; the sense of unity; interpersonal style; psychic style.

A decrease occurred for self-conceptualizations based of territory, citizenship, possessions, resources; physical body self, body image. Curvilinear age changes were found for the use of the categories: sex; name; kinship role; membership in an abstract category; judgements, tastes and likes. The results for self-concept development were in general agreement with Werner's notion that cognitive development proceeds from a concrete to an abstract representation, and with Livesley and Bromley using a British sample.

Thomas (1974) provides material on the content of self-description written by ten-year-olds. Physical appearance ranked first, consisting of 27 per cent of the responses, a reflection of the importance of body image. Kindness and generosity with 17 per cent of the total comments, ranked second. Third came being good at sport with 12 per cent of the comments. Being friendly and loving one's family ranked fourth and fifth with 8 per cent and 7 per cent respectively.

Mullener and Laird (1971) also provide some evidence of increasing differentiation in self-esteem with age. Their subjects were seventh-graders, high school seniors, and evening college students whose ages averaged in the upper twenties. (The groups were reasonably comparable with respect to IQ.) The subjects were asked to use a six-point scale running from 'very true' to 'very untrue' to rate themselves on forty characteristics (for example, 'I think I am good at mathematics'). The statements were chosen to represent five different areas: achievement traits, intellectual skills, interpersonal skills, physical skills, and social responsibility. When measures of individual variation among the five areas were computed, older subjects were found to vary more than younger ones. That is, older subjects might rate themselves very high on intellectual skills and very low on interpersonal skills or physical skills, while children in the seventh grade would be more likely to rate the five areas of competence similarly. However, even the youngest children varied considerably from one area to another.

There are several ways to think about the fact that self-esteem seems to become increasingly differentiated as children grow older. Mullener and Laird suggest that a single global self-concept breaks down into several distinct ones, and that the single global concept ceases to exist.

THE SELF–IDEAL SELF DISCREPANCY

Children not only build up a concept of themselves (what they are like and how they are seen by others) they also construct a concept of what they would prefer to be like. Some children's ideal self is very similar to their concept of their actual self, and they do not aspire to be more than what they believe they already are. For other children the ideal self (sometimes called the ego ideal) is a distant goal, something to be worked toward. It may be modelled on one or several admired persons. Sometimes the ideal self is realistic: sometimes it may be pure fantasy.

What does it mean if the ego ideal is very different from the child's actual self? Clinical psychologists have suggested that a very large discrepancy between the real and ideal selves is an unhealthy sign. A child who feels avoided by other children but wants very much to be popular surely experiences a state of considerable tension compared to either a contented loner or a sociable child with a secure place in a group of friends.

A large discrepancy indicates that maladjustment is likely to occur because the individual sees himself as greatly different from the person he would like to be. An individual with a small discrepancy may be better able to satisfy his needs through attaining his ideals. The relatively frequent occurrence of problems in living that occur during adolescence may be in part the result of this increase in self–ideal-self discrepancy.

Katz and Zigler (1967) and Katz, Zigler and Zelk (1975) have challenged this view, suggesting that a gap between the ego ideal and the real current self is a sign of maturity rather than disturbance. They asked groups of children to respond to a series of statements such as 'I get along well with other people' and 'I feel unsure of myself'. First the young subjects rated the statements in terms of their actual self (the scale ranging from very true to very untrue) and then in terms of their ideal self (the scale ranging from 'I would like this to be true' to 'I prefer that this is not true'). Each subject's answers concerning the real self were combined into a single score, the same was done for the ideal self, and thus a difference was obtained. The ideal-self score was always higher than the real-self score, but the difference was much greater for some children than others. In two studies conducted with ten- to thirteen-year-old children, the older children had higher discrepancies.

Katz and Zigler (op. cit.) also investigated the question of whether a large discrepancy is associated with psychological disturbance. Working in a school system that had separate classes for emotionally disturbed children, they compared the children in these classes with those in normal classes. The disturbed children had lower discrepancy scores. This finding was particularly true of children who had externalizing symptoms—that is, children whose problems included frequent fighting or stealing and inability to settle down and pay attention in class. Thus, setting a high standard for the ideal self is associated with impulse control. Other disturbed children were classified as internalizers: these children suffered from anxiety, depression or social withdrawal. Although they did not have quite as large a gap between their real and ideal self-images as normal children, the internalizers were more similar to the normal children than the externalizers were.

Experience in role taking—skill in taking the perspective of others—helps the child to develop a realistic self-concept. Following this lead, Leahy and Huard (1976) tested children's ability to take the perspective of others. They used a story procedure (adapted from Flavell) in which the child was given a series of nine cartoon-like pictures, one at a time, and was asked to tell the story as the sequence unfolded. Partway through the story a bystander appeared who could not know about the earlier episodes. The child was asked to retell the story from the standpoint of this poorly informed bystander. Some children were able to understand that the first part of the story was privileged information not available to the bystander; they told the story from the bystander's point of view. Other children were unable to do this; they assumed the bystander must, somehow, have access to whatever information they possessed. They could not take the perspective of a person with different experience than their own. The experimenters also asked Katz and Zigler's self-image questions and found that the children with the greater discrepancy between the real and ideal selves were the ones who were the most successful in taking the bystander's perspective. Thus, these findings suggest that role-taking skill is involved in a child's capacity to develop differential concepts of an actual and an ideal self.

During the latter part of the primary school years, then, most children develop a concept of the kind of person they would like to be. In normal children, this image is truly ideal, in the sense that it has more positive qualities and fewer negative ones than the children think they currently possess. We do not know the precise function of the ideal self-image but children probably try actively to shape their own behaviour towards this ideal. The formation of an ideal self-image probably helps children to develop the kind of impulse control that were noted by Katz and Zigler (op. cit.) in their internalizers. Children whose aspirations do not include an ideal self that is in some ways better or more mature than the current self seem to remain impulsive longer than normally developing children, as they lack a control mechanism implicit in the ideal self that maintains socialized behaviour even if at the expense of guilt and conscience of the internalizers with their anxiety symptoms.

Jorgensen and Howell (1969) found that there was an increase in the discrepancy between self and ideal-self between the ages eight and thirteen, as Katz and Zigler (op. cit.) had before them. They suggest that this may be the result of the child internalizing cultural and parental standards.

The ideal self has been studied by Havinghurst, Robinson and Dorr (1946) and they described the changes in the identification figures as the child grows older. The young child is said to identify mainly with the parental figure. During middle childhood, the parent's role declines and is replaced by a romantic or glamorous figure. This may account for the attraction that young adolescents seem to have for rock or film stars in our culture. After the age of fifteen, the ideal self seems to be reconceptualized into a composite of the characteristics of the friends that are significant in the individual's life.

This study also found a relationship between the socioeconomic status of the child and his stage of development through these three categories. Subjects from a lower group were found to progress to the stage of choosing a glamorous adult as the ideal self about two years later than subjects from a middle economic group. This study shows the powerful effect that one individual may have on another; the character qualities of an attractive adult provide models which the growing adolescent strives to emulate.

SUMMARY

This chapter considers some of the developmental aspects of the self-concept. The self-concept is learned through the external and internal sensory information fed to and interpreted by the brain. A phenomenological perspective is emphasized. Neonates seem to possess a greater capacity for interpreting and responding to sensory input than was originally thought.

Erikson proposes a developmental theory which involves self-feeling and identity as central themes. Initially the infant needs to develop a sense of basic trust in others and himself, coming later to recognize his autonomy, and develop initiative and a sense of industry. Successful achievement of these goals provides a basis for positive self-esteem.

The self-concept seems to become explicit when the child is able to define himself in relation to others and consider the way he is defined by others. Mastery of language aids self-conceptualization, with the use of personal pronouns and names clarifying self-identity. Cognitive development is involved in such linguistic and perceptual differentiation of self and others. As they get older, children are able to employ more non-concrete and less egocentric constructs about self. Self-conceptualizations undergo a developmental transformation as the child becomes more able to draw inferences and form hypotheses about self-characteristics.

The main component of the self-concept of the pre-school child appears to be body image. With increasing age, significant others, personal relationships and beliefs and attitudes become more important components.

Children build up an ideal self, often modelled on admired persons. A large discrepancy between cognized and ideal selves has been regarded as an index of maladjustment. However, the increasing discrepancy noted with age may be due to cognitive development, specifically the ability to hypothesize possibilities for self and to acknowledge realistically any personal deficiencies.

Further Reading

Young, L. (1965) *Life Among the Giants*, New York: McGraw-Hill. The author explains what it is like to be a child, and teaches her adult readers how to be children again by helping them understand the world from a child's point of view.

3

Body Image and Appearance

O, that this too, too solid flesh would melt
(*Hamlet* I, ii)

INTRODUCTION

After initial sex-typing at birth (an obligatory, continuous and primary element of the self-concept) body size and shape become the major sources of body image. There are ideal body dimensions which may differ from culture to culture, and from time to time, but most cultures favour big males and smaller females. Positive evaluations of one's body, from others and from oneself, facilitate the overall positiveness of the self-concept and, similarly, negative feelings about the body engender an overall negative self-concept. Jourard and Secord (1954, 1955a, 1955b) were able to demonstrate these relationships in series of studies. Measures of satisfaction with various parts of the body correlated significantly with overall self-esteem. To be referred to as 'skinny', 'fatso', 'four-eyes', 'not as big as his brother was', or 'hasn't the lovely curly hair her sister had', may lower the general self-esteem as these images incorporate themselves into the overall self-picture. A person's height, weight, bodily proportions, health, eyesight, complexion, etc., can all become such intimate constituents of his attitudes to himself that they form a major control of his feelings of personal worth, adequacy and acceptability. No part of ourselves is more visible and sensed than the body. We feel, see and hear a lot of ourselves, never able to leave our body behind. It is an unavoidable part of the person, always available to personal and public scrutiny. A puny, bespectacled child must experience a completely different world from his muscular, tall, athletic and physically powerful counterpart.

Failure to meet the physical standards valued by significant others and by society, has a painfully intense effect on self-concept development.

51

Stop, for a moment, and consider how you respond on first meeting a short, fat person or a tall, thin person. You are likely to expect them to possess certain personality characteristics and behave in specific ways. You are likely to read into their behaviour elements that ensure your expectation is confirmed. The subject interprets your verbal and non-verbal responses to fit in with the cultural expectation and so both parties, to the interaction, firm up the existing stereotypes.

BODY IMAGE AS A SOURCE OF SELF-CONCEPT DEVELOPMENT

The concept of the physical body has been conveyed in self-concept literature by two terms, *body schema* and *body image. Body schema* is the basic identity of the body, a map of position, location and boundary constructed from sense perception and held in the cerebral cortex. The *body image* is the evaluative picture of the physical self. The idea of body image as presently used in psychology was developed largely by Schilder (1935) in his efforts to integrate biological and psychoanalytical thinking. Schilder (op. cit.) defined it as the image of our body which we form in our mind—the way in which our body appears to ourselves.

Each of us carries around a mental image of our own appearance which is more than a mirror image and may or may not approximate to our actual body structure. In fact, the body image, although wholly a psychological phenomenon, embraces not only our view of ourselves psychologically but also physiologically and sociologically.

The complicated constellation of psychological components that determine the 'structure' of the body image, may be classified as follows:

1. the actual subjective perception of the body, both as to appearance and ability to function;
2. the internalized psychological factors arising out of the individual's personal and emotional experiences;
3. the sociological factors—how parents and society react to the individual and the adolescent's interpretation of their reactions;
4. the ideal body image, formulated by the individual's attitudes toward the body derived from his experiences, perceptions, comparisons, and identifications with the bodies of other persons.

Modifications in the actual appearance of the body may cause drastic changes in the body-image through any of these channels.

The organization of body image may begin in the womb with the fetus exposed to proprioceptive sensory impressions from the vestibular apparatus and the receptors in the muscles and joints. Then, after birth, the mouth is the first area to be stimulated by sucking and feeding, and from about three months on, the hand-to-mouth relationship gets under way. The child begins to use both hands and arms to grasp and knead the mother's breast and face, and to explore his own body surface and contact others. At the same time he finds that the hand can substitute for the nipple as a pleasure device and thereby relieve tension. It is on these exploratory movements of the infant's hands that the beginnings of body-image are founded.

In infancy the child's self-concept would presumably be mainly a concept of himself as a physical being, a body image since most experiences are body experiences, sensory and motor. Most early learning involves physical skills too. The first distinctions an infant makes between self and non-self will be rooted in muscular, tactile and kinaesthetic sensations as he throws, touches, bumps, falls, holds and bites. Only when some basic, early, physical skills are mastered—accompanied by positive and negative feedback from close relatives depending on their perception of how well the infant is coping—can the infant extend the boundaries of his environment and interact with a wider range of others.

A welter of body sensations enables the infant to clarify the boundaries, locations and positioning of the body and its parts. These sensations originate from within and without the body, but most come from his explorations of the environment, explorations that are initially random with accidental results but later by design, so that self-awareness through motor activity compliments that derived through sense perception. He can produce effects often on himself by his own actions. The self-concept is not an all-or-nothing perception. It arises gradually with different elements of it being perceived with varying degrees of clarity at different times. But to make self-concept effective on behaviour, the child must perceive himself as a distinct object, distinguishable from other objects. He must also be aware of other perspectives for only through these can he receive and understand evaluatory feedback from others to nourish his self-perception. Physical body is the most public display of the person.

SELF-AWARENESS AS A SOURCE OF SELF-CONCEPT DEVELOPMENT

Physical body is the most public display of the person. Awareness of one's person as a physical entity with shape and other characteristics which can be evaluated by others and oneself, is continuous throughout life. It evolves out of the organism's earliest physiological experiences of sensing and recording. Sullivan (1953) calls this phenomenon 'experiencing one's own body' and sees it as the first stage in the process of differentiating the body from its encapsulating environment. As such it is also the first stage towards self-identity, and the formation of the self-concept.

That infants have no self-concept and that they cannot distinguish themselves from other people is a common belief among psychologists. Many writers have held the opinion that the infant cannot make a clear distinction between what is 'himself' and what is not 'himself' and not knowing where one body ends and another begins implies no boundaries between self and others. So the neonate presumably regards mother as part of himself. There is no evidence for this and since the self-concept is learned developing out of the plethora of sensory experience which impinges on the neonate from outside and inside his own body, right from birth a gradual development of self-awareness must occur. They ought to learn quite soon to tell the difference between their own bodies and those of other people.

They have ample basis for making this distinction—their own fingers hurt when bitten; they experience no such sensation when biting a toy or their mother's fingers. We do not know precisely when infants begin to associate the feelings that come from their own bodily movements with the sight of their own limbs and the sound of their own cries. But it is reasonable to expect that, quite early in life, these sense impressions are bound together into a cluster that defines the bodily self. Of course, a rudimentary understanding of the limits of and the sensations that emanate from one's own body does not necessarily imply an understanding of the existence of other similar bodies. And, therefore young children may not truly distinguish themselves from other selves, even when some initial features of a self-concept are present. If we ask, 'Do infants have or do they not have a self-concept?' we are asking the wrong question. It is not achieved in a single step; it is not something that is either present or absent; it develops by degrees and is a product of more and more complex understandings. We might more reasonably ask how the understanding of oneself grows and changes through a lifetime, and how far a given child has progressed along the path to a mature self-concept.

Self-awareness emerges slowly as the infant explores and manipulates his world often by accident. His maturing capabilities of grasping, picking up, crawling and hitting brings a dim awareness that he can produce effects and widen his learning environment. But all these sensations and motor activities play a role in assisting this initial differentiation of self from 'non-self'. This embryonic self-concept based on limited sensory and motor experiences is of a different kind and quality to the mature adolescent and adult self-concept which involves Piagetian formal operational thinking, the ability to consider ourselves from a variety of different prespectives, to understand how others may perceive us.

Too little research has been undertaken on the development of the self-concept compared to many other attributes. Yet interest is starting to blossom in several aspects of the growth of children's self-concepts. For instance, psychologists are interested in self-recognition: how children learn to know their own faces. They have also been interested in self-definition: how children learn personal pronouns like 'I' and what they mean when they use these words, how children come to understand the self as separate from other people, how children come to identify the self with other people, how children develop an ideal self—a sense of what they ought to be—and how children learn to take the perspective of others.

Research on the emergence of the self-concept has been sparse, however, probably because of the difficulty of specifying what reflects its early development. The few existing studies have usually focused on the reaction of an infant to his own image in a mirror. This appears to be ideal for assessing at least one aspect of the development of the notion of self, the development of self-recognition.

The onset of this ability would seem to be a valid indicator of a rudimentary self-concept in the infant. How early does an infant recognize itself in a mirror or photograph? Obviously it is difficult to answer. Before the age of two years a child may not answer correctly when shown a mirror and asked 'Who is that?' Being unable to respond correctly may merely reflect a poor command of language. Children do appear to recognize their own image at a far earlier age but cannot tell us. Fortunately, questions about self-recognition have been posed in relation to animals, and ingenious nonverbal methods have been devised to explore them—methods that can be used with children as well.

Gallup (1977) discovered that a spot of red dye on the forehead of chimpanzees was reacted to when the animal was placed before a mirror. They touched the marked part of their bodies indicating that they recognized themselves. Only chimpanzees and man have this ability to recognize themselves. Gallup argues that this reflects the presence of a concept of self-identity. He then drew on the Cooley–Mead approach that a person's understanding of their own identity represents a reflection of how they are regarded and responded to by others. The self-concept is an internalization of others' viewpoints. That is, the self develops out of the reflections in a social mirror. If these ideas were valid, Gallup reasoned, then chimpanzees reared in isolation should lack the sense of self-identity that would enable them to learn to recognize themselves. True to the prediction, when chimpanzees raised without social contact were anaesthetized, marked and tested with a mirror, they did not touch the marked portions of their faces, nor did they show any increase in their interest in the animal in the mirror. Thus, in these apes social experience appears to be a prerequisite for self-recognition. This is remarkable, considering that looking into a social mirror does not tell one much about the appearance of one's own face. Presumably, it is other aspects of the self that are reflected.

This suggests that even in infants, the foundation for their self recognition lies at least partly in their limited social experience. Similar experiments to Gallup's have been made with pre-verbal infants. In such experiments the mother applies a dab of rouge to the infant's nose and observers note how frequently nose touching occurs when seated in front of a mirror.

Lewis and Brooks (1974) conducted this self-recognition test on human subjects and observed the reactions of 23 infants ranging from 16 to 22 months when rouge was put on their noses by their mothers while supposedly wiping the infant's faces. If the infants reacted to their own noses rather than to the mirror, self-recognition was inferred. In the Lewis and Brooks study, none of the six 16-month-old infants touched his nose, whereas all eight of the 22-month-old infants did so. This finding supports later observations that mark-directed behaviours first occurred at 18 months and were common by 20 months. For example, Bertenthal and Fischer (1978) hypothesized a five-stage developmental sequence of self-recognition behaviour that could be related to Piaget's concept of object permanence, which presumably is involved in the development of the early stages of self-concept formation, i.e. that one's physical body has permanence. Bertenthal and Fischer tested 48 infants between six and 24 months of age. They hypothesized that self-recognition does not emerge suddenly with one particular behaviour, but develops gradually through a succession of types of behaviours, all of which relate to self-recognition. Accordingly, most of the previous contradictions appearing in the literature can be resolved by the specification of a cognitive-developmental sequence of self-recognition behaviours.

Table 1 Examples of the tasks devised by Bertenthal and Fischer

Task	Procedure	Criterion	Rationale
Tactual exploration	The infant was placed in front of the mirror so that he or she faced the mirror.	Stage 3 Within three minutes (Phase 2), the infant had to simultaneously look at and touch some part of his or her mirror image.	The infant must coordinate his or her own reaching with the image that he or she sees in the mirror.
Rouge task	A dot of rouge was applied to the tip of the infant's nose. After a free-play period, the mirror was brought into the room, and the infant was placed in front of it.	Stage 6 Within three minutes (Phase 2), the infant had to look in the mirror and then touch his or her nose or indicate orally that something was different about it.	The infant must coordinate his or her own body movements with the mirror image of the infant's face and with the infant's schema for what his or her face (or nose) normally look like in a mirror.
Name task	The infant was placed in front of the mirror. The mother stood so that her image was not projected in the mirror and then pointed to the infant's mirror image and asked three times in succession, 'Who's that?'	Stage 7 Immediately following the mother's question (Phase 2), the infant had to state his or her name or use an appropriate personal pronoun.	The infant must coordinate (a) his or her own body movements with the mirror images of his or her body and the mother pointing and (b) the mother's vocalization with his or her own vocalization, and the infant must coordinate (a) and (b) with each other.

No previous research has clearly demonstrated a developmental sequence of self-recognition behaviours. Bertenthal and Fischer's study was designed to overcome these limitations and test for a predicted cognitive-developmental sequence of self-recognition behaviours. A sequence of five steps was predicted on an *a priori* theoretical analysis, and five specific tasks were devised to correspond to the five steps (examples in Table 1). The theory used to predict the sequence was derived in part from Piaget's framework for describing development during infancy, which he called the sensorimotor period. 46 of the 48 infants fitted the predicted sequence. The implication is that self-recognition does not occur suddenly but develops gradually. There was a tendency for object permanence measured by other tests to be in advance of self-recognition. This would seem to suggest that the former is a prerequisite for the latter, which is only one aspect of object permanence even if it is the major one. But there was still a high correlation ($+.84$) between the two, showing the dependence during the early stages of developing a self-concept on cognitive maturation and experience.

Results show that at about 18 months infants show a rapid increase in nose touching indicating a recognition of their own image and the ability to coordinate the mirror image with their own body. The schema or mental image of how their own face looks has been constructed by then, so that the unusual facial marking becomes a noticeable discrepancy. Of course, these experiments do not tell us how fine a distinction children can make between their own face and the faces of other children. If we could somehow show a child a mirror image of a different face with a nose dot, how would the child respond? We can only assume that previous experience with mirrors would have taught the child that no one else's face looks exactly like the child's and that no one else's face makes movements exactly coordinated with the bodily sensations coming from the child's own movements. Thus, self-recognition in a mirror does indeed require the building up of a quite specific schema of one's face and no other.

The growth of the ability to recognize the image of the self in a mirror closely parallels the other aspects of a child's intellectual development, e.g. object permanence, giving further weight to the belief that self-recognition is a conceptual matching process.

Other convincing evidence of self-recognition comes from the labelling reactions elicited from eleven 19-months-old infants and twelve 21-month-old infants by asking 'Who is that?' when presenting six slides: (1) infant's mother, (2) infant himself/herself, (3) 9-month-old male infant, (4) baby same age and sex as subjects, (5) adult female, (6) adult male. Lewis and Brooks (1974) found that the 19- and 21-month-old infants did not label themselves 'baby'; either their proper name was uttered or no label was produced. Moreover eleven of the twelve infants who labelled self and/or same age baby labelled them differentially. The labelling of the self-condition provides the strongest evidence for the existence of self-recognition; seven of the seventeen 19- and 21-month-olds who verbalized in the elicited condition recognized themselves and gave a proper verbal label; they did not mislabel a same-age and same-sex infant.

This early significant learning about his person, through interaction with persons and objects, facilitates the definition of the person as an independent, permanent object. Piaget (1952) claims that the development of object permanence is the major learning in the sensory-motor stage. The main point, however, is that even as early as eighteen months, the self is a concept and the way children think about themselves is closely linked with the thought processes they use to understand other aspects of their world.

Developments in cognitive ability appear crucial, as we shall see later, in the emergence of a stable sex role identity and the changing content of the self-concept at various periods of life.

The conventional view that sensory-motor functions are so important to young children that body is central to self-perception is not always borne out by research. The motor activity would seem to predominate over the sensory mode in self-description, for in a study of pre-school children by Keller, Ford and Meacham (1978), the body image was not predominant. Gellert (1975) too found that body image showed a lack of test–retest stability and may not be stabilized enough to be centrally important to the very young child. As an alternative to the body image importance Keller et al. (op. cit.) proposed that action competencies are the major feature of the self-concept. This is hypothesized from Piaget's (1954) theory in which the child's actions are instrumental in the construction of knowledge of the environment including self-knowledge. They tested this out with a small group (48 strong) of three-, four-, or five-year-olds. Data from open ended completion measures and 'I can/I am/I have' measures indicated the action category (I can) to be a more important dimension than body image (I am) or possessions (I have). More body image responses were obtained in the more structured 'I am' approach suggesting that when prompted young children can produce a good number of body image descriptions but that the frequency of these is low when more spontaneous self-descriptions are required. Keller et al. (op. cit.) claim that evidence from their study suggests that the young child's self-concept is more an action concept than a body image concept. The conflicting results between this study and theory lie in the test items used, because a test is only as reliable as its questions.

By the age of three and a half to four years children appear to be able to distinguish between an outer body or physical self visible to others, and a private inner psychological self-concept that is not accessible to others. It may be that the early mirror recognition at 18 months is no more than the self as a physical body or entity, an outer shape of skin.

Work by Flavell (1978) suggests that children of three can have a rudimentary notion of a private internal self-concept. He gave two-and-a-half- to five-year-old children tests designed to discover what they think other people can see. The experimenter and child sat facing each other around a small table on which a Snoopy doll had been placed. The child was asked to close his eyes. The experimenter would say: 'Now your eyes are closed and my eyes are open' and ask a series of questions: 'Do I see you? Do I see Snoopy? Do I see your head? Do I see your arm?' Children younger than three-and-a-half years old quite often said that the experimenter did not see them. Without exception, however, they believed that the experimenters could see Snoopy. Thus, an egocentric explanation was ruled out that these young children cannot imagine other people's perspectives. However, young children often gave different answers from older ones to questions about their visibility. When a child was hidden behind a screen so that only the child's eyes could be seen through the two eyeholes, the youngest children usually answered 'yes' to the question 'Can I see you?' while older children doubted that they were visible unless quite a substantial part of their bodies could be seen.

In another experiment Flavell (1978) asked the children whether dolls know their names and think about things the way people do. Most of the children said that a doll does not know its name and is not able to think, but that people can. The experimenter then asked: 'Where is the part of you that knows your name and thinks about things? Where do you do your thinking and knowing?' The questions were difficult for some of the these pre-school children, but fourteen out of twenty-two children did give a fairly clear localization for the thinking self, most often saying that it goes on in their heads. The experimenter then looked directly in the child's eyes and asked: 'Can I see you thinking in there?' Usually, the child thought not. Here is an example:

> (Can I see you thinking?) 'No' (Even if I look in your eyes, do I see you thinking?) 'No' (Why not?) ''Cause I don't have any big holes.' (You mean there would have to be a hole there for me to see you thinking?) Child nods. (Flavell 1978, p. 16)

Another child said his thinking processes could not be seen ''Cause the skin's over it'. These answers suggest that children as young as three have a rudimentary concept of a private, thinking self that is not visible even to someone looking directly into their eyes. They distinguish this internal self from the bodily self, which they know is visible to others, although their definition of what is meant by the visible self differs with age. Flavell suggests that the face is necessary to the child's definition of the bodily self and that this conception derives from adult training. He points out that when adults say, 'Look at me,' they usually want the child to meet their gaze. Indeed, if the child does not, the adult may turn the child's face and say 'Look at me when I talk to you'. It is not surprising then, that children come to believe that adults are referring to the face when they use personal pronouns. In contrast when adults use you, they are more likely to mean the whole physical body or any part of the body that can be recognized, e.g. I saw you in the supermarket yesterday. But when this separate internal self-concept first becomes explicit for any individual is not known. For many, it must be a gradual process determined by experiences and cognitive maturation; for a few some critical episode may suddenly clarify the self-concept out of a penumbra of shadowy feelings and cognitions.

RESEARCH ON PHYSICAL APPEARANCE AND SELF-CONCEPT

Research reveals that different body builds do elicit different reactions from others, which feeds back for some people as positive evaluation and, for others, as negative evaluation. On the basis of his body configuration, an individual typically receives consistent reactions from others which provides a framework for his body concept which is a significant part of his total self-concept.

Hippocrates has been credited with beginning work in the field of physique-behaviour relationships suggesting that personality was determined by the relative amounts of your body fluids or humours. Later work this century by Kretschmer (1925) and Sheldon (1942) also sought to determine the relationship between body type and personality. Generally, the suggestion is that three modal types of body build are associated with specific sets of personality characteristics. These are:

Endomorphic build (pyknic)—obese and rounded shape associated with the visceratonic personality characterized by its love of company, good food and comfort, its variable mood swings which in its extreme form becomes the manic-depressive psychosis.

Mesomorphic build (athletic)—upright, strong and muscular associated with the somatotonic personality, characterized by a love of adventure, challenge, and a vigorous approach to life.

Ectomorphic build (asthenic)—tall, thin and fragile associated with the cerebro-tonic personality with its restraint, inhibition, parsimony, frugality and withdrawal which, in the extreme, forms the psychotic state of schizophrenia.

Of course these relationships could well arise from stereotyping and expectancy, wherein say the possessor of a tubby physique behaves in a jovial, happy-go-lucky way in accordance with the stereotype he is aware of, and those with whom he interacts respond to him according to their beliefs about how he ought to act, thus feeding back supportive and confirmatory expectancies about current and future behaviour. This increases the tendency of the tubby person to behave stereo-typically. Staffieri (1957) writes:

> The role of an individual's body configuration in social interactions and the effects of these interactions on self-concept is an important part of the total process of personality development. (p. 101).

In studying body types and personality traits, Wells and Siegel report that characteristic body builds do elicit stereotyped responses in adults. Similarly Staffieri (op. cit. p. 101) has found evidence to suggest that a body type is capable of evoking rather common reactions from both adults and children in the form of attributed personality and behaviour traits. Specifically he found the mesomorph image was perceived as entirely favourable, while the ectomorph and endomorph images were perceived unfavourably. These findings are corroborated in part by Dibiase and Hjelle (1968) who found support for the evidence of social stereotypes among college males in that mesomorphs were perceived most favourably. Caskey and Felker (1971) also found evidence of social stereotyping of female body images in schoolgirls. These authors report that elementary school girls unfavourably stereotype the endomorph and favourably stereotype the ectomorph.

In another study, using five fifteen-inch male silhouettes representing five body builds, Brodsky (1954) demonstrated differential reactions to each silhouette, with white and black student subjects. Since all subjects responded similarly there was evidence of a cultural stereotype to body build. The muscular, athletic mesomorph was consistently ascribed very positive characteristics by both black and white subjects. The image created by the short, obese endomorph was regularly described in negative terms. The stereotyped characteristics attributed to the tall, thin ectomorphic silhouettes were less favourable than those of the mesomorph but not as disparaging as the endomorph's.

Even boys as young as six could apply behaviour stereotypes to body build in Staffieri's investigation. Here the young boys described the mesomorph as aggressive, active, outgoing and possessing leadership skills. The endomorphic build was described as delinquent and socially offensive while the ectomorphic shape was described as shy, nervous, retiring and introverted. The subjects chose the mesomorph and ectomorph child as most popular. The endomorphic child was less likely to be chosen as a friend and such children also possessed negative rejecting feelings about the body image.

Using a social distance index as a measure of social acceptance, Lerner, Karabenik and Meisels (1975) showed that children, four to eight years old, disliked the endomorphic body shape most, while the mesomorph was the most acceptable. The endomorphic body shape would seem to produce, from others, social reactions of rejection, avoidance and withdrawal, while mesomorphy elicits the opposite. Lerner et al. (op. cit.) found this trend increased with the age of the subject.

Personality attributes do seem to be associated with different body types. Kirkpatrick and Sanders (1978) used three body silhouettes to which descriptive adjectives were to be applied by five hundred subjects ranging in age from six to sixty years.

Kirkpatrick and Sanders (1978) showed that the mesomorph was overwhelmingly and consistently viewed as the most positive of the three body types but was rated somewhat more negatively as the age group increased. Participants of ages 6 through 25 rated the endomorph more negatively than the ectomorph, while those of ages 26 to 40 rated them equally. In contrast, the participants over 40 years of age viewed the ectomorph more negatively than the endomorph. Sex of subject had no bearing on the attributes given to the silhouettes.

Research suggests that children are likely to respond to each other on the basis of body image, particularly on initial encounters before they really know each other and can judge properly. The endomorph is generally likely to receive negative feedback about himself while the mesomorph generally basks in the light of favourable responses based on his idealized body dimensions. Even teachers are likely to use body type as a significant basis of their judgements about pupils with both endomorphs and ectomorphs being evaluated by those over twenty-six in a negative fashion and an ectomorphic shape being particularly the stimulus for less than desirable ascriptions from the older teacher.

Lawson (1980) investigated the relationships between self-esteem and peer-group judgements to stereotyped attitudes attached to fat, average, and thin bodies. Eighty-four Australian boys and girls, grades two, four and six, were asked to rate drawings of fat, average and thin persons of their own age and sex, on a fifty-six item adjectives check list. The check list contained positive and negative items in the physical, social, and personal dimensions. Coopersmith's SEI was used to measure self-esteem. Twelve items were taken from the check list and each subject was asked to name classmates who fitted the descriptions.

Consistent with other studies, no sex differences in responses were found in any grade. In each grade the fat figure was received unfavourably and the average figure favourably. Preference for the average figure increased significantly with grade. Grades four and six gave predominantly negative scores for the figure stimulus. No significance was found between the stereotypes attached to the drawing and the same item judgement attached to peers. This result indicates that subjects did not use body build to evaluate familiar others. Also the individual's body build did not seem to affect self-esteem as measured by the SEI. Lawson's study points out that we do not evaluate familiar others and ourselves on the same basis as we make evaluations of a stimulus drawing.

Lawson (1980) appears to be the only published researcher who has investigated the relationship thoroughly. His study takes into account the need for a relevant stimulus model about which subjects can make judgements. Knowledge of and association with the model has indicated that evaluations are context specific. When judging inanimate representations of body shapes, we make a culturally stereotyped evaluation. When the model is a known peer the same evaluation may not hold true. Many of the studies cited have used dolls or silhouettes rather than real peers. How far their findings are generalizable to such real people is unknown.

A study by Bergscheld, Walster and Borhnstedt (1973) suggested that the face was the most important aspect of the body in its influence on the self-concept of their later adolescent sample. This is disputed by Mahoney and Finch (1976) in a rather statistically more elaborate study. They were able to show that for male students, voice, chest and facial features contributed most to self-esteem. For females, overall physical attractiveness accounted for most of the variation in self-esteem between individuals with small contributions from voices, hips, calves and height. This result further confirms the importance of body image for self-concept. The conspicuous absence of those body aspects which might have been intuitively thought to be important for self-esteem—height for males and bust for females—is difficult to explain since the ideal body image for both sexes is imposed unceasingly on young people through advertising, magazines and the like. Is it that the ideal body image is changing so that the conventional findings of two decades ago, of males wanting a large physique and females wanting to weigh less, have gone? (Jourard and Secord 1954; Calden, Lundy and Schlafer 1959.)

It would appear, then, that the mesomorph is regarded as the most favourable physique from early schooldays. Dissatisfaction with the self, derived from body image, would seem to be capable of arising quite early in life.

A child's self-concept is certainly not caused by the possession of a particular body shape, but the shape does affect the feedback he receives in terms of stereotyped responses. The subject himself also knows these stereotypes and will think stereotyped things about himself, too.

The cultural stereotypes of an obese, jovial Sir John Falstaff, a tall, thin Cassius ('a lean and hungry look') and an energetic, strong Tarzan, each conjure up particular expectations of behaviour for the possessor with whom he interacts. Children often employ bodily appearance as a basis for nicknames and are experts at selecting and exaggerating, somewhat cruelly, physical characteristics that stand out. Being the target of such barbs as 'spotty', 'fatso', 'big ears', cannot help any child to feel positive about himself, as a 'defect' generalizes and comes to define the total person by name. Even the possession of a forename or surname which is peculiar, funny or 'derogatory' may provide a child with feelings about his body which are quite different from those felt by a Smith or Jones, or a John or a Mary.

BODY IMAGE AND SEX-ROLE IDENTITY

The hypothesis that physical attractiveness is positively correlated with happiness, psychological health and self-esteem was tested with 211 men and women under-graduates by Mathes and Khan (1975). Physical attractiveness was measured by judges' ratings while, happiness, psychological health (neuroticism) and self-esteem were measured by self-report inventories. Physical attractiveness was found to correlate positively with happiness ($r = +0.37$), negatively with neuroticism ($r = -0.22$) and positively with self-esteem ($r = +0.24$) for women but not for men (who correspondingly rated $r = +0.09$, $+0.03$, and -0.04 respectively). These results were accounted for by the suggestion that physical attractiveness 'buys' more for women students than for men and the most prominent outcomes obtained by physical attractiveness—friends and dates—are of greater value to women under-graduates than men. Thus, an attractive woman may obtain better outcomes from men than an equally attractive man obtains from women. If physical attractiveness as an input is more important to women than men, it follows that the correlations between attractiveness and happiness, psychological health and self-esteem should be higher for women than men.

A second explanation may be that the outcomes which both sexes obtain, as a result of physical attractiveness, that is of friends and dates, are of greater importance and value for women than for men. Because affiliative needs of women have been found to be greater than those of men, friends and dates may be more important to women than men and so positive correlations between attractiveness and happiness, psychological health and self-esteem, exist for women only. Supporting this is the fact that our culture defines as successful a woman who affiliates while a successful man is the man who achieves.

Guy et al. (1980) sought to establish a relationship between body image and another major element of self-concept, perceived masculinity and femininity. This they did, showing a clear relationship for the mesomorph male and the ectomorph female; the mesomorph male was sex-typed masculine while the ectomorph female was sex-typed feminine. The remaining body types for both males and females were not clearly sex-typed masculine or feminine.

The masculine orientation of the male mesomorph image supports earlier findings. Specifically, this body image has been reported to be the ideal male physique. Guy's findings show that the sex-role traits perceived as ideally masculine have also been linked to this body image. Accordingly, it may be argued that the mesomorph male provides a stimulus which is consistent with cultural learning. In particular, masculine traits may be given to this body image through inference termed 'reasoning by analogy'. If the mesomorph male is the ideal body image, then he must also possess the ideal masculine traits.

The feminine orientation of the female ectomorph image also supports past research. Caskey and Felker (1971) have identified the ectomorph as the ideal female body image. This choice has been influenced by our culture's emphasis on physical attractiveness in females, and thinness has come to be associated with physical attractiveness in women. Consequently, reasoning by analogy, it is not surprising that the sex-role traits representing ideal femininity would be linked to the ideal female body image.

The findings are not meant to suggest that one's sex-role orientation is affected by one's body type. However, the existence of a relationship provides support for Staffieri's (1957) notion that individuals may respond to each other in consistent and patterned ways, a self-fulfilling prophecy. If, as Lerner and Korn (1972) suggest, 'the physiognomy of the person stimulus provides a primary salient dimension of others' approach behaviours towards a person' (p. 919), it seems conceivable that such interaction helps in the formation of one's own sex-role orientation.

TEACHERS' AND PUPILS' PHYSICAL ATTRIBUTES

We cannot expect teachers to suspend their culturally learned responses to, and judgements of, such physical stimuli as weight, height, cleanliness, attractiveness, disability, etc. Neither can we expect pupils to suspend their interpretation of and feedback to teachers in terms of the teacher's appearance. Unfortunately, most of the literature focusing specifically on teacher response to the physical characteristics of pupils is anecdotal rather than research-based; relevant research tends to cover the development of self-concept rather than the relationship between teacher behaviour and pupil body concept. Thus, it is within the confines of these research limitations that the teacher's impact on pupil body image can be examined.

A child entering school has already acquired an operating self-concept as a physical entity. The child has had psychological experiences through which reflections of his, or her, physical form and performances have been transmitted. Yet, this concept of physical self is not so set that it is unaffected by new reflections received in the classroom. Generally, it may be reinforced or altered by new psychological experiences.

Pupils carry with them a number of characteristics that may evoke responses from the teacher and the classroom, responses which may influence the formation of self-concept, e.g. sex, body build, race, physical appearance, physical defects or anomalies and age.

While physical disability and ethnic qualities have a dramatic influence on their bearers to meet the ideals and standards of the core or majority culture in body appearance, it must not be forgotten that even minor skin blemishes, spectacles or imperceptible weight differences from the ideal can be a burden, particularly as it is the individual's subjective assessment that these are 'defects' that affect his self-attitudes. In fact, no defect may be apparent to the external observer, but if the unhappy bearer believes he does carry one, then his behaviour and self-concept will be based on that belief. I have seen a teenage, anorexic girl, wafer thin, look into a full-length mirror and claim she was overweight! Objective facts generally matter less than subjective feelings, evaluations and interpretations, which appear as objective to the individual.

Without doubt, physical size and shape do influence the quality of an individual's life by determining the experiences encountered and the self-reflections received. Children's classroom experiences are often dictated by their size or body type. Short pupils spend a great deal of time in front rows; tall pupils fetch material from top shelves and pin up classwork displays; heavy-set girls play the 'grannies' while tall girls play the 'queen'; small boys and girls play the children; stocky boys carry or move the equipment. All of these children know how others perceive their bodies. They know the advantages and disadvantages of their size and shape and may come to rely upon or resent their physical image.

In a study by Walker (1962) mesomorphic children received more favourable ratings from others, and body build was valid for predicting behaviour in these children. He noted that mesomorphs of both sexes are generally assertive, competitive, fearless and impulsive whereas ectomorphs are typically aloof. Teachers were able to predict pupil behaviours associated with physique, particularly for boys. Furthermore, children with certain body types were apparently channelled into specific kinds of activities: one male body group was directed towards more physical, motor activities while one female body group was guided into social behaviours. All this needs further investigation. For example, do parents and teachers consistently stress certain kinds of behaviour according to their perception of the child's body type? Does the school experience affect self-concept differently for pupils with different body types? Is teacher–pupil interaction influenced more by physical characteristics than personality attributes? Do pupils base their image of the 'ideal' body on particular teachers, parents or other models such as sports heroes or heroines? Which teacher behaviour alters or reinforces pupils' body image? We do not yet have enough answers to comprehend fully the role of body image in school. Feeling and intuition still play a large part in our conventional wisdom on this issue.

We might assume, for example, that physically attractive children receive more attention from their teachers. However, this is not always the case. Adams and Cohen (1974) found an interaction between pupil facial attractiveness and the frequency and type of teacher contact with students during the first few days of school. Both kindergarten and 9-year-old pupils rated below average in facial attractiveness by their teachers received more supportive and neutral contact from these teachers than did pupils rated above average. This interaction was not observed with 12-year-old subjects. However, because this study used a small restricted sample (three females teaching upper middle-class boys in a private school) the findings cannot be generalized.

Adams and Cohen (op. cit.) suggest that the observed teachers, recognizing our culture's value for attractiveness, may have been giving forced attention to the younger children whom they perceived as unattractive. The fact that teachers at the upper age level did not respond to the facial attractiveness of pupils could indicate a shift in teacher concerns. Teachers of younger pupils may be concerned about the children's first encounter with school, while those whose pupils are more experienced, may be more concerned about establishing authority and control. Teacher concern for self and task (i.e. concern establishing and maintaining control) can make the teacher less receptive to pupil stimuli such as facial attractiveness. An alternative explanation enables us to interpret the findings according to Combs's (1969) 'helping' dimensions. Assuming a difference between the sets of first and seventh grade teachers, the instructors of the younger children, taking a helping stance, were positive and more open. This allowed them to respond to behavioural cues given by the unattractive pupils—cues not noticed by the other teachers, who were limited by a more closed attitude. The lower age-range teachers may have perceived these cues (facial expressions such as lowered eyes, or body language such as immobility, droop or withdrawal) as indications of fear or lack of self-confidence. Since pupil behaviours were not observed and recorded, this is pure speculation based on the supposition that unattractive children are likely to have negative self-concepts, and that such cues were more prevalent among unattractive students. Perhaps, when unattractive children confront new situations and people, their negative feelings are intensified in anticipation of more unflattering self-reflections.

Unfortunately, we need to question the perceptiveness of some teachers in regard to pupil body concept. A study by Clifford (1975) indicates that infant teachers may be unaware of the important role that the sense of the physical self plays in pupil self-concept development and peer relationships. Passport type photographs of 5-year-olds previously rated according to high/low, male/female attractiveness were attached to simulated reports and distributed to many infant school teachers. On an accompanying opinion sheet, teachers were asked to estimate (on the basis of the information and photographs) pupil IQ, success in peer relations, degree of parental interest in pupil achievement, level at which the pupil's education would terminate and pupil's self-concept. Responses to the questionnaire indicated an attractiveness effect on teachers' estimates of pupil IQ, parental interest and level of future education, with the high attractiveness pupils eliciting more positive responses. However, teacher estimates of pupil self-concept and success in peer relationships were not characterized by a significant attractiveness effect. Evidently, teachers were influenced by appearance when making their own estimates of the pupil, but not when projecting a self or peer perception of the pupil. These teachers seem to believe that appearance plays no part in peer relationships or pupil self-concept.

Clifford (op. cit.) further concluded that teachers, though influenced by first impressions of physical attractiveness, are not necessarily affected by these early impressions in predicting the long-term academic success of pupils. There is evidence in both the Clifford (op. cit.) and Adams and Cohen (op. cit.) studies that pupil attractiveness may colour a teacher's expectations before actual pupil performance data are available. Research does not tell us whether, or to what extent, initial expectations (rather than subsequent perceptions) altered in light of the pupil's performance, are reflected in the teacher's behaviour. Therefore, we can only speculate about the nature of the behavioural dialogues and psychological experiences of the pupils involved in these studies.

When research deals directly with the pupil's value of bodily appearance, however, we can expect changes in the concept of physical self. Cole, Oetting and

Miskimmins (1969) investigated the effectiveness of a group treatment programme in producing self-concept changes among female adolescents with behavioural problems. The ten-week programme focused on physical appearance and social behaviour. Subjects were divided into two treatment groups, one led by professional counsellors, the other by lay volunteers. Comparing before and after the tests indicated that the self-concepts of girls in both treatment groups changed more positively and consistently than those of girls in the control group, who represented a normal female adolescent population. More positive views of physical appearance were clearly associated with more positive views of themselves overall.

The teacher's verbal behaviour should also be considered in relation to the pupil's bodily self-concept. Teachers who refer to a child's continual clumsiness or lack of coordination, or who express preferences for particular physical characteristics are undoubtedly affecting pupil body concept.

SUMMARY

Body image is a basic element in each person's self-concept. Self-awareness of physical body appears to develop around 18 months of age, and arises out of the welter of body sensations experienced by the infant. Cognitive development aids the understanding of the permanence of the physical body.

Research has found that certain body configurations connote specific temperament and personality traits. Such associations are evidently established quite early in life and lead then to the development of stereotyped body images. Mesomorphic (muscular, athletic) body shapes are always highly evaluated. Ectomorphs and endomorphs are generally given negative attributes, particularly the latter shape.

Physical appearance is a very potent agent for attracting particular social responses. This feedback creates, to a considerable degree, the way a person feels about himself. The person learns through cultural stereotyping, expectations and nicknames, that it is not a good thing to deviate too far in body size and shape from the mesomorphic ideal.

Little research exists on teacher response to pupils' physical characteristics, though there is a tendency for classroom experience to be dictated by such characteristics.

4

Children's Self-Concept and Parental Behaviour

The family appears to be the major unit of society throughout the globe even though it can take on various forms. The family unit provides all the initial indications to the child as to whether he is loved or not, accepted or not, a success or a failure, because until schooldays the family is virtually his only place of learning. The first five years of life are seen by most psychologists as the ones in which the basic framework of personality and self-conceptualization is erected. The young child is very vulnerable, with a high degree of physical, social and emotional dependence on the family group. He knows few other people and all his needs are supplied within this group. Thus, parents and siblings become highly significant others, with whom the child interacts daily. These first human relationships teach the child what to expect later in his dealings with others. As the parents handle their infant, satisfying or failing to satisfy its needs for food, love, comfort and security, they have an unremitting influence on it. The child begins to feel the world is either benign and to be trusted, or hostile and not to be trusted. If a child's first interpersonal relationships give him the wrong view of life at the outset what hope is there for the future? Erikson's (1963) views on the role of the parents in helping the development of a basic sense of trust and security during infancy and striking a happy balance between autonomy and dependence in the pre-school child have already been noted in Chapter 1.

Although in reality it is presumptive of psychologists to classify types of parents into neat boxes, much time and effort has been devoted to this. Such packages of child-rearing practices are really half-truths born of tidy minds. Evidence on child-rearing practices is not of very high reliability or validity, derived as it often is from subjective recollections of child and parent. There are fairly consistent trends found, however, in the many researches on the effects of authoritarian, permissive, rejecting and accepting home practices on the child's behaviour and personality. The fact that self-concepts of children are influenced by parental practices is not surprising considering the parents' generally accepted roles as significant others, their dispensations of rewards and punishments, and their modelling and identification functions.

It was Stott (1939) who first noted the pattern of child rearing that promoted positive self-conceptualization after studying 1800 adolescents. Those teenagers coming from homes where there was acceptance, mutual confidence and compatibility between parents and children, were better adjusted more independent and thought more positively about themselves. Those from homes where family discord reigned were in general, less well adjusted.

A perusal of psychological, social and educational writings on the self-concept shows that a wide variety of family variables are supposedly relevant to children's self-concepts. Most frequently mentioned are the following: parents' child-rearing practices; interparental relationships; absence of one parent through death or divorce; working status of the mother; family size and birth order of the children. Theories about most of these variables are poorly developed, ambiguous, and there are few researches on most of them. Therefore this chapter focuses selectively on some of the available research.

It is a generally accepted premise in the psychological literature that the family plays a significant role in the development of a child's self-concept. We tend to assume that parents, serving as models and as sources of reinforcement, mould and shape the child's ideas and feelings about the kind of person he is and would like to be.

Both the theory and the research in this area lean heavily on identification and learning in exploring child development. (Chapter 5 explores identification and sex role self-concept.) The child's dependence on his parents and his affection for them makes many psychologists believe that parents have a unique opportunity to reinforce selectively a child's learning and to influence his general perception of himself, the behaviour to which he should aspire and his self-acceptance (including his negative feelings and limitations).

Parental reinforcement and the rewards of imitating their parents presumably play important parts in shaping children's 'actual' characteristics and behaviours. Partly as a function of these actual characteristics (especially as they are reflected in the child by others' reactions) children develop self-conceptualizations. However, self-conceptualizations about 'actual' characteristics which meet with disapproval from significant others may be excluded or distorted (Rogers 1951). Hence accuracy of self-conceptualization may depend partly on unconditional regard from significant others, especially parents, as Rogers has indicated.

So far as children's over-all self-acceptance is concerned, this is presumably affected greatly by parental self-acceptance, since a self-rejecting parent would be unable to give adequate love and unable to provide an adequate model of self-acceptance. Rogers (1951) stressed the value of the parents' unconditional positive regard for self and child.

Most studies use small numbers of subjects, instruments of unknown reliability and validity and depend on children's and parents' retrospective reports which are notoriously biased, distorted and badly remembered. Hence even the reliability and validity of some of the better known research in this area is suspect and results should be regarded as pointers rather than as definitive facts.

THE COOPERSMITH STUDY

Stanley Coopersmith (1967) in *Antecedents of Self-Esteem* looked at the conditions that enhance self-esteem. The subjects were grouped initially into five levels of self-esteem. His results, however, deal exclusively with only three levels of self-esteem. He discounts psychoanalytic theories and those that support theories of permissiveness. He points to the relationship a child has with his family as critical to self-esteem rather than general social conditions.

Self-esteem, as presented in Coopersmith's study, is the judgement of personal worthiness that is conveyed to others by each individual in what he says and what he does not say; by what he does and what he does not. The self-evaluations that the individual makes and customarily maintains are private and subjective. They can be studied, nevertheless, Coopersmith argues, in their manifestations as overt behaviour.

Assessment measures were used with both the boys and their mothers. Each of the 82 mothers who participated in the study were interviewed for about two hours. The questions covered social background, pregnancy and infancy, developmental history of the child, current parent–child relationships, parent's appraisal of the child and interviewer's appraisal of the mother. In all, there were 182 questions, 116 asking for straightforward information and 66 more open questions (Coopersmith 1967, Appendix D, 'Mother's Interview', pp. 274–9). In addition, the mothers completed a questionnaire of 80 items taken from the Parent Attitude Research Instrument (PARI) (Coopersmith 1967 Appendix C, 'Mother's Questionnaire', pp. 269–73). This scale consists of 14 subscales grouped under three headings: (a) democracy domination, (b) acceptance–rejection and (c) indulgence autonomy.

Information from the child came from his responses to the Thematic Apperception Test (TAT). Thus, information on parent–child interactions was obtained from both the mother and the child and this included information concerning the father's attitudes and behaviours also, since the father was not contacted directly.

To measure the child's self-esteem from the perspective of the subject, a specially constructed 50-item self-esteem inventory, the Coopersmith Self-Esteem Inventory (SEI) was used (Coopersmith 1967, Appendix A, 'Self-Esteem Inventory', pp. 265–6). For each item the child was asked to check whether it was 'like me' or 'unlike me'. Sample items are: 'I'm proud of my schoolwork' and 'Most people are better liked than I am'.

For another measure of the child's self-esteem, teachers were asked to rate each child on a 15-item five-point scale of behaviours, the Behaviour Rating Form (BRF); e.g. 'To what extent does this child show a sense of self-esteem, self-respect, and appreciation of his own worthiness?' (Coopersmith 1967, Appendix B, 'Behavior Rating Form' (BRF), pp. 267–8.)

The 85 subjects were not chosen at random. They met the specification, pre-determined for five identified types of self-esteem. From a group of 1748, 85 boys between the ages of ten and twelve were selected. All the boys were middle-class urban school children who lived with their parents. All the children were identified by the schools as being of normal behaviour and intellect. The subjects were assigned to high, medium and low self-esteem groups on the basis of two criteria; that of their self-esteem score and its match with the ratings of teacher and mother.

An overall pattern of 90 per cent agreement between self-evaluation and behavioural valuation occurred. Verbal and subjective self-attitudes often seemed to be congruent with behavioural expressions as assessed by the other observers. Only high, medium and low esteem groups are discussed by Coopersmith.

Parental characteristics were interpolated on the basis of the mothers' responses and that of the sons. It was concluded that the self-esteem of the mother influenced her choice of husband. The choice of husband, while this was not explicitly stated by Coopersmith, would influence the degree of harmony and the general functioning pattern of the family's relationships.

Statistical results dealing with the relationship between self-esteem and some 58 family variables were presented in tables as percentages of responses that were characteristic of parents of low, medium and high self-esteem boys. The results were expressed in terms of whether the differences were statistically significant or not.

The majority of the significant tests were based on statements made by the mother concerning, for example, her acceptance of the mother role or her ideas concerning the child's right to privacy. These subjective reports make the Coopersmith study more a study of perception by, and of, the parent for self and child, than a study of more objective factors influencing the child's self-esteem.

Of the 58 family variables in this study, 38 are significant at the 0.05 level, fifteen are not significant, while significance or non-significance is not reported for the remaining seven.

Low Esteem Condition

Low self-esteem was closely related to the parental demand for accommodating behaviour. Accommodating behaviours were:

obedience
adjustment of others
helplessness
good grooming
getting along with the peer group.

Success which is predicated upon pleasing others rather than upon concern for achievement seems to lead to low self-esteem.

Twenty per cent of the low self-esteem group came from homes where parents remarried. This particular marital status was negligible in other groups. Conflict between parents was more pronounced in families with low self-esteem subjects. The mothers in these families (76.6 per cent) were dissatisfied with the relationship between husband and son. The mother was much less likely to feel that the father took an active and supportive role in rearing their child. This was taken as an indication of possible conflict in other areas of family life.

Such parents who preferred to keep their offspring submissive and dependent lowered self-esteem and kept children tied to their parents. But such children are psychologically crippled, distrustful of the outside world, lacking self-worth.

Medium Esteem

Analysis of medium self-esteem subjects revealed a number of features common to that particular condition. Parents of the medium-condition group were more likely to be protective and indulgent. They seemed to have lower aspirations than did either high- or low-condition parents. Their more modest goals allowed them to be more accepting of their childrens' performances. They tended to be more anxious about their child's independent actions, e.g. Coopersmith describes hesitancy in allowing staying overnight at a friend's house. The boys were more likely to have more limited private personal experiences away from the family than were other self-esteem conditions. The parents allowed less self-reliance. This group was more dependent on others to supply their self-evaluation than was the high self-esteem group.

High Esteem

Mothers in the high self-esteem group were almost always satisfied (93.3 per cent) with the father's relationship with his son. The boys were likely to concur with their mother's evaluation of the father–son relationship. They were likely to view their fathers as confidants.

Decision-making prerogatives in the homes of high self-esteem subjects were most clearly established. The patterns of authority and responsibility were more clearly delineated than in other conditions. One parent made major decisions. The decision being made, other family members complied with its provisions. Ordinary decisions of everyday life were more likely to be shared. This is in keeping with the support for the decision or family behaviour standard pattern that is found in these families. A pattern of mutual trust and acceptance seemed the rule. Coopersmith states that while fathers most frequently made the major decisions in the homes of the high condition subjects, it was decision making by family consensus that was important.

The high esteem household is one of greater integration and solidarity of purpose. The mother views herself and her husband more positively. The child views the parents as more successful. He feels more confident in patterning himself on the model which they provide. He feels more equipped to deal effectively and decisively with everyday problems. Stress and anxiety are less common. He possesses a more realistic and positive view of his environment and of himself.

High self-esteem boys held higher aspirations than low self-esteem boys—a difference that reflected the greater value parents of the former placed on achieving standards of excellence. These parents established definite standards, provided feedback on level of success and offered guidance on what would be required to obtain success. The high self-esteem child was presented with challenges to his capacities and encouraged to appreciate his strengths and weaknesses. Thus high self-esteem boys had higher goals and were more successful in attaining them. Low aspirations and lack of confidence were characteristic of those who had low self-esteem. Parental expectations (or lack of them) set up a self-fulfilling prophecy (often so noticeable in school).

Coopersmith describes high self-esteem boys as able to approach tasks and persons with the expectation that they will be well received and successful. Their favourable self-attitudes lead them to accept their own opinions and place credence and trust in their reactions and conclusions. This permits them to follow their own judgements when there is a difference of opinion and also permits them to consider novel ideas.

The self-trust that accompanies worthiness is likely to provide the conviction that one is correct and the courage to express these convictions. The attitude and expectations that lead the individual with high self-esteem to greater social independence and creativity also lead him to more assertive and vigorous social actions. They are more likely to be participants than listeners in group discussions, they report less difficulty in forming friendships and they will express opinions even when they know these opinions may meet with a hostile reception. Among the factors that underlie and contribute to these actions are their lack of preoccupation with personal problems. Lack of self-consciousness permits them to present their ideas in a full and forthright fashion.

This assessment of the effect of self-esteem on behaviour is consistent with therapists' observations of depressed patients. Depressed people are a perfect contrast. They lack confidence in their perceptions and judgements, do not expect to be able to influence other people and, hence, hesitate to express their opinions.

Siblings

Do children born into smaller families have higher self-esteem than those born into large families? Coopersmith says not. Family ordinal position, however, does seem to be linked to self-esteem. While 70 per cent of the low and medium condition subjects were not first-born children, only 42 per cent of the high condition subjects were not first-born children. First-born and only children seem to have an environment better suited to self-esteem. The relationship between the amount of attention a child receives from his parents and the family size appears to be complex. Attention, in and of itself does not predetermine the outcome of an individual's self-evaluation.

High self-esteem subjects reported themselves as close to rather than distant from or antagonistic toward siblings. Harmony in this relationship seems to have been generalized outside the family group to non-family playmates. The high self-esteem subjects as a group were socially skilled youngsters who get along well with other children. Coopersmith provides a reasonable explanation for this finding. High self-esteem individuals have less need to bully to prove their worth. Their parents have defined their social condition clearly and realistically. Rules conducive to cooperation are enforced vigorously and concern, attention and love are felt by their offspring. There is consequently little sibling rivalry and jealousy in these well-structured homes.

Children's Friends

Mothers of boys in the high self-esteem group knew over half of their sons' friends. Of the mothers of the low self-esteem group over a third did not know their sons' playmates to any great degree. There is definitely an overlap between the conditions of high and low self-esteem in the degree of reported acquaintanceship between these two conditions. It is certainly plausible that the parental ignorance of the child's friends can be interpreted as distrust rather than evidence of trust depending on the child's assessment of his place and value in the family. Phenomenological independence in the child's decision making is one of the Coopersmith's assumptions in his monograph.

Infant Feeding Practices

Controversy over the relative merits of breast and bottle as sources of infant nourishment persists. Breast feeding is generally assumed to produce happier babies. Coopersmith's research does not support assertions that breast feeding in itself communicates more concern, love and affection to the children than bottle feeding. He finds that it is confidence in the feeding method that aids self-esteem rather than the method *per se*. Guilt and uneasiness in the mother's attitude towards her practices is associated with low self-esteem. Infant practices can be safely subsumed under more general child-rearing practices. Consistency seems to be the key parental characteristic in the high self-esteem group.

Childhood Problem Areas

Questions were included about childhood problem areas. There were situations found in a normal childhood such as:

   bed wetting
   frequent illness
   school-related stress
   thumb sucking
   academic failure.

Two-thirds of the low condition reported problems in contrast to only one-third of the high condition. No indication of the medium condition was found in the report. It is assumed that it was intermediary between the other two conditions. Childhood problems of a repetitive nature are associated with low self-esteem but certainly not predictive or it.

Trauma

Coopersmith could find no evidence to indicate the importance of severe but single traumatic occurrence. While this problem was not clearly defined it was understood that it meant occurrences such as a broken leg or a death in the family. He found no support for dramatic turning points in the formation of self-esteem.

Acceptance

The value, a child has, to an accepting parent in a healthy child–parent relationship is not achieved but is *ascribed.* Being their child is enough in their eyes to guarantee him their love and parental approval. The acceptance of the child is unconditional, regardless of his specific intellectual abilities or physical endowment. Acceptance of the child himself is distinctly separate from any judgements the parents might make about his performance.

The rejecting parent, on the other hand, views the child with disinterest, disapproval and distaste. The child is a legal responsibility and a financial burden. Rejection in the form of a solicitous overprotective concern is as deleterious as neglect and abuse. Low condition mothers were least likely (43.3 per cent) to express warm accepting attitudes towards their children. This contrasts with the medium condition (78.8 per cent) and the high (82.4 per cent) condition groups.

Expressed acceptance cannot, however, be considered a necessary antecedent of self-esteem. Children whose mothers did not express strong indications of acceptance also were found within the high self-esteem condition. Again it is clear that the child's view of whether his parents are accepting is at least as important as the particular child-rearing practice that is employed.

The relating of specific antecedent parental practice to specific personality variables has been made difficult by just this phenomena. No single practice was in itself sufficient or accurate index of acceptance, Coopersmith argued.

Permissiveness and Strictness

Permissiveness was most strongly supported by early adherents of psychoanalytic theory. Greater impulse expression and gratification was suggested. Coopersmith's findings support strictness, however, rather than permissiveness as the chosen child-rearing method. He strongly advocates a clearly defined, structured and enforced set of demands as the central element in adequate and good child-rearing practices. Six times as many mothers in the high self-esteem group as in the other groups believed that strictness had beneficial consequences. They regarded discipline as very important. Nine out of ten of these mothers carefully and consistently enforced established rules. Only six out of ten medium and low condition mothers were as zealous. Demands, clearly stated expectation and enforcement of family rules are much more a part of high condition family life.

The high-esteem child (100 per cent) generally agreed with his parents' discipline measures and opinions. There was only a 60 per cent agreement from the subjects in the other two conditions. High self-esteem subjects were generally more favourably disposed toward the view of their families. Reward was more frequently used, but punishment was perceived by the child in the high condition as deserved and just.

On the other hand, the freedom to explore the environment in an unrestricted and unguided way coupled with consistent permissiveness appears to engender anxiety, doubts about self-worth, low expectations of success and an inability to develop sound social relationships based on mutual respect.

Punishment seems to have been interpreted by the child in the context of other expressions of attentive and respectful treatment. Restrictions appear to make harsh punishment to enforce control unnecessary. The key to self-esteem seems to be favourable but not extreme attitudes of acceptance.

Democratic Practices and the Family

For Coopersmith, the social analysis model terms of democracy and domination are not ideas and concepts that are properly applicable as such to child-rearing practices. By its very nature the parent–child relationship is one of inequality. Six areas of inequality are suggested:

knowledge
skill
experience
control over family material resources
physical strength
financial control.

That the child may be admired and desired by his parents does not offset this disadvantage. Cultural and social mores support the superior–inferior relationship in advocating obedience and respect not a democratic interplay between parent and child. Parent–child relationships of dependency on the part of one and responsibility on the part of the other are very long-lasting. Dissolution of this unequal partnership rarely occurs before the child attains the age of fifteen.

The family inevitably restricts what is subject to discussion and change. Full participation in making decisions cannot exist for young children. Parental respect is shown in their efforts to clarify and justify policies and a willingness to permit free expression of opinion. The caring parent views the child as a separate and distinct individual rather than as an extension of himself, but he does require compliance to the family behaviour role. Rules and expectations sometimes will be changed as the result of family discussion but only when overriding principles are more fully served by the change.

Other Issues

Surprisingly, Coopersmith found no relationship between self-esteem and physical attractiveness, size of family, height, social class or income. The boys in Coopersmith's study appear to have evaluated themselves, their achievements and treatments within the bounds of their own interpersonal environment and had not taken more general and abstract norms of society into account. Daily personal relationships provided the major sources of self-evaluation rather than external standards. This, too, was the conclusion noted by Rosenberg in his major study (see p. 80) and by workers investigating the self-concepts of minority, often coloured, groups (see Chapter 14).

Coopersmith showed, too, that style of drawing, and other creative work differed between boys varying in self-esteem. Boys with high self-esteem were more creative and original in their drawings than those with lower self-confidence, with their drawings characterized by sensitivity and humour. The drawings of boys with medium self-esteem were more restrained and static, less complex and less vigorous. The boys with low self-esteem draw small, distorted figures indicative of their lack of confidence. The figures drawn by the three categories of boys suggested distinct differences in their perceptions of themselves and other people.

Summary and Evaluation of Coopersmith's Findings

The data point to discipline in the home as the most important antecedent to self-esteem. Perceived acceptance and the self-esteem rating of the mother also appear to be critical factors. Being a first-born child was also found to be predictive of high self-esteem. Remarried parents were found to produce the greatest number of low-esteem children. Discord between the parents generally is related to low self-esteem as were repetitious childhood problems such as bed wetting and thumb sucking. The child's own phenomonological individuality had to be considered as a factor in the variance of self-esteem.

Coopersmith found no support for social class, religion or the method of infant feeding as predictors of self-esteem levels. Adler's theory of physical deficiency leading to compensatory striving does not seem to be supported by either the trauma or non-serious childhood problem results.

Unconditional acceptance of the child should be moderated by favourable but not extreme attitudes towards his actual performance. Discipline, firm and fair, and seen as such by the child himself was found to be necessary for favourable self-esteem. Firm and fair discipline practices were marked by attainable standards. Unambiguous and accepted values provided a clear reliable gauge by which the child could judge his performance in terms of success or failure. Success was more likely than failure in the secure and structured homes of the high self-esteem group. Knowledge of general principles rather than of isolated admonitions allowed the child the self-confidence necessary for postitive self-esteem.

Coopersmith focuses primarily on the child's treatment by significant others, a return again to the concept of the looking-glass self. Family members are the significant others whose attitudes matter most when children form their own self-concept in his view, although other workers such as Kirchner and Vondraek (1975) would not accept this view of the parents.

In Coopersmith's results we find some confirmation for the idea of the looking-glass self; parents are a child's social mirror and if children see that parents regard them with affection, respect and trust then they come to think of themselves as worthy of affection, respect and trust. It comes as a surprise to find strict control related to high self-esteem. Coopersmith provides several explanations for this:

1. Firm management facilitates the development of firm inner controls. When parents give children a clear idea of the right way to behave, they are providing clues that maximize successful interactions and minimize anxiety about parental response. Children experience a predictable, ordered social environment and hence feel in control. Low self-esteem emerges from a vague and inconsistent programme of social reinforcement.
2. Clear, firmly enforced rules help children to establish clear self-definitions. Children are compelled to acknowledge forces outside of themselves and to recognize the needs and powers of other people. They are given an opportunity to learn the difference between wish and reality and the distinction between self and others.
3. Children see parental restrictions as proof of parental concern about their welfare. The parent who says, 'Do whatever you like but don't bother me' is transmitting a message which says that the child is not worthy of concern.

Significantly Coopersmith found that parents can combine strictness and democracy and that this pattern, rather than strictness and autocracy, is associated with high self-esteem.

We have been interpreting Coopersmith's findings as if parental practices directly produced high self-esteem but the causal relationship can also go the other way. Many high self-esteem boys said that when they were punished, they usually deserved it and that they usually agreed with the views of their parents. Mothers of these children reported that punishment was usually effective in correcting children's misbehaviour and that they had good rapport with their sons—involving a mutual trust and willingness to accommodate to each other. The high self-esteem boys are relatively easy to live with, self-confident and competent in school and in their social relationships. They share their parents' values and accept their discipline. Surely such children are very easy to accept, love and respect. Perhaps these parents seldom use coercive, punitive methods with these children because they don't need to—the children yield to reasoning. We cannot be sure whether the parents' firm, loving and democratic treatment of these boys has led to their high self-esteem or whether the boys' competence, trustworthiness and cooperative attitude towards their parents have enabled their parents to be loving, firm and democratic. The influences likely run both ways.

The pattern of rearing of high self-esteem boys in Coopersmith's study is a recurrent theme in psychological literature. Such a climate of acceptance coupled with positive non-contingent reinforcement reappears in many situations, for instance, in Rogers's client-centred therapy.

Other studies report similar findings to Coopersmith. For example, Medinnus and Curtis (1963) noted that mothers with high self-esteem have children who also possess high self-esteem. Similarly, low self-esteem children tend to come from families with low self-esteem mothers. It would seem that high self-esteem parents convey confidence, trust, love and acceptance of their offspring which feed the latter's self-concept through feedback and through identification with the attributes of liked parents.

In summing up his results Coopersmith says:

> The most general statement about the antecedents of self-esteem can be given in terms of three conditions: total or nearly total acceptance of the children by their parents, clearly defined and enforced limits, and the respect and latitude for individual action that exist within the defined limits. (p. 236).

Generalizations tell only part of the story, as Coopersmith points out in his summary. Looking at the details of the statistical data, a somewhat more complicated picture of the situation emerges. Consider, for example, the fact that about 12 per cent of the mothers of the high self-esteem group did not enforce limits consistently and with care and that, on the other hand, 60 per cent of the mothers of the low self-esteem group did enforce limits (table 10.3 p. 186). These figures and others would suggest, says Coopersmith, that self-esteem is the result of no single parent variable, but a combination of positive conditions together with a 'minimum of devaluating conditions'—the whole forming a pattern (p. 240).

Wylie (1979) criticizes this study for having too small a sample and for omitting any material from the father. Any information about the father's attitude and behaviour comes second-hand from interpretations made by the mother and son. The more intensive work was done with only white middle-class boys in a fairly narrow age range. We cannot be sure that the same results would have been obtained if his studies had included girls or children from a wider range of ethnic and social backgrounds. It would also be useful to know whether changes take place with age in the way parental methods relate to children's self-concepts.

Another complicating factor is the matter of the grouping of the boys. Originally there were five groups with seventeen boys in each set-up using the combined scores from the SEI and BRF as follows: High-High, Medium-Medium, Low-Low, High-Low, and Low-High. But in reporting results in the 58 tables involving family variables, the five-fold classification is used in only four of the tables, per cent of responses is given for three groups only and the general heading of the groups is 'Subjective Self-Esteem'. No reason for this shift from five groups to three is given (High-Medium-Low) nor is a restatement made concerning the number of boys in each of the three groups.

Wylie (1979) itemizes discrepancies in Coopersmith's text which do not accord with the tabulated figures. For instance, Coopersmith describes the parents of low-esteem children by saying that 'they rely upon harsh treatment to exercise their control over their children' (p. 215). But table 10.5 (p. 192), 'Type of Control Generally Employed by Mother When Rules Are Violated', shows that the difference among the parents of the three groups of boys is not statistically significant.

Despite the continuing interest in the findings of Coopersmith's study, a more sanguine current view is that it is a potpourri of subjective and behavioural variables, replete with confusing and conflicting statements making the validity of the results difficult to assess.

THE ROSENBERG STUDY

This study is reported in Rosenberg's (1965) book, *Society and the Adolescent Self-Image.* He investigated the factors associated with level of self-esteem in over 5000 adolescents. He looked at a wide variety of factors, some related to society's general structure (social class, religion and ethnic group), while other factors were inter-familial such as birth order, marriage rupture, parental interest in child, and so on.

Societal Factors

Rosenberg (1965) commenced to consider the relationship of the social structure to self-esteem and, in particular, considered the effect of social class, religion and race on self-esteem. If a person's self-esteem is influenced by what others think of him, then there is reason to expect those with the highest prestige in society—the upper class—to be more likely than others to accept themselves. At the same time, it must be recognized that Rosenberg is dealing with adolescents. Their location in the stratification scheme is not based upon their personal achievements but upon the prestige of the parents. It is thus possible that, within this age group, the neighbour-hood, family, or peer group, rather than prestige in society, may predominantly influence the individual's feeling of self-worth.

Rosenberg found that children from higher social classes are somewhat more likely to accept themselves than those from the lower social strata. Whereas 51 per cent of the members of the highest class ranked high on our scale of self-esteem, this was true of only 38 per cent of those in the lowest class. It is interesting to note that class differences in self-esteem are considerably greater among boys than girls. Whereas the highest-class boys are substantially (19 per cent difference) more likely than the lowest-class boys to have high self-esteem, the highest class girls are only slightly (6 per cent difference) more likely than the lowest-class girls to have high self-esteem.

Rosenberg was able to show that upper-class parents differed considerably from lower-class parents in their values and behaviour towards their sons but differed very little in their values and behaviour towards their daughters and that these values and behaviours were relevant for the youngster's self-esteem.

Recent studies of social class and parental values have clearly shown that middle-class and working-class parents differ in their child-rearing values and practices. Let us consider here one part of parent–child relationships, the father's relationship with the son and daughter. A study conducted by Kohn and Carroll found that middle-class children were more likely to have supportive fathers than working-class children would have. The main point, however, is this; middle-class fathers were considerably more likely than working-class fathers to support their sons, but middle-class fathers were only somewhat (if at all) more likely than working-class fathers to support their daughters. Mothers, fathers and children all interviewed independently, agreed on this matter, and Rosenberg's data show very similar results.

Adolescents who reported close relationships with fathers were considerably more likely to have high self-esteem and stable self-images than those who described these relationships as more distant. These results suggest that one reason upper-class boys have an advantage in self-esteem is that they tend to have closer relationships with their fathers.

Rosenberg suggests that among subcultural norms there is a complex system of family relationships involving the closeness of the father to sons and to daughters, and that these norms may have a bearing upon the child's self-esteem. But these results, it should be emphasized, are not a direct consequence of the general prestige of the social class in the broader society. Upper-class children do tend to have somewhat higher self-esteem but this is not simply because society evaluates them higher. Factors internal to the family also appear to be involved.

Rosenberg also found that father's job and child's self-esteem only related in one instance. This is the small group whose fathers are in highly authoritarian and violent occupations—so violent, in fact, that the incumbents carry guns. Specifically, respondents whose fathers were members of the armed forces, policemen or detectives, or bailiffs, had unusually low self-esteem.

Fathers in these occupations may well like an authoritarian work structure and be willing to face and use violence. Perhaps the occupational imperatives influence the individual's personality; more likely the personality helps draw the individual to the occupation. Of course, even if these fathers do have authoritarian personalities, we do not know how such personalities influence the self-conceptions of the children. Nevertheless, it is interesting that lower self-esteem is found among children whose fathers are in authoritarian occupations and who use violence to control violence.

Neither religious nor ethnic group membership showed a relationship with adolescent self-esteem. This may be because these are assigned by society and have nothing to do with the adolescent's own accomplishments. Nor need the individual accept the social evaluation of his worth as his personal definition of his worth; on the contrary, there is a wide variety of 'coping mechanisms' that may be adopted in order to save one's self-esteem in the face of social disadvantage.

When we deal with self-esteem, we mean whether the individual considers himself adequate, a person of worth, not whether he considers himself superior to others. Implicit in such a feeling of adequacy is the relationship between one's standard and one's accomplishments, or, to quote the felicitous formula of William James, self-esteem = success/pretensions. Thus, a person who has modest goals and fulfils them may consider himself a perfectly worthwhile person. He will not deem himself superior to others, but he will be relatively satisfied with himself; such self-satisfaction would, in our study, be reflected in a high self-esteem score. Different occupational goals might have similar consequences for self-esteem. It is reasonable to assume that a middle-class youth will be at least as uncertain about his ability to become a lawyer as a working-class youth is about his ability to become a bricklayer. Group-determined goals and standards, as well as accomplishments, must be considered in attempting to account for feelings of self-worth.

Inter-Familial Factors

Broken Homes. Family breakup may result from problems of the parents, but it generates problems in the child. It is a common observation that delinquency and emotional disturbance often appear among children from such broken families. Rosenberg found that a somewhat larger proportion of children of divorced or separated parents had lower self-esteem than those whose families were intact. Children of separated parents were as likely as children of intact families to have high self-esteem, but were less likely to have medium self-esteem and more likely to have low self-esteem. As a group, children whose parents had been separated by death did not differ much from those of intact families. In terms of self-esteem marital rupture does appear to have some effect but the differences were generally small.

Birth Order. Along with parents and friends, the child's brothers and sisters constitute an important part of his interpersonal environment. Not only do they exert a direct influence upon him as members of the same household but their very presence necessarily affects his relationship with his parents. Rosenberg noted that a child's self-esteem in the family had little to do with birth order. What does make a difference is whether the subject has any brothers or sisters, as only children tend to have higher self-esteem.

It is interesting, however, that it is the male only child who is especially likely to have high self-esteem. The only girl, apparently, has no general self-esteem advantage over girls with siblings. Rosenberg, also considered the difference between having brothers and having sisters, and between having older brothers or sisters, or younger brothers or sisters. Among males, if the majority of children are boys, the self-esteem of the respondent tends to be lower than if half, or less than half, are boys. The self-esteem of girls, however, is not enhanced by being surrounded by brothers. Whether the girl is surrounded mostly by brothers or by sisters appears to have little effect on her level of self-acceptance.

Why is the younger boy in a family consisting mostly of older sisters so unlikely to have high self-esteem? Certainly there are reasons for expecting the opposite: in identifying with older sisters, for example, he might develop 'sissyish' characteristics which would make him an object of contempt to other boys. On the other hand, there are many advantages. Perhaps the best approach is to consider how the family is likely to greet the arrival of the boy.

Having had several daughters, Rosenberg suggested, the father would be anxious to have a boy. The family's status, after all, chiefly depends upon the accomplishments of its males and the family's hopes for upward social mobility are likely to be pinned on the son. The longer the son's arrival is deferred, therefore, the more eager the father may be to have a boy. Another consideration is the family name—only the boy can carry it on. The name is an important part of the individual's identity, and in this sense the son represents an extension and continuity of the father's identity, which may be important to the father. In addition, the father may wish to introduce the boy to some of the high points of his own childhood (football, fishing, etc.) which he cannot recapture in the rearing of girls. These, plus the general cultural prescription that 'a man should have a son' may make the father all the more eager to have a boy the longer his arrival is deferred.

Mothers, too, are likely to be anxious to have a boy after having several girls. That the mother does feel unusually warm and affectionate towards the newly arrived boy after having had several daughters is clearly suggested by the study of Sears, Maccoby and Levin (1957). The younger-minority boy, unlike other youngsters will tend to develop a type of self-esteem which is not based on competitive achievement, on outdoing others, or upon social or academic success. Rather, it is a fundamental feeling of worth deriving from the care, and affection of his significant others. In his early years, at least, everything is working in his favour. The father is eager for his arrival, the mother treats him with inordinate affection, the sisters regard him as something precious. Is it any wonder that he should grow up feeling that he is a person of worth?

It should be noted, however, that the younger-minority have significantly lower grades in school than other boys. It may be that a solid, unshakeable feeling of self-acceptance may deter accomplishment. Part of the motivation to work hard in school may be the need to prove one's worth both to other people and to oneself, but his worth has been proved at home.

Parental Interest in Child. Rosenberg selected three areas of parent–child interaction as sources of feedback to the child which would influence his self-esteem. These three areas were:

1. parent's knowledge of child's friends,
2. parent's reaction to child's academic performance,
3. parent–child interaction at dinner table.

These three were selected as they measure interest and concern that the parents have in the child and in his welfare and progress.

Parent's knowledge of child's friends. During the period of middle childhood and adolescence a child's emotions tend to be deeply involved in his friends; indeed friends may be the child's main ego-extensions. The parent's reactions to the child's friends may thus be an indirect indicator of their interest in the child.

Rosenberg found there was little difference in the self-esteem of those who said their mothers knew 'all' or 'most' of their friends but that the self-esteem of these respondents is substantially higher than those who said their mothers knew 'some' or 'none' of their friends. It should be noted, however, that only 8 per cent said their mothers knew 'some' or 'none' of their friends. These responses thus appear to indicate an extreme lack of interest. It is among this exceptional group that low self-esteem is particularly likely to appear.

The father's knowledge of the child's friends is not strongly associated with self-esteem except for the extreme group who said their fathers knew 'none' or 'almost none' of their friends. This small group (8 per cent of the respondents) was clearly more likely to have low-esteem than those who reported that they knew some, most, or all of their friends. Exceptional parental indifference does seem to be associated with low self-esteem in offspring.

Parental interest in academic performance. How a child gets on at school is a specific point of contact between parent and child which may serve as an indicator of parental interest in the child. While it is possible for the parent to be oblivious to what happens to the child in school, total performance is tightly and regularly summarized on the report card. His response to the report card, then, may epitomize his attitude towards the child's achievements and qualities.

In order to learn something about the parent's typical reactions, Rosenberg asked respondents: 'When you were in the fifth and sixth grades in school, what did your mother usually do when you brought home a report card with high grades?' (Check as many as apply.) 'How about when you brought home a report card from the fifth or sixth grades which contained low marks? What did your mother usually do then?' The same questions were asked about the father's reactions.

The parental response to poor grades may roughly be divided into three types: (1) the *punitive* reactions—scolding the child, criticizing him, depriving him of something he wants; (2) the *supportive* reactions—praising him for the subjects in which he did do well, trying to help him in subjects in which he was doing poorly, or discussing the reasons for his poor performance; and (3) the *indifferent* reactions— paying no attention to grades, simply taking poor report cards for granted, or not even looking at the report card.

In terms of Mead's principle of reflected appraisals, those students whose parents were critical or punitive would have the lowest self-esteem; those whose parents were supportive and helpful would have the highest self-esteem; those whose parents were indifferent would be in-between. The results, however, do not bear out these expectations. It is not the punitive responses which are most closely related to low self-esteem, but the indifferent ones. Once again, we find, the proportion that gives the indifferent responses is very small. We may thus assume that they were cases of rather extreme indifference. Those who do report such indifference, however, not only have lower self-esteem than those who report supportive responses but also somewhat lower than those who report punitive responses.

It is interesting to note that those students whose only supportive responses do not differ from those who report both supportive and punitive responses. Both groups, however, have higher self-esteem than those who report only punitive responses; those who report indifferent responses as noted are lowest in self-esteem.

Another possible indication of parental indifference was assessed by the following question, 'If your marks were average or below average, was your mother satisfied with your grades in school?' As expected those students who said that their mothers were satisfied even when their grades were below average, had higher self-esteem than those who reported that their mothers were dissatisfied. More interesting, however, is the fact that the lowest self-esteem appears not among those who report that their mothers were dissatisfied but among those who said, 'She seldom commented on my marks'. Once again maternal indifference is more highly predictive of low self-esteem than overt dissatisfaction. Those students who reported that their mothers and fathers gave supportive responses had higher self-esteem than those who reported indifferent responses.

While many people are inclined to treat the school report card as trivial, it holds a special and almost unique significance in the development of the self-concept.

Among the myriad criteria upon which an individual's worth may be judged, the report card is almost the only objective, unequivocal measure of a certain aspect of the individual's worth. Whether a person is kind, courageous, principled, likeable, etc., may be a matter of opinion, but a report card is a black-and-white, strictly measurable and comparable characterization of the individual. Total parental indifference to the report card is very rare.

It may thus be that most parents who are totally uninterested in the child's school performance are likely to be uninterested in the child. The parent may be punitive—may scold the child, deprive him of something etc., if he does poorly in school, but at least he is interested, concerned and involved with the child. Apparently more than deprecation and chastisement, and certainly more than praise or support is associated with lower self-esteem in the child.

Participation in mealtime talk. This is an everyday event which reflect parental interest in the child. The importance of the evening meal is that it is a constant and frequent point of contact between parents and children. What goes on at the table may well epitomize the total range of parent–child interactions which occurs in other areas of life.

Rosenberg asked the respondents three questions. Do all your family eat the evening meal together? If so how often do *you* participate actively in the mealtime conversation? As far as you can tell, how interested are the other family members in what you have to say on such occasions?

Fewer than six per cent of the respondents said that they 'rarely or never' participated in the mealtime conversation and an equally small proportion of those who did participate felt that others were 'not interested' in what they had to say. These respondents were considerably more likely than others to have low self-esteem.

The student's belief that others are interested in him is thus closely related to his self-conception. His self-conception, of course, undoubtedly contributes to his belief that others are interested. The child who thinks little of himself is automatically inclined to assume that others are uninterested in his opinions and activities. At the same time it is likely that something in the actual attitudes and behaviour towards him contributes to his belief that they are not interested in what he has to say. The student has, after all, interacted with his family hundreds of times. He has thus been exposed to almost innumerable signs as to whether others are interested in what he has to say. Either the yawn when he speaks, interruptions, changing of the subject, looks of distractedness; or, on the other hand, the light of interest when he presents his views, the responses appropriate to his comment, the encouragement to continue, or the request for his opinion on a subject which others have initiated. All these are clear and unmistakable signs that others are interested in what he has to say.

While none of these three areas of interaction may in itself be an adequate reflector of parental interest in the child, the consistency of the results in all these areas suggests that there is a real relationship between parental indifference and low-esteem in the child.

It should be stressed that reports of parental indifference in the child are clearly the exception; very few students gave the 'uninterested' or 'indifferent' response to any of these items. In order to provide the most liberal interpretation of parental indifference, Rosenberg combined all those who reported *any* lack of interest on the part of their parents. Twenty per cent of the sample did report such indifference. This is an exceptional, but not insignificant group; forty-four per cent of these students had low self-esteem compared with twenty-six per cent of the others.

It may be noted that this association between parental indifference and children's self-esteem is not an artifact of associated status or role characteristics. In other words, whatever one's class, religion, sex or wherever one lives, the result is essentially the same: if one's parents are indifferent, one is less likely to have a high level of self-regard.

Similarly, it is not simply a question of whether parents were strict or lenient with the child or whether the respondent feels that the punishment he received as a child was deserved or not. Whether the student says that his parents were stricter or less strict than others, or whether he says that the punishment he received was generally deserved, partly deserved and partly undeserved, or generally undeserved, the result is the same: students who report a lack of parental interest have lower self-esteem than others.

These data thus suggest that extreme parental indifference is associated with lower self-esteem in the child and, in fact, seems to be even more deleterious than punitive parental reactions. It may be that even if the mother is only sufficiently interested in the child to chastise him, even if she is discourteous enough to be unpleasant to his friends, this level of interest is associated with higher self-esteem than is maternal indifference.

Of course, it is probably not simply interest *per se* which accounts for the observed relationships. Very likely such lack of interest in the child goes along with lack of love, a failure to treat the child with respect, a failure to give him encouragement, a tendency to consider the child something of a nuisance and to treat him with irritation, impatience and anger. But whatever other kinds of parental behaviour may be reflected in these indicators, they probably reflect the idea that the child is important to someone else, that others consider him of worth, of value and of concern. The feeling that one is important to a significant other is probably essential to develop self-worth. In all, the work of Rosenberg and Coopersmith show similar conditions facilitating positive self-esteem. It is specific relationships in the effective interpersonal environment that affect self-esteem, those intimate features of home environment that the child equates with success and self-worth, particularly parental interest, concern and warmth. Broader social forces have little impact.

THE SEARS STUDY

In a follow-up study of the children involved in *Patterns of Child Rearing* (Sears, Maccoby and Levin 1957) Sears (1970) reports on the children who were then twelve, with respect to five measures of attitudes concerning the self-concept and one measure of masculinity–femininity. In the original 1957 study, 379 children and their mothers participated but, in the follow-up, when the children were seven years older, only 160 were available for testing. Sears claims that a careful comparison of demographic characteristics and mothers, reveal that the follow-up cases are an accurate sample of the original total. Sears followed Coopersmith's (1967) findings and proposed a hypothesis that parental attitudes toward a child which give him a feeling of being loved, wanted, accepted, and respected should induce a similar attitude in him, that is, being worthy and successful. Thus parental warmth and affection and love-orientated discipline should be associated with high self-esteem while coldness and harsh discipline should be associated with the opposite.

The reasoning is that a mother who is affectionate and loving to her child expresses this through smiling, talking, hugging and gives the child an understanding that he is desirable and sought after. Presumably, such a concept of the self as worthy develops over many years and only gradually gets translated into specific verbal judgements such as those agreed or disagreed with on the various test instruments used with the present twelve-year-olds.

The self-concept measure used by Sears concerned such categories as physical ability, social relations with various others, work habits, academic competence and self-criticism. The femininity scale from the CPI was included to measure gender role, Sears assumes without question that masculinity and femininity are opposites so that low scores on that scale reflect masculinity!

The parental measures were the original ones reported in 1957. These fell into six components: permissiveness, family adjustment, responsible child-training orientation, father–mother dominance, father's warmth and acceptance. The results showed that there were no sex differences between overall self-concept scores and, for both sexes, a high self-concept was significantly associated with high arithmetic and reading achievement with small family size, early ordinal position in family and high paternal and maternal warmth. For both sexes, high femininity was related to poor self-concepts. For boys only, self-concepts were associated with low father dominance in husband and wife relationships.

The mechanism responsible for transmitting these evaluative attitudes is presumably social reinforcement from loved persons who serve not only as reinforcers but as models. They specify in their own behaviour certain attitudes towards the child and he adopts them.

A complication in this otherwise simple prediction stems from the unequal participation of the two parents in the caretaking process and the differences in the roles they play with children of the two sexes. In the first few years of life, the mother is the chief caretaker for both boys and girls. By the age of five, however, the father is becoming more salient in the family interaction process and during the subsequent seven years he is an especially significant model for the boy. If one hypothesizes either a process such as identification (primary for the girl and defensive for the boy) or a sex-typing process based on imitation of an idealized gender model, in part represented by the parent of the same sex, that parent should gain greater reinforcing power than the parent of the opposite sex. The reasoning is that since the same sexed parent is the model whose behaviour and attitudes the child is trying hardest to emulate, he should pay more attention to that parent and respond more readily to relevant cues from him for shaping his own behaviour.

Sears argues that the expected outcome is that the mother's warmth and acceptance would influence the self-concepts of both boys and girls but be more strongly evidenced in the girls than the boys. The father's warmth, however, should be influential for the boy's self-concepts than for the girl's. He enters relatively late into the reinforcing process and never is the approved gender role model for the girl but he does become so for the boy. If he thus gains more reinforcing power, as is here assumed, the boy should show his influence more than the girl.

One corollary to these predictions is that the degree to which a child of either sex has achieved the appropriate gender role should determine, somewhat, the satisfaction of the parents with his behaviour and the amount of warmth and acceptance they express. Hence, one would expect that masculine girls and feminine boys would have poorer self-concepts than more adequately sex-typed children. (An obvious alternative interpretation of such a finding would be that the antecedents of good sex-typing are the same as those for developing good self-concepts.)

It would seem that by the age of twelve the characteristics of the feminine role are generally viewed negatively with consequent effects on self-evaluation. Thus, with girls, a strong sex-typing is possibly deleterious on self-conception while for boys it is a poor sex-typing that has that effect.

The correlations between academic performance and self-concept are for boys $+0.28$ (reading) and $+0.26$ (arithmetic) and for girls $+0.28$ (reading) and $+0.21$ (arithmetic). These figures are consistent with other studies e.g. Coopersmith r of $+0.28$ between IQ and self-concept. When the correlations between the self-concept and various measures of parental behaviour were considered in boys, at least, it seems clear that the warmth factor is the main contributor to a prediction of good self-concept. In girls, maternal permissiveness seems to be just about as predictive as warmth.

There is no support for the hypothesis that warmth of the same-sex parent would be the more influential for each sex of the child. As far as the self-concept score is concerned, the two parents appear to have exerted about equal influence. Indeed, an important point is revealed when the children are divided into four groups based on whether their mothers and fathers were above or below the mean score on warmth. For both sexes of children there were no significant differences in self-concept among three of the sub-groups: warm-warm, warm-cold, cold-warm. For both sexes, however, the fourth group (cold mothers, cold fathers) was significantly poorer in self-concept than the other three groups; by t test, the six differences between the cold-cold and the other three groups (both sexes) were all significant. Evidently one warm parent is sufficient, on average, to produce a good self-concept.

In sum, then, Sears's study supports the consistent finding that parental warmth and acceptance are significant determinants of the child's self-esteem and it makes little or no difference to boys or girls whether these parental qualities are exhibited by the mother or father or both. With respect to father dominance, the r of -0.33 with boys' self-concepts is the largest one obtained in the study. The r for girls was approximately zero.

The apparently deleterious effect of father's dominance on the boy's self-concept agrees with one of Coopersmith's (1967) findings. From interviews with his boy subjects themselves, he obtained the boys' perceptions of which parent was dominant in the decision-making role in the family, in controlling the child ('telling him what to do') and in administering punishment. Low self-esteem was somewhat associated with the father's dominance on child control and punishment, although unrelated to decision-making dominance. In the present instance, the measure of dominance was obtained from the mother interviews of seven years earlier, rather than from a current report of the boys themselves. Again, it is not known whether the reported role of dominance was consistent through those years, but it is notable that such different measures of the antecedent variable yield such similar results.

One crucial question cannot be answered from either source of data, however, whether father dominance had a bad effect on self-concept or mother dominance had a good effect. Since the role-dominance scale was bipolar, high father dominance was the same as low mother dominance.

In line with Rosenberg, Sears's study (op. cit.) also revealed the advantage of being an only child. The hard realities of family life are that parents have only so much time and energy to devote to their children. Hence, the more children there are, the greater the competition for parental attention, or for the kinds of admiration and expressions of acceptance which seem to influence self-concepts.

Furthermore the battle is unequal, for a first child has a period without competition, while later children not only have competition from the beginning but have the everlasting handicap of being smaller, younger, less effective, than their older competitors and, at any one time, may have less talent for making themselves seem worthy of admiration within the family. Thus it is to be expected that the only, and the eldest, children would have better self-concepts than the middle and the youngest, and that the larger the family the poorer would be self-concepts regardless of ordinal position. These predictions are fairly well supported by Sears's data. With respect to family size, for boys the r with the self-concept score is -0.20, for girls, -0.28. The larger the family the poorer was the child's self-concept.

The Sears (1970) study provides more evidence to support Coopersmith's earlier findings that parental warmth is related to high self-concepts in children. In Coopersmith's study, the warmth was measured concurrently with the children's self-esteem. In this instance, the warmth was measured seven years earlier when the children were five years old. The two findings were not replicative, therefore, but supplementary. They suggest that whether maternal warmth is measured in the child's early life or when he reaches age twelve, there is a tendency for warm and accepting mothers (and fathers) to have children with high self-esteem.

The proposition that father's warmth would be more closely related to son's than to a daughter's self-concept was not supported. The powerful intrusion of the father into the controlling and decision-making activities of the family was associated with poor self-concepts in boys but was irrelevant to those of girls. Coupled with Coopersmith's somewhat similar findings with respects to boys, the search for a more precise theory of the father–son relationship needs promoting. However, future investigation must note the basic contamination in the so-called father measures in both these studies. Coopersmith secured his information from the sons and Sears's came from the mothers. Any single agent reporting for both himself and someone else can provide correlational data relating his own feelings about himself to his perception of another's behaviour, but cannot provide *any* independent measure of the other's overt actons. Likewise, the mother's perception of the father cannot be a measure of his behaviour independent of her perception of them both.

In sum, the present data suggest fairly clearly that a child's self-concept at age 12 is significantly related not only to his own academic competence (as measured three years earlier) but to several aspects of the family which already existed when he was five years old. When six of these measures are used as independent variables in a multiple correlation for which the summary self-concept measure is the dependent variable, the r for each sex of child is 0.53. The six measures are reading, achievement, number of children in the family, ordinal position (for which point biserial r's were used), mother warmth, father warmth and father dominance.

Warmth is difficult to define and yet the findings from most child-rearing studies suggest that warmth is an important aspect of being a parent. A warm parent is one who is (1) deeply committed to the child's welfare; (2) responsive to the child's needs; (3) willing to spend time (within limits) in joint enterprises of the child's choosing; (4) ready to show enthusiasm over the child's accomplishments and acts of altruism; and (5) sensitive to the child's emotional states.

Unconditional acceptance of the child is the characteristic shared by all these aspects of warmth. The message is that nothing—neither the child's naughtiness nor the parent's anger—threatens the parent's basic commitment and enduring love for the child.

OTHER STUDIES

In a very small scale study employing only 21 boys and 21 girls aged 8 to 11, Dickstein and Posner (1978) explored the parent–child relationship. The quality of the child's relationship with his parents was based on criteria of interest in the child, involvement in rule making, etc., assessed by a Parent–Child Relationship Questionnaire designed for this study. This 13-item scale required the child to respond to questions such as: 'Does your mother know who most of your friends are?' The child responded along a five-point scale ranging from 'knows who all are' to 'knows none'. Six questions pertain to the mother and six to the father, while one question asks of the general home atmosphere: 'Are the rules at your house flexible?' The test–retest reliability of this scale when measured after a five-month interval was 0.51, which is rather a mediocre level. The questionnaire could be valuable if further work improved its technical qualities.

Dickstein and Posner found, as hypothesized, that the quality of the parent–child relationship in the child's view were significantly correlated ($r = +0.47$). Furthermore, when the Parent–Child Relationship Questionnaire was separated into a father scale and a mother scale, the correlations between the separate scales and self-esteem proved to be significant as well.

Although, all the correlations were significant when the total sample was considered, separate analyses for male and female subjects revealed important sex differences. First, the data for the boys showed a strong relationship between self-esteem and the parent–child relationship ($r = +0.50$), while for girls this relationship was not statistically significant ($r = +0.35$). The most interesting finding, however, concerns the differential effect of the sex of the child and the sex of the parent on the size of the correlation between self-esteem and the parent–child relationship. For boys, self-esteem was significantly related to the quality of the relationship with the father ($r = +0.49$), but not with the mother ($r = +0.34$). The converse held for girls. For them, self-esteem was significantly related to the quality of the relationship with the mother ($r = +0.53$) but not with the father ($r = +0.21$).

Because of the reasonably high correlations between the mother and father scales ($r = +0.45$ for boys, $r = +0.49$ for girls) Dickstein recalculated the correlations between self-esteem and the mother–child and father–child relationships. It was hoped that a more accurate set of correlations would emerge through ignoring spurious inflation or deflation of correlations due to the subjects responding similarly to questions concerning their two parents. The results of this second analysis were even more clear-cut than those of the first. For boys, the correlation between self-esteem and the father scale, adjusted to exclude the mother scale remained high ($r = +0.40$). On the other hand the correlation between self-esteem and the mother scale, adjusted to exclude the father scale, dropped to $+0.16$. The results for the girls remained very close to the original correlation ($r = +0.51$) for the correlation between self-esteem and the mother scale. By contrast, the correlation between self-esteem and the father scale was reduced to near zero ($r = +0.06$). It is clear that it is the relationship with the same sex parent that is mainly responsible for the correlation between self-esteem and the parent–child relationship. Any correlation between self-esteem and the opposite sex seems to be mainly an artifact between the scales for the two parents.

In a study of the antecedents of self-esteem in Australian university students, Watkins (1976) found that there were significant relationships between self-esteem and father's educational status and between low self-esteem and conflict between parents. These results confirm earlier findings of Rosenberg (1965) and Coopersmith (1967).

In the only cross-cultural study available on this issue, Ziller et al. (1968) investigated differences between Pakistani Asian, Indian and American children and the implications for self-esteem. The latter was measured by the topological Self Social Construct Test. The extended family of the Indian child is presumed to affect his self-concept. In this form of social setting the child will have many parent surrogates. The child may be nearly as close to his aunts as to his mother and, indeed, all females of the joint family may be thought of by the child as having essentially similar or even identical functions. In this way, the child is not disciplined by, or responsible to, a single individual. Warmth, acceptance and closeness are extended to all Asian children. The Indian child is more highly valued by the extended family, more enmeshed in the family matrix which largely determines the child's social universe; he or she is inseparable from parents and parent surrogates, is less separated from parents in terms of status barriers, and tends to be the focal point of the family's reason for being.

Thus Ziller et al. (1968) found that the Indians had higher self-esteem and closer identification with parents and teacher than the American sample. Ziller et al. argue that the difference of Indian self-identity and family-identity being interwined contrasts with the USA where the nuclear family places high self-esteem in jeopardy. The Indian students also showed higher self-acceptance.

Graybill (1978) looked at child-rearing practices of mothers from the child's perspective. This adds further evidence to the Coopersmith (self-report measures) and Sears (interview data) studies, by using another perspective. Although, using only 52 children over a wide age-range (7 to 15 years) the findings did support the work of Coopersmith and Sears in showing the relationship between maternal child-rearing behaviours and a child's self-esteem. The fact the maternal behaviours were assessed differently in this study from the perspectives used in previous studies adds further strength to this conclusion.

Consistent with previous findings, children with high self-esteem viewed their mothers as accepting, understanding and liking them. Also consistent with previous findings, children with high self-esteem did not have mothers who used drastic forms of psychological pressure as punishment (i.e. withdrawal of love, guilt etc.) to control them.

The most recent backing for the influence of parental variables such as punishment, control and support on the self-esteem of children comes from Growe (1980). Mother's behaviour was correlated more highly with children's self-esteem than father's. Boys' self-esteem was more closely associated with the perceived behaviour of the parents than was girls' self-esteem.

Earlier results linking maternal warmth to high self-esteem are supported by the present findings. Greater support and milder punishment from mothers enhance the self-esteem of children of both sexes. Children who perceive their mothers' behaviour towards themselves as expressing a positive evaluation will tend to internalize this view.

Maternal and paternal protectiveness were related to lower self-esteem in boys but not in girls and the difference between the correlations was statistically significant. Boys treated protectively by parents have difficulty achieving the mastery and self-sufficiency expected of males in our culture and, consequently, they suffer from lower self-esteem. Overall Growe's results reaffirm the link between parental support and self-esteem in children. Other researchers have thought that birth-order or family size might be among the objective family variables related to children's self-conceptualizations and, like Rosenberg, were disappointed.

In 1969, Kohn and Schooler analysed data from the US National Occupation Study to determine whether there was a relationship between birth order and the person's self-concept. The data used as a basis for this analysis were but one part of a large study which they conducted on the social and psychological consequences of occupation experience. Interviews were conducted by the National Opinion Research Centre with 3101 men, representative of all men throughout the United States employed in civilian occupations. Birth-order differences were examined by dividing subjects into the following five groups: (a) first born; (b) first half but not first born; (c) middle child in odd-sized families; (d) last half but not last born; and (e) last born. In all analyses effects of family size were controlled through covariance and only-children were excluded. The dependent variables, based on analyses of the responses in the interview which, on average, lasted two and a half hours. Aspects of the self-concept which were among the 21 dependent variables listed in the study were: (a) self-confidence; (b) self-deprecation; (c) a sense of control over fate; (d) anxiety; (e) believes ideas conform to those groups to which one belongs; and (f) compulsiveness. No statistics are given in this study so it is not possible to determine exactly how scores were computed or groups were compared with each other. In commenting on this study Schooler says that no significant birth-order effects were found for these dependent variables and

> this lack of findings is, in fact, a record of sorts, since given the large number of cases and the relative discriminatory power of the dependent variables, nearly all other analyses with this body of data have produced some pattern of results regardless of whether the independent variables represented occupational conditions, background factors, or even aspects of family structure such as family size, intactness of family and having a mother who worked. (p. 170)

In other words, birth order was not an independent variable for these self-concept dependent variables. On a related issue, Schooler (1972) comments that 'analysis of responses of 1516 men in the sample who had children between 3 and 15 years of age also failed to reveal any differences related to birth rank of the child in child-rearing values or in the reported display of affection or anger.' (p. 171).

These null findings agreed with Bachman's (1970) large multivariate study of 2213 tenth-grade boys and with Rosenberg's (1965) survey of 5024 New York State high school students, using the Rosenberg Self-Esteem Scale, although Sears (1970) found a birth-order effect.

In discussing his own results and the results of many other studies concerning the influence of birth order Schooler (1972) raises the question as to why birth order has had such a fascination for researchers 'given the few replicable findings that have emerged from this relatively large body of research' over the past 30 years. He suggests that this may have been because birth order has been considered to be a seemingly simple independent variable, when, in fact, it is not. He concludes by suggesting that to be fruitful, the study of birth order necessitates dealing with the complexities such as the sex of siblings and family density.

Bachman (1970) included family size in his study of tenth-grade boys mentioned above which Schooner did not. Bachman reports, 'We did find, as did Rosenberg (1965) a tendency for only children to be slightly higher than others in self-esteem'. Nystul (1976), and Stotland and Dunn (1962) could not produce evidence relating to this association either. In view of such negative results, it would seem that a clearer understanding of birth-order effects would emerge if such variables as sex, and closeness in age, of siblings was taken into account.

The sex of the child has most often been considered when the relationship between parental behaviour and self-esteem has been examined. In addition there have been conflicting reports regarding the relationship of parental behaviour and the sex of the child. Maccoby and Jacklin (1974) in reviewing the pertinent literature, note few differences in parental treatment of children according to the sex of the child.

However, the impact that parents can have on a child's self-concept may be affected by the sex of both. For example, a boy's self-concept depends to some extent on the level of affection existing in his relationships with his father. Mussen et al. (1963) showed in a cross-cultural study that boys whose fathers showed insufficient paternal affection were less secure, less confident and less well socially adjusted than those boys whose fathers manifested sufficient affection.

Bronfenbrenner (1961) notes a sex difference in the effects of parental treatment leading to independence, responsibility and leadership in adolescents: 'affiliative companionship, nurturance, principled discipline, affection and affective reward appear to foster the emergence of leadership in sons but discourage it in daughters.' (p. 326)

An explanation may be that these characteristics of responsibility and leadership are rewarded highly in males but not strongly expected in females, who are not likely therefore to receive much reinforcement for displaying them. As we have already argued earlier in this chapter, the expectations and characteristics of femininity and masculinity are different in our culture so that the same parental treatments may have different effects on boys from girls. Different practices are also required to develop the required (if stereotyped) sex-role self-concepts. For instance, love-oriented child-caring is more effective in developing healthy self-conceptualization in girls. (Sears, Maccoby and Levin 1957). On the other hand, with boys, parents are likely to invoke more physical punishment, be more permissive of aggression and stress independence and achievement. Parents seem to direct boys to control their environment; for girls their aim is to protect them from the environment. This may help to explain why girls manifest more cooperation, obedience and social adjustment than boys. Although love and warmth is necessary for boys to develop self-esteem, a different balance of discipline and firmness against affection is necessary from that offered to girls. As Coopersmith showed, boys need consistent parental discipline in concert with love-oriented strategies. Just as assertiveness in girls is less valued by others, so is dependence and lack of self-assertion in boys.

In a more recent study Elrod and Crase (1980) extended investigation in this area by examining the relationship of reported behaviours of both parents to self-esteem of children with sex of child as a variable. Accordingly, the following questions were asked: (a) Do parents behave differently towards boys and girls? (b) Does parental treatment of boys and girls relate to their self-esteem? (c) Does one sex have higher self-esteem than the other?

The subjects were 49 boys and 45 girls enrolled in six nursery schools or day-care centres, and their parents. A modified version of Woolner's Preschool Self-Concept Test (Woolner 1966) was administered individually to the children. Each child was shown ten plates on each of which were two pictures representing opposing characteristics that children would recognize. For example, a plate might depict a child engaged in an activity in which a child was dirty and one in which a child was clean. Verbal statements accompanied the presentation of each picture. The child was then asked to choose the person he was and the person he would like to be, and could respond to that question on the modified self-concept test by pointing to the same picture twice or to two different pictures. The items corresponding to each picture were then simply scored 'agree' or 'disagree' and a total of 'agree' and 'disagree' scores were computed. A high number of agreements between self-score and ideal-score in this self-concept test was defined as high self-esteem while a low number of agreements was defined as low self-esteem. This is a reliable and valid scale. A parental behaviour inventory to assess child-focused behaviours of parents was completed by both parents of each child. The analysis of the resulting data revealed that mothers interacted more with the children than the fathers did, and that while fathers interact more with their sons than with their daughters, mothers interact equally with both. As with previous research findings, the mother's behaviour correlated significantly with the daugther's self-esteem but not with the son's. However, in contrast to previous findings, father's behaviour was negatively correlated with son's self-esteem as well as daughter's self-esteem. The behaviour of mothers helping their daughters' self-concepts can be usefully categorized in the following way: active involvement with the child, giving immediate assistance to the child, and imposing limits on the child. (cf. Coopersmith 1967: with boys.) These results suggest that high self-esteem in girls is related to the mother's communication that she values the child through action and deeds. In contrast, however, the behaviours of fathers which related to low self-esteem of sons also involves limiting immediacy of assistance. Thus, in several cases, behaviour of mothers towards daughters correlated significantly with high self-esteem while that same behaviour by fathers towards sons meant low self-esteem. The specific behaviours included restricting the kinds of food the child eats, insisting that the child speak politely, and going immediately to the child when seeing him hurt. Likewise, mothers helping their daughters recognize another person's point of view related significantly to high self-esteem, while the same behaviour on the part of fathers related to low self-esteem of daughters. The data indicate that mothers' behaviour relates to high self-esteem in girls while neither parents' behaviour relates to high self-esteem in boys. One might speculate that the same behaviour of mothers and fathers is perceived differently by sons and daughters and the same behaviour of mothers and fathers towards daughters is perceived as having different meanings. Is it possible that these divergent perceptions are the result of early differential treatment of boys and girls by mothers and fathers?

The analysis of the data also demonstrates that boys have a significantly higher self-esteem than girls.

The paradox that certain behaviours of mothers are related to high self-esteem in girls, while similar behaviours of fathers are related to low self-esteem in boys and girls is only interpretable through a phenomonological approach, in that boys and girls actually perceive this behaviour in different ways.

Far more research is needed on the effects of the interaction of each parent with boys and girls on the offspring self-concept, in order to resolve the dichotomy of the existing research findings. This research needs integrating with work on the expectations and learned characteristics of femininity and masculinity in our culture, for there is no doubt that subtle variations in parental treatment towards boys and girls will have some effect just as the same parental treatment of boys and girls will have different effects as they view it from their own sex-role perspective.

MATERNAL DEPRIVATION

The concept of maternal deprivation is a muddled one and encompasses a wide range of events from institutionalization, through distortions of maternal care, to temporary separation as a result of hospitalization and, finally, the lack or loss of attachment to a particular individual. In many cases, several of these events have occurred in differing degrees and combinations causing difficulty in isolating specific cause–effect relationships. The inevitable concomitants of maternal deprivation also have confounding effects. For example, where separation is due to death, the trauma of death itself might produce effects independent of the separation. Nor can control groups be found easily. There are no children in institutions who have not been separated from their mothers; controls with the same diseases as hospitalized children are difficult to come by.

Despite methodological problems of small samples, descriptive case studies and poorly defined variables of institutionalization and deprivation, studies of maternal deprivation provide strong evidence, in an extreme form, of the effects of early experience and learning on relationships, with others and on self-perception.

Early social interactions, involving the possible development of strong attachments to a consistent figure and the feelings generated from these, all act as prototypes for the engagement in, or avoidance of future interactions. As we have emphasized, it is in these first social contacts that the child discovers how people react to him and how in return, he responds to them. In a wide range of family environments, parents generally provide a fund of security, support and acceptance, enabling the child to develop a fairly positive view of himself, to be willing to enter into social relationships, and to feel confident and competent.

However, some child-rearing backgrounds, particularly those characterized by maternal deprivation in its many forms, tend to suggest to the child that the world is not benign but hostile and not to be trusted. Emotional and social deprivation stunt the child's own social and emotional development.

If a child's first relationships give him the wrong view of life, what hope is there for the future? It would seem that love and acceptance from intimate, continuing and consistent contacts with at least one adult are essential for a child to develop into a socialized being, able to channel his emotions in such a way as to ensure a positive self-concept and adequate handling of later family-life and citizenship.

Goldfarb (1945) demonstrated that an institution-reared group of children showed a 'profoundly deviate personality type' (p. 20). As well as being physically and intellectually retarded, such children were characterized as being: '. . . more isolated from other people and less able to enter into meaningful relationships . . . and to be marked by an unusual degree of apathy of emotional response.' (Goldfarb 1945. p. 20.)

Bowlby (1946) labelled this personality as the 'affectionless character'. Many of his studies (e.g. 1951, 1953, 1960) have indicated that after a succession of transient attachments to a series of nurses, each of whom eventually disappears out of the child's life, the child eventually begins to act as if neither mothering nor contact with others has much significance for him. After losing mother-figures, to whom he has given trust and affection, he commits himself less and less to succeeding ones, becoming increasingly self-centred and avoiding social relationships. Any social contacts made are fraught with hostility and aggression since having received little love or acceptance, it is difficult then to give these. The aggression is also a defence against the fragility of the self-concept which has been given little positive direction or content.

The monkeys of Harlow and Harlow (1962) demonstrated similar findings. Severe maternal deprivation for these animals gave rise (when later placed with normal monkeys) to exaggerated aggressive responses and the inability to make friends and develop adult heterosexual behaviour. Any female so treated, who later became pregnant, ignored and abandoned her offspring.

It is not difficult to hypothesize the development of a low self-concept and an isolated, affectionless and hostile personality through failure to develop consistent attachments to parents or caretakers. Such contacts as there have been will have usually been impersonal, cold and inconsistent. A sequence starts with the feeling of rejection, real or imagined, from which develops a negative self-appraisal; this then generates tension and a rejection by others. The interpreted reactions, reinforce the negative self-concept and attitudes towards others. Consequent hostility towards others and towards self becomes pronounced in attitude, in word, and, often with such a child, in deed.

The child is thus denied through both external events and his own, often faulty, interpretation of experience any learning of the art of social living and any experiencing of meaningful relationships with others. People have been a source of frustration rather than a fount of reward to such a child and do not acquire reward value. The adult is not viewed as a potential source of love and acceptance; the child does not expect it and, moreover, has been weaned off giving it. Erikson's 'basic trust' has not developed. Maternal deprivation, thankfully, is a rare form of child-rearing but it does again indicate that experiences that affect the burgeoning self-concept and so cause a devalued self, create an inability to accept others. Bowlby saw this relationship when he claimed:

> to the extent that it involves privation or deprivation of a relationship of dependence with a mother figure, it will have an adverse effect on personality development, particularly with respect to the capacity for forming and maintaining satisfactory object relations. (Ainsworth and Bowlby 1954. p. 2)

Research on child-rearing clearly indicates that parents who are harsh, inconsistent and do not show love for the child are most likely to bring up children who find it difficult to develop positive self-attitudes and adequate personal relationships. Such extreme distortions in attachment are lessons that tell the unfortunate child that he is unloved, unacceptable, a failure and of no concern to any one.

In a related study, Rosen (1978), using an unpublished self-concept scale, compared the self-concepts of a group of women who abused their children with a group who did not. The *t* test analysis of the self-concept data indicated that the women who abused their children had significantly lower and less consistent self-concepts than the non-abusers. They also experienced a greater incongruence between the way they viewed themselves and the way they would like to be.

The inconsistency of self-concept, i.e. no firm sense of who they are but an ever shifting and contradictory set of attributes may serve as sources and consequences of the extreme frustration which leads to violence when socially appropriate avenues for social enhancement are unavailable.

The large self–ideal discrepancy which distinguished the child-abusers has often been theoretically considered as a valid index of maladjustment and it demonstrates this in Rosen's study.

ABSENT PARENTS

In a recent article, Lifshitz (1975) proposed that identity, or self-concept, develops as a function of successive comparisons and contrasts between self and father and mother. According to Lifshitz, self-perception can be seen as a body situated between two distinctively perceived poles, father and mother. If one parent is absent, Lifshitz proposes that the child may be drawn towards the existing pole or the parent who remains to care for the child. If this model of self-concept is correct, then these notions seem to follow:

1. Individuals who are brought up in intact families should have self-concepts that are directly related to their perceptions of their mothers and fathers.
2. Individuals who are brought up in families in which the fathers are absent— regardless of cause—should have self-concepts that are even more strongly related to their perceptions of their mothers, but not significantly related to perceptions of their absent fathers.
3. Individuals from father-absent homes who have subsequently been raised by stepfathers should tend to overcompensate, because of increased fear of rejection, by more strongly aligning their self-concepts in accordance with how they perceive their stepfathers. That is, a strong, positive correlation should be found between these individuals' self-concepts and how they have come to perceive their stepfathers.

The results of a study by Parish and Copeland (1979) lend support to Lifshitz's model, for college students from intact families tended to develop self-concepts that were significantly correlated with how they evaluated their mothers and their fathers (+0.37 and +0.20 respectively).

Also in accordance with Lifshitz's model was the finding that individuals from father-absent families more strongly identified with their mothers (+0.48) and their stepfathers (+0.76) but not with their fathers (+0.02). Loss of a father results in increased emotional distance between the absent father and his children. As children redefine their feelings towards one or both parents, they generally come to feel closer to their mother. This allegiance to mothers, and to stepfathers too, may be fostered by feelings of uncertainty within the children who seek some of the stability they have lost. While the data may not provide clear insight regarding the possibility of the fear of rejection by children in families with new parents, it may suggest that these children overcompensate to gain needed stability.

Another possible explanation for the significant relationship between the self-concepts of individuals who have lost their father and their evaluations of their mothers and stepfathers, is that mothers and stepfathers who are left with the children after losing the father tend to assert themselves in order to gain compliance from their children as they grow up. Such coercive techniques may foster greater dependence in their children and create individuals who wish to conform to the expectations of those who are in authority rather than to face punishment and/or rejection. However, as in all correlational research, the underlying causes and effects cannot be clearly stated.

In a subsequent study, Parish and Dostal (1980) continued the investigation of Lifshitz's (1975) proposal that the child's self-concept develops as a result of successive comparisons and contrasts between the child, father and mother, by computing evaluations of self and parents by children from intact and divorced families. In total, 537 children from intact families and 102 children from divorced families participated. It was hypothesized that, in divorced families, the longer the period for comparison and contrast between real father and stepfather, the greater the movement of the child's self-concept towards the stepfather's perceived self-concept and away from the real father's self-concept.

It was found that the children who came from intact families had self-concept scores (i.e. self-evaluations) that were significantly correlated with their evaluations of their mothers ($r = +0.34$) and their fathers ($r = +0.37$). For the children from divorced families, the self-concept scores were found to be significantly related to their evaluations of their mothers ($r = +0.44$) but not their evaluations of their fathers ($r = +0.17$). Notably 72 of the 102 children from divorced families had stepfathers and as predicted, the self-concepts of those children were significantly correlated to their evaluations of their stepfathers ($r = +0.23$).

Since 47 of the children from divorced families had undergone this experience during the last two years, the self-concepts of these children were correlated with the various parents. Interestingly, the self-concepts of these children correlated with their evaluations of their mothers ($r = +0.34$). For those who are already in the care of stepfathers ($n=33$), their self-concepts were also found to be correlated significantly with their evaluations of them (i.e. their stepfathers, $r = +0.34$).

The notion that an extended period of comparisons and contrasts results in movement towards the mother and stepfather and away from the absent father, as proposed by Lifshitz, received only partial support in this study. Specifically, while overall evaluations of fathers by children from divorced families did not correlate particularly with evaluations of self, there was nevertheless significant correlation between evaluations of self and father for those children whose parents had divorced within the previous two years.

As indicated above, children from divorced families were found to express self-concepts that were significantly correlated with their evaluations of their mothers and stepfathers. Interestingly, for those who had experienced the divorce of their parents within the previous two years, there appeared to be an early alignment with their stepfathers and a relationship between their self-concepts and evaluation of their mothers. It appears that children from divorced families quite rapidly identify with remaining or new parents possibly in an attempt to overcome uncertainty and re-establish parent–child relationships. This rather rapid alignment of the self-concepts of children from divorced families seems to contradict Lifshitz's gradual movement hypothesis and should tell counsellors and parents how children's self-concepts and perceptions of parents develop and change following their parents' divorce.

The impact of divorce and subsequent absence of the father may leave the children feeling bitter towards the absent father, and make them more reliant on their mother and stepfather.

AUTHORITARIAN PRACTICES

It is apparent from the review of previous research that permissiveness and/or lack of concern for the child does not help the emergence of a positive self-concept. The overbearing authoritarian parent equally fails to nurture self-esteem in the child.

The work of Brunswick (1948), Gough (1950), Kutner (1958) and many others have shown that authoritarian parents like things clear cut and unambiguous. Thus, any punishment or discipline is not diluted with tenderness, acceptance and reasoning. They may actually perceive the child at certain times as 'all bad'. This parental behaviour transmits to the child that he is poorly accepted, bad and disapproved of. The responses of children of authoritarian parents are more intense than those of children of non-authoritarian parents, since frustration from their developing, confused and generally negative self-concept is added to ordinary drive. In addition, such a child develops expectancies of punishment in new or unclear situations with the corollary of anxiety and discomfort. Hence the child becomes persistently anxious in a wide range of what are to him ambiguous situations.

Authoritarian parents' own needs take precedence over those of the child. They often assume a stance of infallibility. On no account can they be wrong or thwarted, unlike permissive parents who seem to avoid confrontation with children, leaving the latter without guidelines.

Hence, both authoritarian and permissive parents tend to inhibit a growing child's opportunities to engage in vigorous interaction with others. Unrealistically high standards that cannot be met or expecting little from the child prevent a healthy self-concept emerging. Parental restrictiveness, rigidity or lack of interest make the child feel he is not loved or accepted. Punishment from a cold, disinterested or even revengeful parent can be interpreted as, 'I am being punished because they don't love me'. However, the child punished by a warm, caring parent is likely to argue 'I am being punished because what I did was wrong'. The authoritarian parent generates a vicious circle of hostility and counter-hostility in the parent–child relationship. The child's self-concept is replete with resentment and anger which can be displaced so easily onto scapegoats. Social withdrawal and shyness can also mark such a child, a child who fears to do things for fear of failure, criticism and punishment. Thus a child in such authoritarian surroundings becomes prejudiced against himself, feeling inferior, weak and dependent. These self-feelings are likely to be displaced onto others so that low levels of self-esteem are positively associated with low levels of esteem for others, a point taken to more depths in Chapter 14. An authoritarian family structure can make a child feel insecure, inferior and worthless. Since irrational authority is the rule, independence and spontaneity are snuffed out, and respect for the child's feelings is lacking. These feelings or weakness and worthlessness have a debilitating effect on self-concept.

Mussen and Kagan (1958) conclude that severe parents conflict more with their children. Hence the children have more experiences with their parents in which yielding or conforming reduces anxiety. Consequently, through generalization, these children adopt yielding as a way of life and distrust other people, which Mussen and Kagan (1958) speculate, 'may be generalised responses stemming from original fear and distrust of parents' (p. 60).

The authoritarian parent sets rules, requirements and restrictions. However, these controls are established by fiat. The message is, 'Do it because I say so'. Such parents are highly concerned with maintaining parental authority and value obedience for its own sake. They may use fairly severe punishment if the child is defiant. The word 'arbitrary' springs to mind. The parent's authority is exercised with little explanation and with little involvement of the child in decision-making. The parent claims the exclusive right to determine the conditions of the child's life and expects that the child will recognize this.

The child of authoritarian parents is pictured as being quiet, obedient, unassertive and rather joyless—a girl or boy whose impulses are under control but who lacks the buoyancy, tough self-confidence and empathy for the give-and-take of peer-group play.

CHILD-REARING PRACTICES AND PREJUDICE

The work of Adorno (1950) and Frenkel Brunswick (1948) established the characteristic parental practices that lead to prejudice in children:

> Prejudiced subjects tend to report a relatively harsh and more threatening type of home discipline which was experienced as arbitrary by the child. Related to this is a tendency apparent in families of prejudiced subjects to base inter-relationships on rather clearly defined roles of dominance and submission in contradistinction to equalitarian policies. In consequence the images of the parents seem to acquire for the child a forbidding or at least a distant quality. (Adorno et al. 1950 p. 385).

Later research by Kates and Diab (1955) and Epstein and Komorita (1965) confirms the strong correlation between parental rigidity and authoritarianism and children's prejudice.

We have seen in many studies (e.g. Rosenberg 1965, and Coopersmith 1967) that children, whose parents were uninterested in their activities (for example their performance in school and their friends) denigrated themselves. Extreme parental indifference worsened self-appraisal even more than did excessive punishment or control. Indifferent parents gave the child little love, respect or encouragement, regarding him instead as something of a nuisance. The child whose parents treat him as unworthy, says Rosenberg, accepts that assessment. He comes to internalize, in other words, the views of his significant others.

If authoritarianism and conservatism induce poor self-esteem and, in consequence, foment prejudice then, perhaps, it is because authoritarian parents demarcate boundaries more sharply than do parents of high self-esteem children. Authoritarian parents, quite possibly, show less love and affection for the child and demand more obedience and conformity. Probably, too, such parents are neurotic, anxious, and disparaging of themselves. They transmit to their children not only prejudiced, authoritarian and ethnocentric attitudes but, also self-deprecating opinions.

Bagley and his associates (1979) reported on a study designed to test the relationship between parental authoritarianism, self-esteem and prejudiced attitudes in children of authoritarian parents. Forty-eight fathers were asked to complete a schedule which measured their authoritarian control of their 13–14-year-old sons as well as measures of conservatism and racism. The technique of stepwise multiple regression showed that father's authoritarianism was a strongest predictor of son's self-esteem and, indirectly, of his level of racism. The father's authoritarianism correlated with son's self-esteem $+0.428$ ($P < 0.01$). The most important variable was not father's racism as such, but his authoritarianism which influenced his son's racism, via the medium of self-esteem rather than through the direct learning of racial attitudes.

FROM HOME TO SCHOOL

The pupil's adaptation to the school environment depends on the existing state of the pupil's developing self-concept and the nature of the psychological experience and concomitant reflections of self, provided by that environment and the significant others within it. Whether the change from home to school environment benefits or harms a child, the transition itself is very likely to cause some stress to many children.

The child's ability to deal with this stress depends to some extent on his or her 'social competence' which is evidently related to the child-rearing behaviour of parents. Baumrind (1967) divided pre-school children into three groups according to their social competence. Pattern one children identified as the most mature and competent boys and girls, had parents who were essentially firm, loving, demanding and understanding. Pattern two children, labelled as discontent, withdrawn and distrustful (dysphoric and disaffiliative, in Baumrind's terms) had parents who were firm, punitive and unaffectionate. Pattern three children described as immature, dependent, lacking in self-control and tending to withdraw from novel experiences, had mothers who were moderately loving but unable to control their children, and fathers who were ambivalent and lax in performing their parental role.

The parents of pattern one (mature) children balanced high nurturing with high control. They gave reasons for their actions, encouraged verbal give-and-take, made high demands, communicated clearly, used power openly without manipulation and exhibited an ability to maintain control without inviting rebellion or passivity from children. Baumrind noted that restrictiveness and control are not synonymous. In his interpretation, control interacts with warmth to encourage a mature self-concept in children while restrictiveness leads to inhibiting, dependent and submissive behaviour.

Pattern one children, presumably, had psychological experiences in the home that reflected their unconditional acceptability as individuals, that interpreted children as active and valued participants, and that helped them internalize socially acceptable standards of behaviour. Pattern two, on the other hand, most likely had psychological experiences that reflected their unacceptability, interpreted them as passive and informed them that power and control are exercised exclusively and absolutely by adults. Pattern three children were probably reflected as acceptable but given neither a consistent interpretation of their role nor information from which to develop goal-achieving behaviours.

It can be assumed that pattern one children, armed with social competence, would be least troubled by the transition from home to school. Even these children, however, may encounter difficulty if the school and home environments are very different. Though these children may have a positive image of self and role, they may find that 'socially acceptable' standards of behaviour acquired in the home are, in fact, acceptable only in the society from which they come. The working-class pupil, to whom conflict generally represents a *physical* threat, may find that the physical methods used so effectively at home are unacceptable in the middle-class school. A middle-class pupil, who has learned to deal with conflict by using language and ideas rather than physical behaviours, has already learned how to cope in the style approved of in the new environment.

Parents who have been counselled on being effective parents show differences in attitude, particularly acceptance and trust, from parents who have not. The former, as a result of effective counselling were more accepting of their children's feelings and behaviour and trusted the child more (Summerlin and Ward 1978). This had an effect on their offspring's self-concepts which rose to a higher level. This is not too surprising in view of the parental variables, highlighted, as important in Coopersmith's and in Sears's studies, and again emphasizes the vital effects of parents' understanding and accepting—though not necessarily condoning—their children's behaviours. Such programmes are few and costly but the potential effect of modifying parental behaviour towards children is not doubted in the enhancement of children's self-concepts and consequent behavioural consequences, particularly academically and socially.

SUMMARY

Child-rearing practices are seen as crucial in self-concept development because:

1. The self-concept is learned and comes particularly in young children, from

feedback from parents who are the most consistently present, significant others, at that stage.
2.   The child has a physical, emotional and social dependence on parents so that they are in a unique position to influence the child's learning about himself. Almost infinite variations can be found in the way parents carry out their child-rearing functions.

Many investigators have stressed the significance of parents in the development of self-esteem and the importance of the early years. Specific parental behaviours, for example, by mothers (Coopersmith 1967), warmth (Sears 1970), interest and concern (Coopersmith 1967; Rosenberg 1963), limit setting (Coopersmith 1967), and democratic child-rearing practices or home atmosphere (Coopersmith 1967), have been significantly related to self-esteem in children.

The most important dimensions of child-rearing practices that affect the self-concept level of the offspring are:

1.   Permissiveness–restrictiveness. Some parents exercise close, restrictive control over many aspects of their children's behaviour; others give the children almost complete freedom; many find a balance somewhere between the two extremes.
2.   Warmth–hostility. Although, almost all parents feel affection for their children, they vary in how openly or frequently their affection is expressed and in the degree to which affection is mixed with (or even out-weighed by) feelings of rejection or hostility.
3.   Interest–indifference. There are few parents who are completely uninterested in their children but such behaviour has gross debilitating effects on the child's self-concept. Criticism and punishment is less damaging than outright indifference.

There seems to be little influence on self-esteem from birth order but there is a tendency for a child's self-esteem to be related to the quality of the relationship with the same sexed parent. Maternal deprivation provides a context in which the child interprets himself as being of little worth and poorly accepted. There is a significant relationship between the self-concepts of children and their mothers when the father is lost. Such children come to identify with the stepfather the longer he is in the home.

Severely authoritarian child-rearing practices inhibit the child's development of self-esteem and can lead to the projection and displacement of low feelings of self-worth onto outgroups, particularly ethnic minorities.

Interpersonal relationships within the family are far more important than societal factors of social class, religious persuasion or ethnic group membership.

Futher Reading

Borgatta, E. F. and Lambert, W. W. (eds.) (1968) *Handbook of Personality Theory and Research in Child Development,* Skokie Ill.: Rand McNally, chapters 4, 5.

Bowlby, J. (1966) *Child Care and Growth of Love*, London: Penguin. A leading researcher reviews the effects of early environment on the child's ability to love and be loved.

Coopersmith, S. (1967) *The Antecedents of Self-Esteem*, San Francisco: W. H. Freeman. An investigation of the conditions and behaviours which affect the developing self-concept in pre-pubertal males.

Ginott, H. G. (1965) *Between Parent and Child*, New York: Macmillan. A handbook of practical suggestions for dealing with daily problems in child-rearing.

Medinnus, G. R. (ed.) (1966) *Readings in the Psychology of Parent–Child Relations*, New York: Wiley.

Rosenberg, M. (1965) *Society and the Adolescent Self Image*, Princeton: Princeton University Press.

5

Sex-Role Self-Concept

INTRODUCTION

A child's sex is both a biological and a social fact. When an infant is born the first question asked is 'Is it a boy or a girl?' Stereotypes influence adult perceptions of newborn infants. When seen for the first time through the viewing window of a hospital nursery infants known to be boys are seen as strong and robust while girls are perceived as soft and delicate even when there is no basis in fact for such attributions (Rubin, Provenzano and Luria 1974). In another study on infants, Condrey and Condrey (1976) showed a college audience a videotape of a nine-month-old's reactions to various situations. Some students were informed it was a girl, others that it was a boy. When the infant showed a strong reaction to a jack-in-a-box, the reaction was labelled 'fear' if the infant was thought to be a girl and 'anger' if it was thought to be a boy. So expectations and cultural stereotyping impinge on the child as soon as it is born. The clarification of a few terms would be useful at this juncture.

Sex is the ascription to an individual of maleness or femaleness on the basis of biological features such as gonads, hormones and external genitalia.

Gender or sex identity is the individual's knowledge of being one sex or the other. The individual's sex is an integral part of his or her personal self-concept from the earliest moments of awareness. A child is named, dressed, treated and spoken of as a girl or a boy. The use of the inappropriate pronoun in reference to itself is speedily and consistently corrected by adults. In fact, the concept of self is gender-differentiated. Thus, the first aspect of its identity that the child is aware of is its gender and thereby his or her similarity to the parent of the same sex as well as to peers of the same sex. Once gender identity is established, many processes may contribute to further sex-role development. Being classified either as a boy or girl is an unavoidable central core of the self-concept.

As Thompson (1975) argues, there are three processes in gender development: learning to recognize there are two sexes; inclusion of the self under one category or other; and the use of a label to guide sex-role preferences. Thompson found that two-year-old children used simple, physical cues, like cranial hair and clothes, to distinguish the sexes; by the age of thirty months many children were aware of their own sex and those of others and were showing a preference for same-sex pictures; by the age of thirty-six months they were using gender labels to direct their preferences.

106

The establishment of gender identity is strongly influenced by the gender assigned to the child. Gershman (1967) points out the fact that the parents are clear in their belief that the infant is either male or female has permanent consequences for the child in terms of behaviour and expectations. Any repeal of gender is tantamount to a violation of personal identity—for Paul to become Paula is not simply a matter of change of gender but a change of person involving a total reconstruction of sex concept.

Levi-Ran (1974) demonstrated the power of firm gender identification for the establishment of personal identity. As Lewis (1977) argues, the infant manifests a self-concept towards the end of the first year. This concept, however primitive, enables the infant to separate social objects into 'me', those 'like me', and others, and subsequently to differentiate more finely amongst the category of 'like me'. This schema of the self as a physical body or entity also stems from this discrimination of self from others, and precedes the differentiation of the sex roles and consequent sex-role behaviour.

Sex-role identity, or sex typing is the identification with the behaviour that the culture labels masculine or feminine. A person does not necessarily adopt all the sex-typed behaviours of his or her sex, but enough to be readily identifiable as masculine or feminine. Sex roles constitute the sum of those interests, attitudes, behaviours and expectations which an individual, as a result of being male or female in a particular society, holds, enacts and fulfils. Thus sex-role identity may also be considered as sex-role self-concept, i.e. the evaluated self-image fits the demands of the masculine or feminine stereotype. So the individual's perception of his or her own degree of masculinity or femininity is based on how far the individual fits the publicly shared beliefs about appropriate sexual characteristics.

The assumption is either implied or expressed, that the prevailing stereotypes about the sexes shape the self-concepts of males and females. Just how this happens is unclear. Various authorities talk vaguely in terms of social pressures to conform to sex-role standards, of the incorporation of sex-role sterotypes into self-conceptions, of imitating, cultural conditioning, rewards and punishments.

Identification is a necessary process involved in achieving sex-role identity or a sex-role self-concept. Psychoanalytic theory was the source of the concept of identification. Identification is essentially an unconscious process that enables a child to think, feel and behave along similar lines to his or her significant others. More specifically the child starts to behave as though he were that other person. Earliest and most potent identifications are with parents, though of course peer-group members, teachers, pop stars, etc. will later be identified with. Some of the young child's developing self-concept, especially appropriate sex-role behaviour, derives from identification with people significant to him. Burns (1979) provides a brief outline of some of the major theories of identification as it relates to sex-role identity.

BIOLOGICAL DIFFERENCES

There is evidence to suggest that biological influences are also at work to account for sex-role behaviour and its variable strength between individuals. (McGuinness 1976).

From birth males are better equipped physiologically than females for a physically active life (Hutt 1972b) with a higher basal metabolic rate, greater muscle develop- ment, a greater capacity for carrying oxygen in the blood (as haemoglobin levels increase) and they are altogether more efficient at neutralizing the by-products of exercise and work. The action of the male hormone provides these advantages. Pre-school boys engage in physical activities more often than girls (Brindley et al. 1973) and the preferred activities of young boys is some sort of physical pursuit (Hutt 1974, 1978a) even indoors. The greater tolerance of adults towards boys' physical and athletic activities, their restlessness, and their untidiness may reflect an intuitive achnowledgement of inherent biological characteristics.

The higher incidence of rough play among boys is closely paralleled by similar behaviour among monkeys. There is no evidence to make us believe that sub- primate parents deliberately train their infants in accordance with sex-role stereotypes. So a biological element rather than solely social pressure may be involved. It is known that if females of sub-primate species are given extra dosages of male hormones prior to birth, they too play in a male way. Human girls who are prenatally androgenized (receive excess male hormones) tend to be tomboys. These girls like rough outdoor games and sports and playing with boys, and they are less interested in playing with dolls than their normal sisters (Ehrhardt and Baker 1974). All this does not mean that the hormones present before birth directly cause a child to be aggressive or rough in play. Prenatal hormone levels may simply establish a predisposition to learn certain behaviours readily, so that rough-and-tumble play, for example, seems more interesting (or less frightening). Most normal boys are probably characterized by this. The strength of this presetting undoubtedly varies from child to child, and the child's social experience, of course, quickly begins to influence the child's interests and activity preferences. Social experience and biological presetting are probably interwoven. A given experience can have a different effect on one child than it has on another, depending on biologically influenced temperamental factors.

In the socializing process, components of nature and nurture are inextricably intertwined. Parental expectations and perceptions affect interaction with children soon after birth.

Moss (1967) showed that in the first few weeks of life boys tended to be picked up and cuddled more, but that this was partly because they tended to be more irritable. By six months of age, however, girls are cuddled more than boys and thereafter girls have more physical, vocal, and visual contact with their mothers (Messes and Lewis 1972). Moreover, mothers encourage more independence and autonomy in sons than in daughters (Hoffman 1972). By eighteen months Weinraub and Frankel (1978) demonstrated that the interaction of the same-sex parent was greater than that of the opposite-sex parent with the infant. Caring in childhood is mainly done by the mother who feels more affinity with her daughter, and these attitudes in turn may enhance the affiliative needs (for praise and support) and encourage dependency in girls and autonomy in boys. With their greater confidence, independence and physical activity boys tend to explore their environment, thereby increasing their confidence (Hoffman 1972), while girls tend to be more inhibited and fearful (Hutt 1970).

SEX-ROLE IDENTIFICATION AND FAMILY PRACTICES

Sex-role socialization through the parents operates by identification and differential treatment. In other words, the child will model himself or herself on a same-sex person in the family and will be dealt with differently by family members and other social institutions as a function of the child's sex. These two processes are closely tied together and provide mutual reinforcement. However, identification is seen as more important, creating a firm link between the person and the perceived standards required in society. Differential treatment is only used when parents need to; there is little chance that enough different instances would occur in which relevant behaviour would be subject to various types of reinforcement to develop thorough sex-role socialization.

It is generally accepted that boys and girls are socialized differently in our culture. Differences in toys, in the furnishing of bedrooms, in clothing, in subtle and not so subtle expectancies of behaviour given verbally and otherwise, are all part of the traditional social conspiracy to ensure that boys and girls function according to the stereotype. Perhaps few teachers and parents are consciously aware of their moulding of the child to meet specific sex-role standards. Much of the differential treatment is a reflection of the adults' own life.

Whether there are different behavioural predispositions in male and female babies at birth, is not certain because differential responses to the neonate from parents and others start immediately and mask any innate differences. In any case there is not just a one-way communication from parent to child but reciprocal interaction.

Although the development of sex-role identity is life long, the process is particularly active in the infant and adolescent periods. In the infant period, the child learns a basic set of appropriate behaviours and learns to inhibit a set of behaviours that are inappropriate by society's standards. Girls are taught to be ladylike and not to play rough games or to fight. Boys are taught that they are to be strong and that they are not to play with dolls. Although these kinds of learnings and teachings are very subtle, there is considerable evidence that they are effective.

Learning the difference between male and female behaviour begins early. By the age of two children can identify male activities as such with a high degree of accuracy; and at two and a half, children can identify items by appearance and task according to sex with 75 per cent accuracy for both male and female items (Vener and Snyder 1966). At three, they can judge a wide range of activities according to sex appropriateness (Schell and Silber 1968). Sex differences in preferred play activities and in actual play are also noted by the age of three (Fagot and Patterson 1969).

The child who does not possess attributes which society labels at any particular time as male or female is faced with a wealth of feedback which indicates to him that he does not belong. The boy who has long or short hair (whichever is not the current societal stereotype of maleness) is faced with an image which clashes with the prevailing stereotypes. A similar process operates with all physical characteristics which are sex stereotyped. The girl who is taller than the majority of boys or the boy who is shorter than most of the girls must overcome stereotyped notions. Numerous other physical attributes, such as facial hair, secondary sexual characteristics, voice range, etc., carry stereotypes of maleness or femaleness and become important at adolescence.

Although these physical characteristics are difficult, it is perhaps more difficult for children to deal with emotions and desires which are judged inappropriate for their sex. Girls who are angry and aggressive not only must deal with the behaviour, but must handle the feedback that labels them 'tomboys'. The boy who is fearful must not only deal with the emotion but with the constant feedback that he is 'like a girl'. The sense of identity and belonging is a part of self-concept and tells the child he or she belongs to a group, either males or females. This is a prelude to being an autonomous member of the group.

By the age of three a child is fully conscious of its sex. While children of that age do not understand the biological criteria of sex determination they know what sex they are because other people have told them so many times. However, learning the behaviour and roles of male and female is more difficult, and children vary in how closely they conform to stereotyped masculine or feminine behaviour or interests. When offered an opportunity to play with materials appropriate to the opposite sex, boys of pre-school age are more likely to choose strictly male activities and toys than girls are likely to choose feminine ones. When the adult experimenter goes out of the room, boys will experiment with the feminine objects while for girls the presence or absence of the experimenter makes little difference (Hartup and Moore 1963). It is as though boys are interested in these things but know that they must not play with them when anybody is watching—a clear sign that they have learned to expect negative feedback for showing such interests. The consistency of individual children's sex typing may not be strong, particularly in play behaviour and a number of writers have argued that masculinity and femininity are not opposites—that there is considerable overlapping in the qualities regarded as characteristic of a given sex (Bem 1974; Sears, Rau and Alpert 1965). When these researchers assessed feminine and masculine sex-typing independently, they found that some individuals rated high and some low on both sex's characteristics, although the majority of people had more same-sex than cross-sex characteristics. Bem has used the term androgynous for people who achieve high scores on both masculinity and femininity scales.

Why some children are more sex-typed than others and why a young boy fears being thought of as an effeminate weakling far more than a young girl fears being labelled a tomboy seem to result from social pressure applied in child-rearing. Distinctively different environments are provided for boys and girls by parents. They are given different clothes, toys and positive reinforcement for different types of behaviour. But parents also provide strong negative responses to obvious signs of cross-sex behaviour. A very young boy who tries on his mother's high-heeled shoes or puts on lipstick may be regarded with amused tolerance or gently ridiculed, but such behaviour in an older child is regarded as outrageous rather than funny. Fathers react especially strongly to any such signs of feminine tendencies in their sons. A possible interpretation of such reactions is that many men experience emotional revulsion over signs of homosexuality in other males. They may interpret certain kinds of feminine interests or actions as signs of developing homosexual tendencies in their sons and react to these tendencies in the strongest terms. Goodenough (1957) reports the abhorrence of one father who was asked whether he would be upset by signs of feminine tendencies in his son. 'Terrifically disturbed—could not tell you the extent of my disturbance. I can't bear female characteristics in a man' (p. 310).

Little girls are allowed more latitude for cross-sex interests and play, but they too are pressured to behave in sex-appropriate ways—again primarily by their fathers. Many fathers react warmly to signs of femininity in their daughters. Fathers then appear to play a crucial role in exerting pressure for appropriate sex-typed behaviour.

The importance of fathers in the development of children's sex-typed behaviour is further emphasized by Hetherington's (1967) studies of the relationship between parents' attitudes and attributes and children's characteristics. She found that pre-school and kindergarten girls who were most stereotypically feminine had fathers who were warm and assertive, and approved of feminine behaviour in their daughters. Boys who were most highly sex-typed had fathers who were dominant (in the sense that they tended to win when there were differences of opinion with their wives). Thus, the fathers' attitudes and behaviour had an effect on the degree of sex typing in both boys and girls, although each sex was influenced differently. The mothers' attitudes and behaviour, by contrast, showed little relationship to sex typing in children of either sex.

Boys are generally under more pressure than girls, particularly over the showing of emotion. But having emphasized social pressure we can also recognize that society does allow each person a flexible range in playing out his or her sex role. A shy quiet boy who avoids rough play can still have friends and acceptance as long as he does not dress as a girl and avoids feminine mannerisms. Children learn a lot about sex roles by observation, particularly of parents; children tend to imitate those who are readily available, powerful, warm and nurturant. Both parents generally possess these qualities in relation to their children so there are all the conditions for promoting imitation in the family.

But who should a boy preferentially imitate his father or a girl imitate her mother? The answer appears to be that children—at least under the age of six—do not. A review of the evidence (Maccoby and Jacklin 1974) found very little relationship between parents' own sex-typing and that of their children, and recent work confirms this conclusion (Smith and Daglish 1977). The most 'masculine' fathers do not have the sons who are more 'masculine' than other men's sons, and the same applies to the femininity of mothers and daughters. Hetherington (1967) found that children of both sexes imitate and have personality characteristics that are similar to the parent who is dominant, but this need not be the same-sex parent. In addition, Hetherington found little relationship between children's femininity or masculinity and their tendency to imitate either parent. These facts contradict the earlier theories of people like Freud.

Luckily most parents want their offspring to develop appropriate sexual identities, and consequently subtle pressures are applied like reinforcement of the 'right' behaviour and selective presentation of toys, clothing and hobbies. Additionally, young children want to be accepted by parents, siblings and peers, a need which equally directs behaviour along relevant avenues. For instance, a little boy uses his toy screwdriver to pretend to mend things just as he sees his father do; a little girl washes her doll's clothes just as she has seen her mother do with the family washing. Little direct teaching is required for either sex-typing or identification. But many subtle pressures are applied to guide the child into behaving in ways culturally relevant to his or her biological sex. From birth many parents clothe infant boys in blue and infant females in pink. At Christmas and birthdays boys are given what are conventionally regarded as boy's toys, e.g. trains and guns. Little girls become the happy recipients of dolls and sewing sets. So by the end of the pre-school years most children are well aware of what sex they are and what is expected of them. Much of the play activity of children can be viewed as a rehearsal for adult roles.

Parents and other significant persons frequently make verbal comments to reinforce appropriate behaviour such as 'You are a big boy now, no crying when you are hurt,' or 'Stop that, Helen, little girls do not play with guns.' Such specific reinforcements do not and cannot provide the complete repertoire of sex-role identity without functioning with other processes such as imitation, cognitive stage, etc. Kagan (1964) reports that as early as three, boys are aware of some of the activities and objects that our culture regard as masculine. Among girls, however, preferences are more variable up to puberty. many girls between three and ten years of age do prefer masculine games, activities and objects; whereas it is not usual to find many boys who prefer feminine activities during this period. This difference in game preference is matched by a relatively greater frequency of girls stating a desire to be a boy or wanting to be daddy rather than a mummy when they grow up (Brown 1957).

Rosenberg and Sutton-Smith (1960) tested children aged between nine and eleven for games preferences. The results suggest that girls were more masculine in their game choices than they had been earlier. There are class differences in the game choices of children. Rabban (1950) asked children (aged three to eight) in middle- and working-class homes to select the toys they liked best. The choices of working-class boys and girls conformed more closely to sex-typed standards than the choices of middle-class children, suggesting that the differentiation of sex-role is sharper in working-class families. Working-class mothers encourage sex-typing more consistently than middle-class mothers. Moreover, the difference in sex-typing between the classes is greater for girls.

The middle-class girl, unlike the middle-class boy, is much freer to express an interest in toys and activities of the opposite sex. This finding agrees with the fact that, among girls, there is positive correlation between the educational level of the family and involvement in masculine activities (Kagan and Moss 1962).

The masculinity and feminity of children from homes without fathers have been studied, and traits considered masculine, such as aggressiveness, have been measured in both boys and girls. Pintler, Sears and Sears (1946) found no difference in aggression between father-present and fatherless girls; Loeb and Price (1966), however, found that girls from divorced families were more aggressive. The data concerning differences in aggression for boys in father-based and father-present homes have also been inconsistent. Fatherless boys have also been shown to be less masculine on traits other than aggression (Santrack 1970).

The influence of the child's age at the separation of the parents has been found to be critical for children five years or younger. Hetherington (1972) found boys who were separated from their fathers during their first four years to be less aggressive and more feminine than boys who were five years and older. Bahm and Biller (1971) also reported that boys whose father had left before they were five had less masculine self-concepts than boys whose father had left after that time.

The loss of a parent may affect the amount of identification with one or both parents and these changes in degree of identification with the parents may influence the adjustment of the adolescent. Lazowick (1955) found low levels of parental identification were associated with high levels of anxiety, and high levels of self-esteem in girls were reported to be associated with high levels of parental identification Lynn (1972) proposed that sons have to learn masculine sex-role behaviour on their own and not through identification with the father; the girl, however, is able to learn feminine behaviours by identifying with her mother. He felt this was because mothers are usually with the children more than fathers are. Although Lynn's proposal has been supported (Ward 1973) considerable research indicates that the father may be crucial for both sons and daughters to learn their appropriate sex roles and behaviours.

Stephens and Day (1979) concluded that no particular advantage concerning sex-role identity followed from an adolescent girl residing with her mother rather than with her father following their divorce.

SEX ROLE STEREOTYPES

In most Western societies, the following are identified as appropriate to the male role: self-confidence, responsibility, maturity, independence, decisiveness, powerfulness, leadership, achievement motivation, aggressiveness and protectiveness toward women and children. Women, on the other hand, are frequently described as the bipolar opposites of men. As such, they are described as warm, passive, nurturing, selfless, emotional, obedient and have a developed intuition. Additionally, despite the fact that women now constitute 41 per cent of the nation's workforce, female roles continue to be stereotyped primarily in terms of domestic responsibilities; and female competency is portrayed in terms of fulfilling supportive, expressive roles to assist husband and children rather than self.

Bakan (1966) proposes *agency* and *communion* as two fundamental differences between most males and most females. *Agency* is characteristically masculine and is represented by objectivity, self-assertion, mastery and repression: *communion* is feminine and is represented by subjectivity, interpersonal relatedness, cooperation and openness. Parsons (1955) similarily has made the distinction between instrumental and expressive roles for males and females respectively. Moffett (1975) supports this dichotomy with findings using a semantic differential.

Of the 40 self-description means, 27 (68 per cent) were significantly ($P < 0.05$) different from a theoretical mean of 4. The men described their actual selves as slightly active, tough, rational and dominating. The women described their actual selves as slightly tender, active, conventional, and tense. The men described their ideal selves as quite relaxed, active, outgoing, tough, slightly dominating, calm, rational, and humorous. The women described their ideal selves as quite relaxed, active, outgoing, slightly tender, humorous, calm, rational, and imaginative.

Generally, there were more similarities than differences between men and women in their actual and ideal self-description. On the dimensions showing sex differences more men described themselves as agent than did women, supporting Bakan's hypothesis and previous research.

Prescott (1978) found a similar dichotomy with a sample of over 400 adolescents. Males scored higher on scales relating to strength, power and activity. Females scored higher on scales such as generous, dependable and honest.

Sears (1970) in a study of 11 year-olds found that high self-concepts were associated with small family size, early ordinal position and high parental warmth. For both boy and girls feminity characteristics were associated with low self-concepts. The femininity characteristics were those of occupational and recreational choice, timidity and social conformity. It would seem that by the age of eleven children feel that women's work, activities and anxiety are not valuable possessions compared to male ones. Thus high self-concept males are very masculine in outlook, while for women to have high self-concepts means denying some basic elements of feminity since to be feminine is to be inferior.

In a study of how children learn appropriate sex roles, Brim (1958) described sex-role behaviour in terms of their congruence with Parson's descriptions of instrumental expressive roles. Judges evaluated 58 traits taken from the Fels Child-Behaviour Scales and the California Behavioural Inventory for Nursery-School Children. Thirty-one of the fifty-eight traits were considered to be specific to either instrumental traits identified by Brim's judges with the traits found in the literature as descriptive of sex-role stereotypes reveals a correspondence between male appropiate behaviour and instrumental roles, and female appropriate behaviour and expressive roles.

Despite the Women's Liberation Movement and the increased awareness of sex-role stereotypes, and the rhetoric of social change and equality which abounds in 'women's' literature, the traits described as instrumental (male) and expressive (female) by Parson's in the 1940s and by Brim in the 1950s appear to apply equally well today. The 1972 Broverman et al. study also reports strong support for traditional sex-role stereotyping. Burns (1977) too has shown that little, if any, change has occured and Hoffman (1972) states '... views reported almost twenty years ago relative to sex associated traits persist today among college students' (p. 7).

Characteristics relating to traditional sex roles show great resistance to change, with feminine ones (e.g. passivity and dependency) showing a high degree of stability from childhood to adulthood in females but not in males. Boys and girls who are equally dependent in childhood diverge at adolescence in response to different social pressures. The boy perceives sexual pressure to become independent and manly; the girl, on the other hand, can continue to be passive and dependent because of traditional concepts of femininity. These sex-role stereotyped characteristics are usually uncritically accepted and incorporated into the self-concepts of males and females.

One reason why most studies of adolescents' self-concepts find boys more positive than girls is because, in general, masculine attributes are more highly valued than feminine ones (e.g. Sheriffs and McKee 1957). Broverman et al. (1972) in a thorough survey show that women tend to incorporate aspects of femininity negatively evaluated by the rest of society (e.g. passivity, incompetence) alongside more positive ones (e.g. warmth, expressiveness). Adult males parallel the male child by possessing higher self-concepts than their female counterparts. The concepts of the ideal male and ideal female are fairly congruent with accepted sex-role stereotypes, hence it is not surprising that female self-concepts tend to be less positive than the male's, as the female stereotype contains items judged socially as less positive. A female has a built-in disadvantage, even in attaining the ideal. She is trapped if she is not a stereotype—for derogation from others can occur—but if she does achieve the ideal for a woman then she has a self-concept containing some less than positive traits. Tolor, Kelly and Stebbins (1976), however, have shown that women who reject their sex role are more assertive and have more positive self-concepts. In other words, unusual psychological strength in a woman is associated with high self-esteem which allows the woman to free herself from stereotyped restrictions on her self-perception.

Most girls derive a sense of esteem through social adequacy. Boys can establish their sense of self-esteem in various ways: by direct sexual expression, by independence and autonomy, by asserting competence to achieve in various competitive areas such as athletics, intellect, leadership in school affairs, responsibility in a job. Girls' greater dependence on society validating their femininity means that being popular and being frequently asked out are more critical to them than to boys (Douvan and Adelson 1966; Kagan 1964). Popularity validates feminine self-worth, a guarantee to them of future marriageability.

In a study of adolescents, Connell and Johnson (1970) noted that high sex-role identification males have greater feelings of self-esteem than lower sex-role identification males ($P < 0.01$) and high sex-role identification females ($P < 0.05$). However, it was also found that low sex-role identification females apparently feel just as adequate and worthwhile as high sex-role identification females, while low sex-role identification males had significantly lower feelings of self-esteem than females regardless of the sex-role identification level of the females ($P < 0.05$).

In general, the results of this study suggest that, for the early adolescent at least, the male role is more rewarding than the female's, regardless of whether it is adopted by a male or female. Society's definitions of the male role emphasize mastery and competence, whereas society defines the female role negatively as dependent and submissive. Consequently the female may be positively reinforced for adopting certain male characteristics (e.g. competence), or she may be positively reinforced for fitting into the stereotype that society has structured for her. The male has a much less ambiguous choice; the male role is the only sex role for which he can receive consistent positive reinforcement. Two other conclusions were also suggested by the results of this study, (1) the peer group's reaction to one's sex-role identification is an important determinant of the early adolescent's adequacy; and (2) teachers and parents apparently respond primarily to factors other than appropriate sex-role behaviour in reinforcing the early adolescent.

Dickstein and Hardy (1979) explained the significant relationship they found between self-esteem and sex-role behaviour through the differential socialization of males and females. The American male is encouraged to be logical, independent, aggressive, competitive, and successful. These 'competency' traits may cause the male to evaluate himself in terms of his good behaviours and his success experiences. For example, taking advantages of others may be necessary to achieve success in some instances and because the male is not trained to be sensitive to the effect he has on others, he may fail to evaluate himself on these 'bad' behaviours. In contrast, the American female is encouraged to be gentle, tactful and sensitive to the feelings of others. These 'warm and expressive' traits may prompt the female to evaluate all her behaviours by their effect on others. Her total self-evaluation depends not only upon her good deeds, but on avoiding of doing harm, emotionally or physically, to others. Thus, the women's self-esteem may be more strongly linked to the effects of her actions on others than is the man's.

Lower self-concept scores may also accrue to girls because they appear to be more willing to disclose their weaknesses. Bogo, Winget and Gleser (1970) noted that boys obtained higher scores on 'lie' and 'defensiveness' scales than girls. Such scales reflect the extent to which the individual disguises his 'true' feelings and presents a more favourable picture of himself than he ought. A more extensive and detailed survey of research on self-concept differences between boys and girls may be found in Maccoby and Jacklin (1974).

Wilson and Wilson (1976) were also able to show that males and females have different sources for their self-esteem. Male self-esteem derives from success in vocations, positions of power and competition. Female self-esteem derives from success in personal goals, body image, existential concerns and family relationships. The clustering of these sex differences by source of self-esteem appears to characterize sex-related socialization patterns. They also found that these sex-linked sources contribute in different weights for different individuals. This raises the serious question of the usefulness of a global measure of self-esteem. Additionally, the male and female differences in measured self-concept scores may be an artifact of the measurement technique. That is, the statements included in any self-concept scale are bound to affect mean sex, social class or any other variable score if those scale items are more favourable to one component of the variable than the others. Hence, a rating scale containing items more favourable to girls than boys cannot but help generate higher self-esteem for girls. This may be an explanation for Bledsoe's (1964, 1973) results which are two of the few studies that have revealed higher self-esteem for girls than boys just prior to adolescence. Bledsoe (1964) originally suggested that the earlier maturity of girls and their frequent contact with women teachers and mothers enables them to develop a more satisfying self-image, with early schooling stressing qualities of neatness, docility and conformity—a woman's world where boys are less successful. In his subsequent study in 1973, as a result of analysing responses to individual items, Bledsoe (1973) discerned that the rating differences favourable to girls were those connoting 'goodness', e.g. polite, clean, kind, sincere, cooperative, friendly, unselfish, etc. These qualities, Bledsoe suggests are usually associated with females rather than male stereotypes. So the content of an assessment instrument may well be determining the results to a large extent rather than revealing real differences between groups or individuals. This again points to the necessity of interpreting results with caution.

The centrality of personal achievement to self-concept in boys, and the importance of personal attractiveness and popularity to girls appear repeatedly in the findings of Douvan and Adelson (1966). When asked what makes them feel 'important and useful' the boys said work and achievement, the girls acceptance, popularity and praise from others. Similarily, the achievement theme appears in the worries boys report, while girls more commonly worry about peer acceptance and popularity. When the chance to be a success is pitted against security, most boys choose the opportunity to achieve. The achievement issue is not simply less important for girls, it is different. Girls are not without their ideals, but these dreams are not of personal achievement or success; they are of attracting and retaining love. The critical question for boys was: 'What is my work?' while for girls it was 'Who is my husband?' For some women who do attend college, peer-group pressures for popularity with men often continue, and more attention is often focused on the weekend date than the lifetime career plan. Pressure for early marriage for women may be lessening now, but the primacy of relating to men instead of to work continues. The female peer group promotes no viable identity for women outside of definition through male relationships. Alternative views, promulgating individual assertion and achievement, are provided by some sources, such as women's movement reference groups and magazines such as *Ms.* and *Spare Rib,* but such values touch the lives of relatively few young women compared with the peer culture.

CULTURAL CHANGE

If the notion that sex-role stereotypes reflect sex-related functions and behaviours in society is accepted, then it might be expected that the convergence of socially permissible behaviours of men and women this century will eventually break down the stereotypes. The fact that the stereotypes continue to exist is presumably due to a cultural lag.

If it is agreed that today's society is changing with respect to prescribed sex-role behaviours, it is pertinent to ask what factors tend to accelerate or retard the rate of change. Cross-cultural studies of primitive societies suggest that societies with large, cooperative family units emphasize sex-role differences in child-rearing. Societies with small, isolated families consisting only of parents and children, on the other hand, give less emphasis to sex-role differences since both mother and father have to be able to take the other's role in emergencies. Other factors which appear to influence sex role stereotypes are social class and education. Thus, clearer and earlier awareness of sex-role patterns has been found among working-class children than among middle-class children (Rabban 1950). Similarly, parental roles in middle-class families are less differentiated than in working-class families (Bronson, Katten, and Livson 1959). Also, the older and the better educated a mother is, the less she insists that boys behave in a masculine manner and girls in a feminine way (Sears, Maccoby, and Levin 1957).

Presumably, then, the trends in today's society towards small families, white-collar work, and increased education and participation of women in economic activities all tend to accelerate the rate of change in acceptable sex-role behaviours.

Variations in family organization, parental education, parental social class and work history of the mother might be examined in future as factors which influence not only the extent to which people's attributes are perceived as linked to sex, but also the degree to which stereotyped traits influence self-concepts.

Presumably, as stereotyped sex differences are reduced, individuals will increasingly tend to see the personalities of others not as stereotypically masculine or feminine, but rather as individuals. Sex stereotypes will tend to be replaced by individual differences in the perceived as well as in the perceiver.

Although sex-role stereotypes may have originated from physiological sex differences of strength and child-bearing, these differences no longer appear to be so important in today's society. However, while strength may indeed be less important in today's urbanized, computerized society, other physiological sex differences are still operating. For instance, female superiorities of attention, perceptual speed and accuracy are well documented (McGuinness 1975). These differences may be due to the differing effects of the estrogens and androgens on the sympathetic central system. If this is correct then some stereotyped differences involving the sympathetic nervous system, such as the tendency of females to be more talkative than males, may persist. Further research is needed to determine those sex differences that stem from physiological factors and those that stem from social training. Physiological differences may, in the end, limit the eradication of sex-role stereotypes.

MASS MEDIA AND SEX-ROLE IDENTITY

Television offers a diet of stereotyped sex roles for children to devour. Cowboys, gangsters and other adventure shows most often feature males while females are relegated to ancillary and domestic positions. Women are sometimes specifically presented as sexual objects with no other function than adornment and enhancement of the male image. Men are often portrayed in aggressive roles, e.g. in detective and western shows, where the moral of the story usually is that the more aggressive man wins in the end. Situation comedy again reveals conventional roles. The highly exaggerated picture presented by television is alarming since many children are glued to the television set out of school hours.

Since the sex roles portrayed on television are so highly stereotyped and distinct for the two sexes, Frueh and McGhee (1975) supposed that the amount of time children spent watching television would be related to their sex-role development, and indeed found this to be the case for both boys and girls.

Other powerful socializing agents are represented by books and magazines. The sex-role expectations purveyed by these are that boys and men are more highly valued than girls and women; that boys are active and achieving while girls are passive and emotional. As Weitzman et al. (1972) point out 'children's books reflect cultural values and are important intruments for persuading children to accept those values. They also contain role prescriptions which encourage the child to conform to acceptable standards of behaviour' (p. 1126).

The Weitzman et al. (1972) survey looked at sex-role portrayal in American children's literature. They report that females were under-represented in the titles, central characters, pictures and stories of every sample of books examined. Most children's books are about boys, men and male animals and most deal exclusively with male adventures. Even when women can be found in books, they often play insignificant roles, remaining both inconspicuous and nameless.

The ratio of titles featuring males to females was 8 : 3; only two of the eighteen books were stories about girls and in nearly one-third of books there were no women at all. Boys were portrayed as active and adventuresome, girls as passive and immobile, most often found indoors, often performing service activities. Books to read and heroes to be worshipped are often geared to peer-group values. For example, my daughter read the whole set of Sue Barton books simply because all her friends were reading them. Such books reinforce the values of feminine domesticity and passivity. Peer pressure led to the acceptance of such books and their values. The peer group, therefore, acts as a primary influence for the processing and dispersal of sterotyped materials produced in mass media culture. Football stars, for example, gain their psychological reality for boys through their idealization in their peer culture.

An American survey in 1972 by Women on Words and Images reported in Tavris and Offir, (1977) looked at 2750 stories from 134 children's books and found that the traits Americans value were mostly portrayed by men and boys.

> Boys make things; they rely on their wits to solve problems. They are curious, clever and adventurous. They achieve; they make money. Girls and women are incompetent and fearful. They ask other people to solve their problems for them . . . In story after story, girls are the onlookers, the cheerleaders . . . even accepting humiliation and ridicule. In 67 stories, one sex demeans the other—and 65 of these involve hostility of males against females. (Tavris and Offir p. 177).

Holter (1970) describes investigations of adolescent books in Scandinavia.

> Males are presented as more aggressive, objective and emotionally neutral than girls . . . boys are active, initiating and ready to explore the world outside the family, whereas girls are passive . . . devoted to the family and inclined to stay at home . . . Besides being passive, helpful and interested in people (the girl) can be a competent and independent heroine when no boys are present. (p. 205).

It is little wonder that sex role stereotypes are so slow to change and that children's self-concepts include strong elements of sex-role attributes.

THE SCHOOL, SEX-ROLE IDENTITY AND SELF-CONCEPT

The effect of the school environment on sex-role self-concepts can be immense. Firstly each teacher, like the parents, will transmit their own specific sex-role expectancies, and reinforce appropriate behaviours, punishing inappropriate ones. This may occur as part of controlling behaviour, or as part of the teaching curriculum, in which early reading material, text books, and careers advice provide very definite stereotypes about sex roles. The assignment of tasks in the classroom reflect the opportunity for sex-typing as do the range of subjects provided for each sex. Expectations of performance in maths, science, art, reading, etc. all transmit a message about sex-role standards. The norms of the classroom—quietness, literacy, conformity are female rather than male. An analysis of children's books as we have seen reveals conventional sexual stereotypes being taught alongside reading.

At school and in the playground each child is faced with a stereotyped peer culture with its own values and activities, and must relate to it or risk ostracism and scorn. Sex-role conflict cannot be avoided if the school, which is, of course, an institutional representation of the traditional values of the dominant middle-class ideology. Generation gaps and culture/subculture differences which occur among teachers, pupils, parents, and school administrators often involve the definition of sex roles, attitudes toward sex and sex-appropriate behaviour. Conflicts over sex discrimination in dress and behaviour codes, curriculum content and activity restrictions reflect the less than universal agreement about sex roles and sex-appropriate behaviour.

Concern about the school's effect on female self-concept has recently been expressed in charges that curriculum content, through sex stereotyping, discourages females from making a contribution to society in traditional male areas. Concern has been expressed for the self-concept development of boys. As child-rearing and teaching are primarily in the hands of females, it has been suggested that young boys are deprived of male models necessary for learning the male role. The school environment is considered as 'feminine'—requiring conforming, submissive, and passive behaviours associated with the traditional female role rather than the male. The assumption is, of course, that male teachers do not demand conforming, submissive behaviour from the pupils! Clearly, these 'feminine' behaviours are really pupil role behaviours, considered necessary and expedient in learning situations. In fact, the behaviours criticized as 'feminine' in school (conformity, silence, obedience) are those imposed by the armed services in order to 'make a man out of you' during training! Perhaps the issue has more to do with bias against women acting in authority a male prerogative. So just as teachers must learn to work with the partially socialized children they receive, the children have to accommodate to teachers with well-developed ideas about sex role and pupil role.

Levitin and Chananie (1972), for example, found that student teachers and infant teachers had well-defined sex-role expectations of their students and defined their preferred pupils as orderly, conforming and dependent. They also indicated rather sharp distinctions between their preferred pupil role and their perception of the male sex role. Davidson and Lang (1960) and McNeil (1964) found that elementary teachers gave girls higher ratings than boys on general behaviour and motivation, and Good and Brophy's (1972) sample of teachers tended to express concern for low-achieving girls while rejecting low-achieving boys. Fagot and Patterson (1969) found that nursery-school teachers reinforced almost only 'female' behaviours in both boys and girls (86 and 97 per cent respectively). Jackson and Lahaderne (1967) observed that over 80 per cent of sixth-grade teachers' prohibitory responses were with boys, while the boys received only slightly more instructional and managerial responses than girls. Meyer and Thompson (1956) partially corroborated these latter findings with another sample of sixth-grade teachers. Brophy and Good (1970) also found that first-, seventh-, and eighth-grade teachers were more likely to have negative contacts with boys than girls.

Studies of reading performance have also focused on differences in teacher behaviour related to the sex of pupils. McNeil (1964) investigated teacher behaviour and pupil-reading performance using an automatic instruction sequence followed by a teacher instruction. After the automatic instruction, the performance of boys was slightly superior to that of girls. However, after the teacher's instructional sequence, the boys' performance lowered significantly, while the girls' performance did not. Pupils reported that during teacher instruction, boys received more negative comments and fewer opportunities to perform, leading McNeil to conclude that teacher behaviour is related to pupil performance in beginning reading.

Palardy (1969) found that male pupils learn to read more slowly than girls when the teacher has previously expressed a belief that girls acquire reading skills more rapidly than boys. Such teacher expectations will be further considered in Chapter 9.

Findings such as these indicate that boys and girls do not have equal access to the typical teacher's expectations about pupil role. Boys are pressured to accommodate to a pupil role which conflicts with their sex role and, perhaps more perniciously, girls are pressured not to deviate from their female sex role. None of this would have much operational meaning, however, unless children were aware of the teachers' expectations, and teachers behaved in accord with these.

When examining the interaction between the sex role, self-concept, culture and schooling, top priority is placed on the covert curriculum for two reasons. First, it is the respository of stable and unexamined interactions between sex role and institutional folkways; and second, given schooling as it currently exists, action directed at the official curriculum is almost inevitably superficial. Official curricular change will take hold only when adjustments are made in the hidden support system. Changing the content of children's readers would have little or no effect without corresponding change in the teacher's expectations, for example.

Educators often argue for realism in expectations of what schools can accomplish. Without support from the larger society, the schools probably cannot do much. However, we have the opposite fear that, due to their inherent conservatism, schools may be falling behind the evolving sex-role sensibilities of everyday society. Unless the schools make adjustments, they shall not participate in the new sex-role biculturalism and may even provide informal opposition to sex-role matters now supported by law.

Teachers need to recognize that their preoccupation with a narrow pupil role forces them to be custodians of those children who do not fit the idea. If teachers prefer to see themselves as more than custodians, then they should encourage children to be learners as well as pupils. Teachers should also attempt to control their own sex-linked expectations and behaviour. This is an aspect of conciousness raising and should be an integral part of any teacher-training programme. It would be helpful for teachers to move sex role to the overt curriculum by making it proper educational fare for social studies or literature lessons. This approach would place sex-role culture under the conscious scrutiny of children, who stand to lose most through its unexamined and unquestioned acceptance.

When the author was a pupil, children entered school through doors marked *Boys* and *Girls*. Though such doors no longer exist, school is still divided on a sexual basis. The classroom is not the realm of female teachers intent on feminizing the masculine population; it is a bastion of conventional values, preserving traditional sex roles, encouraging sex-appropriate activities through controlling behaviours. It is possible that this reinforcement of sex-related behaviours and roles has an adverse effect on learning, directing the potential of both boys and girls, and creating strongly differentiated sex-role self-concepts.

As we have already noted, boys are more strongly orientated to achievement than girls, as achievement is a stronger component of their sex-role self-concept. It would seem possible to hypothesize that female pupils would be more vulnerable in academic competition and reveal a lack of confidence in their own abilities.

There are several possible reasons why female students, even though they feel generally as comfortable as men about their own competence, should express less self-confidence about how they will perform. The simplest explanation is that they are more hesitant about bragging, so that though they really feel self-confident they do not say so.

Another reason may be that women do not define themselves in terms of success on these kinds of tasks and are willing to accept a wider range of performance as being consistent with a favourable self-image. There is evidence that women are more acceptant of others, despite any weaknesses they may have (Berger 1968) and they may have a similarly more tolerant attitude toward their own performance. Another way of putting this is to say that their aspirations are lower.

A further possible reason why female students may lack confidence in their performance on a forthcoming task is that they do not feel so in control. In recent years, measures have been developed for the 'locus of control', and individuals may be characterized by whether they feel that the events affecting them are the result of luck or chance (externalizers), or whether they feel they can control their lives through their own actions (internalizers). The sexes do not differ consistently on these scales through the grade-school and high school years, but in college there is a trend for women to be externalizers. That is, they believe their achievements are often due to factors other than their own skills and hard work.

We have seen that parents and mass media act as models for imitation and identification. Teachers too are significant others who commonly present themselves to children as models of competence and desirable behaviour. Asking children to 'watch the way I do it', then, 'do it just like me' is a standard pedagogical formula assumed to be effective, whether used explicitly or implicitly. The effectiveness of modelling, however, depends on the child's willingness to imitate, and the available research indicates that children imitate same-sex teachers more than opposite-sex teachers. Portuges and Feshbach (1972), for example, found that third- and fourth-grade girls imitated filmed female teachers significantly more than their male peers did. Friedman and Bowers (1971) compared five categories of verbal behaviour of female teachers of young children with the verbal behaviours of their students, and found that girls more closely resembled the teachers than boys on four of the five categories. Unfortunately, neither of these studies included male teachers to test the converse. In another study, Madsen (1968) found that nursery-school boys imitated the film aggressive behaviour of familiar male teachers more than girls did. The girls, incidentally, were more non-imitatively aggressive than boys were. Instead of punching, hitting and throwing a doll, the girls used more so-called feminine aggression, such as pushing, shoving, slapping, pinching and squashing.

One should be wary of inferring too much from these three studies, but they suggest that children between the ages of three and nine tend not to imitate opposite-sex teachers. Since less than ten per cent of teachers of the under-tens are male, it would seem that boys and girls do not have equal access to the teacher as a model of competence and behaviour. The ubiquity of the female teacher at the early stages places unfortunate constraints upon both the teacher and her pupils. Her sex detracts from using her as a model for approximately half her class. While many boys instructed in their sex-role cannot imitate their female teachers, most girls lose the option of *not* imitating their teachers.

We should seriously consider the contribution that male teachers may make to the sex-role environment of the classroom. There is no sizeable body of research indicating male teachers differ spectacularly from female teachers or that they favour boys over girls. It may be that the combination of male and female teachers would be optimal for young children, especially if two modelling possibilities were provided. The female teacher should be a model of female competence for girls, that is, a blend of instrumental competence and comfortable female identity. The male teacher should provide the complementary model for boys, that is, a mixture of nurturance and secure masculine identity. None of this is to suggest that the female teacher be cold or the male teacher be incompetent or that any other role manipulations take place. The contention is simply that the presence of male and female teachers would give children equal access to the teacher's modelling value.

Giving young children more male teachers is doubly valuable. First, there should be advantages for young girls because of their relative willingness to imitate male models. The male teacher could make his sex-typed competencies available to young girls through both modelling and direct teaching, thereby enhancing their already manifest tendency toward biculturalism. Second, there remains the problem of most boys' reluctance to imitate female models. Since male teachers of young children are generally quite nurturant, they could provide effective models of biculturalism to young boys. By involving themselves in female- as well as male-typed activities, they could show boys that interest in feminine activities does not constitute a threat to masculine identity (Baumrind 1972). It should be mentioned, however, that male teachers are not to be seen as the special property of boys any more than female teachers are of girls. Teachers of both sexes would be expected to make their sex-role cultural resources available to all children, irrespective of sex.

SUMMARY

Cultural expectations and stereotyping impinge on the child as soon as it is born. There are some biological differences between the sexes which help sex-role behaviour and identity, but these are mainly effected through differential treatment by parents and others and modelling by the child.

Differential identification with parents and teachers, acquisition of sex-typed skills and proper sex-role experiences all determine the degree to which an individual labels himself or herself as masculine or feminine. Appropriate sex-role identity demands a same-sexed parent whose behaviour is relevant, who is nurturant and rewarding, and an opposite-sexed parent who also supports and rewards the correct identification.

Evidence across different researches is largely consistent, revealing a common core of stereotyped characteristics. Females are described as warm and sensitive, socially skilled and inclined toward interpersonal and artistic interests. Males are described as competent and logical, possessing self-confidence, direct in manner and dominant. These expressive and instrumental traits are incorporated into the self-concepts of females and males respectively.

Such stereotypes are slow to change in our culture. Girls generally show lower self-esteem than boys by adolescence. This may be due to the tests being biased towards boys or because traits associated with femininity are less valued generally by society. Boys establish their esteem through achievement in many areas; girls derive their self-esteem mainly through social competence.

Television and books strongly reflect sex-role stereotypes and thereby help to perpetuate them. Within school, teachers transmit sex-role expectancies and the curriculum tends to reinforce this. Young boys are deprived of male models in school, which tends to be a 'feminine' context. Male teachers provide an alternative model for girls and reveal to boys the possibility of nurturant behaviour in a male.

Further Reading

Hutt, C. (1972) *Male and Females,* Harmondsworth: Penguin.

Hutt, C. (1978) 'Sex Role Differentiation in Social Development', in McGurk, H. (ed.) *Issues in Childhood Social Development,* London: Methuen.

Maccoby, E. E. and Jacklin, C. N. (1974) *The Psychology of Sex Differences,* Stanford: Stanford University Press.

Mischel, W. (1970) 'Sex Typing and Socialisation' in Musen, P. (ed.) *Carmichael's Manual of Child Psychology,* vol. 2, New York: Wiley.

6

Adolescence and the Self-Concept

INTRODUCTION

Adolescence brings with it both consolidation and change for the existing self-concept. A number of factors promote self-concept modification during this period, though findings are somewhat equivocal over the conventional view that adolescence is stormy and stressful, with all that that implies for the self-concept. The features of adolescence that suggest, at first appearance that some modification of the self-concept is unavoidable are: 1) the physiological and physical changes in body build as a function of puberty which lead to changes in body image; 2) the maturing of cognitive and intellectual skills (e.g. achievement of formal operational thought) which bring a more complex and differentiated self-concept involving an appreciation of both real and hypothetical possibilities; and 3) the demands of various aspects of society including parents, peers and school which may conflict and involve role changes and fundamental decision making about occupation, values, behaviour, etc., presenting role conflict and status ambiguity.

Rosenberg (1965) claims that Western society has no clearly defined expectations of the individual during adolescence. This results in adults responding to teenagers in ambiguous ways, requiring demonstrations of independence and self-confidence on some occasions but obedience and dependence at other times, without the contextual reasons being all that apparent.

In this chapter the theoretical and research evidence concerning the adolescent self-concept are discussed, particularly the conventional approach as exemplified by Erikson (1963) and the validity of the concept of identity crisis. The effect of changes in body image and sex-role identity are considered also.

Adolescent behaviour is often paradoxical. Revolutionary fervour can quickly give way to conformity; demands for independence alternate with requests for support; the enthusiastic, hard-working teenager on one day is the mindless drifter the next. These rapid changes seem to occur because adolescence is a period of transition between childhood and adulthood. Specifically it is between the onset of puberty and the achievement of socially sanctioned maturity. The latter can be regulated by many criteria such as age permitted to marry, or vote, or drive a car or be responsible for one's own actions in a legal sense, all of which can be varied by government from time to time. The transfer from adolescence to adulthood is difficult to define.

This transition from childhood to adulthood is affected by a number of inter-acting pressures. Some of these pressures are biological, involving puberty, body change and emotional expression. Other pressures stem from the expectations and demands of society, particularly parents, peers and school. These pressures some-times advance the adolescent towards maturity quicker than he or his significant others would like; at other times they retard the progress towards maturity to the chagrin of the young person. It has been wisely said that adulthood occurs two years earlier than most parents would like but two years later than most adolescents would prefer.

TWO GENERAL THEORIES OF ADOLESCENCE

Coleman (1980) classifies the explanations of the problems of this transition period into two: psychoanalytic explanations and sociopsychological explanations. The former has focused on the psychosexual development of the individual and the youngster's emotional ties within the family. The latter approach seeks an explanation in the social context within which the individual functions, empha-sizing roles, status, role conflict, ambiguity and social expectations.

The Psychoanalytic Perspective

The psychoanalytic approach concentrates on the rise of instinctual forces at the onset of puberty which upsets the psychic balance of the latency period, resulting in emotional upheaval. This awakening of the Freudian genital stage leads to the breaking of emotional ties with parents, as appropriate love objects are sought outside the family.

Two major psychoanalytic writers have expounded on the psychological bases of adolescent storm and stress. Blos (1962, 1967) described adolescence as 'the second individuation process', the first having been finished by the beginning of the fourth year of life. Blos saw both periods as having common elements. In both, the child has to adapt to becoming more mature, there is vulnerability of personality, and psychological disturbance if the tortuous path of change is not accommodated to psychologically. In this comparison, Blos appears to discern a parallel between the transition from dependent infant to more self-reliant, independent and autonomous pre-school child, and the movement from the pre-pubertal child locked into the family web to adult independence. This latter transition involves acceptance of independence by adolescent and parent, and the renunciation of child–parent ties, the mainspring of emotional nurturance. The internalized parent needs to be displaced in the disengagement to make room for a future love object, a marriage partner.

Although there are notable similarities between the two struggles for independence, the outcomes are dramatically different. The two-year-old almost always
loses and the adolescent not only almost always wins but *must* win.

Another contribution of Blos's approach to understanding adolescent psychology
is the significance of regression. The adolescent, he argues must behave appropriate
to earlier periods of development since independence and individuation require the
severing of close emotional family attachments. This can only happen, Blos believes
by a reactivation of the origins of these infantile involvements. 'The adolescent has
to come into emotional contact with the passions of his infancy and early childhood
in order for them to surrender their original cathexes; only then can the past fade
into conscious and unconscious memories.' (1967, p. 178).

A number of examples of regression in adolescence are detailed by Blos. For
example, the adolescent's idolization of famous people, especially pop stars and
celebrated sports personalities, a parallel to the idealized parent of the younger child.
Another example of behaviour in which we can recognize reflections of earlier states
is the emotional condition in which the individual becomes totally submerged by, or
'at one with', another. In this condition, the adolescent might become almost
completely absorbed in such abstract ideas as Nature or Beauty or with political,
religious or philosophical ideals.

A further example of behaviour derived from early childhood is ambivalence, or
the vacillation from one behaviour to its opposite, a seemingly incomprehensible
part of adolescence. The rapid shifts from hating to loving, from accepting to
rejecting, from anger to joy, all part of the emotional instability of early years with
their contradictions in thought and feeling, are reactivated again in adolescence.
Adolescent rebellion represents the conflict between loving and hating, between the
desire for independence and the need for dependence when the harsh light of reality
illuminates the daunting prospects ahead. Sometimes, the rebellion and non-
comformity can be a defence mechanism. If the adolescent can perpetrate the
rationalization that parents are old-fashioned, restrictive and out of step, then the
breaking of old emotional ties is easy. There is nothing to be lost; home can be safely
rejected and independence gained.

The experience of separation and loss that can occur at adolescence had been seen
as paralleling that adult phenomenon of mourning and grief which accompanies the
death of someone close. Blos terms this state 'object and affect hunger' which results
in the adolescent need for intense emotional states such as delinquent activities,
drugs and mystical experiences and short-lived, but intense, relationships, as a
means of coping with the inner emptiness. Even the need to do things 'just for kicks',
simply represents a way of combating the emotional flatness, depression and loneli-
ness which are part of the separation experience. 'Object and affect hunger' finds
some relief in the adolescent gang or peer group, a substitute for the adolescent's
family, within which he may experience all the feelings for individual growth such as
stimulation, empathy, belonging, role playing, identification and the sharing of guilt
and anxiety.

So, the psychoanalytic approach views adolescence as being the period of vulnerability of personality due to instinctual upsurges in puberty. A maladaptive and
vacillatory behaviour is emphasized to deal with inner conflict and stress, as

emotional bonds developed from infancy have to be broken to establish mature emotional relationships outside the home. Furthermore, a period of identity and diffusion is postulated as adolescents attempt to become autonomous individuals. The total picture is one of turmoil which is, perhaps, to be expected from psycho-analysts whose contact with adolescents has been with those referred for treatment.

The Social Perspective

The sociopsychological perspective on adolescence focuses on socialization and role. It is concerned with the ways in which the standards, values and beliefs of a particular society affect the expectations and prescriptions of behaviour appropriate to roles such as teenager, parent, son, daughter, etc. Socialization and role become problematic in adolescence since the cognitive ability of the adolescent, the greater choice of roles available and the expanded environment offer a wider range of socializing agents. Altering the relative effectiveness of former agents provides more choice, a chance to experiment and greater opportunity for doubt and indecision. Role change is an important feature of adolescent development.

First, growing independence from authority figures, involvement with peer groups and sensitivity to the evaluations of others, provoke role transitions and discontinuity of varying intensities, as functions of both social and cultural context. Second, pubertal change increases the need for reassurance and support for one's view of oneself. Third, the effects of major environmental changes, such as changing schools, moving from school to further education, leaving home or taking a job, all permit involvement in a new set of relationships, different and often greater expectations, a substantial reassessment of the self-concept and an acceleration of the process of socialization.

The transition of adolescence therefore involves socialization into new roles, and with role change may come upheaval, discontinuity, role conflict and role choice. For the pre-adolescent, roles are ascribed by others, but for the adolescent choice and interpretation of chosen roles are offered.

Adolescence is perceived as culturally created phenomenon. It did not exist in Britain a few generations ago, because education was short and one's working life commenced early. Even today in many primitive societies adolescence is unknown with transition from childhood to adulthood happening in a few hours at a ritual ceremony. In Western society, however the lengthening of education required for an advanced technological society has created an interval between physical maturity and adult status and privilege. While such a transition period provides a young person with a longer time to develop skills and prepare for the future, it produces a period of conflict and vacillation between dependence and independence, between child roles and adult roles. The adolescent becomes a 'marginal' adult.

But as well as role change, the adolescent has to cope with role conflict, a situation in which the adolescent is trapped between the mutually incompatible expectations of two roles, say daughter and girlfriend. The daughter feels she ought to stay in at night to keep her widowed mother company but, as a girlfriend, is expected to go out each evening with the boyfriend providing him with love, affection and care. The adolescent's transit through the period is likely to be effected by consistent, or inconsistent adaptive or maladaptive expectations concerning his roles held by significant others. In a discussion of adolescent socialization, Baumrind (1975) talks of 'reciprocal role assumption', by which she means how prior role assumptions by other members of the family effect the role that another member may assume. The perception influences the role behaviour.

Socialization is perceived as more uncertain in the contemporary setting, too. Elder (1975) draws attention to several social-change issues which may create problems for adolescents. Young people are more dependent as more stay longer in education, and there has been a decline in the role of the family while the peer group becomes increasingly important as parents abdicate responsibility. Finally, the adolescent is exposed to a garish blast of conflicting values, standards and role expectations through the plethora of mass media, youth organizations, political organizations, student and trade unions, etc. Both Elder (1975) and Bronfenbrenner (1974) see uncertain socialization and alienation as making it hard for the young person to learn adult roles.

Compared to the psychoanalytic viewpoint then, the psychological approach looks at stress and tension as resulting from conflicting pressures from external society and not from internal emotional instability. They do hold one belief in common and that is the conventional concept of adolescence as a turbulent and stressful period of development, with consequent effects on how the adolescent views and evaluates his current self-image.

ERIKSON'S PERSPECTIVE

A perspective that links these two approaches would seem to be Erikson's (1963) socio-pyschoanalytic synthesis in which biological maturing and drives interact with social roles, expectations and demands throughout the life cycle, evoking crisis at each stage, a major crisis being that of adolescent identity formation.

The concept that crises can serve as opportunities for personal growth has been developed particularly by Erikson. He describes a series of overlapping stages in life, each of which is characterized by a specific crisis in personal and social relationships, and all of which contribute to the development of a sense of identity. Crises and the development and maintenance of identity in fact share a common characteristic; the individual has to choose between one or more possible alternatives. Thus, following Erikson's formulation, the developing child passes as we have noted, through successive crises in terms of basic trust versus mistrust; autonomy versus submission, associated with shame and doubt; personal initiative versus fear of disapproval and guilt. This leads up to the adolescent crisis of identity formation versus identity diffusion, or the development of a negative identity based on opposition and rebellion but not yet on the choice of an identity truly one's own. Each successive crisis, if successfully survived, leaves the individual more capable of making a satisfactory personal choice at the next stage, and hence ultimately in adolescence when identity formation becomes the central issue. This will be considered in more detail later in this chapter (p. 142).

PUBERTY, BODY IMAGE AND THE SELF-CONCEPT

The word 'puberty' comes from the Latin *pubescere* which meant to be covered with hair. In English, the word refers to the total biological changes that take place in the growing adolescent. These changes affect the way the adolescent is viewed by others as well as his view of his total self-concept and especially his body image.

The biological changes in puberty usually are sequential but the age at which they begin, the length of time they take to complete varies markedly, with individuals. Factors which influence timing aspects of development are primarily heredity, health and environment. In contemporary Western Europe and North America, the average range for the onset of puberty is from ten and a half to thirteen years of age for girls. Boys, on the average, are two years behind girls developmentally. Thus the average age for the onset of puberty in boys is between twelve and a half to fifteen years of age. The growth spurt that signals puberty varies widely in intensity, duration and age of onset among perfectly normal children, a fact not always understood by adolescents and their families and often a source of needless concern. Youths who enter puberty later than the average range often face special concerns which will be discussed later.

The growth spurt is the most obvious signal of the onset of puberty. At this time, all parts of the body increase in size with the exception of the brain, skull and reproductive organs. The order of increased growth is typically sequential starting with leg length and body width. While many youths are waiting for the increase in trunk length, which occurs about one year later, they may appear to be all legs and may feel uncoordinated and perplexed by this new version of themselves. Physical strength increases at this time. While, before puberty, boys and girls had equal strength, after puberty, boys' strength will have exceeded that of girls. This is because boys gain more muscle bulk, and have a greater increase in the number of red blood cells which carry oxygen to the muscles. Their lung capacity increases to a greater extent than for girls. The heart grows rapidly in both sexes at this stage. Both sexes have an increase in body hair with subsequent maturing of reproductive organs. The female has an increase in fatty tissue which the blossoming bosoms and curving hips make more evident. The male on the other hand, becomes more muscular, has coarser textured skin and develops facial hair. Their voices start the process of changing which by its rambling inconsistency may prove embarrassing. Problematic skin changes brought on by the growth of sebaceous glands do not discriminate against either sex.

The changes in hormonal levels that accompany puberty are partly responsible for the mood swings. The interest in the opposite sex is stimulated by the presence of the hormone androgen which is present in both sexes during adolescence and in adult life. This interest in the opposite sex is at the core of the social and affective changes in adolescence. Early maturing boys and girls will start dating while later maturing boys and girls still congregate in the same-sex groups giggling at the opposite-sex groups or at those more mature peers who are dating.

Body Image

I can help you to lose weight.
Are those adolescent spots and skin eruptions losing you your girlfriends?
Contact lenses are less unsightly than glasses.
Men! Build up your body and get a healthy he-man look at our health centre.
No more looking up to everybody when you wear our built-up shoes.

These are all typical advertisements. You know of many more like them, focusing on the need to fit some ideal physical stereotype of masculinity and femininity at particular ages. Our society places considerable stress on body and bodily appearance, resulting in cultural aspirations (sometimes engendered by advertising agencies) for being the 'right' weight and height, and for having the correct dental, skin, hair and body-odour conditions. Appearances do count in the evaluation of self and others because first impressions count most of all and body appearance is the predominant first impression. It is only through further contact that evaluation can include personality.

Male and Female Satisfaction with Body Image

Erikson (1968) places major emphasis on the adolescent's physical attributes as a source of identity and self-concept. To Erikson, personality development and identity formation represent a synthesis of the biological, psychological, and sociological components of the person. Consequently, each sex must use their bodies (and specifically their genitals) in a biologically appropriate—i.e. adaptive manner to achieve complete synthesis, and concomitantly successful self-definition. For a female, biologically appropriate use of the genitals requires a 'taking in' or an incorporation of a male. While this incorporation may be either literal and/or symbolic, the suggestion is that females should view their bodies as the basis for attracting and incorporating others. Females should therefore view their bodies' utility in terms of interpersonal physical attractiveness because the more attractive the female feels she is, the more likely she is to attract a male to her, and hence increase the chance of attaining an adaptive, incorporatively based sense of self.

For males, however, biologically appropriate genital use requires a 'pushing out', or an intrusion, into objects in the environment. These objects may be animate (e.g. females) or inanimate, but in either case this intrusive orientation suggests that to the extent males can feel that they effectively push out into their environment an appropriate, positive sense of self will develop. Thus, males should view their bodies as instruments for manifesting their individual physical effectiveness, i.e. the basis for their attaining the ability to competently intrude upon the world external to them.

These theoretical speculations suggest that the adolescent female's evaluations about herself (her self-esteem, her self-concept) should relate more to her attitudes about her body as a physical attraction, than to her attitudes about her body as an instrument of individual effectiveness. Conversely, the adolescent male's self-concept should be more highly related to physical effectiveness than to physical attractiveness.

As we have seen in Chapter 5 on sex-role self-concept, support for such divergent social expectations exists; both male and female late adolescents stereotypically define male behaviours in terms which describe a 'competence' cluster and female behaviours in terms which describe a 'warmth-expressiveness' cluster (Broverman et al. 1972). Moreover, Kagan and Moss (1962) report that childhood behaviours found to be continuous through adolescence were those characteristics congruent with socially traditional sex roles. Thus, across this period males tended to show continuity in aggressiveness, while females show passivity and dependency.

If such divergent sets of behavioural prescriptions define the male and female roles respectively, then the more a male sees himself as emitting competent and effective behaviours, and the more a female sees herself as possessing the attributes to express warmth and security, their self-concepts should be more positive. The more a male can 'use' his body to demonstrate his 'individual' effectiveness, and the more the female can attract others with whom to be warm and expressive, secure and dependent, the more will their behaviours conform to societally rewarded expectations.

Accordingly, we see that a major source of females' self-concept is interpersonal, implying the saliency of their bodies as a stimulus for the attraction of others, while a major source of males' self-concept is individual, implying the importance of their bodies for instrumental effectiveness. The results of recent research are consistent with these derivations.

Lerner, Karabenick, and Stuart (1973) measured male and female late adolescents' feelings of 'satisfaction' with twenty-four parts of their body and related overall mean satisfaction to a measure of self-concept. In both male and female groups satisfaction with the body was a moderate predictor of self-concept. However, since it is possible that males and females could be satisfied with their bodies for different reasons (e.g. the body is satisfactorily attractive or effective) Lerner and Karabenick (1974) asked an independent group of male and female late adolescents to rate how physically attractive they thought each of the twenty-four body parts were. Inter-relation of mean attractiveness ratings and self-concept scores indicated that the former ratings played a more prominent role in predicting females' self-concepts than predicting males' self-concepts. As expected, the correlation between mean attractiveness and self-concept was significant, although moderate for females, but was not significant for males. However, Lerner and Karabenick did not ask subjects to rate the effectiveness of their body parts, and so the contribution of such ratings to the prediction of males' self-concepts, as well as those of females remains unknown.

Lerner, Orlos and Knapp (1976) addressed themselves to that issue. Male and female late adolescents were asked to successively rate twenty-four parts of their own bodies for both physical attractiveness and physical effectiveness. For females it was expected that the former ratings should be more important than the latter in predicting self-concept, while the reverse pattern was expected for males.

Moreover, the assessment of physical effectiveness and physical attractiveness attitudes in both male and female adolescents allowed for an important, related comparison to be made of the congruence of these types of attitudes within each sex. That is, it is known that adolescent males view as most attractive that male body type which is also most instrumentally effective: the mesomorph.

The athletic looking, muscular, and strong-boned mesomorph is positively stereo-typed with both instrumentally functional and personally approved traits, and adolescent males with such a body type show better self-concepts than adolescent males without. However, there is some evidence that among females the female body viewed as most attractive is not the one seen as most effective. Staffieri (1957) found that elementary-school girls viewed a body type closer to ectomorphy as most attractive. However, no appraisal of the relation between attractiveness and effectiveness attitudes *per se* has been conducted among adolescent females. Thus, a secondary purpose of study by Lerner et al. (1976) was to assess if the implications of the above data could be supported in the present study's late adolescent sample. Specifically, this second set of expectations involved the prediction that, more so than with female adolescents, among male adolescents a body part that is seen as advancing effectiveness is also seen as something which enhances attractiveness.

Lerner et al. (1976) used 124 male and 218 female nineteen-year-olds in the study subjects rated twenty-four body characteristics in terms of how physically attractive and how physically effective they assumed these parts to be. Subjects also responded to a short self-concept scale. It was expected that attractiveness attitudes should contribute more to the self-concepts of females than should effectiveness attitudes, while a reverse pattern of interrelatedness was expected for males.

Consistent with a presumably greater interpersonal than individual personality development of orientation, the females' self-concepts appeared more strongly related to their attitudes about their bodies' physical attractiveness than its physical effectiveness.

The males' data, however, appears to be consistent with an orientation towards physical effectiveness. The converse of the above findings pertaining to the females' data obtained with the males' results. These findings suggest that for these males, self-concept was more highly related to body attitudes pertaining to 'individual' physical effectiveness than 'interpersonal' physical attractiveness.

The correlation between the effectiveness ratings of the twenty-four body part items and male self-concept was 0.58 while the corresponding relation between the attractiveness ratings and self-concept was 0.50. The correlation between the attractiveness ratings of the twenty-four body parts and female self-concept was 0.52 while the corresponding result between the effectiveness ratings and self-concept was 0.37.

The body parts found to be the most significant predictors of the female self-concept were face, waist, bust, teeth and mouth. These were only significant when rated in terms of attractiveness. However, the prediction of the male self-concept were body parts rated not in terms of attractiveness but of effectiveness such as height, body build, thighs, mouth and width of shoulders.

Of course, these sex differences reflect only a relative orientation difference within each group. Thus, the present data in Lerner's study may not be construed to mean that attractiveness is irrelevant to males (or effectiveness to females). Rather, we see only a differential, sex-related emphasis in orientation and, in fact, find considerable correspondence in each sex group's rating for attractiveness and effectiveness. This congruence is quite high for males, significantly greater than that for females, and may reflect a confounding in our society between the male physique type having the structural requisites of physical effectiveness—the mesomorph—and the male physique stereotypically seen as the most attractive—again the mesomorph.

The issue of whether 'anatomy being destiny' leads to either greater interpersonal or individual personality development depending on one's sex, or whether 'mechanically', socially mediated systems of rewards and punishments produce such personality differences, remains unresolved. More data from within the above extremes will need collection before final decisions can be reached.

The adolescent's view of their appearance and self-concept was the subject of a study by Musa and Roach (1973). Their subjects were 119 boys and 83 girls in junior high school from an American mid-west industrial city. The subjects compared their own appearance to that of peers in the ladder device developed by Cantril (1965). Other tests given were the personal adjustment half of the California Test of Personality which measured six components of adjustment, self-reliance, sense of personal worth, sense of personal freedom, feeling of belonging, withdrawing tendencies and nervous symptoms. The 'sense of personal worth' component was used to study total self-concept.

The findings of the study showed that 41.5 per cent of the boys and 43.4 per cent of the girls rated their appearance equal to their peers. More boys (34.7 per cent) rated their appearance better than peers, while only 27.7 per cent of the girls did. A larger number of the girls (28.9 per cent) than boys (23.7 per cent) rated their personal appearance lower than they rated their peers' appearance. Boys (43.7 per cent) were more satisfied with their appearance than girls (12.2 per cent). The girls that wanted changes wanted them in hair, weight, clothes and figure. Boys wanted changes in clothes, face, hair, and weight, in that order. Both boys and girls who rated themselves higher or equal to peers in appearance had a higher rate of personal worth while boys and girls who rated themselves lower than peers in appearance had low ratings.

Gunderson (1956), in a study of older adolescent males showed that deviation from preferred height and weight had a pervasive negative influence on self-esteem and similar findings in seventeen to twenty-one year-old women were reported by Jourard and Secord (1955b). Jones and Bayley (1950) reported that two-thirds of the adolescents they studied expressed a desire for some change in their physique.

The results of a study by Simmons and Rosenberg (1975) gives credence to the view that given the great cultural emphasis placed on female beauty, girls would care more about their appearance than would boys. In fact, in late adolescence 36 per cent of girls say they care 'very much' about how good looking they are in comparison to only 24 per cent of boys. At the very same time as they care more, teenage girls are less likely to perceive themselves as physically attractive: e.g. in late adolescence only 16 per cent of girls can be classified as 'satisfied with their looks' in comparison to 35 per cent of boys.

These differences between boys and girls generally do not occur in the 8 to 11 year-old group; they first appear in early adolescence. Thus the changing body image that occurs in adolescence seems to be more of a problem for the girl than for the boy. She suffers from the conjunction of attitudes that is most detrimental to the overall self-image; she is more likely to feel she is succeeding in an area about which she cares very much—in this case her looks.

The results from Mahoney and Finch's (1976) study suggest that the relative importance of different body parts for self-esteem are not those previously thought to be so. Only a small number of body parts in their study contributed to self-esteem. The correlations for males and females between global body cathexis and self-esteem were +0.45 and +0.37 respectively.

The variable which contributes the most to self-esteem is general appearance or overall physical attractiveness in the case of both sexes. Examining specific body aspects, there is a clear tendency for facial features and 'major' body aspects to contribute the most to self-esteem in both studies, an observation that supports the conclusions of Bergscheld et al. (1973, p. 126) that for both sexes, face is the most important with regard to self-esteem and that, for males, the body part that had the second strongest impact on self-esteem was the chest; for females, the second most important factor was the mid-torso reflecting their worry about weight. Closer analysis of the individual body aspects involved revealed, however, that for males only six of the original twenty-three body aspects actually account for variance in self-esteem. For females, only seven of the original twenty-one body aspects remain. For males, the body aspect which contributes the most to explaining variance in self-esteem, is voice, followed by chest and facial features. For females, overall physical attractiveness is the aspect which accounts for the most variance in self-esteem with voice, calves, height and hips minimally contributing.

This study further indicates that female body aspects generally thought to be important to self-image are not important to self-esteem (bust, waist, weight). Even though females may be dissatisfied with these body aspects to the point of desiring to be different the degree of satisfaction appears irrelevant to self-esteem. This is also the case for males with the absence of weight and height as contributors to self-esteem. However, the subjects were post-school students hence the body worries of adolescence may have been over for them.

Menarche

Puberty has long been recognized as a developmental landmark. Menarche, on the other hand, while probably experienced by girls as the single most important event of puberty, has received scant attention. A treatment of menarche as a normative crisis in girls' development is conspicuously absent from the literature. Further empirical observations of the impact of menarche are rare. Although Offer (1969) has written extensively on the development of normal adolescent boys, no comparable body of the data exists for girls.

At present, Kestenberg (1961) comes closest to providing a framework for understanding menarche as a normal developmental crisis. Kestenberg describes the first menstruation as the most important event of adolescence for girls, and focuses on the positive aspects of menarche. Drawing mainly from the clinical materials,

Kestenberg has described the period preceding menarche as one of confusion and 'disequilibrium'; the pre-menarcheal girl had difficulty organizing and communicating her thoughts. With the onset of menstruation, however, there is a dramatic change; according to Kestenberg, the post-menarcheal girl is able to express herself more clearly, and her thoughts appear better organized. In particular, Kestenberg has suggested that menarche has an important role in organizing the adolescent's girl's image of her own body and her sense of identity as a woman. Pre-menarcheal confusion about sexual identity and body image gives way to post-menarcheal acceptance of womanhood with a corresponding reorganization and articulation of body image (Kestenberg 1961).

Interviews with normal adolescent girls, both pre- and post-menarcheal, support Kestenberg's formulation. Post-menarcheal girls report that they experience themselves as more womanly and begin to contemplate their future reproductive roles. Greater definition and acceptance of the body as feminine as well as clarification and acceptance of the self as female are normal consequences of menarche for girls. Associated with these changes is a general awareness and differentiation of male and female bodies (Haworth and Normington 1961).

The first menstrual period, experienced by the average British girl at about twelve and a half years of age, occurs late in the developmental sequence of adolescence. It follows the period of maximal growth spurt and the emergence of secondary sex characteristics by as much as two and a half years.

Although the actual feminizing changes of puberty thus begin long before and continue long after menarche, it seems that the onset of menstruation—a sharply defined biological event—is the particular time at which the psychological and biological changes occurring through adolescence are organized and integrated. Menarche provides 'proof' of womanhood; not until the first menstruation do adolescent girls seem to accept or assimilate the feminizing changes of puberty.

As yet, there seems to be no systematic empirical research to complement the clinical literature relating menarche to changes in body image and girl's acceptance of themselves as females. There is, however, a good deal of work concerned with general developmental changes in body image, particularly sexual identification and differentiation. A consideration of this work provides useful background for the present investigation as it explored specifically the significance of menarcheal status for body image and acceptance of the feminine self.

One developmental prediction supported by the results of several investigations is that progressive awareness of sex differences and greater acceptance of one's sex role increase with age and are reflected in increases in the degree to which male and female human figures are drawn as sexually different (Haworth and Normington 1961).

In addition to these studies, one investigation has examined the relationship of body image to a rather broadly defined stage of puberty. Dreyer et al. (1971) compared the figure drawings of pre- and post-pubertal boys and girls. Results indicated greater sexual differentiation in the drawings produced after the onset of puberty. These data are consistent with the clinical reports that post-menarcheal girls have a more sexually differentiated body image than pre-menarcheal girls. Similar results emerged from the work of Koff et al. (1975).

A methodological problem in this research is that puberty and age are confused. What are interpreted as body image changes associated with puberty, may in fact be changes related to increase in age. Yet the post-menarcheal girls' greater satisfaction with female identity than the pre-menarcheal points to menarche as a pivotal event for the reorganization of the adolescent girls' self-concept.

Yet the psychological significance of menarche is all but ignored in our culture. Rather than regarding menarche as a critical maturational crisis with enormous emotional impact, our culture attempts to treat it as a hygienic issue. The adolescent girl is cautioned to learn to care for herself at 'that time of the month' to avoid embarrassment. The failure of our culture to recognize the psychological importance of menarche is reflected, perhaps, in the paucity of theoretical, clinical and empirical study of this aspect of adolescent girls' lives. The data in this study, in particular the changes observed in the figure drawings associated with the onset of menstruation, are consistent with the view that menarche is a turning point in the adolescent girls' acceptance of herself as a woman. Clearly, there is a need for an expanded framework within which to study such psychosocial consequences of menarche.

With adolescence, the extensive alterations in both size and configuration of the body require radical reorganization of the body image. It seems that the onset of menstruation, as an unequivocal event (at least for normally developing girls) has the potential for greater impact as a focus of the body image than do other, more gradual, changes associated with puberty.

RETARDED AND DEVIANT PHYSICAL DEVELOPMENT

Ordinarily, during childhood and pre-adolescence, the body image changes slowly. Gradual alterations in appearance and height are easily absorbed in the picture the child has of his body. Then, with the upheaval of adolescence, the pace of change is so greatly accelerated, that there is need for radical reconstructing of the body image.

The growth process tends to be asymmetrical. Physical changes do not always take a sexually appropriate course and any delay in the onset of puberty is regarded by the immature boy as evidence of impaired virility. The presence of this discordance in growth often tends to intensify the usual instability found in adolescence, further stimulating anxiety and feelings of inadequacy. Incongruous secondary sexual development, as in boys with gynecomastia, usually has a deleterious effect. The more obvious the defect is, the more likely that personality adaptations are distorted.

More important than the objective handicap of late or inappropriate sexual development is the social disadvantage at which it places the deviant adolescent. Deviancy from the group elicits a highly negative response from his peers and almost guarantees that he will be treated differently. Adolescents accord highly discriminatory treatment to persons with physical handicaps. Such persons enjoy lower status in the group, are frequently ostracized, fail to receive their share of attention from the opposite sex and are often treated with open contempt and hostility.

Adolescents take advantage of their rivals' shortcomings in the race for status in the group and for favour in the eyes of the opposite sex. The individual's response to his own deviation is largely a reflection of the social reaction to it. During adolescence, when he is so dependent on a peer group for status, he tends to accept the value that the group places on him as real. The advertising media, magazines, films, television and hero worship of athletes have by direct or indirect means contributed also to glorifying the ideal body and degrading the deviant.

The adolescents intensified awareness of his body stems partly from the consciousness of his own physical development, partly from the inflated emphasis assigned to physical traits by schoolmates and partly from increasing identification with culturally determined standards.

Deviant Physical Development

In a study of the body image of disturbed adolescents Schonfield (1963) found three types of subject group. First were those seen in the endocrine, plastic surgery and pediatric clinics with actual inappropriate sexual development—boys with enlarged breasts; obese boys with apparent feminization due to fat distribution; boys and girls with puberty delayed beyond sixteen years of age; and boys and girls with short stature, ranging from dwarfism to short normals. Some of these adolescents showed overt disturbances of behaviour adaption, but others did not until they were further questioned.

The second group of adolescents had no physical abnormalities but still were overtly concerned over their sexual adequacy. These adolescents showed disturbances of body image through emotional problems ranging from transient difficulties of adjustment, conduct disorders, learning problems anxieties and psychosomatic symptoms, to psychoneurotic reactions. Others repressed their concern and expressed anxiety over their body image only after prolonged psychotherapy. The third group of adolescents were those using a physical defect as a rationalization of a more basic personality defect of social ineptness.

The adolescent who lacked relative stability as a child due to disturbances of parent–child relationship, prolonged illness and problems of adjustment, frequently failed to develop a proper basis for self-concept. When such an adolescent has to integrate the changes in body structure inherent in even normal pubescence, he experiences greater anxiety than those who are well adjusted. The less effectual his adaptations are in early childhood, the poorer are his adaptations to even normal adolescent body changes or minimal deviations in maturation and body configuration. When maturation actually deviated from the normal strong reactions could be noted to the disturbance of body image (Schonfield op. cit.)

Physical abnormalities which may have been present since childhood, develop a new significance in adolescence. Several case studies known to the author of adolescent males who had serious negative feelings about their body images follow. In all cases the devaluing of the physical self-concept led to maladaptive behaviour and poor academic performance. But with sympathetic and empathetic treatment from staff and professional intervention by a therapist, there were clear and positive changes in self-conceptualization with consequent changes in behaviour.

Adolescent Case Studies

B was seen by his doctor at sixteen years of age because he claimed he had a persistent cough. Examination revealed no symptoms to explain the cough but did reveal an appreciable enlargement of his breasts. He then admitted that the presenting affliction of a cough was a rationalization for his visit and was really worried about his masculinity. he was then seen in subsequent interviews by a psychologist who initially noted that B would not talk about his body image as he was not yet psychologically ready to face it. At later interviews, he began to express concern that he was turning into a woman and that he spent many hours examining himself to see if it was progressive, rather than studying his schoolwork. His work at school was suffering from lack of attention and declined to such a serious level that a previously prognosticated academic future was in jeopardy. He withdrew from all activities that involved physical exposure and close peer group relationships. Yet, paradoxically, he tried to prove masculinity and virility in obnoxious ways such as defiance of school rules, bullying younger children and general insubordination, he had to be the big man. After supportive psychotherapy, and surgery, B returned to his previously acceptable social and academic behaviour.

F was referred for psychological examination at fourteen. He had become a disruptive influence in the class using a variety of attention-seeking devices and the headmaster's report talked of him as impatient, highly strung, argumentative, domineering and little liked by his classmates as they found him difficult to get on with. His academic record revealed that, despite an IQ of 148, he was working well below his capacity. Physically, he showed a marked difference in maturity for a chronological age of fourteen. He was only the height of an average ten-year-old and his general physical development was pre-pubescent. This discrepancy was determined as the root cause of his behaviour for, though he initially denied concern over his height, pubertal status and muscular development, he discussed these issues at later therapy sessions revealing his worries and feelings of inadequacy. He also felt rejected because of his body image. He responded well to psychotherapy sessions and to oral androgens given by his doctor to stimulate sexual maturation and growth in height, so that social and academic adjustment in school were achieved.

W had been obese since the age of nine without any apparent worry until, when nearly fifteen he reported his awareness of being physically different from other boys in his class. Rep Grid constructs showed that he perceived peers as virile and mature while he saw himself as flabby and immature. He had become seriously disturbed with his body image and had refused to undress for PE and swimming and started to attend school on an irregular basis. As far as could be ascertained he had not been subject to any ridicule or criticism about his obesity from pupils or staff at school. His behaviour was now based on his own interpretation of his appearance and of his failure to achieve the 'ideal' body image presented by his peers. Psychotherapy and cooperation with a dietician changed his self-attitudes. When last seen, at seventeen years, he was assessed by the therapist and the school as a mature, sensible person with a good personality adjustment.

Retarded Physical Development

While such intensive case studies show that personal and social adjustment during adolescence may be profoundly influenced by rate of physical maturity, there are not enough systematic data on the relationship between the adolescent's physical status and his underlying motivations, self-motivations, self-conceptualizations and interpersonal attitudes. There is, however, a small body of evidence which demonstrates that early-maturing boys differ from their later-maturing peers in both overt behaviour and reputational status. In one study (Jones and Bayley 1950) in which a staff of trained observers assessed a large group of adolescents on a number of personality variables, boys who were consistently retarded in physical development were rated lower than those who were consistently advanced in physical attractiveness, grooming and matter-of-factness; and higher in sociability, social initiative (often of a childish, attention-seeking sort) and eagerness.

On the basis of these findings, it may be inferred that adult and peer attitudes toward the adolescent, as well as their treatment and acceptance of him, are related to his physical status. This means that the sociopsychological environment to which late maturers are subjected and, consequently, the social lessons they encounter may be significantly different from that of their early-maturing peers. As a consequence they acquire different patterns of overt social behaviour. It seems reasonable to hypothesize that groups differing in physical status will also differ in more covert aspects of behaviour and personality.

Indirect evidence, relevant to this hypothesis, comes from an investigation of the long-term consequences of physical acceleration or retardation during adolescence. Jones (1957) found that group differences in physique had practically disappeared by the time early- and late-maturing subjects reached their early thirties. Nevertheless, young adults who had been physically retarded adolescents differed from those who had been accelerated in several important psychological characteristics. In general, the adult subjects could be described much as they had been during adolescence. Those who had been early maturers scored higher in the good impression, socialization, dominance, self-control (low score on impulsivity), and responsibility scales of the California Personality Inventory, while those who had been slow in maturing scored higher on the flexibility scale. On the Edwards' Personal Preference Schedule, early maturers scored significantly higher on the dominance scale, while the late maturing were high in succorance. Jones concluded that the early maturers present a consistently favourable personality with regard to important social variables. The early-maturing adult males had made successful vocational adjustments, were more self-controlled, more willing and able to carry social responsibility. The later-maturing group were more dependent, rebellious, touchy, impulsive, self-indulgent, insightful and had not made good vocational adjustments. These differences in later adjustment suggest that the sociopsychological atmosphere in which the adolescent lives may have profound, immediate and enduring effects on his personality structure as well as on his overt behaviour.

In another study, Mussen and Jones (1957) investigated the relationship between self-concept, motivation, and interpersonal attitudes of thirty-three late- and early-maturing boys. The study concluded that the boy whose physical development is retarded is exposed to a sociopsychological environment which may adversely affect his personality. They found that being in a disadvantaged position in athletics, as well as being regarded and treated as immature, may lead to a negative self-concept, increased feelings of rejection by others, prolonged dependency needs and rebellious attitudes towards parents. These researchers stated that these late-maturing boys were more likely than their early-maturing peers to be personally and socially maladjusted during late adolescence. The one positive comment that Mussen and Jones made about the plight of late-maturing boys was that they were more sensitive to their own feelings and more ready to admit and face them openly.

The physically accelerated boys, on the other hand, are likely to experience an environment which is much more conducive to good psychological adjustment. Hence, their psychological picture, as reflected in their TAT stories, is much more favourable. By the time they were seventeen, relatively few early-maturers harboured strong feelings of inadequacy, perceived themselves as rejected or dominated by parents or authorities, or felt rebellious toward their families. As a group, they appeared to have acquired more self-confidence and had probably made stronger identifications with mature adults. Hence, they perceived themselves as more mature less dependent and in need of help, and more capable of playing an adult male role.

In contrast to the dramatic effects bodily change has on the male self-concept in adolescence, physical change, whether early or late, has a much less potent influence on the self-concepts of adolescent girls. This difference may be due to the male cultural norm of tall, brawny masculinity, whereas early maturing for girls contains no prestigious advantage. In fact, early maturation can be a calamity: the girl will stoop to hide her height, or wear sloppy jumpers to disguise her developing breasts. Early-maturing girls are perceived as listless, submissive and lacking poise (Tryon 1939) and are judged to have little popularity among their peers (Jones 1958). This picture contrasts very much with that painted of early-maturing males. The early-maturing girl is, of course, three to four years ahead developmentally of the average boy, and had to seek social outlets with much older males. Thus the slower-maturing girl is likely to enjoy more social advantages with her male age peers.

In a similar study to the one conducted on males, Jones and Mussen (1958) compared early- and late-maturing girls in terms of their self-conceptualizations, motivation and interpersonal attitudes. They found that early-maturing girls had more favourable self-concepts and were less dependent, but the relationships were far less clear than for males, for whom physical strength and sport were so important. The feminine sex-role stereotype does not have such a high premium placed on total physical make-up, though specific physical elements are important, e.g. attractive face, well-endowed bosom, etc. A girl need only possess one of these qualities to elicit positive responses; a deficit in one aspect can be more than compensated for in another. Girls are expected to make themselves attractive and are judged on how they look, whereas boys are expected to perform feats with their bodies. Total physical make-up, rather than specific aspects, is more important. On the existing evidence it is possible to speculate that maturing in adolescence has a less dramatic effect on girls than boys because the former have greater flexibility for altering or changing their looks through a sensible use of cosmetics, padding, etc. but the latter can do little to alter their performance. But despite the camouflage of cosmetics, the psychological damage caused may never be eliminated completely.

Frank Barron, in his *The Shaping of Personality* (1979), takes a different view than Mussen and Jones about late maturers. He believes that often the later maturer is working toward a more complex integration in adulthood. He referred to the Oakland Growth Study (1979), a long study that began in 1932. The subjects were interviewed in junior or senior high school and again at age forty to fifty. When the interviews were compared, Livson, concluded that among the most healthy and best adjusted subjects in middle age there were many who had severe sexual identity conflicts in adolescence or were non-conformists in that regard. This shows a more positive forecast for late-maturing youths.

Mussen and Jones (1957), like other researchers, concluded that early maturers have an easier time in adolescence. There are generally two reasons given. First they look more adult sooner and are respected by their peers and often are given more freedom by adults which provides an environment which promotes self-image and self-confidence. The second reason is that they get over the tension and anxiety caused by pubertal changes earlier and they are able to cope with other problems of adolescence much sooner and more effectively than late maturers.

The striking similarity between the various research findings derived from different kinds of tests and collected at widely separated periods of time, lends support to Jones's (1957) conclusion that adolescent advantages and disadvantages associated with late, or early, maturing appear to continue into adulthood to some extent. It seems clear that many attitudes of adolescent personality (patterns of motivation, self-conceptualizations, and attitudes to others) characteristic of late- and early-maturing boys are relatively stable and durable, rather than situational and transitory.

One important factor which seems absent from these studies is the criterion which standardizes the meaning for the terms late- and early-maturing adolescents. The small size of their sample seems to lead one to believe that they overgeneralized their conclusions. There is no mention of early-maturing adolescents who have difficulties because people expect too much of them. The other early maturers not mentioned in the study are the precocious adolescents who by their physically mature looks find themselves in situations which call for more maturity (experience) than they possess, and who may make poor choices which are hard to change later. Certainly further investigation of late- and early-maturing adolescents is needed.

ERIKSON AND THE SENSE OF IDENTITY

Erikson (1963) has claimed that the major task confronting the adolescent is to develop a sense of identity, to find answers to the questions 'Who am I?' and 'Where am I going?'. The search for personal identity involves deciding what is important or worth doing and formulating standards of conduct for evaluating one's own behaviour as well as the behaviour of others. It also involves feelings about one's own worth and competence.

Adolescents' sense of identity develops gradually out of the various identifications of childhood. Young children's values and moral standards are largely those of their parents; their feelings of self-esteem stem primarily from the parents' view of them. As youngsters move into the wider world of the secondary school, the values of the peer group become increasingly important—as do the appraisals of teachers and other adults. Adolescents try to synthesize these values and appraisals into a consistent picture. To the extent that parents, teachers, and peers project consistent values, the search for identity becomes easier.

The concept of identity itself requires careful consideration. A person's identity, like any other psychological characteristic, can no longer be thought of in terms of the person in isolation, but must be seen in the social context of his relation to others, originally his family. In other words, it has both personal (subjective) as well as social (objective) aspects, and the two are closely interrelated. William James made this distinction as early as 1890. He referred to the personal aspects of identity as the 'consciousness of personal sameness' and contrasted this with the social aspects, that a man has as many social selves as there are individuals who recognize him and carry an image of him in their mind. We tend nowadays to speak of the part a person plays in relation to others as his social role and to distinguish this from what he feels himself actually to be, sometimes referred to as his true self, or personal identity. These two aspects of identity formation can be regarded as self-realization and social definition. In fact, there is a close relationship between the two. The less well established or unified a person's sense of inner identity or self-realization is, the more likely he is to assume a variety of contradictory roles in his outer behaviour. Someone with a more consistent sense of personal identity is likely to reveal this even in the various social roles he has to assume. Conversely, the achievement of mutually satisfying interpersonal and social roles increases self-confidence and the sense of self-realization.

Out of these distinctions arises the need for each individual to make choices, both between different aspects of his inner self, and between these and the outer roles he assumes in a social context. These conflicts between self-realization and social definition which are most striking in adolescence recur throughout life, and tend to be most marked during crises. One's identity is in fact not finally established in adolescence but the process of identity formation continues throughout life. Both self-realization and social definition continue to remain problems which demand conscious reappraisal. In this sense we continue to create our own personal and social identity; the term identity *creation* may, therefore, be more appropriate than the term identity *formation* which suggests a more passive process. The importance of both the personal and social aspects of identity, and their interrelationship, is best expressed in Erikson's definition of identity.

'The conscious feeling of having a personal identity is based on two simultaneous observations: the immediate perception of one's self-sameness and continuity in time; and the simultaneous perception of the fact that others recognize one's sameness and continuity.' (1959, p. 23). According to Erikson, then, in order to achieve a sense of identity 'the young individual must learn to be most himself where he means most to others—those others, to be sure, who have come to mean most to him'. (1959, p. 102).

It frequently happens that, upon reaching the age when a choice of identity is necessary, a young person is unable to do so. At this point a person may take what Erikson calls a psychosocial moratorium, 'a prolongation of the interval between youth and adulthood', during which the young person lives somewhat purposelessly, waiting to find himself. In the United States, the psychosocial moratorium has been institutionalized in the form of a system of higher education that allows young people to forestall the identity crisis until their middle twenties.

In the fusion of the psychoanalytic and sociological perspectives, adolescence becomes a period of physical maturity and social immaturity. Because of the complexity of the present social system the child reaches physical adulthood before he is capable of functioning well in adult roles. Adolescence becomes extremely difficult because the new physical capabilities and new social pressures to become independent coincide with many impediments to actual independence, power, and sexual freedom.

The resulting status ambiguities, that is, the unclear social definitions and expectations, can be seen as causing a corresponding ambiguity of self-definition. In addition, the need to make major decisions about future adult roles on the basis of what he is like at present, heightens the adolescent's self-awareness and self-uncertainty even more (Erikson 1959).

From society's viewpoint, these external and internal pressures to plan for a future career, to beome more independent and to establish relationships with the opposite sex, all direct the individual away from his family of origin toward the creation of a new family. In the course of adolescence he changes from a dependent whose prime emotional attachments are to his family, into a person capable of embarking on an independent existence, ready to establish his most important emotional allegiances outside of his present family. With all these physical, emotional social changes, it is small wonder that theorists assume that this period is difficult for the child's self-image.

Erikson has had a considerable effect on how adolescence is viewed, and on the implications that stage of development has presumably for every teenager. He employs emotive phrases such as 'identity crisis' and 'the psychopathology of everyday adolescence', and argues that turmoil is a normal expectation in adolescence with the crisis points more likely occurring towards the end of that period.

From this perspective, adolescence is accepted as the time when each person needs to re-examine and re-evaluate himself physically, socially and emotionally, in relation to those close to him and to society in general. He labours to discover the various facets of his self-concept and then be himself, since former ways of defining self no longer seem appropriate.

Adolescence is seen by Erikson as a 'psycho-social moratorium' when choices of career, of values, of life style, of personal relationships have to be made in the face of conflicting evidence and values often on the basis of inadequate knowledge within a restless and uncertain society. Within this confusion of values many adolescents give each other mutual support through the discomforts and turmoil of identity crises in endless coffee-bar chats and by trying out various roles stereotyping themselves as mods, rockers, hell's angels, students, etc. , and likewise stereotyping their 'opponents', parents, teachers, police as the 'out group'; the peer group and peer culture supplant the family as an anchor. It 'provides a haven in which the delicate task of self-exploration and self-definition can be accomplished' (Douvan and Adelson 1966, p. 352).

One way of approaching the identity problems is to try out various roles. Many experts believe that adolescence should be a period of role experimentation in which the youngster can explore different ideologies and interests. They are concerned that today's academic competition and career pressures are depriving many adolescents of the opportunity to explore. As a result, some are 'dropping out' temporarily to have time to think about what they want to do in life and to experiment with various identities. Communes, and such religious groups as the Jesus Movement and the Hare Krishna sect often provide a temporary commitment to an alternative life style; they give the young person a group to identify with and time to formulate a more permanent set of beliefs.

The search for identity can be resolved in a number of ways. Some young people, after a period of experimentation and soul searching, commit themselves to a goal and proceed towards it. For some, the identity crisis may not occur at all, these are adolescents who accept their parents' values without question and who proceed toward a career consistent with their parents' views. In a sense, their identity 'crystallized' early in life.

Other adolescents may go through a prolonged period of identity confusion and have great difficulty finding themselves. In some cases, an identity definition may ultimately be worked out after much trial and error. In others a strong sense of personal identity may never develop.

It was comparatively simple in earlier times, in less sophisticated societies, to form a stable self-image and identity, since potential identifications were limited. But now there are a bewildering number of possible identifications; the stage is wide open. A confusion of identifications and images pulsate out of the mass media and pop culture kaleidoscope. Garish images, often inconsistent with models in the surrounding subculture, can be overwhelming for some and stimulating for others in their search to establish a stable and unique self-concept.

What adolescents must avoid in this developmental period as Erikson sees it is self-diffusion. Arthur Miller sums it up in *Death of a Salesman*, 'I just can't take hold, Mom. I can't take hold of some kind of life.' A young person can scarcely help feeling unable to give consistent direction to his life when the body changes in size and shape so rapidly, when gentital maturity imburs body and imagination with surges of emotion, when adult life lies ahead with such a diversity of conflicting possibilities and choices.

Identity diffusion, has four major components in Erikson's formulation.

Intimacy. The individual may fear commitment or involvement in close interpersonal relationships because of the possible loss of his or her own identity. This can lead to stereotyped, formalized relationships, or to isolation.

Diffusion of time perspective. Here the adolescent is unable to plan for the future, or to retain any sense of time. This problem is thought to be associated with anxieties about change and becoming adult, and often consists of a decided disbelief in the possibility that time may bring change and yet also of a violent fear that it might.' (1968, p. 169).

Diffusion of industry. Here, the young person finds it difficult to harness his or her resources in a realistic way in work or study. Both of these activities represent commitment, and as a defence against this the individual may either find it impossible to concentrate, or may frenetically engage in one single activity to the exclusion of all others.

Negative identity. The young person selects an identity exactly the opposite to that preferred by parents or other important adults. The loss of a sense of identity is often expressed in a scornful and snobbish hostility towards the role offered as proper and desirable in one's family or immediate community. 'Any aspect of the role or all of it—be it masculinity or femininity, nationality or class membership—can become the main focus of the young person's acid disdain.' (1968, p. 173).

These elements will not all be present in any one adolescent who is undergoing an identity crisis.

Whether this feeling of self-diffusion is fairly easily overcome or whether delinquency, neurosis or outright psychosis occur, depends to a considerable extent on previous experience. If the course of personality development has been a healthy one, self-esteem has accrued from the numerous experiences of success in tasks and acceptance by others. Along with this, the child has come to the conviction that he is moving towards an understandable future in which he will have a definite role to play. Adolescence may temporarily upset this assurance but a new integration for such a person is not hard, and when it is achieved the adolescent sees again that he belongs and that he is on the proper path.

The course is not easy for adolescents who have had a past diet of negative feed-back or for those whose security had been broken by distortions in childrearing practices. Already unsure of themselves, they find their earlier doubt and mistrust reactivated by the physiological and social changes that adolescence brings.

Erikson regards it as important that children can identify with adults since, for him, psychosocial identity develops out of a gradual integration of all the identifi-cations a child is able to make. If there is a conflict between the identity models a child is exposed to, however, problems can arise—as with a black child in a white society, or a child taught Christian beliefs at a church school whose father is a criminal. Identity involves recognizing the consistency of one's self and being recog-nized by others as being who you are.

The change to formal operational thought may have some relevance to the problems of the adolescent for he is no longer tied to an egocentric perception of experience. He is able to consider experience more objectively and evaluate possi-bilities. He has a growing awareness of the points of view of others and can make more realistic consideration of their motives. The codes of behaviour presented by adults and hitherto accepted with no real understanding can be appraised and set alongside other possible codes. This ability for formal thought produces insecurity as they abandon the life-raft of previously accepted behaviour and roles, and challenges them and their parents to cling to new and sometimes incongruent forms of behaviour.

Physical maturity clashes with social immaturity to provide disturbances as the adolescent seeks to make choices in a complex society full of status ambiguities for him. The adolescent can become ill at ease, jittery and show nervous mannerisms that give the impression of immaturity and silliness. Unfavourable social reactions to these lead to feelings of social inadequacy and inferiority. The expression of emotions on the spot gives an impression of impulsivity and immaturity as does too frequent, too violent and apparently unjustified emotional outbursts.

It would thus seem 'normal' to have some emotional upsets in adolescence. The adolescent has just left childhood behind but still has not found himself a secure, definitive identity as a responsible adult. Under stress there is a tendency to revert to the security of childhood dependence on parents. But, at the same time, he feels ashamed of this need for his parents since most of the pressures on the adolescent are pushing him towards independence and winning acceptance as a responsible adult. What the parents think of him now becomes less important than what his con-temporaries and other adults think of him. For example, the well known 'quick change' moods of the adolescent could be partly explained by the following sequence. The adolescent in asserting his independence, is difficult, awkward and challenging and pushes his parent to the point where that are almost ready to kick him out of the house. This frightens him so he becomes very friendly again to placate his parents. The relationships become more tender and close and, as this is too like the childhood relationship he is trying to throw off, he becomes difficult and awkward again.

Obviously, the strain on the parents and teachers of the adolescent is consider-able. They have to be able to respond to the changes of relationship in a reasonable way to allow the adolescent to become independent and, at the same time, exert reasonable control and set down reasonable limits to his behaviour. It is not surprising then that adolescence can be a stormy emotional period for everybody concerned. Most of the emotional problems, however, are mild and transient and usually self-limiting or may require just a small amount of psychological counselling.

By late adolescence the battle to become an adult has been won but the victory has not yet been consolidated. The adolescent has largely left behind the dependency of the child, can see for himself as an adult responsible for himself and for the consequences of his behaviour. He has set up a framework to judge himself as an adult. He finds that his behaviour is more consistent and predictable in a given situa-tion and not so likely to be swayed or overwhelmed by his emotional reactions to that situation. He can now enter into deeper relationships with others, relationships in which he is not so likely to re-enact his childhood dependence on his parents. He can now accept his own awareness of full physical maturity and his sexual role and feels others will also accept him as a mature person. He has a good idea of what sort of person he wants to be and what he wants to do with his life. On the whole he has developed fairly consistent personality characteristics which are unlikely to change suddenly, but, of course, there will be gradual changes as experiences involving self-attitudes continue.

But Erikson bases his views, which have been taken up as a standard developmental feature for all adolescents, on clinical cases. He acknowledges that his evidence may not be validly generalized to all adolescents.

'Whether, and in what way, disturbances such as are outlined here also characterise those more completely placed somewhere near the middle of the socioeconomic ladder, remains, at this time, an open question.' (1968, p. 25). Despite this, Erikson has had a considerable effect on how adolescence is viewed.

STUDIES EXPLORING QUANTITATIVE ASPECTS OF ERIKSON'S THEORY

Erikson tends to concentrate on qualitative issues in identity formation, and it has been left to others to test out the notions. Marcia (1966) has been a prominent investigator in this concern, and using incomplete sentences and semi-structured interviews has attempted to chart four identity stages, which are:
1. Identity diffusion. The individual has not yet made any commitment to a set of beliefs or a vocation nor has experienced an identity crisis.
2. Identity foreclosure. The individual has not experienced a crisis but, nevertheless, is committed in his or her goals and beliefs, largely as a result of choices made by others.
3. Moratorium. This is the crisis stage. The individual is actively searching among alternatives in an attempt to arrive at a choice of identity.
4. Identity achievement. Here the individual has experienced a crisis but has resolved it on his or her own terms and is firmly committed to an occupation and ideology.

These four identity stages may be seen as a developmental sequence but not necessarily in the sense that one is the prerequisite of the others. Only the moratorium stage appears to be essential for identity achievement since the searching which characterizes it precedes a resolution of the identity problem. In Marcia's original research (1966) he found that as students moved through the four years of college the proportion of those with identity diffusion declined, while the number of identity achievement subjects steadily increased.

Additionally, Marcia showed that those young people who had reached identity achievement were more resistant to stress when doing tasks and were less vulnerable in their self-esteem when provided with negative information about themselves. Results of a futher study (Marcia 1967) indicated that this group had higher self-esteem in general than those in the other three categories.

Other investigations indicate that those students with identity diffusion are most likely to conform when in groups. Toder and Marcia (1973) and Waterman et al. (1971; 1974) noted in a four-year study that in their first year at college around half of the students changed their identity status, but at the end of the fourth year, stability was very apparent. Those who attained a firm identity at the end of the first year. maintained it, and very few students remained in the moratorium status.

Matteson (1977) and Coleman (1980) criticize Marcia's categories, particularly the view that identity crisis is a single event. Matteson argues that: 'there is considerable evidence that adolescents undergo a series of crises and that at one particular time, one content area may be stable while another area of life's decisions is very much in crisis. A separate analysis of each content area of the interview is needed. (1977, p. 354 f.).

Most of this work has been based on American college students and has provided no insight into the identity problems of teenagers in general. Matteson (1977) attempted to assess exploration and commitment in four major areas—occupation, values, politics and sex roles. The results reflect the value of investigating different areas of life independently, and distinguishing between exploration and commitment. Weinreich (1979) has studied identity diffusion among adolescents in Britain from immigrant communities. He used the repertory grid technique and results show immigrant girls, especially those from Pakistani families, to have the highest levels of identity diffusion. To sum up, it would seem that while some teenagers have identity problems, research based on Erikson's notions has not been able to provide any conclusive evidence for a normative crisis. Only around thirty per cent of teenagers at any age level reveal some disturbance and many of these have had 'problems' of various sorts in their earlier years such as distortions in parental care, academic or social difficulties. It would seem, too, that it is early adolescence with the onset of puberty rather than Erikson's proposal of late adolescence that is the location of identity problems. To suggest as Erikson and Marcia do—that without some sort of crisis no firm resolution of identity is possible—seems to fly in the face of the evidence. Most adolescents from stable backgrounds given the sort of support, acceptance and encouragement from home and school emphasized repeatedly in this book appear to adapt gradually to the evolving physiological and social changes demanded of them.

Reference to the identity problem suggests a single common crisis of adolescence. But since every person at the beginning of adolescence, or at any other level of development, is an individual, different from every other, the particular identity 'crisis' he faces is in many respects a highly personal one. It differs as a problem in its total pattern and its details as seen by the young person himself. It is personal in the nature and the degree of inner conflict and effort it involves, and it is individual in the pattern of its resolution—in changes which may ensue.

EMPIRICAL STUDIES OF ADOLESCENT SELF-CONCEPT

Aside from theory derived from psychiatric case histories, there is little evidence to refute or support the argument that the child's self-image changes from childhood to adolescence. Since most work on adolescent disturbance has been clinical in nature, several fundamental questions on the self-image remain to be answered. First, do data support the belief that the adolescent's self-image differs from that of younger children? If so, could one term this difference a 'disturbance', that is, a change which would cause the child some discomfort or unhappiness?

Second, if there is an adolescent self-image disturbance when does it begin? This question is crucial to the evaluation of certain theoretical notions. Erikson (1959) tells us that the adolescent must deal with the issues of a career decision and the establishment of his own family. While these concerns may be salient to the 18 or 19 year-old, they do not concern the 12 year-old. Conversely, it is the younger adolescent who is confronted with the body-image changes of puberty.

An early study by Engel (1959) provided the first indication that the self-concept might well be fairly stable. Using a Q-sort technique for the assessment of self-image, she administered the test to boys and girls at 13 and 15 and then again when the subjects were 15 and 17. The results showed a relative stability of the self-image between 13 and 15 as well as between 15 and 17.

Highly significant overall correlations between the first and second testing provided the evidence. Engel also showed that twenty per cent of the sample who showed a negative self-image were significantly less stable in their view of themselves than the majority who expressed a positive self-image. This is an important point to which we shall return. Other longitudinal studies of this kind are rare in the literature. However, both Tome (1972) and Monge (1973) do provide support for Engel's conclusions. Their studies, although cross-sectional, investigated the structure of the self-concept at different stages during adolescence, and both writers argue against any major change or reorganization of the self-concept during the years 12 to 18.

Engel's (1959) study is important on two counts. First, only a low proportion of teenagers showed self-concept disturbance and, second, it was those students who had negative self-concepts on first testing who continued to show instability and disturbance throughout the longitudinal study. Those with positive self-concepts initially remained at that level showing no signs of any identity crisis.

Piers and Harris (1964) who investigated the level of self-esteem in 9, 12 and 16 year-olds, showed that, while 9 and 16 year-olds had similar levels of self-esteem there was a significantly lower level of self-esteem in the 12 year-old age group. Carlson (1965) on the other hand, looking at self-esteem levels at 12 and at 18 found no difference at all between the two age levels.

Several dimensions of self-image were measured in a cross-sectional study of 1917 children aged 8 to 17 by Simmons, Rosenberg and Rosenberg (1973). The early adolescents (12 to 14) have a consistently lower self-image than the younger children (8 to 11). They are less likely to rate themselves very favourably on the qualities they consider important. In some cases, such as being 'good at making jokes', the differences are minor; for others they are large. There is little difference between early and later adolescents in this regard; the consistent and clear difference appears between childhood and early adolescence, with the early adolescents likely to say that they are performing well with respect to their self-values.

It may be argued that there are lower self-ratings on these qualities simply because adolescents are more 'realistic' while younger children tend to 'inflate' their self-qualities. Other analyses of these data have shown that compared to older children, elementary-school children do tend to inflate the prestige of their racial and ethnic status and their father's occupation (Simmons and Rosenberg 1971). Perhaps the adolescent does become more realistic about what he is like, but this does not mean that the adjustment to reality is not distressing for him. As Blos (1962, p. 192) has noted: 'The difficulty of relinquishing the inflated self-image of childhood is usually underestimated'. The results show a general pattern of self-image disturbance in early adolescence. The data suggest that, compared to younger children, the early adolescent had become distinctly more self-conscious; his picture of himself has become more shaky and unstable; his global self-esteem has declined slightly; his attitude toward several specific characteristics which he values highly has become less positive; and he has increasingly come to believe that parents, teachers, and peers of the same sex view him less favourably. The data show early adolescents to be significantly more likely to be psychologically depressed.

The course of self-image developments shown in this study after 12 to 14 is also interesting. In general the differences between early and late adolescence are not large. There is improvement in self-consciousness, stability and especially global self-esteem, but no improvement in assessment of specific qualities or in the perceived self. The main change occurs between the 8 to 11 year-old children and the 12 to 14 year-old children.

For almost all the dimensions considered here, disturbance continues to increase after 12, but in most cases the high point of disturbance occurs either at age 12, 13 or 14. In fact stability of self-image and global self-esteem seem to improve after this point, particularly in late adolescence, while disturbances in self-consciousness and in specific self-esteem seem to level off and remain at early adolescent levels. The sole area of increasing disturbance in later adolescence involves the children's perceptions of the opinions of significant others.

Placing the rise in self-image disturbance at some time after the twelfth birthday would seem to agree with the assumption that puberty is the chief determinant of this disturbance. But are there factors in the social environment which may also be responsible for these changes?

One important environmental change occurs for most children at this time. They generally begin their last year of elementary school (the sixth grade) when they are 11 and the first year of junior high school (the seventh grade) when they are 12. Does the movement into junior high school itself contribute to the increase in self-image disturbance?

Obviously, one cannot examine the effects of change in environment by comparing sixth and seventh graders since one does not know whether such differences are because the seventh graders are in junior high school or simply that they are older. It is, however, possible to unravel the effects of age maturation and school contexts by comparing children of the same ages. Some of the 12 year-olds in the study were still in elementary school and the rest in junior high school.

The 12 year-olds in junior high school had lower global self-esteem, lower specific self-esteem, higher self-consciousness, and greater instability of self-image, than their age-peers in elementary school. For example, 41 per cent of the 12 year-olds in junior high school indicated low global self-esteem while only 22 per cent of those in elementary school did; 43 per cent of the former showed high self-consciousness compared to only 27 per cent of the latter. All but one of these differences are statistically significant beyond the 0.05 level. If these findings are valid, they are certainly a vivid illustration of the way a social context can affect individual personality.

Alban Metcalfe (1978) was able to discern a similar finding in England between pupils who changed to a secondary school at eleven and those of the same age who remained in their middle school. The explanation in both these cases seem to be that the child remaining in his middle school is among the biggest and strongest while those who transfer to a new school find themselves very small fish in a large pond. Thus, movement into junior high school at puberty is a significant event for the child. He moves from a protected elementary school, where he usually has one teacher and one set of classmates, to a much larger, more impersonal junior high where his teachers, classmates, and even his rooms are constantly shifting. He moves from a setting where the teacher is a parent-surrogate, to a more impersonal environment. Here he is expected to behave more independently and more responsibly, and he must make his first career decision—whether to take an academic, commercial, or vocational course.

Thus, the transition into junior high school seems to represent a significant stress along several dimensions of the child's self-image; while ageing from 11 to 12 and 12 to 13 does not in itself appear stressful. Within the same school class, age makes little difference; but within the same age group, school makes a great difference.

In sum, the data indicate increased self-image disturbance associated with the transition from elementary to junior high school. The reason does not appear to be solely the age change (with its associated biological changes). Perhaps puberty does not in itself disturb the self-image but heightens vulnerability to environmental circumstances which threaten the self-concept. Only futher research can determine what it is about the junior high school experience that is stressful for the self-image.

The existence of a definite self-image disturbance around 12 years of age in the Simmons, Rosenberg and Rosenberg (1973) study agrees with the findings of Offer (1969) who studied a somewhat older adolescent group (14 to 18), and who reports that both parents and adolescents agreed that the greatest amount of 'turmoil' in their lives occurred between ages 12 to 14. The finding that instability of the self-picture increase during adolescence might appear to support Erikson's (1959) views on adolescent problems of ego identity. However, Erikson seems to place the ego identity crisis in late adolescence; whereas Simmons et al.'s data indicate a rise in instability during early adolescence.

The largest sample used to study the presumed changes in self-concept during adolescence is the 6000 students aged 12 to 17 in the investigation of Ellis, Gehmen and Katzenmeyer (1980). This was a cross-sectional study employing a random sample of 1000 students in each year. The purpose of the study was to determine whether or not specific elements of the self-concept as measured by specific sub-scales remain stable.

All the subjects took the Self-Observation Scale which includes eight scales: school affiliation, self security, social confidence, peer affiliation, family affiliation, self-assertion, teacher affiliation scale and self-acceptance scale. The results showed a stability across the adolescent age span of seven of the scales. The only scale that revealed any change was self-acceptance.

The primary basis of the self-acceptance scale shifts from self-perceptions regarding external standards to self-perceptions regarding internal standards of personal happiness. During the 13, 14 and 15 year age span, the individual rates him or herself primarily according to external standards of achievement. At approximately 16 the individual's idea of what is important to the self is recognized. When the individual is 17 or 18, he or she rates himself or herself according to internal standards of personal happiness. It would seem that the role of significant others become less important.

Some extensive surveys of adolescent boys and girls have been conducted by the 'Survey Research Center' of the University of Michigan (Douvan and Adelson 1966). The data for these studies were obtained by interview involving some 1045 boys and 2005 girls aged 11 to 17. Careful sampling techniques were used in the selection of the subjects. The individual interviews lasted from one to four hours, and were conducted at the schools. This means, of course, that the study was limited to students in school, which would rather under-represent children in the population at large.

The findings of this research, then, refer specifically to ordinary nonpathological, school-attending youth of the late 1950s. The tendency in ordinary American youth, generally was not to turn their backs on the prospect of a life in the world of adults and become alienated without a goal in relation to society. On the contrary, the adolescent revealed the urge towards the independence of adulthood; the future was, by no means, a remote or irrelevant prospect. In one form or another, the future orientation appears again and again as a distinguishing feature of the youngsters who are making adequate adolescent adjustments. (Douvan and Adelson 1966, p. 341).

This forward thrust was found to be common to boys and girls but its style and focus differ markedly between the sexes. Boys were concerned with quite different kinds of future activity than were girls. Boys' choices were concrete. They thought in terms of specific work roles in relation to their own interests, tastes and capabilities. The findings suggested clarity of vocational goals and with real notions of what it takes to achieve them.

Girls, on the other hand, according to this study were not strongly oriented toward jobs and vocational activities. Their focus was upon the interpersonal and social aspects of future life. Marriage was the common goal, with special concern in their thinking with the roles of wife and mother. Their choices of vocations were those which express their feminine interests and which would to place them in settings which will bring them in contact with prospective husbands. Again, the results indicated a relation between clarity of goal aspiration and personal adjustment.

A clear concept of her adult femininity, or feminine goals and interpersonal skills, functions for the girl like the vocational concept for the boy. It bridges the worlds of adolescence and adulthood, brings the future concretely into current life, and allows the future to contribute meaning and organization to adolescent activities and interests. Girls who have relatively clear notions about the goals in adult femininity show a high degree of personal integration. Those girls who specifically reject a feminine future are the troublesome adolescents. (Douvan and Adelson 1966, p. 343)

Another difference which showed up between the sexes was in relation to the need that was felt to detach oneself from the family and become independent. In the first place, the researchers saw in general a less dramatic, and less conflicting process than tradition and theory hold. They also noted a significant sex difference. The urge to be free and 'to be one's own master is almost exclusively a masculine stirring' (p. 343). The girls of the study, up to the age of 18, showed no significant drive for independence.

Closely associated with the urge for independence was the issue of the importance of the peer group. A conclusion of this study was that in theory the importance of the peer group to the ordinary adolescent has been much exaggerated.

With respect to the search for personal identity, Douvan and Adelson (1966) characterized this problem largely in terms of differences they noted between the two sexes. They concluded that 'there is not one adolescent crisis, but two major and clearly distinct ones—the masculine and the feminine' (p. 350).

Douvan and Adelson (1966) drew a distinction between present and future self-identity, a distinction which may illuminate the issue of stability or instability of the adolescent self-concept. Erikson seemed more concerned with the present identity whereas Douvan and Adelson argue that the level of stability–instability may arise out of the ability of the adolescent to integrate his future image into his current identity. Coleman and his colleagues (1977; 1980) have attempted to pursue this possibility in research terms. In the 1977 study, working class youths completed missing sentences task specifically designed to differentiate between future and present orientations. The responses revealed that while the proportions of each age group expressing a negative present self-image remained the same, the numbers expressing negative sentiments and anxieties, concerning their future self-image increased markedly in those approaching the school-leaving age. Phrases such as 'dreary', 'dead', 'depressing' and 'a dreaded age' were common among 16 year-olds to describe their future.

For example, the percentage expressing negative responses to the statement, 'sometimes the future seems. . . ' rose from 20 per cent at 12 years to nearly 60 per cent at 16 and for 'if I think about when I am older. . . .' the percentage for those two age groups rose from 14 per cent to 35 per cent.

More recently, Miller and Coleman (1980) have established that concepts of the future self are affected by the sex of the adolescent. Boys express greater anxiety about the future than girls, and social class as well as the imminence of leaving school also play a part. This research project is still in progress at the time of writing, and firm conclusions cannot yet be provided.

Linked to this future identity problem is the current likelihood of unemployment for many school leavers. More adolescents leave school, today, to join the ranks of the unemployed than ever before. Employment and career become central to an individual's self-concept in middle adolescence as a source of values and structure to life. A person's work is an integral part of his identity. To be unable to get a job puts into question one's capacity to carry responsibility for oneself. As many of the young unemployed reportedly feel, they have become statistics no longer individuals. They feel looked down upon, ineffective and different. In not having an occupation, the person has no social identity and has invalidated most of the basic expectations which he had of himself. The social evaluation of one's work forms a central feature of one's identity. To be mature, stable and adequate is to be able to cope with external reality and its demands. The pre-eminent demand of the middle adolescent is the entry into the world of work.

COGNITIVE DEVELOPMENT AND ADOLESCENT SELF-CONCEPT

The ability to integrate future identity and perspective into the present may depend on cognitive development. Some theorists argue that cognitive development enhances the adaptiveness of the self system. The cognitive structural limitations of the child, narrow the child's field of awareness and constrict his ability to understand himself. The adolescent's greater cognitive maturity enables him to be aware of a broader array of experiences and to conceptualize himself from perspectives unavailable to the pre-adolescent. Generally, theorists agree that the developmental constructs of differentiation, abstraction and integration underlie the changes which occur in the self-system as one matures.

In spite of this theoretical rationale, there are relatively few studies which investigate the adequacy of this cognitive developmental model of the self-system, but what research there is has supported this theory. Montemayer and Eisen (1977) studying subjects aged 9 to 18, concluded with age. In addition, the older adolescents referred more to beliefs and personality characteristics than did younger ones. Livesley and Bromley (1973) have evidence which supports Montemayer and Eisen's results. Further, Livesley and Bromley found that the ability to integrate personality characteristics does not appear until adolescence. These researchers contend that the major development after the age of 15 is an increased awareness of covert and psychological determinants of behaviour. The major limitation of these two studies is that the responses were coded in terms of their content meaning, rather than the cognitive processes which yield the product.

Dixon and Street (1975) and Mullener and Laird (1971) found greater self-differentiation with age during adolescence. However, these studies also were flawed methodologically, confounding verbal facility and experiential differences with the cognitive capacity of differentiation.

In summary, the limited findings now available suggest that there will be greater differentiation, abstraction, and integration of the self-system as one develops through adolescence. However, the self-system research has dealt with the classification of the content meaning of self-referring statements, rather than with the cognitive processes from which these arise. Bernstein (1980) considered these processes in a study in which he hypothesized that, as one proceeds through adolescence there will be greater differentiation, abstraction and integration. To test these hypotheses, ten middle-class males in each of these three age groups, 10, 15 and 20 years old, were employed as subjects.

Three free response, self-reliant tasks were presented. Three major hypotheses were supported but it was an abstraction that was the most important process in that the ability to abstract determined the level of differentiation and integration.

Inhelder and Piaget (1958) argued that abstraction is one of the major cognitive developments occurring during adolescence. In other words, the enhanced ability to abstract appears to be of central importance to the greater differentiation of oneself and one's world and to the integration of a more comprehensive self-system.

In addition, developing the capacity to abstract appears to contribute to a transformation from the child's dependence upon surface qualities as behavioural determinants to the adolescent's greater awareness of personality and dispositional determinants of behaviour. Significant linear trends with age were obtained by Bernstein (op. cit.) for decreasing the responsiveness to specific overt behaviours of others and for increasing the reference to one's own beliefs and personality.

Although the study does find evidence supporting an increase in references to personality characteristics for behaviour after age 15, it is not statistically significant. The older adolescent's greater awareness of personality determinants of behaviour seems to be based upon more fundamental cognitive structural changes in the ability to abstract (Berstein op. cit.).

At best, the youngest group, the least advanced in the capacity to abstract, was able superficially to integrate their self-concepts (40 per cent of the 10 year-olds showed this capacity). This evidence seems to conflict with Livesley and Bromley's (op. cit.) conclusion that the ability to integrate first appears in adolescence. Contributing to the disparate findings are Livesley and Bromley's lack of an objective assessment of integration and the more structured approach used in the present study, which ostensibly allowed more advanced cognitive processes to be exposed systematically. What may appear to be listing of self-concepts may, in effect, be the product of a superficial integration. For example, a 10 year-old mentioned in tasks (a) and (b) that he fools around, likes to talk to his friends, can aggravate people sometimes, tries to be helpful and to do his best, is shy with those he does not know well, and sometimes gets mad at people. His summary statement illustrates a superficial integration: 'I think I'm fairly easy to get along with, and helpful, and I always try and do my best.'

A major transformation in the development of the adolescent self-concept appeared after the age of fifteen through sudden increases in the ability to abstract and integrate information about the self. This facilitated the crystallization of self-identity in later adolescence.

To what extent this evidence can be attributed to societal influences upon cognitive structure is unknown. Bruner (1964) suggests that environmental demands force the adolescent to acquire more adaptive cognitive operations. The conditions in Western society require some, but not all, adolescents to consider the future, themselves and society in new perspectives in order to choose adult roles. An individual may not develop more advanced modes of reasoning if the problems he confronts do not demand abstract solutions.

ADOLESCENT SELF-ESTEEM AND THE FAMILY

Taking a lead from the three extensive monographs in the area of family interaction on self-concept (Rosenberg 1965; Coopersmith 1967; Bachman 1970) and from the social-psychological theory of Mead and Cooley which stresses the importance of social interaction in the development of the self-concept Gecas (1971) examined the relationship between parental control and support, and adolescent self-evaluation. In this respect this study is similar to those of Rosenberg, Coopersmith and Bachman, and is a repeat of their works. Support as well as control are expressions of parental concern and interest in the child and, both, are hypothesized to be positively associated with the child's self-evaluation.

In a sample of high-school boys and girls in New York State, Rosenberg found high self-esteem to be related to parental interest in the child, interest in his friends, his academic performance and his contribution to mealtime conversations. Similarly, Bachman found high self-esteem, in a national sample of tenth-grade boys, to be positively associated with 'good' family relations. 'Good' family relations meant such things as affection between family members, common activities, fairness and inclusion of children in family decision making. Coopersmith, dealing with a slightly younger population (fifth and sixth graders), found three general conditions associated with high self-esteem in the child: (a) parental acceptance of the child; (b) clearly defined and enforced limits on the child's behaviour and (c) the respect and latitude for individual action that exists within the defined limits. Coopersmith's findings are of special interest in the emphasis they place on parental control, along with parental acceptance and affection, as a variable affecting the child's self-esteem. Taken together, the findings of Rosenberg, Coopersmith and Bachman, as well as a comparative study of Puerto Rican and American youth by Gecas et al. (1970), point to the importance of certain parental behaviour patterns for the development of the child's self-evaluation—primarily to the importance of parental support and control.

However, the Gecas (1971) study goes beyond past studies on these variables in its treatment of the dependent variable: self-evaluation. Self-evaluation, or self-esteem, is typically treated as an undimensional variable, referring to the individual's conception of himself in terms of various qualities and attributes, that is in terms of various focuses. There is a considerable advantage in anchoring the individual's concept of himself to key contents or focuses of self-evaluation. One reason for this specification is that these dimensions of self-evaluation may be differentially related to other variables, such as parental support and control.

Two contents of focuses of self-evaluation which appear to have theoretical relevance as well as empirical generality are the dimensions of power and worth. These refer to the person's feelings of competence, effectiveness and personal influence, and his feelings of personal virtue and moral worth, respectively. Becker (1962) views the individual's feelings of power as the key element in his psychological stability. He argues that man as an active animal defines himself largely in terms of the effect he has on his environment. When this feeling of confidence in one's power breaks down it is often accompanied by serious repercussions throughout the self. Becker considers alienation and schizophrenia to be two manifestations of the person's feeling of powerlessness. Adler (1927) considered the 'will to power' as the *modus operandi* of man as a social being. Similarly, a person's feeling of moral worth, is an important element in his self-conceptualization and psychological make-up. Various psychological disorders, especially psychotic depression, are characterized by feelings of worthlessness, personal contempt, and conceptual-izations of oneself as an evil, wretched person (Diggory 1966; Sullivan 1953). In fact, research on the self-concept has tended to equate self-evaluation with this moral worth to the neglect of power.

Both dimensions of self-evaluation (SE) were expected by Gecas (1971) to be similarly related to parental support, a positive relationship. But SE-worth is expected to be more strongly related to control than is SE-power, although there should be a positive relationship for both.

Gecas (1971) used over 600 sixteen year-old adolescents in his study of the relationship between two dimensions of parental behaviour: support and control and the adolescents self-evaluation, as measured on a fivepoint semantic differential. It was hypothesized that both parental support and parental control would be positively related to adolescent self-evaluation.

Of the two categories of parental behaviour considered, parental support was found to be consistently related to the adolescents' self-evaluation, while parental control was not. This was generally the case for both boys and girls as well as for working-class and for middle-class groups.

The findings reported here suggest that children who are raised in families that are affectionate and supportive will develop higher evaluations of themselves as persons: that is, they will tend to think of themselves as competent and worthy individuals. When the affection and support comes from the mother, this is especially true for their view of themselves as persons of worth; when it comes from the father it will have a stronger impact on their evaluations of themselves as competent and effective individuals (a finding compatible with Parsons's (1955) conceptualization of family structure in terms of 'instrumental' roles for husbands and 'expressive' roles for wives).

The failure to find a relationship between parental control and self-evaluation raises questions concerning both the theoretical importance of control as an explanatory variable and the adequacy of the measures of control used in the study. There are reasons to suspect that the impact of parental control is considerably more complex in its effect on self-evaluation than was measured by the study instrument. Coopersmith (1967), for example, criticized the unidimensional idea of control used in personality studies. He suggested that parental control is likely to contain cross-cutting components of firmness and flexibility when it contributes to the development of high self-esteem in the child. Firmness in the sense of imposing well-defined rules and regulations on the child combined with flexibility which allows the child freedom within these boundaries. Failure, in Gecas's study, to take into account the flexibility–rigidity component in measuring control may have diluted the effect of control on self-evaluation.

A further shortcoming of this research, however, is the tendency to treat self-esteem in different situations as a general characteristic of the individual, similar to intelligence or creativity. The degree to which self-esteem varies with time or with social context is an empirical question which has not been adequately explored, even though the variable nature of the self-concept has been a common theme in the social-psychological writings of Mead, Cooley and James, who consider that a person has as many selves as there are groups about whose opinions he cares.

Little has been done in exploring situational variations in self-esteem, in evaluating the salience of social contexts for self-esteem for specific populations, and in examining the relationship between the evaluative behaviour of significant others and a person's self-esteem in different social contexts. So in a second study Gecas (1972) deals with three questions concerning adolescents' self-esteem focused on the context of self-evaluation. The three questions were:

(a) To what extent does the self-esteem of the adolescent vary according to the context: classroom, family, friends, with opposite sex, with adults, and is the pattern the same for boys and girls?

(b) Do some dimensions of self-evaluation upon which self-esteem is based, e.g. peceived power and self-worth, vary according to context?

(c) To what extent are antecedents of self-esteem, e.g. parental support and control, context-bound in their influence? Support was defined as parental behaviour which expresses a positive effect between parent and child. Control refers to those parental behaviours which circumscribe, limit, structure or direct the child's actions.

There are a number of implications in approaching self-esteem contextually Gecas argues. Since social contexts vary in importance, in commitment and in other ways mentioned, they should be associated with different levels of self-esteem for the individual. However, the problem may be more complicated than this. Different aspects of self-esteem may vary depending on their relationship to aspects of the social context. The perception of oneself as powerful is affected by the power configurations which exist in specific social contexts. For example, Gecas suggests a power configuration in which the individual is a subordinate, such as an adolescent in school, is likely to be associated with lower feelings of personal power than those contexts in which he is an equal i.e. with peers.

Gecas (1972) attempted to answer the three questions above in a study which examined through a phenomenological perspective the effect of different contexts on the level of self-esteem expressed by 600 adolescents and on the relationship between certain parental behaviours and adolescent self-esteem. Five contexts were considered: classroom, family, friends, with the opposite sex and with adults. It was found that adolescents' self-esteem measured by a five-point semantic differential was especially pronounced on the power dimension of self-esteem and less on the self-worth dimension. Friends also ranked as the context in which adolescents felt 'the most real', while in the classroom they felt least 'real'. Parental support (and to some extent, control) was found to be significantly related to self-esteem only when adult contexts were used, i.e. family, classroom and with adults. These were not antecedents of self-esteem when the context for the adolescent was his peers. This research suggests that social context is an important independent variable of self-esteem and cannot be assumed to be constant.

What are the implications of Gecas's findings? We can conclude from these that there is variability as well as stability in adolescent self-esteem across contexts and that the variability is more a function of the power dimension of self-esteem while stability is more characteristic of the self-worth dimension. A person's feeling of self-worth, once established may be more easily transported across social settings and become less dependent on continued reinforcement. Power, on the other hand, may have to be more frequently re-established as one moves across social contexts. But, to the extent that these two dimensions are related (and they are) the fate of one will eventually affect the other. We would not expect to find a person who is very high on SE-worth and very low on SE-power or vice versa.

This variation indicates that some contexts in the adolescent's social environment are more important sources of self-esteem and feelings of authenticity than are others. Although this study does not presume to measure alienation *per se*, a rather complicated concept, the findings can be interpreted as relevant to the topic. To the extent that alienation is subjectively feeling unauthentic and powerless, we can ask: in which context do adolescents feel most alienated or least authentic? The answer, based on the salience ratings of contexts and the levels of self-evaluation, would have to be the school, or more accurately, the classroom. This is hardly surprising and is congruent with the critiques of our education system which see it as irrelevant to the real needs and interests of young people about to embark on their working lives, and too bound up with evaluation in which only a few can derive feelings of success. Conversely, adolescents seem to feel most authentic with their peers.

This agrees with much of the research on adolescents which points to a shift from parents to peers as frames of reference and sources for self-evaluation (Kirchner and Vondraek 1975). However, the claim that adolescents become alienated from their families is not supported, since 'family' was selected almost as often as 'peers' as the context in which they felt most authentic.

A third conclusion from these findings is that parental support is context-bound in its effect on adolescent self-esteem. Its effect was strongest in the family but it also carried over to other contexts similar to the family in authority structure, e.g. the school and adults. In other words, parental support is related to adolescents' self-esteem primarily in adult contexts. It could not be considered an antecedent of adolescent self-esteem in the peer contexts, at least not in the power dimension. The supportive environment conducive to the development of high self-esteem in the family (parental control was a much weaker antecedent variable) has a very limited effect on the adolescent's self-esteem level when he is with his peers. Undoubtedly, the self-esteem built up in one context will to some extent carry over to other contexts, especially with respect to feelings of self-worth, but this effect is limited. In a previous paper, Gecas reported finding a strong positive relationship between parental support and adolescent self-esteem (1971). This relationship as well as those reported by Rosenberg (1965), Coopersmith (1967) and Bachman (1970), needs to be qualified in the light of the present findings. Future studies of self-esteem need to take into account not only dimensions of self-evaluation but also the contexts within which these evaluations take place.

Another conventional belief is that there is a generation gap between parents and adolescents which leads to conflict, which in turn leads to alienation and identity diffusion. However, research on conflict between parents and adolescents reveals a far more comforting picture. Bandura (1972), Douvan and Adelson (1966) and Fogelman (1976), all report mutually satisfying relationships with but a few minor conflicts. Most teenagers tended to value and accept parental advice rather than reject or despise such views. Generally, teenagers felt their relationships with parents became easier as they passed though adolescence, trusting each other more. There was little evidence of slavish conformity to peer groups either, with most adolescents being quite selective and discriminating in their choice of reference groups. In Fogelman's (1976) study of over 11 000 British teenagers, only 10 per cent of parents reported conflict of a frequent nature and this tended to be over dress and hair. Rutter (1976) found only 5 per cent of his young people felt alienated from their parents.

How can parents and teachers help young persons through adolescence? The primary task is for adults to adopt a phenomenological stance and try to see the world from the standpoint of the adolescent to understand his behaviour and feelings. This counsel, of course, applies to all relationships not merely ones where adolescents are concerned. It is, too, a counsel of perfection; one can never see things as another sees them but useful approximations can be made if an honest attempt is made, even though you must always be on the outside looking in.

The provision of increasing independence of choice and action within a consistent framework of rules is necessary. As we noted in Chapter 4 all young people want some guidelines within which they can operate. Complete independence is anxiety provoking, even to adults. The provision of guidelines is interpreted as meaning that someone cares for them. There must be some structure without being too constructive; this provides controlled opportunities to demonstrate competency. Explanations must be given to adolescents about the changes that are about to occur or are occurring in the physical, sexual or emotional areas. Worries, ambiguities and inconsistent feelings and behaviours can be reduced and understood if these young persons are prepared by more information being given to them. The late-maturing male needs to be reassured that he, too, will have a growth spurt and catch up; the girl needs to understand her mood changes. They must come to see all these changes in shape, size and feeling as normal and this cannot be done if explanations are simply limited to the physiological level. They must have opportunities to talk about their emotions, feelings and attitudes in an accepting and warm relationship, so that they come to understand how mature adults cope with these issues and handle their emotions. Adults still act as models to be imitated. This implies that significant adults must become mature examples.

Adults can help adolescents to make decisions by showing them that adult decisions are not choices between absolute wrong and absolute right. Adolescents tend to be plagued with doubt over their decision making because choices are usually between things that are less than ideal, or between conflicting but correct choices rather than between perfection and anything less. They need to see through discussion and example that adult decisions are based on perceptions of the situation as it really is, and not on some ideal. This does not mean that judgements are to be made without standards but it does mean that standards must have something to do with real activities of life.

Finally, adults must always encourage any attempt towards more mature behaviour, self-understanding and coping. Such positive feedback not only increases the probability of repeated, successful behaviour but informs the young person that he is approved of, accepted and worthwhile, despite the changes he is undergoing.

SUMMARY

Various theoretical stances suggest that adolescence is a period of stress due to, amongst other things psychosexual development, emotional upheaval, role conflict, status ambiguities and unstable social values. It is a period of discontinuity between childhood and adulthood. Erikson sees the task of adolescence as that of self-definition of identity formation. Changes in body image, in peer and parent relationships, in cognitive skills and in relationships to society at large all combine to effect a re-evaluation of each young person which has implications for change and development of the self-concept. All of these changes, taking place as an integrated process in a relatively short time, constitute a complex and often difficult problem—perhaps more aptly, a set of difficult problems—for the child and for those about him.

Body image becomes an important factor in adolescent self-concept development as puberty occurs, and much adolescent self-worth derives from perceiving that one's body fits the norm. Deviant and retarded physical development can have deleterious consequences on self-concept.

Research on the conventional view of adolescence as a period of stress tends to reveal it rather as a period of stability, with any crisis occurring in early adolescence, rather than later as Erikson claimed. Cognitive development aids the adolescent in understanding himself and his world, enabling him to integrate all his experiences into a more comprehensive self-concept, as well as permitting a more mature view of the ideal–self discrepancy.

Further Reading

Blos, P. (1962) *On Adolescence,* London: Macmillan.
Coleman, J. (1980) *The Nature of Adolescence,* London: Methuen.
Douvan, E. and Adelson, J. (1966) *The Adolescent Experience,* New York: Wiley.
Erikson, E. (1963) *Childhood and Society,* New York: Norton.
Livesley, W. J. and Bromley, D. B. (1973) *Person Perception in Childhood and Adolescence,* London: Wiley.
Offer, D. (1973) *The Psychological World of the Teenager,* New York: Basic Books.

7

Significant Others and Feedback

O wad some Pow'r the giftie gie us
To see ourselves as others see us!
Robert Burns, 'To a Louse'.

Man wishes to be confirmed in his being by man, and wishes to have a presence in the being of the other . . . secretly and bashfully he watches for a Yes which allows him to be and which can come only from one human person to another. It is from one person to another that the heavenly bread of self-being is passed. Buber (1965, p. 71)

INTRODUCTION

Burns's couplet expresses a concern about self-knowledge and its origins that is both ancient and modern. When people are asked how they know that they possess certain characteristics, a typical answer is that they have learned about them from other people. A more formal theoretical statement of this view had been articulated by the influential school of symbolic interactionists. This school proffers the idea of a 'looking-glass self' and asserts that one's self-concept is a reflection of perceptions about how one appears to others. The assertion has received widespread professional acceptance and is intoned with catechistic regularity in many leading texts on social behaviour.

Throughout this text the role of feedback from significant others is stressed at appropriate points. Parents, peer group and teachers have all been allocated an important feedback role.

THEORETICAL CONSIDERATIONS

According to Cooley (1912) from early childhood our concepts of self develop from

163

seeing how others respond to us: 'In the presence of one whom we feel to be of importance, there is a tendency to enter into and adopt, by sympathy his judgement of ourself' (p. 175). Mead (1934), the major theorist of symbolic interactionism, amplified and expanded the view of the self as a product of social interaction: 'The individual experiences himself as such, not directly but only indirectly, from the particular standpoints of other individuals of the same social group, or from the generalized standpoint of the social group as a whole to which he belongs' (p. 138). Essential to the genesis of the self is the development of the ability to take the role of the other and particularly to perceive the attitude of the other towards oneself. Mead's looking-glass self is reflective not only of significant others, as Cooley suggested, but of a generalized other, that is, one's whole social and cultural environment. Later Kinch (1963) summarized the symbolic interactionist theory of self by noting that it basically involves an interrelation of four components: our self-concept, our perception of others' attitudes and responses to us, the actual attitudes and responses of others to us, and our behaviour.

In recent years, self-theories have been proposed that do not insist on the primacy of social others as sources of information about the self. Bem (1967, 1972) has asserted that self-perception is a special case of person perception:

> Self-descriptive attitude statements can be based on the individual's observations of his own overt behaviour and the external stimulus conditions under which it occurs . . . As such, his statements are functionally similar to those that any outside observer could make about him. (1967, p. 185.)

There is some evidence that individuals' self-perceptions are similar to their perceptions of how they are viewed by others in general (Miyamoto and Dornbusch 1956; Quarantelli and Cooper 1966).

The term 'significant others' means those persons who are important or who have significance to the child by reason of his sensing their ability to reduce insecurity or to intensify it, to increase or to decrease his helplessness, to promote or to diminish his sense of worth. Significant others play a confirming role in defining the self. Parents are presumed to be the most significant others in an infant's environment. Later teachers and peer group join in.

The role of the significant other is one of reflection, but not in the sense of casual mirroring. The person seeking an image of self, selects a significant other and values the representation of the self reflected by that significant other. The accuracy of the reflected image depends on the capabilities of the significant other; unfortunately, accurate reflection is not even a minor consideration in selecting and valuing a significant other.

The selection of the significant other appears to be forced by limited options: the choice must be made from those persons who can interact with the image-seeking self. The most important point, however, concerning the selection and valuing of a significant other is that the process involves unequivocally influencing the developing self-concept. Becoming a significant other in a child's life is not simply a matter of assuming the role. Either one is a significant other or one is not; there is no option of declining. While willingness to act as a significant other may improve, and unwillingness impair, one's performance in that capacity, the role is always conferred, never assumed. The parent, the teacher, the religious leader, a relative or a peer are the most likely choices for the role of a significant other.

To function properly, a significant other requires not only the opportunity and capacity to interact with the person, but also the ability to reflect a stable, integrated image of that person. Here again, accuracy is not the criterion used by the child in placing value on the reflection supplied by the significant other. To the child, the image reflected by the significant other always has impact, though it can be incorporated into the developing self-concept only it if is consistent, stable and does not contradict the existing schema or construct. The significant other may be uniformly accepting and consistently reflect a positive image to the child, or constantly rejecting, reflecting a negative image. In either case, the reflected image becomes a prime source of psychological experiences necessary to the formation of a self-concept.

In addition to reflecting an image of the child, the significant other also interprets experiences and events for the child through the feedback they provide.

Reinforcement is necessarily involved in feedback, which can, depending on its form and content, increase the probability of a response being made again, or decrease the probability of a response. Feedback which is pleasant and agreeable, telling the child that what he is doing is good and valuable, informs the child that he is competent and of worth. Feedback which is unpleasant and disagreeable informing the child he is doing badly, performing incompetently, or wrongly, teaches the child that he is incompetent and worthless. A smile, verbal praise, a pat on the back or a present are all examples of positive reinforcement which will enhance the recipient's self-esteem. A grimace, verbal criticism, a smack or deprival of some desirable event or object serve to lower self-esteem. But it must always be remembered that the reinforcement must be viewed from the point of view of the recipient. For a youngster of five to receive a couple of coloured paper stars stuck underneath some correctly computed sums, may well be highly reinforcing and beneficial to his self-concept. The same tokens of success given to a teenager would cause ribald remarks. For a youth of 16 who is soon to leave school the verbal praise of a teacher given in front of the rest of the peer group with whom the youth wishes to have some standing is likely to have the opposite effect to that which the teacher intended. The youth will avoid performing well for fear of further negative feedback from his friends who ostracize him as 'teacher's pet' and lower his standing in the peer group.

So reinforcement seen as positive by the recipient will encourage similar behaviour and positive self-feelings; reinforcement construed as negative or punishing will cause a more denigratory self-attitude. We come to evaluate ourselves through the subjectively perceived responses of others to us. People can also give feedback to themselves. Simply achieving something even without others knowing about it can be reinforcing. We can feel a sense of pride and competence, or criticism and failure through self-evaluation of our own efforts. Once children have identified with parents they are able to respond to themselves in their thoughts in the same terms as they have experienced their parent actually do so in the past when much younger. How often in the day do you say to yourself, 'Good, I managed that quite well,' or 'No, I mustn't do that,'? But the role of feedback from others seems primary since the internalized self-referent feedback is learnt through having experienced it at an earlier time. If all a child has heard has been negative comments then he will likely learn this habitual form of response to himself in his internal self-referent feedback.

The principle would seem to be that children must be given positive feedback wherever possible to insure the growth of positive self-feelings which then permit the willingness to experience and try a wider range of acceptable behaviour. The parent and teacher can manipulate the environment and the tasks presented so that reasonable success is assured (Chapter 16).

It is surprising, however, that there is no empirical literature substantiating these arguments. Naturalistic studies of self-concept and perceived or actual assessments by others use subjects from the captive environment of the school. The subjects in these studies are typically in at least the third or fourth school year. Studies of controlled feedback almost exclusively use undergraduates. Since the pre-school years are so vital to theories of the development of self-concept, it seems imperative that this period be examined empirically. However, this is easier to say than to do. Trickett (1972), for example, has noted the difficulties encountered in assessing the self-concept of first graders, which means that new and imaginative methods are necessary here. Furthermore, recent work raises the questions about whether young children possess the abstract concepts necessary to process information from others and use it in forming perceptions of themselves. A naturalistic study of parent–child evaluative interactions might be desirable to discover just what kind of feedback is given in the earliest stages of life.

FEEDBACK AND THE YOUNG CHILD'S SELF-CONCEPT

If the child is going to develop a sense of competence, important people around him should emphasize the new things that he has learned and the possibility of additional learning, rather than how incompetent he is.

The young infant also begins to achieve a sense of worth. Early parental care for the infant contributes to this sense of worth by showing the infant that the parents are attuned to his needs. The fact that parents will act to give comfort instead of pain tells the infant that he is of worth. The infant also receives confirmation that he is of value and worth in the sight of his parents by the verbal and physical expressions of love which they show him. These are indirect ways of saying, 'You are worthwhile.'

The neonate has no self-awareness, since all his behaviour is dominated by the need to satisfy bodily needs and not by any reference to a self. Therefore the earliest feedback to the infant about how people feel about him lies in the reduction of physiological needs. As the infant is being fed, changed, bathed, he also receives a message that he is valued and accepted. Fondling, caressing, smiles and 'baby talk' dispensed by mother (and father too!) are communications indicating that the infant is esteemed. Through this a person learns to seek out the feeling of being valued by others, since it is associated in the past with the reduction of physiological discomfort.

All humans need love, acceptance and security—most of all young children. The receipt of love and acceptance is very satisfying, but to know whether he is receiving any the child must observe the face, gestures, the verbalizations and other signs of significant others, usually parents. Each experience of love or rejection, each experience of approval or disapproval from others causes him to view himself and his behaviour in the same way. During early childhood the child anchors his perception of himself very much in his own direct experience of physical self and of the reactions of significant others, particularly his parents, to him.

Most personality theorists and research workers agree on the role of significant others, particularly parents, as an influential source of information about oneself. Since few things are more relevant to the young child than how people react to him, it is not really surprising that the reflections of himself in the eyes of significant others ('the looking-glass self') play a crucial role in the self-concepts the child acquires. Parents have the greatest impact in the developing conception of self as they are the fount of authority and the most likely source of trust. Murphy (1947) says therefore that it is vitally important to save the child from acquiring an unlovely view of himself. This self-portrait is gradually modified and rebuilt according to the experiences the child has had and the adjectives he hears used to describe him. But it shows diminishing returns as the picture becomes well established. Thus the child becomes less and less a perceptual object and more and more a conceptual trait system.

Snygg and Combs (1949) have also emphasized the vital effects of constructing how significant others evaluate one.

> As he is loved or rejected, praised or punished, fails or is able to compete, he comes gradually to regard himself as important or unimportant, adequate or inadequate, handsome or ugly, honest or dishonest . . . or even to describe himself in the terms of those who surround him . . . He is likely therefore to be affected by the labels which are applied to him by other people (p. 83).

During the first few years of life, parents are necessarily a significant influence on the development of their offspring's self-concept. This is because the infant and pre-school child has a narrow environment within which to operate—essentially the home. Thus parents become the primary models for imitation, identification processes, and the learning of socialized behaviour. They also function as the primary source of feedback, evaluating and responding to the child's behaviour, so that the latter comes to know how he is regarded. The mother is usually more influential than father as she spends longer with the child, taking the major responsibility of caring for it and satisfying its basic needs.

The parents influence the sense of belonging, the sense of competence, and the sense of worth through their behaviour and role as model, feedback agent and evaluator. The early learning of the child is strongly influenced by the primary model available to him. Some psychologists have attempted to explain the whole process of identification (the emotional attachment of a child to his parents and the adoption of the parent's behaviours and values as his own) by attributing this process to imitation (Bandura 1965; Kagan 1958). The model that the parents present in their treatment of the child, and in their treatment of themselves and each other teaches the child how he should treat himself.

For example, children frequently use the same words and inflections that the parents have used when talking to the child. 'I'm a good boy. I put my coat on all by myself,' is likely to sound very much like the parent who has previously said to the child, 'You are a good boy. You put your coat on all by yourself.'

Each individual receives a plethora of feedback cues from the environment, and some of these cues are provided in the interactions of the individual with his environment. Individuals do things, and the consequences or outcomes of the actions provide their own feedback. The child attempts to climb some steps and falls. The facts that he ends up on the ground and is hurt provides him with natural feedback on his activities.

A second type of feedback requires that another human agent functions in the situation. Much of the feedback from parents and other humans to infants gives 'moral' or 'worth' meaning to the results of the activities. The girls who knocks over a cup receives immediate feedback on her competence in the sense that the cup falls and breaks. It takes another human to add the dimension of morality or worthiness. This is added in such a statements such as, 'You are a bad girl!' Notice that this statement does not deal directly with the girl's behaviour. Even though the statements may have brought about by knocking over a cup, it has gone beyond the behaviour and has attached meanings of worth to the individual.

The parent also acts as an evaluator. Although the infant can receive a natural evaluation of his efforts by observing what happens when he attempts something, the adults in the situation many times provide a verbal evaluation. 'That is very good.' 'You can't do it.' 'What a big boy!' Adults have many such verbal evaluations that they offer to children. One of the difficulties which parents face is that, as a general rule, children of all ages want to do many things which are too advanced for them. But unfortunately, parents frequently do not want their children to do many things which the children are perfectly capable of doing. The child wants to climb on the climbing frame which is probably a little too high and difficult for coming back down, and the worried mother does not want the child to climb at all for fear that he will fall. The child wants to put his own soup into his mouth but the mother continues to feed him because she does not want a mess. Too frequently, adults give negative evaluations rather than positive, making the failure, the weakness and the naughtiness stand out rather than the success, the strengths and the acceptable behaviour which so often are taken for granted.

For example, the occasional wet bed by a boy of three can be so overemphasized by parents as naughty, wrong and even dirty that this has a far greater effect on his view of himself that the many 'dry' nights he has managed which were not praised to the same extent because it was expected of him. We all tend as parents and teachers to highlight an isolated event and by implication the associated feelings that should really by played down. There is a human failing to reinforce the wrong behaviour. Children are given more attention and notice when they are naughty or fail; when satisfactory they are relatively ignored which neatly extinguishes the behaviour and the consequent positive feelings. The environment also offers the child the psychological experiences of exploration, limitation and self-impact. The child who trusts the environment can be open, accepting, autonomous and explorative, and through these behaviours can continue to acquire the confidence and competence which reinforce a postive self-concept. The child who mistrusts the environment because of negative psychological experiences in early years will tend to limit self-initiated activities which could provide him or her with new experiences and positive reflections. These self-imposed limitations reinforce the already negative and perhaps unrealistic self-concept the child has acquired through earlier psychological experiences.

The child who feels he is accepted warmly and loved by his parents is informed from infancy that he is a 'happy baby', a 'strong boy'. This parental love and attention establishes his worth in his own eyes. He hears and feels evidence of his parents prizing him. This is augmented as he grows older by comments about his performances, 'Mummy was very pleased that you tidied your bedroom this morning,' and 'Teacher told me you have learned your tables well'. Another child, of course, may hear nothing but that he is a nuisance, that he never does anything right or is always careless. These labels are negative in character, and become attached by the child to himself. He has learned a negative view of himself. This learning about self goes on all the time. Teachers, youth leaders, peer-group members and neighbours can teach children to value or undervalue themselves depending on how they respond to the child. Respect, attention, care and acceptance teach any person that he is of value and lead to a positive self-concept. Most of us try to maximize the postive view we have of ourselves and try to avoid hearing or feeling negative aspects of ourselves, or putting ourselves in situations where failure, guilt, shame or rejection are likely to accrue to us. When criticism has to be made of a child, it must be made in a generally supportive relationship, or self-protective techniques will deny, distort and rationalize the criticism, instead of it being accepted and integrated and acted on.

One little coloured boy asked 'Why do the others call me "Paki"? I know it isn't a nice name.' This boy was struggling not only with the meaning of the word but with understanding the implications of the word as applied to him and the non-verbal intentions of the tone and manner in which it was uttered. This would then lead to an attempt to accomodate this meaning and implication into his existing self-concept. New and discrepant views of oneself can be disturbing.

We learn to feel towards ourselves the way we interpret others feel towards us. The implications of this for parents, teachers and youth leaders, etc. is that they must treat all others, particularly young persons, with consideration, respect and acceptance. But of course from a phenomenological perspective, it is not the intention of the parent or professional that really counts, it is the client's perception that really matters, how he interprets the content of the interaction.

RESEARCH ON THE ROLE OF FEEDBACK

General Issues

Evaluations by self and others have most often centred on global measures of self-concept, although some investigations have examined more specific aspects of personality and behaviour. Overall these studies show modest to strong correlations betwen individuals' perceptions of themselves and the way they assume others perceive them. Schrauger and Schoeneman (1979) review research on the relationship between self-perceptions and evaluations from others. They show that many investigations have sought support for the idea of the looking-glass self in naturally occurring interactions. One group of studies has focused on the proposition that individuals' self-perceptions should be highly congruent with the way they think others perceive them. Most analyses were correlational, subjects of study were usually asked to describe themselves along a number of different dimensions. Their presumed significant others were then asked to rate them along these same dimensions. Correlations were then computed between the two sets of ratings, with the usual result that subjects' self-ratings were strongly correlated with the ratings of them by the significant others. Unfortunately, such results are not very instructive. They do not demonstrate a sound causal connection between others' views toward self and self-conceptualization. Such correlations could quite well result from the person's conceiving of himself in a specific way and convincing others of that identity.

Much more convincing are experimental studies demonstrating that with a systematic alteration of a person Y's overt communication of what he thinks of Z, Z's self-conceptualization changes accordingly.

The demonstration of a relationship between people's self-perceptions and how they feel others see them is not sufficient in validating the symbolic interactionist position. It is necessary, in addition, to demonstrate congruence between self-perceptions and others' actual perceptions of the person, and also between other's perceived evaluations and others' actual evaluations. A large number of studies have examined the former relationship. Although many of these studies are of questionable statistical and conceptual significance (Wylie 1974), the overall pattern of the conclusions drawn by these investigations suggests much less agreement between self-judgements and actual judgements by others than between self-judgements and perceived judgements. Approximately half the studies reviewed show no significant correlations between self-pereceptions and others' evaluations.

One would not necessarily believe that there should be total agreement between self-concept and direct feedback from others because such feedback may be infrequent and/or ambiguous. In addition, although norms regarding the evaluation of other people's behaviour probably vary widely across different subcultures and situations, strong sanctions are often maintained against making direct appraisals, particularly when they are negative. In some of the only research on the communications of evaluations, Blumberg (1972) found that people report inhibiting the direct communication of all types of evaluations to others, particularly if it is negative or if the recipient is not well known. Barriers to direct expression can be found in intimate relationships as well as in more impersonal social interactions. This 'not-even-your-best-friend-will-tell-you' phenomenon had been noted by Goffman (1955), who pointed out that unfavourable evaluations of close associates are typically given only when directly solicited and that in such a situation, chances are that the asker has already made some negative self-appraisal. Perhaps, this accounts in part for the popularity of sensitivity training, in which people have the privilege of finding out what others really think of them and of assertiveness training, in which they can learn to communicate their true feelings about others.

It would also seem that self-conceptualization is vitally affected by social comparison. As Festinger (1954) has pointed out, people have a constant need to evaluate their abilities and test the validity of their opinions. Since there are few yardsticks to aid in such evaluations the person will compare himself with others in order to reach conclusions about himself.

While social comparison theory has generated a considerable amount of research most of it has dealt with the effects of comparison in the evaluation of particular skills and opinions. It also seems clear that people are often concerned with their personal attractiveness and general value as human beings. They may frequently compare themselves with others in their immediate environment (and in the media) to judge their own personal worth. Thus, for example, to find oneself dishevelled when those around are tastefully dressed may be humiliating. Or, for the typical student to discover that he has obtained the highest score in his class may boost his self-esteem. Rosenberg (1965) reports that high-school students have lower self-esteem when living in ethnically mixed neighhourhoods than when living in homogeneous ones. Likewise Clark and Clark (1939) found that black children attending integrated, northern schools show more self-hatred than those in segregated southern classrooms. In both cases, respondents in the ethnically and racially mixed environments may have had more opportunity to compare themselves with their more affluent and better established neighbours (see Chapter 14).

Mirror versus Model Explanations

There are two popular and, to some extent, competing explanations of the development of the self-concept, which can be identified as the 'reflection' or mirror theory and the 'imitation' or model theory. The first position is associated with G. H. Mead, C. H. Cooley and William James, and is an integral part of the symbolic interactionist tradition. This view holds that the self-concept is a product of the reflected appraisals of others, especially significant others.

The second theory is derived from social learning theory, most notably from the work of Bandura and his associates (1963a; 1963b). This position, which we call modelling theory, states that a child acquires most of his behavioural characteristics, and from these his attitudes, through the process of imitating various others in his environment. Attitudes towards the self develop in the same way as attitudes towards other subjects; i.e. through the incorporation of the behaviours and attitudes of significant others in the social environment. Identification is the term usually associated with this process which Bandura considers as simply one type of imitation which can be classified as vicarious processes. A child who identifies with a parent, for example, is acting in a manner characteristic of all modelling behaviour: i.e., acquiring self-attributes through the perception and incorporation of the attributes of another.

For Bandura, the mechanism which links modelling behaviour to self-concept formation is self-reinforcement. Bandura, in reviewing some of his own research, states that people generally adopt the standards for self-reinforcement exhibited by exemplary models, they evaluate their own performances relative to that standard, and then, as their own reinforcing agents, reward themselves according to the internalized standards. In expounding his theory of self-concept from social learning, Bandura defines the self in terms of the relative frequency of positive to negative self-reinforcements, so that a negative self-concept would be one that has a high frequency of negative self-reinforcements. If we substitute the word self-evaluation for self-reinforcement, Bandura's definition would be congruent with Cooley's. Futhermore, this substitution is tenable in that self-evaluations are necessary in order for self-reinforcements to be made.

In summary, these two theories, rely on two different processes to account for the development of self-conceptualization. The mirror theory stresses the evaluative responses of others; that is, the feedback others give to a person as to how he appears to them. The modelling theory focuses on the conditions under which a person adopts as his own the characteristics of another.

The available empirical research supports both explanations. Research emanating from the symbolic interactionist tradition has consistently found that a person's self-conceptualization is associated with the idea held of him by others, especially significant others. Thus, the central hypothesis derived from the mirror theory is that parental evaluation of child is positively related to the child's self-concept.

On the other hand, research stemming from behaviouristic psychology supports the notion that self-concept develops through modelling behaviour and the internalization of standards and attributes of the model. Therefore, the central hypothesis from the modelling theory is that parental self-concept is positively related to the child's self-concept.

In addition, it becomes important to ask under what conditions—e.g. age, sex of child, sex of patient, etc.—might one process prove to be more strongly related to the child's self-concept. For example, Bandura (1965) suggests that the modelling relationship should be stronger for the parent and child of the same sex; while mirroring, should be stronger between the parent and child of the opposite sex. Since there is usually considerable social pressure exerted on the child to develop sex-appropriate characteristics, there is pressure on the child to identify with (model) the same-sex parent. The rationale for expecting the opposite tendency in mirroring relationships is a direct consequence of the pattern suggested for modelling. The establishment of identification bonds (modelling) usually leads to admiration and respect which often impairs easy and warm interaction both on the part of the parent and of the child. By contrast, since identification occurs less in opposite-sex parent and child relationships, the interaction can be freer and more open. As a result, the child may be more influenced in his self-concept by the evaluative responses of the opposite-sex parent.

Research on parent and child interaction has consistently shown that girls have a greater tendency to be influenced by parents and to conform to their expectations than do boys. This evidence fosters the expectation that girls will mirror and perhaps model parents more than will boys. From both model and mirror frameworks we would also expect that younger children living at home would show stronger tendencies for their respective relationships than older children who are away at school.

Gecas et al. (1974) explored the 'modelling' and 'feedback' alternatives with 300 families in the USA using the semantic differential technique involving evaluation, potency and activity scales to produce measures of self-concept (of each family member), parents' perceptions of their children, and children's perceptions of parents. Gecas then compared the correlations for the various relationships to determine which process, mirror or modelling, had the greater effect on the children's self-concepts. He found that for every comparison the mirror correlations were stronger; that is, the relationships between evaluations of child and child's self-evaluations are stronger than those between parent's self-evaluations.

Of the three dimensions of evaluation considered, the differences between the mirroring and modelling coefficients are greatest on the activity dimension ($P<0.05$ and 0.01 for girls), smaller on the power dimension and smallest on the worth dimension. This suggests that the development of a behavioural self-concept—an image of oneself in terms of power and action—may be more dependent on the responses of one's social environment than on the models present in that environment. This is consistent with Becker's view that man as an active agent defines largely in terms of the effect he has on his environment. Similarly, Foote and Cottrell's concept of 'interpersonal competence', which they define as the ability to produce intended effects and White's 'sense of efficacy', both stress the importance for the self of being a causal agent in the environment. And the most direct evidence of being a cause is observing the consequences of one's actions, such as the responses of others.

How are these relationships modified when sex of the child is considered in combination with sex of parent? Both mirror and model correlations are consistently higher for girls than boys, supporting the expectation that females are more dependent on, and susceptible to, parental influence than are males. The average correlations for modelling are $+0.16$ for girls and $+0.06$ for boys, while those mirroring are $+0.28$ and $+0.17$ and boys respectively.

We would expect that mirroring processes would be stronger for cross-sex parent and child relationships, while modelling would be stronger for same-sex relationships. The findings only partially support this expectation. Boys' self-evaluations are slightly more strongly related to their mothers' evaluations of them, than they are to their fathers' evaluations, at least on the power and worth dimensions; and girls' self-evaluations tend to mirror fathers more than mothers. This gives tentative support to the notion that the most important self–other relationship for the child's 'looking-glass self' in the family is the cross-sex parent and child relationship.

Modelling correlations, on the other hand, do not support the expectation that they would be strongest along the same-sex lines. On all of the evaluation dimensions, father appears as the more influential model for both boys and girls. The average correlations on modelling are 0.14 for father compared to 0.07 for mother. One later explanation of this finding is that power may be more relevant than gender for modelling processes. That is, children may be more strongly inclined to identify with and model those persons in their family whom they perceive as having the most power. In most American families this is the father. Bandura and Walters (1963) have, in fact, identified power as one of the more relevant characteristics of a model, and in psychiatric literature this tendency has been conceptualized as 'identification with the aggressor'.

When we consider the age of the child we find that younger children tended to model their parents more than older children. This is consistent with the rather common observation that children begin to identify less with parents as they get older and their scope of relations expands. We do not find the same tendency for the mirroring influence of parents. The correlations indicate that parental influence was stronger for older children on power and activity. As parents decrease in importance as significant others for the child as he grows older and leaves home, we would expect a decrease in influence on both modelling and mirroring processes. Failure to find this pattern for older children on the power and worth dimensions suggests that either the categories of 'older' and 'younger' child are not different enough in age to make a difference on these variable, or the method of discovering parental influence on child's self-concept is weak.

A few words of methodological caution are warranted at this point. First, the generally higher correlations for mirroring relationships may be an artifact of the methodology, in that the correlated scores in these instances were child's descriptions of self and parent's description of child. Two persons describing the same object should obviously correlate more than two persons describing different objects. Thus, the higher correlations for mirroring may be a result of knowledge rather than influence. On the other hand, the perceptions we have of people often have little correspondence to the nature of the person as such, but they do have implications for the way we act towards those persons. It is often these actions which create the person we imagined we perceived. In this sense, socialization of the child by the parent becomes the creation of a social reality, or to use a more colourful expression, a 'self-fulfilling prophecy'.

Second, the correlations for both the modelling and the mirroring relationships were lower than expected: model correlations ranged from -0.14 to $+0.31$ and mirror correlations from -0.05 to $+0.41$. This means that most of the variance in self-concept is unaccounted for by the familial factors we have considered. Thus, while the data do favour the 'looking-glass' idea of self-concept formation, the findings are more suggestive than they are conclusive of the relative importance of mirroring versus modelling processes.

This 'mirror' relationship between the child's level of self-esteem suggests the causal relationship runs from others' views of self to self's view of self. However, there is already a self-concept which is evaluating this feedback. Kahle et al. (1980), using a three-year longitudinal study with an adolescent sample, demonstrated that it was the existing level of self-conceptualization that interpreted the feedback and brought it into congruency with the existing self-concept. Incongruent feedback tended to have little effect on modifying the self-concept. This suggest that the correlation between feedback and self-concept is a function of distortion, and other defences to enable the self-concept to receive consistent information about itself. The self-concept is a somewhat opaque screen protecting itself and enabling the possessor to behave in known, acceptable and consistent ways, even though the subjective beliefs and evaluations are objectively incorrect.

Sources of Self-Esteem in Children

Kirchner and Vondraek (1975) argue that as it is difficult to measure the self-concept in young children unskilled in verbal ability, a more realistic and profitable approach is to investigate the sources of self-esteem at that age. One major root they study is esteem perceived from others. The subjects were 282 pre-school children, and perceived sources of self-esteem were assessed by a 'Who Likes You Scale'. This provided data on the specific sources and the number of sources mentioned.

The esteem sources in descending order of the percentage of subjects mentioning one or more sources in the category are child friends 52 per cent; sibling(s) 49 per cent; mother 46 per cent; father 33 per cent; other extended family 17 per cent; grandmother 13 per cent; day-care staff 12 per cent; grandfather 9 per cent; pet 7 per cent; and other adults 6 per cent. Less than 5 per cent of the children mentioned sources in the remaining categories of experimenter, self, nobody, everybody, television or fantasy characters and public servants. The percentage total exceeds 100 because of multiple responses.

Data concerning mother and father as esteem sources were analysed to determine whether a relationship existed between mention of one parent and mention of the other. Results indicated that the mention of neither or both parents occurred significantly more often than mention of one parent independent of the other.

Because about 40 per cent of subjects resided in one-parent homes, additional analyses were performed if the frequency of mention of mother and father was associated with whether both parents or either parent was present in the home. Results showed that mention of father was significantly related to whether both parents, only mother or only father was present. Father was mentioned by 64 per cent of the children in father-only families, by 37 per cent in two-parent families and by 23 per cent in mother-only families. The mention of mother, however, was not significantly related to whether or not she was present in the home. Mother was mentioned by 43 per cent of the children in father-only families, by 44 per cent in two-parent families and by 50 per cent in mother-only families. Females mentioned significantly more esteem sources (M = 4.78) than males (M = 3.48) regardless of chronological age.

The four esteem sources most frequently mentioned (child friend, sibling, mother and father) were further analysed for possible age and sex differences. There were no significant age differences in frequency of mention of these sources but significant sex differences appeared in the mention of three of these sources. Females cited mother and sibling(s) as esteem sources more frequently than males did.

The finding that no significant relation existed between age and the number of esteem sources mentioned argues against the notion of the test being an index of verbal fluency. Also, the correlation between number of sources cited and family size was sufficiently small to rule out availability of others in the home environment as an important response determinant.

The prominence of peers and siblings and their precedence over parents as perceived sources of self-esteem are the most interesting findings of this investigation. These findings are of particular importance to self-concept theory in that they suggest the potency of age-mates as contributors to the development of self-regard and thus challenge the tenet to self-theorists that the growth of self-esteem in early childhood centres round the parent–child relationship.

Similarly, that peers and siblings exceeded parents as esteem sources is important to developmental theory generally. This finding conflicts with the common assumption the peers do not appreciably influence development, however, with a growing body of literature that peer contact may have considerable impact on developmental phenomena much earlier than has generally been supposed. We can see this in Bronfenbrenner's (1971) position regarding the relative potency of peer versus parent influence on child development and behaviour in contemporary American society.

The finding that peers constituted the prime source of esteem for the present sample is also relevant to the debate between Borke (1972) and Chandler and Greenspan (1972) regarding the age of onset of social decentration and the capacity of young children for emphatic awareness. The Piagetian position that social egocentrism does not decline until later childhood has fostered the view that children tend to perceive age-mates as 'obstacles' or 'inanimate objects'. This view has also been encouraged by excessive reliance on observational methods where adult observers evaluate the affective quality of peer interactions from the vantage point of adults. The present results suggest that, in fact, young children have strong, positive affective responses to age-mates and are supportive of Borke's (op. cit.) contention that traditional thinking about young children's interpersonal perceptions should be reassessed.

The fact that mother was mentioned as an esteem source by a substantially higher percentage of subjects than was father is congruent with studies indicating that both male and female children regard fathers as more punitive, more threatening, and less friendly than mothers. The significantly more frequent mention of neither or both parents than the mention of one parent only, regardless of family type, may be most parsimoniously explained as an instance of paired-associate learning. The strength of the associative bond between the words 'mother' and 'father' probably overrides differential percepts of parents as esteem sources in many young children in a test. More provocative, however, is the finding that father was mentioned significantly less often in mother-only families than in father-only and two-parent families and that parallel results did not occur for mention of mother. A number of factors, none differentially supported by available data, might account for these results, including the child's perception of the cause of parental absence, the child's age at the time of onset of parental absence, and/or frequency of contact with the absent parent.

The significant sex differences found in this study, that young females report more esteem sources and mention esteem sources within the immediate family more frequently than males, agree with reports of sex differences in social percepts among older children. Previous researchers have proposed the following factors to account for observed sex differences in interpersonal percepts: (a) more favourable treatment of females than males by significant others, (b) greater response to social desirability by females than males and (c) sex-linked genetic dissimilarities.

The relative absence of age differences in the four major esteem sources may reflect the fact that this study dealt with a single developmental period. It seems probable that comparable studies with older age groups would show age-related changes in frequency of mention of esteem sources. Whether age affects the number of sources cited and how the number of sources cited relates to level of self-esteem requires future investigation.

This study by Kirchner and Vondraek (op. cit.) strongly supports the view that commonly held assumptions concerning development in early childhood must be reconsidered. Specifically, this investigation points out the need to re-evaluate the relative impact of peers and parents on the development of self-esteem in young children. This study also provides additional evidence for reconsidering the impact of peers on development in early childhood and for increased attention to the child's phenomenal field.

The crucial area does seem to be peer interaction. Peers approximate in size and age, whereas at home there exists an age hierarchy with even brothers and sisters being older or younger. So differences in competence at home are expected, but in the peer group the child need only show he is at least equal with others. At home he must be love-worthy, within the peer group he must be respect-worthy, competitive and competent. The penalties of failure are self-concept components of humiliation, rejection and derogation from self and others. These different expectations between home and peer group are due to the former placing a high premium on behaviour, while the latter place it on performance. In fact, behaviour that is unacceptable for parents may well be ignored in the peer group, or even accepted if the child is, say, a good footballer.

In the upper primary school years the child's self-concept continues to modify as it is influenced by his expanding social environment. The new levels of self-expression obtained from more advanced schoolwork, new levels of attainment and competency, extracurricular activities and complex group activities generally raise self-esteem, and most pre-adolescents see themselves as capable of accomplishing all the tasks set them. Abilities and talents are usually evaluated in terms of school standing, peer acceptance, athletic pursuits and popularity. All prefer activities which test their prowess. Thus, at this stage of life the self-concept is based on social relationships and comparative performances. The child has an increased sensitivity to the approval and disapproval of significant others, especially peers and teachers. The development and encouragement of special interests, e.g. art, craft, music, or sport, assist socialization and maturing. Therefore, school allows the development of new skills, providing the individual with more chances to compare himself with others and perceive others' evaluation of him. In-group and out-group categories become available, encouraging the labelling and categorizing of others and self.

School then continues and augments the processes that are involved in developing a self-picture, as Staines (1958) has shown so well in his study of the subtle influences of teachers through their verbal and non-verbal communications to pupils. Even teachers' ordinary comments are fraught with a hierarchial evaluational and emotional content for children. School provides new models in the peer group and new demands and expectations. These models provide standards against which the child can evaluate himself. He finds that some of his peer group do better or worse than him in academic, sporting, artistic and many other fields. Comparison cannot be avoided.

Standards set by parents or teachers are vitally important for the development of self-esteem, since standards provide a means of measuring self-progress, validating competence and showing that others have interest in the individual. A lack of any requirement to meet standards suggests that parents and teachers have no concern for the child and is not worth bothering about (Coopersmith 1967).

The fairly direct feedback that parents, children, adolescents and students commonly convey to each other has been shown in several studies to affect the individual's self-concept (Videbeck 1960). An instance of this is described by Guthrie (1938). A group of male students played what was intended as a joke on a dull, unattractive female student. They treated her for a time as though she was tremendously popular and attractive. The shocked students found that within a year she developed an easy manner, confidence and popularity. Such a manner increased the eliciting of positive and reinforcing reactions from others. Similar feedback cycles lie behind many of the self-concepts and behaviour patterns of all of us.

Wooster and Harris (1973) predicted that the frequent moving of children of armed service personnel would impair the development of their self-concept, since some major sources of the self-image such as comparison with significant others, learning from others' reactions and role playing, are more restricted than in 'static' children. Frequent changes of teachers, peer groups and neighbours would prevent the development of stable reference groups. The researchers found a low level of conviction in the views the 'mobile' pupils hold about themselves, the pupils were unsure of their parents' affection, saw themselves as of little value as friends, and doubted their success outside school. In general his changing sources of self-information leaves the 'mobile' child bewildered and unable to cope with the tasks of making judgements about himself.

There is little question but that the peer group has an enormous impact on the final embellishments that are fixed on to the core self-attitudes in adolescence. The peer group is important at this stage because it replaces the family as a major source of feedback; it also provides self-esteem, mutual support, standards, opportunity to practise and rehearsal of tasks preparatory for adulthood. The peer group is a place within which an identity may be secured, since the growing child must become less like his parents and more like his peers. Suprisingly, external standards and societal norms do not exert anywhere near the influence of interpersonal relationships with relatives and friends (Coopersmith 1967; Rosenberg 1965). One way to improve self-conceptualization, even if only slightly, might be to alter the interpersonal environment so that the person can associate more with people who can become significant others and whose interests, abilities and backgrounds are more similar to his. This may require the development of new interests and a deliberate willingness to make friends with those whose skills and background are similar.

In a study designed to test Sullivan's view that a close friend (chumship) increases a child's sense of self-esteem, Mannarino (1978) found, using the Piers–Harris scale, that children with a close friend possessed significantly higher self-concepts than those without one. This finding was accounted for in terms of Sullivan's (1953) notion that a chumship provides the opportunity for the pre-adolescent to realize that he shares common thoughts and feelings with his friend. Thus, his own sense of self-worth is mutually validated.

Thus, as Sullivan theorized, a chum relationship can enhance the self-worth of the pre-adolescent. As two youngsters communicate openly, the pre-adolescent realizes that he shares certain ideas and feelings with his chum and begins, perhaps for the first time, to appreciate the common humanity of people. No longer perceiving his own thoughts as entirely unique, or idiosyncratic, he can resolve some of the uncertainty of his personality. As noted earlier, Sullivan labelled this process 'consensual validation of the self'.

Sullivan's explanation seems plausible, especially in the light of some research concerning the bases upon which pre-adolescents choose their friends. Byrne and Griffitt (1966) reported that similar attitudes, interests and tastes were important reasons given for selecting best friends during this period. In relation to Sullivan's theory, selecting best friends for these reasons would enhance the process of consensual validation. As the pre-adolescent interacts closely with individuals who can reinforce his own attitudes and ideas, his feelings of self-worth will increase because he knows that he possesses certain qualities common to other human beings, such as attitudes, interests and feelings.

A pre-adolescent without a close friend does not have the opportunity to communicate intimately with a peer, and his self-worth is not thus validated. He will accordingly possess lower self-esteem than one who has formed a chumship.

Research suggests that children may not concern themselves with social comparisons until around the age of eight (Nicholls 1979). In two studies presented by Ruble and Boggiano (1980) children's achievement related self-evaluations were little affected by relative comparisons until they were seven or eight. Such works seem to conflict with other reports, for example, Masters (1971) reported that even nursery-school pupils are influenced by social comparison as measured by self-reinforcement after a child has been differentially reinforced relative to a peer. These apparently conflicting results may be due to the importance of different facets of social comparison developing at different times.

For example, children's initial comparisons seem to be at an overt physical level, such as equalizing the number of rewards received (Masters 1971), and do not involve inferences that are removed from concrete differences, such as self-evaluation or behaviour based on self-evaluations. Younger children's focus of attention was most likely directed externally towards the specific features of the task that they (as actors) were engaged in. Thus, their assessment of performance based on direct experience with the task, may have dominated evaluations and such salience effects are likely to be especially pronounced in young children. Furthermore, young children's perceptions that their abilities are unstable or rapidly changing may make information on their relative performance essentially meaningless, in that their concern is more with how to improve their skills (e.g. to get more correct answers) than with evaluating their current level of competence.

It is possible that children younger than eight use social comparison information for self-evaluation in more familiar settings where comparative information is repeatedly available. However, these findings suggest that the role of peers in the self-socialization process undergoes significant *qualitative* changes as well as *quantitative* ones. That is, children's initial comparisons are apparently not concerned with self-evaluation or self-definition but, rather with ensuring that they are getting their fair share of rewards or with desiring to be similar to others. Thus, until children recognize that the outcome of comparisons have deeper implications for the self, competition or comparative evaluation may have little-lasting impact.

Studies of Controlled Feedback

In studies of controlled feedback subjects typically describe themselves on the attributes assessed by the tests, then take the tests, receive feedback about their performance either immediately or within a week or two, and finally reappraise themselves. This procedure has been used not only in specific efforts to assess the symbolic interactionist position, but also in studies examining the effects of change in self-evaluation on other aspects of behaviour, with change in self-evaluation often examined as a manipulation check. In the second type of study, feedback is based on the subjective impressions of other individuals who have not specific knowledge of objective assessment results. These studies have varied in the extent to which the other person is presented as having expertise in the topics considered.

The most elementary question typically asked in this research is, 'Will individuals modify their self-descriptions in the direction of the feedback they receive?' The most elementary answer is, 'Usually'.

Such changes have been shown for numerous populations and for many different attributes. Videbeck (1960) was among the first to demonstrate this phenomenon in a direct way. He studied thirty speech students each of whom read aloud six poems in the presence of a 'visiting expert' in oral communication. At random, without regard to actual performance, half the subjects received from the expert a positive appraisal, informing them of their superiority in controlling voice and conveying meaning. The other half of the subjects each received a rather negative appraisal of the same qualities.

Before and after the experiment, subjects made a number of self-ratings. These estimates were of three kinds: first, their adequacy in controlling voice and conveying meaning, that is, the attributes specifically appraised by the expert; second, their adequacy in areas related to those appraised but not specifically covered by the expert; and third, unrelated abilities, such as their adequacy in social conversation. If reflected appraisal is important in moulding self-conceptualization, those receiving the positive evaluations should come to rate themselves as more adequate after the session than before. Likewise, subjects receiving the critical appraisals should show a reverse effect. The greatest change in self-ratings should be found on items reflecting the content of the appraisals, less change should be found in ratings of related abilities, and the least change should be revealed in estimates of unrelated abilities.

Subjects who received a positive appraisal showed a general increase in their feelings of self-adequacy, an increase that was strongest for attributes directly appraised and weakest for unrelated aspects. Subjects who received a negative appraisal revised their self-estimates in a negative direction, with the impact varying directly with the relevance of the content to the appraisals. Harvey and Clapp (1965), however, found that students changed their self-ratings on a set of bipolar adjectives more when they had received positive feedback than when they received negative feedback from classmates.

In another study, junior high-school boys were given feedback about the physical skills by either one or two experts (Haas and Maehr 1965). Initial post feedback ratings did not differ as a function of the number of raters, but self-ratings made six weeks after the experts' judgements showed greater changes on the attributes evaluated for these students judged by two experts.

Other studies by Shrauger and Lund (1975) and Regan (1975) equally produce effective changes from varying feedback. In almost all cases changes in self-perception have been judged by modifications in verbal self-descriptions made immediately following others' evaluations and in the presence of the evaluator.

Muller and Spuhler (1976) observed that college freshmen who had been told that they scored very low on a foreign language aptitude test scored lower on a subsequent self-concept test and learned a paired-associates task more slowly than a control group who received no test information. Muhler and Spuhler suggest that anxiety may have been induced when the positiveness of self-concept was lowered, and the anxiety, rather than self-concept impaired learning.

Giving individual information about himself in a negative judgemental fashion may heighten anxiety. It is possible that Muller and Spuhler used such a negative, judgemental tone in lowering self-concept, thereby producing heightened anxiety, which in turn reduced performance on the paired-associate task. Had they provided the same information in a supportive fashion, perhaps, learning would not have been impaired even though self-concept was lowered. To answer this point, Sharp and Muller (1978) systematically manipulated the self-concepts of college students regarding ability to learn a foreign language and then measured performance on a paired-associates task. Sixteen subjects were randomly assigned to each of four treatments: self-concept raised, self-concept lowered therapeutically, self-concept lowered without support, and a control group. Self-concepts were raised or lowered by providing each subject with a false score on a foreign language aptitude test. When self-concept was lowered therapeutically, a very low aptitude score was presented supportively and the acceptability of low foreign langauge ability was emphasized. When a self-concept was lowered unsupportively the low score was presented in a way that emphasized the unacceptability of low ability. Each subject then learned a paired-associates task. The mean learning task performances for the raised, therapeutically lowered, and control groups were equal to one another but were superior to the performance of the unsupportively lowered group.

The importance of this finding for schools is that when negative information is provided in a supportive manner, there is not necessarily a detrimental effect on learning since self-concept accuracy is more important than its level. However, when essentially the same information was presented in an unsupportive manner, a significant impairment to learning was detected.

These results, like Muller and Spuhler's (op. cit.) suggest that college students are more likely to internalize other-provided, negative descriptions of self, than they are positive descriptions.

Educators should be primarily concerned with enhancing self-descriptive accuracy rather than simply positiveness. Enhancing positiveness of self-concept without regard for its accuracy may be counter-productive. The results of this experiment indicate that teachers and counsellors can adjust self-concept downward in order to achieve self-descriptive accuracy without impeding learning if adjustment is made in a supportive and reassuring tone.

Although controlled feedback from others typically produces some changes, other factors are involved. For example, the credibility of the source, personalism, the audience effect, attentional focusing, original level of self-esteem, anxiety level, etc., the whole area is a morass of interacting variables that almost defy isolation. Some of these factors will now be briefly considered.

FACTORS AFFECTING FEEDBACK

Audience Effect

It should be noted that empirical investigations of Mead and Cooley's looking-glass-self hypothesis have explored almost exclusively the impact of direct feedback from others. There may, however, be several less direct but equally important effects of others' judgements on self-perception. Simply being in the presence of others may influence the manner in which people behave (Goffman 1959) and presumably come to evaluate their own behaviour. At a conscious level one might deliberately enhance socially desirable and minimize socially undesirable behaviours when in the presence of others and such changes could influence how one saw oneself. Less deliberately controlled aspects of behaviour may also be affected by the presence of others as suggested in studies of audience effects on performance and self-evaluations of competence (Shrauger 1972). Also, as Mead's (1934) notion of the generalized other implies, the physical presence of others is not imperative, so long as the perceiver can manage a mental impression of them.

Shrauger (1972) studied the effect of the presence of an audience on persons varying in self-esteem while they performed a concept attainment task. When individuals must engage in some activity requiring skills in the presence of other people, some are able to perform with little effect on either their emotional state or their competence and, on occasion, with an actual enhancement of their performance. For other people, however, the presence of an audience seems to lead to discomfort, a devaluation of their efforts and interference with an effective performance. One potential determinant of differential reactions to being observed by others is one's level of self-esteem. Shrauger's study was designed to explore how the favourability of one's perceptions of oneself is related to the way of responding to the presence of others.

The person who expresses general confidence in himself should, (provided this reflects more than a defensive posture) be expected to be less affected by others observing him. The basis for this assumption is the notion that high self-esteem people should operate under less stress. While the specific motives aroused by situations involving others' presence may vary, it is assumed that one central source of the heightened arousal which an audience presumably produces involves anxiety regarding the quality of one's performance and the prospect of being evaluated. People who are uncertain about their competence would be particularly susceptible to such stress. Individuals scoring high on measures of self-esteem have reported less general anxiety on self-report inventories than individuals with lower self-esteem (e.g. Worchel 1957). Thus, if an audience does arouse concern about evaluation, subjects with low self-esteem are likely to be operating in such situations under relatively high levels of anxiety. Since high levels of anxiety are found to interfere with performance on complex tasks, one would expect that low self-esteem individuals might show more impairment in performing such a task than would high self-esteem subjects who are presumably not so anxious.

Shrauger (1972) found that although general self-esteem was not related to actual performance, high general self-esteem subjects thought that they had performed better and were more confident of their responses than low general self-esteem subjects. Analysis indicated that this difference tended to be greater with the audience present. Subjects were also divided into high and low specific self-esteem groups on the basis of their pre-task estimates of their performance. High specific self-esteem subjects performed better than low specific self-esteem subjects. Low specific self-esteem subjects performed significantly more poorly with the audience than without one, while the presence or otherwise of an audience had no significant effect on high specific self-esteem subjects.

The results support the general notion that one's self-esteem is related to the way one reacts to the presence of an audience. They also suggest that the manner in which self-esteem relates to performance in this situation depends on whether one considers a general or a task-specific measure of self-esteem. Specific self-esteem is more predictive of differences in actual performance: both general differences across conditions and differential changes as a function of the presence of an audience. General self-esteem shows no systematic relationship to actual performance, although it does tend to predict how favourably one perceives one's performance, again both across conditions and as a function of the presence of an audience.

This audience effect would seem to be due to the presence of a stimulus that increases self-focus attention and makes the performer more self-conscious. Being a teacher in front of the classroom audience, or being a pupil surrounded by an audience of peers, with an authoritative master of ceremonies looking on, are situations where the audience effect increases self-focused attention, a deleterious effect for performance for those without a secure self-concept.

Attentional Focusing

A recent series of experiments (Brockner 1979; Brockner and Hulton 1978) also suggest that the important factor in performance was the low self-esteem students' focus of attention during that performance. Low self-esteem people did quite poorly in the presence of stimuli designed to increase self-focused attention (e.g. an audience, a mirror and a video camera). However, the low self-esteem person's performance was enhanced considerably by a set of instructions intended to increase task-focused and decrease self-focused attention. These latter data have implications for breaking the vicious cycle of low self-esteem. It seems entirely possible that if low self-esteem people improve their task performance their self-opinions may begin to become more positive.

Brockner (1979) suggested that the attentional focus manipulations produced differential levels of anxiety for those with low self-esteem. That is the self-focusing stimuli appeared to make those with low self-esteem more anxious, whereas the task-focusing instructions, by reducing self-consciousness, were thought to make them less anxious. Brockner also presented evidence consistent with the notion that anxiety and performance were inversely related—Buckner observed that the low self-esteem people's performance does not always have to suffer in the presence of self-focusing stimuli. Low self-esteem were placed in front of a mirror and were also instructed to concentrate on the task. It was found that these subjects made significantly fewer errors than low self-esteem people who performed the task in front of a mirror but were not told to focus on the task, the former group's level of self-focus, and therefore anxiety, was reduced.

Additional evidence for the inverse relationship between self-esteem and self-consciousness stems from recent findings in the objective self-awareness literature. Ickes, Wicklund and Ferris (1973) observed that subjects who completed a self-esteem inventory in the presence of a self-focusing stimulus (a mirror) rated themselves significantly lower than subjects completing the inventory without a mirror. Futhermore, self-focusing stimuli cause subjects to behave as low self-esteem people 'naturally' do. For example, there is some evidence that they are rather persuasible (Janis et al. 1959). Using two very different conformity procedures, Duval (1976) and Wickland and Duval (1971) both found enhanced persuasion in the presence of self-focusing stimuli.

Mischel, Ebbesen and Zeiss (1976) developed a paradigm to investigate the influence of success and failure experiences on subsequent selective attention to information about the self. College students were assigned to success, failure, or control experiences on an achievement task and subsequently required to attend to their assets or limitations. Successful subjects attended more to their personality assets and less to their liabilities than did subjects who failed or formed the control.

Research indicates that low self-esteem people show greater anxiety in a test (Dunn 1965). Test anxiety in turn has been shown to impair performance particularly under conditions that could cause self-focused attention, such as the presence of an audience (Ganzer 1968). The test performance of high self-esteem persons is less likely to be adversely affected by self-focused attention because they are simply not as self-focused as low self-esteem persons. This allows them to devote more attention to the task. Also even when high self-esteem people are self-focused in a test the experience is probably not as anxiety provoking as it is for low self-esteem people. The possession of high self-esteem appears to enable the student to focus on the academic task rather than on himself when solving problems. Extraneous cues concerning self-evaluation are ignored in order to focus on more crucial considerations (Mossman and Ziller 1968). Low self-esteem hindered full attention to the task as the student was more concerned with his own feelings and expectations of failure and how others would react to his performance. This suggests that the enhancement of self-esteem is vital in school if pupils are to work effectively on academic matters so that self-doubt does not hinder performance. It is not that low self-esteem pupils are on the whole less intelligent but that they themselves are central in their thoughts rather than the task. Their attentional focus must be changed.

The attentional focus on self often brought about in education by the presence of an evaluator (e.g. teacher, parent, self) or of an audience (e.g. other pupils) evokes stress and anxiety. These can have a debilitating effect on performance leading to lowered self-esteem, negative feedback and more stress.

Feedback and Anxiety

Negative feedback about performance can lower self-esteem and impair later performance, possibly through the mediation of anxiety. Relationships between self-concept and anxiety are usually negative, that is, low self-concept is related to high anxiety. In a study involving 10 to 12 year-old pupils, Lipsitt (1958) found that children with low self-concepts were significantly more anxious than were children with more positive self-concepts. From his study of female college students Mitchell (1959) concluded that the better the self-concept the less anxiety is shown. Lampl (1968), Wittrock and Husek (1962), Coopersmith (1967) Many and Many (1975) all provide similar findings to those above.

Those with low self-esteem are more adversely affected by stress than high self-esteem people according to Schalon (1968). He produced stress from experimentally induced task failure by specifically informing his subjects that they were not trying and ought to put more effort into the task and that they had done less well than 50 per cent of a comparable group.

Anxiety is primarily aroused in social relationships as it is directly linked to individuals' assessments of others, and discrepancies in evaluations by self, and others, are an important precipitant of anxiety. From a psychodynamic point of view, anxiety involves both phenomenological and physiological components. In terms of subjective experience anxiety represents an unpleasant affective state with feelings of apprehension and dread. Physiological symptoms of anxiety include heart palpitation, sweating, tremor, and a variety of other body manifestations. Sullivan (1953) in particular has emphasized that anxiety is aroused within one's relations with other persons. In infancy, anxiety is transmitted by the 'mothering' one through a variety of non-verbal cues. More generally anxiety is associated with disapproval, real or imagined, from significant others. Thus anxiety is viewed as arising from perceived threats to the self system. Similarly Rogers (1951) contends that 'psychological' tension occurs as the individual has experiences that cannot be readily assimilated into his or her current self-structure.

Comparable inferences can be drawn from a symbolic interactionist perspective. For these theorists, social participation is made possible as the individual comes to define and respond to his own line of activity from the perspective of others. One implication is that when discrepancies occur between appraisals by others and the individual's self-evaluation, anxiety is likely to be an important emotional consequence for the individual.

Within this general theory at least four distinct hypotheses can be proposed. Here,

Miller's (1963) distinction between 'self-esteem' and 'subjective public-esteem' proves useful. Self-esteem (SE) refers to individuals' evaluations of their own attributes. Subjective public-esteem (SPE) refers to individuals' perceptions of the evaluations of themselves held by significant others within a given social context.

(a) A first hypothesis is that anxiety will be associated with low SPE. To the extent that the individual believes that significant others hold a negative opinion of him and are likely to react to him with criticism and disapproval, anxiety is likely to be high.

(b) Second, low SE is likely to be associated with high anxiety. That is, anxiety will be aroused when individuals feel inadequate or ineffective when coping with life.

(c) Third, anxiety might be expected to be high when SPE is both discrepant from SE and more negative than it. Here, anxiety would presumably be precipitated by threats to self-esteem stemming from negative perceived appraisals between SPE and SE which imply potential contradiction of the individual's view of self, will be associated with high anxiety, regardless of whether SPE is more negative or more positive than SE. When SPE is more negative, the individual is faced with pressures towards decreased SE. When SPE is more negative, the individual is faced with pressures towards decreased SE. When SPE is more positive than SE, the individual is likely to feel incapable of living up to others' expectations.

Minimal research has focused upon relationships of anxiety to discrepancies between public-esteem and self-esteem. However, in a directly relevant study Felker (1969) hypothesized that high anxiety would be shown when self-evaluations are more favourable than evaluations of the individual by others, and that anxiety would be lowest when self-ratings are more negative than ratings of the individual by others. Teacher ratings, peer ratings, self-ratings, and Children's Manifest Anxiety Scale scores were obtained for a sample of fifth graders. As predicted, low anxiety was found when self-ratings were more negative than peer ratings. However, anxiety scores were not unduly high when self-ratings were more positive than peer ratings. Felker also found that evaluative ratings by peers were more strongly associated with anxiety than were self-ratings.

Lundgren and Schwab (1977) too found, that increasing discrepancy between self-esteem (SE) and perceived self-esteem (SPE) are related to increasing levels of anxiety.

The most feasible interpretation would appear to be that discrepancies between SPE and SE, whichever their direction, constututute a threat to the individual. When SPE is more positive than SE the individual is likely to experience others' views and expectations as exceeding his or her own capacities, and feel threatened because he cannot live up to these expectations. When SPE is more negative than SE, the perceived appraisals of others constitute a direct threat to valued attributes of self. Thus, absolute SPE–SE discrepancies prove a more sensitive predictor of anxiety than do directional discrepancy scores.

In summary, the findings as a whole point to two important interpersonal factors in anxiety: (a) low self-esteem; and (b) discrepancies between self-esteem and subjective public-esteem, regardless of their evaluative direction. The sources of anxiety would appear to differ for these two variables. Low SE presumably involves the expectation that one lacks abilities to cope effectively with other people. SPE–SE discrepancies, on the other hand, are likely to induce feelings of threat and uncertainty due to the potential contradiction of the individual's self-evaluation or to anticipated loss of esteem from significant others.

Susceptibility to Persuasion

Self-esteem is generally negatively related to susceptibility to persuasion with high self-esteem providing protection from social influence (Janis et al. 1959). This general finding has been modified by the work of Nisbett and Gordon (1967) who reported that such a negative relationship only holds when the persuasive message is easy to comprehend and relatively implausible. The more difficult the feedback is to understand and the greater the plausibility, the higher the level of self-esteem needed to avoid being influenced.

Objective Appraisal and Credibility

Bergin (1962) found that the credibility of feedback influenced the relationship between discrepancy and self-perception changes. With a high credibility source, increases in discrepancy resulted in greater changes in self-relevant attitudes, whereas for a low-credibility source the tendency was for greater credibility to produce less change. Although not wholly consistent, other results have suggested that when other's evaluations are reportedly based on objective test data, self-perceptions change more as the discrepancy from initial perceptions increases.

Although many factors may differentiate these studies from one another, they are generally consistent with Bergin's argument about the role of credibility and suggest that for feedback that diverges substantially from one's views to have a strong effect on self-evaluations, it must be perceived as being based on clear objective information.

A determinant of assuredness may be the clarity of the criteria against which attributes are judged. A person is more likely to have a firmly established self-appraisal of an attribute that has a very clear public definition. One reason for children's potential susceptibility to self-concept moulding may be their lack of clear criteria for defining particular characteristics.

This may also account for the clinical observation that negative global self-perceptions (e.g. 'I am rotten' or 'I am a total failure') are resistant to change without exploration of what these attributes actually entail.

The credibility of feedback and its apparent objectivity in school mean that it should have quite a potent effect on self-esteem. This has been shown to be so in the many research studies considered in Chapters 8 and 9 where the expectancy effect and the relationship between achievement level and self-concept, are discussed.

When an appraiser appears to have expertise in any given situation, we are mc likely to place our trust in his evaluations. In effect, he is more credible. Research into changes in attitude has shown that the more credible the communicator, the greater will be his impact on our conceptualization of self. This is one reason why family members and teachers are particularly influential in determining self-conceptualization. If parents communicate to their son that he is 'irresponsible', he may well come to see himself in this way; after all, he may tell himself, no one has better knowledge of his behaviour. And for the same reason, he may come to see himself as 'brainy' because the teacher has told him so.

Personalism

All too often, others communicate things to us without seeming to be truly aware of us as individuals. Their appraisals of us appear insincere, based to serve their own ends, or the result of lazy disregard for detail. How many times have students accused college administrators of just such impersonalism, while the administrators find the students equally impersonal? On the other hand, there is the communicator who appears to take into account our every action, who attends to the subtleties in our behaviour and modifies his appraisal accordingly. This type of communicator may be called personalistic and should have a greater influence over our views of self.

One experimental study has attempted to demonstrate such an effect. This study (Gergen 1965) concentrated on the person's esteem for self. Female subjects were interviewed by an attractive girl a few years senior to them. During the interview it was the subject's task to rate herself along a variety of dimensions. The interviewer subtly showed signs of agreement whenever the subject rated herself positively and signs of disagreement whenever the subject rated herself negatively. Agreement was signalled by smiles, nods, and an occasional brief statement such as, 'Yes I think so too.' Disagreement was expressed by silence, frowns and occasional verbal statements. Prior to the interview, half the subjects were instructed that the interviewer would be simply practising a set of interview techniques and that all her behaviour was prescribed for her (impersonal condition). The other subjects were told that the interviewer had instructions as to her behaviour and that it was her main task to be as honest as possible during the interview (personalistic condition). Both before and after the interview all subjects were given a test of self-esteem and told to evaluate themselves as honestly as possible.

The results of the study showed that subjects who received the impersonal appraisals showed little increase in self-esteem as a result of the interview. On the other hand, subjects who received the personalistic appraisals showed strong increase in self-esteem—a difference exceeding that found in a control group interviewed with reflected appraisal. In other words, persons are more strongly affected when others appear sincere, uncalculated and attuned to them as individuals.

Group Aspirations

The group's aspiration is pertinent in influencing the extent to which the individual evaluates objective failure feedback as a failure and an objective success as a success, assuming, of course, he expects that the group will become aware of his performance.

Stotland et al. (1957) considered the two kinds of reference a person is influenced by, in placing the goal line of his aspirations. One reference is a source of pressure from other persons or groups to perform in a particular fashion on that activity. The other involves pressure from the person's own expectations concerning his likely performance in that activity, arising from past experiences. Stotland et al. (op. cit.) examined the effect of a specific level of achievement upon an individual's evaluations of his performance when the achievement is relative to a level of aspiration established by a group and when the achievement is also relative to the member's stabilized expectations about himself as represented by his self-esteem.

When a person evaluates his level of achievement he refers not only to the expectations of other persons but to the concept he has of himself as well. The degree of an individual's self-esteem therefore, is expected to affect the way in which an individual evaluates his performance in a particular situation.

Persons who have high self-esteem, we assume, differ from those who are low in the way they react to an immediate experience which has been a test of their abilities. Cohen (1959) has reported that persons with high self-esteem, as compared to those with low, are characterized by tendencies to protect themselves from negative self-evaluation. It is not clear why this should occur. Perhaps people with high self-esteem have learned to overlook their objective failures and to concentrate upon their successes in building their self-concept, or, perhaps, they have consistently performed in accordance with their ideals and hence are less threatened by an experience of failure. In any event, it would be expected that persons with high self-esteem would be able to evaluate an objective failure as a small failure and an objective success as a large success. Persons with low self-esteem, however, because they do not protect themselves from negative evaluation, are more likely to evaluate an objective failure as a very poor performance and a success as a small success. All the subjects in Stotland's (op. cit.) study were aware of the criteria for a successful performance of the task.

The results suggest that people who were successful did not tend to evaluate their performance in the light of the group but that those who failed were affected by the group's expectations. Successful people clearly evaluated their performance as highly successful regardless of whether the task was relevant or irrelevant, the group's expectations were high or low, or the group's expectations were an important concern to them or not. People who failed, however, evaluated their performance low if the group had high expectations, and they evaluated their performance high if the group had low expectations. The effect of the level of expectations upon the evaluation of their performance was also greater the more the people were concerned about the group's expectations. These results occurred when the task was relevant, but did not occur when the task was irrelevant.

Why did the wishes of the group determine self-evaluations for persons who failed more than ones who succeeded? A failure, presumably, has an important property which is not present in a success. The person who has failed cannot be sure how the group will receive his report that he has failed. An audience for a report of failure, especially when it is an attractive group, is likely to create some embarrassment for the reporter. Uncertainty regarding the consequences of a report of failure makes the person who has failed highly sensitive to the opinions and evaluations of the others. Thus, social reality is more important to a person who fails than to a person who succeeds. The greater the relevance of the task, the more the person who has failed feels impelled to evaluate himself in accordance with the group's expectations. The person who has succeeded, in contrast, can be quite sure that his report of success will be favourably received regardless of the group's level of expectations. He does not need the group for social reality and is quite ready to evaluate a success as a success regardless of the group's wishes in the matter. The results and their interpretation suggest that even though an objective, nonsocial basis for self-evaluation is available, a person may evaluate himself by comparison with others if he has failed in a task which is relevant to the group.

It is noteworthy that relevance or irrelevance of the task, exclusive of the group's expectations, did not affect the evaluation that a person placed upon a failure experience in Stotlands et al.'s study. These results indicate, we believe, that 'letting a group down' on a relevant task is no more conducive to poor self-evaluation than failure on an irrelevant activity. The evaluation a person assigns to his performance is primarily affected by the group's level of expectations, where the task is relevant.

The results indicate that persons with high self-esteem dealt with their experiences in a way that helped them to maintain their high self-esteem. They tended to evaluate themselves better after a failure than individuals with low self-esteem, regardless of the level of the group's expectations. Those with low self-esteem reacted to their experiences in a way that made it difficult to improve their self-esteem. They not only evaluated a failure very low but they became more concerned with the group's expectations when an unfavourable evaluation was most likely for them. Those with high self-esteem, in brief, reacted to their experiences in the group in the best way to protect themselves from unfavourable evaluation.

Salience of Characteristic Judged

Also relevant in assessing the importance of feedback from others is the extent to which the effect of feedback generalizes from attributes to other characteristics. The three studies that have examined this effect used expert sources and systematically varied the relatedness of secondary attributes to the focal dimension (Haas and Maehr 1965; Maehr et al. 1962; Videbeck 1960). They found not surprisingly, that judgements changed more on the dimension that was evaluated than on the one that was not (Maehr et al. 1962) and that those changes that did occur in other dimensions dissipated over time (Haas and Maehr 1965). Therefore, relatively little information exists regarding the manner and extent to which content-focused evaluations are generalized to other characteristics of oneself.

There is ample evidence of changes in self-perceptions following controlled feedback in laboratory settings. However, the importance of these findings is unclear because of the short-term nature of most assessments.

THEORIES OF SELF-ESTEEM

The high-self-esteem person in this book has been conceptualized as liking or valuing himself, as well as seeing himself as competent in dealing with the world he perceives. The person with low self-esteem is seen as disliking and devaluating himself, and in general perceiving himself as not competent to deal effectively with his environment.

Two competing theories have been proposed to explain in what ways high self-esteem and low self-esteem persons are likely to respond to positive and negative feedback. These are the self-consistency, and the self-esteem theories.

Self-Consistency Theory

The central theme of self-consistency theorists is that an individual's actions, attitudes, and his receptivity to information from other people are strongly affected by a tendency to create and maintain a consistent cognitive state with respect to his evaluations of himself. Various reasons are given for this cognitive tendency including economy in the organization of one's perceptions (Heider 1958), the reduction of dissonance (Festinger 1957), predictability in relationships with others (Secord and Backman 1964).

As elaborated by Secord and Backman (1961), a state of self-consistency or congruency is said to exist 'when [his own and others] behaviours imply definitions of self congruent with relevant aspects of the self-concept' (1961, p. 23). Given a state of inconsistency or incongruency involving relationships with another person, the individual may change his concept of himself, change or misperceive his own actions, or in a variety of ways transform his relationship with the other person. Concerning the latter, he may interact only with those whose behaviour validates his self-concept or misperceive an attempt to change those actions of the other person which produce the inconsistency. Finally, Secord and Backman (1961) propose that inconsistencies may be eliminated by selective evaluation of other people, and they predict that the individual 'tends to increase his liking for [others] who behave toward him in a congruent fashion, and to decrease his liking for those who behave in an incongruent manner' (p. 25).

The self-consistency notion has played a role in other theoretical approaches to interpersonal relationships such as Heider's (1958) balance theory and Newcomb's (1961) symmetry model. It also has been central to the thinking of humanistically oriented self-concept theorists such as Lecky (1945) and Rogers (1951, 1959). Although these positions contain many differences in their focuses and in their implications for action involving self and others, the common characteristic which concerns us is the proposal that relations between evaluations of self and others are mediated by a tendency toward self-consistency. For individuals with high evaluations of themselves or some aspect of self, positive evaluations are consistent, whereas for individuals with low self-evaluations, positive evaluations are inconsistent and negative evaluations are consistent. Therefore, the prediction from the self-consistency theories is that high self-evaluators will react more favourably to approval than to disapproval and that low self-evaluators will react more favourably to disapproval than to approval.

Self-Esteem Theory

The self-esteem stance assumes that the individual has a need to enhance his self-evaluation and to increase, maintain or confirm his feelings of personal satisfaction, worth and effectiveness. Although this need is assumed to be general, at any given time it may show itself with respect to a particular aspect of one's self-evaluation rather than to more global feelings about the self. Futhermore, the need varies with the degree of personal satisfaction or frustration the individual experiences. The self-esteem need also varies with individuals. It is assumed that this variation is reflected in attitudinal measures of self-esteem and that persons with high self-esteem are relatively more satisfied with respect to this need than persons with low self-esteem.

As was the case with the self-consistency theories, the self-esteem need is responsive to evaluative information the individual gains from his own behaviour and comparative or reflected appraisals from other people. Coping effectively with the tasks and problems he encounters in his physical and social environment as well as gaining information from others that he is liked and respected or that his actions or characteristics are highly evaluated produce satisfactions for his self-esteem need. Data from a variety of social psychological studies, including, for example, studies of social influence (Hovland and Janis 1959) self-presentation (Jones 1964) and self-comparison (Morse and Gergen 1970), have been interpreted in terms of this direct relation between self-esteem needs and social acceptance or rejection.

The critical question for purposes of comparison with self-consistency theories is what predictions self-esteem theories make regarding the individual's reactions to positive or negative evaluations received from other people. Besides the self-consistency theories, the major sources of change in thought or action involve the individual's evaluation of himself, his choice of activities or social roles and his relationships with these others. The difference is that these changes are designed to enhance self-esteem rather than to achieve self-consistency.

In general, one would expect people to respond favourably (i.e. like, support, agree with, etc.) to positive evaluations of themselves which are assumed to satisfy esteem needs and to respond unfavourably (i.e. dislike, attack, disagree with, etc.) to negative evaluations of themselves which are assumed to frustrate esteem needs. Specifically, low self-esteem individuals are expected to respond more favourably to positive evaluations from others and more unfavourably to negative evaluations from others as compared to high self-esteem individuals. This prediction, first articulated by Dittes (1959), follows from the assumption that low self-esteem people have greater needs for esteem enhancement and are, therefore, more satisfied by the approval of others and more frustrated by the disapproval of others than are high self-esteem people. A summary of these two hypotheses is illustrated below:

Subject's 'original' self-concept level	Feedback evaluation of subject	Hypothetical pleasurable state (+) or aversive state (−) created by:	
		Enhancement theory	Consistency theory
High	Positive	+	+
Low	Negative	−	+
Low	Positive	+	−
High	Negative	−	−

Table 2   Comparison of Consistency and Enhancement Theories.

However, Secord (1968) proposes that there is an asymmetry involved: restricted 'negative evaluations have the property of spreading to other related aspects of self which have a positive valence' (p. 353), whereas there will not be similar spreading from positive evaluative input to other aspects of the self having a negative valence. This could explain why the negativity of a self-referent input to the subject could have greater impact than would be predicted on the basis of its dissonance only and greater than a positive evaluative input of presumably equal dissonance.

If Secord's idea is correct, the subject who devalues self in one restricted respect and is given an inconsistent favourable evaluation in that particular respect does not experience general self-enhancement; instead he or she experiences a given amount of dissonance on a restricted dimension and a little increment in self-evaluation. By contrast, the subject who evaluates self highly in that one respect and receives inconsistent unfavourable evaluation concerning that particular aspect of self would experience general devaluation in addition to experiencing the given amount of dissonance.

Empirical Evidence

The critical test between the self-esteem and self-consistency theories involves manipulating or measuring the individual's evaluations of himself and the evaluations he receives from other people, then measuring the feelings he expresses to or about his associates, their characteristics or actions.

Backman and Secord (1962) asked each member of a college sorority to select from a list of sixteen adjective pairs the five adjectives most characteristic of herself, to indicate which five adjectives each other sorority member would attribute to her, and to rank the other members according to their attractiveness. Interpersonal congruency was measured by the degree of overlap between the adjectives a subject selected for herself and those she estimated would be attributed to herself by others. More congruency was obtained for the subject's ratings of the sorority members most liked by the subject than for the members least liked by the subject. From results obtained in a longer investigation, Newcomb (1956) reported that interpersonal attraction was closely related to the perceived agreement between a person's self-description and his estimate of how others would describe him.

In experimental studies as contrasted with correlational studies of the self-consistency theory, evaluations from others (which were manipulated) actually were received rather than estimated by the subject. In one study, Wilson (1965) led subjects to believe that they had failed on a task. Then either by having subjects make their own decisions (personal decision condition) or by having these decisions made for them by a 'chance' procedure (chance decision condition), he brought about the decision that subjects would not proceed with a second task. After this decision, subjects received a bogus comment, supposedly written by their partners, which in half of the conditions described a subject as competent and implied that he should accept the second task, and, in half of the conditions, described him as incompetent and implied that he should not accept the task. Wilson found that, of the subjects in the personal decision conditions, those receiving a negative note rated their partners as more accurate and slightly more attractive than those receiving a positive note. For subjects in the chance decision condition, those receiving a positive note rated their partners as more emotionally supportive, more attractive and slightly more accurate, than those receiving the negative note.

The most widely cited study of self-consistency and interpersonal evaluations is Deutsch and Solomon's (1959) test of derivations from Heider's (1958) balance theory. In their 2×2 design, self-evaluation was manipulated by informing subjects that they had either succeeded or failed on each of two tasks and evaluations from others, were manipulated by having each subject receive a note from one of her team-mates stating either, e.g., 'You are the person I most prefer to have on my team again', or 'You are the person I least prefer to have on the same team with me again'. Analysis of evaluating ratings each subject made of her note-sending team-mates showed first, a 'positivity' effect, that is a tendency for subjects to rate more favourably the positive note sender than the negative note sender, and second a self-consistency effect, that is an interaction between self-evaluation and evaluations received from others in which the tendency for such a positivity effect was obtained only for subjects in the high self-evaluation treatment. Low self-evaluators tended to rate the negative note sender slightly though not significantly, more favourably.

Skolnick (1971) performed a similar experiment to Deutsch and Solomon but failed to get similar results. He first attempted to manipulate self-regard by manipulating task success, after which he gave notes to half the subjects in each self-regard group saying the team wanted them, while to half he gave notes saying the team did not want them. The low self-regard subjects (task failure group) showed a great difference in evaluation of positive and negative note writers than did the high self-regard subjects (task success group) but the interaction did not reach the 0·05 level. This insignificant trend fails to reproduce Deutsch and Solomon's results and supports the idea that the stronger self-enhancement needs of the low self-regard subjects made the self-enhancement influences override the consistency influences rather than the reverse.

The procedure of Jacobs, Bergscheld and Walster (1971) may be viewed as similar to that reported in the preceding two publications with the addition of a third ('ambiguous') level in the second self-regard manipulation. First, the self-regard levels of male college freshman were manipulated by bogus favourable or unfavourable personality test feedback and psychiatrists' evaluations of their personalities. In the second self-regard manipulation, they were exposed to either a clearly accepting, or clearly rejecting evaluation of themselves which had supposedly been made by a college female who had judged their social skills on the basis of listening to five taped telephone calls which the subjects had been induced to make. Both subjects with high and low initially manipulated self-regard evaluated this female more favourably if she supposedly clearly accepted them as opposed to clearly rejecting them. This difference was somewhat larger among subjects with initially lowered self-regard.

Although the latter trends were not separately evaluated for significance, they are similar to results reported by Skolnick (1971). Thus, they are in the direction predicted by the assumption that low self-regard subjects have greater self-enhancement needs so that enhancement tendencies override consistency influences. Subjects with initially raised self-regard evaluated the ambiguously accepting female about as favourably as the clearly accepting one. Those with initially lowered self-regard evaluated her more favourably than the clearly rejecting female, considerably less favourably than the clearly accepting female, and significantly less favourably than did the high self-regard subjects. The authors suggest that the person with low self-regard feels less favourable towards the ambiguously accepting person because he is less able to interpret her behaviour as accepting. In other words, it appears that the subjects with low self-regard found clear acceptance the most desirable of the three even though it is the most dissonant from their allegedly low self-regard level. If, as the author believes, the ambiguous acceptance is perceived as less favourable by the low self-regard subjects than by the high self-regard subjects, it makes such ambiguous input less rewarding to the former, even though more nearly congruent with their low self-regard. Accordingly, the trends obtained from the subject's responses following an ambiguous acceptance also tend to support the idea that the low self-regard subjects had stronger self-enhancement needs, and the enhancement influences overrode the consistency influences.

Dittes (1959), too, found the self-consistency theory wanting when, in an experiment set up to test it, the prediction was not fulfilled. Dittes (1959) varied original self-regard levels not by experimentally manipulating it but by choosing groups who were high, medium and low on an idiosyncratic measure of extent self-regard. One-third of each self-regard group was told by note that their acceptance by the group was well above average, one-third that it was average, and one-third that it was below average. A post-manipulation check using an idiosyncratic self-evaluation index suggested that the manipulation had affected the subjects' self-regard. Congruent with the idea that low self-regard subjects have especially strong self-enhancement needs which will override consistency influences, the originally low self-regard showed a significantly greater attraction to the positive and average than to the negative note writers, while the originally average self-regard and high self-regard subjects showed successively smaller differences of this kind, both differences being insignificant.

Finally, Shrauger and Lund (1975) divided their groups into those with high and low self-esteem. Then, following an interview of each subject by a supposed graduate student in clinical psychology, the experimenters gave one-third of each self-esteem group bogus feedback from the interviewer to the effect that they were 'self-aware' (supposedly a favourable evaluation), or not 'self-aware' (supposedly an unfavourable evaluation). The remaining one-third received no feedback. Subjects then rated their perceptions of the favourability of the interviewer's attitudes towards them; the interviewer's objectivity, competence, and degree of emotional bias in making judgements; and their emotional reactions toward the interviewer. The subjects' rated emotional reactions towards the interviewer gave entirely null results. The ratings of interviewer objectivity, competence, and bias failed to support self-enhancement views in that it was the high self-regard subjects who tended to rate favourable interviewers as more objective, competent, and unbiased than unfavourable interviewers, whereas low self-regard subjects showed little difference in these ratings of favourable and unfavourable interviewers. However, as in Deutsch and Solomon's study, the subjects did not give significantly better ratings to unfavourable evaluators, even though the unfavourable evaluators' feedback would supposedly be more congruent with the subjects' unfavourable self-evaluations. Thus, the evidence is not clearly in the direction to be expected if consistency effects override self-enhancement effects.

This brief survey of some of the relevant studies suggests that in general the evidence tends to favour self-esteem theory over self-consistency theory. In a fuller survey Shrauger (1975) found of the sixteen investigations reviewed, ten support self-esteem theory, and suggested that there are serious problems of interpretation or reproduction with the experimental studies often cited as support for self-consistency theory. Futhermore, the self-esteem evidence becomes more impressive when one considers the variety of different procedures and measures used in these studies. In addition comment on the 'counter-intuitive' quality of many predictions from cognitive consistency theories and some of the implications of self-consistency theory are often subject to this general confusion. Many authors working primarily within a cognitive consistency framework have acknowledged the discrepancies between cognitive consistency motivations and self-esteem, self-enhancement, or even achievement motivations, and have expressed such reservations. Rosenberg (1968) for example, observed that one of the most important failings of the consistency approach seems to be the experimental affirmation of this hard, intractable fact; the need for (or trend towards) 'the maintenance of internally consistent affective cognitive structures is often subordinated to man's penchant for trying to think well of himself and optimistically of his prospects' (p. 384).

However, two recent British studies attempt to clarify the issues still further. The first by Colman and Olver (1978) offers support for the self-consistency notion because their low self-esteem (SE) subjects preferred a neutral to a positive evaluator. However, their results could be consistent with those of studies employing positive and negative feedback conditions and finding support for the self-enhancement notion, because it may well have been the case that low SE subjects in the Colman and Olver study would have disliked a negative evaluator the most, had one been used. Aitkenhead (1980) argues that by using only two feedback conditions previous research has assumed that the two theories are mutually exclusive. Aitkenhead makes the case, however, that both the need for self-consistency and for self-enhancement operate simultaneously in an individual. She criticizes the use of only two levels of feedback as an inappropriate test of this hypothesis because whenever results are 'significant' one theory must be accepted at the expense of the other.

If both needs operate simultaneously in an individual, then low SE individuals face conflict. Acceptance of positive feedback means that the need for self-enhancement is satisfied at the expense of the need for self-consistency: acceptance of negative feedback implies the reverse, Aitkenhead points out two ways in which low SE subjects can partially satisfy both needs rather than satisfy one at the expense of the other. The first is to reach a compromise by most preferring a neutral evaluation. The second is that in some reactions to evaluations they could allow one need to be satisfied whereas in other reactions they could allow the other need to be satisfied. Previous research has tended to employ only one dependent variable (e.g. liking of the evaluator or assessments of his competence) yet reactions to feedback are so complex that assessment of only variable may prove misleading, and so it is hardly surprising that inconsistent results have emerged.

Shrauger's (1975) review points out that studies measuring subjects' liking of the evaluator generally support self-enhancement theory whereas those measuring subjects' assessment of the evaluators' competence have generally supported self-consistency theory. In a low SE subject, the need for consistency may predominate in the latter case because it is illogical for someone to say he has performed well when the objective results, or past experience, indicate otherwise. On the other hand, affective reactions (such as liking) need not have a rational basis and in this case the need for self-enhancement prevails with the low SE subjects liking the positive evaluator the most.

Aitkenhead's (1980) study examines the possibility that both needs are operative, and tries to discern if low SE subjects attempt to reach either, or both, of the two types of compromise. It does so first by including a neutral (as well as a positive and a negative) feedback condition and second, by assessing several reactions to the feedback. If low SE subjects react most favourably to the neutral feedback for some of the dependent variables, evidence for the first type of compromise will be found. If these subjects react in accordance with self-consistency predictions for some measures and in accordance with self-enhancement predictions for others, then evidence for the second type of compromise will be found.

Specifically, it was hypothesized that low SE subjects will like the positive evaluator the most (showing self-enhancement), but will think the neutral evaluator to be the most competent (showing the first type of compromise here).

In sum, this experiment has several aims. The first one is to include a neutral feedback condition in order to assess the adequacy of the consistency and self-enhancement principles and to distinguish between liking of the consistency and self-enhancement principles. The second aim is to distinguish between liking the evaluator and assessments of his competence, and the third is to look for evidence of consistency and self-enhancement in other aspects of the subjects' response to feedback.

Using nurses receiving feedback from doctors as subjects, the findings agreed with the suggestion that neither the need for self-enhancement nor the need for self-consistency alone operates within an individual. Which need, if either, has the greater effect upon human behaviour depends upon which aspect of behaviour is being investigated.

It was suggested that low SE subjects may partially satisfy both the need for self-enhancement and the need for self-consistency (given that they cannot completely satisfy both simultaneously) by reaching a compromise. This can be in either, or both, of two possible ways. First, by most 'preferring' a neutral evaluation and secondly, by 'preferring' a positive evaluation in some aspects and a negative one in others.

The results provided no unambiguous support for self-enhancement theory: on no variable did low SE subjects react significantly more favourably to the positive than to the neutral feedback. Whilst low SE subjects liked the positive evaluator the most, as predicted, this result was not significant. However, in general little distinction was made by the subjects between the positive and neutral evaluations (exceptions are that high SE subjects remembered most of the neutral feedback and also that high and medium subjects were less satisfied with an average than a good mark). This may be because nurses regard doctors as being of high status and therefore would not derogate them when they receive an average mark, which, after all, is not that bad.

Status of the evaluator would seem a useful variable to investigate in this area. It could be argued that self-enhancement was operating in those cases (e.g. liking competence), where the neutral and positive evaluations were preferred over negative ones by low SE subjects.

From the recall scores low SE subjects remembered most of the negative feedback, and in the marks expected next time low SE subjects expected no more marks following success than high SE subjects did following failure. These results are in line with self-consistency predictions. Taken together with those findings supporting self-enhancement theory, it may be concluded that low SE subjects seek to satisfy both the need for self-enhancement and for self-consistency. They do this by reacting in a extremely complex way to feedback, satisfying one need along some dimensions and the other need along others.

It is worth noting here, however, that a motivational explanation of the recall and expected results is not the only possible one. Miller and Ross (1975), in an excellent review of studies concerned with attributions of results, point out that in many instances findings could be accounted for purely in terms of rational, non-motivational thought processes based upon past experience. It is quite reasonable to assume that one performs in the same way one has normally performed.

As the neutral evaluator was never clearly preferred by low SE subjects, evidence for the first type of compromise was not strong. Low SE subjects showed a different trend from the other subjects by regarding the neutral evaluator (as opposed to the positive) as most competent (as predicted) and an average mark as most justified; these effects were not significant.

Aitkenhead's conclusion suggests that co-existence rather than mutual exclusion is the best way currently of examining the self-enhancement self-consistency controversy.

IS HIGH SELF-ESTEEM ALWAYS WHAT IT SEEMS?

Cohen (1959) argued that different ego defences are employed by individuals with high and low esteem and Silverman (1964) predicted and found a similar interaction. Cohen's theory states that individuals with high self-esteem defend their confidence by avoidance, whereas the characteristic defences of low self-esteem individuals are expressive, for example, projection. That is, a high self-esteem individual will tend to avoid unfavourable feedback about the self altogether; a low self-esteem individual distorts it. Moreover, the low self-esteem individual tends to respond to failure by identifying with others, under the assumption that their beliefs and actions are more successful in satisfying needs than his own. All of this leads to the prediction that high self-esteem individuals should be made less easily influenced by failure, due to their use of avoidance, while the reverse should be true of subjects with low self-esteem.

The effect of a successful manipulation is not to alter self-esteem but to trigger ego-defence mechanisms which differ for individuals at different self-esteem levels.

Stotland et al. (1957) found that self-esteem affected evaluation of one's performance when failing but not when succeeding. Individuals with high self-esteem rated their failure performance significantly better than did individuals with low self-esteem.

A genuine high self-esteem person should be less concerned to avoid or repudiate failure, since failure is not particularly threatening. People with genuinely high self-esteem may be better at ignoring failure, or they may be more likely to try to improve areas of relative failure rather than repudiating evaluations in those areas.

Defensively high self-esteem individuals ought to do more than react to success or failure; they ought to attempt actively to change their public definition after failure, to gain approval when possible, and to encourage social situations to maximize their self-enhancement. Self-presentations are one way of manipulating social situations to gain approval (Jones 1964). Schneider (1969) found that subjects who were told they had failed were significantly more self-enhancing in their public presentations than were successful subjects. It was also found that failing individuals with high self-evaluations showed high positive correlations between positiveness of self-presentation and need for approval scores (as measured by the Marlow-Crowne Social Desirability Scale). In other words, individuals with high self-esteem and great need for approval (which is our concept of the individual with defensive high self-esteem) exhibited particularly positive self-presentations in reaction to failure. The higher the need for approval, the more positive was the self-presentation of the failing, high self-esteem subject. Thus for the defensive individual, it seems that a self-presentation strategy of positiveness may be used to maintain the high level of self-esteem that he reported.

This was found to be so in Schneider and Turkat's (1975) experiment, where defensive high self-esteem individuals presented themselves more positively than genuine high self-esteem.

Individuals in reaction to negative information, while there were no differences in reaction to positive information. To the extent that positive self-presentations indicate a need for approval, it appears that defensive high self-esteem individuals may be differentiated from genuine high self-esteem individuals by their stronger need for approval in the face of negative information.

When failing, defensive high self-esteem individuals will be strongly affected by and more dependent upon the evaluations of others for their feelings of self-worth. Thus, they would be more concerned with the presentation of a socially desirable appearance than individuals with genuine high self-esteem. As we have seen, the reaction to challenging or threatening information is to compensate with a positive self-presentation. The genuine high self-esteem individual seems to be less dependent upon the evaluations of others for his feelings of worth.

Discrediting the source, too, may be sufficient to reduce whatever threat a high self-esteem person may find in a negative evaluation. If he can do this, he may not need to modify his effective reactions to the evaluator or his interpretations of the evaluator's reaction to him (Shrauger and Lund 1975).

SUMMARY

The role of feedback from significant others is emphasized as the main way an individual learns about himself. The theoretical emphasis has always been on the Cooley–Mead formulation of the 'looking-glass' hypothesis, while the 'modelling' explanation of Bandura is not as strongly supported by research. Feedback can be seen as reinforcement in behaviourist terms, but in a phenomenological sense it is the individual's subjective interpretation of the meaning and relevance of the feedback that really matters.

The roles of parents, peers and teachers as significant others in the life of the child is emphasized, though parents may not be as important to the school-age child as significant others as was thought. Peers take precedence over parents as sources of self-esteem.

Few controlled experiments exist in which feedback is deliberately manipulated, but such effects are usually strongly demonstrated. A variety of interacting variables affect the way in which feedback from others is interpreted, e.g. credibility of source, presence of an audience, salience of characteristic involved, anxiety level, extant self-esteem level and so on.

The study of the ways in which persons with differing levels of self-esteem respond to evaluative feedback from others suggests that self-enhancement theory has more research support than self-consistency theory. High self-esteem, however, may be a defensive technique for some individuals who use avoidance and repudiation to maintain such high levels.

8

Self-Concept and
Academic Achievement

*A person who doubts himself is like a man who would enlist in the ranks of his
enemies and bear arms against himself. He makes his failure certain by himself
being the first person to be convinced of it.*

Alexandre Dumas *The Three Musketeers,* (1844)

> *Our doubts are traitors*
> *And make us lose the good we oft might win,*
> *By fearing to attempt*

(Measure for Measure I. i)

INTRODUCTION

Children enter school with a predisposition towards achievement or failure already
fertilized by the qualities of parental interest, love and acceptance offered them. This
fairly firm picture of his self-worth provides the child with an array of self-
expectations about how he will cope in his school work and how others will react to
him as a person. Each pupil is already invisibly tagged, some enhancingly by a diet of
nourishing interest and affection, and others crippled by a steady downpour of
psychic blows from significant others denting, weakening and distorting their self-
concepts. So children enter school with a self-concept already forming, but still
susceptible to modification. Teachers cannot work on a malleable lump of clay and
mould it to a form which they believe is best, they have to work on a young person
who has a self-concept already formed out of his previous experiences. What the
teacher must do is to ensure the child's passage through the rigours of formal
education without damage to the child's self-esteem. For the child who comes to
school with essentially negative views of himself the teachers' aim is to employ the
academic and social learning experiences school provides to reteach the child a view
of himself that includes competence, worth and belonging.

It is generally accepted that to modify a person's self-concept, to any large extent
requires a major act of therapy or some quite traumatic event. However, in school

where many other new learnings and experiences are daily happenings it should not prove difficult to modify the self-concept alongside these other learnings and as a result of them.

EDUCATION INVOLVES EVALUATION

The wider range of interactions that are possible following the child's entry into school around the age of 5 produce a new set of learnings that can enhance or debilitate the existing self-concept. School implies increased independence from parents, allows more exploration of the physical and social environment, and places more emphasis on the child's own performances. He is in charge of himself at a time when more evaluation, academic, social, and physical is going to accrue. So self-evaluation is more central, ubiquitous and unavoidable. A new feedback agent, teacher, also enters the fray.

School is a context in which evaluation is pervasive, continuous and systematic. Most children are evaluated many times each day in contests not of their own making or choosing and in which there are few winners. It would be fascinating to attempt a tabulation of the number of times a pupil is evaluated each day in school. Even if there were no examinations and no grading, evaluation would still be present for a child knows, himself, how well he is doing and can see what other children are like. Neither can he avoid non-verbal feedback from teachers and peers. As an adult it is possible to choose to do those things one is interested in and competent at. At school this choice is almost non-existent. Even if an activity is not rewarding, or if it is one at which competence is low, then the rule in school is to spend more time on it.

Schools stand for even more evaluation than the child has faced already at home. Appraisal of academic work, of sporting ability and of social behaviour cannot be avoided. Most pupils face daily reminders of their potentials and limitations; rewards, punishments, success and failure are on offer on a lavish scale.

William James (1890) wisely pointed out: 'With no attempt there can be no failure; with no failure no humiliation. So our feeling in this world depends entirely on what we back ourselves to be and to do.' (p. 313). Unfortunately, most children have little choice about the areas in which they must perform, and suffer evaluation, or in which they wish to make their mark on the world.

In a stimulating paper Jackson (1968) observed that although every child experiences the pain of failure and the joy of success long before he reaches school age, it is only when he enters the classroom that his achievements (or lack of them) become official in the sense that a public record of his progress begins to accumulate and he himself must accept that pervasive spirit of evaluation that will dominate his school years.

Self-evaluation begins as we have seen long before children reach the school and the high or low self-esteem that becomes apparent in school generally originates in previous psychological experiences within the family. The school, however, offers new psychological experiences which ultimately will affect the individual's self-esteem. Pupils who have successfully negotiated their first five years may encounter problems in school if their previous experience has not equipped them with the concepts, values and behaviours necessary for success in the classroom.

THE ACADEMIC EMPHASIS

The most dominant value operating in the educational system is academic achievement. In the classroom, teachers interpret this to the pupils. They apply academic standards to the pupils' daily efforts and products. The self-concept becomes permeated with values and standards for academic behaviour.

There will be pupils, of course, who have low potential for academic achievement and they may compensate for this by valuing the approval given for arduous and continuous effort.

High achievers—pupils whose high potential is realized in performance or whose performance exceeds their potential—are rewarded by the classroom value system. Low achievers, regardless of potential or effort, are either unrewarded, or rewarded for behaviour other than academic achievement. If academic achievement is to serve as a source of self-esteem, it must first be valued; to acquire this value the pupil must be recognized and affirmed as an achiever who has positive impact on significant others and the environment. This may require that the pupil be given: (1) psychological experiences which offer a new basis for self-evaluation; (2) a clear understanding of the values and standards by which to judge performance; and (3) the skills necessary for evaluating his or her own work.

Children are the recipients of two different school curricula at their most impressionable period of life. One is the explicit curriculum of the school while the other is a curriculum which is implicit in the interactions of persons within the school. The former curriculum is what the scholar is conventionally expected to learn, it is visible and the school's resources are mainly directed towards the students' learning of the academic syllabus. The latter curriculum is more covert and is the affective and social curriculum by which each student learns who he is, what others think of him and how he comes to view himself. Judgemental processes relative to self are the central features of this implicit curriculum. There are few occasions in education when a pupil is not being judged in detailed terms by teachers, by peers or by parents, or even by himself, against standards set by external authority. No matter how well or how poorly he does, he is aware of his standing since educational judgements are mostly based on relative performance. Such judgements are made frequently since the education system emphasizes competition as the main motivational technique.

While some individuals may need more pass–fail experiences before they come to accept a particular view of themselves, this is only a matter of degree. Given a sufficient number of unsuccessful experiences, almost everyone must eventually succumb to an acceptance of a self-view which is negative or inadequate. Similarly for the successful encounters, given enough of them, one must eventually come to view oneself as positive or adequate.

A few successful or unsuccessful experiences may not have a major effect on the self-concept—in fact, it is possible that occasional experiences which can be turned by the individual into successful experiences may be of special significance in strengthening the individual's self-image. However, it is the frequency and consistency of adequacy or inadequacy over a period of years which has its major effects on self-concept.

The provision of successful educational experiences is no firm guarantee of a generally positive self-concept but it does increase the likelihood that such will be the case. On the other hand, unsuccessful school experiences, more than likely, guarantee that the individual will develop a negative academic self-concept and a general negative self-concept.

Glasser, in his book *Schools Without Failure* (1969), argues that the whole of our society today is dichotomized between those who identify with success and those who identify with failure. He criticizes schools and the role they play in blocking the achievement of a success identity. Schools tend to reward those children who perform well and expose those who are unable to compete while emphasizing academic material and giving little encouragement to learning about oneself.

Need achievement appears to differentiate people with more favourable self-esteem from those with less favourable self-esteem (Bedeian and Touliatos 1978). The inextricable link between self-esteem and achievement was emphasized by Bardwick (1971) who noted that the striving for success is the striving for self-esteem.

In traditional classrooms verbal intelligence has generally been recognized as the major, if not the sole basis for determining who is capable and likely to succeed. Teachers in these classrooms have generally failed to teach children to recognize, use and value their other skills and abilities. Consequently, many children who are not in the top quarter in verbal intelligence feel that they are incapable and are virtually doomed to failure. Many traditional schools have also favoured the use of the marks competition between children and fear of failure as a means of motivating children. The schools have thus set up a system for generating negative self-concepts and low self-esteem—a system that virtually guarantees that a great many children will feel they are incapable and have not succeeded. It should, therefore, come as no surprise that there is a regular and consistent decline in children's self-esteem between the second and the seventh school years (Morse 1964). Apparently, the longer today's children are in traditionally structured classrooms, the more likely they are to feel they are failures and ineffective in achieving academically valued goals and skills.

Given the heavy emphasis on competition and the pressures applied by teachers and most parents on children to achieve academically, it is not surprising that most children use academic attainment as an important index of self-worth. The evaluations of others become self-evaluations so that an unsuccessful student comes to feel incompetent and inferior. The child's world is largely the world of school; his basic tasks are largely school tasks; it is the most salient area of his life, but it is open to inspection by significant others. It is no wonder that with the unavoidability of academic pursuits, the cultural stress on success and the ubiquity of assessment and competition, life in school is a patent influence on self-esteem.

A survey of adolescents' experience of school after they left, conducted by Richer (1968), provides an unavoidable impression that for these less academic youths, the post-school period was a time when they recovered from the emotional and devaluing effects of education.

Many of the respondents made clear that they were now able to be themselves; they were accepted by workmates and friends. Now people took you for yourself, 'just as you are'; in your own right, happy, relaxed and not too serious. Your good and bad habits were both accepted. Thus after leaving school it was possible to be yourself, to be 'just ordinary'. Richer's (op. cit.) young people like to be liked. Many are shy and anxious at school and are often secretly ashamed of their lack of success. Accepting the picture of oneself presented by the school meant for most seeing that one was 'not very brainy'. Despite this, members gave many illustrations to show that they were 'not as dim as teacher made out'.

In general, school made Richer's respondents feel a failure. They were depressed to recall school experiences and had not felt satisfied with themselves on leaving school. This was very much reflected in the tone of the taped responses. For this reason, members were glad to have their parents remain away from school, they did not want them to share their shame. Parents who did visit school or supported it by pushing disliked homework were rare. It was also noted that large schools offered comparatively less opportunity for the personal success of the less able and the average child.

Members were conscious that after they had left school they began to grow up. Now 'You had to think for yourself'. They had begun to cope with their own problems, to express themselves and gradually to become self-controlled, 'smartening yourself up', as they took on new responsibilities and responded to the challenge of work. That school is failing these less able pupils both academically and as persons is evident in this survey. Education was seen as an agency for social control.

Boys appear to have more problems on entering school than girls. First, the latter are more mature than boys on average and this is maintained as far as mid-adolescence. Second, as we saw in Chapter 5, school is a female place initially, as most teachers are female for the younger ages. Besides this, Kellogg's (1969) study of school-related objects found that items such as chalk, books, desks, etc., were regarded by children as being 'female'. Hence, in their early schooldays, boys may be working in an environment better suited to girls. Third, girls, possibly because of their faster development, tend to excel in a wide range of school tasks. All this suggests that boys may have to handle more failures in a 'female' environment making the maintenance of a positive self-concept more difficult. But for both sexes beginning school has a depressing effect on self-concept level, which suggests that what goes on in school is not considered in terms of its effect on the affective characteristics of the child but only in terms of its cognitive effect. Yet the influence of these two effects is reciprocal.

Many writers (Felker 1969; Williams 1976) have noted the fourth-grade (at nine years old) slump in self-concept scores in American schools. It would seem that, at that age, stress enters the educational curriculum. This is not surprising as one views the typical educational programme in many primary schools; for at that time in pupils' lives they are expected to be rather well regimented into a certain academic mould imposed by teacher, peer and parent pressures for school success. This is especially true in the 'skilled' areas of reading, mathematics and language. In the 9 to 10 age group fun and games in school end and desk tasks become predominant. Text-books and workbooks are used exclusively for content skill development while curiosity and imagination gradually wane or wither. Certainly, as Torrance (1962) found, further development of the ability to think fluently, flexibly, originally and elaboratively decrease markedly unless such growth is the objective of a school programme. Usually it is not; school begins to take positive qualities out of pupils and are not, on the evidence available, enhancing self-concept in the early years of schooling despite the fact that a positive self-concept is one of the most vital elements for academic success.

SELF-CONCEPT AND ACADEMIC ACHIEVEMENT

Prior to the 1950s, few psychologists and educators made a systematic study of what factors influenced school performance. They were so engrossed with their new toys of intelligence measurement that the focus was primarily on the intellectual basis of educability. Home background, social class, child-rearing practices, motivation, personality, cognitive style, etc., were not considered until well after the second world war.

Yet comments and views on the relationship between academic performance and personality have been made intuitively in school reports and staffroom chat over many generations of pupils and teachers. Such comments as 'is positive in his approach to work', 'cannot concentrate', 'diffident about his abilities' and 'worries about being a failure' have graced many school reports. Such intuitive and anecdotal material seems concerned with the relationship between scholarship and the pupil's image of himself and the behaviour that perceived image generates. We must however leave the safe refuge of anecdote and subjective opinion and seek out reliable evidence to support the belief that personality (particularly a person's attitudes to himself, his feelings of competence and worth) influences school achievement. It is to this end we turn.

In a major study of personality and motivation in relation to school achievement, Cattell, Sealy and Sweney (1966) found that of the total variance in school achievement 21 to 25 per cent were accounted for by a culture-fair intelligence test, 27 to 36 per cent by personality traits and 23 to 27 per cent by motivational traits. The findings suggest that the level of prediction of school achievement could be doubled by adding measures of personal traits to measures of ability and trebled by the addition of motivational measures. Since the self-concept is both a personal and motivational variable its overall contribution to the variance of academic achievement should be quite high. Physical, social and emotional development are of equal concern to the educator, and this widening of purpose injects self-concept development as a central theme in non-cognitive development. This is also linked with the all too recent awareness that academic development and progress cannot be considered in isolation from other aspects of human development.

The impelling writings of Combs (1965) and Jersild (1952) in America, and Staines (1958) in Britain on their research into classroom practices gave the impetus to the consideration of the self-concept as both an influence on and an outcome of the performance of pupil and teacher, though its importance had passed unnoticed by those focusing solely on the inculcation of academic knowledge and skills. Many studies have been reported in the literature relating academic performance and self-concept. A complete catalogue would become rather tedious and boring. So a sample of the major findings will be covered, since all tend to tell the same story.

Global Self-Concept and Achievement

Performance on Coopersmith's Self-Esteem Inventory (SEI) is found to be related to various measures of achievement. Coopersmith (1967) reports an $r=0.30$, significant at the 0.05 level, between his SEI score and grade-point average in children aged 10 to 12. Morrison, Thomas and Weaver (1973) report an $r=0.34$ ($P=0.01$) between SEI score and grades on an objective test on material about learning theory. Morrison and Thomas (1975) report an $r=0.26$ ($P=0.05$) between total SEI score and proportion of thoughts contributed to a class discussion; an $r=0.40$ between school, self-esteem subset and contributed thoughts. Correlations ranging from 0.35 to 0.45 were found by Trowbridge (1972a) between SEI scores and reading level scores for children within different socioeconomic levels. In a study by Rosenthal (1973) the mean SEI score of dyslexics, 61.8, differed significantly from that of controls, 75.5.

Concerning the SEI, Coopersmith (1959) reported a correlation of 0.36 between SEI scores and the Iowa Achievement Test and a correlation of 0.30 between SEI scores and Iowa Achievement Tests with sociometric choice partialled out. Both correlations are significant at the 0.01 level. Simon and Simon (1975) obtained a significant correlation of 0.33 between SEI scores and Scientific Research Associates' Achievement Series for 10 year-old boys and girls. Significant correlations of 0.30 and 0.42 were also reported by Lewis and Adank (1975) between the SEI and raw scores from the Stanford Achievement Test for 9 to 11 year olds who were enrolled in classrooms with an individualized instructor's programme and a self-contained programme respectively. Trowbridge (1972b) correlated SEI scores and the most current reading test scores of children in experimental and control classrooms. The target area classrooms were composed of disadvantaged children. She found a significant correlation within the target area classrooms of 0.33 and a significant correlation within the nontarget area classrooms of 0.38.

The manual for the Piers–Harris test (Piers 1969) includes correlations between an 80-item version of the test and an unspecified achievement test for boys and girls in the fourth and sixth grades. All of the correlations were significant, ranging from 0.32 to 0.43, except the correlation for sixth-grade girls, which was only 0.06. A study by Piers and Harris (1964) also obtained significant correlations of 0.19 and 0.32 between a 95-item version of the Piers–Harris and an unspecified achievement test for children in the third and sixth grades respectively.

In a representative national sample of 2213 tenth-grade boys attending American public high schools in 1966, Bachman (1970) found a significant correlation of 0·23 between an idiosyncratic self-esteem score based on Rosenberg's Self-Esteem Scale and self-reported grades for the ninth grade and a significant correlation of 0·48 between self-concept of schoolwork ability and self-reported grades.

An analysis by Bachman and O'Malley (1977) based on a sample of about 1600 young men from the high-school class of 1969, showed that self-esteem is positively correlated with educational success. The study also showed that educational accomplishments seem to have greater importance or centrality for self-esteem during the high-school years than during the 5 years beyond high school.

In a further study, the same two workers (O'Malley and Bachman 1979) questioned over 3000 male and female students. Again it was shown, paralleling the findings from the 1969 students, that educational accomplishments undergo a reduction in importance for self-esteem after leaving school. This suggests that school performance is very salient for the early teens. The self-esteem education performance relationship was similar between the two cross-sectional populations studied eight years apart. 0·27 from the 1969 students and 0·28 from the 1977 ones.

Chang (1976) found a significant relationship between teachers' ratings of the child's self-concept and the child's academic achievement, while Ellerman (1980) using Australian primary-school children found that children doing poorly in school increasingly come to hold a more negative view of themselves. In Gill and D'Oyley's (1970) investigation involving 1424 ninth-grade students in five Toronto high schools, correlations of 0·42 for boys and 0·35 for girls were obtained between scores on an idiosyncratic perceived self scale and final average marks. Williams and Cole (1968) found significant correlations between Tennessee Self-Concept Scale measures and achievement in basic subjects (average $r = +0·33$) and emotional adjustment ($r = +0·62$).

Some large cross-cultural studies by Smith (1969) provide strong indications of the contribution of self-concept elements to academic performance. From data collected on 37 samples comprising 5777 nine to eleven year olds, Smith found that the variables which provided the highest correlations with academic performance related to self-attitudes and personal motivation. The use of these self-concept elements enabled Smith to more than double the accuracy of prediction of performance and of dropping out of school in his samples.

Specific Academic Self-Concept and Achievement

The relationship between self-concept and academic achievement, however, is most pronounced when measures of academic self-concept are employed. Global self-esteem indices do not usually reveal so strong a relationship. The major specific measure of academic achievement is Brookover's Self-Concept of Ability Scale. Brookover and his colleagues carried out a number of related studies in a longitudinal programme.

Three major hypotheses were tested by Brookover, Thomas and Patterson (1964), namely (1) self-concept of ability in school is significantly and positively related to the academic performance of students even with an ability dimension controlled; (2) self-concept of ability in school is differentiated into specific self-concepts which correspond to specific subject areas in the school programme and these specific self-concepts are better predictors of academic performance in the relevant area than is the general self-concept of ability; and (3) self-concept of ability is significantly and positively correlated with the evaluation that one perceives significant others to hold of one's ability.

Brookover's Self-Concept of Ability Scale was administered in two parallel forms. The first was designed to measure self-concept of ability in general; the second to measure self-concept of ability in four school subject areas: mathematics, science, social studies and English. Though the references were changed the substance of the questions remained the same in both forms. The questions included for example, 'How would you rate yourself in school ability compared with those in your class at school?' The pupils were requested to tick one of these five alternatives: (1) I am among the best, (2) I am above average, (3) I am average, (4) I am below average, (5) I am among the poorest. The correlation between the grade point average and general academic self-concept with IQ controlled was $+0.42$ and $+0.39$ for boys and girls respectively. The specific self-concept of ability correlations (Table 3 below) are significantly higher for males in maths, social studies and science; for the female pupils the correlation is significantly higher in social studies. On the other hand the correlation between specific self-concept and achievement in English is lower than the correlation between general self-concept of ability and achievement in English. Thus the findings indicate that generally the specific self-concept of ability is a better predictor of academic performance for males but not for females. Although this sex difference may be a reflection of the particular school community, it is interesting to recall that maths and science are subjects usually considered as important areas of achievement for male pupils. But on this argument it would also have been expected that self-concept of ability in English would have been a better predictor for girls.

Table 3. Self-Concept Achievement Relationships (Brookover et al. 1964)

| | Correlation coefficients | | | | | | | |
| | *Maths* | | *English* | | *Soc. Studies* | | *Science* | |
Variables Correlated	*M*	*F*	*M*	*F*	*M*	*F*	*M*	*F*
General SC with grade	0·50	0·52	0·44	0·52	0·51	0·50	0·52	0·48
Specific SC with grade	0·59	0·54	0·43	0·47	0·56	0·58	0·61	0·51

Brookover tested the third hypothesis by interviewing the under- and over-achievers and finding out how each perceived what significant others feel about his ability. The correlation of student self-concept and how the student felt others viewed him was $+0.58$. So this major research showed:

1. There is a significant and positive correlation between self-concept and performance in the academic role; this relationship is substantial even when measured IQ is controlled.

2. There are specific self-concepts of ability for specific areas of academic role performance, which differ from the general self-concept of ability. These are, in some subjects, significantly better predictors of specific subject achievement than is the general self-concept of ability.
3. Self-concept is significantly and positively correlated with the perceived evaluations that significant others hold of the student; however, it is the composite image rather than the images of specific others that appear to be most closely correlated with the student's self-concept in specific subjects.

Brookover, Le Pere, Hamachek, Thomas and Erickson (1965) found correlations between achievement and self-concept of ability ranging from 0·56 to 0·65 in a study of 12 to 15 year-old pupils, in this study general self-concept of ability and self-concept of ability in mathematics, English, social studies and science were compared to grades in each subject area. Correlations between self-concepts of abilities and grades ranged from 0·30 to 0·60.

In the third and final phase (Brookover, Erikson and Joiner 1967), by which time the students were 17 years old, the authors were able to note that: the correlation between self-concept of ability and grade point average ranges from 0·48 to 0·63 over the six years. It falls below 0·50 only among boys in the twelfth grade. In addition the higher correlation between perceived evaluations and self-concept tends to support the theory that perceived evaluations are a necessary and sufficient condition for the growth of a positive or high self-concept of ability, but a positive self-concept is only a necessary, but not a sufficient, condition for achievement. The latter is further supported by the analysis of the achievement of students with high and low self-concept of ability. This revealed that although a significant proportion of students with high self-concepts of ability achieved at a relatively lower level, practically none of the students with lower (less positive) self-concepts of ability achieved at a high level (p. 142).

In research by Anderson and Johnson (1971) involving 114 Hispano American and 49 Anglo junior and senior high-school students, self-concept of ability scores were used to predict students' most recent semester grades in English and mathematics. In an analysis of self-concept of ability and seven home background factors the coefficients for self-concept of ability were 0·3097 for English and 0·3059 for mathematics. Self-concept of ability was found to be the most significant of the predictors. Joiner, Erickson, Crittenden and Stevenson (1969) obtained correlations in three different schools between general self-concept of ability and achievement. The correlations obtained were 0·51 in an Indiana school for the deaf, 0·32 in a Michigan school for the deaf, and 0·53 in a public school group.

Jones and Grieneeks (1970) identified self-concept of academic ability as the best predictor of achievement from among a range of non-intellectual variables. The correlation of academic self-concept with achievement was +0·43 and with the scholastic aptitude test was +0·42. This self-concept of ability scale (Brookover) was a better predictor than scholastic aptitude tests, a normally accepted standard measure in America.

Mintz and Muller (1977) examined the correlations between academic achievement and factor specific, as well as global, measures of self-concept for 314 fourth and sixth grade boys and girls divided into grade level groups with and without

Spanish surnames. The Primary Self-Concept Inventory was used to measure self-concept on six scales; physical size, emotional state, peer acceptance, helpfulness, success and student-self. A global self-concept score was derived by totalling the scores on the six scales. The two specific measures of self-concept that were most reflective of school performance, success and student-self, tended to show low positive correlation (0·26 and 0·39 respectively with achievement). The global measure, tended to show no relationship to achievement.

The results of this study and Brookover's investigations indicate that a factor specific model of self-concept is of greater utility in assessing the relationship between self-concept and achievement than is the undifferentiated or global model. It also emphasizes the fact that academic performance is related to those factors of self-concept most specific to academic performance. That is, success and student-self factors more frequently correlated with achievement than did other factors. The correlations between achievement and self-concept may have been spuriously low, however, in Mintz and Muller's study because the Primary Self-Concept Inventory (PSCI) was designed to identify the child with a low self-concept. It was not designed to differentiate between levels of high self-concept. Furthermore, a rather global measure of achievement, total achievement as measured by a standardized achievement test, was used. Brookover et al., as we have noted, show somewhat greater correlations when more specific or immediate measures of achievement are used. Additionally none of the factors measured by the PSCI is specifically a school achievement factor. Brookover et al. (1964) used school achievement specific measures of self-concept.

In a study of the developmental changes in self-concept in America using a cross-sectional approach involving nearly 1500 children from 5 to 14 years old, Larned and Muller (1979) found that self-concept level remained stable in relation to physical self and peer relations. It was the academic self-concept that revealed a fairly drastic decline. They were also able to show that it is the academic self-concept which bears a closer relationship to academic performance than other areas of self-conceptualization do. Physical maturity self-concept was the only measure to show different developmental patterns for boys and girls. These patterns appeared to reflect physical size and growth rate differences between the two sexes. Small sex differences occurred in academic success self-concept, academic success self-esteem, and school adaptiveness self-concept. However, the developmental trends for the two sexes on these scales seemed to be approximately parallel.

Torshen (1969) reports that academic self-concept (general) correlated +0·46 with overall teachers' grades while for the same students it correlated +0·33 with overall achievement test scores. The higher relation between academic self-concept and teachers' grades can be attributed to the fact that teachers' judgements (and marks) are communicated to the student on a daily basis while standardized tests may be used rarely during an academic year. Furthermore, teachers' judgements tend to emphasize the student's relative standing in the class or school. This is the peer group against which the student typically compares himself, especially in reporting his academic self-concept. The standardized test scores refer to a larger population (typically the national distribution) and this is only rarely the group against which the student judges his own progress. Thus, the student's view of himself is likely to be most directly influenced by the frequent judgements about himself as a learner that he receives in school and especially those judgements made by teachers and peers in the school and his parents and siblings in the home. These tend to be relative judgements in that each student's learning is compared with the learning of other students in the same class or school.

Such teachers' judgements have a cumulative effect on academic self-concept. This was studied by Kifer (1973) who followed the relation between academic self-concept and teachers' marks over grades 1 to 8 (pupils of 5 to 13 years old). Kifer selected students who were in the upper fifth of their classes by their teachers' marks. He also selected other students in the same classes who were in the lowest fifth of their classes in marks in the same grades. Each of these students completed Brookover's Self-Concept of Ability Scale.

Only slight differences in academic self-concept between the successful and unsuccessful students were apparent at the end of grade 2. Somewhat greater differences appeared at the end of grade 4, while the differences at the end of grade 6 and at the end of grade 8 were very marked. The academic self-concept of students is clearly influenced by the number of years in which the students have been judged and graded by the schools. This is most clearly apparent for the extreme students.

In addition to the extreme students, Kifer (op. cit.) also studied the relation between academic self-concept and teachers' marks for the whole set of students in grades 5 and 7 (10–12 year-olds). The correlation between teachers' marks and academic self-concept at grade 5 was $+0.23$ while at grade 7 it was $+0.50$.

The academic self-concept is an index of the student's perception of his previous school history of himself in relation to the achievement of the other learners in his school class. It is, undoubtedly, based on the feedback he receives from grades, tests, teachers, parents and peers about his schoolwork. The more evidence the student receives, the more likely it is that his academic self-concept will be predictive (and determinative) of his future academic achievement, unless some major change takes place in either student or school.

It is evident in these studies that academic self-concept is relatively clearly defined by the end of the primary-school period. The size of the correlations indicate that, for the extreme students (upper and lower fifth) on academic achievement, the relationships between academic self-concept and school achievement are rather strong, with little overlap in academic self-concept between these extreme groups.

It is the middle groups of students who may be least affected by their school achievement as far as academic self-concept is concerned. They receive enough positive evidence of their basic adequacy to balance the negative evidence, or at least they can take some comfort that they are as adequate as most of their peers, though many turn to other areas of activity and to other aspects of themselves to find more positive signs of their personal worth and adequacy.

There are, even in school, aspects which may be classified as non-academic self-concept, concerned with self-appraisals with regard to athletics, relations with boys and girls, relations with others and appearance.

There is low but positive relation between the academic and non-academic categories of self-concept. Torshen (op. cit.) found a correlation of $+0.35$ for 10 year-olds while Kifer (op. cit.) reports correlations of $+0.31$ and $+0.35$ for 10 and

12 year-olds respectively. Kifer also observed that the general self-esteem of the successful students remained relatively high over the eight years of school while the general self-esteem of the unsuccessful students dropped markedly from nine years of age and was still declining by the end of the eighth year in school. The evidence suggests that individuals who are low in academic self-concept may be high, average, or low in non-academic self-concept. It is likely that individuals who are low in both are in great difficulty and this may be true for up to one half of the students who are low in academic self-concept.

It is possible for some individuals who are low in academic self-concept to get considerable comfort from a positive, non-academic self-concept. However, the academic self-concept is important in its own right in determining whether or not the individual will voluntarily engage in other school-related activities when he is free to do so. Also, a low academic self-concept increases the probability that an individual will have a general negative self-concept. It is always open to those who do not do well in school to degrade and minimize the salience of academic success and obtain their self-esteem through other activities, e.g. athletic, delinquent, etc. In any case, thinking, caring parents and educators would not wish to encourage pupils of limited academic potential to appraise their overall work in terms of scholastic success. Every child possesses some strength, some positive attribute which can be made the basis of enhanced self-evaluation given the guiding hands of supportive significant others.

Self-Concept and Underachievement

Some research on the relationship of the self-concept to school achievement has been concentrated on the underachieving student. Combs (1964) conducted a study with high-school boys to determine whether academically capable but non-achieving high-school boys tend to see themselves and their relationships with others in ways that differ from those students who make a happier and more successful adjustment to school. Each of the boys in the two groups of twenty-five 16 year-olds had IQs of 115 or better. He found that underachievers saw themselves as less adequate and less acceptable to others and they also saw peers and adults as less acceptable. This is consistent with the view that an individual is inclined to project his feelings about himself on to others. Combs concluded that underachieving but capable high-school boys differ significantly from achievers in their perception of self, of others and in general and emotional efficiency.

In an investigation to explore possible relationships between academic under-achievement and self-concept. Fink (1962) studied a group of older students which included twenty pairs of boys and twenty-four pairs of girls. They were matched for IQs (all in the 90 to 110 range) and each individual student was judged as an underachiever or achiever depending on whether his marks fell above or below the class average. One achiever and one underachiever made up each pair. The self-image of each pair was rated as adequate or inadequate by three separate psychologists, based on data from three personality tests, a personal data sheet and a student essay: 'What will I be in twenty years?' The combined ratings of the three psychologists showed significant differences between achievers and underachievers with achievers being rated as far more adequate in their concepts of self. Fink (op. cit.) concluded that there was a strong significant relationship between self-concept and academic underachievement and this relationship was stronger for boys than for girls. In view of the fact that boys focus more on achievement than girls to acquire self-esteem (Chapter 5) the conclusion does not seem surprising.

Walsh (1956) conducted a study involving twenty elementary school boys with IQs over 120 who were 'under-achievers' and who were matched with twenty other boys who had similar IQs but who were high achievers. She found that bright boys who were low achievers had more negative feelings about themselves than did high achievers. In addition she noted that low achievers differed reliably from high achievers in (1) feelings of being criticized, rejected or isolated; (2) acting defensively using compliance, evasion, or negativism; and (3) being unable to express themselves appropriately in actions and feelings. Borislow (1962) used semantic differential scales to get an index of over-all self-regard and to obtain the subjects' more specific evaluations of themselves as students. Although 'achievers' and 'under-achievers' did not differ in general self-evaluation, some positive findings were obtained with the more restricted, idiosyncratic measure of 'self-evaluation as a student'. Achievers exceeded underachievers in 'self-evaluation as a student', both before and after the tests. In two groups reporting low scholastic achievement motivation, achievers exceeded underachievers in 'self-evaluation as a student' after the test with no significant difference appearing before the test.

Shaw, Edson and Bell (1960) also reported finding that bright underachieving male high-school pupils had more negative self-concepts than equally bright but achieving students. Shaw and Alves (1962) confirmed these findings. In addition, the low self-concept under achievers were less accepting of their peers.

From these, and other studies, it seems fairly clear that achievement in school is indeed related to basic personality structure, particularly as this involves a student's performance in the academic area and in his broader social world as well. There is general agreement that, as a group, underachievers tend to have less adequate self-concepts than do normal achievers.

Most experienced teachers can recite a great many examples in which a student's concept of his abilities severely restrict his achievement, even though his real abilities may be superior to those which he demonstrates. It is not infrequently that some students will insist that they cannot do a task almost before they have an opportunity to examine the nature of the work. Nor is it unheard of for some students to offer an apology before they answer a question, such as: 'I'm not really sure but . . .' or 'This may seem a foolish question but . . .'.

Some people have firm images of themselves as people who cannot learn foreign languages, chemistry, statistics or some other subject. It is interesting to ponder whether a person cannot learn a subject because he does not like it or whether he does not like it because he cannot learn it. The answer is academic and not readily apparent but the two factors appear to vary together; that is, they are correlated. It is probably true that a person's attitude toward a subject is an overriding factor. On the other hand, there is no denying that his attitude is often reinforced by his poor performance. Combs (1952) exemplifies this point that a particular self-perception, can so easily become self-validating. For example, a child is likely to avoid reading and thus the very experience which might change his concept of self is bypassed. Worse still, the child who believes himself unable to read, confronted with the necessity for reading is more likely, than not, to do badly. The external evaluation of his teachers and fellow pupils, as well as his own observations of his performance, all provide proof to the child of how right he was in the first place! The possession of a particular self-concept tends to produce behaviour that corroborates the self-concept with which the behaviour originated.

These notions of an inability to learn appear to be self-fulfilling prophecies. That is, the types of experiences that might alter the notions a student holds about himself are deliberately avoided. Instead of obtaining more practice in an area of weakness, the student withdraws from the subject. As a result low ability is perpetuated.

Self-Concept as Predictor of Achievement

Those doing well will not only internalize a positive view of themselves but, also enjoy more satisfactory relationships with peers, teachers and parents as a result of their success. This, in turn, increases the child's motivation to approach academic tasks with confidence and persistence. In such a way, then, self-concept can become a predictor of academic performance. The studies already mentioned in this chapter reveal correlations that imply some ability to predict attainment from a knowledge of self-concept score. This predictability is increased when specific self-concept subject area scales are used in relation to relevant specific subject area performance. However, the array of correlations linking self-concept level and achievement while positive and statistically significant, tends to hover between the region of 0·20 and 0·50, a level which is not all that striking, indicating only that up to a maximum of 25 per cent of the variance in academic performance can be 'explained' in terms of self-concept level. The above statement is meant to be cautionary rather than damning, since the opening remarks of this chapter suggested that the self-concept was only one of a number of variables that affect academic performance. Hence, it would be surprising to find the self-concept having an overwhelming influence. But, it is certainly too important to be disregarded and must be ranged alongside those other usual explanations of IQ, social class, parental interest, etc.; all of which need to be invoked to produce an over-all picture of why some children succeed while others fail.

Self-concept has been found to be closely associated with the prediction of achievement in reading, a basic and necessary competence. Black (1974) reports correlations of +0·58 for a retarded reading sample, with poor achievers tending to show a significant decrease in self-concept scores with increasing age.

Stenner and Katzenmeyer (1976) reported a strong relationship between the Intermediate Level Self-Observation Scales (SOS) and teacher-rated reading (TRR) achievement. Six of the seven intermediate scales were shown to be positively and significantly ($P < 0.0001$) related to TRR after controlling for family income and ethnicity (a seventh scale School Affiliation, was negatively—$P < 0.0001$—related to TRR). Employing a national sample of 3054 fourth, fifth and sixth graders, the seven intermediate SOS scales combined to yield a multiple correlation of 0·48 with TRR.

In a companion study using a national sample of 2481 first, second and third graders, Katzenmeyer and Stenner (1977) found all four of the Primary SOS Scales to be positively and significantly related to TRR after controlling for family income and ethnicity. In their 1976 study, Stenner and Katzenmeyer applied two IQ tests, six achievement tests and the Self-Observation Scales to 225 pre-adolescents. Again self-concept was shown to add significantly to the prediction equation for achievement over and above the contribution of non-verbal intelligence. The SOS accounted for 22 per cent of the variance in reading achievement and combined with non-verbal intelligence to account for 34 per cent of the variance in reading achievement.

The SOS correlated to a significantly greater degree with achievement area than with non-verbal IQ, thus supporting the conceptual independence of the two constructs (self-concept and ability) and illustrating the incremental value each gives to the other in predicting achievement.

Self-conception can affect performance at an early age, too, as Wattenberg and Clifford (1964) show. They found that unfavourable self-conceptualization and achievement is already in many children before they enter first-grade. They studied 128 kindergarten students in two schools, one serving a working-class neighbourhood, the other a middle-class one and measured the intelligence, ego-strength and reading ability of all the students when they were in kindergarten and again when these same students finished second grade. They found that measures of self-concept and ego-strength made at the beginning of kindergarten were more predictive of reading achievement thirty months later than were measures of intelligence. In other words the self-attitude of the kindergarten student was a more accurate indication of his potential reading skills than his intelligence test scores.

In a longitudinal enquiry into the relationship between reading difficulties and antisocial behaviour, reports on the self-concepts of a group of Scottish children at the beginning of their school career, when they were between $4\frac{1}{2}$ and $5\frac{1}{2}$ were taken by McMichael (1977).

The results of this study serve to support those of Wattenberg and Clifford. McMichael (op. cit.) also found that an unfavourable view of the self and poor achievement were already established in many children while they were in kindergarten. Measures of self-concept at this stage were closely related to levels of reading readiness and behaviour problems later at school entry. Subsequent reading failure is likely to reinforce rather than cause low self-esteem.

Bridgeman and Shipman (1978) addressed themselves to a similar question; what is the relation of measures of self-esteem obtained in head-start year, kindergarten and first grade, to reading and mathematics achievement in the third grade (8 years old)?

The early self-esteem scores contributed significantly to predictions of third-grade performance. However, the predictive variation in the scores may have represented differences in task understanding and attentiveness rather than differences in self-esteem. Some children might have listened carefully to each item and considered both alternatives before responding, whereas others might have chosen quickly.

Thus attention to the self-esteem scale and to teacher in the classroom is a possible explanation of the relationship.

The personality characteristics and attitudes towards achievement of two groups of fourth- and fifth-grade children differentiated in reading ability were analysed by Zimmerman and Allebrand (1965). Subjects in this study consisted of 71 'poor' readers and 82 'good' readers equated as nearly as possible for age, sex, ethnic background and intelligence. Compared to the bad reader, the good reader was found likely to describe himself as well-adjusted, motivated and striving for success. This is in contrast to the picture presented by bad readers who, according to the investigators, would willingly admit to feelings of discouragement, inadequacy and nervousness and whose proclaimed goals are often ephemeral or immediate, especially in avoiding achievements.

The feasibility of using self-concept measures along with intelligence measures to improve the prediction of achievement has been explored. We noted earlier that Brookover's work and that of Mintz and Muller (1977) indicate (1) that self-concept measures that reflect school success are more closely related to achievement than are either global self-concept measures or specific self-concept measures that are reflective of other areas of the child's school experience (e.g. peer relations, physical maturity, or school adaptiveness); and (2) that a self-concept measure that specifically reflects success within a given academic area will maximize the correlation between self-concept and achievement within that area. This, in turn, suggests that the prediction of area specific achievement scores would be maximized with the use of subject area specific measures of academic success self-concept.

However, if self-concept is to be used to improve the prediction of achievement, it must contribute to the degree of prediction already attainable through more conventional means. One of the most effective predictors of achievement is intelligence. Thus, if self-concept has potential practical value as a predictor, it should by itself or in combination with intelligence account for a greater proportion of the variance in achievement scores than does intelligence alone.

Brookover et al. (1965) correlated grade point average with intelligence and the combination of intelligence and general academic success self-concept. They found that the combination accounted for approximately 10 per cent more variance in grade point average than did intelligence alone. However, they did not report the correlation between subject area achievement and the combination of intelligence and subject specific measures of academic success self-concept. Nor did they examine the relationship between achievement and the combination of intelligence and general as well as subject area specific measures of academic success self-concept. Gose, Wooden and Muller (1980) attempted to determine whether such a combination of intelligence and self-concept measures can account for substantially more variance in achievement than intelligence alone.

Two self-concept scales specifically indexing academic self-concept were employed as well as an IQ test and achievement test battery. The results of this research are consistent with those of earlier studies in that only academic success self-measures were consistently correlated with academic achievement. Furthermore, those self-measures that specifically reflected success within a given academic area tended to maximize the correlation between self-concept and achievement within that area. Achievement was found to be related to academic success self-concept, but not to physical maturity, peer relations, or school adaptiveness self-concepts. Achievement in the subject areas of reading, language and mathematics was most directly related to self-concept measures that were specifically reflective of academic success in these subject areas. In each of these areas, the combination of intelligence and the related academic success self-concept measure accounted for more achievement variance than did intelligence alone. This last finding was interpreted as evidence suggesting that subject area specific self-concept measures might facilitate the prediction of academic success.

Specifically, the addition of the self-measures to the intelligence measures increased the proportion of accounted for achievement variance from 0·77 to 0·81 for reading, 0·42 to 0·61 for language, 0·52 to 0·66 for mathematics and 0·72 to 0·77 for total achievement.

SELF-CONCEPT AND ABILITY

In a complex study concerned with the investigation of factors that facilitate the prediction of behaviour, Terborg et al. (1980) considered ability and self-esteem in relation to reward systems. Dunnette (1973) had proposed that even when constraints to performance are removed, knowledge of individual ability will not always predict individual performance. This is where motivation concepts become important because Dunnette argues that the primary effect of motivation could be to enhance the expression of individual ability. Motivational research should be concerned with the identification of factors that help the display of individual ability differences. Extending Dunnette's work, Terborg (op. cit.) made the following predictions. First, there will be a significant predictive relationship between measures of job-related ability and measures of job performance. Second, there will be greater effort and better performance in situations in which rewards depend on performance rather than where they do not. Third, because of the facilitating effects of dependent rewards on the expression of ability, ability will be a more valid predictor of performance where rewards depend on performance than where they do not. The former provides a reason for a person to display whatever ability he or she possesses. When rewards do not depend on performance, there is one less reason for a person with high ability to display his or her potential. Consequently, even though ability and knowledge of rewards may simultaneously affect performance, Dunnette predicts a greater difference in performance between high and low ability people when rewards depend on performance.

Since, individuals are motivated to perform and behave in a manner consistent with their self-esteem, Terborg further predicted that self-esteem will be positively related to both effort and performance and self-esteem will function as an individual difference factor that will facilitate the expression of ability. Therefore, ability will be a more valid predictor of performance for individuals with high self-esteem than for those with low self-esteem. People with low self-esteem should not be motivated to do well and, as a result, their *ability* differences will not be reflected in *performance* differences. But, because people with high self-esteem should be motivated to do well, their ability differences *will* be reflected in performance differences. Self-esteem is predicted to operate in a manner similar to differences in dependent and independent reward systems, in that both have the potential to facilitate the expression of ability. Finally Terborg (op. cit.) predicted that self-esteem will be a more valid predictor of effort and performance when rewards do not depend on performance than when they do. In the former situation there may be no reason for a person with low self-esteem to perform well, whereas there is a personality reason for people with high self-esteem to perform well. Consequently, in this situation, self-esteem should be a valid predictor of performance.

When rewards depend on performance, however, there is a reason to perform well. Although, this should provide additional motivation for high self-esteem people, they already may be functioning at high levels. The major impact, then, of dependent reward systems may be on the motivation of low self-esteem people to exert greater effort and attain higher levels of performance than they might otherwise attempt.

Terborg's results reveal a significant correlation between ability and self-esteem ($r = +0.48$) and that the sequence of the relationship was ability → perfor- mance → self-esteem since the relationship between performance and self-esteem should be reduced when ability is partialized from both but relationships between ability and performance should be unaffected by the partializing out of self-esteem.

This finding suggests that if we are interested in predicting performance at one point in time, the measurement of self-esteem may be redundant with ability. But the value of self-esteem becomes evident when we attempt to predict changes in performance over time or reactions to task success and failure. Given task failure, a person with high self-esteem is predicted in the short run, to approach the task again and to engage in behaviour required for task success. We expect greater effort and better performance on the second attempt. Knowledge of only a person's ability does not lead to predictions of change in effort or performance because ability is relatively stable and it would not be expected to change with one attempt at performance.

Actual IQ and ability levels must interact with self-evaluation since differing ability levels likely bring in their wake different experiences of success or failure in academic tasks. Many researchers have discerned positive relationships between IQ and self-concept (e.g. Coopersmith (1967) reports $+0.28$; Piers and Harris (1964) report $+0.48$). But this relationship may not be as straightforward as it might seem for students can distort their perceived ability and achievement levels by deliberate defence of naïvety. For example, a pupil may evaluate his own performance, comments and scores mainly in terms of more limited reference groups, e.g. the special class, the subculture or the gang. The reference groups may simply be those which happen to be available or they may be chosen by the individual. If the reference group is relatively low on achievement and ability, the pupil whose standing in a heterogeneous group is low may consider his abilities and achievements to be sound enough in this more limited group. This, as we shall discover in later chapters, is the position that research finds, which delinquent pupils and black pupils use to maintain and even enhance their self-esteem over the majority pupil culture. Such limited referents actually insulate some sub-cultures from the mainstream criteria.

While achievement indices are reasonably easy to come by in the school system e.g. teachers' marks and comments, class positions, acceptance on courses, etc., ability indices are hard to locate by pupils save inferences by achievement. Distortion of perceived self-concept is possible in an upward direction since low-achievement can always be self-excused by low interest, low motivation, poor teaching, teacher's bias, etc., thus protecting self-concept of ability. This distortion would produce a negative skew to the distribution of self-concept of ability scores, as few pupils tend to report themselves at the lower end. Statistically, this would tend to lower correlations between self-concept of ability and attainment scores.

ATTRIBUTING ACHIEVEMENT AND FAILURE

Determinants of academic achievement and failure are perceived as different for high and low self-concept children. Weiner (1971) has suggested that the self-perception of success and failure can be understood in terms of the relative weight a person accords the following factors: ability, difficulty of task, luck and effort.

An analysis of luck and effort shows that these explanations for success and failure are changeable and unstable. People are most likely to use luck or effort to explain success and failure that is inconsistent with past experience or unexpected. By contrast, difficulty of task and ability are generally stable explanations for success or failure that is consistent with past experience and is expected.

Most people attribute consistent failure to 'low' ability and high difficulty of task. Failure following consistent success is most often attributed to bad luck. Failure following alternating success and failure is most often attributed to lack of effort and bad luck.

Success can also hinder performance if it is experienced by people with very low self-esteem. Female college students were tested on a task involving motor coordination. It was arranged that all students would succeed. For most of the students this experience of success led to better performance on later trials of the task. This was not true for students who had weak feelings of self-acceptance and low self-esteem. Students with low self-esteem who experienced success and were led to attribute the success to their personal skill did not improve their performance in later trials. These students were apparently made uncomfortable by the unexpected experience of success and they regulated their future performance so that this success would not continue (Maracek and Mettee 1972).

When students with low self-esteem were led to attribute their success on the tasks to luck, the results were very different. The students did not appear to experience the same discomfort of unexpected success. They derived some personal satisfaction from the success because they did not have to take full responsibility for that success as a result of their personal skill. These students did not hold back their performance on the tasks during future trials.

Ames (1978) put boys and girls into pairs and gave them tasks to complete in which one of the pair succeeded and the other failed. Results showed that high self-concept children attributed success more to their high ability and engaged in more positive self-reinforcement following success than did low self-concept children. In competitive settings, high self-concept people perceive themselves as more capable and engage in more self-congratulatory behaviour than low self-concept people. Likewise, the effects of failure were more devastating in a competitive setting leading to increased self-therapy by the high self-concept child but to increased self-punishment by the low self-concept child.

Ames and Felker (1979) devised a study in which they hypothesized that differences in self-concept should be reflected in how persons categorize incoming information, that is, how they interpret the nature of a test. In their study a test was characterized as involving both skill and luck components, high and low self-concept children were expected to interpret the causal nature of their performance in a dissimilar manner. That is, high self-concept children should focus on skill and low self-concept children on luck when they explain a successful performance, but lack of luck should be emphasized by high self-concept children and lack of skill by low self-concept children when they attempt to explain failure. In both instances, the child's motivation is directed towards maintaining her or his prior self-evaluation by taking responsibility for outcomes consistent with the prior self-evaluation and denying responsibility when the results are inconsistent.

It was argued that self-concept reflects a relatively stable self-evaluation based on consistent patterns of social and achievement-related experiences, and, as such, should reflect an attributional disposition toward explaining achievement events in relation to their own abilities. Thus, self-concept was viewed as a trait that should involve differences in attributions to a stable internal factor. As a consequence, ability, rather than effort, was investigated as the critical attributional factor differentiating high and low self-concept children's causal perceptions of achievement events. Attributing success to one's stable ability by high self-concept children maintains a high level of confidence in their abilities and their own positive self-image. Conversely, low self-concept children, by attributing failure to stable low ability, maintain a low level of confidence and confirm their negative self-view. Thus children who differ in self-concept should attribute self-consistent events to a stable dispositional trait such as ability, while events that are not self-consistent should be attributed to external causes such as luck.

Ames and Felker (op. cit.) used 156 children in their study. They all completed the Piers–Harris SC Scale and six puzzles drawn from a stack at random. The instructions were intended to create an ambiguity over the causal determinants of one's performance. Thus children could perceive their performance on the task as predominantly caused by their own skill or by luck.

These results suggest that when a task is characterized as involving skill and luck, the causal explanations of high and low self-concept children involve a differential bias towards using skill to succeed. Whereas high self-concept children appeared to take credit for their success, low-concept children tended to reject success by taking little personal responsibility for the outcome. Within attribution theory, success outcomes ascribed to ability or skill have important consequences for one's resulting achievement behaviours and self-esteem (Weiner 1974). Ascribing success to ability—an internal factor that is stable over time—by the high self-concept children should augment further achievement directed behaviours and should produce greater satisfaction with their performance. Supporting this latter prediction, the data showed that high, more than low, self-concept children engaged in some form of positive self-reinforcing behaviour following success.

From an attributional perspective, the low self-concept child seems to maintain his or her low self-appraisal by attributing success to luck, an external cause that implies no need for changing one's prior self-evaluation and that generates minimal positive self-feelings. Success experiences appear to have significantly less reward value for low than for high self-concept children, evidenced by their lower level of self-reward. Thus, compared with high self-concept children, there seems to be considerably less internal incentive for low self-concept children to exhibit persistent achievement-oriented behaviours.

Contrary to expectations, there were no differences between the self-concept groups in their causal attribution for failure outcomes. Both groups tended to use the ability cue (lack of skill) to explain their performance. Additionally the self-concept groups did not differ significantly in the amount of reward they felt was deserved for their performance. The low self-concept children, however, did give themselves more punitive statements than high self-concept children.

Attributing failure to one's lack of skill may be expected to produce lower expectancies of future success and motivate the child to avoid further contact with the task (Weiner 1974). However, it might be conjectured that while both self-concept groups attributed their failure to the internal factor of skill, high self-concept children may have seen skill as less stable and as capable of being remedied, whereas low self-concept children saw their failure as due to a general lack of ability. It should be noted that unstable skill implies lack of immediate understanding, mood or fatigue and does not necessarily imply lack of effort. Using the construct of 'skill', rather than 'ability', in the task instructions and dependent measures may have actually helped alternative interpretations.

By attributing failure to unstable skill, high self-concept children would be more likely to persist in task-oriented behaviours, while low self-concept children, attributing failure to stable low ability, would perhaps withdraw. It is the attribution of failure to stable low ability that involves more negative consequences, as it implies a negative self-labelling that is more likely to be associated with anxiety arousal and emotional dysfunction (Kuiper 1978; Storms and McCaul 1976). Supporting the above analysis is the higher degree of self-criticism observed in the low self-concept children following failure as compared to those with high self-concepts (see also Ames 1978). Chronic self-criticism can be maladaptive by contributing to feelings of discouragement or depression (Bandura 1977; Kanfer 1971) and by inhibiting achievement behaviours (Masters and Stanrock 1976). It thus appears that a punitive self-reinforcement mechanism distinguishes low from high self-concept children after failure.

In conclusion, two critical factors that are considered important for achievement, directed behaviours—beliefs about one's ability—and self-reinforcement mechanisms, have been shown to be strongly related to self-concept. The findings suggest that attempts at modifying low self-concept must be concerned with both cognitive and self-reinforcing responses to achievement outcomes and must involve training these children how to interpret and deal with success as well as failure feedback.

SEX DIFFERENCES IN THE SELF-CONCEPT–ACHIEVEMENT RELATIONSHIP

A significant relationship between self-esteem and academic achievement was found by Primavera, Simon and Primavera (1974) for 11 year-old girls (r ranges from 0·21 to 0·50) in seven academic achievement tests but only in one test ($r = 0·25$) for boys. They suggest the source of this sex difference lies in the fact that the school plays a greater role in the affective quality of a girl's self-esteem because it is a major source of approval and praise for her whereas boys can seek approval through athletics and other more stereotyped male behaviours. It is probably true that this qualification is related to age and it is quite possible that academic achievement and self-esteem may be related for high-school and college males since it is at this level of education that academic achievement becomes an increasingly important source of social approval for the male. The results of this study strongly indicate a need for a revaluation of data in this area with reference to sex and age differences. It should be pointed out that the sex differences found here cannot be accounted for by differences in levels of self-esteem, since self-esteem scores for males and females did not differ significantly from each other.

In contrast, Bledsoe (1964) had earlier found significant correlations for boys between self-concept and attainment but not for girls. Bledsoe argues that these differences are due to boys perceiving traits and abilities measured by attainment tests as more important in their self-esteem than girls.

The inconsistent sex difference is as yet unexplainable though it may be caused not, as Bledsoe (op. cit.) suggests by the content of the achievement tests favouring the boys but, rather, by some self-concept scales containing items more appropriate for endorsement by boys than girls and, others, more relevant to girls than boys.

Perhaps such sex differences are a result, too, of the social expectations for males in Western society, especially in terms of academic progress and ambition. Female self-concepts focus on different areas from male ones. Veness (1962) noted that girls are more concerned with personal appearance and social relationships than boys who showed more concern with academic progress.

As we noted in the chapter on sex-role self-concepts (Chapter 5) girls are less oriented towards achievement than boys as a result of socialization. This appears to lead to girls feeling uncomfortable and anxious if they achieve, since it undermines their self-concept as a stereotyped female.

Fear of success is present in women when they are uncertain of the reactions they might receive for being successful. Because of the fear of rejection, women are often reluctant to compete. Females in single-sex high schools had significantly less fear of success than female students in co-ed high schools. Females who had also attended single-sex elementary schools were the least afraid of success. It has been argued that females in single-sex schools do not have to suffer the negative reactions resulting from competition with males (Winchel, Fenner and Shaver 1974).

Male pupils tend to attribute success to ability, but female pupils attribute success to luck (Nicholls 1975). It is not surprising that as a result of different socialization experiences, boys and girls develop important differences in self-perceptions of success and failure in school. Dweck (1974) showed that boys and girls receive the same amounts of positive and negative evaluations by teachers, but the nature and goal of these positive and negative evaluations are strikingly different. A large proportion of the negative evaluations received by boys were based on their conduct in class and have nothing to do with the intellectual quality of their work. Negative evaluations received by girls, in contrast, were based largely on the intellectual quality of their work. This discrepancy in negative evaluations leads to some important differences in socialization. Boys do not interpret the teachers' negativity as a reflection of their lack of ability. Girls, on the other hand, become quite sensitive to negative feedback as an indication of lack of ability.

Positive evaluations by teachers are also used differently for boys and girls. Boys are given positive evaluations almost for the intellectual quality of their work. Girls more often receive positive evaluations for good behaviour and other nonintellectual aspects of performance.

DIRECTION OF INFLUENCE

Since all the studies reported in this chapter tend to be correlational in design, causality cannot easily be determined. Does a positive self-concept provide a student with the attitudes and approach to his work that are likely to ensure success, or does academic success nourish and augment positive feelings a student comes to hold about himself? An armchair analysis suggests that both these causal relationships exist, each helping the other. Studies that attempt to isolate which variable is the independent one are inconsistent in their findings. In order to provide convincing evidence of the effect of self-concept on behaviour, self-concept must first be systematically manipulated and then changes in behaviour observed, or cross-lagged panel analysis used. Using systematic manipulation, Gabbler and Gibby (1967) showed that behaviour can be affected by false feedback indicating failure. The subjects had never before failed in school. An experimental and a control group were both administered three tests: an English grammar test, the Gibby Intelligence Rating Schedule and a test of word fluency. Three days later both groups were again given a test of word fluency, but just before the test, members of the experimental group received slips of paper indicating they had failed the previous test. The scores of the experimental and control groups were then compared. The results indicated that under the stress of failure even quite able children performed less effectively. Furthermore, as shown by self-referrent statements, children in the experimental group tended to regard themselves less highly, tended to believe that they were not as highly regarded by significant others in their lives, and showed a decrement in intellectual productivity. The negative effect of failure was manifested in both the reported self-concept and the measured cognitive function.

Performance modifying self-concept was also shown in Calsyn and Kenny's (1977) cross-lagged panel analysis. They analysed data from a longitudinal study of 556 adolescents to compare the self-enhancement model with that of the skill development approach. Self-enhancement theory suggests that self-concept variables affect level of academic performance. Hence, to improve achievement levels the self-concepts of ability of pupils need to be made more positive through various feedback mechanisms, e.g. counselling and reinforcement. The proponents of the skill-development model claim that academic self-concept level is primarily a consequence of academic attainment. For this method of teaching, personalized instruction and curriculum structure are seen as keys to improved levels of self-concept of ability. Calsyn and Kenny's results were clearly supportive of the skill development model in which academic achievement is causally predominant over self-concept of ability. Perceived evaluations and feedback from others follow as a consequence rather than precede as a cause of level of self-concept of ability.

However, other studies support the opposite argument that self-concept affects academic performance, and improvement in the latter is preceded by self-concept enhancement. For example Brookover, Le Pere et al. (1965) attempted to discover whether enhancing the academic expectations of low-achieving adolescents would improve school attainment. The enhancement was undertaken:
1. by increasing positive parental feedback to the students
2. by having an 'expert' inform the student about his ability and
3. by creating a significant other (a counsellor) whose high academic expectancies and evaluations might be internalized by the student.

The first approach was the most successful. As parental perception changed in a positive direction, so too did the self-perceptions of the students. However, improvement was not maintained when the treatment ceased. Lawrence (1971, 1972), using several counselling approaches with retarded readers, demonstrated a significant gain in reading attainment over control groups. Again, it would seem that modification to self-perception has a considerable effect on academic performance. At the present state of knowledge it seems reasonable to assume that the relationship between self-concept and academic attainment is reciprocal, not unidirectional. Academic success raises or maintains self-esteem, while self-esteem influences performance through expectations, standards, recognition of personal strengths, higher motivation and level of persistence. There is a continuous interplay between the benefits gained from self-esteem increasing the likelihood of increased competencies and academic success, and the influence of academic success on increasing confidence, expectations and standards. This is obviously a beneficent cycle if both or even one of the sides of the equation is fairly positive; however, a destructive cycle is set in motion when one or both are at a low level, with low self-esteem undermining confidence and setting low expectations or with poor performance levels reducing self-esteem. It is a highly complex egg and chicken situation.

Since it is difficult in practice to separate out the reciprocal effects of level of self-concept and academic performance, many workers, however, look at each variable of the self-concept performance relationship separately. This does not imply a lack of understanding about the reciprocal nature of the effects but reveals a weakness in available research techniques, and in practice workers are content at present to describe the conditions under which either factor may be the dependent variable, with the other the independent variable.

CONCLUSION

A plethora of research studies communicate a consistent message that differences in academic performance are associated with differences in self-concept level. Many more studies telling the same story could be cited but this flood would dampen the ardour of any reader if described at any length. Findings summarized by Purkey (1970), La Benne and Green (1969) and Wylie (1979) all point roughly in the same direction. Children whose self-concepts do not include the view that they can achieve academically tend to fulfil that prediction. Judging by the results of literally dozens of studies there seems ample support for the position that children who have clearer and more positive appraisals of their ability to perform in school and have more positive views of themselves and their capacities actually do better in their studies than those with more uncertain or negative views of themselves. While caution must always be exercised in making any firm conclusion, since consistent findings have emerged from correlational studies using a variety of scales to measure various aspects of self-concept and achievement, we can say that the relationship between self-concept and academic performance is a valid one. Purkey (1970) was led to conclude that 'overall the research evidence clearly shows a persistent and significant relationship between the self-concept and academic achievement' (p. 15).

SUMMARY

Entry to school widens the range of possible self-evaluations, and teachers are in a position to modify the existing self-concepts of the child though the latter's previous experience already makes him consider himself in particular ways. Children meet more evaluation in school than ever before and cannot opt out of the system even though failure and incompetence may be their hallmark. Up to the present, few workers have considered schooling in terms of its effects on the affective charac- teristics of the child. The slump in self-esteem around 9 years of age suggests that school is stressful and is failing to meet the affective needs of young people.

Studies using a wide variety of self-concept and achievement measures reveal a consistent picture of a significant positive though low association between the two factors. The correlations tend to run higher when academic self-concept rather than global self-concept is involved in relation to specific subject area achievement. The correlations tend to hover around 0·30 to 0·50 over-all. Self-concept is also positively associated with underachievement, and with the prediction of achievement in such skills as reading in primary-school children. In this latter case, self-concept is a better predictor of future achievement than intelligence is.

High self-concept pupils take credit for their successful achievement by attributing it to ability. Low self-concept pupils reject success by attributing it to the impersonal factor of luck. Both types see failure as a result of lack of ability but the high self-concept child sees ability as potentially improvable; the low self-concept child does not. Girls tend to attribute success to luck rather than to ability.

It is reasonable to assume that the relationship between self-concept and achievement is reciprocal. Research shows both that performance can influence self-concept, and that self-concept manipulation can modify performance levels. The findings reported in this chapter are indicative of the role of the self-concept as an influence on, and potential predictor of, scholarship. They reinforce the notion that educators in general would do well to attend more directly and discriminatingly to the self-perceptions of students at all levels.

Further Reading

Covington, M. V. and Berry, R. G. (1972) *Self-Worth and School Learning,* New York: Holt, Rinehart and Winston.

Hamachek, D. E. (ed.) (1965) *The Self in Growth, Teaching and Learning,* Englewood Cliffs, New Jersey: Prentice Hall.

Purkey, W. W. (1970) *Self-Concept and School Achievement,* New Jersey: Prentice Hall.

9

Teachers' Expectancies

You see, really and truly, apart from the things anyone can pick up (the dressing and the proper way of speaking, and so on), the difference between a lady and a flower girl is not how she behaves, but how she's treated. I shall always be a flower girl to Professor Higgins, because he always treats me as a flower girl, and always will; but I know I can be a lady to you, because you always treat me as a lady, and always will.

Eliza Doolittle to Colonel Pickering
George Bernard Shaw *Pygmalion* (1912)

INTRODUCTION

Chapter 8 has revealed the rather pertinent and important relationship between self-concept and academic performance, and since we are well aware from the studies in Chapter 7 that feedback from significant others is a vital factor in determining self-concept level, this chapter and the succeeding ones look at research of school experiences that modify self-concept and ultimately performance levels. We consider the role of teachers' feedback, expectations, methods, school organization, teacher training and self-concept enhancement activities for pupils. This chapter looks specifically at teachers' feedback and expectations.

Purkey (1970) recounts an anecdote by H. F. Lowry called 'The Mouse and Henry Carson'. This story is a good illustration of some points about academic performance, teachers' expectations and self-concept formation. A mouse fouled up a computer just as the College Entrance Examination Board's data on one Henry Carson was being marked. Henry, a rather unsure mediocre student, was given very high scores by the faulty computer. His potential was reassessed by teachers and Henry responded to their re-evaluation by developing both as a student and as a person. As Purkey notes 'Once he became aware of his potentialities and he began to be treated differently by the significant people in his life, a form of self-fulfilling prophecy took place. Henry gained in confidence and began to put his mind in the way of great things.' Lowry ends the story of 'The Mouse and Henry Carson' by saying that Henry became one of the best men of his generation.

This story illustrates the ways in which pupils view themselves are influenced greatly by the ways in which others respond to them and that the expectations engendered are very important to performance in school.

The school/college context is essentially one of interaction. A milieu is provided in which individuals evaluate each other; teachers judge pupils, pupils judge each other and teachers. This cycle of appraisals, consequent feedback, interpretation of feedback and subsequent responses fuels the existing self-concepts of the participants by functioning as expectations of performance, often self-validating in effect.

The Model Student

Part of this expectation effect is that teachers tend to have their own model of what an 'ideal' student should be like. Becker (1952) first raised this notion. His interview data produced a picture of the ideal pupil as one who cooperates with teacher, who is eager to learn, behaves well, and causes no trouble in class. But as a corollary, pupils who do not match that model become classified as less than ideal and the stereotype of the lazy, dull, badly behaved, hostile child so well depicted in Lacey's (1970) work emerges and attracts different expectations from teacher, since the evaluation is less favourable. The ideal pupil fulfils an important function in the teacher's own self-concept, since such a pupil lends support to the teacher's role. This strengthening of his role confirms the teacher's beliefs and self-evaluation because his classroom performance becomes a more satisfying one. Those pupils who do not conform, and hence do not support the teacher's self-image are evaluated by the teacher as deviant, hostile, indifferent and delinquent. Such feedback to pupils produces a self-fulfilling prophecy (Hargreaves 1967; Lacey 1970).

For pupils to learn in school, it appears self-evident that they need sufficient confidence, in themselves and in their competencies to make some effort to succeed. Without self-confidence it is easy to succumb to apathy, dependency, and loss of self-control. The classroom result is that some students will expect the worst in every situation and will be constantly afraid of doing the wrong thing or saying the wrong word. The real problem of negative self-esteem is hidden beneath the label 'unmotivated' far too frequently. We have noted already from Coopersmith's (1967) study on the antecedents of self-esteem (in Chapter 4) that there are pervasive and significant differences in the experiential worlds and social behaviours of persons who differ in self-esteem. People high in their own estimation approach tasks and people with the expectation that they will be well-received and successful. While feeling worthless is not the same as being worthless, its impact on student classroom behaviour is often the same. Students often report that they take little part in some teachers' lessons because of the tone and content of the comments the teacher directs at the pupil if the pupil is wrong in his answer. The best way to avoid the sarcasm, the sneer, the telling off, is to opt out and not reveal yourself. Students are then labelled as apathetic, inattentive, lazy; they may involve themselves in disruptive behaviour. Research on classroom discipline, for example, reveals a significant relationship between low self-concept as a learner and student misbehaviour in the classroom (e.g. Bogert 1967; Branch, Damico and Purkey 1977). The latter study evaluated disruptive and non-disruptive middle-school students (grades five through eight) on their professed and inferred academic self-concepts. Those students identified by their behaviour as disruptive had significantly lower self-concepts as learners than did students identified as non-disruptive. The theoretical implication drawn from the study was that the negative feelings about oneself as a learner may be a contributing factor in student disruption. Related research in the area of juvenile delinquency has indicated a strong relationship between negative self-concept and delinquency (Chapter 15).

Teachers' Feedback

Most teachers tend to be tuned into what pupils do wrong. That is, a considerable part of the role of some teachers is 'catching' pupils as they make errors, lose attention, forget books etc. Pupils in turn see teachers as people to try and 'get by' through deceit, withdrawal, avoidance etc. Read this sequence and make a response to item 4:

1. A student has not spoken in your class for several weeks.
2. You ask a question which he volunteers to answer.
3. He gives you the wrong answer.
4. Your next statement is . . .

If we are 'tuned in' to correctness, we will say or do something which indicates he is wrong, and we probably won't hear from him again for several weeks. However, if we are sensitive to success, we will respond to his efforts to participate in class, which was his primary role in all probability. Such a teacher would say something like, 'That's a fine try', or 'That's very close. Let me ask it another way.' Whatever she said would be directed towards enhancing the student's feeling of success. That is what keeps him 'alive'.

   If this process of adequate or inadequate appraisals with regard to learning tasks is generalized over a large number of tasks over time, eventually the object of appraisal for the student becomes partially shifted from the school subjects or the school to the person.

   For the individual to work and study in an environment in which the majority of learning tasks over a period of years is accompanied by self-appraisals and external appraisals as adequate, is to develop in the individual a general sense of adequacy, at least in connection with school activities. Similarly, if most of the encounters with learning tasks are accompanied by appraisals of inadequacy, the individual is likely to develop a deep sense of inadequacy in connection with school activities.

   In many cases, the feedback from teachers may simply confirm what the pupil already thinks. Consider the case of a student who believes he is disliked by teachers. If a student is already convinced he is disliked by all teachers, it is perfectly consistent for him to respond by being unfriendly and uncooperative. Teachers in turn may interpret his bored and hostile appearance as meaning that the teacher is dull and ineffective, hardly a flattering evaluation of one's professional competence. If the student maintains an unlikeable self long enough, it will be virtually ensured that most teachers will begin to respond to him in negative ways. He will then have proof that he is disliked. Although he has 'written his own script', it is doubtful that he will realize that it was his own behaviour which was responsible for the outcome.

Whatever the origin, once the belief is accepted into the student's concept of self, he can be expected to look for signs that it is correct. Psychologists call this 'biased scanning'. People engage in biased scanning because their images of self provide them with a degree of security, hence they are motivated to seek information which confirms their accuracy. As a general rule, information consistent with self-concept is eagerly accepted; inconsistent information is either ignored, interpreted, or rejected.

We have already seen that the student can confirm his belief that he is disliked by behaving in unlikeable ways. He can also engage in biased scanning to interpret the teacher's behaviour to confirm his beliefs. So, when the teacher smiles, it is not a sign of friendliness and warmth, but rather an indication that he is laughing at him. When the teacher attempts to include the student in a class discussion by calling on him, he perceives the real motive is to humiliate him publicly. By remembering that meaning is in people, and not in words and gestures, it is possible to understand how the student can interpret the teacher's greatest efforts to be accepted as indications of rejection. Once the feeling of inadequacy, failure and low self-concept of ability have been forged then these affect future behaviour. Pupil and teacher fed expectations of failure lead to withdrawal.

Zimmerman and Allebrand (1965) demonstrated that bad readers lack a sense of personal worth and adequacy to the point where they actively avoid achievement. For bad readers, to study hard and still fail provides unbearable proof of their inadequacy. To avoid such proof, many students deliberately choose not to try. Their defence against failure is secretly to accept themselves as failures! It is better, from the students' viewpoint, not to read at all than to read poorly; it is better not to try than to be embarrassed or humiliated.

Glock (1972) stated the situation succinctly: 'A negative self-image is its own best defender' (p. 406). Actions taken that are incompatible with one's self-image are likely to result in psychological discomfort and anxiety. The result is that everything a person experiences is filtered through, and mediated by, whatever self-concept is already present in the individual. There is little agreement about what is good teaching or about what happens when teaching occurs, though data point to the attitudes, evaluations, expectancies and warmth of the teacher as a primary force in influencing students' perceptions of themselves as learners. Of course the effects of feedback from significant others is recognized in other fields besides education. If a doctor told his patient that his heart was not as strong as he would like, then the behaviour and self-attitudes of the patient would be considerably affected. In theory the interpersonal relationship is seen as crucial in developing self-attitudes (Rogers 1951). In a range of institutions clients are induced to conform to notions of how they ought to behave from the deliberate and accidental feedback of professionals (e.g. Goffman 1961). In *One Flew Over The Cuckoo's Nest* (Kesey 1962) a nurse reminds the other staff 'this is an institution for the insane . . . it is important to get patients adjusted to surroundings'.

The teacher's task is then a dual one, each part interlocked with the other, of helping children understand how they can learn and how capable and worthy they can be.

Purkey (1978) defines the teacher as an inviter, who sends invitations, through formal and informal, verbal and non-verbal, conscious and unconscious ways to students to see themselves as able, valuable and acceptable. Good teaching, he sees, is inviting students to view themselves positively, enabling them to grow and realize their potential. Conversely Purkey defines a 'disinvitation' as an interaction that tells a pupil he is incapable, worthless and not acceptable.

RESEARCH ON TEACHER EXPECTANCY EFFECTS

The reason why feedback from significant others is so important in modifying self-concepts is that it contains others' definitions and expectations of us. We readily accept their judgements and so come to behave in accordance with those definitions. This process is a self-fulfilling prophecy. The unwitting influence that people have on each other, on their behaviours and on the views they hold about themselves has a considerable impact on educational performance through the mediation of self-conceptualization.

The completion of the cycle between teacher input and pupil output is formed by expectancy effects. If the learner thinks of himself as inferior, his actions will tend to be those of an inferior person and will confirm to his teacher and peers the reasonableness of treating him as inferior.

Several studies substantiate the notion that low expectations tend to place a functional limit on performance and self-concept. For example, Aronson and Mills (1959) showed that persons are generally unwilling to accept evidence that they are better or worse than they themselves have decided. Those who found themselves doing well experienced considerable discomfort and tended to make their performance consistent with their expectations. Students who did poorly, but expected to do so, were more satisfied and contented than even those who did well but had not expected to do so. As the standards of performance fall, so does the attitude toward the importance of the subject, followed by lowered aspirations and motivation. Furthermore, maintenance of the cycle is guaranteed by the tendency for the individual to interpret any actions from others in the light of his own self-view. If he views himself negatively, any actions (irrespective of the motives of the doer) will emerge through a negative filter. One of the first studies to reveal a teacher expectancy effect was that of Perkins (1958). The study involved 10 to 12 year-old children from seven schools. They were asked to sort statements such as, 'I look on the bright side of things', 'I understand the kind of person I am' and 'I am not a fast runner' and to nominate up to four classmates, including themselves, for each statement. Teachers were asked to nominate four children using twenty-five similar statements. This rather simple methodology showed that the teachers were as accurate as their pupils at predicting children's perceptions of each other.

Similar results were obtained by Davidson and Lang (1960) who attempted to determine what the relation was between children's perception of their teachers' feelings toward them and the variables: self-perception, academic achievement, and classroom behaviour. They found that children's perception of their teachers' feelings towards them correlated positively and significantly with self-perception. The child with the more favourable self-image was usually the one who perceived his teachers' feelings towards him as more favourable.

The more positive the children's perception of their teacher's feelings, the better their academic achievement is, and the more desirable their classroom behaviour as rated by the teacher becomes. The children indicated that they perceived themselves in very much the same way as they thought their teachers perceived them. Moreover, those children who said they thought well of themselves were regarded by the teacher as well-behaved and of high ability. Davidson and Lang stress the importance of the interaction between the child's self-concept, the perceptions the teacher has of that self-concept and the child's behaviour (p. 112):

> The child who achieves well and behaves satisfactorily is bound to please the teacher. She, in turn, communicates positive feelings toward the child, thus reinforcing his desire to be a good pupil. Which of these variables serves as the primary determinant is a fact difficult to ascertain. It seems rather that they reinforce each other.

Pygmalion in the Classroom Experiment

In a famous (some may say infamous) study by Rosenthal and Jacobson (1968) the researchers addressed themselves to the question, do children perform in the way teachers expect them to perform? Furthermore, once teachers have made up their minds about the capabilities of a pupil to what extent does this decision influence their treatment of the pupil?

Rosenthal and Jacobson selected 'Oak School', an elementary school located in an urban, working-class San Francisco community. Three teachers from each of the six grades were chosen as subjects for the experiment. This involved giving information concerning students' intelligence test scores to the teachers early in the year. Test scores were not represented accurately to the teachers. They were told that the test which actually measured intellectual ability, was a measure specifically designed to identify which students were likely to 'bloom' intellectually during the coming school year. Several pupils in each of the 18 teachers' classes were randomly selected to be the 'bloomers'. The teachers were told that these students could be expected to make unusual learning gains. At the end of the first year the 'bloomers' had gained significantly more IQ points relative to the control children. This was due mainly to changes in one first grade classroom where the 'bloomers' improved their relative IQ by 15 points. There were no significant gains for grades 3 to 6. Indeed, in only two of eighteen classes (one first and one second grade) did 'bloomers' show any significant increase in IQ. In one third-grade class they even deteriorated. Nevertheless,

Rosenthal and Jacobson believed that they had demonstrated expectancy effects between teachers and pupils and they speculated on the reasons (p. 180):

> Teachers may have treated their children in a more pleasant, friendly, and encouraging fashion when they expected greater intellectual gains of them.... Such communications together with possible changes in teaching technique may have helped the child to learn by changing his self-concept image, his expectations of his own behaviour, and his motivation, as well as his cognitive style and skills.

These results then apparently demonstrated to the researchers' satisfaction that teachers' expectations, induced by the false knowledge that some of their students would improve dramatically, acted as self-fulfilling prophecies.

Rosenthal and Jacobson attempted to explain their findings in terms of the probable ways teachers treated the designated 'bloomer' students. This explanation is consistent with the theory that differential expectations are communicated through differential teacher behaviours toward different students. Teacher behaviours rather strangely were not actually measured in the study. Hence the conclusion that the observed difference in learning gains was directly attributed to teacher behaviour was attacked with great zeal. In the ensuing years, numerous attempts to repeat the findings of the original study have been inconsistent in their findings. Experimentally induced expectation effects are apparently more difficult to obtain than Rosenthal and Jacobson's study suggests. Thus the educational community remains in dispute, with some constituents firmly convinced of the validity and generality of the Pygmalion effect while an equal number of sceptics who, largely on methodological grounds, reject the original results as accidental.

Snow's (1969) review brought out some disturbing features of Rosenthal and Jacobson's interpretation of statistics. First among these was the nature of the intelligence test scores used in the research. According to the teachers who administered the tests (a rather dubious procedure) the average IQ of the first grade pupils was 58. This is almost moronic level! There is no evidence that they were and one can only conclude that the test was of doubtful reliability and validity. In any case the instrument used, the Test of General Ability (TOGA), has no norms below 60 and it is evident that some unjustified extrapolations were made. Thorndike (1968) was quite scathing and wrote of the study, 'It is so defective technically that one can only regret that it ever got beyond the eyes of the original investigators'.

Brophy and Good (1974) have reviewed and synthesized the bulk of the research literature on teacher expectations and have concluded that there are indeed instances in which true expectancy effects occur. That is, there is substantial evidence, from naturalistic rather than experimental studies, that teachers form inappropriate expectations of their students. Such expectations manifest themselves through shifts in students' performance levels in the direction of the inaccurate expectations. Studies reviewed by Brophy and Good demonstrate irrevocably that teachers treat individual students differently and in ways that are often self-defeating, although these effects are not generally indicative of a Pygmalion effect. Rather, the effect occurs only when certain specific conditions are present. Brophy and Good (1974) describe them in the following sequence:

1. Early in the school year, using the school records and/or observations during classroom interaction, all teachers form different expectations regarding the potential and characteristics of the students in their classes.
2. Teachers begin to treat students differently in accordance with their expectations. Where teacher expectations are inappropriate and rigid, treatment of the students will be inappropriate.
3. Pupils treat teachers differently because of their different personalities, and they also respond to the teachers because the teachers treat them differently.
4. Thus, in general, each student will respond to the teacher with behaviour that complements and reinforces the teacher's expectations of him. In the case of students towards whom the teacher holds inappropriate and rigid expectations, the students will tend to be conditioned to respond with behaviour that helps to reinforce the teacher's expectations.
5. If continued indefinitely, this process will cause students towards whom the teachers hold inappropriate and rigid expectations gradually to approximate those expectations more and more.
6. If continued over the course of the school year, differential treatment of teachers of different students will show effects on both process and product measures. Where teachers' expectations are appropriate, or where they are flexible so that any inappropriate aspects are quickly corrected, the teacher–student interaction will be largely predictable from knowledge of the student's general personality and specific classroom habits. His achievement relative to that of his classmates will be highly predictable on the basis of his previous achievement. In other words the classroom behaviour and academic achievement of such students will be 'about as expected' (p. 39f).

The sequence presented by Brophy and Good should provide a useful framework for teacher self-examination as well as a skeleton model from which the researcher can develop tenable hypotheses for experimentation.

Other Studies that Produce Expectancy Effects

In a study of streaming that is referred to in more detail in Chapter 12, Barker-Lunn (1970) found that the A stream pupils had as high a self-image as children who were near the top of the B and C streams. Under-achieving children in mixed-ability schools had a poor self-image and seemed ashamed of their apparent 'stupidity'. Teachers constantly compared them, much to their detriment, with the more able members of their stream or class. One teacher in the study remarked, in front of the class, 'I don't like teaching dull children; I wasn't trained to teach them. Those are my bright children over there,' pointing to a row by the window, 'the average are in the middle and the dull children are over there'. Not surprisingly, interaction with teacher and the teacher's rating of the child's ability significantly predicted self-esteem (Barker-Lunn 1970).

A number of American studies have found that self-esteem aligns with stream position (or track position, in American terminology). Pupils in low streams, perceiving themselves as failures, are likely to drop out of school and engage in antisocial activity. Rather similar findings emerged from Hargreaves's (1967) study in an English secondary modern school. Hargreaves found a 'drop-out sub-culture' of D-stream boys, largely a reaction to academic failure and the negative views of teachers. Rist (1970) in an observational and longitudinal study of a black kindergarten teacher in America and her thirty black pupils, found that 'permanent' seating assignments made on the eighth day of school coincided with the social class of the students. The teacher grouped the children at three tables, explaining that they were seated according to their ability to 'learn'. The occupants of Table 1 were from families with higher incomes, higher education levels, fewer children, and both parents in the home. These children were better dressed, neater and cleaner than those at Tables 2 and 3. They talked and interacted more easily with the teacher in what the investigator calls 'Standard American English' than children at the other two tables who spoke in a dialect. As the school year progressed, they interacted considerably more frequently with the teacher and received more positive responses and privileges from her. The teacher presented lessons directly to Table 1 and described children at Tables 2 and 3 as 'not having any idea what was going on in the classroom'. While some children from Table 2 and 3 scored higher on an end-of-year IQ test than some children at Table 1, when the pupils moved on to the first grade, they retained the 'ability' grouping assigned them on the eighth day of kindergarten. This ability grouping, reinforced in first grade by performance records, accompanied the pupils into second grade. Rist concludes from observation of teacher–pupil interaction that the children's learning experiences reinforced the original 'ability' grouping, producing a self-fulfilling prophecy. While this study focused on only one teacher and her pupils, and is thus inadequate for generalization, educators and researchers can speculate about the factors at work here and examine them further.

Mazer (1971) found that pupil socioeconomic status is also related to teacher expectations of pupil performance. After giving teachers from various backgrounds photographs of pupils with accompanying descriptions of their socioeconomic status, Mazer asked them to estimate each student's performance on a 5-point scale covering 12 variables. The photographs (of male and female, black and white pupils) were switched among the SES descriptions. Results indicated that the socioeconomic status of the pupil, rather than sex or race, differentiated the performance predictions. The teachers' background and experience did not affect the estimate in any measurable way.

Labelling and grouping can exacerbate the development of a negative self-concept particularly as many categories are potent instruments for social regulation and control. Labels can degrade, hurt, exclude undesirables, and justify all manner of behaviour towards those pejoratively labelled. Rist (1970) claims that many children are 'locked in' to a particular life style, treatment and self-evaluation by early labelling as retarded, hyperactive, slow learner or maladjusted, etc. Many studies reveal that teachers respond to pupils in terms of such labels, and express negative attitudes to these children (McGinley and McGinley 1970; Stevens 1971). For example, Frericks (1974) demonstrated the effects of telling prospective teachers that a classroom of students, seen on videotape, were 'low-ability' students. A control group watched the same videotape but was told that it showed 'normal students in a normal classroom'. After watching the videotape, both groups of prospective teachers completed a scale designed to measure their attitudes toward the videotaped students. Compared to the control group, the experimental group of prospective teachers who had been told the students were 'low ability' viewed them as less responsible, possessing less self-control, more prone to rudeness, and showing less capacity to engage in an abstract level of discussion. These findings agree with those of other studies, which indicate that labelling and grouping can carry a number of penalties.

Rubovits and Maehr (1973) selected pupils, both black and white, from the same ability group and arbitrarily assigned them 'gifted' and 'ungifted' labels. These pupils were then taught microlessons by student teachers who had been informed of their gifted or ungifted status. Results showed significant differences in teacher behaviour on dimensions of race and giftedness. While all pupils received a similar amount of teacher attention, the quality of teacher attention differed for the two groups of children. Gifted pupils were called on and criticized more often, but the most amount of criticism came during teacher interaction with the gifted black students. Gifted white students were called on, praised, and criticized more often than the ungifted white students, and in subsequent interviews with the student teachers, gifted white students were most frequently named as 'most liked', 'brightest', and 'most probable leaders' of their class. Black students were given less attention than were whites, were ignored more, praised less and criticized more by all the teachers. And, interestingly, the gifted black pupils received more negative attention than the nongifted blacks. Since all pupils had been selected from the same ability group, these teacher behaviours were not based on actual pupil performance differences.

Palardy (1969) asked 63 first-grade teachers to report their beliefs about the rate at which first-grade boys learn to read. Among the 42 teachers who responded to the questionnaire, he identified three groups. Group *A* consisted of teachers who believed boys learn to read at an equal pace with girls. Teachers in Group *B* thought boys considerably slower than girls in learning to read, and Group *C* teachers believed boys to be somewhat slower. For research purposes, Group *C* was dropped, and comparisons were made between the two extreme groups. A reading pre-test administered to all pupils showed no differences among them. On the post-test, however, boys taught by Group *B* teachers scored significantly lower than girls, while there were no significant differences between the scores of boys and girls taught by Group *A* teachers. These results suggest that pupil performance can be depressed as well as raised by teacher expectations. Both groups of teachers managed to support their beliefs.

Palfrey's (1973) report on the expectations for their pupils held by two head-teachers, revealed an alarming influence of such expectations on pupils' self-concepts. Two small secondary schools, one boys' and one girls' in a Welsh coal-mining area, were involved in the study. The headmaster of the boys' school saw his pupils as unlikely to have any high scholastic or occupational aspirations and equally unlikely to be favourably disposed towards school or to accept its norms. The headmistress of the girls' school took quite a different view. She maintained a fairly traditional school regime, trying to encourage pupils by awarding prizes, merit marks and so on. She believed that most of her girls would get a worthwhile job on leaving school, whereas the boys' school head thought that very few of his pupils were likely to find themselves in worthwhile employment. The self-concepts of fourth-year pupils in each school reflected similar attitudes towards their future. Palfrey argues that these differences in what we may call headteacher style were important factors influencing their pupils' self-concepts. He expected that the boys would have measurably lower self-concepts than the girls. The pupils seemed to agree with their respective headteachers about their future jobs. As many as 55 per cent of the girls thought that they would get a good job after leaving school whereas only 20 per cent of the boys thought so. It has to be said that this study has considerable weaknesses. There are no statistical tests of the results and no control group was employed.

A simple observation schedule was used by Ensor (1976) to record teacher–pupil dyadic interactions in four separate classrooms. Two groups of pupils in each classroom were identified; those with a high self-concept of their abilities (SCA) and those with a low SCA. Ensor found that the high-SCA children received more favourable communication from their teachers, initiated more acceptable behaviour patterns with their teachers and were more favourably evaluated by their teachers. In turn the low-SCA children received more behavioural criticisms from their teachers, initiated less acceptable behaviour patterns with their teachers and were less favourably evaluated by their teachers than their high-SCA counterparts.

Nash (1973) noted significant positive correlations between the teachers' perceptions (based on Kelly's personal construct theory of personality) and the pupils' own estimates of their class positions. A rank order of relative ability within the class was also found, derived from the pupils' estimates of each other's positions, and this too was found to correlate positively and significantly with the teachers' perceptions of their pupils. In a study of feedback on a maths test, Callison (1974) administered to 28 eight year-olds the first half of the Piers–Harris Self Concept Scale followed by a maths test. One half of the group were told they had made high scores on the maths test; the other half were informed they had performed poorly. The second half of the self-concept scale was then completed. The children given negative feedback showed a significant decrease in self-concept score on the second half of the Piers–Harris scale compared to the first half. Pupils given positive feedback showed no significant change, possibly because their sound maths performance had been expected by them and was no surprise. This study demonstrates the power of even one single instance of negative feedback to exert considerable influence on the self-concept. Other support for the expectation effect comes from a study by Burstall (1970) concerned with the teaching of French to low-ability children at primary school. She developed and administered a scale measuring the attitudes of teachers towards teaching French to such children. After two years she found that low-scoring children in the sample of slow learners were found to be concentrated in a small number of schools where the teachers had expressed a negative attitude towards the teaching of French to low-ability children.

Children bearing first names judged desirable by teachers tend to have more positive self-concepts (Garwood 1976). First names were also found to lead to different expectations so that name stereotyping plays some role in the classroom.

Harari and McDavid's (1973) research too pointed to the direct influence of the name-stereotyping phenomenon in teaching practices. Harari and McDavid asked experienced teachers to grade children's essays (previously judged as comparably equivalent, neither good nor bad) which were linked to authorship by a selected desirable or undesirable first name. Essays written by students with desirable first names received significantly higher scores than the same essays bearing undesirable first names. The indication is that students' first names are related to teachers' expectations of students' achievement behaviour.

These findings suggest that children with first names which teachers consider desirable may have better self-concepts and higher achievement scores than students whose first names are considered undesirable by teachers.

Studies That Failed to Produce Expectancy Effects

One thorough investigation repeating the Pygmalion experiment by Claiborn (1969), failed to find any evidence for expectancy effects. Twelve first-grade (6 years) classes were divided equally into 'biased' and 'unbiased' groups. In the 'bias' groups teachers received a list of some 20 per cent of the students who could be expected to show 'intellectual blooming'. These students were chosen at random. Two months later re-tested showed no relative gains in learning among the experimental group and no changes were observed in the teacher–pupil interactions. The author concludes, reasonably enough, that this failure to repeat the findings of Rosenthal and Jacobson points to the need for further research before the expectancy phenomenon is accepted as a psychological fact, though the time span of the study was rather short for the effects to show through.

Fleming and Anttonen's (1971) study also failed to show expectancy effects. The study involved thirty-nine teachers of 7 year-olds. The sample of more than 1000 children was divided into four groups. Different information about the tested abilities of each of these groups was given to the teachers:

1. traditional IQ scores,
2. IQ scores inflated by 16 points,
3. no IQ score, and
4. Primary Mental Abilities Test.

The children were tested at the start and at the end of the study. The hypothesis, that children with inflated IQ scores would show greater relative gains in learning than others, was not upheld. There were no significant differences of any kind. On the question of expectancies they comment (p. 251):

> the way in which teachers influence pupil behaviour appears to be a far more subtle and complex phenomenon than some have suggested. The body of knowledge and attitudes of teachers about testing, their personal characteristics and their ways of dealing with children seem to be far more critical for pupil growth than intervention *per se*. The present study suggests that teachers assess children, reject discrepant information, and operate on the basis of previously developed attitudes towards and knowledge about children and tests.

In order to explain such inconsistent results, Hargreaves (1972) has made a significant attempt to draw together in a theoretical perspective the relationship between teachers' expectations, self-concepts and pupils' academic achievement. Hargreaves argues that three variables, the teacher's notion of the pupil's ability, the pupil's own idea of his ability and whether or not the pupil regards the teacher as a significant other, all help to bring about the self-fulfilling prophecy effect. In Hargreaves's scheme the pupils most likely to fulfil the teachers' expectations will be (a) those who are perceived as bright by the teacher, who perceive themselves as bright, and who perceive the teacher as a significant other and (b) those who are perceived as dull by the teacher whom they regard as a significant other.

Where the perceptions of the teacher and the pupil are incongruent and where the teacher is not seen as a significant other there is unlikely to be a manifestation of the expectancy effect. Hargreaves's scheme relates entirely to what is perceived by the teacher and the pupil. The scheme certainly offers an explanation for both the positive and the negative results of the experiments into the expectancy effect. It may be that children reported to their teachers as 'spurters' and so perhaps treated favourably will develop enhanced self-concepts and improved performance provided that they regard the teacher as a significant other. If this is correct, and it sounds reasonable, then there is clearly little point in attempting further expectancy studies without taking into account the pupils' existing self-concepts and the extent to which they regard the teacher as a significant other. It may be too that the age of the pupil affects the chances of expectations becoming a reality. Certainly the effect is stronger with younger children, so caution is required in generalizing to secondary schools or colleges. Primary-school teachers, after all, spend hours in the presence of their pupils daily, with numerous opportunities for influence that the high-school or college teacher never has. This increases the importance of a single teacher's expectations in the primary-school classroom. In the early school years children develop academic self-concepts and are not equipped to weigh the credibility of teachers as more mature students are. In this sense, the impact of expectations on students' performance may be reduced in a high school or college.

HOW IS THE EXPECTANCY EFFECT COMMUNICATED?

Generally, the expectancy effect occurs when the teacher is regarded as a significant other and reveals his perception of the pupil in verbal and non-verbal ways.

By Verbal Communication

While occasionally a tired or frustrated teacher may declare to a student that he or she is incapable of learning, the message is not usually stated so directly. Rather, the verbal signals are likely to be more subtle. Brophy and Good (1974) suggest that differential treatment emerges through the frequency and quality of verbal contacts between the teacher and the individual student.

Teachers tend to communicate low expectations to pupils by calling on low-achievers less frequently than on high achievers. Therefore, the low-achieving student is deprived of a critical opportunity to demonstrate or acquire knowledge in the classroom. Even when the student volunteers an answer, he or she is less likely to be chosen than a high-achieving student. Studies reveal that the difference becomes more pronounced as pupil numbers increase. It seems reasonable to assume that, over time, the student adapts to this treatment by attempting less and less.

More striking instances of the way teachers communicate their expectations lie in the quality of verbal exchanges. Praise and criticism are staple teacher responses to pupil performance. Differences in expectations, however, dictate widely varying patterns for high and low achievers. For the low-achieving student, the prospects are, at best, mixed. Some teachers praise any response such a student makes without regard for accuracy or appropriateness. While the teacher's intentions are probably sympathetic, Brophy and Good (1974) aptly note that praising inaccurate responses may only emphasize the student's academic weaknesses. The reactions of the low achiever's peers to his or her undeserved praise are likely to offset any positive effects on future performance. Students value accurate feedback from their teachers. Overpraising inadequate responses does little to develop academic self-esteem and may damage credibility with pupils.

In contrast, some teachers frequently are overly punitive toward low achievers. Studies reveal two ways in which this tendency may be verbalized in classes. One way low expectations are communicated occurs when teachers praise the correct responses of low-achieving students less frequently or vigorously than those of high-achieving students. Sometimes, correct responses are even ignored. Can the student in this circumstance fail to infer that he or she is not expected to perform adequately?

Criticism also becomes a vehicle of a teacher's expectations for a student's performance. Low-achieving students are substantially more likely to be criticized for incorrect responses than their high-achieving peers. The inappropriateness of this teacher behaviour can hardly be overstated. It is one thing to correct a wrong answer and quite another to criticize a student for attempting to respond. The disproportionate amount of criticism given these students conveys a message that they are failures. As Brophy and Good (1974, p. 331) state,

> The situation is clear for lows in certain classes: if they respond, they are more likely to be criticized and less likely to be praised; thus, the safest strategy is to remain silent and hope that the teacher will call on someone else.

Children need positive verbal and non-verbal reinforcement just as they need nutritional food. Treated with apathy and indifference they become apathetic and indifferent. Extinction of responses to the school environment occurs as the school environment ceases to provide positive reinforcement. Just as a child who is not receiving adequate meals is more vulnerable to illness so a child who is feeling some-what negative about himself is more susceptible to the effects of even more negative feedback.

Even run of the mill comments can be interpreted by a child as reflections of himself and converted into vital self-concepts. For instance the teacher might say,

> Peter, I want you to play the King in our play, you always stand tall and straight; John you can be the jester, just behave as you do when you are acting

the fool in class; Stephen you will have to be the page boy—there are no lines to speak this time—you forgot your lines in the last play so this part should suit you fine.

Such comments reveal significant others' expectations and beliefs about one. The child learns that this is him, tall and regal, or a fool, or an incompetent learner in the example above. He is apt to produce behaviour in line with this conception of himself—he will live up to his reputation.

Canfield and Wells (1976) use the term 'killer statements' to describe the means by which a student's feelings, thoughts, and creative behaviours are 'killed off' by another person's negative comments, physical gestures, or other behaviour. These actions may be little more than a teacher's suddenly stiffened spine when a child of another race touches him—or as elusive as a teacher who seldom calls on certain children in the classroom. But they may be far more overt involving a verbal barrage telling the child he is worthless, or incapable, or irresponsible. I have heard teachers say to a child such things as:

'I have never met a pupil as stupid as you.'

'Unless you have something sensible to say which is never, just sit quietly.'

'You are not to be trusted.'

'You are not worth me wasting my time on.'

What damage such statements inflict on the child's feelings about himself is unknown but there can be few who find such negative experiences a spur to their performance and who are capable of fighting back to prove the teacher wrong in the long run.

By Non-Verbal Communication

But with every verbal message we communicate our real feelings with non-verbal output or 'body language'. We may speak with our tongues but we communicate with our whole bodies (Argyle 1975). The non-verbal message lies in the teacher's tone of voice, physical appearance, body stance, facial expression, gestures and physical proximity. Eye contact, especially looking directly at a particular student, can signal, 'I am sincere in what I say, and my words are aimed directly at you.' A warm tone of voice, a neat physical appearance, a friendly smile, and direct eye contact all communicate that the student really is accepted. A teacher's aloof behaviour, forced smile, tightly crossed arms, or indifferent manner may say more clearly than words, 'I don't care for you'.

Students are quick to spot conflicts between what teachers say and what their non-verbal behaviour communicates. It is easy to lie to a pupil verbally about their performance and your acceptance of them. It is almost impossible to lie with non-verbal signs; they make real feelings obvious.

Two other important non-verbal signals constantly available in the classroom are time and spatial relationships. Low achievers are often given less class time (e.g. opportunities to answer questions) than their peers, although private contacts with their teachers (e.g. tutorials) are about equal for the two groups of students. In a typical lesson, however, teachers appear unwilling to wait for low-achieving students to respond to questions who are also quickly passed over if their answers are incorrect. High-achieving students, by contrast, are likely to have more time to answer. Should they answer incorrectly, the high achievers are given more second chances to improve their responses. The teacher's apparent willingness to devote more time to the high-achieving students suggests a difference in performance standards. Students cannot fail to recognize this difference and infer something about their academic worth from the teacher's use of time.

Similarly, spatial relationships reveal teachers preferring students whose achievement level is high. Brophy and Good (1974) summarize studies which indicate that, when a teacher establishes a seating pattern for a class, low-achieving students are placed further away from the teacher. This physical message of space is ultimately translated into a psychological message of rejection for some students, particularly the low achievers. Their distance from the teacher decreases the likelihood that they will be noticed as individuals. Thus another element is added to a cycle perpetuating mediocre performance. The students with the greatest need for the teacher's attention and efforts are in the least desirable position to obtain them.

Brophy and Good's (1974) synthesis of studies on the communication of expectations depicts a grim reality of classroom life. Some students are, by virtue of a teacher's expectations, given an impoverished atmosphere for learning. This discussion should alert you to some of the ways in which teachers not only reveal, but repeatedly reinforce, their expectations for student performance, and their view of the student himself which the student so easily comes to accept as valid.

HOW TO COUNTERACT THE NEGATIVE ASPECTS OF THE EXPECTANCY EFFECT

It would seem that the expectancy effect functions when the pupil accepts the teacher as a significant other (Hargreaves 1972) and when the perceptions of both pupil and teacher are reasonably congruent. A bright child who is informed he is incompetent will tend to disregard the message and possibly devalue the person communicating it. Hence the greatest effect on pupil self-concept occurs when a child receives what to him is proof of his low ability, poor performance or other negative attribute from the teacher in her role as a significant other. It has been argued by many workers that the expectancy effect is harmful even to those with positive self-esteem who receive congruent messages. This is because even this is seen as unfair and discriminatory in that it 'artificially' raises the achievement of pupils who are highly thought of. The high achievers get an extra bonus and the poorly achieving ones an additional handicap. The message for ordinary teachers is that unexplored assumptions about pupils' potential are possibly influencing their interactions with their pupils in ways which, for some, at least, will be unhelpful to them. And we can suppose that a teacher who is aware of her attitudes and who has made herself conscious of how they influence her actions is more likely to give all her pupils equal opportunities within her class.

The impression is often created by research into teachers' expectations that teachers are peculiarly insensitive towards the children they teach, continually misperceiving and misinterpreting the reality of the classroom. This, of course, is a gross exaggeration. It may, however, be accurate for a few teachers and it is not unreasonable to suppose that it does apply to the interaction of some teachers with some of their pupils.

Interact Evenly with All Pupils

Probably without being aware of it, some teachers tend to interact unevenly with their pupils, communicating positive feedback to some, negative to others, while neglecting yet others. The problem of favouritism and its negative influences on both self-concept and school achievement has been documented by House and More (1974) and Insel and Jacobson (1975).

A way to reduce or eliminate favouritism is to be systematic rather than to rely on a random pattern of interaction in which the teacher will most likely call on those students thought to have the correct answer. Through rotating assignments, seating charts, check sheets, or other means, the teacher tries to ensure that each student is invited to participate, that the teacher's attention is equally spread, and that time is taken for some personal contact with all students.

Talk with All Pupils

It is difficult to overestimate the importance of the time reserved for one-to-one contacts with individual students. Although it may be difficult with large classes, it is vital that the teacher squeeze in a few moments for semiprivate chats. These chats last just a few seconds, but they can be powerful in their effects on pupil self-attitudes. This habit of trying to reach all students is particularly important for relating with the quiet, submissive, subdued student who can easily be overlooked and ignored.

Teachers should always be prepared to listen and attend to pupils. By this he shows concern and acceptance. How can a pupil feel of value and accepted if a teacher continues to mark some work, keeping his eyes glued to the paper while the pupil is carrying on a conversation with him? The teacher merely signals disinterest and a lack of concern.

Praise Pupils Realistically

Praise should be based on honest performance. While praise generally produces increases in effort compliments tossed out to students with little or no justification quickly lose all meaning. Researching the dangers of excessive praise shows that many young people simply 'tune out' the frequent verbal praise of adults (Brophy and Evertson 1976), a result probably due to the unrealistic amount of praise distributed by some teachers, parents and friends.

The importance of realistic praise has been demonstrated by Rowe (1974), who found that students ranked poorest by teachers actually received more verbal praise than those ranked best. It was difficult, however, to determine what the lowest students were being praised for; as much as 59 per cent of the praise did not appear attached to correct responding. Rowe commented that the lower students generally receive an ambiguous signal; in other words, what these students did or did not do seemed unrelated to the praise they received. In comparison, top students received less verbal praise, but the praise they did receive was more pertinent to their responses. What Rowe's research means for teachers is that actions taken to encourage academic achievement and self-regard must be realistic and relevant to honest performance. To inform a child that although he is still getting many of his spellings wrong, he has now learned correctly a couple of last week's spelling mistakes and that this is a pleasing improvement, will do his self-esteem, his self-expectations and his future performance more good than lavishly expressing delight at how good a speller he has become when he knows he is not from the objective proof of this week's spelling test. Few students are fooled by this sham; the student knows who he is and what he is and what he can do based on actual experience. No pass mark can make him deny his experiences when he must work alongside his classmates each day. This does not mean that the student does not want to get a good mark or want to believe that he is doing his work satisfactorily. Whatever he wants to believe must ultimately be tested against the reality of his experiences. Teachers who behave in this fashion probably do so out of a false notion of kindness. Teachers use a variety of ruses to encourage poor achievers not to feel too bad about themselves. They may divide their class into three or four groups, call them after colours or species of bird, but never make any reference to the ability level of each of these groups. This game teachers play amuses the students. Each student is not only aware of which group he is a member, but he is also able to rank the groups according to ability. Where ability grouping is used throughout an entire school, the students have little difficulty in distinguishing the various ability levels. The kindest approach, however, would be to be completely honest with the students.

When children have the security that the teacher accepts them for what they are as worthy beings, there is no need to give false praise or to disguise the facts with a coating of sugar. If children know the teacher is on their side, they can profit from the truth about their achievements and constructively build upon the knowledge of their needs and current weaknesses. Indeed, there is no other way to assist them in appraising their present progress and establishing plans in terms of what is to be accomplished next. Confronting reality in an atmosphere of warmth and acceptance is imperative for an accurate view of self. For example, Sharp and Muller (1978) report that when self-concept was lowered by presenting failure information in a supportive manner, subsequent learning performance was not affected, but when it was lowered by presenting failure information in a critical manner, subsequent learning was impaired. This suggests that although a decline in the positiveness of self-concept resulted from the supportive presentation of realistic negative information about academic ability, academic performance was not similarly affected.

Set Tasks to Suit Individuals

In terms of prescriptions, Good and Brophy (1973) argue persuasively that the notion of one standard for all students is arbitrary and inappropriate. Teachers must exploit every opportunity to individualize instruction. All students should satisfy the minimal performance standards for a curriculum, but provision should be made for students to work from their level towards realistic rather than arbitrary goals. Furthermore, teachers must become convinced of the value of rewarding each student for gains that are made in respect of individuals' desires. There is no reason why students must always be compared to a total class or group. Somewhere in the curriculum and during each day, students must be given opportunities to work to their own expectations, and they should be rewarded when they make significant gains in these endeavours.

The weakest link in the vicious circle of teacher's expectation and the self-fulfilling prophecy which is the best place to overcome it, is academic performance which can be manipulated by the teacher providing realistic tasks and expectations within the pupil's capabilities. However, success cannot simply be equated with getting work finished. Attaining high scores for which little effort is required to ensure full marks can be boring and frustrating, as it provides no positive experience. Similarly, work that is too difficult, quite beyond the knowledge and competency of the pupil, is equally frustrating and anxiety provoking. Hence, successful experiences need to be perceived phenomenologically from the point of view of the pupil. This perspective suggests that success has two components: first, a clearly delineated goal that is potentially attainable, and second, progress towards that goal. Of course, the teacher guides the child to suitable goals and provides an environment in which the child is led forward academically in stages, competing against his previous best rather than against externally imposed standards he may never be able to attain. Even the most handicapped child can be successful.

Innovations intended to foster a positive self-concept and high self-esteem have been introduced into schools, but many of these innovations have little theoretical or experimental support and tend to be ineffective. For example, educational innovations that focus on the open classroom or allow the child complete expressiveness or exploration do not neccessarily foster a positive self-concept or self-esteem. Such well-intentioned procedures often establish conditions that are likely to leave the child feeling uncertain of his skills and strengths as he has no standards to refer to.

So the axiom, nothing succeeds like success, can work in the classroom. Reinforcement can be provided for all pupils by programming work to suit individuals, by placing demands on students which can be met without fear of failure. Therefore the task cannot be too easy as this removes satisfaction, or too hard as this causes anxiety and failure. There must be a slight mismatch between existing performance and what will be required to succeed. Hunt's (1971) proposals about intrinsic motivation seem very relevant here. Teachers must accept individual differences rather than assume that most pupils can attain the same levels at the same time.

The mandate is clear: to help a child develop a positive self-concept, one must help him select experiences which provide a challenge, and at the same time help him maximize his opportunities for success.

This is more easily said than done, because it demands that there can be no pre-determined standards for an entire class. Each student must be viewed as a separate entity and learning tasks must be tailored, as far as possible, for each student even though the entire class is being taught at the same time. To insist that the class standards exist is to ignore the fundamental principles of child growth and development which state that children grow, develop and learn at differing rates.

CONCLUSION

A teacher can get more out of a student – and lead him to get more out of himself—by building him up through encouragement than by destroying him. We need to stress the positive, the fact that we expect him to succeed rather than give the impression we would be surprised if he succeeded. It is particularly important that the child's first attempts at a task are successful. Some degree of failure is inevitable, but he should not fail too soon, nor too often. The child faced with unrealistic goals or impossible demands will either have to incorporate failure as a part of his self-image or avoid conflict by being uninterested. This pattern is far too common in schools. Every teacher is in his own way a psychologist. Everything he does, says or teaches has, or could have, a psychological impact. What he offers helps children to discover their resources and their limitations. He is the central figure in countless situations which can help the learners to realize and accept themselves or which may bring humiliation, shame, rejection and self-disparagement.

Although the teacher can exert considerable influence on the shaping of a child's self-concept, ultimately that self-concept is constructed by the child himself. The teacher's treatment, beliefs and expectations are part of the child's experiences and thereby influence the child's developing self-concept. The issue here is how the teacher's actions are interpreted by the child. Thus we must give the child a major part in the formation and modification of the concepts that he holds. The teacher can provide experiences and guidance but the child's interpretation of the teacher's actions and their significance plays an important role in how the child reacts to these experiences. Although teachers can attempt to provide children with successful experiences, unless the child believes he is responsible for the successes and can attribute them to himself, they do not become part of the self-concept (Weiner 1970). Nor do children necessarily accept all kinds of treatment and information to the same extent or passively. Children sift, reject, seek, and avoid information; they interpret experiences in light of the concepts they have formed; they do not accept information from adults they do not trust or who have rejected them as readily as they do from adults who have accepted them and they trust. Studies of teachers' expectations, whether experimental or naturalistic, suggest that certain teachers' characteristics are related to the likelihood that they will form the rigidly inappropriate expectations for a student's performance that are the cause of Pygmalion effects. These characteristics may be considered in terms of a teacher's attitude to self. Teachers need to be sensitive to the biases and stereotypes they hold and examine these seriously in relation to their behaviour in the classroom. After all, it is the 'teacher expectation of pupil' and the vicious circle it triggers that will determine largely the child's self-image, and ultimately academic success or failure. We will be considering such teacher characteristics, teachers' preferred teaching styles, and teacher training in relation to teachers' and pupils' self-concepts in the following chapters.

SUMMARY

In this chapter the central place of the teacher as an agent influencing the developing self-concept of the student is emphasized. Teachers tend to have a model of what an 'ideal' pupil should be and pupils come into the school context with an existing level of self-esteem predisposing the pupil to function at a particular level. This interaction between teacher expectation and pupil performance tends to firm up the pupil's existing level of self-concept of academic ability. In this way both teacher expectations and pupil self-concept become self-fulfilling prophecies.

A child who is confident and has high self-esteem when he enters school will want to maintain this positive self-concept both in his own eyes and in the eyes of others. He attempts to fulfil the expectations he perceives teachers have of him and, in attempting to live up to them, provokes favourable reactions from his teachers. Teachers' favourable judgements are likely to enhance his self-image even more. Thus the vicious circle is set in action and we have the makings of an ideal, successful pupil—or a typically unsuccessful one, in the case of a child who starts off with a low degree of self-esteem. The cycle is self-perpetuating. High esteem leads to success and approval from others. This in turn enhances self-esteem. If a pupil commences with low self-esteem, unfavourable reactions from teacher confirm his and the teacher's original expectations. If teachers anticipate poor work, they usually get it. Teachers typically communicate their performance expectations for students through the quantity and quality of their verbal interactions with individual students. Non-verbal signals of teacher expectations are expressed through the degree of attention given individual students, the quality of feedback and physical proximity permitted.

When teachers believe that students are able, valuable and worthwhile, and when they view teaching as the process of intentionally inviting students to see themselves in positive ways and to reach beyond their present performance, then pupils are more likely to have a clear picture of their potential as human beings and to realize what they can achieve. No person can take advantage of an opportunity if he cannot be brought to believe that he has possibilities for growth and can operate successfully.

Such Pygmalion effects are neither simple nor universal. The popular notion that many or most teachers exert such drastic effects on student performance is erroneous. While teachers' expectations are unavoidable in the classroom, self-fulfilling prophecy effects do not necessarily occur. Pupils must accept the teacher as a significant other if expectations are to have even minimal influence. The efficacy of expectation may also be mediated by the age of the pupil, with increasing age reducing the effect. To avoid selling students the idea that they are incompetent, thereby cheating them of any possibility of success, teachers must provide honest appraisal and evaluation, while at the same time avoiding too obvious a comparison with other students. Confrontation with reality in an atmosphere of warmth and acceptance is imperative if one is to get an accurate view of self. False praise for poor performance is ineffective. Pupils must be provided with valid educational experiences in which they can have success and from which they can draw the inference that they are successful.

Teacher expectancies and goals for the student must be set individually; each student must be given experiences that are congruent with his own particular abilities, needs and interests.

Further Reading

Elashoff, J. and Snow, R. E. (1971) *Pygmalion Reconsidered,* Ohio: Jones.

Brophy, J. E. and Good, T. L. (1974) *Teacher–Student Relationships,* New York: Holt, Rinehart and Winston.

Hargreaves, D. H. (1972) *Interpersonal Relations and Education,* London: Routledge.

Insel, P. and Jacobson, L. (1975) *What Do You Expect?* Menlo Park, California: Cummings.

10

Teachers' Self-Concepts

The more that a person accepts himself, the less is he threatened by the experience of being known by others. Jourard (1971, p. 76)

INTRODUCTION

Throughout this book, there has been theory and research presented consistently to suggest that low self-concept children are anxious, touchy, self-rejecting, feel unworthy, have difficulty in interpersonal relationships and generally show poor social and emotional adjustment. It would therefore seem a reasonable supposition to infer that teachers and student teachers who are low in self-esteem equally have more difficulties of an emotional and social nature in their school related activities, show anxiety and stress, and, in general, will be less able teachers, eliciting less respect from colleagues, and less able to promote positive self-esteem in their charges.

One of the disturbing features of the plethora of research into teacher education and teacher effectiveness, is the relative absence of studies investigating the role of teacher self-concept on teacher behaviour and effectiveness. There is no reference in the monumental *Second Handbook of Research on Teaching* (Travers 1973) to either self-concept or self-esteem despite the fact that the handbook reviews many hundreds of studies.

Research on teacher education and teacher effectiveness is pervaded by a primitive simplicity and a reluctance to acknowledge the complex of human motivation and behaviour. No real understanding of teacher effectiveness can be gleaned without taking into account

1. motivational aspects of classroom behaviour,
2. that teacher and pupil behaviour are reflections of attitudes and values derived from outside the classroom confines,
3. that teaching is not a science or a mechanistic activity but is a process of inter-actions capable of many interpretations and outcomes, and

4. that pupils and teachers are not passive agents in an instructional system but humans replete with the same drives, needs, strengths and weaknesses they use in the world outside.

In other words any account of teaching and learning that does not invoke the fundamental human nature of classroom interaction and behaviour is an invalid one. Teaching behaviour is an extension of daily behaviour in that it exemplifies the ways a person habitually copes with tasks and with people.

We have seen that self-concept and achievement are clearly associated and that teachers' expectations serve to enhance, maintain, or worst of all diminish, pupils' self-esteem. So now we turn to the teachers themselves.

It can be assumed that teachers generally intend their behaviours to have a positive effect on pupils and that negative consequences of their actions are therefore inadvertent. Intent, however, does not matter to the child. It is the child's interpretation of the teacher's behaviour to which the child responds. Because of the social origin of the self-concept, the quality of the interpersonal environment within the classroom also monitors the self-attitudes of many pupils. The teacher–pupil encounter is permeated on the teacher's side by his general outlook and philosophy of life. We have concentrated on pupils up to now, but, of course, teachers also possess self-concepts which affect their own and the pupils' behaviour, their ability to build sound relationships with the pupils, their style of teaching, and their perceptions and expectations of themselves as teachers and of children as learners.

When reminiscing about childhood days, most adults can recount a story beginning, 'Once I had a teacher who . . .' usually about some incident that had a tremendous impact on them. Such incidents tend to be interpersonal ones involving, for example, support, raised self-esteem and concern, or humiliation in front of the class, embarrassment, unfairness in evaluation and destruction of self-confidence. The teacher's power to humiliate or humour, to hurt or to heal is beyond doubt.

CHARACTERISTICS OF EFFECTIVE AND INEFFECTIVE TEACHERS

In a study of the effect of the teacher's personality on classroom interaction Bowers and Soar (1962) found that the best predictive scales on the MMPI for being a 'good' teacher as assessed by observers in the classroom, were (a) the psychopathic deviate, low scores indicating maturity, responsibility, and personal and social loyalty; (b) schizophrenia, with low scores indicating warmth and interest; (c) hysteria, with low scores indicating little distortion in perception.

Studies by Hart (1934), Bousfield (1940) and Witty (1947) suggest that at all levels of teaching it was the teacher's personal style of communicating what he knew that affected the response of the learners to the teacher as a person and the achievement levels reached. Teachers who were aloof, overbearing and unable to interact with the learners were assessed most negatively by the latter. Similarly, other workers, e.g. Cogan (1958) and Reed (1962) have found that it was the effectiveness of the teacher in creating a warm, supportive interpersonal environment which helped student performance.

Moreover, pupil behaviour is a major outcome of teacher behaviour since the teacher is a necessary though not sufficient condition for purposeful pupil performance, and pupil behaviour is a response to the way the teacher provides situations for learning in which the pupils are initiates.

For example, Ryans (1961) demonstrated that in elementary school, high positive relationships exist between observed 'productive pupil behaviour'—alertness, participation, confidence and responsibility—and observed patterns of behaviour in the teacher which reflect understanding, empathy, warmth, friendliness. In secondary schools the same relationships were found to exist but were not so pronounced. Spaulding (1963) showed that the self-concepts of pupils were apt to be more positive in classrooms in which the teacher was 'socially integrative' and 'learner supportive'.

A basic assumption derived from self theory is that persons behave in ways consistent with their beliefs. It follows then that what teachers believe about themselves is a critical factor in their effectiveness. Lembo (1971) summarizes the self view of influential teachers suggesting

1. The teacher sees himself as being competent to cope with life's challenges and problems. He believes that he is capable of accepting each phase of living, of rolling with the punches. He does not view himself as having major failings.
2. He sees himself as being accepted, needed and wanted by others. He believes that his judgement and skills are valued and that others see him as being a worthy person. In short he has high self-esteem.

Using the Piers–Harris self-concept scale Cheong and Wadden (1978) examined the effects on fourth, fifth and sixth grade pupils' self-concept when they were taught by two extreme, significantly different groups of teachers: one group were the most experimental or the least dogmatic, and the other were the least experimental or the most dogmatic. The result of the study was that pupils who were taught by the most experimental group of teachers had significantly higher self-concepts than pupils who were taught by the least experimental group of teachers.

Of 92 teachers in a study by Cummins (1960) seven were found to have attitudes to themselves and their pupils which had the dangerous potential of blighting the lives of their pupils. This pernicious influence was indexed by these seven low-esteem teachers claiming the following items were characteristic of their teaching:

1. Rejects those students who do not like her.
2. Puts students to the test whenever possible to strengthen him.
3. Spurs student to greater effort by making him ashamed of his inadequacies.
4. Introduces considerable competition into her classes.
5. Anticipates students' efforts to cheat in examinations.
6. Conditions students to face the hard realities of adult life.
7. Protects students from a natural tendency toward delinquency.
8. Punishes student in proportion to the seriousness of his offences.

Heil, Powell and Feifer (1960) related student achievement to interaction between different teacher and student personalities. They compared the various teacher–pupil personality combinations in terms of pupil's achievement, teacher's knowledge, and classroom settings. Using scores from achievement tests as their criterion measure, they found that the well integrated (healthy, well-rounded, flexible) teachers were most effective with all types of students. Two other identified types of teacher (fearful and turbulent) were only successful with certain students.

All the above studies are American and contain elements of unreliability in that one of the factors, 'good' or 'effective' teaching (terms which may not be synonymous or easy to define), was derived from observers' assessments. However, the same trends seem to be apparent in that interpersonal relationships appear to be strongly affected by attitudes to self and others.

Effective teachers then appear to differ from ineffective ones by demonstrating:

1. a willingness to be more flexible;
2. an emphatic ability, sensitive to the needs of pupils;
3. an ability to personalize their teaching;
4. an appreciative reinforcing attitude;
5. an easy, informal, warm, conversational teaching manner; and
6. emotional adjustment, self-confidence and cheerfulness.

In other words, effective teachers create a different learning environment from ineffective teachers.

EFFECTIVE TEACHERS HAVE POSITIVE SELF-CONCEPTS

That teachers can be clearly differentiated in terms of their teaching style and its effectiveness on pupil attainment and attitudes has much empirical support, but what causes these personal differences in teaching style? If the teaching style can be identified, can those responsible for producing teachers develop it in their protégés? A substantial clue to the basis of the differences can be found in the literature. For instance, Ryans (1961) found that teachers reported to have high emotional stability frequently named self-confidence as a dominant trait in themselves. They also preferred active contact with people. Those with low emotional stability scores preferred not to have contact with others, possessed less self-confidence and were more authoritarian. In a review of several studies, Combs (1965) was able to conclude that good teachers can be clearly distinguished from poor ones with respect to the following perceptions about people:

1. The good teacher is more likely to have an internal rather than external frame of reference. That is, he seeks to understand how things seem to others and then uses this as a guide for his own behaviour.
2. The good teacher is more concerned with people and their reactions than with things and events.
3. The good teacher is more concerned with the subjective and perceptual experience of people than with objective events. He is, again, more concerned with how things seem to people than just the so-called 'facts'.
4. The good teacher seeks to understand the causes of people's behaviour in terms of

their current thinking, feeling and understanding rather than in terms of forces exerted on them now or in the past.

5. The good teacher generally trusts other people and perceives them as having the capacity to solve their own problems.

6. The good teacher sees others as being friendly and enhancing rather than hostile or threatening.

7. The good teacher tends to see other people as being of worth rather than unworthy. That is, he sees all people as possessing a certain dignity and integrity.

8. The good teacher sees people and their behaviour as essentially developing from within rather than as a product of external events to be moulded or directed. In other words, he sees people as creative and dynamic rather than passive or inert.

We may conclude that the ways in which teachers perceive themselves and perceive students influence how effective their teaching will be. According to Combs (1965) a positive self-concept is a necessary prerequisite for the creation of a supportive classroom environment. This conclusion corroborates an earlier finding by Combs and Soper (1963) that self-confident teachers generally exhibit classroom behaviour that fosters positive pupil self-concepts.

Teachers who feel personally or professionally inadequate, or who dislike teaching, may allow these feelings to colour the classroom dialogue. They may be overtly controlling, authoritarian and defensively hostile toward their pupils. Or they may be excessively and inappropriately non-directive, easily diverted from teaching tasks and indifferent to pupil performance and products. The point is that extreme feelings, or self-concerns, will produce extreme behaviour of one type or another, ranging from hostility towards pupils to unmerited praise and flattery; from low acceptance of pupil ideas to unguided pupil leadership; from a high frequency of convergent questioning to unstructured efforts to pool pupil ignorance.

In a study of teachers' values by Rosenberg (1955) 57 per cent of 'people-orientated' individuals remained in the teaching profession during the two-year period of the study, while only 2 per cent of 'non-people-orientated' individuals did so. In a study of emotionally handicapped children, La Benne (1965) found a highly significant relationship between the teacher's self-concept and the pupil's perception of himself in the classroom, as did Edeburn and Landry (1974) whose self-accepting teachers tended to produce more positive self-concepts in pupils than teachers low in self-acceptance. Schuer (1971) found a significant gain in academic achievement level in disturbed and maladjusted pupils who saw their teachers as possessing a high degree of unconditional regard for them.

Research tells us that positive self-concepts in teachers helps not only their own classroom performance as a confident, unanxious, respected guide to learning, but also pupil performance which flourishes in all respects when the pupil has someone who projects trust and belief in their capacity and has a warm, supportive ethos to enhance his view of himself as someone of worth. Expectancies from such teachers lead to high pupil self-esteem and performance.

As we will see later (Chapter 11) student teachers rated high on teaching practice tended to show significantly higher self-concepts than those rated low

(Garvey, 1970). Success in teaching is certainly associated with a positive view of oneself, confidence and adjustment.

In the broadest sense of the word, good teachers see themselves as good people. Their self conceptualizations are, for the most part, positive, tinged with optimism and coloured with healthy self-acceptance. The self-perceptions of good teachers are like the self-perceptions of any basically healthy person, whether he be a good electrician, a good manager, a good experimental psychologist, or whatever. Clinical evidence has told us time and again that any person is apt to be happier, more productive and more effective when he is able to see himself as positive.

Many of the positive characteristics of successful teachers discovered by previous research experts seem to coincide with Maslow's (1954) notion of the self-actualizing person, whom he sees as a fully functioning, psychologically healthy individual possessing acceptance, spontaneity, autonomy, a democratic nature and creativeness. In the development of his theory, Maslow suggests that the self-actualizing person is indeed the most effective teacher. This relationship has been investigated by at least two previous empirical studies conducted by Murray (1972) and Dandes (1966) both of whom report the self-actualizing teacher as more effective.

Murray (1972) attempted to assess the effect of teacher's self-actualization on his students' perceptions of the teachers' expressed concern. It was hypothesized that students of self-actualizing teachers would perceive their teachers as creating a more growth-promoting atmosphere than non-self-actualizing teachers.

Support was found for this hypothesis and students are aware of the existence of a potentially productive climate. Many studies (e.g. Mason and Blumberg 1969) indicate that the value of learning as perceived by the learner seems to be associated with the quality of the interpersonal relationship which exists between teacher and learner. Hence teachers who feel positive in themselves are likely to create the best learning situations.

These personality characteristics which appear to separate effective from ineffective teachers are clearly related to the self-concept. The role teachers have to play must heighten their awareness of themselves and of others, for teaching is a sharing of self with others. Hence attitudes to self and to others would seem to be of vital importance in influencing interpersonal behaviour in the classroom and as a corollary in influencing preferred teaching style.

ACCEPTANCE OF SELF AND OTHERS

The psychological events occurring within the classroom resemble therapy. The teacher as a significant other must feel and demonstrate unconditional acceptance of the pupil as a person just as the Rogerian therapist does for the patient. In order to do this the teacher must feel secure and not defensive about himself in personal and professional roles.

The extent to which teachers accept themselves, their role and the pupil determines the extent to which they can function positively in the role of significant other. Teachers who are comfortable and not defensive can acknowledge their own limitations while accepting those of their pupils. They can be sympathetic and supportive of pupils while at the same time constructively critical of their performance. This enables such a teacher to use his power as a significant other to produce positive change in pupils. The dialogue between pupil and teacher is more extensive and uncontrolled than a therapy context, and subject to many influences outside the control of either pupil or teacher. So while a theoretical framework assumes that teachers function for the most part as significant others, we must take care not to give them all the blame nor all the credit for the self-concepts of their pupils.

It appears plausible that a person who has low self-esteem and possesses low self-acceptance, would find it difficult to relate easily and sociably with others. He would more likely derogate others as he does himself. Attack is the best form of defence when one is susceptible to evaluating negative feedback from others as congruent with one's opinion of oneself. Additionally, projection allows one to acknowledge that there are people inferior to one, thereby enhancing self-esteem. Thus, it comes as no surprise to find that there are consistently found strong and positive relationships between self-esteem and acceptance of others which, at the extreme, demonstrate a major role for self-concept in determining prejudicial attitudes. The theoretical background to this relationship and the research findings, are vitally important in the educational context since teachers and pupils must interact. To promote pupil self-concept, teachers must be able to adopt the Rogerian counselling principles of warmth, acceptance and genuineness and only teachers who are sufficiently secure in themselves can effect these. Both teachers and pupils need to respect and accept each other and feel free from threats to the self for effective educational processes to function.

Teachers with less positive self-concepts are more likely to demonstrate less than positive acceptance of others who are different, e.g. handicapped, coloured, low social class, low ability children. Pupils, too, can make life pleasant or nasty for other pupils depending on their own self-concept level. It is noted in Chapter 14 how strong the relationship is between acceptance of self and acceptance of others (e.g. Burns 1975).

The possession of positive self-attitudes helps the construction of warm, supportive attitudes towards others, which acts as a therapeutic mechanism to promote the development and continuity of positive self-attitudes in the others. Davidson and Lang (1960) showed that pupils were well able to evaluate their teachers' feelings towards them and those who saw the teacher as one who presented favourable regard to them were the possessors of more positive self-concepts and higher academic performance. Staines (1958) has been able to identify teachers whose verbal input into teaching enhanced pupil self-concepts. Combs (1965) indicated that effective teachers have a more positive attitude to themselves than do less effective teachers.

If a teacher's basic psychological state is one of fear then this teacher is anxious and suspicious in the teaching context and in relationships with pupils, colleagues and parents. Such mistrust likely stemmed from early experiences with authoritarian parents. As a result the teacher may identify with all identity figures and authoritarian roles, adopting negative and controlling behaviours as well as seeking approval from those in command.

If the teacher is to participate in developing individuals with positive self-concepts who function effectively, he must act as a model for this kind of behaviour. The classroom then becomes a social learning environment as well as a place for cognitive gain.

EFFECTIVE TEACHERS FROM THE PUPILS' PERSPECTIVE

Teachers who are effective in influencing pupils' self-concepts for the better tend to possess two major characteristics, credibility and personalism, as seen from the pupils' perspective.

Credibility

Essentially, credibility refers to what students think of you as a teacher. McCroskey, Larson and Knapp (1971) suggest that the attitudes others have toward us consist of several dimensions including competence, character, and intention. When students evaluate the competence of a teacher, they ask if he is qualified by experience and ability to 'know what he is talking about'. When they evaluate a teacher, they wish to know if he is basically honest and fair. They also wish to know his intentions and may ask, 'Is he concerned about me, or just himself?'

To be effective in helping students develop more positive self-concepts teachers must persuade students to view themselves in new ways. Research into the process of persuasion has revealed that a would-be persuader must be perceived in positive ways by those he wishes to persuade (Chapter 7).

Personalism

The most frustrating part of any learning experience is when you are treated in an impersonal way as at registration or sitting examinations in a large hall with many others. As each name is called on the register, or each seat allocated for the examination, the student can feel like an object or a number filed away in a bureaucratic system. We can label such conditions and such communication as 'impersonal'.

A teacher is impersonal when he does not take into account the details which make each pupil a unique human being. The teacher who cannot remember a name or which of his courses the student is attending, conveys that he attaches little significance to the student's existence. Evaluations from such impersonalistic teachers, even very positive ones, are likely to have little impact on a student's self-concept. 'After all', the student is likely to ask, 'Why should I believe this teacher's evaluation of me is accurate when he doesn't even know who I am?' A personalistic teacher, by contrast, convinces us that he is genuinely interested. The personalistic teacher remembers details about us, and in interactions is sensitive to our moods and feelings. In short, when we are convinced that a teacher has a sincere concern for us, and an accurate picture of who we are, we are greatly influenced by that teacher's appraisal. An experimental study by Gergen (1965) discussed in Chapter 7 illustrates this.

COUNSELLING FOR TEACHERS

Although we know that if teachers possess characteristics of empathy, warm acceptance genuineness, and self-worth they can help the growth, development, maturity, improved functioning, improved coping and more functional use of the latent inner resources of the individual pupil, research tends to indicate that few teachers possess high levels of such therapeutic characteristics. Aspy (1975) and Wolf (1971) both found that although different teachers possess different variables such as accurate empathy, interpersonal respect and genuineness which make a difference in the school-related lives of teachers and students, the majority of teachers tend to exhibit minimal levels of these characteristics!

Again in Schultz's (1972) study mean teacher helpful behaviour was well below the mean of the Carkhuff scale. Carkhuff (1969) himself has reported similar findings, and it becomes apparent that if teachers are to be directly responsible for the implementation of affective encounters with children or others, training will be necessary to increase their functional capacity along the dimensions central to helpful communication.

Strenuous and extensive efforts need to be made to prepare teachers who will be sensitive to others, and who view teaching as a human process involving human relationships and human meanings. We need to introduce and expose teachers to sensitive processes and subtle complexities of personality structure. Teaching about group processes does occur in teacher education but, for the most part, in an abstract theoretical vein, unconnected to the students' real needs. Intensive group experiences and counselling can change the self-esteem and self-acceptance levels of participants in a favourable direction. These techniques could be used in both the initial training of teachers and in-service courses. As self-attitudes are learned they can therefore be favourably changed. More importantly for teachers engaged in interpersonal relationships, the same therapeutic climate that brings changes in self-concept also creates increasing levels of acceptance of others. In this way group dynamics and other counselling processes effect a two-pronged attack on the low self-concept person, making him more competent and secure in himself, as well as helping improved interpersonal relations which act as feedback to the blossoming selves of both teacher and pupil. Despite the obvious importance of producing teachers with positive self-attitudes little research has been undertaken and few courses have been operated to modify teacher self-concept.

In the USA during the past two decades teacher educators have turned their attention to their responsibility for developing teachers who are psychologically healthy persons. They have become increasingly aware that concentrating on cognitive development alone is not enough.

One landmark in this growing concern for the personal needs of teachers was Jersild's *When Teachers Face Themselves* (1955) which stresses that teachers should confront their deeply experienced personal needs and provide appropriate gratification for them. This concern with the teacher as a person has been paralleled and influenced by an emphasis on positive mental health or self-actualization by psychologists such as Maslow, Rogers, Combs and Snygg, Jourard and others. Mental health courses have become popular in colleges of education, and workshops for teachers are beginning to focus on teachers as people. But courses in mental health tend to concentrate on gaining information about mental health rather than experiencing personal growth, and the high cost of the special projects devoted to the personal development of teachers has severely restricted the number of teachers who could participate in them. There is a need in teacher education for reaching large numbers of people with specific experiences aimed at self-actualization, at a cost that is realistic.

In his study of self-actualizing people, Maslow (1968) found that his subjects, in comparison with people in general, were characterized fundamentally by a more efficient perception of reality and more comfortable relations with it. A critical part of reality is oneself; because self-actualizing people tend to know themselves better and to be more accepting of what they are, they are freer from the defences and perceptual distortions that tend to thwart effective behaviour in less healthy people. Increased self-understanding and self-acceptance are often the growth outcomes of successful therapy; but therapy, even group therapy, is not generally available in teacher education.

McClain (1970) reports on a mental health course in training that has provided not only the usual cognitive experiences but that has also focused on personal growth for the students. The course described in McClain's report was designed to help self-actualization through increased self-understanding for a whole class at a time. It included readings on mental health as one means of enhancing self-understanding, but in order to ensure personal involvement and (it was hoped) personal growth, the major focus was on the individual student's written analysis of personality test data about himself.

Within the psychoanalytic field, Horney has made a case for self-analysis for those who do not have the services of a therapist. Taylor (1955) has shown that repeated introspection can bring about some of the self-insights anticipated in therapy. An assumption behind this course has been that analysis of extensive personality test data should produce more self-insights than introspection alone. Jourard (1958) developed the idea that a person comes to understand and discover himself only as he discloses himself to another. McClain's (1970) course provided for self-disclosure in the written self-analysis in this case, disclosure to the professor. Feedback of personal test data can enhance self-understanding if the one who receives the information is free to react to it with the one who gives it. With today's large classes, it is not feasible to arrange individual conferences for students to express their reactions, but the written self-reports in this project gave the students an opportunity to express their personal responses to the data. However, these reports were aimed at more than acceptance of personal information; they were designed also to produce self-insights in depth by requiring the cognitive work of finding personal meanings in the data and of communicating those meanings to a reader.

McClain (op. cit.) found that the discussion of self-feelings and attitudes in the mental health course increased self-actualization scores, and decreased the discrepancies between self-concept and ideal self-concept scores.

The highly consistent results from three independent measures of self-actualization were offered as evidence that the experiences of the mental health course helped student teachers make progress toward self-fulfilment. Finally, there were unsolicited reports from the students themselves that the experiences in the course have resulted in personal enhancement. In nearly all of their written reports and in many informal conversations, they said that they were more comfortable with themselves and felt hopeful about their ability to cope with their life problems, according to McClain.

Just as sensitivity, encounter and training group experience can aid a wide range of others to develop more positive feelings for self and others, so too can such experiences function for teachers, and student teachers. Effective teachers who can develop pupils cognitively and as individuals are those who are positive in self-attitudes themselves. Chapter 16 details a set of useful sensitivity exercises devised for college undergraduates which lead to this positive enhancement and understanding of self.

Perkins (1958), using a Q-sort method among 9 and 11 year-olds, has demonstrated that teachers' perceptions of children's self-concept are, in general, positively and significantly related to these children's expressed self-concepts, i.e. most teachers accurately perceive the self-concepts of the children in their class. However, different groups of teachers perceived their pupils' expressed self-concepts with varying degrees of accuracy. It was found that teachers who had completed three years of an in-service, part-time child-study programme showed a greater correspondence between their perceptions of children's self-concepts and these children's expressed self-concepts than did those who had not taken such a child study programme. He suggests that this occurred because the former teachers had greater sensitivity to, and provided for, children's needs far better than the latter group.

The guide to learning must be a secure person. Little headway can be made in understanding others or in helping others to understand themselves unless he is endeavouring to understand himself. The person with low self-esteem sees those with whom he interacts through the bias and distortions of his own needs, fears and anxieties. Only when the teacher has self-awareness and sufficient self-esteem can his own needs (e.g. for recognition, importance, power, etc.) be reduced so that teaching is based on the needs of the children and not those of the teacher. While informal education relieves the teacher of the burden of omniscience, it adds the burden of fallibility, a situation in which the teacher must feel comfortable in admitting to children: 'I don't know much about this. Let's see if we can find out together.'

It seems from this evidence that there is some relationship between intensive group experiences among teachers and students and improvement in the teacher–student relationship. Obviously, shared personal experiences between staff and students are only one way in which a better relationship can be created but the responsibility for enhancing this must go beyond the confines of traditional classroom behaviour and role relationships. An improved teacher–student relationship creates a better learning environment too (Cooper 1975). Mason and Blumberg (1969) found that high-school students judged by independent assessors to have learned the most rated the perceived relational responses of their teachers significantly higher than those students judged to have learned the least. Emmerling (1961) found among 600 pupils and 20 teachers that those teachers receiving high empathy scores were also assessed as significantly more pupil centred, more open to their experiences and more effective in the classroom as judged by the students themselves.

James Hannum (1974) conducted a study designed to help two teachers who felt excessively self-critical to increase their positive self-thoughts and decrease their negative self-thoughts, in other words, to improve their self-esteem. An intensive experimental design involving four phases was employed. Each phase—Baseline, Thought Stopping, Positive Intervention, and Follow-up—lasted approximately two weeks. During all phases of the experiment the teachers observed their positive and negative self-thoughts with the help of wrist counters. Classroom observers coded instances of overt positive and negative behaviour of the teachers. A positive intervention, which used stimulus cues to prompt positive self-thoughts, was effective in increasing the positive thoughts of one teacher. The results of thought stopping (thinking the word 'stop' to inhibit unwanted thoughts) were mixed by two self-report measures and, to some extent, by the external observations of teacher and student classroom behaviour. Teachers reported the reinforcing effect of positive self-thinking; using the wrist counter to record a positive self-thought may have functioned as a reinforcing event. The following conclusions seem warranted:

1. Both interventions (thought stopping and the positive intervention) were associated with changes in the frequency of self-thoughts.
2. Changes in the self-thought frequencies were supported by similar changes in two other self-report measures.
3. Corresponding decreases in overt negative behaviour and increases in overt positive behaviour were found in each case.
4. The techniques of self-observation used in this study were feasible for teachers to use in the classroom.

Questions can be asked on the usefulness of concentrating on self-thought as a means of changing self-esteem rather than teaching a person to be able to cope better. Low self-esteem (high self-criticism and low self-positiveness) can be viewed in two ways, and the intervention chosen may therefore vary accordingly. In one case, the self-criticism may be the result of actual problems and hence it is a realistic response to one's situation. Here an intervention focused upon learning helps behaviours that would take precedence over dealing with the self-critical thoughts. Self-criticism would be expected to decrease as the ability to cope increased.

Self-criticism may occur even though a person appears to be coping well with the environment if the person's evaluative standards are far too strict or harsh. In this latter case, intervention on overt behaviours is unnecessary. The intervention should focus rather on the self-critical thoughts themselves, as in this study, seeking to change the patterns of self-evaluation. The two teachers in this study were chosen not because of classroom problems, but because they indicated they were much too critical of themselves and wanted to change. The possibility of using this technique in the classroom is advantageous over normal group therapy since teaching time is not lost by the teacher being absent, and the cost for the increasing numbers who could be involved in such a programme is relatively lower. However, specialized approaches are not essential, for as Jersild (1955) suggested, the teacher can gain a deeper understanding of his self-concept by asking himself questions like the following:

1. 'Do I regard myself as a crystallized and complete person or one who is still learning and growing?' The latter is one who can critically examine new experiences and is willing to immerse himself into the intellectual and social challenges inherent in the teacher's role. Rogers (1956) has suggested that the continuous development of an individual must include his willingness to be part of a process that is ever changing. Some mistakes are inevitably part of the learning process, but the developing person is one who can be disappointed and learn something from it.

2. 'Do I possess flexible self assurance?' Research in effective teaching consistently demonstrated that successful teaching is related to emotional maturity and self-assurance. Such teachers show more spontaneity, initiative and empathy and fewer negative attributes such as conflict with others, emotional coldness and rigidity in behaviour. If teachers can replace fears and anxieties by self-assurance which can cope with both good times and bad then they are able to be flexible to meet new and dynamic classroom challenges for up to six hours each day with a group of up to forty lively young minds.

3. 'Do I tolerate diverse points of view? Am I comfortable when a pupil takes issue with me? Have I sufficient intellectual flexibility to avoid such dogmatic assertions as, "The only way to teach maths is . . .; the only good text on this topic is . . .; there is only one way to learn this . . ."'. Lack of appropriate perception toward diversity may be shown by irritation when controversial issues are discussed. Lack of tolerance for diversity of opinion may also be reflected in a desire to give 'the answer' quickly in a discussion rather than encourage the clash of differing perspectives and the probable accompanying sharpening of intellectual abilities. With desirable perspective the teacher will encourage an atmosphere where each student will not be afraid of being labelled foolish if he proposes an unconventional idea even if it is extreme.

4. 'Do I see myself as a person able to accept positive criticism, as part of my personal and professional development, and openly discuss my personal and professional problems?'

As the teacher looks in on himself he inevitably sees areas of doubt and uncertainty in his search for meanings and values. The comprehensive study by

Jersild suggests that excessive personal tension may appear in disproportionate resentment, competitiveness, discouragement, efforts to impress or placate, to play the game and play it safe.

Jersild (1955) found that teachers regarded it as useful to discuss their real professional problems in a shared human experience with intimate involvement. Some questions the teacher could profitably raise with himself in order to understand the perceptions he has of his pupils might include the following:

1. Am I aware of my pupils' perception of the environment, especially their feelings, attitudes, beliefs and perceptions about me? Do I see myself through my pupils' eyes?
2. Am I person oriented rather than event or object oriented? Do I like to build personal relationships with my pupils, working alongside them, or maintain an impersonal, disinterested, distant approach? Am I more concerned with the subject matter than with the pupils' needs and perceptions?
3. Do I search for the cause of pupils' difficulties rather than merely being content to consider the child incapable? Do I modify constructively the 'failing' pupil's programme of work so that he is more likely to gain some success, understanding and a sense of achievement? Do I believe in individual differences so that lessons are structured in which each is expected to perform according to his abilities and not to some arbitrary class standard?
4. Do I foster a love for learning and an interest in my subject through my teaching behaviour?

By using these and other similar questions the teacher should gain more insight into his own teaching behaviour; he will begin to think and reflect, an essential start to discovering and understanding oneself and others. Self-understanding precedes understanding of others. All those whose work places them in constant daily transactions with others have an obligation to try to understand themselves, but as Jersild (1955) points out, to gain self-knowledge, one must have the courage to seek it and the humility to accept what one may find. Without self-knowledge a society can only be erudite, never wise. We should not leave such a vital element of learning to sheer luck. It ought to be one of the objectives of a thorough education.

The aim of moving teachers' self-concepts in a positive direction is admitted unashamedly to be that of helping teacher and student growth as a humanistic educational endeavour. As to what we mean by humanistic education and self-growth, we investigate this below.

PHENOMENOLOGICAL PSYCHOLOGY AND HUMANISTIC EDUCATION

In the field of education there is at present a renewed interest in the affective or humanistic dimensions of teaching behaviour, which is compatible with placing a higher priority on learning than teaching. This concern for humaneness, originating from diverse sources, expresses itself in a variety of moods and philosophies.

In his collection of writings dealing with this topic, Carl Rogers (1969) presents the freedom-to-learn notion and directs special attention to the personal qualities and behaviours of teachers concerned with the accomplishment of such student freedom. He prescribes no particular pattern and, in so doing, supports Comb's (1965) view that each teacher must discover effective ways to use his peculiar talents to maximum advantage, the developing process of teaching rather than the mechanistic and structured approach.

Possibly the most concise statements on humanistic education come from the originator of humanistic psychology, Abraham Maslow (1968) who differentiates between intrinsic and extrinsic education by defining intrinsic education as that which changes the person and enables him to move toward his unique potential; and extrinsic education as education that is an end in itself. We noted earlier in this chapter that students of self-actualizing teachers would perceive their teachers as promoting growth (Murray 1966). The findings of this study support the hypothesis that students perceive self-actualizing teachers as more concerned than non-self-actualizing teachers. It is assumed that self-actualizing people who are teaching have chosen to do so of their own free will, that teaching affords them opportunities for self-enhancement. Maslow (op. cit.) refers to the self-actualizing person's need for a particular type of work, which is perceived not as a deficiency need (D-need) but as a being need (B-need), a situation providing for growth of one's unique self. Furthermore, the self-actualizing teacher, by enhancing the attractions and minimizing the dangers, may create growth for his students. This goes beyond the creation of a positive classroom climate to involve using this climate as a means to student growth rather than merely as an end in itself.

It cannot be denied that non-self-actualizing teachers may provide a potential growth/learning climate for some of their students, but this will be for fewer students.

Real learning according to phenomenological psychologists involves the total person rather than merely providing him with facts to be memorized. True learning experiences enable the learner both to discover his own unique or 'idiosyncratic' qualities and to find in himself those features of caring, doing and thinking which make him one with all mankind. Learning in this sense is becoming, and becoming (learning how to be) fully human is the only true learning.

Acknowledging the central role that schools have in our society, the phenomeno-logical and humanistic psychologists claim that educators have the major responsibility of helping students to become more fully developed persons. In this context, the roles of both students and teachers are markedly different from those in traditional classrooms. The student is seen as having a very active role throughout the educational process, including decisions about what is to be learned as well as how and when it is to be studied. The teacher is characterized as a helper who provides a climate in which the student can feel free to develop emotionally as well as intellectually. Of low importance are the most usual notions of the teacher as an authority and source of information.

It was not until 1969 that Rogers published his proposals for education. He made extensive use of his own personal learning experiences in proposing educational practices. One of the fundamental themes is that teaching does not seem to be an interesting or an important process to Rogers but that the student's learning is tremendously important and interesting. But even here it seems to Rogers that the only valuable kind of learning is that which involves self-discovery, self-appropriated, self-initiated learning. This prompted him to theorize that there are two kinds of learning, and to propose that only one type is really appropriate. His delineation of these two types of learning will show that to some extent Rogers is almost as sharply critical of cognitive discovery learning as he is critical of more behaviouristic principles.

Rogers's two basic types of learning which are cast at the extremes along a continuum of personal meaning are 'cognitive learning' and 'experiential learning'. By cognitive learning he refers to those kinds of associate processes which are in practically all traditional psychological learning theories, including some aspects of cognitive theories. This kind of learning requires that the student absorbs some body of knowledge; there is some tendency to emphasize rote factual learning, but Rogers even seems to include more complex associative processes and objectives as well. In contrast, Rogers depicts experiential learning as something which is personally and emotionally meaningful as well as cognitively relevant.

Rogers (1969, pp. 221–37) drew from his psychotherapy theories to identify guidelines as to what constitute personal involvement and kinds of experimental learning. The most fundamental idea is that one must be oneself, without apologies and defensiveness, but with sensitivity and congruence. Such learning occurs when we keep communicating with our own internal feelings and beliefs and also with those of other people whom we encounter. In a sense, one's own experience must be seen as trustworthy and as one's only criteria against which we assess life's experiences. It is extremely satisfying learning to be real (congruent) in relating to others and in encountering persons who are also real.

Rogers sets for education, as he has for psychotherapy, the goal of enabling students to become fully functioning individuals. He holds that the real challenge of education is to find what it takes to produce whole communities of learners who maintain their curiosity about life—a curiosity found universally in infants and too infrequently in adults—and who thirst for continuing education without any sticks or carrots to motivate them. Education for Rogers, and for most humanistic psychologists, must be changed so as to 'free curiosity; to permit individuals to go charging off in new directions dictated by their own interests; to unleash the sense of inquiry; to open everything to questioning and exploration; to recognize that everything is in a process of change' (Rogers 1969, p. 105).

Rogers assumes that all persons have a natural inclination to want to learn. Moreover, he assumes that they will continue their motivation to learn throughout their life unless conditions stifle such a desire. The main idea here is: 'Human beings have a natural potentiality for learning' (Rogers 1969, p. 157). But they will only really learn and understand those things that are meaningful to them.

The real concern should be with those experiences which make it possible for the student to integrate the new information and ideas as part of himself. Rogers assumes that one should avoid those experiences which call for drastic change in one's self-perceptions, as such changes in self-structure can only come about in an emotionally supportive climate when external threats seem to be at a minimum and the classroom is not necessarily like that. He criticizes the allegedly common assumptions that the main truths about the world are already known and that education thus consists of accumulating bricks of factual knowledge and that learning is a passive process. He would see learning as optimally occurring when the student participates responsibly in the learning process and when learning involves 'a continuing openness to experience and incorporation into oneself of the process of change' (1969 p. 163). Evaluation too should be student based so that self-criticism and self-evaluation are primary. Underlying all his writings is the theme that experiential learning as an educational objective can be attained only to the extent that the student himself is involved in the learning process.

Acceptance of these assumptions about the nature and the importance of experiential learning, implies that the teacher's role has been greatly overestimated. Rogers advocates emphasis on the facilitation of learning so that his principles of instruction centre on how one can create an intellectual and emotional climate which will facilitate experiential learning. Not too surprisingly, since these principles were derived from psychotherapy and not education theory they contain many of the same notions that Rogers claims help therapy sessions.

Rogers contends that instruction should be scheduled and planned in accordance with the manner in which pupils are likely to meet problems. Once the student is aware of a problem requiring a solution, the main role of the teacher is to create a climate in which the pupil will feel free and stimulated to learn. Rogers (1969 pp. 164–6) lists ten guidelines for creating such an emotional and intellectual ethos.

1. The teacher must communicate his trust in the students from the very start.
2. He must help students to clarify and articulate their individual and group objectives.
3. He must assume that pupils have intrinsic motivation that will enable them to pursue their studies.
4. He must act as a resource person who makes available the widest range of learning experiences possible for the objectives selected.
5. He should be a resource person for each individual.
6. He should learn to recognize and accept emotional messages expressed within the group.
7. He should be an active participant in the group.
8. He should be open in expressing his feelings in the group.
9. He would maintain empathic understanding of group members' feelings.
10. Finally, he must know himself.

Examples of Practical Methods

Rogers (1969) has identified seven practical methods which in his opinion can facilitate experiential learning.

1. Students should be given the option of participating in an open and free classroom experience, or in the more traditional structured approach.
2. The student and the teacher should develop contracts agreeing as to what is a

meaningful unit of work. In some cases these contracts are also tied to academic grades contingent on the student completing an agreed amount of work at an accepted level.

3. Rogers recommends inquiry training or discovery learning with the aim of understanding and learning how to learn rather than rote learning.

4. Classroom learning can be made personally relevant by having real life experiences simulated in the classroom. Simulation techniques have been used to teach how different political and governmental organizations operate, show the economic aspects of business operations, etc. He favours the approach not only because it captures the interest and the enthusiasm of students but because it gives much of the responsibility for learning to the students.

5. Sensitivity training groups or basic encounter groups are primarily designed to help persons learn about themselves as humans. The learnings include how they feel about themselves and about other people. He characterizes the group as being almost autonomous and having no initially formalized structure until group members evolve their own purposes and working procedures. The object is mainly to help individuals to explore their feelings and to share them with other group members. Rogers reports that they have been used with elementary students as well as adults and that they typically result in increased ability to handle freedom and responsibility.

6. Facilitator learning groups are essentially relatively autonomous student-directed study groups with between seven and ten members. It is a technique which is used with larger classes when it is not otherwise feasible to have extensive student participation in discussions.

7. Given Rogers's strong objections to externally dominated instruction it is surprising to find him advocating the use of programmed instruction. Nonetheless, he does; but he is careful to point out that there are many different ways in which one can use programmed instruction. In brief he sees a role for those many instances in which the student encounters 'gaps in his knowledge, tools which he lacks, information which he needs to meet the problem he is confronting. Here the flexibility of programmed instruction is invaluable' (Rogers 1969 p. 140). Warning against indiscriminate use of programmed instruction (as a substitute for thinking, for example), he proclaims 'that it is one of the most powerful tools which psychology has as yet contributed to the field' (Rogers 1969 p. 141) when it is used to achieve flexibility in education.

The phenomenological psychologists have thus not only raised questions about the methods of instruction advocated by other instructional theorists, but they have also raised questions as to who should set goals for the individual and who should determine educational objectives, and have emphasized the need for examining value systems and the relevance of education for society as a whole. There is a tendency, however, to make the assumption that only by feeling free when learning will a student later be free and creative in real life. This is plausible; it should be submitted to empirical test, however. Additionally, proponents of this approach— like all the others—hold that their theory is unlimited in the range of students and subject matter to which it is applicable. This too needs to be tested. A final criticism is that while we can accept the idea that a person may be 'expert' about his own needs, feelings, beliefs, etc. with regard to psychotherapy, and that the client rather than the therapist should have the major responsibility in the psychotherapeutic relationship, one may question whether the student is 'expert' about educational objectives to the extent that he can know better than professional educators what he should learn. This seems to be one centre of controversy around which more empirical evidence will be required before we can do more than speculate.

SUMMARY

A large collection of research on 'effective' teachers consistently reveals that compared to 'ineffective' teachers, the former have higher self-esteem, feel more positive about themselves, are free from self-doubt and anxiety, and have a positive impact on pupil self-concept and academic performance. Teachers who *accept* themselves are also more likely to accept others, and teachers who *reject* themselves are more likely to reject others. Thus the teacher's attitudes towards himself are an important and basic determinant of whether children will be enhanced or devalued through their contact with him. Teachers who have positive attitudes about themselves and feel confident about their abilities as teachers are more able to relate to others and express their competencies in the classroom. In other words, it is the quality of the relationship that seems most important, and this depends to a large extent on what the teacher is like as a person.

Deliberately planned efforts to guide teachers towards a better understanding of themselves and their interpersonal relationships are rare, but they do work as research on sensitivity and training group effects show. Carl Rogers presents the freedom-to-learn notion and directs special attention to the personal qualities and behaviours of teachers concerned with the accomplishment of such student freedom. The principles of humanistic psychology support the idea that the only true learning is that which totally involves the student as a person.

Further Reading

Brophy, J. E. and Good, T. L. (1974) *Teacher–Student Relationships,* New York: Holt, Rinehart and Winston.

Kraft, A. (1975) *The Living Classroom: Putting Humanistic Education into Practice,* New York: Harper and Row.

Hamachek, D. E. (1965) *The Self in Growth, Teaching and Learning,* Englewood Cliffs, New Jersey: Prentice Hall.

LaBenne, W. D. and Greene, B. I. (1969) *Educational Implications of Self-Concept Theory,* Pacific Palisades, California: Goodyear.

Purkey, W. W. (1970) *The Self and Academic Achievement,* Englewood Cliffs, New Jersey: Prentice Hall.

Rogers, C. R. (1969) *Freedom to Learn,* Columbus, Ohio: Charles E. Merrill.

Smith, P. B. (1980) *Small Groups and Personal Change,* London: Methuen.

Torrance, E. P. and Strom, R. D. (1965) *Mental Health and Achievement,* New York: Wiley.

11

Teacher Education

INTRODUCTION

If we want education to benefit the whole person, and if the teachers necessary for this need self-acceptance, empathy, genuineness, an ability to accept others and freedom from self-doubt, anxiety and defensiveness, as well as teaching skill and academic knowledge, then teacher training is the area where the most effective inter-vention can be made. Initial training is the obvious place to provide experiences that will enhance the self-concept of the trainee rather than attempting to change teachers' attitudes and styles of teaching later when they are set in their ways. Two issues need tackling here. First, the syllabus needs to contain more than just academic material to be taught and a 'tips for teachers' survival kit. Integrated throughout must be self-development, for only out of this can a teacher become someone who is able to help others to develop. Second, the teacher-training experiences, particularly the practice periods, need to be so structured that self-esteem rather than self-doubt are engendered. All teachers know only too well how stressful the initial foray into the classroom can be for a student who is inexperienced, faced with new challenges to many personal competencies, and teaching those who are but a few years younger than themselves.

More emphasis is required in teacher training and on in-service courses on the psychological morale of the student teacher and qualified teacher. Emphasis has mainly been placed in studies of teacher training and teacher effectiveness on intelligence and academic knowledge; less emphasis has been placed on such factors as self-esteem and mental health. More student teachers than one ever suspected, apparently, are burdened with low psychological morale. All this suggests that the length and organization of the practice and the roles of both supervising tutor and teacher need close investigation. Traditionally the tutor and supervising teacher have seen their role as one of preparing student teachers for a professional career in school. Little attention has been paid to their almost equally important role as 'counsellors', ready and competent to discuss the student's emotional and social problems that result from stressful classroom interactions. Of course the majority of supervising staff do, when they see a student in difficulty, intervene and counsel the student. But often such intervention is too late and is not carried out in a very effective manner by well meaning but untrained staff. Students need to be prepared before the event, before wading into the turbulent water of the practice period, not pulled out and resuscitated just before they drown in a sea of self-despair, humiliation and failure.

All this suggests that careful consideration needs to be given (1) to the inclusion of some form of counselling as an essential part of a teacher training programme; (2) to supervisors being trained to be more aware of the emotional problems of student teachers and to taking action sooner; and (3) to screening teacher training applicants for emotional suitability since those who possess low self-esteem and experience psychosomatic symptoms are at risk in the intense personal atmosphere of the classroom. Effective teaching is a function of a healthy self-concept if all the research is to be believed. Hence, how a trainee teacher develops in college in terms of personal adjustment is as important as how he develops in academic prowess. Learning about self and others is as important as learning factual curriculum material, for all teachers are teachers of others not just teachers of some definable part of the curriculum.

STUDENT TEACHER SELF-CONCEPT

An investigation into the effect of certain selected variables upon the self-esteem of 157 student teachers at the University of Birmingham, was conducted by Doherty and Parker (1977). The subjects were administered two specially constructed questionnaires to measure their self-esteem, the Eysenck Personality Inventory, and a further questionnaire to elicit details of their family circumstances, academic achievement, area of study etc. The most efficient predictors of self-esteem scores were the neuroticism and extraversion scales of the EPI. Neuroticism scores correlated significantly, although inversely, with self-esteem scores ($r = -0.48$). There was a very significant positive correlation between extraversion scores and self-esteem scores.

These student teachers thus tended to be stable extraverts, characteristics intuitively one would hope for in such a professional where neurotic and introverted persons would prove incompetent or even harmful in close interpersonal relationships.

In a second study (unpublished) by Doherty (1979) the self-concepts of 174 student teachers at Birmingham University were related to a number of aspects of teaching behaviour rated by supervising teachers (e.g. class control, relationships with pupils, degrees of stress manifested, lesson preparation, flexibility in teaching style, variability in classroom performance, absenteeism during teaching practice). The student teachers themselves completed self-esteem scales, and scales concerning psychosomatic symptoms and self-concept stability, before starting the practice.

Self-esteem seemed significantly related to the number of psychosomatic symptoms experienced by the student, and to stability of the self-concept. Students low on self-esteem experienced significantly more psychosomatic symptoms, and had more unstable self-concepts. A surprisingly high proportion (around 25 per cent) of the student teachers seemed to suffer from low psychological morale.

Self-esteem was also significantly related to overall teaching competence, social integration with other members of the staffroom, degree of emotional stress experienced while teaching, and the number of emotional problems encountered which stemmed from teaching practice.

In all of these areas, students with low self-esteem were rated significantly lower than students with high self-esteem i.e. they were rated as being less competent at teaching generally, less integrated with other members of the staffroom, more under stress while teaching, and as experiencing more emotional problems stemming from teaching practice. There was also evidence that students with low self-esteem tended to be rated significantly lower on other aspects of teacher behaviour. The general trend of means in nearly every case pointed to the superiority of the high self-esteem students.

Soares and Soares (1968) concerned themselves with the nature of the student teacher's self-concepts as teachers—whether positive or negative, and how much in either direction—and whether congruence exists between this self-concept and the reflected self in the view of the college supervisor and the cooperating teacher. If images are positive, there is a good chance that the student-teaching experience and those with whom the students worked had a constructive influence. But should significant differences exist, or the images be negative, then the students are probably not profiting as much from their teaching experience as they should. The following questions were tested:

1. After student teaching, do the student teachers have positive self-concepts as teachers?
2. Are there significant differences between the students' self-concepts as teachers and the concepts they believe their supervisors have of them? Between their self-concepts and the concepts they believe their cooperating teachers have of them? Between the concepts they believe their supervisors have of them and those they believe their cooperating teachers have?

The results showed that there is a greater correspondence between the student's self-concept and his judgement of his supervisor's rating of him as a teacher, than between his self-concept and his judgement of his cooperating teacher's rating. It is interesting to note that the cooperating teacher spends more time with the college student, yet, the student's perception of himself is significantly closer to the rating of his supervisor, who sees him only three or four times during the practice. It may be that the supervisor carries more weight, since he grades the student, or projects greater prestige because he has status.

Garvey (1970) investigated the role of self-concept on success in teaching practice. Using the Tennessee Self-Concept Scale, Garvey found that those students rated high in student teaching do, as one might anticipate, report higher self-concepts, especially in relation to identity (what I am); show less confusion, uncertainty and conflict in self-perception, particularly in scores on net conflict and total variability scales; and demonstrate less similarity to patient or disturbed groups and more to well-integrated groups.

The results of this modest exploratory effort suggest the desirability of investigating, and also the relationship of, self-concept information to success in first-year teaching. Scores such as those available from the Tennessee Self-Concept Scale, administered following employment, might be helpful to those responsible for placement and in-service education of novice, and perhaps more experienced, teachers.

Crane (1974) investigated the relationship between acceptance of self and acceptance of others, and adjustment to teaching. The first two were measured by specially constructed scales. Adjustment to teaching was measured by several inventories and a tutor's rating. One part of the study involved the identification of three groups of student teachers, comprising those who appeared to be well-adjusted to the course and to teaching, those who had seriously considered withdrawing from the course and those who had actually withdrawn. Crane's hypothesis that there would be a significant relationship between acceptance of self and acceptance of others, and adjustment to teaching, was strongly supported by the evidence. Acceptance of self and acceptance of others (scales combined) correlated consistently and significantly with four different estimates of job satisfaction in three samples of students. These combined scales also differentiated significantly between the three groups described. Crane's evidence would seem to suggest that the student who shows a high degree of acceptance of self and acceptance of others will tend to be better adjusted to teaching.

Milgram and Milgram (1976) found self-concept differences in student teachers in primary, elementary, secondary and special education. Self-concept, intelligence and academic achievement were examined in the four teaching levels using the Tennessee Self-Concept Scale, a group intelligence test and school grades. Data showed no differences in academic achievement or intelligence but there were differences in self-concept. Secondary student teachers reported a more positive self-concept than primary or elementary, with special education trainees reporting the least positive concept of all. This difference might be because people who choose to teach adolescents, who potentially can challenge their teachers' intellectual and interpersonal authority, must have a relatively positive self-concept if they are to feel comfortable and competent in dealing with pupils. By contrast, people with less positive self-concepts feel competent to teach young children. This is unfortunate because the lower levels and special education deserve their equal share of student teachers with positive self-concepts. If the trend was reversed, in time the adolescents, presumably with higher self-concept, would possibly not be as challenging.

TEACHER TRAINING AND ITS EFFECT ON SELF-CONCEPT

Some educators consider teaching practice to be the most important training experience for student teachers (Shaplin 1961). In the words of these educators teaching practice is the *raison d'être* for the whole of the student teacher's education. Every component in the curriculum is geared towards making a student teacher into a teacher, and it is during practice teaching that this teacher education is used in real teaching situations. Moreover, it is in teaching practice that a student teacher engages in the role behaviour which will, at a later time, distinguish him as a full-fledged, legitimate teacher.

The effect of teaching practice upon the self-concepts of student teachers has been of particular and recent concern. It may be argued that one of the most important tasks for practice teaching is to socialize student teachers into the profession so that they develop self-concepts as competent teachers. Howard (1965 p. 453), for example, argues that 'the most important task for a student in a teacher education programme is to feel like a teacher.'

In essence, Clifton (1979) argues that teaching practice is a marginal situation and, as such, the student teacher's greatest concern is simply surviving. This perspective is provocative but it may stimulate further thought and research.

In terms of this conceptualization, a few research studies show that the self-concepts of student teachers either stay stable during teaching practice (Covert and Clifton 1979; Gregory and Allen 1978) or slightly increase (Brim 1966; Clifton and Covert 1977; Smith and Adams 1972). On the other hand, a large number of other studies suggest that, as a result of teaching practice, the self-concepts of student teachers decrease rather than increase. These studies are important because they suggest that teaching practice, as it is now conducted, may not be as instrumental in producing competent teachers as we may have thought.

In the United States, Walberg (1966) was one of the first researchers to discover that the self-concept of student teachers decreased as a result of teaching practice. In a pre-test post-test design using the semantic differential, Walberg showed that there was a significant decrease in the self-concept scores for a group of student teachers following a block of teaching practice. This study was conducted in a number of schools within Chicago's inner city, and Walberg explained his findings by the fact that many middle-class student teachers trained in urban schools suffered from 'culture shock'. Inadequate facilities, poorly motivated pupils, uninterested parents and behavioural problems all contributed to the rigours of reality in that context. One is led to believe that the unanticipated sociological realities of these schools produce less positive teaching attitudes and lowered self-concept.

However, a rival psychological hypothesis and some evidence (Walberg 1967) suggest that conflict between the personality need—to establish rapport with children—and the role demands—to establish authority and discipline in the professional role of the teacher during teaching practice—lowers self-concept. The sociological hypothesis states that the shocking reality of working-class morality and behaviour lowers the novice teacher's self-concept; the anthropologist would speak of it as culture shock during the rites of passage; and the social psychologist would talk of personality–role conflict lowering self-concept.

Walberg's succeeding study (1968) attempted to furnish evidence for these hypotheses by determining the presence or absence of lowered self-concept in student teachers in middle-class schools.

Other purposes of the study went to examine the effects of tutoring for self-concept development in pupils and teaching attitudes and to contrast these effects with those of practice teaching. Tutoring has evoked a great deal of interest among educators and students inside and outside the profession of education. It presents education students with the real teaching task—producing learning in an individual—and makes relevant the child-centred teaching principles espoused in professional courses.

Two groups of female students training to be primary-school teachers were involved. One group undertook a normal teaching practice; the other group were also required to tutor deprived individual children in arithmetic. Semantic differential scales were used to assess self-concept before and after the practice and tutoring experience. The authors reported a decline in the professional aspects of self-concept in neat, pedagogical, identified, pupil-centred, egalitarian and neo-progressive, democratic teaching attitudes. There was an increase in personally fulfilling aspects of self-concepts and controlling attitudes (expressive, narcissistic, controlling and puritanical). These results support the hypothesis that middle-class students trained for middle-class pupils have declining self-concepts when they encounter the social realities of poverty in the inner-city schools. On the other hand, student teachers in affluent, suburban schools, although declining on some aspects of professional self-concept and attitudes, appear to derive more personal satisfaction from their teaching. The declines in professional self-concept in all groups of student teachers is interpretable in the light of the psychological hypothesis which suggests that the conflict between the personality need to be close to children and the role demand to establish authority and discipline as teacher brings about lowered self-evaluation in the professional role of the teacher.

In contrast to the student teachers, each of the tutors in the study worked with one or two children in slum schools, many of whom were truants or had other school behavioural problems. The changes in this group were unlike those in the student teachers of this study or in the previous research. In the personal intimacy of tutoring, the students became less controlling and authoritarian and more pupil-centred. An obvious explanation is the greater attention one can give to individual differences in tutoring as contrasted with teaching.

A number of implications for teacher training follows from these findings. Should education students tutor throughout the college years? If so, what kind of children should they tutor? Should students observe in middle-class schools only? To what extent should teacher education at a college or university be split into separate programmes for urban and suburban teaching? To what extent can the experiences of professional education courses and the realities of teaching be brought closer together? How far do selection and training experiences relate to problems of role adjustment and the very high rates of attrition in novice teachers? In short, how do we do the best possible job of preparing good teachers for different kinds of children?

Walberg's findings were seen as evidence that college and university courses are oriented towards teaching middle-class pupils and as a result student teachers are shocked by the realities of teaching working-class pupils. In an extended series of studies initiated by R. F. Peck, researchers found that the concerns of pre-service teachers could be grouped into definable developmental and sequential stages (Peck and Tucker 1973). The first stage in the sequence revealed that pre-service teachers are primarily concerned with self and self-protection. Later stages in the sequence showed a shift from self-concern to concern for the task of teaching, and finally to concern for pupils. After analysing the reported concerns and observed behaviours of pre-service teachers during their teaching practice, Fuller (1969) concluded that student teachers who were preoccupied with personal concerns and self-protection, or who were worried primarily about their image as achievement-oriented authority figures (task and self as performer), did not have sufficient freedom from 'self' to allow them to see or remedy the needs and concerns of their pupils. Pre-service teachers with positive self-concepts and 'reasonable' self-confidence, however, exhibited a flexibility that allowed them to encourage pupils to be autonomous and accept pupils' ideas.

Other researchers in Australia (Coulter 1974), Canada (Gaskell 1977) and the USA (Freibus 1975), using both questionnaire and multivariate analysis and participant observation techniques, have found similar results. That is, all of these studies also pointed to the fact that for student teachers teaching practice is generally associated with the development of less positive self-concepts.

All of these results suggest that self-concept is a factor in student-teaching success. Providing appropriate amounts and kinds of field experience might be one of the steps in enhancing self-concept prior to the teaching practice.

These findings may merely confirm what teacher educators and supervisors have long suspected, that success in student teaching is affected (but not necessarily determined) by a positive view of oneself, lack of confusion in self-perception and good adjustment.

Further study with other student teacher groups and with in-service teachers is obviously necessary to establish more about the relationship of specific self-concept scores to professional performance ratings. Application of multiple regression and analysis of variance techniques to larger collections of data might prove fruitful. Efforts should concentrate on establishing which self-concept scores prove especially useful in working with individuals in counselling, teaching and supervising. This would help produce teachers able to exercise and to provide for their own pupils what Rogers (1969) has labelled 'freedom to learn' (Chapter 10).

TEACHING PRACTICE AS A MARGINAL SITUATION

Educators have long recognized that there is a great deal of stress associated with teaching practice. But it would seem that before we may be able to improve the situation we must have a proper explanation of why teaching practice causes the self-concept of student teachers to become deflated. And so far such an explanation has eluded us.

One explanation may imply that lowered self-concepts resulting from teaching practice may simply reflect more realistic self-concepts. That is, practice teaching may force student teachers to consider teaching as a pragmatic vocation rather than as an idealistic one, and as a result the student teachers may adjust their self-concepts accordingly. Nevertheless, a more intriguing explanation may be that teaching practice is a marginal situation as Clifton (1979) suggested. That is, teaching practice may not be integrated in a systematic way with the functioning of the school, and the lack of integration may cause the self-concepts of student teachers to become deflated. While recognizing that the first explanation may have some substance, there seems to be considerable evidence to support the second.

The concept 'marginality' has been used to define roles within an institution which are peripheral to the main functioning of that institution (Stonequist 1961). That is, a marginal person is one who is not integrated into the formal structure of the institution and, as a result, does not contribute to the achievement of the desired goals. More specifically, a marginal person may be in a situation which is structured so that it is not integrated within the institution. As a result, the individual who is in the situation cannot contribute to the achievement of the desired goals. In this sense, a marginal situation is a situation in which there is no clear set of rules which legitimate the person's behaviour, and as a result his role is not related to the achievement of the desired goals of the institution.

In the case of teaching practice, the lack of legitimacy may be identified by two connected factors. First, student teachers do not have authority in the classroom, and second, they do not know the rituals of the classroom. These factors are interrelated in the sense that not having authority means that the student teacher can never participate in forming all of the rituals which are continually being evolved as new situations arise. Because the student teacher never knows all of the rituals, he or she is continually reminded of those they do not know by both pupils and cooperating teachers. This further illustrates their lack of authority. We will look at these issues more closely.

First, student teachers do not have an official position in the school. Their position is artificially created, usually after the school year has begun, and it is extinguished usually before the school year ends. Because student teachers do not have an official position in the school they cannot rely upon authority which is ascribed to such a position. At least one student teacher had made this quite explicit in answering a question about the nature of teaching practice:

> It's not real, especially my relationship to the kids. They know I'm a student teacher. They think it gives them license to get away with more. I'm not the supreme authority like the regular teacher is (Freibus 1975, p. 12).

The concern expressed by this person, however, seems to be shared by many student teachers. Generally, student teachers realize that they have little authority in the classroom, derived in part from the fact that they only spend a small proportion of the school year participating in the activities of the school.

Moreover, the fact that teaching practice is a short-term exercise leads student teachers not to emphasize long-range planning, getting to know the pupils or assuming responsibility (Gaskell 1977). Thus, for student teachers the lesson becomes the basic unit of work. As a result, student teachers usually spend an inordinate amount of time preparing each of their lessons. But they are unlikely to see how the lesson fits in with the pupils' general academic programme. In this respect Goodlad (1965, p. 268) notes:

> The prospective teacher observed a social studies lesson, for example, but has no basis for understanding how and why the class got there or where it is going; often, as a consequence, his perspective is rudely distorted.

At the same time, a student teacher reported:

> When you are assigned individual lessons, you can teach the lesson beautifully—you can get all kinds of concrete material. It's just isolated, though; you've got no way of integrating it with other facets of the curriculum (Loosemore and Carlton 1977, p. 415).

In response to this type of behaviour another student teacher said:

> I think it is very important to try to begin the school year with the students and not come in the middle of the school year. It just seems to me you are making that kind of situation even more artificial if you don't start out with them (Gaskell 1977, p. 14).

The lack of authority, which may be derived from an official position and the fact that teaching practice occupies such a relatively short period of time means that student teachers often feel as if they are intruders into the classroom. The learning experiences of the pupils have been defined and shaped before the student teacher enters the classroom and will be developed and extended after he has left. As a result, it is not surprising that both teachers and pupils often regard student teachers as disruptive to the normal progression of events, and when this happens student teachers cannot help feeling frustrated and dissatisfied with their teaching practice experiences.

The second reason for the difficulties encountered by student teachers is the fact that they are often seen by both their cooperating teachers and the pupils as being neither experts nor competent. Student teachers are continually being coached and evaluated, and as both they and the pupils know, a competent and expert person is not continually being coached and evaluated, especially in front of pupils who are supposed to be his subordinates.

The coaching may begin even before the student teachers start their teaching practice. In their classes at the university or college student teachers are reminded that they are going to participate in a 'teacher's classroom' and they must act accordingly. For example, Kaltsounis and Nelson (1968, p. 279) report that student teachers are typically reminded of their behaviour by such words as:

> Don't forget that you are guests in the school to which you are going. Remember that you are there to learn. The class into which you are going belongs to Miss So-and-So. Do not upset her routine. Make sure you check with the teacher on everything you must do.

Not only does this remind the student teachers of their behaviour in the classroom but it informs them in a very subtle way that they will not have authority in the classroom. The classroom will 'belong' to their cooperating teacher and they will be there to learn and to follow directions even if it deviates from what they have previously learned in their university courses.

Educators have recognized that there is a certain degree of stress associated with teaching practice, but they may not have realized how severe this stress may become or that what they observed as stress may be in effect significant depreciation in their student teachers' self-concepts. If this is true, it seems to contradict the established goals of teaching practice. That is, it has often been assumed by educators that teaching practice is very important in that it provides training for the actual teaching roles the student teachers will assume in the future. More importantly, teaching practice also serves as a forum for assessing the teaching performances of student teachers. However, these performances may be so different that teaching practice may not indicate very much about the way a student teacher will behave as a fully-fledged teacher.

ORGANIZATION OF TEACHING PRACTICE TO IMPROVE SELF-CONCEPT

Factors identified as contributing to changes in self-concept, usually a decline, seem to be quality of interaction between experienced and prospective teachers (Krasno 1971); quality of supervision (Burgy 1972; Goodlad 1965; Soares and Soares 1974); tempering of idealism by reality (Wright and Tuska 1966); conflict between personality needs and role demands (Walberg 1968); and speed of induction into teaching and school (Coulter 1974; Clifton 1979), length of practice (Tattersall 1979) and existing self-concept level (Crane 1974). Taken as a whole the research leads to the conclusion that a primary cause of the usual decrease in professional self-concept was a conflict between students' unrealistic and idealized perceptions of themselves as teachers, and the realities of schools, the patterns of behaviour they were forced to conform to, and their lack of skill in teaching. Some conflict of this kind is probably inevitable, but the effects could be modified by factors such as speed of transition into teaching, level of support from supervisors, and length and continuity of the experience.

In order to make sure that teaching practice has greater significance in the training of teachers it must be integrated in better ways with schools (Clifton and Covert 1977). This goal may be achieved in part by having student teachers participate continually in school throughout the school year. At least this may mean that the student teachers would learn and understand the important rituals of the classroom. Beyond this, however, it may be important to ensure that student teachers have authority in the classroom. This may be achieved not only by having student teachers spend more time in teaching practice, but also by structuring the practice so that they are recognized as holding official positions in the schools. At the same time, it may be important to ensure that student teachers are recognized as being competent by both cooperating teachers and pupils. All of this entails substantially revising the way student teachers are educated. Finally, if we are serious about improving the education of teachers, researchers must monitor teaching practice to be certain that the desired goals are achieved.

Several writers have linked anxiety to aspects of self-concept (Coopersmith 1967; Felker 1972) and argued for the notion of an optimal level of anxiety in teachers. Too little anxiety might lead to tolerance of unsatisfactory situations in schools and inadequate preparation for teaching, while too much might cause undue stress and tension and interfere with performance. Greenstein and Greenstein (1973) linked anxiety to discrepancies between initial idealistic views of teaching and the realities of the classroom, and Lortie (1975) associated high levels of anxiety with the usual abrupt transition into teaching. Because of these links between self-concept and anxiety, it was considered that an examining of anxiety might be useful in interpreting the changes in student teachers' professional self-concepts.

Gregory and Allen's (1978) programme of teacher training in Canada was designed to reduce the debilitating impact of anxiety derived from teaching on the self-concepts of the student teachers. This programme has a number of features which differ from what is generally considered traditional (Channon 1971) and which might be expected to reduce anxiety and the usual negative impact of the practice on professional self-concept. On the other hand if the effects of the practice are inevitable, as has been suggested by some researchers, the extended time in schools should increase the negative effect. The untraditional features are: (1) induction into teaching is gradual and at a rate that is considered appropriate for the individual concerned. (2) Orientation meetings at the beginning of each term are held for the classroom teachers and university supervisors who work with the students in the schools. Both the orientation meetings and the supervision workshops are well attended and favourably received, a response providing reasonable grounds for believing that supervisors are generally familiar with and sympathetic towards the programme and their intended role in it. (3) The extended periods of time in classrooms allow for gradual introduction to teaching, the development (as distinct from testing) of teaching skills, and accommodation to the realities of the classroom. (4) While there is considerable emphasis on discussion of teaching and formative evaluation, assessment is not emphasized and grading is done on the basis of pass or withdraw. (5) The teaming of students in the initial practice provides additional peer support and possibilities of observing and sharing difficulties with other inexperienced colleagues. (6) Most of the university supervision is done by teachers on leave from local school districts. This tends to reduce the philosophical differences which are sometimes found between teachers and permanent university staff. It has an additional advantage in that supervision is the sole responsibility of these individuals and does not have to compete for time and emotional commitment with research or other activities.

In summary, the Professional Development Programme examined by Gregory and Allen (1978) provides a gradual introduction to teaching, good support from supervisors and other students, and longer periods of time in schools than most other programmes. Because of this it was predicted that the normal decrease in professional self-concept would not be found.

The selected students completed a semantic differential instrument to measure the effect of the practice on student teachers' professional self-concepts. This produced scores of seven factors (warmth and supportiveness, creativity, nonconformity, orderliness, satisfaction, clarity, energy and enthusiasm) for each of four concepts related to self-concept *myself,* and *myself as I would like to be* (personal concept); *myself as a teacher,* and *the teacher I would like to be* (professional concepts). A measure of teaching anxiety, was also completed.

The results clearly support the prediction that was made. There were no significant declines on any of the factors. On the other hand there were a number of increases that were large enough to be considered significant. The tendency to increase self-concept was strongest for the group which spent a full term in the schools and weakest for the group whose shorter six-week practice was interrupted by periods of workshops and seminars. However, the results must be considered as lending support to the idea that the length of the practice is one of the major variables influencing self-concept. If this pattern of results was confirmed in other studies, there would be a strong indication that the normal practice of four to six weeks' duration would have the negative impact on self-concept that has been found in other studies, even when there is high-quality supervision and a gradual transition to teaching. The first and most obvious point to emerge from this study is that the generally found decline in self-concept after student teaching is not inevitable.

The second point to consider is whether changes that did occur could be particularly associated with any specific aspects of programmes. In this study, the greatest increase in professional self-concept (actual) was found for students on the full term practice, and this effect was sufficiently powerful to increase students' personal self-concept (actual) as well. The elements which distinguished this practice from the practice experiences were an individual placement, the length of continuous practice and the fact that it was preceded by a previous practice. Other supportive mechanisms and a gradual transition were common to all groups. Which or what combination of these variables were most influential could not be conclusively determined from the data in Gregory and Allen's study. However, it should be noted that individual placements and previous practices are common to many of the short-term practices studied in other research, in which declines in self-concept have been almost universally found. This, coupled with the tendency towards a decline in professional self-concept after three weeks of the shorter six-week practice with a subsequent recovery, suggests that the most influential variable was the length of continuous teaching practice under conditions which provided a high level of support. This interpretation is admittedly speculative, but if it is correct, and student teachers' professional self-concept is considered important, there must be some doubt about the wisdom of the widespread use of several short teaching practices. Additional studies in which comparisons could be made between practices of different lengths at several institutions might provide more conclusive data on this point.

Tattersall (1979) focused his research on the changes that occur in student teacher self-concept during the period of an extended practice of three months as reported by Canadian student teachers.

It was hypothesized that significant decreases in teaching anxiety would occur after 9 and 12 weeks, that actual professional self-concept and actual self-concept would increase significantly after 12 weeks, that ideal professional self-concept and ideal self-concept would be stable, and that the professional self-concept and self-concept discrepancy scores would decrease significantly after 12 weeks.

The Parsons Teaching Anxiety Scale measured teaching anxiety and the Elsworth–Coulter Semantic Differential provided scores on seven dimensions and the total scale of each of four components of self-concept. Respondents also provided open-ended descriptions of important incidents that had occurred during the practice.

Pre-tests were administered during the first two days of the practice. The 195 respondents were assigned randomly to one of four post-test groups, established as homogeneous by analysis of variance, for testing at the end of week 3, 6, 9 and 12 respectively. Tattersall detected potentially serious mid-practice stress with a beneficial effect the longer the practice continued. This is consistent with the previous study of Gregory and Allen (1978).

A new programme to train teachers providing greater integration between what was observed and practised in schools and what was taught in a faculty of education was evaluated by Clifton and Covert (1977). The basic question addressed by this research was whether student teachers who completed one year in an experimental programme differed in any significant manner, in motivation to become teachers and in self-concept as teachers, from a control group of student teachers who completed one year in the regular teacher-education programmes.

Clifton and Covert (1977) argue that for prospective teachers, the meaningfulness of their education is related to the degree of integration between what they observe and practise in the schools and what they are taught in the teacher-training institution. They evaluated an experimental programme of training teachers which was to provide a greater degree of integration between what student teachers observed and practised in the schools and what they were taught in the faculty of education.

In addition to their course load, which was the same as that of students in the regular programmes, thirty experimental students spent at least one afternoon a week, throughout the academic year, observing and practice-teaching in the various schools. Each student teacher was assigned to a specific school and to a specific supervising teacher but had ample opportunity to observe in other classrooms. This allowed the student teachers to participate in the establishment of the classroom environment at the beginning of the year and to see how this environment developed and changed throughout the year. Moreover, it allowed the student teachers to play a legitimate role in the classroom activities. They were integrated into the school programme as active participants rather than simply as 'student teachers' who participated in the classroom activities for a two- or three-week period during teaching practice. The amount of time they spent in the schools allowed them to know many of the pupils and teachers on a personal basis. As a result, they not only participated in the regular classroom activities, but also participated in such things as field trips, sports days, and staff meetings.

The professors who participated in the experimental programme consciously attempted to relate the knowledge, skills, and intellectual competencies they were attempting to teach with the experiences the student teachers were having in the schools. For example, readings and discussions were geared to what was actually happening in the classrooms. Furthermore, lessons were planned in the university classrooms and then tried out in the school classrooms. Discussions about these lessons took place both before and after they were implemented. There was a continuous attempt to maintain a high level of integration between what was taught in the university and what was practised in the classroom. In the regular programmes student teachers completed their second-year courses before they engaged in student teaching. That is, the students completed their theoretical work before their practical work and as a result there was little integration between the two aspects. Furthermore, there was little liaison between their professors and their supervising teachers. Beyond this, students in the experimental programme spent significantly more time in the schools than students in the regular programmes. Students in the experimental programme spent at least 60 hours in the classroom during the academic year, plus two weeks in regular teaching practice sessions at the end of the academic year. Except for occasional visits, student teachers in the regular programmes went to the schools only during their regular teaching practice sessions. Finally, student teachers in the experimental programme received considerably more individual attention than student teachers in the regular programmes. Not only were they assigned advisers, which was not so for other students, but their university classes were approximately half as large as the classes for other students.

The measure of self-concept as a teacher was constructed from five items on a semantic differential. There were no significant differences between the two groups on the pre-experimental tests. The post-practice tests produced significant differences between the two groups for both dependent variables. That is, on both motivation to become a teacher, and self-concept as a teacher, the students in the experimental programme had significantly higher mean scores than students in the regular programmes. This research suggests that the amount of productive time a student teacher spends in school and the integration between what is observed and practised there and what is taught in education institutions has a significant effect upon the development of his motivation to become a teacher and his self-concept as a teacher.

Scherer (1979) attempted to determine whether secondary student teachers who had selected an early field-based experience (Project Interaction) would differ significantly in self-concept and performance during student teaching from those who had not selected the early field-based experience. It was also designed to test self-concept as a correlate of teaching performance ratings.

The value of participation in such early field-based projects has been argued in much recent literature. Such phrases as 'integrate theory into practice,' 'gain direct knowledge of pupils in schools and community settings,' and 'demonstrate growing ability to perform as a teacher,' recur in numerous programme descriptions. The results suggested that participation in an early field experience, Project Interaction, did affect self-concept positively.

A further suggestion to help teacher trainees come to feel more positive about themselves would be the introduction into teacher-training schemes of sensitivity/encounter group exercises undertaken before teaching practice. The sort of exercises employed by Stanton (1979a) which we discuss in Chapter 16 would seem a useful starting point. Any group therapy that enabled the students to feel more secure in themselves, more able to cope, more positive towards themselves and others would almost certainly enable more students to cope with the personal and interpersonal rigours and realities of teaching. It must be better than the present convention of entering school with a prepared academic and methodological crust that offers only minimal protection to a vulnerable and unprepared person. In situations where pure academic knowledge and methodology fail or have limited application to the prevailing classroom conditions, the person is exposed as a person. In any case we have seen in Chapter 9 that even the use made of the academic material and its method of presentation cannot be divorced from the type of person presenting it. Like beauty in the eye of the beholder, knowledge depends on the people involved.

SUMMARY

Institutions designed for the training of classroom teachers have two important functions. The first is to provide the prospective teachers with the skills, knowledge, and intellectual resources necessary for functioning in the classroom. The second function is to initiate the socialization of student teachers into their prospective occupational role; that is, to initiate them into the role of 'teacher'. This socialization involves the development of motivation to become a good teacher as well as the development of a self-concept as a competent teacher. This latter function is as important as the first, since teachers need to be better types of people in all sorts of ways if pupils are to develop as proper people.

Success on teaching practice does seem to depend on the possession of an adequate level of self-esteem with those low in self-esteem being less adjusted to teaching, less able to accept others in close interpersonal supportive relationships and showing more emotional stress in teaching.

It is argued that teaching practice is marginal; student teachers do not fill roles which allow them adequately to legitimate their behaviour. More specifically, they do not have authority in the school, and they do not know the rituals of the classroom. As a result, they tend to feel like they are impostors and their self-concepts suffer.   *How can school help?*

Programmes involving high levels of support from supervisors and school staff, gradual transition into teaching, extended teaching practice and previous experience in fieldwork contact with children appear to offer the best chance of avoiding the debilitating effect of practice on self-concept. The application of group therapy and sensitivity training exercises to strengthen self-concept would seem an appropriate innovation in teacher-training programmes.

12

School Organization
and Teaching Approaches

The organization of the school and classroom has been investigated to determine whether the type of organization or style of teaching, influences the self-concepts of the pupils and whether particular types of classroom organization are preferred by teachers of varying levels of self-esteem.

TRADITIONAL VERSUS CHILD-CENTRED APPROACHES

Most schools are organized in such a way as to provide continuous competition and evaluation. Purkey (1970) suggests this process of shaping behaviours increases negative feelings about oneself. Ruedi and West (1973) described the traditional environment as requiring all pupils to work in the class on the same subject at the same time as instructed by the teacher. Interactions between teacher and students usually occur as a group. To promote the idea of the group, the desks face the front. At times, the teacher divides the class according to ability. Tests are given to everyone simultaneously over material covered. The classroom is characterized as structured.

In comparison, the open environment is more flexible. Teaching is usually conducted individually or in small groups. Students progress at their own speed. Tests are taken at the completion of a unit. Students are free to leave the room. The focus of the desks vary and are usually not towards the blackboard. The noise level is higher in these classrooms than in the traditional ones since subjects are free to confer with one another and to move about the building. Reports and grades are not given, instead conferences with parents are used. The environment is characterized as individualized. It is generally proposed on an intuitive basis that, in contrast to traditional modes of formal education, open informal schools explicitly emphasize the following: (a) individualizing the curriculum; (b) employing intrinsic motivation; (c) fostering cooperative learning in the classroom; (d) promoting personal interactions between teacher and student; (e) transforming the role of teacher to that of resource person; and (f) using play in learning. In so far as academic achievement is concerned in informal schools, it is seen as a consequence of heightened student interest engendered by the achievement of these primary objectives.

From these assumptions, several specific hypotheses follow. Relative to students in formal schools, students in informal schools should (a) show more positive attitudes towards their school and learning in general; (b) show more positive attitudes towards teachers and other school authorities; (c) feel more positively about their role as students, having higher academic expectations; (d) possess higher self-esteem; (e) more frequently transfer their school experiences to the home and the community; and (f) assuming confirmation of the former hypothesis, perform better at such traditional academic tasks as spelling, grammar and creative writing.

None of these hypothesized differences was found by Groobman, Forward and Peterson (1976) when formal and informal pupils were compared on measures of self-esteem, academic expectations and performance. The only difference was that 'informal' pupils had more favourable school attitudes. But the impact of this on other school variables was not immediate. Perhaps more time is required for such effects to happen.

Results from Ruedi and West's (1973) study showed that there was no significant difference in self-concept, or in the factors of interpersonal adequacy, autonomy and academic adequacy in the two types of schools. The only positive effect found in favour of open schools was the more favourable attitude towards school compared to a traditional environment.

Allen (1974) investigated the effectiveness of open area classrooms in terms of self-esteem and student performance with self-contained classrooms. No significant differences were found between levels of self-appraisal between the two classroom types. This does not mean that open areas have no helpful effect. It may require a lengthy longitudinal study to reveal a cumulative effect over a number of years and this has yet to be done.

Franks, Marolla and Dillon (1974) found significantly higher self-esteem scores in an open-school group using competency based measures. Wright (1975), however, found no evidence of self-esteem differences between the two treatment groups (open versus traditional).

A favourable attitude towards school is, sometimes, cited as a result of the open classroom and evidence showing gains in this area has been presented by Ruedi and West (op. cit.) and Groobman, Forward and Peterson (op. cit.). Favourable school attitude may be valued in its own right but it is not the same as self-esteem and should not be confused with it.

Positive results were found, however, in the Cockerham and Blevins (1976) study. They investigated the relationship between the type of school and self-concept of American Indian youths in Wyoming, USA. The study compared 43 Indian students from an open school with 116 Indian students from a traditional school and 184 white students from a traditional school.

Results showed that there was a positive relationship between the type of school and a positive self-concept. Indians from the open school had a more positive self-concept than either white or Indian students from traditional schools.

Cockerham and Blevins (1976) suggest the reason for these findings is that open schools seem to clash less with Indian practices and customs than traditional schools, e.g. cooperation and sharing.

A more recent study (Klaus and Hodge 1978) could not produce any significant differences in self-esteem between open and traditional school classrooms. So, in general, differences in self-concept between pupils in formal and informal classrooms in American research are small and do not favour the latter, as intuition might suggest.

However, the major criticism of the studies dealing with open versus traditional schools is that school settings vary widely in actual practice, and so threaten the external validity of any research (Klaus and Hodge 1978). Only with extreme settings where all involved are deeply committed to the philosophy of the organization do hypothesized differences emerge. For example, Purkey, Graves and Zellner (1970) explored the impact of an innovative, team-teaching, completely ungraded elementary school on the professed self-esteem of pupils in that school.

Several practices of the experimental school used are worth noting. Pupils were continually regrouped on the basis of individual differences as growth occurred and progress made. Pupils could be promoted or reassigned any day of the week.

Provisions were made for individual differences without attaching the stigma of failure and without placing a child outside his normal peer group. There were no failures in the school and all pupils were grouped by the number of years they had attended school. Children were permitted early to participate in setting their own learning goals with teacher and child working together. The professional competency of teachers is thus used efficiently and teachers work together in teams with a team leader. Extended day programmes included art, music, fine arts, mathematics, science and a number of clubs. During a typical day, parents, with the help of volunteer workers, ran many of the school's activities. These and many other practices grew out of the firm commitment of the experimental school to a humanistic approach to education. The school provided successful experiences and maximum freedom for exploration for all children. Academic failure and having to repeat a year were eliminated.

A neighbouring elementary school was selected for comparison purposes. This comparison school was traditional and typical in design and in curriculum with conventional grade levels and self-contained classrooms.

Two hypotheses were formulated: (1) Pupils enrolled in the experimental school will evidence greater self-esteem than pupils enrolled in the comparison school. (2) As grade level increases, measured differences in self-esteem between the two groups of pupils will increase. Coopersmith's Scale was applied, and the first hypothesis was confirmed. Results indicate that over the four-year span of ages in the study there was a highly significant difference between the scores of the two groups. Pupils in the innovative school scored, on average, almost a full point above the pupils in the comparison group.

The second hypothesis of the study was that as a grade level increased, the differences in self-esteem between the pupils in the two schools would increase. This hypothesis was also confirmed. Pupils in the experimental school showed relative stability in self-esteem up to ten years of age, then showed a marked increase in mean self-esteem score at eleven. Pupils in the comparison school showed a steady decrease in mean self-esteem scores to ten years of age and then stabilized at that level.

The general findings of this study indicate that pupils in an innovative and humanistically orientated elementary school have more favourable self-esteem than pupils in a comparable but traditionally orientated elementary school. Although results do not take into account the length of time an individual pupil was exposed to the experimental school, the data suggest that prolonged exposure to the environment of the innovative school does have a positive influence on the professed self-esteem of children aged eight to twelve.

The innovative school was unique with commitment to its philosophy from all involved – a rare condition. Yet it does indicate what can be achieved in self-esteem development. However, Purkey et al. (op. cit.) do not indicate the relative academic achievement of the school and this is just as important. In view of the general relationship between self-concept and achievement, it could be reasonably inferred that more children in the innovative school were performing in line with their ability than in the conventional school.

The dichotomy of traditional and child-centred classrooms are in reality models at the extremities of the dimension of teaching approaches. In between these extremes is a mixture of aims, methods, teacher and pupil roles that defies any clear classification of teaching methods. The extremes have been described, but these rather simple stereotypes suggest that across the range of teaching styles there will be different expectations placed on pupils, and different feedback content which presumably affects self-concept. Bennett's (1976) study reveals that teachers aim to promote a variety of outcomes in their pupils depending on their particular teaching style.

Bennett was unable to find any evidence that self-concept changes resulted from changes in teaching style during the year of his study, but there was evidence that anxious and insecure pupils found informal classrooms rather stressful. Such children seem to function best in a structured and organized environment. In an extension of the Bennett study, Jordan (1980) showed that when six classrooms taken from the extremes of the dimension were considered in more depth with sociometric analysis included and with greater control exercised over intervening variables there were significant differences in self-esteem. Self-esteem did not relate to achievement in any of the informal classrooms in the case studies, whereas significant correlations were obtained in two formal classrooms.

It would seem that in formal classrooms self-esteem is closely tied to achievement since this is the only area positive feedback is given in. It is perfectly possible to develop and maintain high levels of self-esteem in an informal class irrespective of performance since other criteria are also used to judge others and self.

STREAMING

Acland's (1973) survey of research on streaming in primary schools suggests that those opposed to streaming argue their case on the enhancing effects of not streaming on pupil self-concepts. Supporters of streaming claim that bright pupils in mixed ability classes give daily reminders to the less able of their inadequacies so helping to undermine those children's self-confidence; others, with opposing views, argue that streaming lowers the aspirations of all children, other than those in the top stream, and that the lower-stream children moderate their abilities and consequently develop poor self-concepts. Barker-Lunn (1970) noted that it seemed quite common for teachers not to enjoy teaching low-ability children (see Chapter 9).

An important study of streaming in primary schools conducted by Barker-Lunn (op. cit.) for the National Foundation for Educational Research concerned itself in part with the self-concept in relation to internal school organization. The study involved both a cross-sectional component employing all four years in 84 junior schools, and a longitudinal component over one year involving 5500 7 to 8 year-olds in 72 schools.

There were three variables involved: (1) Teacher-type (i.e. whether the teacher believed in streaming or not); (2) School organization (i.e. whether the school streamed the children or not) and (3) Pupil (whether the child was above average, average, or below average in ability). Results of the study showed that neither school organization nor teacher type affected development of self-concept in children of above average ability.

However, both these variables affected children of average and below-average ability. Specifically, pupils taught by teachers who were in favour of their schools' organization had better self-concepts than pupils taught by teachers who were mismatched. That is, those students taught by 'non-streamers' in unstreamed schools were better off than their counterparts taught by 'non-streamers' in streamed schools. The poorest self-concepts were held by pupils taught by 'streamers' in unstreamed schools. Pupils taught by 'streamers' in streamed schools generally held quite positive self-concepts.

Barker-Lunn reports that most of these British schoolchildren had a clear self-image of their ability. If they were in a streamed school, the 'stream' they were in influenced their self-concept. 'Top-stream' children had positive self-concepts but a considerable number of lower ability children had poor self-images and expressed shame at not being clever. Explicit or implicit comparisons between low and high ability children in unstreamed classes are unavoidable and result in the slower children feeling inferior and of less personal worth than the brighter members.

In a streamed school, a boy in the top stream reported, 'We are very clever in this class'. Even a child in a lower stream could say 'I am the best in the class and still am'. So, streaming is placing like with like and enables even slow children to have more positive attitudes to themselves than when placed with unstreamed classes where there are far brighter children and where often the slow child would comment along the lines 'We're useless at schoolwork'. Children do seem to develop a clear image of their performance relative to others in the group. All this raises doubts about mixed-ability classes. In a follow up, Ferri (1971) found that in secondary schools both boy and girl slow learners had developed more favourable self-concepts. Ferri claimed that this change arose for such pupils no longer being in classes with wide ability ranges and hence being able to show competency when compared to others of similar ability. The work of Barker-Lunn and Ferri appears to indicate that grouping procedures themselves affect self-concept and that high achievers tend to report more frequently positive self-concepts than do low achievers. Also it is apparent that the teachers' attitudes and expectations are vitally important in that teachers who favour streaming but teach in an unstreamed school create a 'streamed' environment. As Wiseman (1973) saw, teachers are far more important in terms of their attitudes and expectations than organizational structures. Emmett (1959) and Thomas (1974) agree. In Thomas's study a similar level of self-evaluation was revealed across three streams: a result of the teaching climate of the whole school which appeared to be democratic, and warmly supporting of every child.

What streaming does is to exacerbate the expectation effect. The top streamers glow in the reflected appraisals of their teachers: the not-so-fortunate pupils in the lower streams function at the level expected of them, thus validating the teachers' expectations and judgements. The danger with streaming is this disturbing tendency to establish and reinforce the child's concept of his ability and perpetuate it. Like a disciplined army, the streamed battalions move through the educational battlefield without any individual breaking rank.

However, it does appear that the child who is less able might benefit more from streaming as far as his self-concept is concerned. Dyson (1967), in America, investigated the relationships between acceptance of self, academic self-concept and two procedures used to group seventh-grade students for instruction. The two facets of the self-concept were indexed for 323 heterogeneously grouped students and 244 homogeneously grouped students. Regardless of grouping procedures used, high achievers reported significantly more positive academic self-concepts, while these concepts for low achievers were significantly less positive ($P < 0.01$). No other significant differences were found. It was concluded that grouping procedures do not significantly affect either personal or academic self-concept, but success in school significantly influenced the academic self-concept regardless of the grouping procedure used.

The effect on the self-concept of pupils who were accelerated (moved up a year) or decelerated (held back a year) was investigated by Storey (1967). Feedback to potential accelerators and decelerators must be somewhat different. For, from their earliest interaction with the school environment level, the potential accelerators have, in the main, been receiving highly favourable feedback. They have learned the song 'Anything you can do, I can do better'. The child who is to become a decelerator has been learning the 'Anything I can do, you can do better' version, for his feedback has been largely unfavourable.

The child who is accelerated has different feedback, for he now finds himself 'promoted' into an older, more mature, and more experienced group. The competition is keener both in and out of the classroom and, consequently, his feedback now informs him that he is average rather than superior, which lowers self-concept as Storey (op. cit.) found.

SELF-CONCEPT AND SCHOOL SIZE

Barker (1964) proposed a relationship between school size and the behaviour of students. In earlier studies, Barker found that students from small schools are likely to participate in more activities, take greater part in a greater diversity of activities and feel a greater obligation to participate (Barker and Hall 1964). Barker argues that the smaller the secondary school, the more pressure is put on pupils to participate in non-academic activities at school.

Few authors have attempted to relate participation in school-sponsored activities with feelings of personal worth. In an early study of the adolescent peer group, Coleman (1961) found that participation in valued school activities was related to greater peer approval and satisfaction with one's role. More recently, Rosenberg (1965) has been able to demonstrate a relationship between measured self-concept and participation in school activities. Neither of these authors related such results to the sort of school the students were attending. Such an effort would provide further insight into how the school environment influences students.

Grabe (1976) following Barker's thesis investigated school size and participation in non-academic activities on self-esteem level. Grabe found that self-esteem was inversely related to participation in small schools. Barker had originally linked participation to school size in a rather mechanical fashion. Grabe's expansion concerns the psychological impact of being able to meet the pressures exerted by peers towards participation. Feelings of personal worth were related to the student's ability to respond to the pressures and obligations of the school. Grabe's (1976) investigation uses the example of a student in a small school who may feel humiliated at not making the basketball team. In contrast, a student from a large school would not suffer such embarrassment as only a few among thousands make the team.

Moreover, younger students feel less pressure, as failures among these students, in such a situation, are more common. In fact, Grabe found the frequency of participation was most closely related to differences in self-concept among small schools' top classes. As a result, Grabe suggests that these top-class students in smaller schools may need special help in dealing with their feelings of personal worth.

TEACHERS' PREFERRED TEACHING METHODS

The different approaches to teaching preferred by teachers differing in self-attitudes and in attitude to others are those theoretically expected to be favoured since a teacher low in self-concept will try to reduce the need for personal relationships, thereby adopting traditional methods. These place the teacher in an unambiguous position with regard to his role and status, pursuing essentially impersonal relationships in task-oriented rather than in person-oriented behaviours. The progressive approach, with its more intense personal relationships, is threatening to those with negative attitudes to self and others. Conformity, rigidity and status preservation are necessary for them. But the person who has a positive self-concept has no need to defend; an unstructured, highly personal contact offers no threat. He can relate to, accept, and work alongside all pupils irrespective of their characteristics and behaviours. This is not to say that such a person condones whatever the pupil does or is, but rather he does not reject an individual out of hand because of some particular attribute.

Burns (1976) was able to show this association quite clearly. Student teachers who preferred child-centred methods of teaching rather than impersonal traditional approaches tended to possess significantly more positive self-concepts than the student teachers who preferred the more formal methods. Since teachers with low self-concepts favour a more traditional approach, with its evaluation and competition, and the possession of such low self-concepts engenders a relative restriction in establishing warm personal relationships, then it is likely that many of their pupils would be more liable to develop less positive self-attitudes in this atmosphere of competition, impersonality and inflexibility of teaching style, and these would have consequent effects on their performance.

The NFER studies of Barker-Lunn (1970) that we referred to earlier also revealed that a teacher's beliefs about teaching—'progressive' or 'traditional'—seems to affect the self-concepts of the pupils in her classes. The result of this appears to be particularly detrimental when the teacher is required to teach in a system that is incompatible with her beliefs.

Since we now know that a teacher's beliefs about and preference for certain teaching approaches are a function of the teacher's own self-concept so we can argue that one way in which the teacher's self-concept influences those of her pupils is through her educational philosophy. As part of this philosophy, teachers differ in the amount of talking they allow. Some restrict pupils' talking to answering their questions, while others allow more verbal interaction and discussion. Teachers who allow pupils to talk in class are more likely than their colleagues to encourage the expression and interpretation of feelings, and when students express their feelings, they create opportunities for self-concept change.

In fact, according to a study by Anandam, Davis and Poppen (1971), freedom to speak of one's feelings can improve not only a pupil's self-concept but the entire classroom climate. Third-grade pupils were divided into two groups, the first of which was given the opportunity to express feelings and were encouraged by the teacher to do so. The second group was exposed to a more intensive programme of interpersonal skill development involving both teacher and peer encouragement. Measures of self-concept, social dependency, and 'individuation' (differentiating the self from others) showed an insignificant difference in favour of the second group. However, indices of classroom climate revealed significant differences between Groups I and II indicating that two very different environments had evolved during the course of the programmes. The teacher of Group I encouraged spoken feelings but gradually limited such expression to a particular time of the day. Group II, on the other hand, pursued its more intensive programme with enthusiastic support from both teacher and pupils. At the end of the two programmes, Group II had increased pupil involvement in the lesson and the interaction of teacher with pupils and between pupils and had decreased the amount of individual desk work significantly more than Group I. These findings support the idea that teachers can create the kind of classroom environment they want.

Creating opportunities for children to express their feelings in the classroom is presumed to be an effective way to help them develop more positive and realistic self-concepts. Sharing feelings helps one identify the self in relation to others, and examining negative feelings presumably helps one remove blocks to cognitive and affective processes.

Pupils' talk depends on the teacher talking less. Trowbridge (1973) revealed how the ratio of teacher's talk to pupils' talk was a reflection of the teacher's self-concept. It was found that teachers with lower self-concepts talk more and also provide less opportunity for their charges to talk than teachers with higher self-concepts. The correlation between proportion of the time teacher talked and teacher's self-concept was -0.624. Teachers with higher self-concepts tended to spend less time on routine activities than those with lower self-concepts. These routine activities were handing out books, collecting work, taking the register, etc. There was also a positive and significant relationship between the teacher's self-concept and the tendency to use divergent and evaluative thinking. Teachers with low self-concepts were more likely to use convergent thinking and memory in their classroom teaching. As Trowbridge concludes, the evidence points to the teacher's self-concept telling us much about the way he teaches. An increase in divergent and evaluative thinking in the teacher's style of teaching may be brought about by making the self-concept more positive. All of this supports the basic rationale that one might expect teachers with more positive self-concepts to feel freer to allow pupils to develop divergent and evaluative approaches to schoolwork. Teachers who are unsure of themselves are more likely to stick to stereotyped formal lessons, involving memory, questions with one answer and convergent thinking, as Burns (1976) found.

So teachers with positive self-esteem are those more likely to develop self-esteem in their charges. When teachers encourage pupils to do more than simply give an answer, affective gain as well as cognitive gain is possible. For example, various workers have attempted to see if self-evaluative strategies would enhance self-conceptions.

When a student answers a teacher's question, the teacher typically judges the student's answer as correct or incorrect and may even reinforce him if he has correctly responded to the question posed. The student's only contribution to this interaction is his answer. It is quite possible, however, for the teacher to more directly engage the student in the evaluation process by asking him to judge the correctness of his own answer ('Do you think your answer is correct?') and to reinforce himself ('Don't you think you did well on that question?'). The former type of evaluation (other-evaluation) involves judgement and praise of the student by another person, which in this case is the teacher. The latter-mentioned type of evaluation (self-evaluation) consists of self-judgement and self-praise.

Regarding self-praise, Felker and Thomas (1971) asked children to rank nine positive and negative statements—e.g., positive: 'I'm smarter than most kids', negative: 'I always fail', as statements they would typically say to themselves during school work. These investigators found that those who ranked positive statements higher than the overall class mean had significantly better self-concepts. Furthermore, Felker and Stanwyck (1971) have shown that after performing school tasks, children with high self-concepts tend to make statements about themselves which are more positive than those made by students with low self-concepts. Hence, it seems that saying positive things about oneself in relation to performance in school is one behavioural manifestation of a positive self-concept. Inducing this kind of behaviour (self-reinforcement) in students, therefore, might be expected to enhance their self-concepts relative to students experiencing reinforcement by another person, usually the teacher. Coons and McEachern (1967) and Felker (1972) point to this possibility in their respective studies wherein students who were induced to make positive statements about themselves attained a more positive attitude toward themselves, as indicated by a significant increase in the number of endorsements of self-accepting statements.

The other component of the self-evaluation strategy, self-judgement regarding the correctness of one's answers to test questions, should represent less of a threat academically than judgement of correctness by another person, which is associated with the other-evaluation strategy.

Brady et al. (1975) tested out the comparative effect of self and other evaluation on self-concept. Seventy-eight fourth-grade children were randomly assigned to one of two evaluation groups which read and answered questions on textbook material. One group (self-evaluation) judged the correctness of their answers and reinforced themselves, while the other group (other evaluation) was judged and reinforced by the teacher. The results further suggested that boys who evaluated themselves tended to experience reduced anxiety and have enhanced self-concept more than boys who were evaluated by others.

The educational implications of the various studies by Felker, and Brady positing a distinction between strategies of self and other evaluation is paralleled by that between leadership styles. The authoritarian teacher being more task oriented would be expected to favour the other evaluation (teacher centred) strategy, while the democratic teacher being more person-oriented would likely favour the self-evaluation (student centred) strategy. Research in the area (Anderson 1959; Brophy and Good 1974) indicates that, while there are no academic performance differences due to variation in leadership style, there are relatively clear-cut affective differences. More specifically, democratic classrooms are characterized by greater cooperation by students, less competitiveness and greater enjoyment by students than are authoritarian classrooms (Brophy and Good 1974). A somewhat similar pattern emerged in the Brady et al. experiment. While there were no cognitive performance differences related to the type of strategy of evaluation employed, there were certain affective differences, in that the student-centred reduced the boys' tendency to lie and enhanced their self-concepts more than teacher-centred evaluations. It seems then, that the affective outcomes associated with the student-centred evaluation strategy are quite harmonious with those associated with democratic classrooms. The formal classroom with its emphasis on teacher assessment and comparison with others, is a stressful place for low self-concept children. Cohen and Cohen (1974) showed that compared with high self-concept pupils, those with low self-concept register greater dislike of 'doing tests', 'mathematics', 'working with another boy or girl' and 'working with a group of children'. At the same time, they give a significantly greater liking rating to 'watching television' and to their ratings of 'listening to teacher' and 'art and craft'.

How do we account for these observed differences? If we dismiss the idea that children with low self-concepts are merely indolent and prefer passive activities such as listening to the teacher tell a story or watching a television show, and call to mind that our sample of junior school teachers, in general, practised grouping by ability and used the recording of marks as part of the reward structure of their classrooms, then one possible explanation of the differences might include the following observations. Relative to his high self-concept classmate, the low self-concept of ability child is unhappy in both curriculum activities where his performance is publicly visible and/or teacher judged (e.g. mathematics, doing tests, acting) and in organizational settings where he is grouped on some criterion of superiority or inferiority in doing a particular skill. In anonymous and unjudged situations, on the other hand (watching a television programme, listening to the teacher) the low self-concept child is presumably less likely to have his self-concept of ability 'damaged' and registers his greater liking for such activities.

Cohen and Cohen's data suggest that for the child who (relative to his classmate) is numerate, literate, independent and not over-anxious when under stress, the formal competitive classroom in which work is regularly set, marked, tested and appropriately rewarded provides a climate for the maintenance and enhancement of a high self-concept. Because the creative arts are less readily assessable and indeed less often formally assessed, subjects such as craft, art and music appear to offer little by way of enhancing or demeaning self-esteem. The converse holds for the child who relative to his classmates is less numerate and literate, and tends to react anxiously to the stress of competitive classroom organization. In this latter case such organizational ingredients are a sure recipe for damaging what may be already a low self-concept of ability. Barker-Lunn's (1970) findings show that children of below-average ability have the poorest academic self-concept, poorest teacher relationships, poorest social adjustment and are the most anxious in the classroom.

Stern (1942) reviewed thirty-four studies comparing directive and non-directive instruction in their influence on two types of learning results: (a) attitude change towards self and others, and (b) gain in cognitive knowledge and understanding. With regard to the latter, he concluded that in general the amount of cognitive gain is largely unaffected by the democratic or autocratic style of the instructor. However, when he summarized the findings related to attitude change towards self and others, he noted that irrespective of whether the instructor was concerned with attitudes towards self, towards other participants in the class or towards outgroups, the results generally indicated that undirected teaching helped a shift in a more favourable acceptant direction. This is to be expected, bearing in mind the results of client-centred therapy and counselling. But it is likely to be the teacher with positive self-concepts who is more willing to try out more non-directive informal teaching (Burns 1976) and hence only that sort of teacher who can change pupil self-attitudes in a favourable direction.

It must be noted, however, that such phrases as child centred versus teacher centred, formal versus informal, democratic versus autocratic, have been used in this text, as in most research reports, as loose synonyms to reflect a crude dichotomy between differences in teaching approach and the amount of pupil involvement in the processes of education, and only really label extremes on the continuum of teaching styles. Most teachers do show flexibility, using a ratio of formal to informal teaching to suit the particular context. It is the low self-concept teacher who would appear to be the most inflexible and rigid, sticking to known and safe techniques.

What the evidence on school organization and teaching style points to is that it is not only the form of organization that matters but the attitudes, values and personal philosophy of the teaching staff involved in articulating the system, the sort of expectations they hold for particular types of pupil, the teaching style and organization they feel most comfortable with and the attitudes they hold about themselves. These matter because it is personal encounter rather than organizational form that comprises each pupil's contact with education. It may be that if governments, administrators and head teachers wish to develop particular school organizations and teaching methods then it is necessary for the teachers involved to possess sufficiently positive and robust self-concepts to make them work.

The basic educational philosophy of the teacher looks as though it resides in the level of his attitudes to himself. It might well be that depending on the sort of educational system desired, one part of the selection procedure for potential teachers should be an index of self-concept. That is, so long as instruments capable of assessing self-concept that are acceptably reliable and valid can be devised. If informal, highly personalized, unstructured teaching approaches are required then those teachers lacking doubts about self-worth may ensure the functioning of the system far better than those who have low levels of self-acceptance. The latter may only be effective in an approach requiring formal teacher-imposed subject matter and impersonal relationships. Obviously, these dichotomies between types of teacher and types of method are crude but the implication is certainly there. One can surmise that many innovations in the methodology of teaching and in the internal organization of some schools have foundered on, among other things, the failure of teachers to work the innovations in the way they were meant to do, because teachers have been either unwilling or unable to adapt (e.g. Barker-Lunn 1970). Low self-esteem functions like blinkers, limiting the perspectives from which the teacher's role is viewed. Thus constrained, the teacher with a low evaluation of himself would find it difficult to undertake another type of role. A change from formal to informal style creates a threat to the self-concept, since the latter style is more demanding, both intellectually and emotionally, exposing personal inadequacy and insecurity. The progressive approach to teaching places more demands on the teacher, as he has to be a better type of person in a great variety of ways.

An interesting analysis of schools by Lewis and Purkey (1978) presents two contrasting models, the family school and the factory school. They argue that the ethos and organization of each influence the quality of life and interaction in the classroom and the development of the self-concept of the denizens. Lewis and Purkey feel that, too often, schooling approaches the factory model. In this model the role of the school is to mass-produce a product acceptable to the consumer (the public). Workers (students) in the factory school have relatively little control over their world, and are required to be obedient, conforming and busy. They are crowded together in large groups and have arbitrary time schedules to control their entries and exits. Their work consists of relatively basic skills to be measured by standardized tests. Quality control is maintained by constant supervision, regulations to ensure desired learning and frequent performance testing.

The factory school in its extreme form provides pupils with an environment where (1) they are expected to conform, be dependent and busy; (2) other people and the clock dictate their interests and activities; (3) they are placed in large groups and processed impersonally; (4) they are continuously supervised, evaluated, rewarded or punished on the basis of performance; and (5) each individual pursues tasks for institutional rewards. Obviously the quality of life in the factory school can contribute to dehumanization, alienation and psychological failure.

The family model which Lewis and Purkey admire, is warm, cooperative, accepting and positive. Mutual support and concern for other group members is central. Feeling welcome and worthwhile is encouraged, enhancing the self-concept while structure and rules allow freedom within limits accepted by all members. Positive expectations and encouragement increases academic achievement in parallel with the self-concept.

Nowhere are we arguing for a permissive 'free' school. An unstructured, spontaneous environment without any clear expectations is detrimental to the self-concept and performance of pupils in school just as it is in the home. Alongside the qualities of warmth, cooperation and acceptance, the teacher must place firm expectations for each child and a structure flexible enough to allow for individual initiative and responsibility. This atmosphere signals to pupils that others have concern for them and have confidence in their abilities to achieve and to assume responsibilities.

SUMMARY

Child-centred informal schooling only seems to produce more self-esteem gains than traditional schooling when the pupils have a prolonged exposure to it. Over the short term of most studies, significant differences generally do not emerge. While high achievers generally show more positive self-concepts than low achievers, streaming appears to help the latter develop more positive self-esteem than they do in unstreamed schools.

The attitudes of teachers seem more important than the classroom organization. If teachers are not at home in the organizational structure, e.g. teachers who favour streaming but teach in an unstreamed school, then many pupils' self-concepts suffer. Teachers' level of self-concept influences their preferred style of teaching, with low self-concept teachers tending towards traditional, formal methods and showing low flexibility in teaching style.

Teachers with positive self-concepts provide a different classroom environment than their low self-esteem colleagues; it is an environment characterized by more pupils talking, more creative and divergent thinking and more teacher and pupil interaction and support at an individual level. This promotes affective development, encouraging pupils to involve themselves in realistic self-evaluation.

Small schools place more demands on all students to take part and compete in academic and non-academic activities than larger schools where the inept can avoid

Can a teacher who finds formal, traditional teaching methods also have a high self-concept?

public display. This suggests that small schools have a greater effect in enhancing the self-concepts of the successful and lowering the self-concepts of the unsuccessful.

The existing evidence on school organization points not only to the form of the organization having an effect on pupil self-concept, but also to the strong impact of teacher attitudes and values, particularly teachers' self-concept which influences teaching methods and the expectations that teachers hold about particular types of pupils.

13

Special School or Mainstreaming

HANDICAP

There has been little work done on the effects of handicap on the self-concept, though it might be argued on the basis of what has already been said that self-dissatisfaction, low self-esteem and self-rejection could well be the outcome of physical disability. Only one major piece of research exists on this issue, that of Richardson, Hastorf and Dornbusch (1964). They obtained self-descriptions from handicapped and healthy ten and eleven year-old children in order to examine the effects of physical disability on a disabled child's concept of himself. The picture produced from the taped self-descriptions of handicapped children emphasized the physical restrictions imposed by the handicap, its psychological impact, the deprivation of social experience and the limitations on involvement in the social world. Lack of social involvement and experience led to an impoverishment of the child's skill in interpersonal relations. It appears that for these children, direct experience in social interaction is a prerequisite for the full development of perceptual categories dealing with human relationships.

The handicapped children were very realistic in their self-descriptions. Although they shared in the peer values, they were aware that they could not live up to the high expectations placed on physical activities. Physical disability does not have the same consequences for boys as for girls. For example, handicapped girls may turn to non-physical recreation, where they are not disadvantaged, but this alternative is perhaps less acceptable to the boys because physical activity is more highly valued among them. Possibly because of this, they expressed more difficulties in inter-personal relations and made more use of humour to gain some measure of acceptance. Handicapped boys, also, expressed more concern about aggression than did handicapped girls, possibly as a consequence of being more often targets of physical aggression which is used less by the girls. Both handicapped boys and girls showed greater concern with the past than did healthy boys and girls, possibly, because of the greater uncertainty and threat in the present.

Children with physical handicaps are likely to encounter a variety of responses to their bodies: curiosity, pity, avoidance, ridicule and, with it all, the message that one is different. Many exceptional children are able to put their plight into words. They can express their awareness of physical difference from other children and can reveal their self-concept and some of the factors which have contributed to their life problems. In this the children talk of the primary importance of parental attitude, of siblings and the peer group, and of teacher attitude. Two case studies of handicapped children follow.

Case Study One

Billy, ten years old. He was referred to the school psychologist because of being 'withdrawn' and because of non-participation in school learning or school activities. A tall boy, he was promoted each year, the teacher said, 'Because he would stand out if we kept him back with the smaller children.' When seen by the school psychologist, Billy claimed that he could neither write, read, spell, nor do arithmetic. Not only that but he even refused to try.

His parents reported that the boy had always been 'different'. He was slow to walk (18 to 20 months), slow to feed himself and was clumsy. The father admitted he had been extremely disappointed in his son: 'Who wouldn't be? He can't do anything like other boys his age. He gets into fights but is beaten up. He can't play football and he can't do things I ask him to'. The other children in the family were 'rewarding' but, 'Billy sticks out like a sore thumb.' This the father said was because of the boy's awkwardness; always knocking things over and spilling things and messing things up and his 'acting like an infant' when out socially. Other children his age refused to play with him because of this. It grieved both the father and the mother that the boy played with five and six year-old children.

A review of school cumulative records and a conference with the teacher revealed that Billy sat quietly in class—often with his head on his desk. Each teacher had accepted him as a challenge but had given up after a few months of school.

Seen in four interviews, Billy demonstrated that he could read, write, spell and do simple arithmetic at a seven year-old level. In revealing this, Billy began to talk about himself and why he refused to do school work. He spoke of his awkwardness and of his poor motor coordination, of his light and dark and grey spells (it was noted that Billy had frequent petit-mal seizures and frequent mild subliminal lapses in attention), and of how no one, not even his parents, had ever understood his problem or accepted or liked him. Of school he said, 'My teacher slapped me in the face because I couldn't remember what she just told me. I've hated school ever since first year. They [teachers] don't understand me.' He talked about being different from others and feeling inferior.

The physical and neurological examinations revealed difficulty with gross motor coordination, a mild visuo-motor perceptual problem, and the petit-mal epilepsy. Billy had the potential for average intellectual functioning, but was severely educationally retarded. The physical (neurological) problems which Billy had were compounded by felt parental rejection and felt rejection by teachers and the peer group. He reacted to this with discouragement and depression. His statements summarized his interpretation of the feelings of others toward him and indicates why he had given up in school learning and in life generally.

Case Study Two

Jane, eleven years old. Jane was referred by the family doctor because she was doing poorly in school and making a poor social adjustment. She had periods of depression, a variety of somatic complaints for which no physical basis could be found. The parents added very little to this and felt that she feigned illnesses. They claimed that she had developed normally in every respect, and they were at a loss to explain the poor school and social adjustment.

Jane herself assumed an air of normality but she had signs of cerebral palsy. Denial of the palsy was written all over her responses to comments and questions. While attempting to accomplish fine motor tasks her athetoid movements became increased and control diminished. She said, 'I have a stomach ache and I think I'm going to be sick. I want to go home.' She spoke of her awareness of her difference from other children, of her parents' attempts to treat her as if she were a normal child, of their seeming to demand that she be normal, and of her confusion arising from her parents' shielding and protectiveness. Jane realized that in ways she was like other children, but early recognized that people changed on meeting her and looked at her curiously. In discussing her various aches and pains she said, 'My mother says she has them when I get her upset. I get them too when I'm upset.' And again, in this context, 'I'm scared when Miss S calls on me. I can't read and I cry and the boys laugh at me and make funny faces.' The teacher brought out that the children were afraid of Jane and would avoid her. At times they would tease her unmercifully. In the summation interview with the parents they revealed their early awareness of the cerebral palsy. In summary, Jane a girl with athetoid cerebral palsy, presented a confused self-concept. On the one hand she was sick all of her life, spoiled, and in her eyes something very special. Parental denial and strivings for normality put undue pressure on her. On the other hand, she was aware of the physical limitations and of the parental reaction and the reaction of others to her condition and felt extremely unworthy and inadequate. Her pattern of maladjustment was neurotic with psychosomatic symptomatology and learning impairment.

Both of these children knew that they had normal abilities for learning. Both wanted to learn and in this be like other children. However, their physical appearance caused adverse reactions which they interpreted as rejection. The use of symptoms and behaviour in the face of anxiety and fear or as protection against their own hostile expression was self-defence. Sensitive, and constantly on the defensive, they so tenaciously protected their feelings about themselves that they dared not participate. They tried their best at times but were hurt by criticism, teasing, failure, etc. Billy, for example, in talking about his first teacher said, 'I was trying my best, but she was too angry to see it. She hit me when I didn't answer.' I stopped trying to answer and hoped that she wouldn't ask me questions. After a while she didn't.'

The most important hurt is that of felt rejection by parents. This rejection is not deliberate but based on parental feelings evoked by having a child who in their eyes is not perfect or the image of their expectations. Parents usually try quite hard to meet the needs of the child but finding themselves psychologically blocked from accepting him they set up their line of defence. Such parents in describing the child do so in a superficial and intellectual way: the emotional bonding is missing in their recitation. Similarly parents who describe their children accurately often do so in a dispassionate way and give the impression that they are living with a group of symptoms rather than the child.

It is this quality of parental self-protection and distortion that the child reacts to as if he were rejected. The parents are unable to meet the emotional needs of the child so bound up are they with their own emotional response to the child. The child too has learned to make an adjustment to his family that is fairly protective of himself but this is interrupted by the advent of schooling. From the relative security of the home, the child enters an arena that demands group conformity, full attention to learning and all under the leadership of a strange adult figure. The child looks for psychological and physical safety, that is, mothering qualities in the teacher. The child will act and react according to previously learned patterns that worked at home. But the teacher tends not to behave as parents have. As emotional and attitudinal handicaps develop so the physical ones decline in importance.

It was of interest to note that these children want things to be better and can spell out how the school and the home can provide the needed security. They show some confusion in this because of the reaction of others to them. They have a good awareness of physical difference and of their potential for learning, and they feel in many respects to be like other children. Many such children question their self-concept because it is now incompatible with the negative attitudes of others. To protect what he had, Billy defended himself by a complete withdrawal from hurtful learning. To outward appearance he was so well insulated that there was a grave question regarding his ego strength. Jane used crying and physical symptoms to avoid the pain of participation and possible failure.

It has been found, that children who have been 'different' from birth and whose parents have reacted adversely accept their physical self. They have found that they can learn and that they can do things to their own satisfaction, close to their potential. There is recognition that generally they cannot do as well as their peers. They ask only to be understood and accepted as they are.

By contrast, the child who was born 'normal' and who developed a normal self-concept, but then receives an ego blow (paralytic poliomyelitis, physical injury, or so forth) wants to be returned to his original physical self. The acquired 'difference' has broken down a previously adequate physical and psychological image of the self. In this, the child reacts to the reactions of parents and others, but mainly on the basis of the personal narcissistic blow.

In considering the physically different child, Cutter (1962) points to the feelings of inadequacy, unworthiness, and confusion that these children have about themselves, and holds that this confused self-concept derives from the lack of understanding and consequent negative feelings of parents, teachers, children and others with whom they come in contact. In a study of normal, hard-of-hearing, and orthopaedically handicapped children, Heilizer (1962) found that these groups perceived themselves differently, and the nature of their self-perceptions was directly related to the types of experiences they had had as a consequence of their handicaps.

In the above case studies, the school representatives in their own ways expressed the conviction that the children were brain damaged or mentally retarded. Mistakenly, they assumed that this alone was the basis of the learning deficit. They felt that such children could be helped only through specialized approaches to teaching. Their preoccupation with organic factors, some vague 'brain damage', caused them to lose focus in trying to treat the symptom. In doing so, they lost the child. The teacher's use of a limiting diagnostic label represented a defence against her failure to understand and teach the child. Sometimes, the child's physical difference stirs up a personal subconscious problem in the teacher. For example, Jane's athetosis was repulsive to her teacher; she found herself psychologically blocked from teaching children with physical differences.

When parents, teachers and others discover the real child behind the physical difference and behavioural symptoms, the emotionally determined learning difficulties can be overcome. It is difficult to convey the feelings of inadequacy, unworthiness, and confusion that the physically different child has about himself and the underlying theoretical and dynamic considerations. The child's confused self-concept derives from the lack of understanding and consequent negative feelings of the parents, teachers, children and others. Of key importance is the help given the parents towards an understanding of themselves and their child, and the close collaborative working relationship with the school and teacher.

Many handicapped and retarded children enter school with a negative self-concept derived from impaired rearing. Parents may intuitively sense that their child is mentally or physically different or severely emotionally disturbed, and they develop intense feelings of failure and personal inadequacy. The presence of the child in the home furthers these feelings. The parents react in accordance with their individual and collective security and maturity. Mature parents, though hurt, are able adequately to accept the child and meet his physical and emotional needs. Less mature parents, or parents who have conflicts in their relationship, react quite differently. They have normal parental feelings for the child but feel guilty because of incomplete or ambivalent acceptance of the child's condition. The child may appear to be normal in specific respects and deviant in others. The parents have difficulty in equating the differences. They are confused by this and by hollow reassurances of relatives and well meaning friends. They witness failure of their many efforts to meet the needs of the child. The repeated frustrations lead to mounting negative feelings and to a parent's giving up in some situations. The guilt, anxiety and confusion call forth self-protective defences which partially block him from giving freely of himself to the child or to the other parent. One parent may play down observed signs of deviation in attempting to make things easier for the spouse and for himself. However, the similarly upset spouse may interpret this as indifference, callousness or lack of concern, and react strongly. One parent may claim complete blame for the condition and bear the burden in masochistic fashion. He may so dote on the child that the other parent reacts by feeling shut out of his own family. The child in turn reacts as if he interprets as rejection the well-intentioned but inadequate supply of love, acceptance and understanding. Thus the stage is set for conflicts in the family. With many children who have physical differences, the total learning maladjustment picture is greater than can be accounted for on the basis of the physical limitations present. The learning problem frequently is in part or wholly a secondary process due to emotional factors. Anxiety, fear of achieving, fear of failure, unhappiness or depression, repressed motivation, negativism or personality disorganization can impair learning and increase the burden on self-evaluation of a handicapped or retarded child.

Our culture values 'overcoming' as opposed to 'giving in to' difficulties and defects. Many parents want their handicapped children to behave as if they were not handicapped and encourage them to devote all their physical and emotional energy to proving that they are just as capable as other children. Less frequently, parents generalize the impact of a handicap in one area to all aspects of physical behaviour. In either of these circumstances, the child may be unable to acquire a realistic image of his or her true capabilities.

The same situation may occur in school. Teachers find that handicaps and illness, real or imagined, have effects in the classroom. The teacher faced with an allergic pupil, for example, may experience internal conflict about how to respond. The teacher who does not 'believe' in allergies may refuse to acknowledge or enforce restrictions requested by parents or doctors. On the other hand, the teacher may respond with exaggerated compliance to the requests. It is not uncommon to overreact to a child's handicap in order to satisfy the teacher's own need to project a nurturant image. Neither of these reactions helps the child to develop a realistic self-image.

Perhaps more important than the interaction between teacher and handicapped child, however, is the response of other pupils to that interaction. The teacher's behaviour not only shapes the pupil's reaction toward handicapped students but also defines the nature of physical incapacity in general. Since young children have limited experience with illness and physical disability, their knowledge of these things is gathered in large part from the teacher's reactions to pupils with such problems. Children who perceive that the teacher's attitude towards a handicapped pupil is negative may fear that they too can lose the teacher's approval and their own self-esteem through an illness or accident. Children who see handicapped pupils receiving special attention, or valuing, may imitate illness or trauma in order to obtain similar treatment.

Clearly, the teacher's attitude towards handicapped students has considerable impact. Yet research indicates that teachers may be unaware of their specific behavioural responses to these pupils. Studying a population of pre-service teacher training to become physical or special education instructors or physical therapists, Wolfgang and Wolfgang (1968) found a discrepancy between expressed attitudes about various handicaps and actual behaviour towards handicapped children. Although the teachers' attitudes were overwhelmingly positive, their behaviour, assessed with social distance measures, varied according to the nature of the child's handicap. In the classroom, teachers placed themselves closer to children with temporary handicaps (e.g. a broken limb) than to children with permanent, uncontrollable handicaps (e.g. amputation, epilepsy) and farthest away from pupils with controllable, physical problems (e.g. body odour, obesity). These teachers were evidently perceiving the handicap rather than the child. Such a perceptual block can blind teachers to behavioural cues which under normal circumstances would guide their responses. Projecting their own feelings into the situation, teachers can misjudge the pupil's needs. A badly scarred little girl, for example, dropped way behind in her reading. The remedial reading teacher questioned her and found that she had stopped performing up to her capability because the new teacher never called on her in class. The new teacher explained that she did not want to 'embarrass' the child by calling on her and thus drawing attention to her.

This child was receiving a false impression of her ability, as many handicapped children do. Keeve (1967) studying pupils excused from physical education classes due to previous trauma or past diagnosis of chronic disability, found that several of this group were in reality no longer handicapped. They were instead perpetuating 'phantom' handicaps. By continuing to excuse these pupils from physical education classes, Keeve concluded, the school administration was supporting their false body concepts and, perhaps, reinforcing a maladaptive mechanism that would become an inappropriate response to stress in adulthood.

Whether real or 'phantom', a handicap undoubtedly colours a child's school experience. Unintentionally, teachers and peers can communicate to handicapped children that they are unacceptable. Teachers, for example, may allow a child's cleanliness, or physical defects, to determine the degree and frequency of their contact with that child. Teachers' behaviours that tell children that they are not nice to be near, or to see, or to hear (e.g. consistently placing them in the back row of school photographs, ignoring them in lessons) reflect a negative image of those children's bodily selves. It is behaviour demonstrating that one is pleasant to see, hear or touch, that carries a message of acceptance and positive value.

SPECIAL PLACEMENT (SPECIAL CLASS OR SCHOOL)

The main current issue concerning the self-concept of children requiring special educational treatment, whether through physical or intellectual deficiencies, is how to set about that task of producing not only cognitive and academic gain, but also realistic self-esteem levels. The issue resolves itself into the question of whether educating them within normal classrooms (mainstreaming) or in special classes/schools is more beneficial for their educational and personal development.

Administrators in the area of special education have assumed that such a child should be placed in a segregated setting where he would have a chance for success among comparable peers. The inference is that normal class placement (or mainstreaming) confronts such a child with standards so out of reach that he has no substantial basis for self-evaluation.

Among the myths too seldom challenged in the field of mental retardation and handicap, is the belief that children so classified must always accrue a negative self-concept. In view of the failure and frustration which appear to be the lot of the retarded and handicapped, the concomitant presence of low self-esteem seemed a reasonable assumption. Special schools not only enable such pupils to feel academically adequate in terms of the norms of those schools but also are able to meet the emotional and social needs of the student because closer relationships in small classes between teachers and students are developed.

It is generally claimed that in the normal classroom, children with severe learning difficulties cannot achieve 'normal' standards. Thus there is little chance of their having rewarding experiences in the normal school environment. These children are, in fact, put at an unfair disadvantage because of failure to meet expectations. All too frequently they are thrust into an educational environment in which they are expected to achieve at a level beyond their capabilities or to perform as though they did not have the often insurmountable difficulties they are faced with. Under such circumstances, the development of positive self-attitudes becomes extremely difficult. As a result, remedial and handicapped children have been usually segregated from their peers in special schools or classes. Research tends to show that, in general, such policy has positive effects on the child's self-concept though opponents intuitively believe that such stigmatization would inevitably lower self-esteem.

Lawrence and Winchell (1973) reviewed research on the self-concepts of retarded children and felt that segregation increased feelings of academic adequacy but were very guarded as to whether segregation was beneficial to global self-feelings. In a major study, later, Smith et al. (1977) suggest that pupil improvement in special class groups was in the academic self-image aspect rather than in the global self-concept.

The important influence of type of school on self-attitudes is suggested by a limited study of slow-learning adolescents in which Higgins (1962) found a significant difference between the self-perceptions of children attending a special school and those attending a normal school. Children in the special school perceived themselves more positively in the school than those catered for in the regular classroom of the normal school who, by contrast, tended to perceive themselves in negative terms.

Schurr, Towne and Joiner (1972) found that taking students out of regular classrooms and placing them in special classes tended to increase their self-concept of ability. They administered Brookover et al.'s Self-Concept of Ability Scale to ESN students, twice, while they were attending regular classes and four times a year during the first and second years of their special classes placement. SCA scores showed a significant ascending linear trend during the first and second years of special class placement. The means of an ESN control group tested only twice during the second year of special class placement to examine possible effects of repeated testing were not significantly different from the group tested four times that year. This rules out repeated testing as an explanation for the ascending trends. Also the self-concept of ability scores of a small group of students reassigned to normal classes after spending one year in the special class decreased after one year of attending normal classes again. These findings agree with the idea that persons will tend to evaluate themselves against a restricted reference group which seems relevant to them.

Battle (1979) found that special-class placement enhanced self-esteem. It would seem that special class placement reduces the anxieties and frustrations of children with learning problems and consequently fosters positive feelings of self-worth. A

British study by Lewis (1971) also found enhancement of self-esteem after admission to ESN special schools.

This would indicate that the social and emotional developmental aims of the day special schools are being fulfilled. The immediate interpersonal environment of the classroom appears to be the effective reference against which actions and performances are measured and a relative status determined. Broader and more complex sociocultural standards have, presumably, not been perceived and this may cause damage to self-esteem in post-school life, Lewis (op. cit.) cautions.

Parish et al. (1980) reveal that the inclusion of exceptional children in normal classrooms is not a panacea for their social and emotional difficulties. Attitudes of such pupils to themselves were not positive and normal pupils held them in low esteem too. Parish et al. (1980) concur with Lewis in finding that the earlier the ESN child enters the ESN school, and the longer he spends there, the more likely he is to have high self-regard. This is probably due to the reduction of time spent in a progressively scholastic normal school where his limitations would be increasingly highlighted and the extension of the period in the special school amongst similarly handicapped children.

Whilst accepting that the ESN day special school class is not the only reference group to which the ESN child relates himself, it is worth remembering that the two most potent sources of influence, the family and the peer group, set standards of behaviour which do not differ appreciably from the demands of his ESN classmates. Thus the ESN child, coming mainly from culturally deprived areas mixes again with children of similar social and educational backgrounds in an environment geared to low levels of expectation which ensure a high degree of success. In such a school a high level of self-regard is hardly a surprising discovery despite the common assumption of widespread self-denigration.

Three things stand out in this research on special placement.
1. Generally self-concepts improve when the standards of evaluation are not those of the normal child.
2. There is a positive correlation between length of time spent in a special class or school and self-concept level.
3. Caution is expressed that whilst the day special school provides a sympathetic, controlled environment in which self-confidence and self-regard are successfully nurtured, the segregated nature of the school is also providing an unrealistic yardstick of human behaviour.

THE MAINSTREAMING APPROACH

Clearly a positive self-concept is necessary to a satisfactory state of mental health but equally a realistic awareness of the normal world is also appropriate. In order to prevent shock to the psyche which many special-school children experience upon leaving school and looking for work, and from which a few never appear to recover, many authorities now favour including handicapped and educationally retarded children in normal classrooms. Research has tended to look at schemes where special-school children have been integrated for only part of each school day, being withdrawn to special classes for the rest of the day, rather than at total integration.

Assignment of children with learning problems to self-contained, special classrooms may result in stigmatization of the child with a lowering of self-concept. This concern for the special class child's self-concept, coupled with mounting suspicion that special-class assignment does not mean accelerated academic achievement, supports the mainstreaming movement where children with learning problems, previously assigned to self-contained classrooms, are placed in regular classrooms. While controversy mounts about the efficacy of mainstreaming special-class children, there is a dearth of evidence on the impact of the experience on the children's self-regard. Although special education has come well on the way to mainstreaming in North America this change has come about because of individual commitment, intuition, a desire for something new, or any other reasons needed to bring about effective change except for hard data.

Research on Mainstreaming

There are but few pieces of work that focus on the effectiveness of mainstreaming. For example, Carroll (1967) compared two groups of educable mentally retarded (EMR) children. One group attended a special segregated classrom for half the day and a normal classroom for the other half while the other group attended a segregated classroom full time. Carroll (op. cit.) found that the results of this study confirm that there was an impact on an EMR youngster's self-perception when he was singled out from a classroom of friends and placed in a different room and, for the most part, a different school.

Those EMR children who remained in a regular classroom one half day had a significant decrease in self-derogation which Carroll interpreted as a more positive self-concept at the end of eight months of this regime. The EMR youngsters who were segregated and had no contact with normal peers during the school day were significantly more derogatory of themselves in the post-test. This was interpreted to mean an increasingly less positive self-concept. This finding is in agreement with that of Meyerowitz (1962) who noted that EMR children placed in segregated settings developed a more negative self-concept than those retained in regular classes.

However, in addition, Carroll's study (op. cit.) revealed that the EMR children in the partially integrated setting made more progress in reading than the segregated group though no differences were found in the areas of spelling or arithmetic.

This piece of work suggests that the partial integration may provide better for the needs of the EMR child than
1. a fully integrated scheme where the specialist help may be missing and evaluation is always against the normal peer group or

2. a fully segregated system where the child builds up unrealistic self-perceptions and has only to live up to the lower expectations demanded in a special school environment.

The partial integration allows for specialist help in basic subjects for part of the day and an opportunity to mix with normal school children, come to terms with the reality of his situation and have somewhat higher expectations applied to him in subjects like art, music, handicraft, etc. where it is feasible for him to reach higher levels of performance. A very valuable offshoot of such a partial integration is that the host pupils and teachers may develop more positive attitudes towards handicapped and retarded pupils.

Influence of Reference Groups

In another report Smith et al. (1977) provide data from several studies on self-concepts of school-labelled learning-disabled (LD) children. During the course of these investigations, some of these children (selected randomly) were integrated into regular classrooms during reading and mathematics periods for half of each school day, while others remained in their traditional self-contained classrooms for the full day. Thus, it was possible to assess experimentally the impact of half-day mainstreaming on children's self-regard, using as controls similar children who were not mainstreamed.

Using the Piers–Harris self-concept scale, Smith and his associates (1977) found that learning disabled (LD), or ESN children did not manifest lower self-concepts and, hence, special class placement and possible stigmatization had not affected their attitudes to themselves. Smith suggests reasons for their robust self-concepts. First, once in the classroom, children were accorded more attention than they received in regular classrooms because maximum enrolment in each class was ten and each teacher received assistance from a part-time teaching aide. The small group also possibly made it easier for each child to feel a part of the whole. Second, academic activities were structured in a manner to preclude the experience of failure.

In the light of these school-related factors, the moderately high mean self-concept score obtained by these LD children seemed somewhat understandable. Furthermore, social comparison theory suggests that in the absence of objective standards of comparison people will use significant others as the basis for estimating self-worth. Also, given the choice of relatively similar and dissimilar others, people more likely select similar individuals as bases for social comparisons e.g. other children in the self-contained classrooms and on the manner in which they were treated in these classrooms.

In a more general sense, LD children in special classes would be expected to base their self-concept social comparisons on other academically handicapped children in the same classroom. When social comparisons are made with other children who possess similar academic handicaps, we see little reason to expect attenuated self-concepts. We might expect that only to the extent that LD children are regularly exposed in school to other normal children, would their estimates of self-worth diminish. The presence of other children without academic handicaps would introduce another basis for comparison. Since this new social comparison group generally would possess superior academic skills, the self-concept of the LD child might diminish at least to the extent that the child used the new reference children when making social comparisons relevant to his or her self-concept.

The impact of integrating a randomly selected subset of these children into normal classrooms on a half-day basis was studied by Smith et al. (op. cit.) who believed that to the extent that the new group is used in making social comparisons self-regard might diminish particularly in relation to intellectual and social status. These partially integrated children were compared with those remaining in the special classes. Self-concept scales were applied on three occasions. Initially both groups were equivalent on total and subtest self-concept scores.

The subsequent testings revealed that the impact of the mainstreaming experiment was to augment considerably the self-concepts of the experimental children. Directionally similar and significant changes also were obtained on subtests indexing intellectual and school status, physical appearance, popularity, happiness and satisfaction. Children remaining in self-contained LD classrooms showed a small initial increase then a levelling off in self-concept. The self-concept change for partially mainstreamed children was seemingly opposite to that predicted on the basis of social comparison theory. However, these results can possibly be reconciled with such a theory.

Morse and Gergen (1970) pointed out that although an individual associates with many others in a day not all those others serve as bases for comparison. Only those who provide information valuable in assessing the individual's position and in planning his behaviour are deemed useful. Additionally, their study suggested that the mere presence of another person who is like oneself may be enough to boost one's self-esteem. Moreover, Festinger (1954) stated that the individual compares himself with those more similar than dissimilar on a specific attribute or ability. The tendency to compare oneself with some other specific person decreases as the difference between his ability and one's own increases. Therefore, both the perceived similarity of other people and the usefulness of comparisons with them apparently figures in selecting individuals or groups to compare oneself with.

A crucial point relevant to the half-day mainstreaming is Festinger's (op. cit.) reference to a person deviating toward the lower end of the ability scale. Provided he has other comparison groups for self-evaluation on this ability he may remain personally and privately quite unaffected by this group. Theoretically, a special-class child who has similar children with whom to make useful comparisons possesses a basis for a positive—or at least not negative—self-concept, even when he is integrated into regular classrooms for part of each day. The special-class child who is integrated into the educational mainstream for part of each day is provided with two peer reference groups. Presumably, the child may exercise relative freedom in selecting which group he uses in relevant self-concept comparisons. Thus he maintains some control over his own self-regard by his choice of comparative reference groups and guides his own fate accordingly. Moreover, Rosenberg (1965) emphasized that the individual may select different reference groups for different self-relevant comparisons. The special-class children integrated into the educational mainstream for part of each day may have used the two available comparative reference groups in maintaining and augmenting their self-regard. For academic-relevant social comparisons, they may have selected the group with children more similar to themselves, i.e., the other academically handicapped children in their special classroom settings. For other comparisons relevant to self-concept, however, these children may have their new, regular classroom reference group. The mainstream integration experience may have imbued the children with an enhanced sense of belonging, or of being more a part of the overall school environment. Assuming that the children liked specific aspects of both classes, then possibly they were enjoying the best of both worlds. The significantly increased self-concept that was measured (even in the absence of substantially improved academic performance) may have resulted from the opportunity to choose their reference group.

If the above interpretation is correct, these results have both theoretical and practical implications. Theoretically social comparison and reference group theory provide a rich foundation from which to derive hypotheses to test in school. These two theories offer the possibility of providing much needed insight into the impact on children's self-regard of the increasingly popular trend toward integrating special-class children into the academic mainstream. Practically, it appears that, under certain circumstances, integration of special-class children into the academic mainstream can lead to increased self-regard. When special-class children are mainstreamed for half of each day, the resulting availability of multiple comparison reference groups may help to increase self-regard, compared with special-class children who remain in self-contained classrooms.

We face, however, the question of what would have occurred had the children been integrated for the entire day. In this case, reference group selectivity would have been eliminated, and the only group available would have consisted of children with potentially superior academic performance capabilities. Under these circumstances, the children's self-regard may well have decreased. A control group of pupils totally integrated into the normal classroom is needed to determine the correct balance needed for both academic and personal development. It may be too that the 'experimental' children realized they were part of an experiment, their teachers certainly did and all this could create a Hawthorne effect.

In order to clarify these issues Smith and his colleagues (op. cit.) included another study. A group of learning disabled children mainstreamed for half a day per week were divided randomly into two groups. When completing the self-concept scale the experimental groups were told to compare themselves only in relation to the pupils in the normal classroom with whom they were for only half a day per week. The other subgroup were free to use either of the two reference groups. Two predictions were made.

Children receiving the manipulation designed to enhance salience of normal classroom group membership, were expected to register no increase in mean self-concept, or even a mean decrease after mainstreaming. The children who could use their special-class group were expected to demonstrate an increase in self-esteem. Both predictions were confirmed. The comparisons exhibited a gain in self-concept. The experimental groups, however, comparing themselves only with normal children, experienced a mean decrease in self-concept. Since all the children were mainstreamed, the manipulation of the reference groups was clearly manifest in its impact on self-concept level. This impact might have shown up even more clearly if instruments tapping the academic self-concept had been used instead of a general self-esteem measure.

The reference group children's restriction consisted of verbal directions to compare themselves only with regular classroom children. Although effective, this manipulation may not be an equal substitute for the actual experience of full main-streaming. The experience of the regular classroom as the role reference group may have had a greater impact on the self-concepts of experimental students. Their self-concepts might have been lowered even further by the actual experience of full integration.

On a given dimension of self-concept, children use similar others to protect their self-concepts from diminution. But when similar others are removed as a source of comparison self-concept declines if those remaining are superior on the relevant self-concept dimension. This investigation therefore supports a hypothesis that comparisons that prove useful are selected to enhance self-esteem. Additionally they support Festinger's hypothesis that persons at the lower end of an ability scale may remain unaffected by a group situation provided they have other relevant comparison groups for self-evaluation.

In addition to adding to our knowledge of social comparison and reference group theory, Smith et al.'s results present important practical considerations for those involved in educational programme planning. Mainstreaming can be a valuable experience for academically handicapped children accompanied by an increase in self-esteem provided they maintain contact with similar others. Sudden, full-day integration into regular classrooms, on the other hand, might be seriously detrimental to the self-regard of the academically handicapped child.

Despite the promise held out in Carroll's (1967) and Smith et al.'s (1977) findings, further research reports both negative and positive effects of mainstreaming on self-concept (Zigler and Muenchow 1979).

INTEGRATING HANDICAPPED PUPILS

Handicapped pupils in the normal classroom present more problems than learning-disabled pupils. Special facilities, teaching techniques and equipment may all be required. Additionally, the perception of very noticeable disabilities by teacher and other pupils may cause discord and difficulty. Learning-disabled children do not stand out so markedly.

The misfortune hypothesis of Dembo, Leviton and Wright (1956) is the most studied and respected hypothesis among students of the psychology of disability. These investigators studied relations between disabled and healthy persons. They observed that the basic relationship between the disabled and healthy depends on their concept of misfortune and that usually both groups devalue a person who has experienced a misfortune. This concept of misfortune and its implications for the conditions under which a person may be devalued also provide a framework for understanding the process of adjustment to misfortune or acceptance of loss. According to this, people who accept their loss value their misfortune differently from those who have not adjusted to their loss. Dembo et al. (op. cit.) further hypothesized that depending upon whether or not the person has accepted his loss, he will interact differently with healthy people. More specifically, they predict different reactions by the physically disabled to the discriminatory attitudes of the healthy depending on the adjustment of the disabled person. If the disabled person has not accepted his loss, he will feel that the negative attitudes of the healthy are justified and valid. He will suffer (feel depressed, anxious, dysphoric, etc.) because of the devaluation but he will still attempt to be like and closely associate with the healthy. If the person has accepted his loss, he does not believe the negative attitudes of others are warranted and he will tend to devalue the healthy evaluator. Also, he will suffer less than the maladjusted disabled person and have less need to associate with and emulate the healthy.

Grand (1972) tested the Dembo et al. (1956) hypotheses and was able to confirm Dembo's theory and show that disabled persons who had not accepted their disability tended to devalue themselves if others around them provided unfavourable feedback.

Disabled persons with low acceptance of their disability also perceive healthy negative evaluators as quite unlikeable. Although this work was with adults it suggests that in the highly evaluative world of the school only those disabled pupils who accept their disability and themselves will be able to deal with the negative evaluation that comes at some time or other in every child's life at school. They are likely to receive more unfavourable evaluations in a normal school (mainstreaming) because they will create more difficulties for teachers, disturb classroom routine and not to be able to take part in normal pupils' social activities. For some healthy pupils, such disabled pupils might be perceived as strange and threatening, causing quite negative responses. Only those disabled pupils who have integrated the disability into their self-concept and accept themselves, are able to cope better with a normal school. If handicapped pupils are to be successfully integrated into normal classrooms, it should be done primarily with those who already accept themselves as they are, not with those who feel unworthy and mutilated. These latter need their self-concepts strengthening through counselling.

Teaching strategies too, even with the self-accepting disabled, must be aimed at providing successful experiences in a warm accepting ethos just as for any other pupil. Pupil members of the 'reception' classes must have positive attitudes to others in order to provide positive feedback to the handicapped and as we know from research (p. 344), such positive acceptance of others derives from positive feelings towards self. There appears to be no unambiguous answer to whether segregated or integrated placement is superior. Zigler and Muenchow (1979) suggest that underlying the concept of mainstreaming is the issue of 'normalization', which they feel is a denial of the child's right to be different or to have special needs. They also criticize mainstreaming on the same lines as de-institutionalization, which often amounts to the trading of inferior care for no care at all. Moreover, without the special education received in special classes some children with special needs may not function effectively in the social world as adults. For example, Zigler and Muenchow (1979) quote a deaf teacher who said that the paradox is that, 'without the education I got in deaf schools I would be hopelessly lost in the hearing world now'. They suggest that social competence should be the ultimate criterion for monitoring the effectiveness of mainstreaming.

A TRAINING PROGRAMME FOR TEACHERS

From what we know of the conditions under which self-esteem and achievement prosper, we can say that whatever the regime (segregated, partially integrated, or totally integrated) it is the quality of the interaction between teacher and pupil, and between pupils that perhaps matters as much. To improve conditions the following seem minimum requirements and one suspects that where exceptional children decline in self-esteem under any organization then these conditions have not been met.

1. Appropriate training for teachers.
2. Extra staff to assist regular classroom teachers with the education of special students.
3. Allocation of sufficient funds to employ an efficient mainstreaming programme.

The first condition is the most important. Ascione and Borg (1980) report on a training programme for teachers designed to enable teachers to modify the self-concept of handicapped children who had been integrated into normal classrooms.

A major problem faced by teachers in mainstreaming classrooms is to help create an environment in which the handicapped child can adjust and learn. Successful mainstreaming will, in part, depend on providing regular classroom teachers with skills relevant to the education and management of handicapped children. A number of studies have shown that handicapped children who meet the requirements for regular class placement often have self-concepts that are significantly lower than those of normal children (Black 1974). Improving the mainstreamed handicapped child's self-concept would appear to be a worthy educational goal especially in light of the significant relationships that have been found between pupil self-concept and both academic achievement and classroom behaviour. Therefore, providing regular classroom teachers with skills that will enhance pupil self-concept may have positive effects on the achievement and classroom behaviour of handicapped children.

The four modules that make up the Self-Concept Protocol series were developed by Borg as materials stressing the practical application of educational and psychological research to the classroom. The seventeen specific teacher behaviours covered in the modules reflect the following general categories of teachers' communication. Ways of expressing anger, for example, by telling the child how misbehaviour makes the teacher feel instead of being sarcastic to the child (module 1); listening skills and objective messages (module 2); forms of praise and giving instructions (module 3); and ways of fostering positive self-perception statements by pupils. Modules 1 and 3 are based primarily on the theoretical work of C. Gordon (1968) and Ginott (1972). No empirical research beyond anecdotes could be found to provide evidence for the desirability of these teachers' behaviours emphasized by these authors. A research base supports the positive effects of teachers' behaviours covered in the modules 2 and 4. For example, reflective listening (restating what a child has said) and accurate empathy are described in module 2. In one study (Stoffer 1970) teacher aides spent between thirty minutes and an hour twice a week for three months interacting with behaviour problem and achievement retarded children in grades 1 through 6. Children whose aides were rated high on nonpossessive warmth and accurate empathy made significant gains in achievement and presented fewer behaviour problems than children whose aides were low on these characteristics. Truax and Carkhuff (1967) found that pre-school children's adjustment to school was positively related to the nonpossessive warmth and accurate empathy displayed to them by their teacher. The most impressive evidence regarding the importance of reflective listening is contained in two studies by Aspy reported by Good, Biddle and Brophy (1975). In the first study, the frequency of grade 3 teachers' reflective listening statements was positively correlated with their pupils' reading achievement. In the second, the pupils of reading teachers trained to use reflective listening made greater gains in reading than the pupils of untrained teachers.

In module 4, emphasis is placed on the teacher-modelling positive self-perception statements and reinforcing such statements made by pupils. Also, Krop, Calhoun and Verrier (1971) showed that a child's self-descriptive responses can be modified in a positive way by reinforcement. Their research suggested that self-concept can be enhanced through reinforcing positive self-perceptions and that such changes are often maintained over time. Therefore, research, albeit limited, supports the desirability of the teachers' behaviours covered in the Self-Concept Protocol Modules.

The Self-Concept Modules were first evaluated as a part of a study reported in Ascione and Borg (op. cit.). Twelve elementary-school teachers in regular classrooms participated in an eight-week in-service course covering the modules. Sixteen additional teachers served as a control group. Teachers were observed before and after the test and so were pupils' self-concepts. Although significant positive gains were made by the experimental group of teachers on the majority of the behaviours, there was no effect on pupils' self-concepts. There was, however, a gain in self-concept that approached significance for a small group of intermediate-grade coloured students. One factor Borg offers as a reason for the negligible effects was the high pre-test self-concept scores of the pupils which left little room for improvement. This would not be expected to be the case in a sample of handicapped children.

Since the main purpose of this research was to assess the effectiveness of these modules in changing the self-concepts of mainstreamed handicapped pupils, the self-concept course was first explained to two teacher-consultants who taught in mainstreaming classrooms. They evaluated the effectiveness of the teachers' behaviours with their handicapped pupils and made suggestions for improving the modules. After the course was taught, the modules were revised, incorporating the teacher-consultants' suggestions. These revised modules were used to test the following hypotheses:

1. Teachers receiving training in the self-concept behaviours will have more favourable adjusted post-treatment scores on the measures of teacher performance than teachers who did not receive the training.
2. Handicapped pupils, in both the experimental and control groups, will score lower on the self-concept measure than normal Anglo pupils on both the pre- and post-tests.
3. The adjusted post-test self-concept scores of handicapped pupils of teachers who received training in the self-concept behaviours will not differ from those of handicapped pupils whose teachers did not receive the training.

Ten volunteer teachers were trained in the self-concept behaviours as part of an in-service course. Eight additional volunteer teachers served as a control group which did not use the treatment. Programme-related teachers' behaviours were observed and a pupil self-concept measure was administered before and after the in-service course. Results indicated that although no changes occurred in programme-related behaviours for the control group teachers, experimental group teachers showed significant increases on six of the twelve programme-related behaviours. No gains in self-concept were made by handicapped children. However, there was some evidence for differential effectiveness of the programme for learning-disabled and emotionally handicapped children.

Analysis of teachers' behaviours in this study indicated that the self-concept programme was effective in changing the frequency of experimental teachers' use of the module skills. The changes were dramatic in some cases: for example, there was near doubling of inviting cooperation and a reduction by half of judging and labelling by the experimental teachers. In other cases, the changes, (though small) reached significance. An example is some teachers' use of reinforcing favourable self-remarks. Neither the experimental nor the control teachers used this skill prior to the start of the study. At the end of the study, the control teachers still failed to display it, while the experimental teachers used it, on average, four times during the observation period (i.e. slightly less than once per hour). Although it is obvious that some behaviours would be expected to occur more often than others (for example, situations that require an instruction would occur more often than situations that produce anger), some variations in the frequency of certain teacher behaviours may reflect the teachers' beliefs about or resistance to using certain skills. For example, many in the experimental group were reluctant to praise their own efforts in front of the class, considering it a form of boasting, even though the self-perception module specifically dealt with this. Significant but small changes occurred for this variable of self-praise. In contrast, most teachers readily accepted the idea that all instructions to the class need not be given in the form of direct commands. Marked reductions occurred for this variable with an equally pronounced increase in inviting cooperation. One way of increasing teachers' practice of behaviours they may be reluctant to use would be to provide more evidence of the effectiveness of the skills, as well as greater monitoring and feedback on the teachers' practice.

The results indicating lower self-concept scores for handicapped as compared to normal Anglo and normal minority children repeat findings in other studies.

Enhancing the self-concept of handicapped children remains an important goal in education and simply placing a handicapped child in a regular classroom may not be sufficient to promote that child's self-esteem.

Although the training programme failed to produce general changes in self-esteem, the analysis of the two groups of handicapped pupils questions whether or not uniform results, regardless of the subject, should be expected. Learning-disabled children in the experimental group showed decreases on two of the subjects which related directly to attitudes toward school and the teacher. In contrast, there was a trend for emotionally disturbed children in the experimental group to increase on two other subjects one relating to peer relations and the other (self-security) relating directly to affective characteristics (e.g. anxiety, fears, worry). The increase in self-security is especially important, since the control group of emotionally disturbed children decreased significantly on this factor. These results, if repeated, suggest that the nondirective approach fostered by the modules may be more appropriate for handicapped children whose disturbance is primarily emotional. Children with specific learning disabilities may profit from more direct approaches with greater emphasis on instructional programming (e.g. tasks that become progressively more difficult, gradually increasing specific instructions instead of choices, etc.).

One additional factor that may have reduced the effectiveness of the programme is the fact that the training programme was conducted toward the second half of the school year. Had it been implemented early in the school year or even prior to the start of school, the children would have experienced greater consistency in their teachers' behaviour as well as longer exposure to them.

SUMMARY

Handicap appears to make the possessors feel less positive about themselves as they are so aware of their differences from normal children. It is so easy for them to feel inadequate and unworthy and then selectively interpret feedback from others in line with this. There is a range of evidence on the effects of special-school placement and integration into normal classrooms on the self-concepts of physically disabled and learning-disabled children. In general both regimes are of value provided the organization of them is sensitive, so that the child not only strengthens his self-esteem but does so realistically. The environment needs to provide for the full emotional development of the child and for emotional support in meeting his everyday problems and experiences. The experiences can be profitably controlled in the school to enable feelings of success, achievement, and adequacy to be a frequent outcome of classroom interaction. Active efforts can also be undertaken to combat the feelings of inadequacy deriving from the environment outside of the school. The importance of the teacher's own attitudes to each child and the role of reference groups in their effect on a child's feelings about himself should not be overlooked.

Programmes for the handicapped are not just a simple matter of allowing the child to achieve less, but they rather allow for achievement and reward within the limits of the child's handicap. Such procedures not only assist in the development of appropriate self-attitudes, but they are an important step in aiding the growth of maximum skills. With success in tasks that are within his ability will come feelings of adequacy in these lessons as well as in peer relationships. The influence of this strengthened self-concept on the child's future development and learning, needs little further amplication. Teachers can be trained in personal and academic skills to deal with the integration of such children into the normal classroom.

So it is not just a new system of educating handicapped pupils by integrating them into normal classrooms, but rather sensitive awareness of the possible self-perceptions of the normal class and the incoming children and the potential results of integration. Each case should be closely evaluated to determine whether an integrated education is the best option in that instance with that particular handicap.

Further Reading

Warnock Report (1978) *Special Educational Needs*, London: Her Majesty's Stationery Office.

14

Self-Concept of Coloured Children and Prejudice

INTRODUCTION: THE CLASSICAL POSITION

Beginning with Clark and Clark's (1940 and 1958) classic studies of racial awareness, there has been continued interest and controversy concerning the relative self-perceptions of advantaged and disadvantaged children. Clark and Clark found that a large proportion of black children indicated a preference for white dolls and frequently identified a white doll as being similar to themselves. These findings were widely interpreted as showing that blacks have negative self-images and generally devalue themselves. A rapid proliferation of child studies followed, modelled for the most part on the Clarks' (1950) example. Researchers such as Radke et al. (1949), Morland (1958), and Butts (1963) all confirmed the basic discovery of lowered self-esteem in black children. The findings appeared to hold for the Northern and Southern states of the USA and for integrated and segregated schools. This conclusion was buttressed by interpretative studies conducted at both the societal and case-study levels. Such celebrated works as Myrdal's (1944) *The American Dilemma* and Kardiner and Ovesey's (1951) *The Mark of Oppression,* provided interpretative underpinnings affirming the thesis that demonstrable psychological 'damage' was present in American blacks caught in a racist society. The Clarks' study (and, indeed, this tradition as a whole) was canonized by the 1954 United States Supreme Court decision in *Brown* v. *Board of Education,* which ordered desegregation.

The classical thesis as explained by Clark (1955) is based on the fact that a child cannot learn what racial group he belongs to without being involved in the larger pattern of emotions, conflicts and desires which are part of his growing knowledge of what society thinks about his race. Thus early in life the black child absorbs the cultural norms, values, and judgements made about his race. Proshansky and

319

Newton (1968) suggested that what the black child learns is to associate 'Negro' with 'dirty', 'bad' and 'ugly', while the white child learns to associate 'white' with 'clean', 'nice' and 'good'. For the black child, these judgements operate to establish his own racial group as inferior to white people.

The assumption in most of these studies is that the black person who feels disdain or hatred for his own racial group, expresses (at some level) disdain and hatred for himself. This assumption led to considerations of the conditions which fostered black self-identity or a particular self-concept which was characteristically black. In particular, this black self-concept was assumed to be the consequence of the experiences of black people. It was also assumed that the self-concept of the black person was the antecedent of his particular behaviour. Research in the area reflected both of these approaches. Pettigrew (1964), for instance, suggested that the 'real tragedy' of the black is that, having been forced to play the servile, passive and inferior role, he came to believe in it as a reflection of his self-image. Pettigrew noted that by judging himself the way others do, the black grows into the servile role, which in time becomes indistinguishable from the person himself. Deutsch too (1960) suggested that black children generally had more negative self-concepts and were therefore more morose, more passive and more fearful than their white schoolmates.

The point which much of this research attempted to establish was that the experiences of black people amounted mainly to an unending source of conflict, which detrimentally affected their self-concepts. Rainwater (1966) gave even greater importance to the family experience. He focused on the black family's central role in transmitting the values and attitudes of and toward society. He suggested that, for most children, growing up involves developing feelings of competence and mastery over the environment, while for the slum child the process is reversed. In growing up, the black child learns what he cannot do. He learns about the blocks and barriers to his mastery of his environment, and he learns most of all the futility of trying. Thus Rainwater concludes by defining the working-class urban black family as the 'crucible of identity'.

All theoretical and research roads led to the hypothesis of lower self-esteem for coloured minority group members in the 1950s and 60s. The notion was so plausible and was summed up in Clark's (1963) assertion that, 'As minority-group children learn the inferior status to which they are assigned and observe that they are usually segregated and isolated from the more privileged members of their society, they react with deep feelings of inferiority and with a sense of personal humiliation. Many of them become confused about their own personal worth' (p. 63).

However, it is important to examine the general nature of the evidence and to analyse its limitations. In most of the studies, children were presented with black and white dolls, pictures, or animals and asked which they preferred, which was pleasant, which one was like them, or other related questions. The most common pattern of results showed that both blacks and whites identify with and favour the white stimuli, although whites do this to a greater degree than blacks. These studies have usually been interpreted as evidence of self-rejection among blacks. The logic of this interpretation contains several links. It is first assumed that black and white stimuli, respectively, represent black people and white people; second, it is assumed that choosing the white stimuli implies a rejection of the black stimuli, and thus the 'rejection' of black stimuli can be taken as evidence of rejection of black people; third, it is assumed that this failure to prefer and identify with black people implies rejection of the self.

Taken together, these indirect measures of black self-rejection are subject to a variety of criticisms. The results of many of these studies may have been affected by variables such as region; the year the study was done; degree of school segregation; the sex and race of the experimenter; the sex, skin colour and age of the subjects; and the sex, colour and other physical features of the stimuli. Additional confusing variables (differential testing experience and differences in intelligence and social class between the black and white subjects) may also have influenced the results of these studies. Another criticism is that the results for blacks actually indicate that they do not have racial preferences, whereas the results for whites demonstrate that they are ethnocentric. Because of these potential criticisms, the results from these doll studies cannot be taken as conclusive evidence of low black self-esteem and self-worth, and black self-rejection.

Another criticism lies in the fact that in their theoretical postulations these earlier workers had taken for granted that the dominant white majority comprised the 'significant others' whose values and reflected appraisals determined the self-regard and other aspects of self-concept in racial/ethnic groups. Baughman (1971), McCarthy and Yancey (1971) and Rosenberg (1973) among others, point out that segregation means that ethnic minority children do not have much opportunity to compare their family, neighbours, peers or selves with the dominant group culture. Therefore, their self-regard is based mainly on feedback from significant others in their own group.

Arguing these more positive views, Barnes (1972) asserts that it is possible for a black child to have or develop a positive actualizing self-concept in this society so long as the black community containing the child and family is characterized by a sense of peoplehood, group identification, black consciousness or pride, and that the family is identified with or belongs to the community. It is argued that when these conditions prevail, the black community serves as a filter against the harmful inputs from the latter.

The final nail in the coffin of the traditional perspective on the lower self-concepts of black people were the research results in the late 1960s and in the 1970s which demonstrated neither significant differences between white and black self-esteem nor a difference in favour of black people. Yet, even in 1973, despite the growing evidence to the contrary, Proshansky and Newton (op. cit.) argued that for the black person there 'are the heavy psychological costs of low self-esteem, feelings of helplessness and basic identity conflict' (p. 176).

THE PRESENT POSITION

Research indicates that in America there is no significant difference between the self-concepts of black and white students. Wylie (1963), Gibby and Gabler (1967), Yeatts (1967), Zirkel and Greene (1971) and Zirkel and Moses (1971) obtained such results for black and white elementary-school pupils. Rosenberg (1965), Coleman (1966), Wendland (1968), Hodgkins and Stakenas (1969), and De Blaissie and Healy (1970) found the same results for secondary-school students. Schulman (1968) and Knight (1969) reached the same conclusion for black and white educable mentally retarded youngsters. Renbarger (1969) reported such results for college and adult students.

Among these and other studies there is even some evidence that the self-concepts of black children may surpass those of their white counterparts. Zirkel and Moses (1971) found the self-concepts of black fifth and sixth graders to surpass, although not significantly, those of the white children in the same classes. De Blaissie and Healy (1970) found the mean self-concept of black students to be significantly superior to that of white students on two of fourteen measures. Hodgkins and Stakenas (1969) found the average of self-concept of black students to surpass significantly that of white students in a study involving subjects from segregated environments. However, they noted that this significant difference was lost when differences in socioeconomic class were taken into account. Hunt and Hardt (1969) found the average self-concept of black students to be higher than that of white students both before and after participation in Upward Bound programmes. Bartee (1967), in a study involving college students, and Soares and Soares (1969; 1971) and Trowbridge (1970), in several studies involving elementary and secondary school students, found the mean self-concept of disadvantaged (predominantly black) students to consistently surpass that of better-off (predominantly white) students. It would now seem that the existence of lower self-esteem for black people is not inevitable, for even in more recent studies the same trend continues. For instance no significant differences in self-esteem between white and black students were found by Edwards (1974) or Stephen and Rosenfield (1979), while Samuels and Griffore (1979) compared the self-esteem of white, black and Hispano pre-school children. No differences were found in the study. Again it would seem that minority children do not have lower self-esteem than white children.

More recently, the champions of the oppressed emphasize the resiliency of minority group members and often view discussions of 'impairment' in family structure and in personality functioning as racist. Blacks are encouraged to internalize the 'Black is Beautiful' credo and to fight actively against discrimination rather than to permit degradation of the self.

Explanations of the Present Positive

Two questions need answering here. Why do the research findings of the 1960s and 1970s seemingly conflict with those of earlier studies? Why does current research indicate that blacks (particularly black children) do not have lower global self-esteem than whites given widespread discrimination, prejudice and poverty?

Methodological explanations. It is possible that early and later studies differ methodologically—in the populations investigated, in the definitions and dimensions of self-image and in the measures used. In fact, all of these discrepancies are relevant. First, most of the early studies have been based on small unrepresentative samples, particularly of nursery-school children (see Clark and Clark 1940, 1958) while the later studies have investigated large random samples, primarily of older children but, also, of adults.

Second, many of the early studies of black children were concerned with attitudes toward being black and toward the black race in general (Clark and Clark 1940, 1958). Recent work, in contrast, has focused on global self-esteem, that is, on one's general feeling of worthiness as a person (Rosenberg and Simmons 1972, Powell and Fuller 1973). It is very possible that an individual may rate the black race as less good in general than the white without feeling that he himself is less worthy as a total human being. While other minority members may be seen as deserving societal prejudice, one may view oneself as an exception. Or at some fantasy level, a person might prefer to be white or light skinned without feeling dissatisfied with himself as a total human being. Such fantasies may assume less significance than the fact that he is well regarded by parents, teachers and peers (most of whom are also black), or that he is skilled at highly valued activities. It is quite possible that there is a difference between global 'self-esteem' measured in the later studies and racial 'self-esteem' measured in the earlier work.

Third, the indicators used in the early and recent studies differ in type. In the early studies, as has been noted previously, the measures were semi-projective in nature, showing that black children preferred light-skinned dolls, pictures or puppets to those with dark brown skin (Clark and Clark 1950; Goodman 1962; Morland 1958). The later studies use more 'objective' attitude tests and scales—e.g. the Tennessee Self-Concept Scale and the Rosenberg Self-Esteem Scale. A reasonable question to ask here is, 'Are these attitude measures valid?' They are designed to measure conscious attitudes. Do they ignore latent attitudes that rapidly manifest themselves in changing situations? In answer, one can only note that the Tennessee Self-Concept Scale and the Rosenberg Self-Esteem Scales have been widely used and reasonably well-validated. For example, those who score low in self-esteem according to the Rosenberg scale also tend to score high on depression and anxiety; to report themselves as less highly thought of by parents, peers, and teachers; to earn less high grades in school; to be school leaders less frequently; and to be less popular in school according to other children (Rosenberg and Simmons 1972; Rosenberg 1965). On the other hand, projective techniques generally possess low reliability and are difficult to validate so the doll technique would tend to produce results which are more dubious than those derived from rating scales.

In a revealing study which compared two well-known self-concept scales, Gray-Little (1979) applied the Coopersmith scale (SEI) and the Tennessee scale (TSCS) to a sample of black and white 12 and 15 year-olds. The 12 year-olds were retested when they were 14. The black subjects were on average less intelligent and lower socioeconomically than the white subjects. The two self-concept scales actually produced conflicting results from the same subjects!

The SEI reveals racial differences; the TSCS does not. One of the reasons for this difference appears to be the fact that the SEI is correlated with a larger number of race-sensitive demographic variables than is the TSCS. Both measures are consistent, however, in showing the major impact that academic variables, such as achievement and IQ scores, have on self-esteem. When black and white students are matched for either of these variables, their self-esteem scores do not differ. Although it is true that tests such as the SEI and TSCS purport to measure the same phenomenon, it is also clear that they are differentially related to a number of factors that affect self-esteem.

The problem is to determine which self-esteem measure to use, especially when one is making racial comparisons. One might easily argue that this should be the one that appears most culture free, that has a weaker correlation with conventional indicators of status and social position, and this would lead to the selection of the TSCS. One might also argue the reverse: that because the SEI is more highly correlated with other conventional measures of status and position, it will be more predictive of success and so it should therefore be used. The latter, culture-bound argument, implies that one's self-esteem should be, for example, a reflection of socioeconomic status. Although it is reasonable that factors such as parental status or school achievement might contribute to a child's self-esteem, many self-concept theorists and researchers seem to work under the assumption that self-esteem is an important feature of personality and should therefore add to the information derived from demographic or academic data. Studies on the self-concepts of black students using the multi-faceted Tennessee Self-Concept Scale do indicate differences between white and black pupils when specific rather than global self-concept scores are reported. The black pupils tended to produce higher physical and personal self scores but lower moral and ethical self scores than whites. The black pupils also tended to score higher on defence and conflict indicative of low self-criticism, contradiction and confusion in self-perception. The Tennessee scale reveals that whether blacks are more positive or less positive than whites depends on the aspect of self-concept under consideration. This is a point to which we will return when considering the role of significant others to the saliency of particular self-concept facets.

Subjects' characteristics such as sex, age and grade have typically varied from one study to the next, with little attention paid to the relevance of these factors to racial differences found (Christmas 1973). Moreover, in many instances important factors such as socioeconomic status and educational achievement—which are probably relevant to self-concept and which are certainly pertinent to discussions of racial differences—have been neither controlled nor co-varied.

The problems resulting from confusing socioeconomic status with racial/ethnic membership are illustrated in studies by Long and Henderson (1968) and Soares and Soares (1969). Long and Henderson found disadvantaged school beginners in a Southern USA community to have lower self-esteem scores than more advantaged children on the Self-Social Constructs Test. Soares and Soares asked fourth-grade through eighth-grade children to rate themselves on a set of twenty points and found that disadvantaged children had higher self-esteem scores than advantaged children. In the Long and Henderson study all the disadvantaged children were black. In the Soares and Soares study two-thirds of the disadvantaged children were black or Puerto Rican, whereas 90 per cent of the advantaged children were white. Neither study made clear whether socioeconomic or racial factors account for the differences in self-esteem scores! Furthermore, in reviewing studies relevant to the present issue (that is, studies that make direct racial comparisons of self-esteem), it becomes clear that not only test and subject characteristics but also contextual variables need to be considered.

Specifically, the racial make-up of the school may be an important determinant of the direction of racial differences in self-esteem. Most of the studies that report higher self-esteem scores for white students or no racial differences were completed in integrated schools (Bridgette 1970; Rosenberg 1965; Wylie and Hutchins 1967). Studies that report more positive self-concept scores for black children seem to have been completed in either segregated schools (Baughman and Dahlstrom 1968; McDonald and Gynther 1965; Wendland 1968) or desegregated schools in which blacks were a majority (Powell 1973; Rosenberg and Simmons 1972; St. John 1975; Soares and Soares 1969).

So the differences between earlier and later research findings could be due to methodological differences rather than to actual change in self-attitudes over time. Moreover, there is always a question about whether the differences between the self-concepts of blacks and whites can be accounted for in any simple fashion. Do blacks have different self-concepts because they are black? Or do these differences exist because they are members of a minority group, or because they are culturally and economically deprived, or because they are undergoing the stresses of a changing social order, or because they are more deviant and disturbed as individuals? Until well-designed experiments controlling all variables but the one under consideration are constructed, no valid answers can be provided.

The interesting puzzle is why blacks are not more likely to have lower self-esteem than whites. Blacks are members of a race that is subject to extensive prejudice and discrimination, their race generally holds a lower rank in society. In a society that values economic success highly, they are more likely to occupy the lowest rungs of the socioeconomic ladder; as children they are more likely to suffer paternal abandonment and to earn lower grades in school.

The assumption of correlation between one's self-esteem and society's evaluation of one's racial or ethnic group, although compelling in terms of common sense, has little empirical support. Rosenberg (1965) called this the stratification hypothesis and found no relationship ($r = +0.04$) between an ethnic group's average self-esteem score and independent ratings of that group's status in society.

Competing Hypotheses

Debate over the proper interpretation of the more recent evidence on race and self-esteem remains active (Adam 1978; Pettigrew 1978), and numerous explanations have been suggested.

One type of explanation assumes that mainstream discrimination and oppression must have their harmful effects on the black psyche, and it is argued that contrary findings reflect inadequacies in research strategy. In particular, it has been suggested that white dominance pushes blacks either to excessive compliance and low self-esteem or to excessive militancy and exaggerated self-esteem, an effect investigators will continue to overlook until they concentrate on measures of dispersion rather than of central tendency.

Other theorists assume varying degrees of autonomy for the black subculture, allowing it to buffer or swamp the negative evaluations of mainstream whites. Powell and Fuller (1973), for example, suggested that the increase in black nationalism with its emphasis on black pride, issued in higher black self-esteem, but the non-comparability of earlier and more recent research (Rosenberg and Simmons 1972) limits possibilities for direct empirical tests of this hypothesis. If we assume, however, that the 'new mood' which emerged in the American black community in the late 1960s had its primary impact upon the young (Caplan 1970; Edwards 1972), then an indirect test suggests itself: there should be a stronger inverse relationship between age and self-esteem among blacks than among whites.

Some analysts do not assume that the black community has only recently begun to buffer negative mainstream evaluations. Myrdal (1944) emphasized the tendency of persons within the black community to blame what appear to be personal failures in mainstream eyes on the white-dominated American social institutions rather than on themselves. McCarthy and Yancey (1971) developed this idea, arguing that blaming escape is primarily available to working-class blacks, but not to middle-class blacks who are more likely to have internalized mainstream criteria (nor to working-class whites, who are less insulated from the dominant culture). We are thus led to expect that working-class blacks will be more inclined to blame the American system than will middle-class blacks or whites at any level, and also that for the individual a direct effect of system-blaming will be the preservation of self-esteem.

Blaming the system is not the only buffer said to exist for working-class blacks. McCarthy and Yancey (1971) suggest that black subcultural norms and values as well as blaming the system help blacks to escape from the burdens of mainstream 'success' criteria, and serve to protect the self-esteem of working-class blacks. The joint operation of these factors should be reflected in an interaction of race and socio-economic status in respect of self-esteem whereby working-class blacks would have higher self-esteem than white workers while the direction of the race effect would be reversed for middle-class persons. In other words, the relationship of socioeconomic status and self-esteem is predicted to be weaker among blacks than among whites.

There have been attempts to synthesize the perspectives that argue for the inevitability of mainstream discrimination's debilitating impact on black self-esteem with those arguing for the buffering effects of the black subculture. Heiss and Owens (1972), for example, qualify the McCarthy and Yancey (1971) hypotheses summarized above by suggesting that the relationship between the self-evaluations of whites and blacks varies according to the particular dimension under consideration. Specifically, they argue that the buffering function of the black community will operate for working-class blacks (and in mitigated form for middle-class blacks) in the spheres of family life and social activity, but not in such spheres at school or work 'where whites have important control over the black man's fate' (Heiss and Owens 1972 p. 363). These authors insist that failure in the measurement process to take account of the many facets of self-esteem is responsible for the misleading conclusion that their minority status imposes no toll on the self-esteem of the blacks.

A kindred line of argument suggests that black Americans maintain their overall self-esteem by playing down the importance of threatening dimensions. In discussing the self-esteem of black, low-achieving school children, Rosenberg and Simmons (1972) introduce the concept of 'value selectivity'. Assuming that black self-esteem is most vulnerable in the white-dominated spheres of school and work, even when socioeconomic status is controlled (Heiss and Owens 1972), this value selectivity concept predicts that such spheres will be relatively less salient to the global self-esteem of blacks than to whites.

Another line of reasoning is that an individual's negative or positive attitude towards himself is influenced less by the larger society and more by opinions of significant others in his immediate environment. The black, particularly the black child, tends to be surrounded by other blacks. Thus, those persons who matter most to him—parents, teachers, and peers—tend to be black and to evaluate him as highly as white parents, teachers and peers evaluate the white child. In addition, although his race, family structure or socioeconomic status may be devalued in society as a whole, in his immediate context most others share these characteristics. Comparing himself to other poor blacks, the black child does not feel any less worthy as a person on account of race or economic background.

In fact, living in a segregated environment as most urban black children are, they may be less aware of societal prejudice than is assumed. Even if aware, they may attribute blame to the oppressor rather than to themselves. Militant black ideology is aimed at just this end, at encouraging the 'sufferers' to externalize rather than internalize blame for their low societal rank and, thereby, protect their self-esteem. Whether the ideology has accomplished this end and actually led to higher self-esteem or whether other factors are responsible for current research findings, the problem of minority status and the self-picture remains an intriguing one.

Hence there are two hypotheses to explain the lack of low self-esteem in a disadvantaged ethnic minority group and neither hypothesis excludes the other. (1) Blame is externalized onto society (blaming the system); (2) the black person's significant others are similar to himself (the significant other or insulation hypothesis).

These two hypotheses suggest (3) that middle-class black children possess lower self-esteem than working-class black children. This third hypothesis follows from the fact that middle-class black children have to compete more on middle-class white criteria (i.e. significant others are more likely to be white) and are less able to blame society for their middle-class position.

System blame hypothesis. It has been usual to assign positive attributes to internally motivated persons and negative attributes to the externally orientated person. However, Hendrix (1980) suggested that an external orientation may be a positive attribute for minority coloured groups leading to more positive self-concepts. Hendrix found a positive correlation of 0·35 between self-esteem and external control.

This research implies that an external orientation on the more general scale for blacks represents the recognition of the existence of external control factors (discrimination, racism, poverty) which influence the success or failure of black people, generally, and to a great extent, control their fate.

Taylor and Walsh (1979) proposed as their hypothesis that when socioeconomic status is controlled, the global self-esteem of blacks is at least as high as that of whites. Taylor and Walsh also argued that lower status black people would blame the 'system' and this helps to maintain positive self-esteem. Their investigation showed that while blacks do have self-concept levels equal to those of whites neither system blaming nor black-pride ideology accounted for self-esteem maintenance.

Black Americans appear to have resources enabling them to maintain a level of self-esteem at least equal to that of whites and these resources are of longstanding existence rather than the product of any recent ideology. These sources of psychic support seem to be available to black persons at varying socioeconomic levels and to operate most effectively at self-esteem maintenance in the spheres of family and social life, relatively remote from white influence, although they also appear to compensate for threats experienced in the white-dominated occupational arena. Findings suggest that black individuals survive threatening and oppressive situations without experiencing radical damage to a more stable self-picture sustained by the resources of more supportive primary groups. This suggests that the second hypothesis is more tenable.

Significant others or insulation hypothesis. The fact that significant others of most black Americans are fellow blacks rather than prejudiced whites is certainly one critical resource serving to sustain black self-esteem. The selection of reference groups within the black community for social comparison undoubtedly serves as a major resource in this regard. The life-styles and opinions of persons in one's immediate environment are much more important than some presumed standards of the larger society.

For one thing, members of an ethnic group will often rank their own group higher than others rank it. Second, group members may tend to react to the disesteem in which they are held by interpreting this as an expression of the selfishness or pathology of the discriminator rather than as inadequacy in themselves. Third, a group member may compare himself with the nationals of his country of origin (or even of his parents), over whom he has considerable material superiority rather than the still more highly prestigious groups in his present country of residence. Fourth, group members living in socially homogeneous neighbourhoods are likely to confine their other associations to people of the same class or ethnic background; hence, their feelings of self-esteem may be based on relative prestige within a class or ethnic group than between groups.

In attempting to explain the changes in the research findings from the 1950s to the 1970s Hall, Cross and Freedle (1972) propose a four-stage process. In the pre-encounter stage, behaviour and basic attitudes towards self are determined by the oppressor's logic. Upon entering the encounter stage, the black person begins to believe 'the world should be interpreted from a black perspective' (p. 159). Carrying this to extremes, he enters the immersion stage in which everything of value must be relevant to blackness: and, finally, the internationalization stage, the person focuses on things other than himself and his own ethnic or racial group and behaves as if he had an inner security and satisfaction with himself (albeit keeping his strong commitment to his own and other oppressed groups). It is not clear how many persons are assumed to pass through these stages; at what ages, or under what conditions transitions would be expected; or what transitional associated variations in self-esteem might be expected. On the whole, however, it appears their argument points towards a favourable level of self-esteem being found among blacks after the pre-encounter stage.

It would also seem necessary to discriminate between personal self-esteem and racial self-esteem explaining the lack of low self-esteem in blacks. The early doll studies (Clark and Clark 1958) looked at racial self-esteem; the present day scales tend to ask questions involving personal self-esteem so that black individuals just like white individuals can indicate they have good qualities and have personal efficacy in their own social environment.

Heiss and Owen (1972) suggest that blacks use different reference groups as bases for their reflected self-appraisals according to the specific kind of self-evaluative area involved. For example, they assume that blacks will use the black group as their self-evaluative standard regarding those particular traits which are (a) of little concern to the whites with whom a black interacts, (b) relatively irrelevant for success in the larger society (e.g. self-evaluation as a parent or self-evaluation of attractiveness to the opposite sex).

A possible implication of this view is that blacks may protectively experience such traits as more salient for their overall self-regard than is the case for traits on which they are more or less forced to evaluate themselves relative to whites or 'the larger society'. Favourable evaluations on the more salient traits could counteract, to some degree, less favourable standings on the less salient ones. Thus, perhaps hypotheses about racial/ethnic differences in self-evaluations involving the more and less salient classes of traits may be more fruitful than is the traditional hypothesis that black status in a white society affects blacks' overall level of self-regard. So it is erroneous to assume that blacks use whites as significant others. To the contrary, Heiss and Owens (op. cit.) suggest that the evaluations of blacks are much more relevant. Since evaluations received by blacks from other blacks resemble evaluations that whites give other whites, one of the assumed causes of lowered self-esteem disappears. Furthermore, the criteria of worth used by blacks may be achievable subcultural ones, not necessarily those of the dominant society, and thus another potential source of low self-evaluation is removed. Heiss and Owens (op. cit.) therefore hypothesize that the self-concepts of blacks are equal to those of whites on some traits depending on the significant others used, subcultural standards, and the opportunity to blame the system. Their results did support the notion that blacks use blacks as significant others. They also use subcultural standards; in fact working-class blacks had higher self-esteem than working-class whites in terms of their evaluation of themselves as offspring, parent or spouse. In the other social classes there were no differences between the self evaluation of blacks and whites on these characteristics. On other traits there is a tendency for whites to rate themselves higher. In summary Heiss and Owens show that the relationship between the self evaluations of blacks and whites varies depending upon the traits involved. Family roles are particularly influenced by sub-cultural factors and the employment of similar significant others. As Coopersmith said earlier (1967):

It is from a person's actions and relative position within [his] frame of reference that he comes to believe that he is a success or failure—since all capabilities and performances are viewed from such a personal context we must know for example conditions and standards within a given classroom, groups of professionals, or a family before making any conclusions about any individual's feelings of worthiness (p. 20).

The system blame explanation did not appear to play much part in determining self-concept of the black subject in Heiss and Owens's study. This is consistent with the finding of Taylor and Walsh (1979) reported earlier.

The findings by Stephan and Rosenfield (1979) that black persons are strongly ethnocentric and that ethnocentrism and self-esteem are strongly correlated for blacks agree with the use of the values and standards of their own ethnic group as a reference group to maintain self-esteem. It would seem that the black consciousness or black pride movement may have had some success in maintaining an acceptable identity and positive self-esteem.

In Rosenberg and Simmons's (1972) study, overall and within each of 3 age groups (8 to 11; 12 to 14; 15 to 19), the percentage of blacks attaining high self-esteem scores exceeded the percentage of whites by at least 12 per cent and the percentage of whites attaining low self-esteem scores exceeded the black percentage by at least 14 per cent. Insulation in segregated environments has preserved or inflated black self-esteem, since only 12 per cent of black children attended predominantly white schools, only 3 per cent lived in predominantly white neighbourhoods, and 99 per cent and 98 per cent of black and white children respectively reported that the majority of their friends were of the same race as themselves. In support of the insulation hypothesis, black self-esteem of secondary-school students seemed to be higher in predominantly black schools.

Rosenberg and Simmons (1972) show that black children do evaluate their own group highly, a mechanism claimed to enhance self-esteem. Asked to rank which of four groups (Jews, white Catholics, blacks, white Protestants) most people in America think is best, 43 per cent of the blacks replied that blacks are considered best. Rosenberg and Simmons note that the lower average school grades that were actually characteristic of the blacks did not seem to counteract the trend toward higher black self-esteem.

School grades seem to make less difference to the self-esteem of black children. This is especially striking among the near-failing pupils; the self-esteem of such white pupils is vastly lower than that of other whites, whereas the self-esteem of such black children is only moderately lower than other blacks. This suggested that blacks, particularly those whose school achievement is low, may more successfully employ certain defence mechanisms. The black child who did poorly in school was less likely than the corresponding white to feel that his school marks represented an accurate appraisal of his intelligence, to believe that his parents considered him unintelligent and to care strongly about the quality of his intelligence. It was suggested that the black child's social environment was more hospitable to the use of these protective mechanisms (Rosenberg and Simmons op. cit.).

Similarly, Coopersmith (1975) summarizes lucidly the evidence that reverses the earlier trends for black children in the USA to have lower self-concepts than white children, thus:

> There is increasing evidence that as long as the child stays within an environment in which his culture is in a majority he is able to sustain positive feelings about himself. . . . The social forces that have sought to segregate the blacks have provided an environment in which these blacks are insulated against direct assaults upon their feelings. In this environment black children are not teased about their racial characteristics, insulted because of their academic performance or demeaned because of the illegitimacy or breakup of their families. Insulated by that environment he has the support to reject the low status to which white society assigns his race. (pp. 161–2)

The segregated schoolchildren's relative confinement to the black community obscures for them some of the status realities of the broader society and the complex connections between performance and conventionally idealized adult goals in a racially-stratified society.

Nobles (1973) too suggests that blacks use members of their own ethnic group as significant others very strongly since the African view of self is an entity that only exists as a consequence of the group's being, 'I am because we are'. There is no distinction between self and others here, and neither is there in the Jamaican Creole use of 'I and I' for 'we'. One's being is the group being—an extended identity, unlike the individual, independent self of the Western culture. Hence close relationships within a black subculture leads to a possible greater use of other blacks as significant others rather than whites.

The use of one's own group as a reference group and as a stable base is further emphasized by Calhoun et al. (1978) who showed that Portuguese immigrant children in the USA had higher self-esteem than Anglo or Hispano Americans. The Portuguese-American families appeared to have close or cohesive family structure. Smith describes this Portuguese 'traditionalism' as 'a reluctance on the part of immigrants and their descendants to give up European patterns and accept American lifestyle' (p. 3). Roles and responsibilities are clearly defined within Portuguese culture, which may provide Portuguese-American pupils with a sense of security which might in turn account for the positive self-esteem common to the Portuguese-American boys in this study.

Social class hypothesis. This hypothesis is closely related to the previous one since insulation among similar significant others is more available to some social class groups than others.

The role of socioeconomic class on the self-concepts of three ethnic groups was demonstrated by Fu, Korslund and Hinckle (1980). At lower income levels there was little difference between the self-concepts of the white, black and Hispano Americans. At middle-income levels there was a significant difference. In general lower self-concepts were found in working-class students. Middle-income minority-group members had significantly poorer self-concepts because their self-evaluation are more majority-group orientated as a result of increased contact with and exposure to significant others from the majority ethnic group who are perceived by society as having higher status.

Children from working-class backgrounds have lower internal standards for judging the adequacy of their achievement and they are also less involved in achievement experiences than middle-class children; hence their poorer achievement is felt to be less of a threat to their self-esteem. Such low standards lead to greater self-satisfaction and less motivation for change. Thus, children in Trowbridge's (1970) working-class group had high positive self-concepts even with low achievement.

Cicirelli (1976) set out to test this social-class self-concept relationship arguing that working-class children have more positive self-concepts than middle-class children because they have lower internal standards for judging their achievement experiences. The resulting data supported the hypothesis. Cicirelli also found that negative evaluation actually raised the self-concepts of the working-class group. This result seems best explained by the theory that working-class children are defensive concerning negative evaluation; threats to self-esteem are blocked out and positive feelings towards the self are exaggerated. If this is true, it implies that children from working-class backgrounds are not impervious to 'middle-class' expectations or standards when they are present; they are well aware of them, rather than having low standards or less expectations. Instead they may be reacting to the fear of not meeting such expectations with defence mechanisms against this kind of anxiety being activated which, in turn, leads to reporting more positive self-concepts than one might expect under such conditions.

Desegregation of Education

An issue pertaining closely to the relationship between self-concept, significant others, insulation and social class is the school desegregation issue in the USA.

The supposed psychological damage to black children due to segregation was the basis for the US Supreme Court desegregation decision in 1954. As St. John (1970 p. 111) pointed out, the empirical evidence prior to the 1954 decision was 'rather slim'. Wertham (1952) for example, concluded that the effects of school segregation were psychologically damaging solely on the basis of psychiatric interviews with 13 black and white children plus previous professional experience.

After 1954, direct empirical data on the effects of school segregation were slow in appearing; however, reports of opinions for and against did not abate. On one side, Bernard (1958 p. 151) insisted that 'inescapable inferiority feelings' were a psychiatric implication of school segregation. On the other side, Gregor and Armstrong (1964) argued that segregated environments insulated the black child from 'psychic tensions' and, therefore, fostered a more substantial self-concept. Katz (1964) reported evidence of such tensions among black male college students when they were working in teams with white students. Moreover, in a review of the research, Fishman (1961) pointed out that the attitudes of segregated black high-school students towards their own ethnic group before the 1954 Supreme Court decisions were found to be more positive than assumed in that decision.

Recent reviews of the literature in this area suggest that the effects of desegregation on prejudice, interethnic contact and self-esteem are complex. Most often, there are no changes, or the effects are negative (Epps 1975; St. John 1975).

There have been a number of studies of the effects of desegregation on black self-esteem. Some of these studies found that desegregation had a negative effect on self-esteem (e.g. Coleman et al. 1966; Bachman 1970; Powell and Fuller 1973) and others found that desegregation had no effect on black self-esteem (e.g. Williams and Byars 1968; St. John 1971; Rosenberg and Simmons 1972). Based on these studies, it appears that desegregation sometimes has negative effects on black self-esteem and never has positive effects. Several of these studies also examined the effects of desegregation on the self-esteem of white students. One study found that desegregation had no effect on white self-esteem (St. John 1971), and one suggests that desegregation may be associated with increases in white self-esteem (Coleman et al. 1966). In a recent study, Stephan and Rosenfield (1979) examined the effect of desegregation on self-esteem with 10 and 11 year-olds. They were tested before and after desegregation. A control group consisting of similar aged children in an integrated school system controlled for maturation and history effects. The total sample consisted of 300 blacks, 487 Hispanos and 528 whites. The attitudes of blacks and whites from segregated backgrounds toward both in-group and out-group members were more negative after desegregation than before.

The fact that the attitudes of blacks and whites from *integrated* backgrounds did not differ from before to after desegregation suggests that desegregation caused the negative changes in attitudes found for the blacks and whites from *segregated* backgrounds. It is likely that school desegregation was more stressful for the students from segregated backgrounds than for those from integrated backgrounds. Students from segregated backgrounds had no previous opportunities to learn the norms that govern interaction with out-group members in school. The effects of the stress created by having to cope with these problems apparently resulted in a generalized negative evaluation of all three groups.

The results for self-esteem revealed only one significant effect involving desegregation. Blacks from integrated backgrounds increased in self-esteem while those from segregated backgrounds decreased. These results are parallel to those obtained by St. John (1971) and can be interpreted in terms of social comparison theory (Festinger 1954). According to social comparison theory, people tend to evaluate their abilities, traits, and emotions by comparing themselves to similar others. As the attitude data suggest, blacks from segregated backgrounds probably experienced considerable difficulty adjusting to the desegregated schools. In contrast, it is likely that blacks from integrated backgrounds, who had extensive prior experience in multi-racial settings, adjusted relatively well. Thus, in this respect, blacks from integrated backgrounds could make a favourable comparison to blacks from segregated backgrounds. These favourable comparisons may then have led to increases in self-esteem for the blacks from integrated backgrounds but to decreases in self-esteem for those from segregated backgrounds.

Bridgette (1970), too, found that whites had significantly higher self-esteem scores than blacks. Bridgette's subjects were in a recently desegregated school in which whites (who were the majority) had vigorously opposed integration. In a similar study, the previous year, Wendland (1968) found blacks to have the higher self-esteem in a segregated school system.

Hodgkins and Stakenas (1969) conducted a study of the self-concepts of black and white high school students in segregated environments. They hypothesized that no significant difference would be found in both the favourable and the unfavourable self-concepts between black and white subjects. However, significant differences were shown to exist between black and white students. A larger proportion of black subjects than white subjects showed self-concept scores above the median, thus providing contradictory evidence to the conventionally accepted notion that children from ethnic minorities suffer from negative self-esteem. Significant differences were also apparent between black and white subjects in the areas of self-adjustment and self-assurance in school, with blacks tending to score higher than whites.

The main purpose of a study conducted by Soares and Soares (1969) was a comparison of the self-perceptions of a sample of 'culturally disadvantaged' students from 9 to 13 years old with the self-perceptions of another sample of similar age range of children who would not generally be categorized as disadvantaged. The ethnic minorities used in this study consisted of black and Puerto Rican students. The 'disadvantaged' children living in working-class areas indicated higher positive self-perceptions than their middle-class counterparts. However, partial explanation for this may have been that the 'disadvantaged' and 'advantaged' students attended neighbourhood schools and were thus only exposed to children of their particular group with little cross-group feedback available. Further explanation of the occurrence of a higher self-esteem in the 'disadvantaged' group may have been due to the possibility of these children finding less difficulty in meeting the expectations of teachers and parents, i.e. these children are not expected to perform well, therefore they find little difficulty in fulfilling this expectation and, consequently, are more satisfied with themselves. The 'advantaged' child may find it more difficult to measure up to expectations because his parents and teachers may expect more from him; thus a lower self-esteem may result. Other studies, e.g. Garth (1963), Williams (1968) and Griffin (1969), found generally insignificant differences with slight differences favouring integrated school settings. Caplin (1968) reported that black and white children attending segregated schools had significantly less positive school-related self-concepts than children attending newly or long-term desegregated schools, but that this significant difference did not hold when self-concept was measured as a global construct.

Rosner (1954), Webster and Kroger (1966) and Denmark (1970) conducted studies of related interest. Rosner (1954) found the expressed attitudes towards ethnic group and self of black and white children in two institutions to be influenced by the majority group of the institution. Webster and Kroger (1966) found that, in integrated urban high schools, black adolescents with white friends had higher self-concepts than those without white friends. Denmark (1970) found the opposite results for black children in an integrated elementary school.

No definite conclusion of the effects of desegregation on black self-concept can be made, yet, since the inconsistent results probably reflect differences in methodology, age groups, length of segregation and desegregation experience, etc.

It could be argued that the first years of desegregation constitute a period during which positive effects are least likely to occur. Desegregation plans often include changes in curricula and the desegregation of the teaching staff as well as the desegregation of the students. Combined with the negative effects of a community's opposition to desegregation of the teachers and students and confusion over school scheduling, it is not surprising that desegregation rarely has initial positive effects on race relations or self-esteem. If desegregation has positive effects, it is probable that it takes up to a decade for them to occur, as students adjust to the new context for self-evaluation.

Even in this brief review, it is apparent that research findings on desegregation are not consistent. Several factors are possibly at play here. One major distinction of note that may bring contradictory results is the use of global self-concept scales in some research and specific academic self-concept scales in others.

Caplin (1968), for example, found a significant difference between the self-concepts of children in integrated and segregated settings in terms of school related self-concept. However, the difference was not evident in terms of a more global social context of personal perceptions. Miller and Woock (1970) attributed Soares and Soares's (1969) unexpected finding in favour of the self-concept of disadvantaged children over those of advantaged children to such a distinction. They stated:

> What seems to be involved in the findings of this study is a distinction between a general self-concept or self-perception, in which disadvantaged youngsters may come off reasonably well, at least when they are in segregated schools and a self-concept of achievement, that is, self measured against the standards and expectations of the school as a middle-class institution. (p. 171)

We have noted this effect in a previous section where Heiss and Owens, for example, argue that black self-esteem levels, relative to white, depend on the particular area of competence under consideration.

A second major source of discrepant results may lie in the factor of school size. In large schools even minority groups may be large enough to constitute a full sub-culture and thus desegregation may not have the same effect as on a minority group in a smaller school. Withycombe (1970) found no significant difference between the self-concepts of American Indian and white children. She found the self-concepts of Paiute Indian first and fifth graders to be related to ethnic-group mixture in the school rather than ethnic-group membership in society.

Rosenberg and Simmons (1972) showed that greater insulation that comes from larger concentrations of one's own ethnic group in school is reflected in higher self-esteem. Work in Britain by Bagley, Verma, Mallick and Young (1979) concurs with this concentration–self-esteem relationship.

Salience of Ethnic Attributes

The hypothesis outlined earlier concerning significant others and insulation would appear again to be quite pertinent to this desegregation issue. In this regard an intriguing hypothesis was proposed by McGuire et al. (1978). They view the person as an information processing machine, conscious of his or her characteristics, particularly distinctive ones such as ethnic attributes, hence their proposed hypothesis that ethnicity is salient in the spontaneous self-concept as a function of one's ethnic distinctiveness in the social environment.

McGuire and his colleagues argue that the distinctiveness theory has particularly rich implications for what one notices in oneself since our potential knowledge about ourselves is very rich, thus imposing a great need for selectivity in self-perception. It implies that we notice in ourselves those aspects that are peculiar in our customary social milieu. One's hair colour becomes part of one's self-concept to the extent that it is peculiar in one's usual social environment: in Finland, say, the brunette would be more conscious of her hair colour than the blonde, while in Italy, say, the blonde is more likely than the brunette to include hair colour in her self-concept. Distinctiveness probably affects the self-concept both directly and indirectly. Directly by our noticing our own distinctive features; indirectly, by others perceiving and responding to us in terms of our peculiarities and our adopting others' views of ourselves. The theory implies that we are conscious of ourselves in so far as we are different and we perceive ourselves in terms of these distinctive features. By altering a person's social environment so that a different physical characteristic becomes distinctive, we can alter that person's self-concept in predictable ways. If I am black in a group of white men, I tend to think of myself as a black; if I move to a group of black men my blackness loses salience and I become more conscious of being a man.

This implies that ethnicity is more salient in people's self-concepts in an ethnically mixed society than in a segregated one and that in an integrated society, ethnicity is more salient in the self-concepts of members of the minority group than of the majority group. The salience of ethnicity in people's spontaneous self-concept is important in multiracial societies for its impact on interpersonal attraction, self-acceptance and inter-group conflict.

The distinctiveness theory has important implications for social policy, implying that as schools integrate, children become more conscious of their ethnicity and more likely to define themselves in terms of it than when in ethnically segregated schools. McGuire et al. (1978) tested the distinctiveness theory's predictions regarding salience of ethnicity in the spontaneous self-concept in school. From the theory four predictions were derived regarding the salience of ethnicity in the spontaneous self-concept, all based on the information value of the trait in the given social environment. The first is that in an ethnically mixed group, members of the minority groups are more conscious of their ethnicity than are members of the majority group. The second prediction is that within any ethnic group, its members become progressively less conscious of their ethnicity as their ethnic group becomes increasingly more predominant. Third, it is predicted that ethnicity becomes more salient as the group becomes increasingly heterogeneous ethnically (that is, as the number of ethnic groups in the setting increases and/or as the distribution of the group members over those ethnic categories becomes more equipotential). A fourth prediction is that for the minority group, ethnicity is more salient in the affirmation self-concept (in response to 'Tell us about yourself') than in the negation self-concept ('Tell us what you are not'). For the majority group, the reverse is the case. Data were obtained through unstructured oral interviews from a total of 560 pupils. Each of the four predictions receive support. Ethnicity does become more important in pupils' self-concept as their environment becomes more heterogeneous in that regard. For children whose ethnic group formed less than 30 per cent of the pupils, 15 per cent spontaneously mentioned their ethnicity. Of those whose ethnic group constituted an intermediate percentage of the student body at grade level, only 4 per cent spontaneously mentioned ethnicity; and when fellow ethnics constituted a preponderant 80 per cent or more at grade level, none spontaneously mentioned his or her ethnicity. This across-ethnic-group trend of decreasing salience of ethnicity with increasing ethnic predominance in the social environment is significant at the 0·01 level.

The topic becomes especially relevant at this time, when increasing efforts are being made to lower barriers that traditionally separated people on grounds of race, sex and religion in school, at work and in other areas. The findings here suggest that such intermixing heightens rather than lowers consciousness of ethnicity (or sex, etc.) and feelings of difference between the integrated groups. By being aware of this cognitive sensitizing effect of ethnic (and other) integration, regardless of the circumstances in which integration is achieved, one is in a better position to use the beneficial effects of this sensitization and mitigate its detrimental ones.

Variables such as social class, IQ, attainment, and sex need controlling to determine whether the independent variable of ethnic group membership is related to self-esteem. It is arguable that many research results confuse these variables.

Gibby and Gabler (1967, p. 147) reflected the over-all situation in their conclusion that 'there are significant differences in self-concept between similar groups of Negro and white children but these differences are dependent on the sex and IQ level of the children as well as on the specific measures being used'.

Response sets, social desirability and experimenter effects are also likely to cloud the issue. Long (1969) for example, attributed Soares and Soares's (1969) finding of the unexpectedly high self-concepts of disadvantaged students to a response set for extremity among disadvantaged children. Greenberg (1970) similarly attributed Soares and Soares's finding (1969) to a possible defensive reaction of disadvantaged children in the academic area. De Blaissie and Healey (1970) found indications in the USA that black and Hispano children were defensive and deliberately tried to present favourable pictures of themselves. Katz (1969) pointed out that the ethnic group of the experimenter may influence the results. Cotnam (1969) found differential results for both black and white subjects according to the ethnic group of the examiner and the purpose given for the testing as did Little and Ramirez (1976) who produced a significant effect on self-esteem with the white tester producing higher positive self-esteem for both white and Hispano adolescents. So it is no wonder that the research on self-esteem in ethnic-minority children whether in terms of a comparison with white ones or in terms of the desegregation issues has produced more heat than light.

ETHNIC-MINORITY CHILDREN AND SELF-ESTEEM IN BRITAIN

In effect all schools in Britain are integrated so that for the most part minority and majority children cannot avoid each other. But because of the uneven geographical distribution of ethnic communities in Britain, some schools may have few, if any, black children in them while others particularly in major conurbations contain large proportions of children from various ethnic communities. Such schools are genuinely multiracial. However, as a result of the policy of parents wishing children to attend local schools, some schools are now tending to become establishments mainly for blacks and Asians, a self-imposed segregation by neighbourhood.

Despite the difficulty of conducting research in Britain on ethnic issues for fear of arousing the ire of those who regard any attempt to discern differences between and problems of different ethnic groups as discriminatory and racist, a number of studies investigating ethnic-minority pupils' self-esteem have been conducted. Although the Department of Education and Science suggested in a Green Paper in 1977 that our society is a multicultural, multiracial one and the curriculum should reflect a sympathetic understanding of the different cultures and races that make up our society, these aims have not been realized in the curriculum; nor do the self-concepts of many black children reflect a curriculum which meets their cognitive and affective needs. Young black children in particular often show more negative feelings about their self-characteristics, including their ethnicity when compared to American research (Milner 1975; Young and Bagley 1979) feelings which may cause difficulty in identity as the child grows older and has to incorporate these negative feelings within a self-concept which attempts to evaluate being black in a positive rather than a negative way (Weinreich 1979). Because of this, and because of the way British society in general regards and treats black people, many black adolescents seem to experience problems in levels of self-esteem. In a review of the literature on this topic the evidence seems to indicate despite a number of divergent findings, that black adolescents (particularly boys) have somewhat lower levels of self-esteem than their white peers (Bagley, Mallick and Verma 1979). An important exception to this generalization is the case of classrooms with a high proportion of ethnic minorities: here the support given by a black peer group seems to be particularly helpful in self-esteem formation, as it has in the USA. At the same time, however, it is probable that many black adolescents have problems in identity formation (Weinreich 1979).

Using a sample of 400 West Indian and English adolescents, Hill (1970) found that although West Indian adolescents did not, in comparison with their English peers, tend to devalue themselves, they were much more likely to see their home and parents in negative terms. Conversely, West Indians saw school in a much more favourable light. The West Indian adolescents too expressed 'a tremendous desire' for whiteness, both for themselves and in their future friends, neighbours and boyfriends or girlfriends. Dove (1974) studied 545 teenagers of various ethnic groups attending three London comprehensive schools. She found that West Indian adolescents showed much more confusion over their ethnic identity than Asian and Cypriot adolescents. Dove suggests that confusion over identity should diminish in blacks over time, especially in those born in Britain.

Hill (1975) in a later study of Birmingham adolescents counters Dove and suggests that the longer West Indian adolescents have been resident in Britain, the more likely it is that they have high levels of neuroticism as measured by the Eysenck scale, in comparison with their English peers. A prolonged exposure to the forces of English racism is likely to have negative effects on the adaptation, identity and self-esteem of black adolescents, especially if they form a small minority in a school dominated by a largely racist ethos.

Lomax (1977) examined self-esteem (by means of a sentence completion test) in a large secondary school for girls in London. In this school two-thirds of the pupils were of West Indian origin and, although these black girls were disproportionately allocated to lower streams, they had significantly higher levels of self-esteem than their white peers. However, black British girls had poorer self-concepts than true West Indian girls. Thus, despite the supportive context of a school in which the majority of pupils are black, a longer exposure to English culture had a depressing effect on self-esteem.

Newly immigrant children often come from materially worse environments than the urban poverty of a British city. They come with the ardour of pilgrims to a promised land expecting the city streets to be paved with gold. The existence of an education system with legitimate mobility lines to success, is a confirmation of these expectations. No wonder first generation immigrants have more positive self-concepts than their peers. Socialization into the reality of the system was probably responsible for the markedly more negative self-images of their children.

Louden (1977) used a self-esteem measure developed by Rosenberg and Simmons (1972) and studied 375 adolescents from various ethnic groups attending secondary schools in the West Midlands. He found that, over all, there were no significant differences in self-esteem between ethnic groups. However, West Indian girls had higher levels of self-esteem than Asian girls, who in turn had higher levels of self-esteem than English girls. Louden found that in general the more blacks there were in a school, the higher were the levels of self-esteem in the black pupils. The relationship was curvilinear, however, and it was the group of West Indians in schools with medium concentrations (between 30 and 50 per cent of blacks) who had the highest levels of self-esteem. Louden suggests that a whole variety of factors in the school may influence self-esteem in various ethnic groups, including the degree to which minority groups are insulated from various types of white racism. So, like American research, the English picture suggests that black pupils can maintain reasonable levels of self-esteem if they live their lives essentially in a black rather than a white world. The longer and greater their exposure to white culture the greater chance of their self-esteem being lowered.

Jones (1977), observing that West Indians are often successful in sporting activities, examined the hypothesis that success in sport would be associated with higher levels of self-esteem in black pupils. The subjects of his study were 1612 English and West Indian adolescents attending London secondary schools. He used the twenty-three item measure of general self-esteem, derived from the Coopersmith scale, and found that both West Indian males and females had significantly poorer levels of self-esteem than their white peers. Jones observed too that the West Indian pupils were much more likely than whites to use the sporting and social facilities of the school in the evenings, using the school rather than the home as a focus of activity. Although West Indian pupils participated more than whites in school sports teams, and excelled in sport generally, this did not enhance self-esteem levels.

Although white pupils who excelled at sport had higher levels of self-esteem, this was a function of their generally higher academic performance level. Blacks, even those excelling in sport, were generally in lower streams, and it was probably this academic debility rather than sporting success which was the most powerful influence on self-esteem. Those West Indians who were in higher academic streams tended to have levels of self-esteem which were equal to those of their white peers in the same stream.

Jones (op. cit.) noted that blacks involved in sports teams with whites did not as a result increase their out-of-school friendships with whites. Teachers saw achievement in sport as part of what they thought was the generally aggressive mode of behaviour of black pupils, rather than a positive element in West Indian behaviour and performance. Bagley, Mallick and Verma (1979) report on a large study of 1900 West Indian adolescents in 39 British schools. With regard to the comparison of self-esteem between black and white, for each West Indian pupil two white controls were drawn of the same sex, in the same class, yielding 147 girls and 126 boys for comparison. In a few classes it was possible to obtain only one control rather than two. This procedure has the merit of controlling for stream, and for the general level of academic achievement. A comparison of means indicated that West Indian boys had significantly poorer self-esteem than the white controls ($P<0.01$). The difference between West Indian girls and the white controls was not significant, however. West Indian girls had significantly better self-esteem than West Indian boys ($P<0.05$). This effect for black girls to have better self-esteem than black males, runs counter to the trend in a number of other studies of self-esteem in white English subjects, in which males have better self-esteem than females.

Asian pupils in the same schools had self-esteem levels similar to English pupils. Bagley, Mallick and Verma (op. cit.) also examined levels of self-esteem in West Indian pupils in relation to their proportions in the school classes studied. The relationship for males was, as in Louden's study, curvilinear, with those in the classes with middle levels of ethnic concentration (between 10 and 29 per cent black) having the highest levels of self-esteem. The relationship for girls was linear, with girls in the classrooms of highest concentration (more than 30 per cent black) having the highest self-esteem, and those in the lowest levels (less than 10 per cent black) having the poorer self-esteem of black pupils in the classroom yielding a value for r of 0·41 ($P<0.05$). This indicates a significant trend for the self-esteem of black pupils to be enhanced as ethnic concentrations increase, a finding noted previously in American research too by Rosenberg and Simmons (1972) amongst others. Bagley et al. (op. cit.) found no significant results in relation to Asian pupils. So for Asian pupils their self-esteem was independent of ethnic concentration in school.

The results of this study show that, in particular, the level of self-esteem in male blacks is below that of female blacks, Asians and whites. This poor self-esteem may be a result of history where the ravages of slavery led to a matriarchal and authoritarian family system which devalued males, and also to the continuance of severe racial discrimination against black males. For example, McIntosh and Smith (1974) found that male blacks applying for junior clerical posts were discriminated against in 48 per cent of cases, female blacks applying for similar posts were discriminated against in 22 per cent of cases. The knowledge of racial discrimination in society filters to the school, and depresses motivation and increases alienation.

If Bagley et al.'s (op. cit.) sample represented a fair picture of the teenagers in multiracial schools, the findings of this study may have a number of implications for multiracial education. In the multiracial school particular levels of self-esteem may emerge from the interactions and the structure of the school. In a further study Bagley, Verma and Mallick (1982) combined the data from this 39-school sample with additional data from four multiracial middle and secondary schools in the London area in an item analysis of the 58 questions which comprise the Coopersmith self-esteem scale. Three ethnic groups were compared: white English; West Indian; and Asian (a miscellaneous group of pupils whose parents originate from the Punjab, Gujerat—sometimes via East Africa—Pakistan and Bangladesh). A further comparison was made with Coopersmith's data collected in secondary schools in India.

West Indian boys tended to have somewhat better self-esteem than their English peers with regard to school-related items, but poorer self-esteem on items concerning relationships with parents. Although a number of significant differences emerged the picture is generally one of similarity rather than of difference. The similarity of means on the item responses is also a feature of the comparisons between the Asian group and their English counterparts and again, although some significant differences between items occur, these differences largely balance one another. Although it is clear that for West Indians and Asians some sources of self-esteem are different, the overall picture is one of similarity, with the possible exception of West Indian males again. An important British study using Clark's doll technique by Milner (1973) repeated and confirmed Clark's gloomy American results. Milner studied 100 black, 100 Asian and 100 white English children aged between five and eight, attending infant and junior schools in Brixton and Southall in London. All the children were attending multiracial schools.

All of the white children chose the white doll in response to the question 'Which doll looks most like you?' but only 52 per cent of the black children and 76 per cent of the Asian children made the correct choice, choosing the black or brown doll respectively. A similar pattern emerged in the family identification tests—35 per cent of the black children and 20 per cent of the Asian children misidentified the black figures. All of the white children would 'rather be' the white figure but so would 82 per cent of the black children and 65 per cent of the Asians. Did these young black and Asian children who failed to identify themselves properly give such responses because they thought they were white? This is a cognitive confusion which results from being members of a minority group, rather than resulting from group and self-devaluation as such. Milner, however, argues against this possibility, since the children did not show cognitive confusion in other areas. He suggests that the pattern of cause is the other way round: because many ethnic-minority children evaluate their group in negative terms, they will in turn deny that they are black or brown, and will say they are white. Thus, group evaluation and self-evaluation are intimately linked. Milner suggests that this identification of oneself as white is a measure of poor self-esteem in his black subjects, and is at the same time a measure of a confused identity. It must be recalled though that this semi-projective doll technique has low reliability and validity.

A study using a different methodology but reaching largely similar conclusions was carried out with random samples of children in East London aged from five to ten (Bagley and Coard 1975). Eighty-eight per cent of the white subjects did not want to change their skin colour, compared with 57 per cent of the 42 black subjects. Sixty per cent of the black children wanted to change their skin colour, their hair colour or texture, or their eye colour, or all three.

Poor personal and ethnic self-esteem was related to educational under-achievement, alienation and prejudice in a study of 11 year-old Londoners by Bagley, Bart and Wong (1979). Children of Jamaican parents seemed to have the lowest self-esteem and achieve most poorly in school.

Weinreich (1979) argues that immigrant children in Britain will show more identity diffusion than white English children. A Moslem girl growing up in England will experience a considerable discrepancy between the values which support the norms of 'dutiful daughter and arranged marriage' at home and those of independence and choice of marriage partner which her English classmates enjoy. There are many contradictions between minority-group models and majority-group models which can have considerable effect on the immigrants' identity. Identity diffusion was actually found to be stronger for immigrants than white pupils, and this was particularly so for girls (Weinreich 1979). He sees the problems of cross-identification of black children as very complex. The black child may not only meet discrimination and be made to feel inferior by the white majority; he even has conflicts identifying with other blacks. He strives to improve his self-image by identifying with significant white persons, but such increasing self-acceptance leads to a rejection of his skin colour. Cross-identification across any boundary (political, ethnic, religious, etc.) must involve rejection of some symbolic aspect of one's formal group.

Educational paternalism, of which Plowden and its positive discrimination is a prime example, has affected our approach to the disadvantaged and minority children possibly to the extent of failing the less disadvantaged. Lomax (1977), in a study already mentioned, examined this point too and suggested that because of the strong support given by school to the most disadvantaged, the less disadvantaged would have lower self-concepts than the more disadvantaged. This hypothesis was supported. The less disadvantaged girls felt greater relative deprivation and frustration, and less support from school. When the less disadvantaged girl did have a positive self-image there was evidence to suggest that this was linked to status achieved in an alternate prestige system that was essentially anti-establishment in nature. The explanation of these results is probably that subjective experiences of deprivation are more related to relative position than to absolute disadvantage. The objectively less disadvantaged people are more aware of their relative disadvantage than the most deprived. Added to this, the most disadvantaged girl received positive support from the school in Lomax's study. Although not a priority school, the concept of positive discrimination was deeply embedded in the school philosophy. Poor girls had both free school dinners and uniform grants—official state support. Immigrants received special help in both social adjustment and language at the local education centres. Remedial work was one of the central pivots of the school curriculum, while the teachers tended to emphasize their pastoral roles to the exclusion of any academic concern. Such care would have been instrumental in producing both greater solidarity and more positive self-images.

The very poor have nothing material to lose. The less poor struggling in a deprived area, with the marks of failure strikingly present around, and little hope of getting out, might well feel the frustration of their situation more acutely. So girls with the fewest welfare problems had the most negative self-images.

Lomax argues that while her study confirms that positive discrimination in the allocation of social and educational resources is highly supportive of the most disadvantaged, this gain does not lead to improved educational efficiency in the system as a whole. This is because the 'gain' apparent for the most disadvantaged children is offset by the 'loss' experienced by their less disadvantaged peers. Also, those children who 'gain' in terms of a more positive self-image, do so by developing a minority in-group value system. Some authorities feel that the identification of West Indians with Africa, of Pakistanis with Pakistan, etc., can provide a source of ethnic pride rather than forcing them to adapt to being 'British'. It frees the immigrant from adopting British values and criteria for evaluating self. However, children cannot continually be insulated against other standards and values and if they are to live and work successfully in Britain they must learn to compete on British criteria. To do this, equality of opportunity and treatment must be available. Most ethnic minority children in Britain live in neighbourhoods predominantly inhabited by their own ethnic group. The effect is that the environment of the minority group child is consonant with the perceptions, standards and interpretations he learns at home. There is considerable evidence that so long as the child remains in an environment in which he is in the majority culture he can maintain positive feelings about himself. The social forces that have imposed segregated living have insulated the minority groups from negative feelings. The black child living within a black environment is likely to find supportive interactions. He is also likely to find other children who do not accept the school judgements of their performance as a valid judgement of his worth. In addition to his own individual defences, the black child's environment makes it comfortable for him to reject the significance of negative judgement by 'white' institutions and thereby continue to feel general positive worth even when not doing well, since academic worth is not one of his pretensions anyway. That black children do not devalue themselves when they perform poorly in school has important implications for teachers and administrators. This finding suggests that traditional assumptions about how to motivate children in school are, at best, incomplete. Children do not necessarily respond to poor performance by intensified effort so that teachers' pressures based upon failure and competition are likely to be ineffective or even counter-productive. There is sufficient social support for the black child from significant others which does not depend on academic success so that the child is unlikely to be motivated by fear of academic failure in what he regards as an essentially white institution. Blacks who try to attain high standards of academic success are often rejected by their black classmates for selling out to the (white) system. Resistance to such peer pressures by being academically successful is likely to result in lower self-esteem than is conformity with one's peers which results in lesser academic performance. There do exist self-esteem building methods to motivate pupils (Chapter 16). We accept that every child has some strength which may not be used or even appreciated in school. The exclusive focus has been verbal comprehension and skill in communication. But other possible strengths include social skills, aesthetic talents and ability to cope with stress. Another assumption of self-esteem educational programmes is that children are inherently motivated to explore, gain information and learn. Rather than being geared to passivity and minimal effort, children will prize activity provided that they are given support, latitude and some expectation of success. In providing such support the educator must recognize and respect the culture of the child, his present level of abilities and interests and then allow him the latitude to make some decisions for himself. This potential of decision making within a caring structure is a major theme in the chapters on child-rearing practices (Chapter 4) and on enhancing pupils' self-concept (Chapter 16). Building up the black child's self-esteem, as with any other person, involves recognition of his strengths, security and support, and reinforcement of developing competencies.

SELF-ESTEEM AND PREJUDICE

Clinical Beliefs

Many therapists have noted the positive relationships between acceptance of self and acceptance of others. Fromm's (1939) thesis was that, as we ourselves are objects of feelings and attitudes in the same way as others, then attitudes to others and to ourselves must run parallel. Adler (1927) claimed that the tendency to disparage others arises out of feelings of inferiority. Horney (1937) asserted that the person who does not believe himself lovable is unable to love others. In a similar vein, Fromm-Reichmann (1949) remarked that, '. . . one can respect others only to the extent that one can respect oneself', and '. . . where there is low self-esteem there is . . . low esteem of others' (pp. 167f).

The work of the client-centred therapists also supports the positive relationship between attitudes to self and to others. For them the basic change in the client lies in the way he comes to perceive himself and, as a corollary, to perceive others. As the number and proportion of positively toned self-references increase, so too do the number and proportion of positively toned references to others (Rogers 1951). Using a small sample of fourteen therapy cases, Raimy (1948) was able to conclude that, '. . . what a person believes about himself is a factor in the social comprehension of others' (p. 154). These parallel changes occurring during client-centred therapy have been empirically tested. Using statements made by ten clients during recorded sessions Sheerer (1949) found 'a definite and substantial correlation (+0·51) between attitudes of acceptance of and respect for self and attitudes of acceptance of and respect for others' (p. 175). Stock (1949), in a similar study, confirmed Sheerer's results with a correlation of +0·38, but of Stock's ten counselling cases, seven had also been used by Sheerer.

Non-Clinical Studies

Only a few studies have been conducted to discover whether this relationship also holds for larger and non-clinical groups. Phillips (1951) using his own questionnaire, demonstrated a correlation of $+0.74$ between attitudes to self and others in a university class. Berger (1952), with his own scale, produced a correlation of $+0.65$ between acceptance of self and acceptance of others for thirty-three evening-class students, and one of $+0.36$ for 183 day students. However the scale used by Phillips was dogged by the acquiescence response set. Berger did attempt to obviate this problem by randomizing positive and negative items in his scale.

Self-esteem is a vital element in coming to any understanding of personal adaptation in social contexts. We all need to gain esteem in some way. So lack of self-esteem will reasonably lead to attempts to re-establish the primacy of the person in relation to others. Devaluing others is a simple but effective way of enhancing self. Visible differences, such as ethnic ones, are particular targets and in some cultures socially acceptable ones.

Trent (1957) in a study on self-acceptance and acceptance of others among 200 teenage blacks in New York, discovered a curvilinear relationship: subjects who were self-accepting or ambivalent about themselves were tolerant of various ethnic groups. But those with the lowest self-concept were the least likely to accept various ethnic groups, including their own.

In a study by Hebron and Ridley (1965) of 189 grammar-school boys in Yorkshire, self-esteem (measured by selecting traits from a prepared list of adjectives to describe the self) correlated $+0.47$ with prejudice, indicating poorer self-esteem in prejudiced subjects. However, prejudiced subjects were more likely than the unprejudiced to perceive themselves as having good manners. The authors explain that the prejudiced prefer conventional norms.

Burns (1975), in a study of 200 English college students training to be teachers, found that Berger's 'acceptance of self' scale correlated $+0.74$ with non-acceptance of immigrants, $+0.79$ with non-acceptance of West Indian students in schools, and $+0.80$ with non-acceptance of Pakistani students.

Another British study, again with teacher-training students, with data from a social distance scale and a semantic differential (Burns 1977) reconfirmed the relationship between self-acceptance and acceptance of a variety of others.

Teachers with low self-esteem are likely to be less able to accept the wide variety of others they necessarily meet in their teaching duties and hence are thereby less able to help these others to develop more positive self-feelings since feedback from teachers informs them they are not all that acceptable.

Some people maintain their self-esteem by denigrating other people, by attempting to establish the inferiority of other people or groups. Ethnocentrism is the province of people who are not fulfilled in other ways. It is the particular province, if the consistent research results are to be believed, of those of low self-esteem who evaluate themselves as of little worth.

Block and Thomas (1955) found that those with poor self-esteem had high scores on Adorno's F scale. Bettelheim and Janowitz (1964) and Jahoda (1975) regarded prejudice as a defence against the discomfort which stems from deep-rooted conflicts about one's identity.

In various studies in British schools Bagley et al. (1979) were able to show that levels of self-esteem can explain a significant amount of the variance in prejudice scores. Poor self-esteem is a significant predictor of racism in both boys and girls. With eleven to twelve year-old boys and girls, the correlations between poor self-esteem and racism was $+0.23$ for boys and $+0.26$ for girls. Similar correlations were obtained for white 15 to 17 year-olds and West Indian teenagers.

Epstein's theory (1955) suggests that a person with a restricted self-theory will avoid threats. Prejudice, low self-esteem and conservatism are likely to characterize such persons. Wilson's (1973) prediction that conservatism and low self-esteem were correlated by Boshier's (1969) New Zealand study in which an r of $+0.51$ was found.

There would seem to be no doubt that a person who is unsure about his own merits, who has low esteem for himself tends to display less acceptance for others than a person who evaluates himself more positively.

Subjects whose self-appraisal were positive in the above studies all appear able to accept and show more positive attitudes towards others, and to lay less stress on ethnic characteristics in evaluative procedures. To a person with a lower level of self-acceptance, however, those who are 'different' seem to pose a real threat. Perceived characteristics, especially ethnic ones, are emphasized and used as the basis of judgement in a rationalization that 'different equals strange equals threat'. There is support in these results for those psychoanalysts who for some time have claimed without empirical justification, that the tendency to disparage arises out of feelings of inferiority (Adler 1927; Horney 1937; Fromm 1939). Affective relationships with others appear to require adjusted personalities so that the psychic economy is not diverted and drained off merely to deal with interpersonal tensions. The results are consistent too with the empirical work performed by the client-centred therapists on therapy cases, and this consistency across 'normal' and 'abnormal' groups suggests that the relationship is probably throughout the whole spectrum of the population. The present results also promote Rogers's eighteenth proposition, which states the relationship in terms of client-centred therapy, from the level of intuitive hypothesis to the realms of empirical proof, and support his speculation that self-rejection could be a major factor in individual hostility, in industrial friction, intergroup relations and even international clashes (Rogers 1951, p. 150).

Since some of the 'others' to whom attitudes have been assessed belong to out-groups and ethnic minorities, it is very apparent that self-attitudes are positively related to ethnic attitudes, and to degrees of tolerance and prejudice. In fact, the strongest relationships between self and other attitudes do occur in respect of specific 'coloured' stimuli (Burns 1977b). Although the various correlations of self-attitudes with the several kinds of others overlap, there is a tendency for the size of the correlations to increase as the relationship moves from that between self with the generalized other, through to that with the 'white' ingroup, and finally to the highest levels of all with the 'coloured' outgroup members. Where specific 'coloured' stimuli are involved, those student teachers with low self-concepts apparently stick rigidly to conventional attitudes, whereas those who have more positive feelings about themselves feel free to divorce themselves from stereotyped convention, strike out on their own and refuse to evaluate others in a negative way because of some ethnic attribute. The lower correlations for the generalized other and for the 'white' stimuli may occur because conventional attitudes and relations to these categories are more fluid, with judgements having less concrete criteria, such as colour, on which to anchor (Burns 1977b).

However, with correlations between self-acceptance and acceptance of a wide variety of others in the various investigations reported above ranging from $+0.23$ to $+0.80$, the residual variances $(1 - r)$ would range from 95 per cent to 36 per cent. Thus variation in measured self-attitudes accounts for only a moderate proportion of the variation in measured attitudes to others. The relationship is not so fixed, or of such a high degree, that individual predictions can be made with any accuracy.

The relationship between attitudes to self and ethnic attitudes exists because the processes leading to the development of both, are the same—child-rearing practices. The antecedents of ethnocentrism have been well documented (e.g. Adorno et al. 1950) and it is these same strict, unaffectionate interactions with parents, where there is little praise or positive evaluation, that lead to the child also learning a concept of himself that is replete with feelings of lack of self-worth and insecurity. By analysing the scores of the high acceptance and low acceptance of self groups to the Semantic Differential scales on the two 'parent' concepts Burns (1975) found several important and relevant mean differences.

The high self-acceptance criterion group saw both parents as more good, tolerant, fair, kind, friendly and valuable than the low self-acceptance group ($p < 0.05$ in all cases). Parental performance which is interpreted as tolerant, fair, kind and good by the child is likely to produce children who are also able to value themselves highly (see Chapter 4).

This not only suggests that the experiences and learnings involved in the various child-rearing practices form the basis of self-evaluation but also that perhaps many of the attitudes a person has towards others come partly by generalization from the attitudes he has to his parents as well as from the internalization of parental attitudes and behaviour. The attitudes a person has for his parents could well be a function of how much they show love for him. If they do show love for him he learns to regard himself highly and need not be preoccupied with the possibility of receiving anything negative such as rejection and isolation. He is less apt to behave defensively and in turn less likely to receive negatively reinforcing behaviour from others which would lower his regard for them. One could further argue that stimulus generalization occurs between learned information about, and attitudes to, oneself and learned information about, and attitudes to, others. In these suppositions, there lies the basis that attitudes towards self condition attitudes towards others. Subjects with high levels of self-acceptance fortified by parental confidence are willing to approach social encounters and expect success. Those with low self-esteem, from previous interpreted experiences, anticipate failure and rejection. This saps motivation to interact with others. Culturally induced prejudices and stereotypes act as rationalizations, and in concert with the displacement of frustration at feeling inadequate, ensure in general a lack of positive responses to others. Child-rearing practices thus appear to condition attitudes to both self and others.

EFFECT OF COUNSELLING ON SELF-ESTEEM AND ETHNIC ATTITUDES

These statistically significant relationships between self-attitudes and many different kinds of others, ranging from specific ethnic minority members, to the generalized other, supply psychology with a principle which is very useful in understanding and explaining the problems of social conflict and hostility which are so detrimental to human relationships. The importance of such an empirical finding is without question. As Rosenberg (1965) concludes, 'The cement of social life does not consist of grand passions or cosmic philosophies. It consists of casual conversations and relationships, small talk, the easy interchange of ideas, and the sharing of minor enthusiasms' (p. 168). The individual's self-concept would appear to play a significant role in all this. What a person thinks of himself does not form a closed system, imprisoned and encapsulated with no relevance beyond the boundary of his own being; on the contrary, it reaches out to manipulate his relationships with others. The self-concept apparently brings to bear a unique prospective for viewing one's relationship with one's social environment.

As attitudes to self are antecedent (however briefly) to attitudes to others, it might well mean that changes in attitudes to others can only come about through changes in attitudes to self. Increased acceptance of foreigners, minority groups or neighbours might best be achieved through some form of group therapy, in which possibilities of altering the individual's acceptance of, and respect for, himself exist when carried out in an ethos of understanding and acceptance. In situations of industrial tension or professional friction the most effective approach might be to deal with the attitudes of the person towards himself rather than searching for solutions through external factors.

Bagley, Young and Evan-Wong (1976) report on such a study they carried out in England with 21 volunteer low self-esteem subjects. A control group matched on prejudice and self-esteem was also involved. Each student was given client-centred counselling for at least one hour a week during three school terms. If the student agreed, his parents were also interviewed by a social worker; any problems were discussed and practical help was offered where appropriate, e.g. one family was rehoused. In the school, particular learning and scholastic problems of students in the experimental group were tackled. As a result of individual testing, two pupils were moved to a higher stream in the second term of the project. Teachers too cooperated in the project, being advised on the necessity for positive feedback to the experimental subjects. Sociometric isolation was tackled too by associating experimental students with popular students in various projects and cooperative activities.

Nine months after the start of the experiment, all subjects completed the same test battery. The main aims of the experiment, to enhance scores on measures of mental health (self-esteem, neuroticism, and suicidal ideation) were realized. The self-esteem levels of the experimental group had moved close to the mean for the remaining 13 year-olds in the school. The mean level of prejudice in the experimental group showed a significant decline, to a level near to that in the remainder of students.

Bagley and Verma (1975) found that the pupils who had at least adequate levels of self-esteem were the ones most likely to benefit from race-relations teaching in attempting to reduce prejudice. Highly prejudiced pupils tend to be resistant to such teaching, and perhaps for them an individualized approach is needed, involving counselling which is not directly related to their racist attitudes, but to the under-lying social and psychological problems which are at the root of their prejudiced attitudes.

The great value of the experimental validation of the basic relationship between attitudes to self and attitudes to others is that the atmosphere of understanding and acceptance which leads to improved relationships with others is the very ethos likely to create a therapeutic experience in itself and consequent self-acceptance for those who are exposed to it. There may be in this relationship—if organized in the correct way in family, group-therapy, classroom, church, work contexts, etc.—a dynamic psychological chain reaction with tremendous potential for solving many of the relationship problems that have always plagued mankind, and which warn of immense social upheaval in the future if little is done to generate more acceptance of others. Psychologists and educators need to devise practical programmes for creating this therapeutic climate in which any members of society can learn to accept them-selves and develop more positive self-concepts. For instance, the recent develop-ment of 'encounter groups', with their climate of trust and healing capacity (Rogers 1970), is a major positive approach designed to allow an individual to understand himself and others (Baynes 1972).

Both child-rearing practices and teaching methods must be based on a policy of the acceptance of all children, providing them with encouragement and success in terms of their individual capabilities. Group-therapy techniques have an appropriate role to play in modifying adult attitudes to self and others but are limited not only because of their cost but also because of the number of people that can be catered for. Although Rogers developed his techniques for those requiring therapy, this approach—with its atmosphere of acceptance and respect—is widely applicable in fact to everyone involved in a work, family or peer-group relationship with others.

SUMMARY

American research before 1970 tended to suggest that many black children had to a large degree internalized the negative stereotypes which the majority community held concerning them, and in consequence had poorer self-esteem than whites. More recent research with children and adolescents in America has, however, challenged this view, indicating that blacks do not have significantly poorer self-concepts than whites. Various explanations have been put forward, including the blaming-the-system and insulation hypotheses. The latter hypothesis is supported by research, in that black children who evaluate themselves according to the standards of their black peers may have high self-esteem. Black rather than white reference groups are important, though this may depend on social class and the particular behaviour evaluated.

Desegregation of education tends to reduce the self-esteem of minority groups as they come against majority group standards and prejudice. Size of minority group in a desegregated setting is important, as insulation in a large minority group protects self-esteem and provides acceptable significant others.

Studies of self-concept amongst minority children in Britain have produced findings which have been both diverse and contradictory, reflecting the contradictions of recent American work. Studies of young black children show that they have considerable difficulty with the formation of an adequate ethnic identity and self-esteem. It appears however that as black children grow older they develop protective sub-cultures and new reference groups which encapsulate their identities from the grosser forces of racism. Problems of identity formation, however, remain. An important structural variable seems to be the degree to which a black adolescent does have a black peer group that can give an adequate sense of ethnic identity. In practical terms, it seems that black children who are isolated in nearly all-white schools are more likely to have poorer self-esteem.

Many studies support theoretical stances in reporting strong and consistent relationships between self-concept and attitudes to others whether group or specific others. This relationship has been shown to hold in a wide range of circumstances particularly in the relationship of self-concept level to the possession of ethnic attitudes. The backdrop to the development of prejudiced attitudes to others appears to be the same type of child-rearing practices that were conducive to the development of low self-esteem. Prejudiced and low self-esteem persons appear to have parents who were authoritarian, unsupportive and unaffectionate.

Counselling appears to have most effect in reducing negative attitude to others on those pupils who were not too negative in their self-attitudes.

Further Reading

Bagley, C., Verma, G. K., Mallick, K. and Young, L. (1979) *Personality, Self-Esteem and Prejudice,* London: Saxon House.

Verma, G. K. and Bagley, C. (eds.) (1975) *Race and Education Across Cultures,* London: Heinemann.

15

Self-Concept and Delinquency

INTRODUCTION

The self-concept provides a perspective for understanding delinquent behaviour which is not possible through sociological analysis; this is the internal frame of reference. If external or demographic variables could entirely predict delinquent behaviour then the self-concept would be redundant. However, given that we cannot predict delinquency with a set of demographic variables, we require a construct that enables the understanding and prediction of behaviour that is not possible from just external information. The self-concept provides us with an indication of the effect on the person of social characteristics, local environment, family character-istics, and the individual's response to them. Delinquency explanations that focus on society, neighbourhood, and family as explanatory variables are fallaciously assuming that all macro social characteristics, neighbourhood characteristics, or family settings have similar effects on all people. What is more important and contained within the self-concept is their *interaction* and the person's *reaction* to them. Self-conceptualization provides a convenient behavioural interface between social and individual events.

Part of this interaction can be identified as a labelling process. Expectations and labelling are fed through feedback to the individual whose self-concept and social identity are thereby modified. In this respect, self-concept is at once both a cause and an effect of deviation, self-concept change (a) being an effect of initial deviation as mediated by social control events, and (b) being also an important precondition of secondary deviation.

Most accounts of this labelling process concentrate on the effects of formal social control events like arrests, commitment to institutions, criminal convictions, etc. However, there is also some notable work on the dynamics of informal social labelling, e.g. Goffman's (1963) writing on stigma management. Two recent efforts by Hewitt (1970) and Kaplan (1975a) in developing what could be called 'self-

351

esteem microtheories of deviance' explicate the self-conception processes left implicit in various interactional accounts of deviance, and focus on self-esteem as a basic motivational mechanism and on evaluative experiences in socialization as the primary causal dynamic. The fundamental propositions tying deviance and self-concept to the social structure are: (1) that commitment to the legitimate social order is a positive function of the adequacy of self-esteem level, and (2) that self-esteem is a cumulative product of socialization which may be distributed across different social sectors or different kinds of interpersonal associations. The motivational model depicted here stresses adaptation to social contingencies keyed on self-esteem maintenance or self-enhancement processes. When the situational structure of contingencies works against self-esteem maintenance, then the theory predicts a tendency to do something else, either individually or collectively, which is unconventional and which provides more positive experiences and hence self-esteem.

Deviance may represent an adaptive response by individuals to situations that inhibit the basic effort to achieve social esteem and self-esteem. When conventional activities prove unrewarding, then activities outside the conventional order provide an alternative source of status. Such accounts focus largely on subculture forms of deviance, where unconventional activities are collectively organized into a subcultural alternative to the social order. This element of collective organization is often described as crucial, since it is the socially supportive reference group that rejects or 'neutralizes' the values of the conventional normative system. For instance, Short and Strodtbeck (1965) assert that in delinquent gangs, the effect of deviance on self-esteem is positive, while outside of the gang, the relationship between deviance and self-concept seems to be negative. So, theoretically at least, the self-concept level of a delinquent should depend on his primary reference group, and on his commitment and marginality to the delinquent subculture. This level of commitment is particularly pertinent in the work of Hall (1966) discussed below, and clarifies the general consistent findings of low delinquent self-concepts when scales are applied to delinquents within what is to them not a normative context.

RESEARCH ON THE RELATIONSHIP BETWEEN DELINQUENCY AND SELF-CONCEPT

The research relating self-concept and delinquency has been consistent in its findings and cross-culturally validated. Fitts and Hamner (1969) in surveying the research conclude that delinquents are a homogeneous group with consistently low self-concepts, and that few delinquents had average or better than average scores. Delinquents were more uncertain, more variable, more negative in their self-concepts and had more personal conflict. They were not defensive, made little effort to portray themselves positively, and had little personality strength for withstanding stress and frustration. Ninety-two per cent of delinquents felt rejected by their parents, as opposed to 13 per cent of non-delinquent siblings (Healey and Bronner 1936). Motoori (1963) found that the existing self-concept of delinquents was significantly different from that of a control group, while their ideal self was quite similar. Epstein (1962) reported that the delinquent female's self-concept is more negative than the non-delinquent female. Fitts and Hamner (1969), however, point out that profiles of non-delinquents showed many deviant signs, but that profiles of delinquents showed significantly greater deviancy. This finding will have significant implications for preventative measures to be discussed later, as it brings up the question of criteria for prediction.

Within the category of delinquents distinction can still be made on various bases. Stewart et al. (1971) found that retarded subjects reported more deviant self-concept than other delinquents. Fannin and Clinard (1965) found a relation between the type of self-concept and the type of behaviour. Working-class delinquents saw themselves as tough, fearless, powerful, fierce and dangerous. Middle-class delinquents saw themselves as smart, smooth and loyal. The delinquency patterns of these two types varied accordingly, with the working-class delinquents committing more violent crimes and the middle-class ones more property offences.

Research on the differing forms of delinquency has been limited and inconclusive. Simon et al. (1974) and Peterson (1972) found no difference in levels of self-esteem between marijuana users and non-users. Demeritt (1970) and Schaeffer (1976) found no difference between general drug users and non-users in self-esteem. Randall (1970), however, found that negative self-concept and low self-esteem are involved in drug usage. Glue sniffers have been described as having low self-esteem (Hansen and Maynard 1973).

No research has been done specifically on teenage alcoholics and self-concept. However, Krug and Henry (1974) and Schaeffer (1976) found that alcoholics possessed lower self-concepts than non-alcoholics, and saw themselves as more aggressive, impulsive, anxious and depressed. Further research is needed to determine if these findings hold for adolescent alcoholics. The cross-cultural validation comes from Lamarche (1968) with data from French Canadian delinquents, Zuriel and Shakad (1970) with Israeli delinquents and Kim (1967) from South Korea. Fitts and Hamner (1969) concluded that regardless of language, country or culture, persons characterized by delinquent behaviour tended to have low self-concepts.

Chapman (1964) studied delinquency in terms of a process of social interaction resulting in persons being alienated from a legitimate value system and being attracted to an illegitimate value system. The process of alienation and attraction was viewed as the result of how persons perceive others and of how they perceive themselves in relation to others. In particular, this research was concerned with (1) how persons perceive 'others' who represent legitimate and illegitimate value systems and (2) how they perceive themselves in relation to the legitimate value system. Chapman proposed three hypotheses: (1) the delinquent will perceive the persons who embody values of an illegitimate social system more positively than the non-delinquent would; (2) the non-delinquent will perceive the persons who embody values of a legitimate social system more positively than the delinquent would; and (3) the non-delinquent will show a more positive self-concept than the delinquent in relation to a legitimate social system. The Kelly Role Construct Repertory Test was the instrument chosen for testing hypotheses 1 and 2, and the Kuhn Twenty Statements Test was chosen for testing hypothesis 3.

These tests were administered individually to twenty matched pairs of male delinquents and non-delinquents, aged 14 to 16, selected from the three public high schools in Springfield, Missouri. All three hypotheses were confirmed. Delinquents and non-delinquents perceived persons who embody values of an illegitimate social system significantly differently from persons who embody values of a legitimate social system. The non-delinquents' self-concepts were significantly more positive than those of delinquents.

In viewing the relationship between delinquency and negative perceptions of persons who embody values of a legitimate social system and negative perceptions of self, the question arises: What is there about negative self-perceptions that lead to delinquency? The negative perception by the delinquent of a school teacher would indicate that the delinquent is being alienated from school and does not perceive school as a means to the achievement of status. The negative perception of a minister would indicate the same for Christianity, and the negative perception of a policeman would indicate the same for the legal system.

The positive perception by the same delinquent of a truant would further indicate that the delinquent is being alienated from school and that he is indifferent to the consequences of truancy. The positive perception of a person who does not like religion would further indicate that the delinquent is being alienated from religion and is indifferent to it, and the positive perception of a person in trouble with the law would further indicate that the delinquent is being alienated from the legal system and is indifferent to the consequences of law violation.

This research of Chapman (op. cit.) has shown that there exists in the sample studied this differential positive and negative response to persons who represent legitimate and illegitimate systems. Delinquents of this sample responded more negatively than non-delinquents to the representatives of legitimate systems than they did to representatives of illegitimate systems. They responded more positively than non-delinquents to illegitimate than to legitimate representations. The delinquents in this study thus indicated by positive and negative responses the possible direction of their movement in two value systems.

The findings of this study appear to bear out theories which call attention to the importance of individual conceptualizations of self, of persons and of social forces in determining the direction and kind of action that individuals will take in differing situations. The delinquent who construes the policeman, teacher, minister, and self as negative does not construe these persons and the systems which they personify as worthy, loved or wanted, and he does not construe himself as worthy, loved or wanted. The delinquent is in search of self-validation or of some group or social system that will be a 'good' looking-glass to mirror the self as 'good' or worthy. If self-acceptance is based upon 'other' acceptance of the self and if the legitimate social system produces only negative images of the self and of persons in the system, the individual will have needs for self-validation through love and acceptance that are not met by the legitimate social system. The delinquent will then reject the legitimate social system for any system that offers an opportunity for fulfilment of his needs.

Thompson's study (1974) of 2000 11 year-old children in British schools illustrates this way of enhancing self-esteem. At this age, children who deviated in various ways felt rejected and undervalued and had poor self-esteem. By the age of

15 they had changed their membership and reference groups, substituting delinquents for teachers and parents as significant others. This is an expected tendency. If we feel isolated, rejected and undervalued, we look around for others in a like condition, expecting from them some support.

Adolescents with low self-identification as students tend to group with others they see as being involved in a delinquent life style (Frease 1972). Just as the proper credentials must be possessed by a person who enters a trade or profession, so it is with a delinquent subculture. The credentials possessed by virtually all delinquents may be low academic performance; and low academic performance may become one of the symbols necessary for entry into the illegitimate system. Furthermore, low academic performance might be taken as a lack of commitment to the legitimate normative structure which stresses the need for high academic performance and high academic self-conception. Therefore, low academic performance may be taken as a sign of solidarity with the delinquent subculture. Furthermore, the coming together of youngsters with similar self-concepts may indicate a mutual search for a solution to their low self-image. A new status system is constructed whereby different rules are employed that allow status conferral and higher self-identification for acts not sanctioned in the legitimate order.

Studies of delinquent gangs clearly portray the operation of these group codes. There have been many studies showing the existence and importance of group standards. The classic studies by Sherif (1935) and Asch (1955), for example, demonstrate that, in a situation where the individual is unable to tell whether his answer is right or wrong, he is almost completely dependent upon the group for selecting a response.

THE ROLE OF IDENTIFICATION AND COMMITMENT

In an interesting paper, Hall (1966) argues for an integration between psychological and sociological approaches to delinquency, the former emphasizing the consequences of inadequate family relationships, and the latter emphasizing deviant subcultural resolutions of society's structural strains. In as much as these approaches appear to be divergent, or at least to view the same object from different perspectives, they have sometimes been thought to be mutually exclusive. Hall (1966) believes a resolution of these supposed differences can be accomplished by using the process of identification to examine the career of the juvenile delinquent.

It is often argued that juvenile delinquents possess low estimations of themselves due to parental rejection and deprivation. For example, from Healey and Bronner's (1936) finding that 92 per cent of a sample of delinquents felt rejected and unloved by their parents, as compared to only 13 per cent of their non-delinquent siblings, it was concluded that these feelings led to a general sense of inadequacy and a low level of self-evaluation, which in turn were important in producing delinquency. Those individuals who became delinquent were seeking emotional satisfactions that they could not find at home. This psychological view of the delinquent has been supported by the Gluecks (1950) among others.

Recent sociological views, however, suggest that the delinquent has joined a delinquent subculture as a solution to the problem of adjustment that often arises because of the disadvantaged position of the working class compared to the dominant middle class. This perspective places the delinquent in a special world which has its own antisocial set of meanings and values to guide perceptions, motivate actions, and provide status and identities. Participation in this delinquent subculture allows the delinquent to gain a high estimation of himself by engaging in behaviour which is rewarded, even if it is delinquent.

From the psychological and sociological approach, one can observe the centrality of two concepts, self-evaluation and subculture. What is of concern in Hall's research is the manner in which the 'push' of low self-evaluation is translated into the 'pull' of membership in the delinquent subculture; the manner in which an individual takes on the attitudes of a pre-existing delinquent group and thus comes to see himself as a delinquent. This process can be seen by examining the relationship of identification with a delinquent subculture to the level of self-evaluation.

The relevance of the process of identification to delinquency lies in the fact that commitment to a particular identity in this instance involves identifying with real or imaginary others from whose perspective criminal behaviour is acceptable. At the same time that the individual comes to identify with delinquent others, he comes to differentiate himself from non-delinquent others. This dual process of identification and differentiation is basic to the validation of the identity. By engaging in this dual process, the delinquent learns who he is and who he is not. Since this learning process constitutes the announcement of a delinquent identity and an identification with a delinquent subculture, delinquents should, for example, want to associate with delinquent models (such as the individual who 'fools around' or gets into trouble) and not want to associate with non-delinquent models.

In addition to specifying models and anti-models of association, the delinquent subculture, as a set of values, beliefs and attitudes, determines the standards by which a member evaluates himself. The delinquent will judge himself by the degree to which he lives up to these standards. As the individual goes through this process of identification, he comes to shift the bases of self-evaluation. Those standards, and the people representing those standards that provided the basis for initial low self-evaluation, are no longer deemed important. It is in this way that the level of self-evaluation can be changed from low to high through the process of identification. It seems likely, therefore, that the delinquent who has a strong degree of identification with the delinquent subculture will tend to have a high level of self-evaluation while those delinquents with weaker degrees of identification will tend to have low levels of self-evaluation.

Against the general view, Hall (op. cit.) argues that since self-evaluation is determined in relation to a set of accepted standards, both non-delinquents and delinquents can have high levels of self-evaluation. The difference, of course, is that non-delinquents judge themselves by conventional standards and delinquents by delinquent standards. In other words, whether a delinquent has a high or low self-concept depends on his degree of identification with the delinquent subculture. Totally committed delinquents should show a complete, consistent, and integrated delinquent self-conceptualization, because this type of delinquent has been stripped, either by choice or sanctions, of all but delinquent roles. More specifically, the totally committed delinquent should (1) conceive of himself in terms of delinquency oriented roles (delinquent identities), (2) possess negative attitudes towards parents, (3) place high value on delinquent associates and activities (delinquent peer-group orientation), (4) reject middle-class success orientations and adopt exotic life-styles and the 'easy life', (5) perceive causes of crime as external to the person, and (6) place an accent on 'kicks' and excitement as models of self-expression. In addition, the totally committed delinquent should have a high level of self-evaluation.

The marginal delinquent possesses both delinquent and non-delinquent identities. Compared to the totally committed delinquent, his delinquency orientation is reduced in qualitative and quantitative terms. Compared to the non-delinquent, the marginal delinquent maintains some conventional identities and values but fails to realize them. The marginal delinquent experiences internal conflict as a result of these inconsistent and contradictory identities. Since he has not been able to completely detach himself from conventional society and its representatives and make the delinquent peer group the primary reference point of self-evaluation, he should reflect low self-evaluation.

To the degree that non-delinquency represents a commitment to 'anti-delinquency', the non-delinquents should resemble the self-conceptualization of the totally committed delinquents in structure. There should be a tendency for non-delinquents to possess an integrated self-concept and a high level of self-evaluation. This type should show positive family relationships, non-delinquent associates, acceptance of middle-class values and represent, in sum, the opposite of the totally committed delinquent.

Hall's all male sample consisted of 23 non-delinquents, 26 self-reported delinquents, 39 delinquents on probation, and 42 delinquents placed in a county institution (Total $n = 130$, all males). The non-delinquents and self-reported delinquents were randomly selected from four high schools. The selected adjudicated delinquents had appeared before the juvenile court for having committed one or more theft offences. All the boys were between the ages of 14 to 16, and from working-class families. The Twenty Statements test was used for self-evaluation.

The results demonstrated that increasing the delinquency orientation has the effect of raising the level of self-evaluation. Delinquents with strong degrees of identification tend to have high levels of self-evaluation and delinquents with weaker degrees of identification tend to have lower levels of self-evaluation. These results suggest a transition process in the career of the delinquent. Attempts to raise self-evaluation of marginal delinquents must be aimed at improving feelings about non-delinquent behaviour since the danger exists that the heightened self-evaluation might only favour elements of delinquent identification.

CRITICISMS OF RESEARCH

Not only are delinquents not a homogeneous group, but neither are non-delinquents. The non-delinquent sample may include 'uncaught' delinquents, which would bias the comparisons of the two. As Fitts and Hamner (1969) pointed out earlier, non-delinquents also have delinquent signs; the question is of degree. Duncan (1966) and Lynch (1968), have noted that fully functioning people have self-concepts that are different from people in general, being more positive, more certain, less deviant, less confused, and less variable. The contrast of these characteristics with both the 'normal' group and the delinquent group suggests that the bipolar classification may hide a question of degree, and provide a limited basis for preventative measures.

Criticisms of research on delinquent self-concepts to do with the sampling procedure and the influence of class variables on the findings have been raised. Hall (1963) presents a critical criticism of this research. He states that the identification with the delinquent subculture will be a better predictor of delinquent behaviour than self-evaluation as long as the adjudication process constitutes the basis of selection. Only some parents in a number of studies allowed the child's participation and these children were more likely to respond in a positive manner. This reduces the number of strong delinquent orientations and creates a bias in the data.

Gergen points out, in considering the nature of self-concept tests, that salience is affected by the stimulus at the moment, the motivation and the amount of training with the concept. Thus the research itself and the effect on the subject's motivation would bias the responding. Chronic delinquents would have more experience with being labelled 'delinquent' and its connotations. These three factors together bias the responses negatively.

Most of the research is done with males which may limit the generalizability of the findings. Coleman (1972) stated that female delinquency was increasing, but there are still four times as many male delinquents as female ones. Research on the female delinquent is therefore necessary. One area that needs investigation is the question of why, if males have higher self-concepts generally than females (see Chapter 5), are there more male delinquents?

Marten and Fitzpatrick (1968) noted that social characteristics such as age, sex, race, and social class help both to determine what kind of crime a person is likely to commit and the proceedings if he is caught. Cloward (1963) adds that delinquents from the upper and middle classes engage in differing forms of delinquency and their access to legal counsel may result in their acquittal or less severe sentence. So the general findings that delinquents have low self-esteem may be an artifact of social and legal variables as well as methodological ones.

SELF-CONCEPT AND REHABILITATION

The self-concept can be used as a focus variable for rehabilitative measures. It provides a means to assess the effects of various treatments, assists in the determination of objectives, and can be used to evaluate progress. There are, however, theoretical and practical problems in basing rehabilitation on the self-concept.

These include the nature of the institution, the nature of the individual, and the post-institutional environment.

In evaluating rehabilitation measures we must consider that it is difficult to generate true changes in people's self-concept in the short term. Short-term efforts have generally resulted in no significant changes (Faunce 1967); intensive rehabilitation measures have produced some effect. This is especially significant in that subsequent behaviour after leaving treatment is highly related to self-concept change during treatment. Fitts and Hamner (1969) concluded that 'incarceration alone produces little change and even intense treatment programmes create only minor differences over short time periods'; it is not sufficient, therefore, to incarcerate. This may even result in intensifying the self-concept problems. The finding of Roberts (1972) in a study of adolescent girls, that those with higher self-images tended not to be reconvicted, whereas lower self-image girls tended to be reconvicted without completing their parole year, indicates that programmes of this sort have high social and personal value.

Research has produced some positive results concerning the self-concept and rehabilitation. If the delinquent gang permits the adolescent to recoup self-esteem lost through defeat in middle class culture and institutions, then by providing success for such delinquents in socially acceptable behaviour and settings should lead to gains in self-esteem and alleviate the need to gain such esteem in antisocial and deviant ways. Such an argument motivated Eitzen's (1976) study on the effects of a behaviour modification programme on delinquent behaviour and self-esteem. The behaviour modification programme was designed to enable them to (1) succeed in the token economy; (2) learn the skills that pay off in social relationships; (3) improve in skills useful for school; and (4) change from socially unacceptable to socially acceptable behaviour.

The research setting was a community based home ('Achievement Place') where from six to eight delinquent boys lived under the guidance of a trained adult couple. The rehabilitation programme was based on a token economy system of reinforcement. In this system the boys received points each time they completed a task and, at a later time, could exchange the points for desirable objects or for privileges. The goal of the 'parents' (2) was to teach the social skills important to be successful participants in the community (e.g. conversation skills, academic skills, pre-vocational skills, manners and acceptance of criticism).

As a group, the boys at admission had much more negative feelings about themselves than did the boys in the control group ($P<0.01$). However, when the mean of the pre-test group was compared with the mean of the post-test group (which was more positive in self-concept than the control group), the delinquent boys were found to have a much more positive self-concept at the completion of their stay ($P<0.01$). This shift in self-evaluation was concomitant with a shift in how the boys perceived that significant others (mother, friends and teachers) evaluated them.

A second research question was whether this improvement in self-esteem by previously delinquent youths was reinforced by the attitudes and actions of significant others (parents, friends and teachers). In other words, if a boy feels that others now view him as more responsible, and more socially skilled than before, then he should begin to view himself differently as well. The results suggested that this assumption is correct, since the perceived attitudes of significant others did shift in a more favourable direction over time corresponding to the actual change in the self-concept of the boys. As was the case with self-concept, the initial means were consistently higher (less favourable) than those of the control group and lower (more favourable) than the control group at the post-test administration of the questionnaire.

If the means for each significant other at the post-test phase are contrasted with the mean for self-concept for that phase, we find that the self-concept of the boys was more congruent with their perceptions of how their friends evaluated them. This finding is not a startling one, given the enormous dependency on peers for approval and self-definition by persons in this age category. However, there was a lag for the other categories, although both were believed by the boys to improve in their evaluations. Thus, with these categories and especially with teachers, the boys had to fight the consequences of their history of delinquency, the labels this history had attached to them and the self-fulfilling prophecies these labels tended to encourage.

Shore, Masimo and Reids (1965) concluded that changing delinquents' feelings about competence generally changed self-esteem for the better. Fitts and Hamner (1969) noted that individuals who show the greatest change through correctional measures tended to have the most negative and deviant self-concepts. They explained this by considering the nature of the self-concept. By initiating changes in the self-concept they were able to change the nature of the self-concept, behaviour and feedback cycle.

At the time of release, subjects who later became recidivists did not differ markedly from the others, but they differed in the direction they were heading. Fitts and Hamner (op. cit.) found that subjects who showed the greatest self-concept change show the greatest behaviour change after leaving the institution.

Fitts and Hamner (op. cit.) stated three characteristics by which the correctional environment must differ from the previous environment. These are:

1. It must convey that the clients are still persons of worth and value despite their previous behaviour.
2. It must help the delinquent to avoid negative behaviour and to find new behaviour that is more rewarding.
3. It must provide opportunity of reward for this new behaviour.

They concluded that the three elements of the interaction cycle (self-concept, behaviour and environment) must be considered in any intervention programme.

In dealing with recidivists we must face the previously unanswered questions: Why are their self-concepts different, what causes these differences, when did they occur, what roles did previous incarceration or subsequent outside experience play? Fitts and Hamner (1969) report that subjects whose self-concept gets worse in the institution are more likely to become recidivist on release.

One criticism of rehabilitation measures is that the pre-test and post-test are by their nature conducted at different times in the incarceration period. The prospect of the incarceration may have a negative effect on the pre-test, while release may have a positive effect at post-test. This cannot be separated out from the actual effects of incarceration either.

The problem of the post-programme environment is stated by Burns (1979) as the expectancy effect of societal figures (peers, police, neighbours, etc.) which confirms their earlier self-concept, and behaviour congruent with this image is likely to occur. This is a further aspect of the labelling problem. Once a person has been labelled delinquent, this leads to a cycle of negative feedback, self-concept and behaviour. The labelling problem was stated clearly by Gold (1973) who concluded that 'getting caught encourages rather than deters further delinquency' (p. 52). The social act of labelling a person as delinquent tends to alter the self-concept of the labelled person towards incorporating the label. This also creates a tendency for significant others to react to the person in terms of the label and this further leads to self-concept change in the direction of 'delinquent'. In the post-institutional environment this can be a very significant effect.

As we shall see in school, counselling can be used in a preventative role to enhance the self-concept (Chapter 16). This same ethos of a helpful relationship replete with warmth, acceptance, empathy and genuineness could make a delinquent or potential delinquent feel safe enough to explore himself. Group counselling, too, may provide an opportunity for the student to interact with other individuals and thus redefine himself through group feedback. The consistent results of the research relating the self-concept and delinquency, the research criticisms, and the preventative and rehabilitative effort that are possible with the self-concept as a focus variable, points to the self-concept having considerable explanatory and predictive value for delinquency.

Ferguson et al. (1977) provided a set of self-concept scales, one for male and one for female, with predictive value for self-concept and delinquency research. Their two scales cross-validated and both predicted concurrent self-reported drug use— beer, wine, cigarettes, marijuana (male only) and LSD (males only). Further research is needed, however, to develop scales with predictive validating for other forms of delinquency such as property offences, violent crimes, and so forth.

The final implication of the correlation of delinquency and self-concept is that of the nature of society. If the self-concept develops in interaction with social factors and leads to delinquency we must consider what this says about the state of society. The implications can easily be extended to a complete questioning of the nature and consequences of social values and goals. For example, high levels of unemployment among young school leavers leads to disillusion and lowered feelings of self-worth, with a possible consequence of increased deviant and delinquent behaviour as the unemployed young people attempt to raise their perceptions of themselves within an in-group setting. Negative identity is preferable to remaining a nonentity and reflects a desperate attempt to regain some mastery in a situation in which society has removed an essential source for a positive identity—being able to earn a living.

SUMMARY

The self-concept is a factor in determining whether a young person becomes a delinquent since delinquency can be frequently an adaptive response to contexts that inhibit efforts to achieve self-esteem in conventional and acceptable ways. Delinquent behaviour with its social identity and peer-group support can provide the missing self-esteem. Delinquents have a two value system and while manifesting low self-concepts when judged on conventional lines may reveal positive self-esteem within the context of the delinquent subculture and reference group. Marginal delinquents generally manifest low self-concepts as a result of inconsistent identifications.

There are considerable difficulties in conducting research on the delinquency self-concept relationship since neither delinquents nor non-delinquents are homogeneous groups. Behaviour modification programmes providing successful feedback appear to allow the recouping of self-esteem and lower recidivism.

16

Enhancing Pupil Self-Concept

Let people realize clearly that every time they threaten someone or humiliate or hurt unnecessarily or dominate or reject another human being, they become forces for the creation of psychopathology, even if these be small forces. Let them recognize that every man who is kind, helpful, decent, psychologically democratic, affectionate, and warm, is a psychotherapeutic force even though a small one.

Maslow (1970, p. 254)

INTRODUCTION

Increasingly various participation based methods of small group training (i.e. sensitivity, therapy, *T*-group, encounter groups, etc.) are being used in industry, the Civil Service, hospitals, the social services and in schools and universities. The initial thrust of these developments was aimed at providing individuals within these settings the opportunity of enhancing their own self-awareness and potential. More recently there have been attempts to adapt these techniques to improve the institutional environment within which these individuals function, on the assumption that this will (in addition to promoting organizational development) provide in the long run greater opportunities for individual personal growth. In education, in particular, there has been a significant movement in this direction. Levine (1973), for example, suggested that there should be more involvement and interdependency in the learning process within educational institutions, and strongly advocated the expanding use of experiential group techniques. Rogers (1970) in his book *Encounter Groups* summed up the position for further innovation in the use of encounter groups and related methods in enhancing the teacher–student relationship:

in our schools, colleges, and universities, there is a most desperate need for more participation on the part of learners in the whole programme, and for better communication between teachers and students, administrators and teachers, and administrators and students. There have been enough

363

experiments along this line so that we know it is perfectly feasible to improve communication in these relationships, and it is nothing short of tragic that education has been so slow to make use of this social invention. (p. 125)

The importance of small group participation for teachers' education programmes has been urged by Jersild (1955) and Combs (1965). All these various possibilities for the use of small group training in education are aimed essentially at developing individual self-awareness, releasing potential and facilitating self-acceptance and acceptance of others. We have already noted the critical relationship between these latter two and the deleterious effect low self-acceptance has on the ability to interact harmoniously and warmly with others whether teacher or pupil (Chapter 14).

The exact nature of self-awareness and what this training should involve, however, needs further clarification. It is not enough to deal with the concept in such global terms as becoming 'aware of oneself'. There is a need to emphasize and operationalize the implications of the cognitive and logical aspects of self-awareness as opposed to the more generalized, mystical interpretations of this often ill-defined topic.

It is the view of humanistic psychology that man is equipped with an innate tendency towards the actualization of his potentialities. However, as Maslow (1968) pointed out, the individual often has trouble discriminating between choices which actualize his potential and those that do not. Self-awareness must involve an understanding of this prior conditioning and how one reacts to it at present. This requires the development of an awareness of one's cognitive capabilities and the logical analysis of one's feelings, thoughts and overt behaviour and their interactions. Furthermore, this involves learning to view oneself as having the capacity and responsibility continually to make choices about one's purpose in life. Becoming more aware of oneself also means realizing that while we do have this capacity for choosing we often allow our conditioning to guide us into making safe choices rather than growth choices. While safe choices seem to require less work and effort, Maslow (1968) pointed out, they are in reality deficiency choices which result in life's problems being made more difficult rather than easier. The environment conditions man to mistrust his logic and to allow himself to be controlled by his emotions. He allows himself to be conditioned to be 'cognitively lazy' and to use his emotions and environment as excuses for his behaviour. The first step in self-awareness is the emphasis placed upon encouraging the individual to view himself as a 'choosing being' who is responsible for his behaviour, emotions and thoughts. The next step involves the recognition of the choices that one is presently making. Involved in this step is an awareness of one's present situation and one's functioning within this situation. Upon recognizing choice one must then work through an analysis of the choices.

To accomplish the task of self-awareness the individual must also take an active role in logically determining how realistic his plans and goals are for him, as opposed to the degree of wishful thinking and denial of reality he is engaging in. This involves the individual's analysing his goals in terms of their global and short-term nature. Simply, are they broad goals broken down into smaller daily goals that provide the structure necessary for working toward more encompassing goals?

When an individual engages in this process of logical analysis of his thoughts, feelings and behaviour, and their interactions, not only does he become more aware of himself, but more importantly he is also actively involved in determining who he is. In other words, he is creating his own meaning and purpose in life rather than passively waiting for life to create it for him. Rogers (1961) spoke of self-awareness in terms of the individual's becoming more self-accepting. The result of self-awareness should not be self-acceptance alone, but belief in oneself and one's ability to make choices regarding who and what one will be: belief in one's ability to become. The person who is actively in the process of becoming is one who sees himself as constantly choosing and as being solely responsible for the life choices he makes. It is to the extent that the individual actively assumes responsibility for his life that he is free. He realizes that freedom does not come easily; that he is free only to the extent that he is responsible. In other words, he sees himself as either creating or limiting his own freedom. He does not excuse his present behaviour in terms of external influences such as previous conditioning or dependency. He refuses to place the blame for any of his behaviour upon others, such as his fifth-grade teacher or his mother and father, etc. Although he is aware that they have affected him in some way, he will not let them control him as he assumes responsibility for himself.

While the use of groups as a therapeutic procedure for the emotionally disturbed dates back to the 1930s, their use as a means of personal and/or emotional growth for normal people is a relatively recent innovation dating back to the late 1940s with *T*-group and laboratory training (Bradford, Gibb and Benne 1964). Since the 1970s, however, there has been a tremendous expansion in the use of groups for this purpose. As a result of this increased popularity of groups to expand the self, numerous encounter techniques have been developed to help self-expansion. While there has been an increase in the number and quality of studies to assess the effects of groups (Gibb 1970), very few well-controlled experiments have been conducted to compare the effectiveness and/or value of different kinds of techniques on personal change and growth.

Many of the pupils and students seeking the help of a student counsellor see themselves as weak, as being unable to discipline themselves either to concentrate on their studies or to live their lives successfully. They had little confidence in themselves, experiencing a sense of inadequacy and an inability to cope with their courses. As self-concept theory has clearly demonstrated (e.g. Combs, Avila and Purkey 1971), the person who experiences such negative self-perception imposes great limitations upon himself, effectively precluding himself from attempting those actions which might reveal to him that he is better than he gives himself credit for being.

The importance of perceiving oneself in positive ways can hardly be overstressed for when one holds such a concept of oneself, one tends to expect success. By thinking in this way, one is likely to bring about this fortunate outcome through the mechanism of the self-fulfilling prophecy (Chapter 9). Success seems to breed success, and failure seems to breed failure. Thus it would appear that the students seeking counsel would have little hope of improving their situation unless they could view themselves in more positive ways. As long as their self-concept remained basically negative, they would continue to distort incoming stimuli in order to maintain that view of themselves, thus preventing themselves from coping more successfully with their studies, and in more general terms, with life itself.

Self-concept change in a positive direction is clearly indicated, then, as one way in which students might be helped to overcome their problems. How to achieve such change is not so apparent. An important lead, however, has been provided by Frank (1972). Writing in a therapeutic rather than an educational context, Frank has expressed the view that people seek psychotherapy not primarily because of specific symptoms but because they are demoralized. That is, they are unable to cope with situations which those around them expect them to be able to handle. This concept seems applicable to the students mentioned earlier. Because of their failure to cope, they felt miserable and depressed, blaming themselves for their inadequacy and experiencing strong guilt feelings.

Frank's approach to coping with this demoralization is quite straightforward. He seeks to restore morale. Once patients recover confidence in themselves, they often have no further need for therapy despite the persistence of their physical symptoms, as they feel they can cope. It would seem, then, if Frank's formulation can be accepted, that one way of helping students would be through morale and self-confidence building, the feeling that one is competent and of worth.

CLIENT-CENTRED COUNSELLING

Theoretical Background

One of the best known counselling techniques involving self-concept change is Carl Rogers's client-centred therapy. His therapy is based on the assumption that maladjustment is the result of attempting to preserve the existing self-concept from the threat of experiences which are inconsistent with it, leading to selective perception and distortion or denial of experience by incorrectly interpreting those experiences. Rogers felt that this incongruence between self and experience would be overcome by the client if he were provided with conditions in which 'he may begin to allow previously denied organismic urges to be a part of his concept of self' (Meador and Rogers 1979 p. 144).

The three conditions that Rogers feels are necessary and sufficient for therapeutic personality change are (1) empathy, (2) positive regard and (3) genuineness (Rogers 1959). These conditions are usually referred to as therapist's attitudes rather than techniques *per se*, hence, the term non-directive, but the conveyance of these attitudes still requires some therapist skills.

1. *Empathy*. Empathic understanding requires that the therapist focus on the client's phenomenal world. This is not done in an attempt to interpret or diagnose. It is simply believed that the experience of being understood promotes personal growth (Meador and Rogers 1979). One way that the therapist can convey empathy is to reflect or mirror what the client says by paraphrasing his remarks in an understanding way. This gives the client feedback that he can clarify or expand on and has been

a major contribution to the field of psychotherapy. Reflective techniques have even been used by behaviour therapists despite their deterministic view of human nature (Rimm and Masters 1979). A scientific evaluation of the effectiveness of this technique in promoting self-disclosure and exploration on the part of the client concluded that reflection of feelings furthered self-exploration and insight while interpretive and structuring remarks did not (Rogers 1961).

Empathy, when expressed verbally, offers the pupil a sometimes intensely reassuring experience of not being alone, and of being understood and accepted for what he is. This component appears to be a key element in the counselling relationships. Some possible behavioural characteristics of the person showing accurate empathy are:

1. He can tolerate the expression of emotion during the counselling.
2. He is able to enter into and describe his pupils' inner subjective world, without losing hold of his own.
3. He is prepared to adjust his perceptions of another person's world, in order to attain increasingly accurate understanding.

2. *Unconditional Positive Regard.* The second condition necessary for personal growth and self-acceptance according to Rogers is unconditional positive regard. The therapist demonstrates this attitude primarily by being non-judgemental. Positive regard is not a 'saccharine optimism toward humanity' but rather a basic human trust in 'the clients' resources for self-understanding and positive change' (Meador and Rogers 1979, p. 152). This unconditional acceptance is a personal characteristic conveyed mainly by non-verbal means, where tones, facial expression, eye-contact and the like seem to convey the feeling component of the relationship.

The major conditions for the child's developing a positive self-concept and self-esteem involve acceptance of the child. Acceptance implies liking and showing concern for the child as he is, with his capacities and limitations, strengths and weaknesses. This acceptance is expressed by interest in the child, concern for his welfare, involvement in his activities and development, support for him in his times of stress, and appreciation of what he is and what he can do. Acceptance is also expressed by recognition of the child's frailties and difficulties and by the awareness that the child can only do so much at this time of his life. Such acceptance does not mean that the parent or teacher necessarily approves of all the child's qualities, but it does mean that the teacher or counsellor can see the child for what he is without being affected by his own feelings of dissatisfaction and desire to change the child. Acceptance is not necessarily indicated by the amount of time the counsellor, teacher or parent spends with the child, but by the feelings, attention and attitudes, expressed during that time. It is the quality rather than sheer quantity of expression that is critical. Children can sense concern, interest and appreciation and are not easily fooled by mere words of praise and affection or by insincere demonstrations of physical affection.

The fact that a child is accepted by the counsellor or teacher as a significant other fosters the child's development of a positive self-concept. Believing that he is basically all right, the child is less likely to deny the strengths he does possess. Recognizing his particular achievements and potential for learning, the child is more likely to achieve at his ability level and to elicit the confirming social and physical feedback on the basis of which he maintains and enhances his self-concept.

The counsellor's acceptance of the child as he is, rather than as the counsellor would like him to be, fosters the child's development of high self-esteem through two mechanisms. First, the child (if he correctly interprets the counsellor's behaviour) will be freed from the fear of being rejected if he exhibits or discusses his own weaknesses and imperfections. In fact, accepted for what he is, the child is not hampered by feelings of doubt and rejection and thus has greater emotional support for any attempts he may make at changing. Thus freed to examine his difficulties without fear of rejection, the child is able to see him clearly. Second, acceptance conveys to the child the fact that he will not be treated more negatively than other children and that he is accepted for what he can do and not in comparison with other children. The counsellor or teacher, in effect, expects the child to succeed in terms of his abilities and accepts his performance in those terms. Accordingly, the child is less likely to internalize or project inappropriately high expectations.

3. *Genuineness.* Genuineness or congruence is the last condition necessary for the self-actualizing process. This involves the therapist being 'real' in the relationship, that is, genuinely expressing his personal responses to the client's feelings in a consistent way (Meador and Rogers op. cit.). Rogers discouraged the therapist from actually going as far as discussing his own personal experiences with the client but other authors disagree with this. Doster and Brooks (1974) found that subjects talked longer and achieved higher levels of self-exploration when interviewers disclosed personal information. Genuineness involves responding to the person in need of help not in terms of his status, his role or some professional stereotype, but naturally and spontaneously, as one might meet a good friend. The pupil seeking aid requires a helper who conveys the impression of personal security and of social ease.

Some possible behavioural characteristics of the genuine person are:

1. His verbal and non-verbal behaviours are congruent with each other.
2. He is willing to be open about himself.
3. He does not draw attention to his status or role.
4. He is consistent in his behaviour when counselling and when he is not.
5. If challenged, he can tolerate it and explain his position without enlisting his 'authority' to put the pupil in his place.

Research Studies

Raimy (1948) studied self-referent statements made by clients throughout the course of therapy. He analysed fourteen complete series of counselling interviews that used a variety of therapy styles ranging from directive to non-directive and found that in successful counselling, clients' self-referent statements changed from predominantly negative or ambivalent to predominantly positive. This supports the hypothesis that successful counselling involves a change in self-concept and Raimy proposed that self-concept is a significant factor in personality organization.

Raimy's original work (1943) expanded on the role of self-concept in counselling and personality organization. He delineated three basic therapists' functions common to most treatment interviews that can produce changes in the structural relationships within the self-concept. The first function is to create a permissive atmosphere to allow the client to relax and self-explore. By this, Raimy meant a more general attitude of permissiveness than did Rogers, in that it can include an 'affectional relationship between therapist and client' (p. 122). The second function of the therapist is to clarify the self-concept of the client. This involves rephrasing, interpreting and asking questions providing they do not distract the client or elicit defensiveness. The third function is that the therapist is a representative of society with professional status and prestige who 'has power to initiate or to stamp with society's approval the re-evaluation of concrete aspects of the self-concept' (p. 121). The stamp of approval may refer to positive reinforcement from the therapist.

Apart from the role of the therapist, Raimy feels that certain other conditions preclude self-concept change. These are motivation on the part of the client, a situation allowing self-exploration, time to organize self-perceptions and an opportunity to test new self-conceptualization in the real world. This last point, the acting out of the self-concept, is the starting point for behaviour therapy, which we consider later in this chapter.

A large number of studies reveal that participants (mainly university students) in small sensitivity training groups feel more favourable towards themselves after the experience (e.g. Larson 1972; Liebeman 1973; Hewitt and Kraft 1973). Participants saw themselves more positively in twelve out of fifteen major studies whereas controls did not. There is a tendency for some loss of this enhanced self-evaluation to occur over time but this is not inevitable.

Zullo (1972) used the Offer self-image questionnaire in assessing the effects of a three-day retreat for senior high-school students. Significant changes were found on the scales for social relations and moral self. The latter change was still present after four months. King (1976) measured self-acceptance among teacher-training students with the Lesser scale. Increases were found after a group met weekly for a term and these were still present three months later. King et al. (1973) obtained a similar effect with undergraduate groups.

In a report focusing on six-month follow-up data, following participation in an intensive two-week residential encounter workshop, Barrett-Lennard, Kwasnik and Wilkinson (1974) noted that each of the following effects occurred for more than two-thirds of the participants.

1. Increased ability to be open and accepting in relationships.
2. In process of developing some new self-awareness and prepared to risk expressing and acting on this.
3. Increased self-regard, self-liking or self-trust.
4. Increased appreciation, regard and concern for the basic rights and worth of others.

From the standpoint of client-centred self-theory, the most central or basic axis of personal change, in these results, is reflected in item 3. It follows from this theory that increased self-awareness or openness to experience is accompanied by changes in actual self-worth or esteem and that these changes lead directly to modifications in behaviour (Rogers 1951, pp. 520–4). Personal exploration and openness were among the aims and processes emphasized in the workshop, and various aspects of development and change in self-awareness are prominent in reported effects. Thus, it is to be expected that consequent changes in self-regard would occur and that associated changes in behaviour and attitudes would follow. A pattern emerged from the obtained classification data which strongly suggested that the workshop experience led to an enduring change in level of self-regard for most of the participants and that this change contributed to associated persisting changes in interpersonal behaviour and attitudes.

Grater (1959) reported an increase of self-acceptance as a function of a classroom that had been made similar to that of a leaderless encounter group. Bessell (1968) reported that some encounter-group techniques, used with elementary-school children, had the effects of: increasing the awareness of self and others, helping the children develop academic skills such as language and mathematics and increase motor skills. Jourard (1971) showed that nursing students who were high in self-disclosure (a prime ethic of the encounter model) had significantly higher grades in nursing classes than did those who were low in self-disclosure.

The major concern of a study by King (1976) was with changes in self-acceptance as it related to different college classroom models. There was one specific hypothesis: self-acceptance will increase as a function of the encounter classroom model. This hypothesis was confirmed. The two traditional classes showed no significant change in self-acceptance, while the three 'encounter' classes showed a significant increase in self-acceptance.

One of the weaknesses of most of the studies reporting self-acceptance changes as a function of an experimental treatment is that there is no follow-up reported to check for stability of treatment effects. King's (1976) study includes a follow-up (three months after the post-class testing) on thirteen of the subjects who could be located. No significant change between post-treatment and three-month post-treatment self-acceptance was found. This indicates that the self-acceptance increase stabilized and had some long-term effect.

Participants in small groups tend to become more open to new experiences and less prejudice against the foreigner or immigrant. Khanna (1971) found that decreases in F scale scores of Tennessee school teachers were still present six months after training. On the other hand Adams's (1970) null finding was also obtained with school teachers. Parker and Huff (1975) report significant reductions in F scale scores after groups for students. Very few of these studies give actual mean scores for their samples, so it is impossible to judge whether the variability of the findings might be because some samples were initially much more prejudiced than others.

Schmuck (1968) reports on an extensive programme which appears to have involved more than 100 hours of training. Children in classes taught by sensitivity trainees showed increases in the influence they perceive themselves to have. Various other changes were also detected but these were found also among those who had other forms of training but no groups. McFarland (1971) found that after two and a half days of training for the teachers, children in their classes perceived a significant increase in attempts by the teachers to include them. Khanna (1971) asked students to use the Leary interpersonal check-list to describe their teachers. After training, the teachers were seen as less hostile and more accepting.

Payne and Dunn (1972) studied the effect of group guidance on the self-concepts of ethnic minority pupils. Three experimental groups (white, black and Hispano) of 10 year-old children were treated to 50-minute weekly guidance sessions. A control group was also used. The analysis of the pre- and post-test differences indicate that the treatment altered the self-concepts of the participants favourably. Payne and Dunn suggest that the guidance sessions provided experiences of positive peer interaction and personal acceptance by others as well as the opportunity for talking about oneself.

Fournier (1977) successfully used a self-enhancement group format with children who have to repeat the first grade. The activities she outlines include encouraging discussion about how the child feels about repeating the year, how they think their parents feel and what will they do if they are teased. Role playing and various reading and verbal games are used to promote positive feelings and develop coping skills.

Caplan (1957) using a Rogerian approach in group counselling with 12 to 15 year-old boys who had histories of conflict with school authorities. Group counsellors tried to create a permissive atmosphere in which they acted as sounding boards for feelings the boys had about school. After one semester of weekly sessions, the Q technique showed an increase in self and ideal self-congruence. Clark (1963) presents three case studies of interactions in training groups in which group members became more congruent by understanding the incongruity of other members and incorporating this new awareness into his own self-concept. Clark and Culbert (1965) found empirical support for the effects of this mutually therapeutic perception in a small training group. Culbert, Clark and Bobele (1968) assessed the effect sensitivity training would have on self-actualization. The study used two groups meeting for one two-hour session for fourteen weeks and both received sensitivity training. One group was made up of subjects who were in the self-actualized range of the Personal Orientation Inventory while the second group had pre-test means more closely resembling normal subjects. The post-test showed that the sensitivity training produced an increase in self-actualization in the subjects in the normal group and had no detrimental effect on the group which initially was quite self-actualizing. McIntire (1973) also found that training groups contribute to self-actualization and that these improvements were maintained at a follow-up one year later.

Bruce (1958) found that pupils who were subjected to a programme that enabled them to understand and develop greater insight into their own behaviour and into the behaviour of people around them showed gains in self-understanding and improved self-acceptance over a control group. There was still considerable discrepancies between self and ideal self in the experimental group, but they displayed lower anxiety and felt more comfortable about the discrepancies. What seems to be important is not the size of the discrepancy itself, as Rogers claimed, but the feelings a person has about it. So what to one person might seem to be a threatening discrepancy became a challenge, an indication of aspirations and a source of motivation to members of the experimental group. Pigge (1970) reports on a study investigating the effects of group counselling on the self-concepts of 9 to 10 year-olds in Texas. Three groups of ten pupils each with a school counsellor had eighteen fifty-minute sessions. A control group not exposed to any group counselling activities was formed. Using a multi-media approach to initiate discussion, a supportive ethos was devised in which students felt free to talk, with little counsellor prompting or structure. The self-concepts of the participants altered favourably but not significantly over the control group. The area most affected positively by the counselling experience involved interpersonal relationships.

Brookover et al. (1967) attempted to improve academic performance of a sample of poorly achieving fourteen year olds by enhancing their self-concept of ability. The most successful treatment involved working with the pupils' parents. Parents were persuaded by the research staff always to give encouragement and praise for any school achievement. This treatment which went on apparently without the knowledge of either the children or their teachers, did result in an improvement in the children's self-concept of academic ability and, produced a parallel improvement in their work. This treatment proved to be more effective than counselling the children. Surprisingly, one experimental group who attended sessions with a trained counsellor actually did worse in many respects than a control group. However, even the favourable results of working through the parents did not persist after the experimental treatment had been discontinued.

Several approaches have been developed for university students. For example, Stanton has conducted a number of studies on enhancing the self-concept of students in Australia (1977). He has used a particular form of experimental group which he terms the self-enhancement group (SEG). Unlike the more traditional encounter group, which often emphasizes confrontation and emotional release through the ventilation of negative feelings, the SEG focuses primarily on activities designed to help participants to think more highly of themselves, to like themselves more as people. Such activities involve acquaintanceship exercises; remembering and sharing successful experiences; self-image projection whereby participants share their images of themselves and receive feedback from others; 'nourishing', in which participants focus on things other group members have said or done which made them feel more positive about themselves; trust exercises of a non-verbal kind; and so on.

Evidence does exist that an experimental group designed specifically to emphasize positive feelings and emotions can succeed in changing people's self-concepts in positive directions (Stanton 1979a). Twenty people, sixteen females and four males, attended a residential weekend under the auspices of the Tasmanian Adult Education Board and participated in the activities listed earlier. Two measuring instruments, a face valid self-concept scale and the Tennessee Self-Concept Scale (Fitts 1955) were administered during the first and last sessions. Comparison of the pre- and post-experience scores provided strong support for the efficiency of the SEG as a means of improving self-concept.

It was considered by Stanton (1979b) that the same approach might be equally successful with low self-concept university students. A residential weekend was possible to organize for only twenty of these students (8 males and 12 females) but one other group, again twenty in number (9 males and 11 females), experienced six two-hourly sessions held on a weekly basis. A further twenty-seven students, who were unable to attend either of the self-enhancement groups, acted as controls.

Whether they attended the residential weekend or the six weekly sessions, students experienced twelve hours of planned activities. Obviously, because they remained together, the 'week-enders' were more able to continue such activities into free time such as coffee breaks and meal times. However, theirs was largely a massed practice situation whereas those students who attended one two-hour session a week were engaged in distributed practice, a schedule thought by many psychologists to produce better results.

The first session began with administration of the counselling form of the Tennessee Self-Concept Scale (TSCS). Following this and in the other sessions the various self-enhancement activities were operated. Comparison of scores on the Tennessee Self-Concept Scale before the self-enhancement with immediate post-experience scores and delayed experience scores (six months later) indicated a significant improvement. A control group showed no such self-concept gains.

The anecdotal reports were useful in providing subjective data that the changes in TSCS scores were reflected in actual behaviour change. Students described specific instances in which they were coping better, both with their studies and with their personal relationships. In particular, the feeling came through very strongly that the majority of students had clarified their goals and were deliberately planning their weekly activities towards achieving these. As they became increasingly purposeful, experiencing some small measure of success, their self-concepts became more positive, with 'I can' statements tending gradually to replace the previous 'I cannot' statements. The trend of both objective and subjective data pointed strongly in the same direction.

A small investment in time (an intensive weekend for one group and six two-hour sessions for the other) helped students develop a more positive self-concept. Self-enhancement group experience might act like a homeopathic medicine, whereby a minute dosage stimulates the body's own vital forces to effect healing. A small 'dose' of self-enhancement might stimulate students to continue the positive development of their own self-concepts.

At the college level, we tend to overlook the personal problems of students. Though we know they do experience such difficulties, we act as though they do not. The model which seems to guide us is that students are information processing machines who listen to our words, read the books and articles we prescribe, perform the experiments we set and give back the appropriate material when requested to do so on tests, assignments and examinations. Unfortunately, adherence to such a model produces many casualties. Students feel inadequate because they cannot handle their studies in a way other people expect of them. They are demoralized by academic pressure and cannot cope. When this difficulty in coping extends to areas outside the academic, as it usually does, they are in real trouble.

SELF-CONCEPT ENHANCEMENT AND READING

In the long run the central goal of self-concept enhancement is to help the child to become his own source of encouragement, motivation and reward. This goal can best be accomplished by improving the specific skills that assure the child that he is indeed capable of learning and achievement. In this regard, reading is probably the most important skill to impart, because reading is the key to so much of the child's learning in other areas.

Individualized contract-based procedures are a particularly suitable vehicle for teaching children competencies while at the same time causing them to assume responsibility for their own growth. In practising this method, teachers meet with children in one-to-one conferences and discuss suitable individual goals and realistic plans for accomplishing each child's goals. Children are given the option for setting up contracts with different demands that receive different grades. Thus a child may read 50 pages of a certain book and receive a C, 100 pages for a B or 150 pages for an A. Within the limits and structure set by a teacher, the child chooses goals and develops plans. These choices are indicated in a contract negotiated by the child. The child carries out the contract, and then may meet the teacher to evaluate the appropriateness of his goals and plans to assess the progress he has made. Using this feedback, the child is asked to negotiate a further contract employing the skills and knowledge previously gained. Lawrence (1971, 1972) has demonstrated that an effective approach with retarded readers is to boost their self-concepts through individual counselling. Lawrence (1973) finds it curious that despite the fact that the retarded reader's most outstanding characteristic appears to be his poor emotional adjustment, remedial reading so often takes the form of a direct attack on the mechanics of reading. Lawrence argues that to improve reading a systematic plan is needed to deal with the child's emotional state, and more specifically, his self-image. Such a systematic approach has been put into effect by Lawrence who has shown that it is possible to improve a child's self-image and ultimately his reading attainment by an individual counselling approach. In his research (1971, 1972) he found consistently that an individual counselling approach involving a warm relationship is shown to achieve superior results to those obtained by traditional remedial reading alone. It concentrates on what is happening inside the child (his emotional state) rather than the usual approach which concentrates on what is happening outside the child (appropriate books and apparatus).

Furthermore Lawrence found that this system of counselling can be used with success by people who have not been professionally trained and who have only a minimum explanation of the procedures involved. He advocates its use in all cases of prolonged reading failure, and in certain other selected cases. Lawrence (1973) outlined his counselling. It is aimed at helping the child regain his curiosity for learning which all children possess unless they have experienced prolonged failure or emotional deprivation.

The counsellor is not trained in any particular school of psychology, or expected to use any interpretative material. She is not going to require a knowledge of psychology: her skills will lie in the factors involved in making human relationships. She will be first of all a good listener and be able to relate to the child intuitively, reflecting his feelings in an uncritical way, and above all communicating to the child that she enjoys the child's company. In this way she is valuing the child and so increasing the child's self-esteem.

The techniques involved do not require so much a training as a briefing. Given first a personality which is sympathetic, warm, intelligent, lively and of sound mental health, all that is required is a brief instruction in principle, which can be learned fairly quickly. Given that it is possible to improve a child's self-esteem in this way, it is not unreasonable to ask why an improvement in self-esteem should have such a dramatic effect as to result in a rise in reading attainment.

We have noted frequently that people behave in ways consistent with their self-concept. To be made to behave in ways foreign to one's habitual way of perceiving oneself is a threat to one's self-image. Remedial schemes in school do just this; they deliberately attempt to modify behaviour to an objective which is out of character to the present self-perception of the child. Only the intellectual component is dealt with. If the child has a self-image that tells him that he is a retarded reader, he is more comfortable in that view, behaves in line with that view and seeks out situations where he does not need to read.

In lessons the teacher is puzzled because he continues to fail, although often appearing to cooperate. In reality he is only going through the motions of learning, experiencing very real difficulty in perceiving himself in the new role demanded by his teacher, i.e. the role of the child who can read well. Seeing himself as a bad reader, he does all he can to confirm that. He does not feel it is possible for him to read, and moreover, not only is it unpleasant to have to conceive of himself in a different role, but it is also unpleasant to have to re-enter the competition of reading, a competition in which he has already failed miserably.

It follows therefore that remedial teaching should be paralleled by a systematic attempt to help the child improve his self-concept. The possibilities of this approach are enormous since pupils not only have self-images of themselves as bad readers, but also as bad at sums, bad at spelling, etc. Conceivably, considerable improvement in all such areas are possible if allied with counselling on the lines Lawrence (1973) detailed in his book, which deserves to be read by all teachers. Other workers have found that self-enhancement programmes of various kinds have beneficial effects on both self-concept and reading ability too.

In an attempt to adapt the principles of non-directive play therapy to the class-room as the medium for non-directive therapy, Carlton and Moore (1966) created and employed self-directive dramatization of stories within the frame of reference of the regular classroom. The work was done by the class teacher with all the children in a regular classroom as a part of the reading programme for the purpose of improving reading and bringing about changes in self-concept from negative to positive.

After testing the technique at different times during a three-year period in laboratory and American public schools with mostly middle-class white children, Carlton secured the cooperation of three other classroom teachers in conducting similar experiments in as many additional classrooms of laboratory and American public schools. Favourable changes in self-concept occurred in all classes, and in all classes but one a positive correlation between self-concept changes and gains in reading achievement was found. Self-directive dramatization of stories as it is used in this study refers to the pupil's original, imaginative, spontaneous interpretation of a character of his own choosing in a story which he selects and reads cooperatively with other pupils in a group which is formed only for the time being and for a particular story.

The experimental groups in a second study consisted of one first, one second, one third, and one fourth grade class in a public elementary school of a large city. The average number of pupils in each class at the beginning of the year was thirty. The pupils came from a low socioeconomic area. Eighty-five per cent of the school population were black. The teachers consisted of one man and three women. Matches for each pupil were selected from other classes in the same school and from classes in another elementary school in the same system. The pupils in the control groups received reading instruction chiefly through the traditional use of the basic reader in small groups or as a whole class. Favourably, changes occurred in self-concept as well as reading ability as before. In addition to enlarging personal experiences, changing attitudes and/or values, and providing an opportunity to talk, group activities have served as an agent of need satisfaction, such as mastering the masculine role, lending peer support, solving personality conflicts, and overcoming shyness and feelings of inadequacy for the underachieving child and for the youngster from ethnic minority groups.

Counselling and Disadvantaged Pupils

Zirkel (1972) summarizes much of the American work on programmes deliberately designed to enhance self-concept and through that the academic performance of disadvantaged children. Self-concept enhancement efforts have been basically limited to tutoring and counselling programmes for disadvantaged children. Research has revealed disappointing results for tutoring and mixed results for counselling. For example, Di Lorenzo (1971) found self-concept enhancement to be one of the five goals shared by all pre-kindergarten programmes for the disadvantaged in New York that were surveyed in his four-year study. However, he found that none of these programmes produced significant differences between the experimental and control children with regard to self-concept. Both Nichols (1968) and Olsen (1969) found no significant overall effect from enrichment tutoring on the self-concept of disadvantaged elementary school students as measured by self report instruments. Talley (1967) found no significant differences in the pre-post measures of the self-concept level of a group of black eighth graders who participated in weekly group counselling sessions during one semester. Hamachek (1968) found that a one-year programme of individual and small-group counselling had a negative effect on the self-concept of a group of low-achieving junior high-school pupils. Herskovitz (1969) also found negative, but not significant, results for an educational and vocational rehabilitation programme for disadvantaged students which included vocational testing and training as well as counselling.

Such overall mixed results may be due to differences in the nature of the subjects and treatment as well as in the type of instrumentation. However, the general disappointing lack of success of tutoring and counselling in enhancing the self-concept of disadvantaged students may be due in part to the unintended stigmatization of such special and separate treatment.

Another probable reason for the apparent failure of many school programmes designed to 'enhance', or 'modify' students' perceptions of themselves is their tendency to overlook the conservative nature of the self-concept. Whether a self-perception is psychologically healthy or unhealthy, educationally productive or counterproductive, students cling to their own self-perceptions and act accordingly. Students who have learned over a lengthy period to see themselves as stupid will experience considerable anxiety over their own successful performance. Several studies have indicated that students who have learned to expect failure are even likely to sabotage their own efforts when they meet unexpected success (Aronson and Carlsmith 1962; Curtis, Zanna and Campbell 1975; Mettee 1971). Jersild (1952) concluded that students are active in maintaining their self-pictures even if by misfortune the picture is a false and unhealthy one. Being right, even about negative feelings toward oneself, can be satisfying.

Taken together, this collection of studies involving a wide variety of samples and variations in humanistic therapy support the contention that changes in attitudes to self can be brought about in young people in this way. Increases in self-concept in client-centred sensitivity or training groups are attributable to a number of factors. Two of the more important factors are: (1) increased motivation to become aware of oneself as the result of group norms emphasizing introspection and openness. (2) The abundance of feedback about one's behaviour which is made available to the individual.

Feedback is considered to be one of the most important factors influencing change in counselling-group members (Campbell and Dunnette 1968; Gibb 1971; Jacobs 1974). Although only a limited number of studies have investigated the overall effectiveness of feedback given in groups, some highly significant findings can be pointed out. In reviews of the group-counselling research literature, Campbell and Dunnette (1968) and Stock (1964) concluded that feedback over and beyond that ordinarily occurring in groups is valuable. More specifically, feedback has been reported to be associated with actual in-group behaviour change (Kolb, Winter and Berlew 1968), to result in greater self-insights (Gibb 1971) to lead to greater in-group sensitivity (Myers et al. 1969) and to increase group efficiency (Stock 1964). Such findings indicate that feedback is an important dimension of the group counselling process. Although the effectiveness of verbal feedback in producing change is supported by research findings, little is known about the most effective conditions under which feedback can be communicated so that it is accepted and utilized in a productive manner. The factors that have bearing on the usefulness of a particular feedback statement have been only partially explored.

Even negative feedback is valuable in unfreezing problematic and habitual patterns of behaviour when it is given in a supportive ethos (Stoller 1968). Such negative feedback puts the recipient in a mild but beneficial state of disorganization that helps to keep the person open rather than closed to the adaptations required by the environment (Lin 1973). This stance indicates that avoidance of negative feedback may not be the best alternative and there is a need to determine how and to whom negative feedback can be given most effectively.

Morran and Stockton (1980) found that even low self-concept students could come to accept negative feedback in a supportive context in which defensiveness is not necessary where psychological trust and safety pervade.

The fact that the process of learning in sensitivity training groups is viewed as centring around feedback is hardly surprising (Chapter 7). Since the turn of the century, learning theorists have proposed the central role of feedback in learning. Feedback is viewed as fulfilling a variety of needs, e.g. reducing tension, providing positive or negative reinforcement and evidencing success or failure, indicating the degree of similarity to a social model, degree of completion of tasks, and so on. Thus, in one form or another, feedback is generally considered essential to the learning process. This leads us on to a consideration of behaviour therapy as a means of self-concept enhancement since this technique too employs feedback as a mandatory principle.

BEHAVIOURAL APPROACHES

Although behavioural techniques do not have their theoretical roots in self-concept theory behaviour modification has equally been shown as effective as its competitor therapies in modifying the self-concept in a positive direction. Eitzen (1976) compared the self-concepts of delinquents in a behaviour modification treatment scheme with a control group.

The rehabilitation programme was based on a token economy system of reinforcement (see Chapter 15). In this system the goal was to teach the social skills important to be successful participants in the community (e.g. conversation skills, academic skills, prevocational skills, manners and acceptance of criticism). Other research has shown that the products of this setting have fewer police and court contacts, better school attendance and grades, and less recidivism than those other delinquent boys from the community who were placed either in the state borstal or put on probation (Phillips et al. 1973). Compared with a control group, the results demonstrated that the behaviour modification treatment group improved significantly in self-concept. They were also perceived by parents, teachers and friends as more responsible, acceptable and socially skilled. So feedback reinforced their new behaviour.

Rimm and Masters (1979) report the successful use of guided behaviour rehearsal and thought stopping-covert assertion techniques in reducing or eliminating self-depreciation and self-castigation.

The effects of selective reinforcement on self-concept was studied by Babladelis (1973). In three systematic studies, attempts were made to modify a complex verbalized self-concept, a simple written self-concept, and a simple verbalized self-concept. In each study therapy was simulated by an interview setting and subjects' past history was taken into account. In the first study, three self-concept measures were used to divide subjects into high, medium or low self-concept groups. Subjects were then randomly assigned to one of three experimental conditions: reinforcement of positive self-statements, reinforcement of negative self-statements or random reinforcement. The second study used the subjects as the first but this time subjects completed an adjective check list while either receiving or not receiving verbal reinforcement. The third study used different subjects and they were asked to choose self-descriptive adjectives with or without verbal reinforcement. In all three studies, results showed no general effect of reinforcement on self-concept although in each case there was a differential effect among high and low self-concept groups in that, in both cases, subjects showed more moderate self-presentations on the retest. On the basis of these results the author recommended caution in using verbal conditioning in therapy (Babladelis 1973).

Another behavioural technique which has been experimentally tested for its effect on self-concept is assertiveness training. Percell, Berwick and Beigel (1974) state that despite the complex and relatively unsystematic approaches used in assertiveness training, the goal is always 'the spontaneous expression of personal rights and feelings, both positive and negative, in a socially acceptable manner' (p. 502). The way in which this could result in an improved self-concept can be understood in Rogerian terms in that it would create greater congruence between self and experience. Also, an increase in self-esteem may result simply from more success in social situations. Percell et al. (1974) report another study which found a significant positive relationship between assertiveness and self-acceptance. In their own study, Percell et al. hypothesized that assertive training would produce an increase in self-acceptance. Two groups of subjects participated in eight sessions of therapy, one getting assertive training and the other acting as a relationship-control therapy group. Results showed a significant increase in self-acceptance in the assertive group as measured by the Berger self-acceptance scale with no significant improvement in the controls. The authors claim the finding shows an effect of a behaviour-modification technique on the cognitive and effective spheres not previously reported in the behavioural literature.

In an early British study on the self-concept, Staines (1954, 1958) showed that it was possible for a teacher to consciously and deliberately change a pupil's self-concept. The teacher behaviours outlined by Staines reveal the strength of the teacher's roles as a significant or salient other who performs the functions of reflecting, interpreting and informing in the behavioural dialogue of the classroom. On the premise that self-concepts are learned structures derived from interaction with others and the environment, Staines formed two hypotheses relating the role of the teacher to the self-image of the pupil. The first of these stated that teachers could be distinguished according to their use of pupil self-referring comments. The second hypothesis stated that change in academic performance and in pupil self-image could be achieved through variations in teaching.

To test the first hypothesis, two pairs of teachers, one at junior high level and the other at primary level, were observed, and their comments were recorded for positive, negative, neutral or ambiguous effect on the 'Self as I Am', 'Other Self', and 'Ideal Self' of pupils. The effect of specific verbal behaviours was determined by three professional judges. The categories that most clearly differentiated individual teachers and teacher pairs were: comments on pupil performance, status, values, and wants, and comments pertaining to classroom management. Primary teachers were further differentiated by their comments regarding pupil physique, pupil traits, and pupil self-orientation. Units of each teacher's commenting behaviour were analysed and the content was related to the following core dimensions of self: salience (a measure of self-consciousness); differentiation (the degree to which self-concepts have been developed and defined by the self); potency (self-adequacy); integrity (self-predictability); insight (the relationship of self-acceptance and rejection (the congruence between the perceived and ideal self). Profiles constructed from scores on the dimensions produced diverse descriptions of teaching styles, suggesting that teachers differ in their effect on pupil self-concept.

In testing his second hypothesis that teachers can teach towards both academic and pupil self-image change, Staines used only the two junior level classrooms. He described the experimental teacher as having a teaching style and an attitude towards pupils that would have a positive impact on pupil self-concept. This teacher, on the basis of several self-construct measures, set self-image improvement goals for each pupil. The teacher also used instructions that provided the events through which pupils could be helped to achieve these affective goals—an illustration of the teacher's assessment expertise being used as a diagnostic and therapeutic tool.

The teacher's role was to affirm each pupil as a worthy, achieving class member and to attend to each child's status needs. In addition to planning instructional methods, the teacher also evaluated pupil performance and products, giving detailed, constructive feedback that avoided the use of single words such as 'good' or 'wrong'. This process was intended to provide cognitive content from which each pupil could acquire the concepts and behaviours necessary to achieve his or her goals.

The results of the investigation indicated that the first hypothesis was supported. Marked differences occurred between teachers in the frequency of self-reference in their comments, particularly in their positive or negative comment on the child's performance, status and self-confidence or potency. The second hypothesis was also supported. A small number of changes occurred in self-traits, but statistically changes were found in two dimensions of the self, certainty and differentiation. Both changes were interpreted as indicating greater psychological security.

A control class taught by a teacher regarded as typically 'sound' and having no awareness of the self-picture as an outcome of education showed significant decreases in certainty about the self and in differentiation. The uncertainty spread throughout the self and was significantly greater than that of the experimental group. Both changes were interpreted as leading to a marked psychological insecurity. These changes, usually indicative of poor adjustment, were the unsought and unnoticed concomitant outcomes of normal methods aimed at securing the usual academic results.

The experiment has shown that good and poor adjustment are linked with the goals and teaching methods of the typical classroom. The changes that occurred in the self-picture are usually accepted as symptoms of good and poor adjustment. Teacher *A*, using the free methods indicated, and stressing the aspects of the self-picture discussed above, was able to make his pupils more sure of what they were like, more accepting of what they were, more able to differentiate themselves and to see themselves with moderation and certainty, more certain of what they wanted to be like, and more aware of what judgements they think others made of them. Such changes are accepted as the marks of good adjustment, and Teacher *A* clearly produced these characteristics in his children. Teacher *B*'s data showed that typical high-pressure teaching, with vigorous personal emphasis with great stress on correctness and on the consequences of failure, and with constant emphasis on the passing of examinations, can lead to significantly greater signs of insecurity. One particular variable which seems to have been neglected is that of the age of the pupil. It has been shown by Livesley and Bromley (1973) that below the age of 7 or 8 years, pupils describe people in terms of external, readily observed attributes, and by 12 they have discovered a number of invariant dispositions and behavioural regularities, so that they begin to see others in the context of personal qualities and surrounding circumstances. The development appears to be rapid in the seventh and eighth years and then slows down, suggesting a parallel with Piagetian developmental trends. This poses the question of whether attempts to alter the self-concept will have different effects on pupils of different ages. Because of this, Harrop (1977) hypothesized in his study that self-concept scores of pupils of different ages would be differentially affected by behaviour modification.

Harrop applied the Piers–Harris scale to 120 children, 24 in each age group from 7 to 11 years of age. Teachers were trained in reinforcement techniques and sought to apply this behaviour modification in an attempt to increase self-concepts of selected pupils. A comparison was made between selected and non-selected pupils. The results indicated that a differential effect occurred. In terms of significance levels, the younger pupils' scores increased significantly more than the scores of the rest of the pupils in their classes, whilst for the older pupils, no such effect occurred. This suggests that pupils between the ages of seven and nine, responded to the treatment, whilst pupils above this age did not respond to the treatment.

There are a number of theoretical considerations that are relevant to this observation. The younger pupils are in the period of rapid growth of person perception identified by Livesley and Bromley (1973) and may well be more open to influence. It could be that sophisticated treatment is required for those older pupils whose understanding has begun to pass (or indeed may have passed) into a more abstract level of analysis. Alternatively, the teacher may be a more reinforcing person to the younger pupils. The decrease in self-concept scores obtained from the younger pupils in the 'rest of the class' group may be accounted for by this alternative explanation, i.e. if the teacher is a powerful reinforcing agent, it may be that although she continues to reinforce the group as before (or even reinforce more than before), the increase in reinforcement to the selected pupils causes a relative deprivation to the 'rest of the class'.

With older pupils, the teacher may be less reinforcing, or the reinforcement used may be too simplistic and inappropriate. At the same time, some complex effect seems to have been occurring, as suggested by the differences in variances produced. In view of the fact that there is a smaller standard deviation in increase scores for the older pupils in the 'rest of the class' than for the same group of younger pupils, it does appear that teachers' treatment of the selected pupils is having less effect on the untreated older pupils than on the untreated younger pupils. This is in accord with the possible explanations previously discussed.

Looking at this experiment from a wider perspective, it can be said that this has been more broadly focused than the more usual kind of behaviour modification investigation. Whilst one can perhaps never claim that the whole pupil has been treated, this is surely a step in that direction. The actual instructions given to the teachers were very simple. This was an essential part of the investigation, since Harrop (op. cit.) did not wish to produce a method of treatment which could only be used by teachers who had served a lengthy technical apprenticeship; and because behaviour modification methods do not generally require a complex approach.

What emerged from this investigation seems to have been a comparatively simple method of treatment for younger pupils, and an underlining of the need to investigate the differential effects of age in investigations aimed at altering pupils' self-concepts.

Muller and Spuhler (1976) provide some experimental evidence that the manipulation of self-concept influences learning. They lowered self-concept of ability to learn a foreign language by providing subjects with negative feedback regarding their performance on a foreign language aptitude test. They observed that these subjects learned a subsequent simulated foreign language task more slowly than did those not receiving negative feedback. However, they were not able to raise self-concepts by providing positive feedback of test results, nor were they able to observe a faster learning rate for subjects receiving positive feedback. Thus, the efficacy of raising self-concept as a procedure for enhancing achievement was not demonstrated.

Felker and Thomas (1971) studying fourth-grade students, found a significant, positive correlation between the number of positive self-descriptive statements emitted during an interview and performance on a self-concept test. D. Allen (1974) successfully used verbal reinforcement to increase the frequency of positive self-descriptive statements in group therapy and observed a subsequent increase in the self-concept test score of the participants. Thus, it appears that increasing the number of positive self-descriptive statements a person makes about himself will increase his measured self-concept.

A study by Lane and Muller (1977) examined the impact of operant reinforcement of positive self-descriptive behaviour on the self-concepts and classroom behaviour of 60 ten year-old students. Three groups wrote a series of eight essays describing their school performance. The first group received written reinforcement for positive self-descriptions of their school performance. The second group received an equal number of reinforcements for general statements. The third group received no reinforcement for written statements. Three areas of self-concept were measured with the Primary Self-Concept Inventory; personal self, social self, and intellectual self. A frequency count was also made of nine classroom behaviours thought to be influenced by self-concept. The first group displayed increases in the frequency of positive self-descriptive statements and in intellectual self-concept but no changes in personal self-concept, social self-concept, or the nine classroom behaviours. The other two groups showed no change in self-descriptive, self-concept, or the nine classroom behaviours.

The findings indicate that the frequency of written positive intellectual domain self-descriptions of low self-concept ten year olds can be increased through operant reinforcement. Changes in measured self-concept were limited to those specific areas of self-concept directly reflective of the kinds of self-referent statements that were reinforced; that is, changes in the intellectual-self domain were observed, while no change in social-self domains occurred. This last phenomenon is supportive of a factor specific model of self-concept in relation to school performance.

The fact that the general reinforcement group showed no greater gains than the control group indicates that reinforcement, when applied to general statements has no significant effect on self-descriptive behaviour or self-concept performance.

Thus, this research indicates that children can quite easily be helped to describe themselves more positively. This in turn reflects itself in higher measured self-concepts. However, these changes do not appear to be associated with measured changes in classroom behaviour. Thus, this study failed to provide support for the widely held notion that changing self-concept will result in behavioural changes. While these results do not refute that notion, they tend to suggest that if such an influence does exist, it is at least moderately difficult to demonstrate. These results suggest that educators should not assume a direct, simple, and powerful causal relationship between self-concept and learning. Furthermore, they indicate that self-concept, just as other specific skills, is more effectively altered by direct, planned and specific intervention techniques rather than global approaches which seek to provide simply a warm supportive atmosphere.

The Rogerian model is consistent with the aims of modern education and our ideas of the value of individuality, but young people may not possess the skills, insight and experience needed for self-discovery, self-awareness and the implementation of the necessary new behaviours required. A totally non-directive model may not be feasible at school level. The alternative directive approach is this behavioural learning model in which the counsellor plays a more active role, reinforcing and shaping behaviour, and planning the steps by which the pupil will attain his goal. There is the implication of imposition by the counsellor, but the programme can be designed to meet each pupil's needs. A combination of the two approaches based on the work of Carkhuff (1969) would seem to employ the best of both, with the counsellor initially providing purpose and direction until the pupil can take over.

VIDEO PLAYBACK RESEARCH

Although the enhancement of a client's level of self-esteem is a frequent goal in Rogerian psychotherapy, this task is typically approached in an indirect and relatively inefficient manner. The need for more direct means of raising self-esteem has encouraged the introduction not only of behavioural therapy but also of technical aids such as videotape and audio playback as adjuncts to therapy. Bailey and Bailey (1973) found that a therapy group did not improve self-concept any more than the control group but that a therapy group with audio playback did. Walter and Miles (1974) found that high gains were made by subjects receiving unstructured feedback, that is viewing without instructions, but that structured feedback was ineffective. Due to the evidence suggesting beneficial results from videotape feedback, Lockwood, Salyberg and Heckel (1978) tried it in a leaderless therapy group and found that the outcome was no better than the control group. The authors conclude that videotape feedback is no substitute for a group facilitator.

Other researchers who found positive results from video playback include: Boyd and Sisney (1967) who found a significant video playback effect following one session and Robinson and Jacobs (1970) found a strong videotape playback effect after only six hours of treatment.

Friedenberg and Gillis (1977) found that self-esteem might be enhanced by means of very direct messages about change of attitude. They based their work on Goldstein's suggestion that much of typical psychotherapy consists of 'efficiency-reducing trappings'. That is, although treatment might be intended to achieve certain goals, no specific methods were employed to realize them. If increased self-esteem were realized, for example, this was most often the indirect result of the accepting, supportive, permissive stance common to most forms of therapy. Despite the acknowledged importance of the goal, few aspects of treatment were specifically directed towards its attainment.

Following Rosenberg (1965), Friedenberg and Gillis argued that self-esteem could be treated as an attitude and that techniques of attitude change might be used to alter it. For this purpose they developed brief videotapes in which a counter-attitudinal, esteem-enhancing message was presented to subjects with low self-esteem. Given under specific conditions of high credibility, this message successfully raised subjects' self-ratings on several measures of esteem.

Because of the pervasiveness of the problem of low self-esteem among clients, findings that simple and straightforward techniques could alter these were encouraging. A second study by Friedenberg and Gillis (1980) sought to assess the effectiveness of this method further. To the extent that it again involved delivering a taped, counter-attitudinal message to subjects having low self-esteem it represented an attempt to validate the previous findings.

Subjects were presented with this message under conditions of either high or low credibility and communicators' attractiveness. A control group of subjects was not exposed to the message, and heard, instead, a tape with no apparent relevance for the attitude of interest. Following exposure to the message, a series of self-esteem measures were completed by both the subject and a clinical interviewer. A naïve judge also assessed the positivity of subjects' self-references from taped segments of their interaction.

An eight-minute videotape was developed from Ellis's (1961) suggestions with regard to those irrational ideas that sustain emotional disturbances. Several of these irrational beliefs were described by remarks that included the persuasive message that the listener was really a better person than he gave himself credit for being and that he should change his ideas about himself accordingly. The speaker was a mature, distinguished individual who spoke in an informative, unemotional manner.

144 college students were exposed to a taped counter-attitudinal message under one of eight experimental conditions. These conditions represented various combinations of high or low levels of communicator's attractiveness and expertise and subjects' ego involvement. Results supported the earlier findings that levels of esteem could be raised by exposing subjects to appropriate messages under conditions of high credibility.

Findings indicate that: (a) it is possible to structure the presentation of a therapeutic message such that subjects' evaluations of the communicator's attractiveness, trustworthiness and expertise are influenced; and (b) presenting the message in the context of high levels of these conditions, can alter effectively individuals' levels of self-esteem. The earlier findings of Friedenberg and Gillis (1977) are thus supported. Moreover, it appears that subjects' levels of ego involvement were not critical to the efficacy of the technique of attitude change. Presumably, level of ego involvement constitutes a major difference between laboratory and therapy settings. It might thus be inferred that techniques of change which have proven effective in the laboratory, where ego involvement of subjects might be low, would have little value in the therapeutic setting. Results suggest that such is not the case. Indeed, although the specific attitude investigated here would appear to be one associated with maximum personal relevance, it was susceptible to procedures for change derived from laboratory studies.

Perhaps, the most impressive aspect of these results is that the method of changing attitude affected esteem in each of the several ways in which it was assessed. Subjects were influenced both to feel and to speak better of themselves and such attitudes were apparent to an observer of their interview behaviour.

So, generally, apart from Lockwood et al.'s (1978) uncomforming result, visual feedback seems to be relatively effective. The reason for this seems to be that the playback patient, as a relatively passive recipient of information about himself may be in a better position to learn than the patient who is learning while closely involved in often dramatic human encounters. If this is true, mechanical feedback would help re-experiencing while at the same time would serve to inhibit influences that impede self-learning.

Unstructured feedback appears more effective than structured feedback as the former promote introspective analyses and concern for the impact of one's behaviour on others. This, then, seems to be the key in the process of increasing self-acceptance. Only if the facilitator is seen as credible, trustworthy and warm does a more structured feedback help as in the Friedenberg and Gillis (1977) study. Without that sort of facilitator, structured video feedback may cause subjects to focus on their inabilities as well as on their merits, whereas the unstructured feedback provides no such focus.

While it would be difficult to conclude the value of videotape feedback from a few studies alone, the general trend of the findings increases confidence in the value of video playback. This suggests that video playback in such areas as micro-teaching could have beneficial effects on self-concept as well as on future teaching performance. It would seem that less emphasis should be focused on the more negative elements of the filmed teaching extract and more placed on the better aspects of the performance. Again the principle of providing positive reinforcement rather than negative reinforcement is suggested as the means of improving self-acceptance. It must also be emphasized that there are individual differences in readiness to experiment and receptiveness to feedback. Some members of training groups take more risks, receive more feedback, and make more behavioural adjustments than others. If this concept of the learning process is approximately correct, these more involved and exposed participants should be those who are more often seen as having changed their behaviour in their normal environment as well.

PHYSICAL CHALLENGE AND HEALTH PROMOTION

Ever since the teachings of Socrates, man has believed in the concept of the body–mind relationship or *mens sana in corpore sano*. The believed benefits of systematic exercise to physical and mental well-being have led to an escalating concern in most western cultures about fitness, health and weight demonstrated by the current fads of jogging, dieting, saunas and health clubs. It has been shown that these beliefs are well founded in improving cognitive functioning (e.g. Ohlsson 1975). They seem equally well founded in the improvements noted in mental health by Griest (1978) who showed that running was as effective a cure for depression as traditional forms of psychotherapy.

Buccola and Stone (1975) reported that aged men became more self-sufficient when given daily exercise. Coleman, Ayoub and Friedrich (1976) said that physical fitness should be a part of the training programme for the mentally retarded. Twenter (1977) argues that any programme which seeks to strengthen a child's self-concept should have some basis in motor development since many children can obtain feelings of success in this area, and every child needs successful play experiences to develop a body image. Physical education and recreation programmes can provide the child who has a learning disability with compensatory successes and satisfactions in play not found in the academic world. For the teacher who is interested in learning the feelings of pupils toward themselves in this area, a very good first step is to observe gross and fine motor performance in the gymnasium, on the playground, in competitive games and when writing. The majority of children with difficulty in physical coordination need help in both developing these skills and recognizing their strengths and weaknesses, so that a general feeling of inadequacy does not permeate and harm all areas of endeavour.

More relevant are the reports that reveal positive changes in measured self-concept as physical fitness improves. Albinson (1974) found that physically active college males tend to have better self-concepts than physically inactive subjects. White (1973) concluded that the self-concept of college males can be raised by increasing their physical fitness levels and Hughes (1974) found the same thing in college females. Johnson, Fretz and Johnson (1968), in their work with children at the Children's Physical Development Clinic at the University of Maryland, found that emotionally disturbed, mentally retarded and brain-damaged children improved in three major factors of self-concept as they improved their physical fitness. Collingwood (1972) found that rehabilitation clients improved their self-concept with physical fitness, and that physical training given to obese teenagers brought about a more positive self-attitude.

Carkhuff (1971; 1972) and Collingwood (1976) suggested that physical fitness can be a significant counselling tool. This idea was further supported by reports from psychiatrists who used distance running as a distinct form of therapy for certain of their patients (Kostrubala 1977). Hilyer and Mitchell (1979) investigated the effects of a systematic physical-fitness programme combined with counselling on the self-concept of college students. The total P (positive) score of the Tennessee Self-Concept Scale (TSCS; Fitts 1956) was used as a measure of overall self-esteem.

Three groups of forty college students were each given different treatments in the experiment. One experimental group received a fitness programme consisting of flexibility training and systematic distance running; a second experimental group received the same physical training plus one hour per week of group counselling designed to reinforce progress made in the fitness programme; and a third group (control) received no physical fitness training or counselling. After a ten-week programme the group receiving fitness training and running made a significant gain in self-concept as measured by the Tennessee Self-Concept Scale. The students were divided into low and high self-concept groups for statistical analysis. It was found that the students who received fitness training and counselling and had low self-concepts on the pre-test measure made positive changes in self-concept significant at the 0·05 level. Only minimal changes in self-concept occurred among high self-concept students.

Among the low self-concept students, the counselling group produced significantly greater gain in self-concept than the control group. Surprisingly, compared with other sub-scales only minor changes in the physical self-sub-scale occurred. Among low self-concept students, the counselling group obtained an increase in total P score two and a half times as great as the running group and four times as great as the control group. Gain in Moral Self for the counselling group was over twice the gain of the running group and five times the gain of the control group. In terms of personal self, the gains of the counselling group were three and a half and two and one-third times the gains of the running and control groups respectively. The gains of the counselling group in identity were three and three-quarters and thirty-seven times the gains of the running and the control groups, respectively. Self-satisfaction score gains for the counselling group were over twice the gains of either the running or the control groups.

Ceiling effects may account for the lack of increase in self-concept scores in high self-concept students. The act of running, of systematically increasing distances and decreasing times, engenders in the student a sense of mastery—an increased sense of control over self and the environment. The counselling used increments of success to reinforce and magnify these benefits that resulted naturally for the activity. The counselling also provided stimulation for overcoming the difficulties and resistance that are part of physical exercise. Furthermore, the counselling helped students clarify the values of the activity and encouraged them to see an increasing number of benefits. It appears that the combination of physical fitness with facilitative counselling can be an effective technique to help persons with low self-concepts gain more positive views of themselves. In short a holistic approach to better overall health, both physically and psychologically, can be promoted through the combination of skills of the physical educator and the counsellor.

Going just beyond physical fitness and pitting oneself against one's physical limits has also been shown to modify the self-concepts of those involved. Clifford and Clifford (1967) studied a group of adolescents in an Outward Bound summer camp. The first such camp was established in Britain during the early days of the Second World War, with the specific purpose of introducing physical challenge into the training of young men as means of developing their character. This philosophy stemmed from the experience with young British sailors in the merchant marine.

Under wartime conditions, an alarming number of them were lost because they seemed to lack the determination to survive. Subsequent wartime experience with graduates of the Outward Bound School established at that time, indicated a greater survival rate for these graduates. Since the war, a number of Outward Bound Schools have been established in Europe and the United States.

On arrival at the Colorado Outward Bound School, for example, boys are assigned to patrols. Each patrol engages in a variety of vigorous physical conditioning exercises, ranging from bathing in a cold mountain stream in early morning to running, axemanship and climbing. The object is to build physical stamina and to push each individual to his physical limit. Patrols compete against one another and considerable pressure is exerted upon each boy to produce maximally. Each boy is also responsible for supporting members of his own patrol. Two main experiences, which are in effect tests of the boy and his training, occur towards the latter part of the month. The first is also a sole survival trip during which the boy spends two days alone in the wilderness. He carries with him a knife, a snare, a string and fishhook, salt, matches and nothing else. The other is a group experience. At the end of his stay the boy and his patrol set off on an expedition. This involves climbing to the top of a mountain, during the course of which all the skills of climbing, axemanship, rope handling and physical conditioning are put to the test, as is the cooperative, supportive emphasis between patrol members.

The psychological assessment of the effects of this type of experience is challenging. It is clear that effects cannot be expected to be uni-dimensional. It is also clear that effects may very well be a function of the state of the boy on entering the programme, as well as a function of the reasons for the selection of such a programme by the boy and/or his parents.

What effects can such an experience have? It is assumed by the sponsors and directors that the feelings a person has about his own worth would be most susceptible to influence. As a result of the emphasis upon physical conditioning and the acquisition of a new set of skills, feelings about competence should be affected. If the challenge has been too great these feelings would be adversely affected, so the primary hypothesis of Clifford and Clifford's study was: 'The experience of being challenged to the limit of one's capacities will result in increased feelings of self-worth and competence.'

Self-concept measures and a semantic differential were administered before training began and again, one month later, at the conclusion of the experience, the hypothesis was upheld. Overall changes in the self-concept did take place in the appropriate direction and discrepancies between the self and the ideal self were reduced. Changes were general rather than specific and were related to the initial of self-evaluation.

In a similar British study Payne, Drummond and Lunghi (1970) monitored the effect of an Arctic training expedition on the self-concepts of thirty-five volunteers aged between 17 and 19. A control group of thirty-four students who had narrowly failed to gain selection to the expedition was chosen. The study aimed to replicate that of Clifford and Clifford on English boys and to extend it in two main directions:

1. A control group was introduced so that any change that occurred could be

reliably attributed to the experience undergone by the experimental group and could not be attributed to the passage of time or being on holiday.
2. Two aspects of personality, neuroticism and extraversion, were measured on both experimental and control groups. These seemed relevant as the effect of the experience could well be a function of the personality of the applicant as well as his reasons for seeking the experience.

The main hypothesis tested, was the experience of being challenged to the limit of one's capacities will result in increased feelings of self-worth and competence.

The interesting fact that emerged from this study was that changes did occur in the participants. That this is due to the experience of the expedition is substantiated by the fact that no changes occurred in the control group. In the total experimental group the discrepancy between their self-descriptions and their ideal self-descriptions diminished by a change in both percepts rather than in one or other. However, when the group is broken down into public-school, grammar-school and police-cadet groups, it becomes clear that this is an over-simplification (though the numbers in the groups are admittedly small). In the public-school group there is a notable diminution in their ideal self at the end of the expedition, whilst the grammar-school boys and police cadets have markedly improved their self-descriptions and are responsible for the significant improvement of this in the whole group.

This does not substantiate the findings of Clifford and Clifford who found that it was the self-rating that changed and the ideal self-rating which remained constant. It does suggest that change occurs in more than one way. It seems that socioeconomic factors and type of school are important background variables in this study.

In a later study, Lambert et al. (1978) examined changes in the self-concepts of college students undergoing a 'wilderness' experience. This was a thirty-day outdoor experience the purpose of which was to provide intense and sustained physical and mental challenges which could be met without failure. Participants showed significant positive increases in the post-test self-concept scores compared to a control group. The few researches in this area do suggest that these sorts of extreme experiences can be beneficial to the participants in terms of their more positive feelings about themselves.

ENCOURAGING SELF-CONCEPT DISCLOSURE

Teachers can acquire an understanding of students' self-concepts in two ways. The first is through self-disclosure, the process of learning about another from the information that person voluntarily provides. The second is observation, the process of drawing inferences about a person's self-concept on the basis of his behaviour.

Student Self-Disclosure

While current knowledge about the process of self-disclosure is far from complete, research findings permit some general suggestions. One-to-one contexts help self-disclosure, as most people feel uncomfortable in revealing confidential information in public. When you disclose information to just one other person, you can monitor closely the responses of that person to what you are saying. If the other reacts in an accepting way, you can continue; if not, you can stop at once. When two or more other people are present it becomes more difficult to attend closely to everyone's responses. The acceptance by listeners of what you are saying is likely to vary too, and the decision to continue or stop disclosing becomes more difficult to make. Even in the one-to-one context self-disclosure is unlikely to be spontaneous as pupils may believe their true identities are not very attractive and that, if they are revealed, others will find them unacceptable and reject them. A common fear also is that, if we reveal ourselves to others, they will have some degree of control over us.

The implication is obvious: students are most likely to share important information about themselves in private conversations. If teachers wish to know students, they must be available for these private meetings. Being available means, however, more than simply spending an extra half-hour in the classroom at the end of the day. It also means being ready to accept, without evaluation, whatever a student may choose to share. Being available also means having a genuine interest in knowing students as distinctive human beings.

Students' self-disclosure can be expected to occur in small amounts which increase as their relationships with the teacher develop in positive ways. An important element in a positive relationship is trust. We are unlikely to share personal information with people who will then repeat it indiscriminately to others. Hence, to build trust, teachers must keep secret any information given in confidence. These conditions that help self-disclosure are the same ones that Rogers promotes in his counselling technique. Acceptance, empathy and trust within a non-threatening environment are the principles derived from Rogers's work, principles adopted so far by school counsellors yet of more potential value in the general school context for the enhancement of all pupils' self-concepts.

There are at least two other variables which can be expected to influence students' self-disclosure quite independently of the teacher's behaviour. The first is age. Younger children are more self-disclosing than older ones. Jourard (1958) noted that young children are relatively unconcerned about revealing their thoughts and feelings to those around them; they say what they think and tell what they have done. Older children have learned the consequences of disclosing. To some statements adults respond approvingly, while to others reactions are disapproving. So children gradually learn to censor the information they reveal about themselves.

The second variable affecting self-disclosure is sex. Boys who honestly express their feelings, particularly feelings of insecurity, run the risk of being labelled as weak and unmasculine as they contravene the sex-role stereotype. Little boys soon learn that 'big' boys act tough, and that self-disclosing is not part of the role.

Teacher Self-Disclosure

Self-disclosure seems a reciprocal process. The teacher who demonstrates trust by taking the initiative in sharing information is likely to find that students respond in the same way. Likewise, the teacher who holds students at a distance, not permitting them to understand her and indicating that they are not trusted, respected or cared about, should not be surprised if students respond in a similar fashion.

The problem that is so difficult to resolve, however, is exactly what is appropriate to disclose. What and how much to reveal is an individual decision for the teacher, but she should strike a balance between over-disclosure and under-disclosure. Over-disclosing teachers relate intimate details of family and personal problems, financial position, and so on. Teachers who reveal innermost thoughts and feelings to their classes are likely to make students feel uncomfortable and embarrassed, even though they may have made such disclosures with the best intentions. Over-disclosers have a problem in not distinguishing what is appropriate to reveal in a given situation, with the result that they reveal virtually anything to anyone. At the other extreme, under-disclosers appear to be little more than robots. They arrive at class, teach and leave. Even though many hours of watching and listening to them may have gone by, pupils feel at the end of the term that they know little more about them than they did before the course began.

In striking a balance three factors should be considered. First, traditional norms do not encourage teachers to disclose themselves to students. Consequently, when students are confronted with an over-disclosing teacher, their expectations are violated and they may be confused as to how to respond. Ironically, because the norm is for teachers not to disclose, students probably feel more comfortable with under-disclosing teachers than with over-disclosing teachers. The second factor concerns the context. As noted before, self-disclosure takes place best with just one other person. Hence for a teacher to do extensive revealing to an entire class again violates student expectations of self-disclosure being a relatively private event. Finally, the third factor concerns the reciprocal nature of showing trust is shared by also self-disclosing. The over-disclosing teacher, then, may make students uncomfortable if they believe they are also expected to engage in extensive self-disclosure before the class.

In searching for the ideal amount of self-disclosure the teacher should ask herself three questions. First, Can I reveal anything about myself which would help students to understand who I am and how I view the world? Second, Will revealing this information cause discomfort on my part or on the part of my students? and third, Will this revelation encourage the pupil to reveal more about how he views himself? If any of these are answered negatively then it is wise not to reveal that particular element.

Observations

While the self-reports of pupils are an invaluable lead to understanding them, there is one major limitation: they depend on what students are willing to reveal. If students have learned that some self-views they hold are unacceptable to others, or if they believe that teachers cannot be trusted, then they reveal only what they believe will be acceptable or nothing at all. Because of these limitations, systematic observation is also needed to gain an understanding of students. Such observations may be most profitable if the following suggestions based on Purkey (1970) are considered.

1. Recognize at the outset that you cannot be totally objective in observing and drawing inferences about another person. You may not be able to suspend prejudices (positive or negative) but you can be aware of how they can influence your interpretation of the behaviour you see.
2. Before drawing conclusions observe the student in as many different situations as possible. It would be usual, for example, to discover that a pupil behaved differently on the playground than in your classroom, and related to peers in a pattern quite different from that followed when interacting with you.
3. Because self-concept may be manifested in a number of ways in a student's behaviour, watch closely, and listen attentively to, the individual. It might be profitable, for instance, to ask yourself how often the individual smiles and what events seem to produce smiles. A person who rarely smiles is often greatly dissatisfied with his or herself and life. Listen to the student's vocal cues. A whining voice or one filled with sarcasm may indicate low self-esteem.
4. Finally, the manner in which a person presents in interactions with others can be especially revealing.

Low self-concept may be indicated by the following:

(a) frequent statements of self-criticism,
  I've never been able to get this right . . .
(b) negative expectations toward competition,
  Why bother? I haven't got a chance . . .
(c) criticism of the achievements of others,
  He's really stupid; it was just luck . . .
(d) unwillingness to accept blame,
  It's not my fault . . .
(e) readiness to point out the failures of others,
  His problem is . . .
(f) inability to accept praise,
  I know you don't really mean it . . .
(g) unfavourable attitudes to school and teachers,
  I don't think teacher likes me . . .
(h) low motivation; will not try,
  I'm not interested in . . .
(i) poor social adjustment, shyness and sensitivity to criticism,
  Everyone is against me.

On the other hand the high self-concept pupil shows optimism about his potential for success in the future, is confident in competence as a person and a student, believes others like him, believes he works hard, sets realistic goals, accepts praise with pride and criticism without hurt and accepts responsibility and initiates new projects and ideas.

After interacting with students over time, the teacher may be able to combine the information they have volunteered about themselves with her observations to determine whether their overall self-concepts are positive or negative, as well as the specific beliefs they hold about themselves and the strength of these beliefs. On this basis the teacher may be able to tell if students have particular problems which are likely to affect their school performance. With this information the teacher may be more able to look at the world through the student's eyes and have greater understanding of their responses to you, to their classmates and to the process of instruction.

CONDITIONS FOR EFFECTIVE TEACHER INTERACTION WITH PUPIL

While pupil self-concepts tend towards consistency in order to protect the individual from anxiety, change in the self-concept is possible, since psychological growth is an ongoing process. These two elements of consistency and growth are encapsulated in the tenet of Rogerian theory that each person has a basic need to maintain, protect and enhance the self-concept, employing the sole motivating power, that of self-actualization. So individuals are always motivated; a pupil can never not be motivated though his motives may not be what we would wish. This view of motivation as an ever-present internal drive which can be dispensed in a variety of ways is a tremendous advantage for the teacher. Rather than wasting time and effort in trying to motivate students, teachers should devote their skills to directing this motivation to educational ends and personal development. Teachers are most likely to achieve this if their students see them as caring, supportive and accepting. 'The individual has within himself vast resources for self-understanding, for altering his self-concept, his attitudes, and his self-directed behaviour—and that these resources can be tapped if only a definable climate of facilitative psychological attitudes can be provided' (Rogers 1974 p. 115). The three main conditions of good effective counselling as presented by Rogers would also seem to be valuable traits for all teachers and counsellors to develop in their interactions, both academic and other-wise, with pupils. But in addition to the three core conditions of empathy, genuine-ness and unconditional positive acceptance there are a number of other conditions which need to permeate the school in order to maximize the effectiveness of teacher and pupil interaction for self-concept and academic gain. Six additional conditions which must be built into the Rogerian ethos in the classroom are considered below.

Make Pupils Feel Supported by the Teacher

Each child needs to feel he is supported by the teacher in the things he tries to do, but not overwhelmed by the teacher's help. This enables the child to see himself as responsible for his own progress and likely to attribute his accomplishments to his own capacities. The teacher should offer advice rather than impose it. In one school I noticed a girl trying to sew a hem. The teacher went over, noticing that it was turning into a major catastrophe and took over completely, rather than giving some advice or a little demonstration and then letting the girl try again.

The teacher showed a lack of support for the pupil in that she showed no faith in the girl to achieve a satisfactory product. The teacher communicated her belief that the girl was incompetent and the girl would not be able to credit herself with whatever favourable accomplishments resulted and would feel she had failed.

Make Pupils Feel Responsible Beings

Just as the provision of a structure of rules within which the child could make decisions appeared consistently as a criterion for positive self-concept development within the family (Chapter 4) so the provisions of adequate choice and decision making within a framework of accepted rules promotes positive self-attitudes and achievement in school (e.g. Lepper and Greene 1975; Maehr 1974; Mahoney 1974). In any case a belief in the ability of people to make intelligent choices is the foundation of democracy. When students are encouraged to make significant choices, they are far more likely later in life to maintain personal integrity in their lives, and in the face of external pressure and manipulation. They are also more likely to support a democratic philosophy of government.

The structure of rules provides support as well as opportunity to explore and choose. Part of the structure is the limits provided by the teacher. Limits indicate a teacher's expectations to the student. As such, limits indicate what the teacher wants the student to refrain from doing and also the accomplishments he expects the student to achieve. The student is given clear and rational statements of behaviours that are not permissible in a learning environment, and the teacher enforces these limits in a firm and consistent manner.

In indicating his expectation that a child should achieve and learn in school, a teacher is requiring that the child plays a certain role in the school. This role is that of a student and carries with it the demand that the child sees himself as a student. Since children tend to function and test adults at very concrete levels of behaviour, specific guidelines are most useful and meaningful to the child in making decisions and evaluating his own performance. To maximize the probability that a child will actually use the limits as guidelines, the teacher should base the limits on realistic and reasonable grounds and set a relatively small number of limits. By basing the limits on realistic and reasonable grounds, the teacher ensures that the limits make sense; accordingly, the teacher is more able to convey the significance of the limits to the children. By setting a relatively small number of limits, the teacher increases the likelihood that the limits can be maintained without making enforcement into a burdensome and tension-building way of life for the teacher and child. Since limit testing is ever present, it is vital that teachers establish limits that are based on the realities of the classroom rather than on abstract considerations or remote possibilities.

The teacher's setting of limits in a form that can serve as guidelines to students promotes the development of a positive self-concept and of high self-esteem by providing the students with standards for judging conduct, avoiding censure and establishing expectations and roles for achieving success. If limits and guidelines are to have significance, they must be enforced by the teacher. Research indicates that the most productive enforcements are authoritative and democratic rather than authoritarian (Baumrind 1968; Coopersmith 1967). The broad limits and guidelines are established and enforced by the adults, and these structuring constraints are explained to the children and sometimes modified in response to the suggestions and needs that the children communicate. The practices that are effective in evoking high levels of performance avoid the use of physical punishment and emphasize rewards (Skinner 1953).

Make Pupils Feel Competent

Our current knowledge of intellectual abilities supports the view that each pupil has a relatively untapped reservoir of abilities for thinking and learning. Intelligence is a dynamic potential developed in association with the perceived environment and is not a fixed entity. The level of mental functioning is helped by a stimulating environment and debilitated by a restrictive and unstimulating one. Both Hunt (1961) and Bloom (1964) considered that most students can grow intellectually to greater levels than they have, provided they become immersed in favourable learning.

Teachers who believe that certain children can neither learn nor benefit from instruction will probably have little success in teaching them, but when teachers have positive views of students' abilities the latter are likely to respond in positive ways. Students develop best in the company of teachers who see them as people possessing relatively untapped abilities and who invite them to realize their potential. This message was implicit in Chapter 9 on teacher expectations.

Teach Pupils To Set Realistic Goals

Performance on a task provides a basis for the evaluation of performance on the next task. However, research on goal setting (e.g. Kay 1972) points to individuals with negative self-concepts setting their goals either unrealistically too high or too low. This ensures that whatever the real outcome it can always be construed as failure. The high goal can never be attained; the low goal is so low that everybody achieves that level 'even me'. As Lecky (1945) and Hilgard (1949) argued, the person attempts to interpret events in terms of his existing self-concept to ensure consistency of feelings and behaviour. Even pupils with positive self-esteem use goal setting to maintain the self as known. In their case, they defend their positive self-concept by attributing failure in achieving a high goal to external events e.g. blame others, bad luck, etc., rather than blaming themselves (Kay 1972). These distortions of reality do nothing towards solving the persistent problems of failure, for eventually a sense of powerlessness pervades the thoughts, self-concept and behaviour of the pupils. They regard everything as against them hence there is no sense in trying to overcome the odds. Distortions in goal setting and denials of blame cannot offer any possibility of long-term self-enhancement potential. Teachers and parents must try to set realistic goals for each child, goals that demand some effort yet which are within the capabilities of the child. In Piaget's terms the child has schemas potentially capable of accommodating to the new material. The discrepancy between what the child can do and what he is being asked to do is not too great a mismatch as to result in anxiety and failure. Instead then of criticizing a child for only getting two out of ten in an arithmetic test and feeding back to him interpretation that he is considered inadequate, incompetent and never likely to get anywhere, why not adopt a pattern of feedback similar to this?

> *Teacher*: Bill, you have two right this morning. This is better isn't it? I am pleased, you only got one right yesterday. How many do you think you can get right tomorrow?
>
> *Bill*: I think I will get three right.
>
> *Teacher*: Good! I think you can, too. Do you know, if you carry on like this you will be getting 10 out of 10 next week?

A goal must be set to motivate the child. It must be an individual goal, realistic in relation to past performance so that success is possible and can be reinforced, thus raising self-esteem and bringing the possibility that the pupil will begin to see himself more as a success and less as a failure. If the goal is set by the pupil in collaboration with the teacher then there is more commitment to it. A goal set by others, imposed and not achieved can be argued away with, 'teacher demanded too much' or 'it was an unreasonable task anyway'. Children do have a tendency to set goals too high due to inexperience, the wish to do well, etc. Such a goal can be used as the ultimate objective with the teacher splitting it down into a series of steps which lead gradually and realistically to the attainment of the goal. Skinnerian linear programming is based on this process though the size of the steps would generally be larger and must be judged on the individual's capability. Learning is a step-by-step process anyway. The child can feel successful, as he is asked for performances that are possible, and self-reinforcement also accrues. The fact that obvious improvement has been made (in that previously stated goals are achieved) prevents the pupil interpreting the well-intentioned positive feedback from teachers, aimed at motivating a child even though he has done poorly, as insincere. The goals that are set need not be restricted to academic performance only. The principle of realistic goal setting can be applied to physical skills in the gymnasium, for physically handicapped children, following school rules, not shouting out in class, or in learning how to interact with others in a responsible and cooperative way, learning leadership roles, etc.

Help Pupils Evaluate Themselves Realistically

This guideline is linked to the previous one for if goals are unrealistic then the evaluation is going to be unrealistic. There is a tendency for those low in self-esteem to judge themselves on the basis of unattainable goals of perfection (Jersild 1963).

Children need help in evaluating themselves realistically as they are in a highly evaluative context and often judge themselves and others more harshly than adults do. Some children give themselves a false negative evaluation in that even though they may score 99 out of 100 this is seen as less than perfect and hence is failure! This is obviously unrealistic. Other children actually do perform poorly and this has to be faced by most at some time or other. Hence some realistic evaluations must be negative but teachers must then help the child use this realistic negative evaluation to provide for a basis of change that will allow later positive performance. Improvement and learning from the experience of true failure can build up an individual's self-concept. Unrealistic evaluations only compound the problems of real failure and lead to generalizing failure to all experiences. A change in performance or learning is not likely to influence unrealistic evaluations. Realistic evaluation should be based on a comparison with past evaluation. The major way of evaluating children is to compare them to similar children on the basis of norms. However, to provide children who will never stand up well to comparison with others with realistic evaluation, it is far better to compare present performance with what was achieved by the child in the past. Johnny may never be capable of being anything but bottom of the class but if his individual performance shows improvement on a day-to-day basis then he deserves credit. This will tend to encourage motivation, interest and positive feelings about himself. But being told you are always bottom is not likely to do any good at all. Children can keep individual record cards on which they chart their progress no matter how slow or slight. When evaluation is based on a comparison with past performance the criterion of perfection disappears. It is always possible to cushion failure with hope, so that while a pupil is realistically made aware of what he achieved or failed to achieve, some positive statement can be made too. It is rare that something on which the child can build cannot be found, e.g. 'Generally your essay was lacking in relevance to the topic but this last section started to get to grips with it. Try to expand this last section now'. Or again, 'You only got two calculations correct, but all your errors were simply careless arithmetical ones; you understood the principle of the technique'. Throughout the evaluation procedure, as much as possible, desist from comparing child with child. Make the child's own past performance the baseline; in other words a system based on the conviction that any improvement is good and is to be encouraged. Each small step should be praised and the pupil taught to regard improvement as the basis for self-praise and self-encouragement.

Encourage Realistic Self-Praise

The main aim of self-concept development is to shift the reinforcement and feedback that enhances self-esteem from a bias towards external agencies to a bias towards internal or self-reinforcement, as a means of controlling the development of positive and realistic self-attitudes. The pupil needs to develop the habit of praising himself, being his own evaluator. This frees the teacher from the role of sole dispenser of reinforcement, and in any case the teacher cannot be aware of everything that is happening in the classroom. Since the self-concept is also learned and internalized, involving the meaning individuals attach to words and phrases relating to themselves, guiding the pupil towards using self-praise not only reinforces the relevant behaviour and the feelings surrounding it, but it also teaches the pupil a new set of self-referent concepts. To say to oneself, 'I succeeded on those physics problems' not only reinforces what was done but equally associates 'success' with 'I' to form a concept of 'I am a success'. The more positive the terms a person can apply to himself derived from realistic performance, goals and evaluation, the more powerful a force it is for moulding a positive self-concept. These overall conditions provide an ethos within which specific classroom practices designed to enhance self-esteem can flourish and work best. But as we have seen (Chapter 12) the ability of any teacher to provide these therapeutic conditions depends quite markedly on the teacher himself possessing a positive self-concept. This allows him to function in a confident way able to accept all pupils as individuals in a supportive and structured environment providing clear and realistic expectations at an individual level.

PRACTICAL EXERCISES FOR USE WITH ALL PUPILS TO ENHANCE THEIR SELF-ESTEEM

Theory is helpful, so is knowledge derived from research but the heart of the matter is what techniques a teacher, counsellor or psychologist can use in a practical way to enhance pupils' self-concepts. Quite a number of exercises have been developed for this purpose and are suitable for use generally as part of school and college counselling procedures, and in many cases in normal classroom contexts. None of these exercises is new and they have often featured in sensitivity and encounter groups as introductory activities. Many of these exercises are used currently in schools in North America.

1. *Acquaintanceship exercises* in which group participants talk to one another on a one-to-one basis, usually centring around questions such as: 'Tell me something about yourself', can be used to begin the group and, when it has been completed, each member of a pair introduces his partner to the rest of the participants.

2. *Positive thinking exercise.* This is aimed at expressing pride in one's accomplishments. It is impossible to dig for weaknesses and self-improvement without a sense of where one's strengths are. We, too, often harp on weaknesses ignoring the very real need to feel pride before permitting criticism (from self or others). Some students, oddly, have a harder time than others in bragging or just talking about their strengths and accomplishments; or perhaps not 'oddly' enough! Certain myths in our culture about 'humility' cause confusion about personal worth, and they must be dealt with. The experiences are short, but rich in potential relief and release when pride is clarified and sanctioned. The exercise involves encouraging pupils to:

Think and feel more positively about self;
Like self;
Laugh at self;
Express pride in self;
Describe personal strengths and weaknesses with greater accuracy.

Discussions at this point can be focused on the following kinds of questions: Is it important to know what you can do well and what you can't? Where is it safe to talk about these things? Do you have to be good at everything? What are the ways others can make you feel good about yourself? What are the ways you can make yourself feel good about yourself? Is there a difference between accentuating your strengths and bragging? What is the difference?

Such discussions provide a basis for students to assess both their own capabilities and potentials, and to distinguish these qualities from their own worth. As students become more familiar with their many and varied strengths and weaknesses, they generally develop a more trusting attitude toward their own capabilities as well as toward other members of the class. They start to learn that even the 'smartest' and most popular students have weaknesses, and that the 'dullest' and most unpopular people have strength. This attitude allows students to begin feeling better about themselves; they are able to begin developing foundations for accepting responsibility for personal thoughts, feelings and actions.

Ask the students to make a statement about a specific item, beginning with, 'I'm proud that'. For example, you might say, 'I'd like you to mention something about your work in school that you're proud of. Please begin your response with, "I'm proud that . . ."' Students may say, 'I pass', if they wish. Those who are unable to think of anything they had done which could be labelled success quickly tend to change their minds as they hear others talking. They come to realize that they have been too hard on themselves through unwillingness to acknowledge their past 'triumphs'.

3. *Self-image projection.* This particular exercise involves the group member writing two personality sketches each on a separate sheet of paper. One of these is a description of how the group member sees himself, and is in fact an outline of the concept he has of himself. He is encouraged to record this as honestly as possible. The second personality sketch is that which the member thinks he projects to the rest of the group. He writes down, in other words, the way he thinks he comes across to other people. No names are placed on these sheets and the 'as you see yourself' personality sketch is folded up and put in a box. One paper at a time is drawn out and read with group members attempting to guess of whom it is a description. The author then claims his sketch and reads his second one, the one describing how he thinks other people in the group see him. Feedback from the rest of the group then follows on this perception. The value of this exercise is that the student discovers that others will see certain potentials and characteristics in terms more favourable than he sees himself.

4. *Weekly report sheets.* Part of enhancing a student's self-concept is helping him

become more aware of the control he actually has over his daily life. Weekly reaction sheets help students see how effectively they are using their time. Hand out a sheet with the following questions to each pupil:

Name ...
Date ...
1. What was the high point of the week?
2. Whom did you get to know better this week?
3. What was the major thing you learned about yourself this week?
4. Did you institute any major changes in your life this week?
5. How could this week have been better?
6. Identify three decisions or choices you made this week. What were the results of these choices?
7. Did you make any plans this week for some future event?
8. What unfinished business do you have left from last week?

A variation on this is to encourage students to keep a daily journal of their reactions (feelings, thoughts, behaviours, 'I learned ...' statements, etc.) to each activity. Keeping a journal has several advantages. It allows the student to keep an account of how he is growing, of what is happening to him, of how uniquely he responds to a given situation. It provides a cumulative statement of who he is, how he sees himself, and how others see him.

The more a person learns about himself, the more he will expand his concept of himself. Many times what is learned in an exercise is overlooked if it is not explicitly stated. After each activity, ask the students to record what they have learned about themselves in the form of 'I learned ...' statements:

I learned that I ...
I re-learned that I ...
I was surprised to find that I ...
I reaffirmed that I ...

5. *Friendship.* One of the factors that erodes self-concept is the inability of some youngsters to make and keep friends. The following activities are designed to help the pupil expand his repertoire of skills in building and enhancing relationships with his peers.

1. Have the class discuss the methods they use to make friends, and act out the best ones.
2. Ask them to write a paragraph beginning with, 'A friend is ...'.
3. Lead a class discussion around the questions: Do you have a best friend? Do you like to do the same things? Did you ever want to do something that he or she did not want to do? What happened? Were you still friends?
4. Ask the students to write a paragraph answering the question: What is there about you that makes your friends like you?
5. Try out the following questions for discussion developed by William Glasser, author of *Schools Without Failure* (1969):

When you first came to school, how did you make a friend? Have you ever moved . . . and had no friends at all? How did you find a friend there? What do you do when someone new moves into your neighbourhood—do you wait for him to come over to your house or do you go over to his house? . . . Do you ever make an effort to help him become friendly with other children?

6. *Words that describe 'me'.* In this particular exercise, participants are asked to write three words that describe themselves. The paper is then turned over and they are asked to write three words which they wished described themselves. They are then encouraged to take one of these words from the second list and to outline specific behaviours that this type of person would exhibit. Group discussion follows on the taking of this particular word as a goal, and using some of the behaviour suggested as a means of reaching that goal. By the time that most group members have participated, a number of generally accepted goals have been established and specific ways of attaining them have been outlined.

7. *Success visualization.* Possibly the greatest power that people have to change themselves is through using the imagination, a viewpoint that has been strongly supported by many writers. Participants are encouraged to visualize the way they want to behave in situations which, in the past, may not have been seen as very successful. At this stage the concept of positive thinking is stressed. Through controlling the thoughts we think, we can convince ourselves that we can, if we so desire, be better than we are. We are what we accept ourselves as being, and we can be what we convince ourselves we can be.

8. *Use of quotations.* Another approach that works very well is to use thought provoking quotations as a stimulus to discussion, self-examination and sharing of experience. The sort of thing here would be on the lines of Abraham Lincoln's comment that: 'Most folk are about as happy as they make up their minds to be' or that of Emerson: 'Most of the shadows of this life are caused by standing in our own sunshine'. By considering such thoughts, participants can be made aware of the tremendous power which they have to control their own thinking and, by doing so, control their feelings. They can come to a realization that often their sense of inadequacy and unhappiness is caused by the suggestions of those around them, and that by reacting in the way they do, they are giving their environment tremendous power over them. One of the things that should emerge during the course of the discussion is the fact that we can choose to make ourselves much more self-confident by thinking more positively. We do not have to think negatively and miserably; we can deliberately choose to change this mode of thinking. So often we do not realize the power we have to make ourselves much happier.

There is no value judgement that is more important to man, no factor more decisive in his psychological development and motivation than the estimate that he passes on himself. At the end of each day, have the students briefly share with the rest of the class the successes they have experienced during the day. Some students will find this difficult at first, but as others begin to share, they too will realize they have had some of the same successes. If a student says he had no success, some of his classmates will chime in with successes they have seen him accomplish. The sensitive teacher will also look for successes to be pointed out to the child with extremely low self-esteem.

A variation of this activity is to have each child share with the class what he feels he has learned that day. In addition to being a great form of review, it provides the student with a sense of accomplishment. Without recall, students are often not consciously aware of all the learning they are accomplishing in and out of school each day. Knowing that he is learning adds positively to a child's self-concept. Negative thinking is virtually synonymous with low self-concept and as students begin increasing their positive type statements and thoughts, an increased level of optimism is usually readily observable.

9. *A classroom newspaper.* The creation of a classroom newspaper is a good way to provide children with the opportunity to see their names and their work in print. Articles can also be written about the children's achievements. Recognition in print of positive services, activities and achievements increases and improves self-concept. Students can select the name of the paper, choose editors and reporters, conduct interviews and draw illustrations. On a school basis, each class could have a reporter, who might change from time to time, to collect and gather material for publication. The writing of the newspaper also helps strengthen written language skills. The newspaper could also be used in various classrooms for reading instruction.

10. *Learning to accept negative feelings.* It is necessary to discuss negative or 'bad' feelings if one is to develop a healthy self-concept. If a child thinks some of his feelings of hostility, aggression, anger and hate are unnatural or 'bad' he will begin to perceive himself as bad or unnatural. Being able to talk about these feelings in the group has two positive effects on the child's self-image. First, it provides him with an opportunity to defuse some of the feelings by talking them out rather than acting them out in a potentially destructive way. Second, as a child sees that he is not the only one who sometimes wishes his older brother were dead or gets angry with his parents, he will see that his feelings are natural and common responses to similar emotional situations that he shares with his classmates. He will discover that it is acceptable to have these feelings—that it is all right to be the person he is.

To get at negative feelings let students 'vote' by raising their hands to indicate their experience with some of the following types of common childhood problems. Maintain an open and accepting environment of trust and empathy as you ask such questions as: How many of you

Are afraid of ghosts; of dogs; of cows? etc.
Ever get scared—when alone; in the dark?
Like to get angry?
Are afraid when your parents get angry?
Sometimes want to destroy everything in sight?
Get so mad you could hit someone?
Think you get bossed around too much at home; in school by your friends; by
    grown-ups in general?

Like one parent more than the other?
Know what you want to be/do when you grow up?
Think school is fun? Think school is hard?
Cry a lot?
Feel that life could be better for you?
Feel that life has not been fair to you?
Would like to change your name?
Feel happy most of the time?
Would like to change something about the way you look?
Have had a scary dream in the last month?
Have a lot of secrets that you keep?
Think people might not like you if they knew who you really were?
Think people would like you if they knew who you really were?
Don't like to talk in class?
Find it easy to make new friends?
Have ever wanted to hurt someone for something they did to you?
Would rather be older or younger than you are right now?
Would like to live somewhere else?
Day dream sometimes?

CREATING A CARING ENVIRONMENT IN WHICH PUPILS ACCEPT THEMSELVES

Whatever exercises are used to attempt to raise self-esteem in pupils and students, the most important ingredient in all of the activities is the ethos within which it occurs. The teacher or counsellor must create an environment of mutual support and caring. Growth is optimized in a supportive environment that contains a little dissonance. We do not have to create dissonance deliberately—there is usually more than enough to go around! The crucial thing, however, is the safety and encouragement students sense in the classroom. They must trust other group members and the teacher to the extent that they can express their feelings openly without ridicule. Furthermore, they must recognize that they are valued and will receive affection and support. This cannot be stated strongly enough. Without the critical environmental dimensions of trust, caring openness and empathy efforts to enhance pupils' self-esteem will be seriously limited.

SUMMARY

Three basic conditions necessary for the enhancement of self-attitudes, according to Rogers are empathy, genuineness and unconditional acceptance. Research reveals fairly consistently that client-centred non-directive counselling and directive behavioural counselling can help to achieve more positive self-concept development.

Video playback appears to have value as a method of providing feedback to enhance self-esteem. Motor development, physical activity and physical challenges can be employed effectively as theurapeutic techniques.

Within the classroom teachers must provide a climate that permits pupils to feel secure and accepted. Only through this Rogerian facilitative ethos can (a) pupils then take advantage of the opportunities offered for self-disclosure (particularly in sensitivity exercises) and (b) teachers provide the other classroom-based conditions that aid pupils in their realistic appraisal of themselves and their performance.

Further Reading

Canfield, J. and Wells, H. (1976) *100 Ways to Enhance Self-Concept in the Classroom,* New Jersey: Prentice Hall.

Gazda, G. M. (1973) *Human Relations Development: A Manual for Educators*, Boston: Allyn and Bacon.

Felker, E. W. (1974) *Building Positive Self-Concepts*, Minneapolis: Burgess.

Combs, A. W., Avila, D. L. and Purkey, W. W. (1971) *Helping Relationships*, Boston: Allyn and Bacon.

Purkey, W. W. (1978) *Inviting School Success*, Belmont: Wadsworth.

Lewis, H. R. and Streitfield, H. S. (1973) *Growth Games*, London: Abacus.

Bibliography

Abercrombie, K. (1968) 'Paralanguage', *British Journal Disorders of Communication*, **3**, 55–9.

Acland, H. (1973) 'Streaming in English primary schools', *British Journal of Educational Psychology*, **43**, 151–61.

Adams, B. D. (1978) 'Inferiorisation and self-esteem', *Social Psychology*, **41**, 47–53.

Adams, G. R. and Cohen, H. S. (1974) 'Children's physical and interpersonal characteristics that affect student–teacher interactions', *Journal of Experimental Education*, **43**, 1–5.

Adams, P. L. (1970) 'Experimental group counselling with intern teachers', *Dissertation Abstracts*, **31A**, 605.

Adler, A. (1927) *The Practice and Theory of Individual Psychology*, New York: Harcourt Brace.

Adorno, T. W., Frenkel-Brunswik, L., Levinson, D. J. and Sanford, R. N. (1950) *The Authoritarian Personality*, New York: Harper and Row.

Ainsworth, M., Bell, S. M. and Stayton, D. J. (1971) 'Individual differences in strange situation behaviour of 1 year olds', in Foss, B. (ed.) *Determinants of Infant Behaviour*, vol. 4, London: Methuen.

Ainsworth, M. D. and Bowlby, J. (1954) 'Research strategy in the study of mother–child separation', *Cournier*, **4**, No. 3 1–38.

Aitkenhead, M. (1980) 'Consistency and self-enhancement', *British Journal of Social and Clinical Psychology*, **19**, 41–8.

Alban Metcalfe, B. M. (1978) 'Changes in self-concept on transfer from primary to secondary school', unpublished MSc thesis, Bradford University.

Albinson, J. G. (1974) 'Life style of physically active and inactive college males', *International Journal of Sports Psychology*, **5**, 93–101.

Allen, D. (1974) 'Student performance, attitude and self-esteem in open area and self-contained classrooms', *Alberta Journal of Educational Research*, **20**, 1–7.

Allen, H. A. (1971) 'The use of cognitive structuring and verbal reinforcements of self reference statements within a short term therapy session to enhance self concept', *Dissertation Abstracts*, **3202A**, 730.

Allport, G. W. (1955) *Becoming: Basic Considerations for a Psychology of Personality*, New Haven: Yale University Press.

Allport, G. W. (1961) *Pattern and Growth in Personality*, New York: Holt, Rinehart and Winston.

Allport, G. W. and Odbert, H. (1936) 'Trait Names: A Psycholexical Study', *Psychological Monographs*, **47**, No. 211, 1–171.

Ames, C. (1978) 'Children's achievement attributions and self reinforcement: effects of self concept and competitive reward structure', *Journal of Educational Psychology*, **70**, 345–54.

Ames, C. and Felker, D. (1979) 'Effects of self-concept on children's causal attributions and self reinforcement', *Journal of Educational Psychology*, **71**, 613–19.

Anandam, K., Davis, M. and Poppen, W. (1971) 'Feelings—to hear or to free', *Elementary School Guidance and Counselling*, **5**, 181–9.

Anderson, J. G. and Johnson, W. H. (1971) 'Stability and change among three generations of Mexican Americans: Factors affecting achievement', *American Educational Research Journal*, **8**, 285–309.

Anderson, R. (1959) 'Learning in discussions', *Harvard Educational Review*, **29**, 201–15.

Argyle, M. (1972) *The Psychology of Interpersonal Behaviour*, Penguin: Harmondsworth.

Argyle, M. (1975) *Bodily Communication*, London: Methuen.

Aronson, E. and Carlsmith, J. M. (1962) 'Performance expectancy as a determinant of actual performance', *Journal of Abnormal and Social Psychology*, **65**, 178–82.

Aronson, E. and Mills, J. (1959) 'The effect of severity of initiation on liking for a group', *Journal of Abnormal and Social Psychology*, **59**, 177–81.

Asch, E. S. (1955) 'Opinions and social pressure', *Scientific American*, Reprint 450.

Ascione, F. and Borg, W. (1980) 'Effects of a

training programme on teacher behaviour and handicapped children's self-concept', *Journal of Psychology*, **104**, 53–65.

Aspy, D. N. (1975) 'The effect of teachers' inferred self-concept upon student achievement', *Journal of Educational Research*, **68**, 386–9.

Ausubel, D. P. and Schiff, H. (1955) 'Some intrapersonal and interpersonal determinants of individual differences in socioempathic ability among adolescents', *Journal of Social Psychology*, **41**, 39–56.

Babladelis, G. (1973) 'Personality and conditioning', *Psychological Record*, **23**, 553–9.

Bachman, J. G. (1970) *Youth in Transition*, vol. 2, University of Michigan: Institute for Social Research.

Bachman, J. G. and O'Malley, P. M. (1977) 'Self-esteem in young men', *Journal of Personality and Social Psychology*, **35**, 365–80.

Backman, C. and Secord, P. (1959) 'The effect of perceived liking on interpersonal attraction', *Human Relations*, **12**, 379–84.

Bagley, C. (1978) 'Self-concept as a pivotal concept in race and ethnic relations', in C. Marrett and C. Leggon (eds.), *Research in Race and Ethnic Relations*, Greenwich, Conn.: JAL Press.

Bagley, C., Bart, M. and Wong, J. (1979) 'Antecedents of scholastic success in West Indian ten year olds in London', in Verma, G. K. and Bagley, C. (eds.) *Race, Education and Identity*, London: Macmillan.

Bagley, C. and Coard, B. (1975) 'Cultural knowledge and ethnic self-image', in Verma, G. K. and Bagley, C. (eds.) *Race and Education Across Cultures*, London: Heinemann.

Bagley, C. and Mallick, K. (1978) 'Development of a short version of the Piers–Harris self concept scale', *Educational Review*, **30**, 265–9.

Bagley, C., Mallick, K. and Verma, G. K. (1979) 'Pupil self-esteem: a study of black and white teenagers in British schools', in Verma, G. K. and Bagley, C. (eds.) *Race, Education and Identity*, London: Macmillan.

Bagley, C. and Verma, G. K. (1975) 'Interethnic attitudes and behaviour in British multi-racial schools', in Verma, G. K. and Bagley, C. (eds.) *Race and Education Across Cultures*, London: Heinemann.

Bagley, C., Verma, G. K., Mallick, K. and Young, L. (1979) *Personality, Self-Esteem and Prejudice*, London: Saxon House.

Bagley, C., Verma, G. K. and Mallick, K. (1982) 'Comparative structure of self-esteem in British and Indian adolescents', in Bagley, C. and Verma, G. K. (eds.) *Self-Concept Achievement and Multicultural Education*, London: Macmillan.

Bagley, C., Young, L. and Evan-Wong, J. (1976) 'Counselling Adolescents', unpublished paper.

Bahm, R. M. and Biller, H. B. (1971) 'Father absence, perceived maternal behaviour and masculinity of self concept in junior high school boys', *Development Psychology*, **4**, 178–81.

Bailey, K. G. and Bailey, R. C. (1973) 'Self concept modification as a function of audio tape play-back', *Psychotherapy*, **10**, 169–74.

Bakan, D. (1966) *The Duality of Human Existence*, Chicago: Rand McNally.

Balester, R. J. (1956) 'Self-concept and juvenile delinquency', *Dissertation Abstracts*, **16**, 1169.

Bandura, A. (1965) 'Influence of models' reinforcement contingencies on the acquisition of initiative responses', *Journal of Personality and Social Psychology*, **1**, 589–95.

Bandura, A. (1977) *Social Learning Theory*, New Jersey: Prentice Hall.

Bandura, A., Ross, D. and Ross, A. (1963a) 'A comparative test of status envy, social power and secondary reinforcement theories of identification learning', *Journal of Abnormal and Social Psychology*, **67**, 527–34.

Bandura, A., Ross, D. and Ross, A. (1963b) 'Imitation of film-mediated aggressive models', *Journal of Abnormal and Social Psychology*, **66**, 3–11.

Bandura, A. and Walters, R. (1963) *Social Learning and Personality Development*, New York: Holt, Rinehart and Winston.

Bannister, D. and Agnew, J. (1976) 'The child's construing of self', in Cole, J. and Landfield, A. (eds.) *Nebraska Symposium on Motivation*, Lincoln: University of Nebraska.

Bannister, D. and Mair, J. M. (1968) *Evaluation of Personal Constructs*, London: Academic Press.

Bardwick, J. M. (1971) *Psychology of Women*, New York: Harper and Row.

Barker, R. (1964) 'The ecological environment', in Barker, R. and Gump, P. (eds.) *Big School, Small School*, Stanford: Stanford University Press.

Barker, R. and Hall, E. (1964) 'Participation in interschool events and extraschool activities', in Barker, R. and Gump, P. (eds.) *Big School, Small School*, Stanford: Stanford University Press.

Barker-Lunn, J. C. (1970) *Streaming in the Primary School*, Slough: NFER.

Barnes, E. J. (1972) 'The black community as a source of positive self-concept for black children', in Jones, R. (ed.) *Black Psychology*, New York: Harper and Row.

Barrett-Lennard, G. T., Kwasnik, T. and Wilkinson, G. (1974) 'Some effects of participation in encounter group workshops', *Interpersonal Development*, **4**, 35–44.

Barron, F. (1979) *The Shaping of Personality*, San Francisco: Harper and Row.

Bartee, G. M. (1967) 'The perceptual characteristics of disadvantaged Negro and caucasian college students', unpublished PhD thesis, East Texas State University.

Battle, J. (1976) 'Test–retest reliability of the Canadian self-esteem inventory for children', *Psychological Reports*, **38**, 1343–5.

Battle, J. (1977a) 'Test–retest reliability of the Canadian self-esteem inventory for children', *Psychological Reports*, **40**, 157–8.

Battle, J. (1977b) 'Test–retest reliability of the Canadian self-esteem inventory for adults', *Perceptual Motor Skills*, **44.**

Battle, J. (1977c) 'Comparison of two self-report inventories', *Psychological Reports*, **41**, 159–60.

Battle, J. (1979) 'Self-esteem of students in regular and special classes', *Psychological Reports*, **44**, 212–14.

Baughman, E. (1971) *Black Americans*, New York: Academic Press.

Baughman, E. and Dahlstrom, W. G. (1968) *Negro and White Children*, New York: Academic Press.

Baumrind, D. (1967) 'Child care practices anteceding three patterns of preschool behaviour', *Genetic Psychology Monographs*, **75**, 43–88.

Baumrind, D. (1968) 'Authoritarian versus authoritative parental control', *Adolescence*, **3**, 255–72.

Baumrind, D. (1972) 'An exploratory study of socialisation effects on black children', *Child Development*, **43**, 261–7.

Bayne, R. (1972) 'Psychology and encounter groups', *Bulletin of the British Psychological Society*, **25**, 285–9.

Becker, E. (1962) 'Socialisation, command of performance and mental illness', *American Journal of Sociology*, **67**, 494–501.

Becker, H. S. (1952) 'Social class variations in teacher–pupil relationships', *Journal of Educational Sociology*, **25**, 451–65.

Bediean, A. G., Teague, R. and Zmud, R. W. (1977) 'Test retest reliability and internal consistency of short form of Coopersmith's self-esteem inventory', *Psychological Reports*, Dec. pt 2, 1041–2.

Bediean, A. G. and Touliatos, J. (1978) 'Work related motives and self-esteem in American women', *Journal of Psychology*, **99**, 63–70.

Bem, S. L. (1967) 'Self perception', *Psychological Review*, **74**, 183–200.

Bem, S. L. (1972) 'Self perception theory', in Berkowitz, L. (ed.) *Advances in Experimental Social Psychology*, New York: Academic Press.

Bem, S. L. (1974) 'Measurement of psychological androgeny', *Journal of Consulting and Clinical Psychology*, **42**, 155–62.

Bennett, N. (1976) *Teaching Styles and Pupil Progress*, London: Open Books.

Bennett, V. D. C. (1964) 'Development of a self-concept Q sort for use with elementary age school children', *Journal of School Psychology*, **3**, 19–25.

Bennett, V. D. C. (1966) 'Combinations of figure drawing characteristics related to the drawer's self-concept', *Journal of Projected Techniques and Personality Assessment*, **30**, 192–6.

Berger, C. R. (1968) 'Sex differences related to self-esteem factor structure', *Journal of Consultative Clinical Psychology*, **32**, 442–6.

Berger, E. M. (1952) 'The relation between expressed acceptance of self and expressed acceptance of others', *Journal of Abnormal Social Psychology*, **47**, 4, 778–82.

Bergin, A. E. (1962) 'The effect of dissonant persuasive communications on changes in a self-referring attitude', *Journal of Personality*, **30**, 423–38.

Bergscheld, E., Walster, E. and Borhnstedt, G. (1973) 'The happy American body', *Psychology Today*, **7**, 119–31.

Bergum, B. O. and Cooper, T. (1977) 'Undergraduate self perceptions of creativity and independence', *Perceptual Motor Skills*, **44**, 187–90.

Bergum, G. E. and Bergum, B. O. (1979) 'Concept of self and academic choice', *Perceptual Motor Skills*, Oct. 79, 535–8.

Bernard, V. W. (1958) 'School desegregation', *Psychiatry*, **21**, 149–58.

Bernstein, R. (1980) 'The development of the self-esteem during adolescence', *Journal of Genetic Psychology*, **136**, 231–46.

Berthenthal, B. and Fischer, K. W. (1978) 'Development of self recognition in the infant', *Developmental Psychology*, **14**, 44–50.

Bessell, H. (1968) 'The content is the medium', *Psychology Today*, **1**, 35.

Bettelheim, B. and Janowitz, M. (1964) *Social Change and Prejudice*, New York: Glencoe Free Press.

Bills, R. E. (1958) *Manual for the Index of Adjustment and Values*, Auburn: Alabama Polytechnic.

Bills, R. E., Vance, E. L. and McLean, O. S. (1957) 'An index of adjustment and values', *Journal of Consultative Psychology*, **15**, 257–61.

Black, W. F. (1974) 'Self-concept as related to achievement and age in learning disabled children', *Child Development*, **45**, 1137–40.

Bledsoe, J. C. (1964) 'Self concepts of children and their intelligence, achievement, interests and anxiety', *Journal of Individual Psychology*, **20**, 55–8.

Bledsoe, J. C. (1967) 'Self concepts of children and their intelligence, achievement, interests and anxiety', *Child Education*, **43**, 436–8.

Bledsoe, J. C. (1973) 'Sex differences in self concept, fact or artifact?', *Psychological Reports*, **32**, 1253–4.

Block, J. H. and Thomas, H. (1955) 'Is satisfaction

with self a measure of adjustment?', *Journal of Abnormal and Social Psychology*, **51**, 254–9.

Bloom, B. S. (1964) *Stability and Change in Human Characteristics*, New York: Wiley.

Blos, P. (1962) *On Adolescence*, London: Macmillan.

Blos, P. (1967) 'On second individuation process of adolescence', *Psycho-analytic Study of the Child*, **22**, 162–86.

Blumberg, H. H. (1972) 'Communication of interpersonal evaluations', *Journal of Personality and Social Psychology*, **23**, 157–62.

Bogert, J. (1967) 'The use of secondary school suspensions as a disciplinary technique', unpublished PhD thesis, University of Tennessee.

Bogo, N., Winget, C. and Gleser, G. (1970) 'Ego defenses and perceptual styles', *Perceptual Motor Skills*, **30**, 599–604.

Borislow, B. (1962) 'Self-evaluation and academic achievement', *Journal of Counseling Psychology*, **9**, 246–54.

Borke, H. (1972) 'Chandler and Greenspan's ersatz egocentrism', *Developmental Psychology*, **7**, 107–9.

Boshier, R. (1968) 'Self esteem and the first names of children', *Psychological Report*, **22**, 762.

Boshier, R. (1969) 'A study of the relationship between self-concept and conservatism', *Journal of Social Psychology*, **77**, 139–40.

Borg, W. R. (1977) 'Changing teacher and pupil performance', *Journal of Experimental Education*, **45**, 9–18.

Bousfield, W. A. (1940) 'Student's rating on the qualities considered desirable in college professors', *School and Society*, 24 February, 253–6.

Bower, T. G. R. (1974) *Development in Infancy*, San Francisco: Freeman.

Bowers, N. and Soars, R. (1962) 'The influence of teacher personality on classroom interaction', *Journal of Experimental Education*, **30**, 309–11.

Bowlby, J. (1946) *Forty-four Juvenile Thieves: Their Characters and Home Life*, London: Bouillere, Tindall and Cox.

Bowlby, J. (1951) 'Maternal care and mental health', WHO Monograph, No. 2, London: HMSO.

Bowlby, J. (1953) 'Social pathological processes set in train by early mother–child separation', *Journal of Mental Science*, **99**, 265–72.

Bowlby, J. (1960) 'Separation anxiety', *International Journal of Psycho-analysis*, **41**, 89–113.

Bowlby, J. (1969) *Attachment and Loss*, vol. 1, Hogarth: London.

Boyd, H. and Sisney, V. (1967) 'Immediate self-image confrontation and changes in self concept', *Journal of Consulting and Clinical Psychology*, **31**, 291–6.

Bradford, L., Gibb, J. and Benne, K. (1964) *T-Group Theory and Laboratory Method*, New York: Wiley.

Brady, P., Rickards, J. and Felker, D. (1975) 'Affective outcome of evaluation strategies', *Psychological Report*, **37**, 311–17.

Branch, C., Damico, S. and Purkey, W. (1977) 'A comparison between the self concepts as learner of disruptive and non-disruptive middle school students', *The Middle School Journal*, **7**, 15–16.

Bridgeman, B. and Shipman, V. (1978) 'Pre-school measures of self esteem and achievement motivation as predictors of third grade achievement', *Journal of Educational Psychology*, **70**, 17–28.

Bridgette, R. E. (1970) 'Self-esteem in Negro and white southern adolescents', *Dissertation Abstracts*, **31**, 2977B.

Brim, O. G. (1958) 'Family structure and sex role learning by children', *Sociometry*, **21**, 1–16.

Brim, B. J. (1966) 'Attitude changes in teacher education students', *Journal of Education Research*, **59**, 441–5.

Brindley, C., Clark, P., Hutt, C. and Wethli, E. (1973) 'Sex differences in the activities and social interactions of nursery school children', in Michael, R. and Crook, J. (eds.) *Comparative Ecology and Behaviour of Primates*, New York: Academic Press.

Brisset, D. (1972) 'Towards a clarification of self esteem', *Psychiatry*, **35**, 255–63.

Brockner, J. (1979) 'The effects of self-esteem, success, failure and self-consciousness on task performance', *Journal of Personality and Social Psychology*, **37**, 1732–41.

Brockner, J. and Hulton, B. (1978) 'How to reverse the vicious cycle of low self-esteem: the importance of attentional focus', *Journal of Experimental Social Psychology*, **14**, 564–78.

Brodsky, C. M. (1954) *A study of Norms for Body Form-Behaviour Relationships*, Washington, D.C.: Catholic University of America Press.

Bronfenbrenner, U. (1961) 'Some familiar antecedents of responsibility and leadership in adolescents', in Putrello and Bass (eds.) *Leadership and Interpersonal Behaviour*, New York: Holt, Rinehart and Winston.

Bronfenbrenner, U. (1971) 'Reactions to social pressure from adults and peers', in Chess and Thomas (eds.) *Annual Progress in Child Psychiatry and Child Development*, New York: Bruner Mazzel.

Bronfenbrenner, U. (1974) 'Origins of alienation', *Scientific American*, **231**, 53–61.

Bronson, W., Katten, E. and Livison, N. (1959) 'Patterns of authority and affection in two generations', *Journal of Abnormal Social Psychology*, **58**, 143–52.

Brookover, W. B., Erickson, E. L. and Joiner, L. M. (1967) 'Self concept of ability and school achievement: relationship of self-concept to achievement in high school', US Office of Education, Cooperative Research Project 2831, Michigan State University.

Brookover, W. B., Le Pere, J., Hamachek, E. D., Thomas, S. and Erickson, E. L. (1965) 'Self-concept of ability and school achievement: improving achievement through students' self-concept enhancement', US Office of Education, Cooperative Research Project 1639, Michigan State University.

Brookover, W. B., Thomas, S. and Patterson, A. (1964) 'Self concept of ability and school achievement', *Sociology of Education*, **37**, 271–8.

Brophy, A. L. (1959) 'Self, role and satisfaction', *Genetic Psychology Monograph*, **59**, 263–308.

Brophy, J. E. and Evertson, C. (1976) *Learning from Teaching*, Boston, Mass.: Allyn and Bacon.

Brophy, J. E. and Good, T. L. (1970) 'Teachers' communication of differential expectation for children's classroom performance', *Journal of Educational Psychology*, **71**, 365–74.

Brophy, J. E. and Good, T. L. (1974) *Teacher–Student Relationships: Causes and Consequences*, New York: Holt, Rinehart and Winston.

Broverman, E., Vogel, S., Broverman, D., Clarkson, F. and Rosencrantz, P. (1972) 'Sex role stereotypes: a current reappraisal', *Journal of Social Issues*, **28**, 59–78.

Brown, D. G. (1957) 'Masculinity–femininity development in children', *Journal of Consulting and Clinical Psychology*, **21**, 197–202.

Bruce, P. (1958) 'Relationships of self-acceptance to other variables with sixth-grade children oriented in self-understanding', *Journal of Educational Psychology*, **49**, 229–37.

Bruner, J. S. and Goodman, C. (1947) 'Value and need as organising factors in perception', *Journal of Abnormal and Social Psychology*, **42**, 33–44.

Buccola, V. and Stone, W. (1975) 'Effects of jogging and cycling programmes on physiological and psychological variables', *Research Quarterly*, **46**, 134–9.

Bugental, J. and Zelen, S. (1950) 'Investigations into the self-concept: 1 the Way Technique', *Journal of Personality*, **18**, 483–98.

Burgy, D. R. (1972) 'Developing good teachers by strengthening student teachers' self-concepts', Eric Ed 087774.

Burns, R. B. (1975) 'Attitudes to self and to three categories of others in a student group', *Educational Studies*, **1**, 181–9.

Burns, R. B. (1976a) 'The concept-scale interaction problem', *Educational Studies*, **2**, 121–7.

Burns, R. B. (1976b) 'Self and teaching approaches', *Durham Research Review*, No.

36, 1079–85.

Burns, R. B. (1977a) 'Male and female perceptions of their own and the other sex', *British Journal of Sociological and Clinical Psychology*, **16**, 213–20.

Burns, R. B. (1977b) 'The influence of various characteristics of others on social distance registered by a student group', *Irish Journal of Psychology*, **3**, 193–205.

Burns, R. B. (1979) *The Self-Concept: Theory, Measurement, Development and Behaviour*, London: Longman.

Burstall, C. (1970) *French in the Primary School*, Slough: NFER.

Butler, J. M. and Haigh, G. V. (1954) 'Changes in the relation between self-concept and ideal concepts consequent upon client centred counseling', in Rogers, C. R. and Dymond, R. F. (eds.) *Psychotherapy and Personality Change*, 55–75, Chicago: University of Chicago Press.

Butts, H. F. (1963) 'Skin-colour perception and self-esteem', *Journal of Negro Education*, **22**, 122–8.

Byrne, D. and Griffitt, W. (1966) 'Similarity and liking', *Psychonomic Science*, **6**, 295–6.

Calden, G., Lundy, R. M. and Schlafer, R. J. (1959) 'Sex differences in body concepts', *Journal of Counseling Psychology*, **23**, 378.

Calhoun, G. et al. (1978) 'An ethnic comparison of self esteem in Portuguese, Mexican and Anglo American pupils', *Journal of Psychology*, **98**, 11–14.

Callison, C. P. (1974) 'Experimental induction of self concept', *Psychological Reports*, **35**, 1235–8.

Calsyn, R. J. and Kenny, D. A. (1977) 'Self concept of ability and perceived evaluation of others: cause or effect of academic achievement', *Journal of Educational Psychology*, **69**, 136–45.

Calvin, A. P., Wayne, A. and Holtzman, H. (1953) 'Adjustment in the discrepancy between the self concept and inferred self', *Journal of Consulting and Clinical Psychology*, **17**, 206–13.

Campbell, D. and Fiske, D. (1959) 'Convergent and discriminant validation by the multi-method matrix', *Psychology Bulletin*, **56**, 81–105.

Campbell, J. P. and Dunnette, M. D. (1968) 'Effectiveness of T group experiences in managerial training and development', *Psychology Bulletin*, **70**, 73–104.

Canfield, J. and Wells, H. (1976) *100 Ways to Enhance Self Concept in the Classroom*, New Jersey: Prentice Hall.

Caplan, N. S. (1970) 'New ghetto man', *Journal of Sociological Issues*, **26**, 59–73.

Caplan, S. W. (1957) 'The effect of group counseling on junior high school boys' concepts of themselves in school', *Journal of Counseling Psychology,* **4,** 124–8.

Caplin, M. D. (1968) 'Self-concept, level of aspiration and academic achievement', *Journal of Negro Education,* **27,** 435–9.

Carkhuff, R. R. (1969) *Helping and Human Relations* vol. 1, New York: Holt, Rinehart and Winston.

Carlson, R. (1965) 'Stability and change in the adolescent self-image', *Child Development,* **35,** 659–66.

Carlton, L. and Moore, R. H. (1966) 'The effects of self directive dramatisation on reading achievement and self concept of culturally disadvantaged children', *Reading Teacher,* **20,** 125–40.

Carpenter, G. C. (1974) 'Mother's face and the newborn', *New Scientist,* **61,** 742–4.

Carroll, A. W. (1967) 'The effects of segregated and partially integrated school programmes on self concept and academic achievement of educable mental retardates', *Exceptional Children,* **34,** 92–99.

Caskey, S. R. and Felker, D. W. (1971) 'Social stereotyping of female body image by elementary school age girls', *Research Quarterly,* **42,** 251–5.

Cattell, R. B. and Child, D. (1975) *Motivation and Dynamic Structure,* London: Holt, Rinehart and Winston.

Cattell, R. B., Sealy, A. P. and Sweeny, A. B. (1966) 'What can personality and motivation source trait measurement add to the prediction of school achievement?', *British Journal of Educational Psychology,* **36,** 280–95.

Chandler, M. J. and Greenspan, S. (1972) 'Ersatz egocentrism', *Developmental Psychology,* **7,** 104–6.

Chang, T. S. (1976) 'Self-concepts, academic achievement and teachers' ratings', *Psychology in the Schools,* **13,** 111–13.

Channon, G. (1971) *Innovation in Teacher Education in Canada,* Ottawa: Canadian Teachers' Federation.

Chapman, I. (1964) 'A comparative study of delinquents and non-delinquents', unpublished PhD thesis, University of Missouri.

Chase, P. H. (1957) 'Self-concepts in adjusted and maladjusted hospital patients', *Journal of Consulting and Clinical Psychology,* **21,** 495–7.

Cheong, G. and Wadden, E. P. (1978) 'The relationship between teachers' experimental and dogmatic attitudes and their pupils' self-concept', *Alberta Journal of Educational Research,* **14,** 121–5.

Christmas, J. (1973) 'Self-concept and attitudes', in Miller, K. and Dreger, R. (eds.) *Comparative Studies of Blacks and Whites in the USA,* New York: Seminar Press.

Cicirelli, V. (1976) 'Effects of evaluating task

competence on the self concept of children from different sociometric levels', *Journal of Psychology,* **94,** 217–23.

Claiborn, W. (1969) 'Expectancy effects in the classroom: a failure to replicate', *Journal of Educational Psychology,* **60,** 377–83.

Clark, E. V. (1976) 'From gesture to word', in Bruner, J. and Gartner, A. *Human Growth and Development,* Oxford: Oxford University Press.

Clark, J. V. (1963) 'Authentic interaction and personal growth in sensitivity training groups', *Journal of Humanistic Psychology,* **4,** 1–13.

Clarke, J. V. and Culbert, S. A. (1965) 'Mutually therapeutic perception and self-awareness in a T group', *Journal of Applied Behavioral Science,* **2,** 180–94.

Clarke, J. V., Culbert, S. A. and Bubele, H. D. (1968) 'Measures of change toward self-actualisation in two sensitivity training groups', *Journal of Counseling Psychology,* **15,** 53–7.

Clark, K. B. (1955) *Prejudice and Your Child,* Boston, Mass.: Beacon Press.

Clark, K. B. (1963) 'Educational stimulation of racially disadvantaged children', in Passow, H. (ed.) *Education in Depressed Areas,* New York: Columbia University Press.

Clark, K. B. and Clark, M. P. (1940) 'Skin colour as a factor in racial identification of Negro preschool children', *Journal of Sociological Psychology,* **11,** 159–69.

Clark, K. B. and Clark, M. P. (1950) 'Emotional factors in racial identification and preference in Negro children', *Journal of Negro Education,* **19,** 341–50.

Clark, K. B. and Clark, M. P. (1958) 'Racial identification and preference in Negro children', in Maccoby, E. P. et al. (eds.) *Readings in Social Psychology,* New York: Holt, Rinehart and Winston.

Clifford, E. and Clifford, M. (1967) 'Self-concepts before and after survival training', *British Journal of Social and Clinical Psychology,* **6,** 241–8.

Clifford, M. M. (1975) 'Physical attractiveness and academic performance', paper presented to annual conference of American Educational Research Association, Washington, D.C.

Clifton, R. (1979) 'Practice teaching: survival in a marginal situation', *Canadian Journal of Education,* **4,** 60–74.

Clifton, R. A. and Covert, J. (1977) 'The effects of an experimental programme on the motivation and self-concept of student teachers', *Canadian Journal of Education,* **2,** 23–31.

Cloward, R. A. (1963) 'Social problems, social definitions and social opportunities', paper given to National Council on Crime and Delinquency, April. Washington, D.C.

Cockerham, W. C. and Blevins, A. L. (1976) 'Open

school and traditional school self-identification among native American and white adolescents', *Sociology of Education*, **49**, 164–9.

Cogan, M. L. (1958) 'The behaviour of teachers and the productive behaviour of their pupils', *Journal of Experimental Education*, **26**, 89–124.

Cohen, A. R. (1959) 'Some implications of self esteem for social influence', in Hooland, C. I. and Janis, I. L. (eds.) *Personality and Persuasibility*, New Haven: Yale University Press.

Cohen, A. and Cohen, L. (1974) 'Children's attitudes towards primary school activities', *Durham Research Review*, **32**, 847–56.

Cohen, L. (1976) *Educational Research in Classrooms and Schools*, London: Harper and Row.

Cohen, L. B. (1978) 'Infant visual perception', in Osotsky, J. *Handbook of Infancy*, New York: Wiley.

Cole, C. W., Oetting, E. R. and Miskimmins, R. W. (1969) 'Self-concept therapy for adolescent females', *Journal of Abnormal Psychology*, **74**, 642–5.

Coleman, A., Ayoub, M. and Freidrich, D. W. (1976) 'Assessment of the physical work capacity of mentally retarded males', *American Journal of Mental Efficiency*, **80**, 629–35.

Coleman, J. (1961) *The Adolescent Society*, New York: Glencoe Free Press.

Coleman, J., Coser, L. A. and Powell, W. W. (1966) *Equality of Educational Opportunity*, Washington, D.C.: US Government Printing Office.

Coleman, J. (1972) *Abnormal Psychology and Modern Life*, Glenview, Illinois: Scott Foresman.

Coleman, J. (1980) *The Nature of Adolescence*, London: Methuen.

Coleman, J. C., Herzberg, J. and Morris, M. (1977) 'Identity in adolescence: present and future self-concept', *Journal of Youth and Adolescence*, **6**, 63–75.

Collingwood, T. R. (1972) 'The effects of physical training upon behaviour and self-attitudes', *Journal of Clinical Psychology*, **28**, 583–5.

Collingwood, T. R. (1976) 'Effective physical functioning', *Counselor Education and Supervision*, **15**, 211–15.

Colman, A. and Olver, K. (1978) 'Reactions to flattery as a function of self-esteem', *British Journal of Sociology and Clinical Psychology*, **17**, 25–9.

Combs, A. W. (1952) 'Intelligence from a perceptual point of view', *Journal of Abnormal and Social Psychology*, **47**, 662–73.

Combs, A. W. (1965) *The Professional Education of Teachers*, Boston, Mass.: Allyn and Bacon.

Combs, A. W. (1969) 'Florida studies in the helping professions', Monographs, **37**, Gains-ville: University Florida Press.

Combs, A. W., Avila, D. L. and Purkey, W. W. (1971) *Helping Relationships*, Boston, Mass.: Allyn and Bacon.

Combs, A. W. and Snygg, D. (1959) *Individual Behavior*, Boston, Mass.: Harper and Row.

Combs, A. W. and Soper, D. W. (1957) 'The self, its derivative terms and research', *Journal of Individual Psychology*, **13**, 134–5.

Combs, A. W. and Soper, D. W. (1963) 'The relationship of child perceptions to achievement in behaviour in the early school years', Cooperative Research Project 814, University of Florida.

Combs, A. W., Soper, D. W. and Courson, C. C. (1963) 'The measurement of self-concept and self-report', *Educational and Psychological Measurement*, **23**, 493–500.

Combs, C. F. (1964) 'Self-perception and scholastic underachievement in the academically capable', *The Personnel and Guidance Journal*, **43**, 47–51.

Condrey, J. and Condrey, S. (1976) 'Sex differences', *Child Development*, **47**, 812–19.

Conger, J. J. (1977) *Adolescence and Youth*, New York: Harper and Row.

Connell, D. M. and Johnson, J. (1970) 'Relationships between sex-role identification and self-esteem in early adolescents', *Developmental Psychology*, **3**, 268.

Connell, W. F., Stroobant, R. E., Sinclair, K. E., Connell, R. W. and Rogers, K. W. (1975) *Twenty to Twenty*, Sydney: Hicks Smith.

Cooley, C. H. (1912) *Human Nature and the Social Order*, New York: Scribners.

Coons, W. and McEachern, D. (1967) 'Verbal conditioning, acceptance of self and acceptance of others', *Psychological Reports*, **20**, 715–22.

Cooper, C. L. (1975) 'The impact of marathon encounters on teacher–student relationships', *Interpersonal Development*, **5**, 71–8.

Coopersmith, S. (1959) 'A method for determining types of self-esteem', *Journal of Abnormal and Social Psychology*, **59**, 87–94.

Coopersmith, S. (1967) *The Antecedents of Self-Esteem*, San Francisco: Freeman.

Coopersmith, S. (1975) 'Self-concept, race and education', in Verma, G. and Bagley, C. (eds.) *Race and Education Across Cultures*, London: Heinemann.

Cotnam, J. D. (1969) 'Variance in self-report measures of disadvantaged young adults as a function of race', unpublished PhD thesis, University of Rochester, New York.

Couch, J. and Kenniston, P. (1960) 'Yeasayers and Naysayers', in Medrick and Medrick (eds.) *Research into Personality*, New York: Holt, Rinehart and Winston.

Coulter, F. (1974) 'The effects of practice teaching on professional self-image', *Australian*

Journal of Education, **18**, 149–59.

Courson, C. C. (1965) 'The use of inference as a research tool', *Educational and Psychological Measures*, **25**, 1029–38.

Covert, J. and Clifton, R. A. (1979) 'The effect of two experimental programmes on the affective states of student teachers', Research Report, 79-001 Institute for Research into Human Abilities, St. Johns Memorial University, Canada.

Cowen, E. L. (1956) 'An investigation of the relationship between two measures of self-regarding attitudes', *Journal of Clinical Psychology*, **12**, 156–60.

Crandall, J. E. (1969) 'Self-perception, and interpersonal attraction as related to tolerance–intolerance of ambiguity', *Journal of Personality*, **37**, 127–1240.

Crane, C. (1974) 'Attitudes towards acceptance of self and others and adjustment to teaching', *British Journal of Educational Psychology*, **44**, pt. 1, 31–6.

Crites, J. O. (1969) *Vocational Psychology*, New York: McGraw-Hill.

Crowne, D. and Stevens, M. (1961) 'Self-acceptance and self-evaluative behaviour: a critique of methodology', *Psychological Bulletin*, **58**, 104–15.

Crowne, D. P., Stevens, M. W. and Kelly, R. (1961) 'The validity and equivalence of tests of self acceptance', *Journal of Psychology*, **51**, 101–12.

Crutchfield, R. S. (1955) 'Conformity and character', *American Psychology*, **10**, 191–8.

Culbert, S. A., Clark, J. V. and Bobele, H. D. (1968) 'Measures of change towards self-actualisation in two sensitivity training groups', *Journal of Counseling Psychology*, **15**, 53–7.

Cummins, R. E. (1960) 'Research insights into the relationship between teachers' acceptance attitudes, their role concepts and students' acceptance attitudes', *Journal of Educational Research*, **53**, 197–8.

Curtis, R., Zana, M. and Campbell, W. W. (1975) 'Sex, fear of success and the perception and performance of law school students', *American Education Research Journal*, **12**, 287–97.

Cutter, A. V. (1962) 'The place of self-concept in the education of the physically different child', *Exceptional Children*, **28**, 146–52.

Dandes, H. M. (1966) 'Psychological health and teaching effectiveness', *Journal of Teacher Education*, **18**, 301–6.

Davidson, H. H. and Lang, G. (1960) 'Children's perceptions of their teachers' feelings towards them related to self perception, school achievement and behaviour', *Journal of Experimental Education*, **29**, 107–18.

Davis, A. J. (1969) 'Self-concept, occupational role expectations and occupational choice in nursing and social work', *Nursing Research*, **18**, 55–9.

De Blaissie, R. and Healey, G. W. (1970) 'Self-concept: a comparison of Spanish American, Negro and Anglo adolescents across ethnic, sex and social class variables', Las Gruces: Clearing House on Rural Education.

De Jung, J. and Gardner, E. (1962) 'The accuracy of self-role perception', *Journal of Experimental Education*, **31**, 27–41.

Dembo, T., Leviton, G. L. and Wright, B. A. (1956) 'Adjustment to misfortune a problem of social psychological rehabilitation', *Artificial Limbs*, **3**, 4–62.

Demeritt, M. (1970) 'Differences in the self-concept of drug users, non-users and former users', *Dissertation Abstracts*, **313A**, 1008.

Denmark, F. L. (1970) 'The effect of integration on academic achievement and self-concept', *Integrated Education*, **8**, 34–42.

Deutsch, M. (1960) 'Minority group and class status as related to social and personality factors in scholastic achievement', Society Applied Anthropology Monograph No. 2.

Deutsch, M. and Solomon, L. (1959) 'Reactions to evaluations of others as influenced by self evaluation', *Sociometry*, **22**, 93–112.

Dibiase, W. J. and Hjelle, L. (1968) 'Body image stereotypes among male college students', *Perceptual Motor Skills*, **27**, 1143–6.

Dickstein, E. and Hardy, B. (1979) 'Self-esteem, autonomy and moral behaviour in college men and women', *Journal of Genetic Psychology*, **134**, 51–3.

Dickstein, E. and Posner, J. (1978) 'Self-esteem and relationship with parents', *Journal of Genetic Psychology*, **133**, 273–6.

Diggory, J. C. (1966) *Self-evaluation: Concepts and Studies*, New York: Wiley.

Dilorenzo, L. T. (1971) 'Which way for pre-kindergarten?', *American Education*, **7**, 28–32.

Dipboye, R. L. et al. (1978) 'Self-esteem as a moderator of the relationship between scientific interests and job satisfaction of physicists and engineers', *Journal of Applied Psychology*, **63**, 289–94.

Dittes, J. E. (1959) 'Attractiveness of group as a function of self-esteem and acceptance by group', *Journal of Abnormal and Social Psychology*, **59**, 77–82.

Dixon, J. C. and Street, J. (1975) 'The distinction between self and non-self in children and adolescents', *Journal of Genetic Psychology*, **127**, 157–62.

Dobson, C., Willis, J., Keith, P. and Powers, E. (1979) 'Further analysis of Rosenberg's self-esteem scale', *Psychological Reports*, April, 639–41.

Doherty, J. (1979) 'The relationship between self-esteem and teaching performance in a group of student teachers', unpublished paper, Education Department, University of Birmingham.

Doherty, J. and Parker, K. (1977) 'An investigation into the effect of certain variables on the self esteem of a group of student teachers', *Educational Review*, **29**, 307–15.

Dorr, D., Rummer, C. and Green, R. (1976) 'Correlations between Coopersmith's SEI and the California Test of Personality for children in grades 4 and 6', *Psychological Reports*, **39**, 221–2.

Doster, J. and Brooks, S. (1974) 'Interviewer disclosure modeling information revealed and interviewees' verbal behaviour', *Journal of Consulting and Clinical Psychology*, **42**, 420–6.

Douvan, E. (1979) 'Sex role learning', in Coleman, J. C. (ed.) *The School Years*, London: Methuen.

Douvan, E. and Adelson, J. (1966) *The Adolescent Experience*, New York: Wiley.

Douvan, E. and Gold, M. (1966) 'Modal patterns in American adolescents', in Hoffman and Hoffman (eds.) *Review of Child Development Research*, vol. 2, New York: Russell Sage.

Dove, L. (1974) 'Racial awareness among adolescents in London comprehensive schools', *New Community*, **3**, 255–61.

Dreyer, A. L., Hulac, V. and Rigler, D. (1971) 'Differential adjustment to pubescence and cognitive style patterns', *Developmental Psychology*, **4**, 456–62.

Duncan, C. (1966) 'A reputation test of personality integration', *Journal of Personality and Social Psychology*, **3**, 516–24.

Dunn, J. A. (1968) 'The approach avoidance paradigm as a model for the analysis of school anxiety', *Journal of Educational Psychology*, **59**, 388–94.

Dunnette, M. D. (1973) 'Performance equals ability and what?', Technical Report 4009, Minneapolis: University of Minnesota.

Duval, S. (1976) 'Conformity on a visual task as a function of personal novelty on attitudinal dimensions', *Journal of Experimental and Social Psychology*, **12**, 87–98.

Duval, S. and Wicklund, R. (1972) *A Theory of Objective Self Awareness*, New York: Academic Press.

Dweck, C. (1974) 'The role of expectations and attributions in the alleviation of learned helplessness', *Journal of Personality and Social Psychology*, **31**, 674–85.

Dyson, E. (1967) 'A study of ability grouping and the self-concept', *Journal of Educational Research*, **60**, 403–5.

Eastman, D. (1958) 'Self-concept and marital adjustment', *Journal of Consulting and Clinical Psychology*, **22**, 95–9.

Edeburn, C. and Landry, R. (1974) 'Self-concepts of students and a significant other: the teacher', *Psychological Reports*, August pt 2, 505–6.

Edgar, P., Powell, R. F., Watkins, D., Moore, R. J. and Zakharov, O. (1974) 'An analysis of the Coopersmith self-esteem inventory', *Australian Psychology*, **9**, 52–63.

Edwards, A. L. (1957) *The Social Desirability Variable in Personality Assessment and Research*, New York: Holt, Rinehart and Winston.

Edwards, A. L. (1959) 'Social desirability and the description of others', *Journal of Abnormal and Social Psychology*, **59**, 434–6.

Edwards, A. L. and Hurst, P. (1953) 'Social desirability as a variable in *Q* technique study', *Educational Psychology Measurement*, **13**, 620–5.

Edwards, D. W. (1974) 'Blacks v. whites. When is race a relevant variable?', *Journal of Personality and Social Psychology*, **29**, 39–49.

Edwards, K. and Tuckman, B. (1972) 'Effects of differential college experience in developing students' self and occupational concepts', *Journal of Educational Psychology*, **63**, 563–71.

Edwards, O. (1972) 'Intergenerational variation in racial attitudes', *Social Society Research*, **57**, 22–31.

Ehrhardt, J. and Baker, P. (1974) 'Fetal androgens, human central nervous system differentiation and behavior sex differences', in Freedman, R. C., Richart, R. H. and Vande Wiele, R. L. (eds.) *Sex Differences in Behavior*, New York: Wiley.

Eitzen, S. (1976) 'The self-concept of delinquents in a behaviour modification treatment programme', *Journal of Social Psychology*, **99**, 203–6.

Elder, G. H. (1975) *Adolescence in the Life Cycle*, New York: Wiley.

Ellerman, D. A. (1980) 'Self-regard of primary school children: some Australian data', *British Journal of Educational Psychology*, **50**, 114–22.

Ellis, A. A. (1961) *A Guide to Rational Living*, New Jersey: Prentice Hall.

Ellis, D., Gehman, W. S. and Katzenmeyer, W. G. (1980) 'The boundary organisation of self concept across 13–18 year age span', *Psychological Measures*, **40**, 9–18.

Elrod, M. M. and Crase, S. J. (1980) 'Sex differences in self-esteem and parental behaviour', *Psychological Reports*, **46**, 719–27.

Emmerling, F. C. (1961) 'A study of the relationships between personality characteristics of classroom teachers and pupil perceptions', unpublished PhD thesis, New York: Auburn University.

Engel, M. (1959) 'The stability of the self-concept in adolescence', *Journal of Abnormal and*

Social Psychology, **58**, 211–15.

Engel, M. and Raine, W. J. (1963) 'A method for the measurement of the self-concept of children in the 3rd grade', *Journal of Genetic Psychology*, **102**, 125–37.

Englander, M. (1960) 'A psychological analysis of vocational choice: teaching', *Journal of Counseling Psychology*, **7**, 257–64.

Ensor, E. G. (1976) 'A comparison of dyadic interactions between high and low self-concept of ability children and their teachers', unpublished MSc thesis, Bradford University.

Epps, E. G. (1975) 'The impact of school desegregation on aspirations, self-concepts and other aspects of personality', *Law and Contemporary Problems*, **39**, 300–13.

Epstein, E. (1962) 'Self-concept of the delinquent female', *Smith College Studies in Social Work*, **32**, 220–4.

Epstein, R. and Komorita, S. (1965) 'Parental discipline stimulus characteristics of outgroups and social distance in children', *Journal of Personality and Social Psychology*, **2**, 416–20.

Epstein, S. (1955) 'Unconscious self-evaluation in a normal and a schizophrenic group', *Journal of Abnormal and Social Psychology*, **50**, 65–70.

Erikson, E. (1959) *Identity and the Life Cycle*, New York: IUP.

Erikson, E. H. (1963) *Childhood and Society*, New York: Norton.

Erikson, E. H. (1965) 'Psychoanalysis and on-going history: problems of identity hatred and non-violence', *American Journal of Psychiatry*, **122**, 241–50.

Erikson, E. H. (1968) *Identity, Youth and Crisis*, New York: Norton.

Fagot, B. I. and Patterson, G. R. (1969) 'An *in vivo* analysis of reinforcing contingencies for sex role behaviours in the pre-school child', *Developmental Psychology*, **1**, 563–8.

Fannin, L. and Clinard, M. (1965) 'Differences in the conception of self as a male among lower and middle class delinquents', *Social Problems*, **13**, 205–14.

Fantz, R. L. (1961) 'The origin of form perception', *Scientific American*, **204**, 66–72.

Fantz, R. L. (1963) 'Pattern vision in newborn infants', *Science*, **140**, 296–7.

Faunce, R. W. (1967) 'An experimental junior high school of the Minneapolis Public Schools', unpublished manuscript Special School District 1, Minneapolis, Minnesota.

Fein, D., O'Neill, S., Frank, C. and Velit, K. (1975) 'Sex differences in pre-adolescent self-esteem', *Journal of Psychology*, **90**, 179–84.

Felker, D. W. (1969) 'The relationship between anxiety, self-ratings and ratings by others in fifth grade children', *Journal of Genetic Psychology*, **115**, 81–6.

Felker, D. W. (1972) 'Prediction of specific self-evaluations from performance and personality measures', *Psychological Reports*, **31**, 823–6.

Felker, D. W. (1972) 'Self-concept and self-administered verbal reward', National Institute of Mental Health Report, Washington, D.C.

Felker, D. W. (1974) *Building Positive Self-Concepts*, Minneapolis: Burgess.

Felker, D. W. and Stanwyck, K. (1971) 'General self-concept and specific self-evaluation after an academic task', *Psychological Reports*, **29**, 60–2.

Felker, D. W. and Thomas, S. (1971) 'Self initiated, verbal reinforcement and positive self-concept', *Child Development*, **42**, 1285–7.

Ferguson, L., Freedman, M. and Ferguson, E. (1977) 'Developmental self-concept and drug use', *Psychology Report*, **41**, 531–41.

Ferri, E. (1971) *Streaming: Two Years Later*, Slough: NFER.

Festinger, L. (1954) 'A theory of social comparison processes', *Human Relations*, **7**, 117–40.

Festinger, L. (1957) *A Theory of Cognitive Dissonance*, New York: Harper and Row.

Fey, W. F. (1954) 'Acceptance of self and others and its relation to therapy readiness', *Journal of Clinical Psychology*, **10**, 266–9.

Fink, M. (1962) 'Self-concept as it relates to academic under-achievement', *Californian Journal of Educational Research*, **13**, 57–62.

Fishman, J. A. (1961) 'Childhood indoctrination for minority group membership', *Daedalus*, **90**, 329–49.

Fitts, W. A. and Hamner, W. (1969) *The Self-Concept and Delinquency*, Research Monograph 1, Library of Congress Catalogue Card 74-104605, 1969.

Fitts, W. H. (1955) Manual, Tennessee Department of Mental Health, Self-Concept Scale, Nashville, Tennessee.

Flavell, J. H. (1978) 'What young children think you see when their eyes are closed', unpublished report, Stanford University.

Fleming, E. S. and Anttonen, R. (1971) 'Teacher expectancy as related to the academic and personal growth of primary age children', Monograph *Sociological Research of Child Development*, **36**, Serial No. 145.

Fleming, J. S. and Watts, W. (1980) 'Dimensionability of self-esteem', *Journal of Personality and Social Psychology*, **39**, 921–9.

Fogelman, K. (1976) *Britain's 16 year olds*, London: National Children's Bureau.

Fourner, M. J. (1977) 'Self-enhancement activity group for 1st grade repeaters', *Elementary School Grade Council*, **11**, 267–76.

Frank, J. (1972) 'The bewildering world of psychotherapy', *Journal of Social Issues*, **28**, 27–43.

Franklin, B. M. (1977) 'Career education and the self-concept', *Teachers College Records*, **78**,

285–97.

Franks, D., Marolla, J. and Dillon, S. (1974) 'Intrinsic motivation and feelings of competency among students', *Journal of Research Development in Education*, **8**, 20–9.

Frease, D. (1972) 'The Schools, Self-Concept and Juvenile Delinquency', *British Journal of Criminology*, **12**, 133–46.

Freibus, R. (1975) 'Socialisation of the student teacher', paper presented at annual conference of American Sociological Association.

Frenkel-Brunswik, E. (1948) 'A study of prejudice in children', *Human Relations*, **1**, 295–306.

Frericks, A. H. (1974) 'Labelling of students by prospective teachers', unpublished paper, annual conference of American Education Research Association, Chicago.

Freud, S. (1905) *Three Essays on the Theory of Sexuality*, Imago Press.

Freud, S. (1933) *New Introductory Lectures on Psychoanalysis*, London: Hogarth Press.

Freud, S. (1949) *Outline of Psychoanalysis*, London: Hogarth Press.

Friedenberg, W. and Gillis, J. (1977) 'An experimental study of the effectiveness of attitude change techniques for enhancing self-esteem', *Journal of Clinical Psychology*, **33**, 1120–4.

Friedenberg, W. and Gillis, J. (1980) 'Modification of self-esteem with techniques of attitude change', *Psychological Report*, June, 1087–95.

Friedman, I. (1955) 'Phenomenal, ideal, and projected conceptions of the self', *Journal of Abnormal and Social Psychology*, **51**, 611–15.

Fromm, E. (1939) 'Selfishness and self love', *Psychiatry*, **2**, 507–23.

Fromm-Reichman (1949) *Principles of Intensive Psychotherapy*, Chicago: University Press.

Frueh, T. and McGhee, P. E. (1975) 'Traditional sex-role development and amount of time spent watching TV', *Developmental Psychology* **11**, 109.

Fry, P. S. (1976) 'Success, failure and self other orientations', *Journal of Psychology*, **93**, 43–50.

Fu, V., Korslund, M. and Hinkle, D. (1980) 'Ethnic self-concept during middle childhood', *Journal of Psychology*, **105**, 99–104.

Gable, R. K., LaSalle, A. J. and Cook, K. (1973) 'Dimensionability of self-perception: Tennessee Self-Concept Scale', *Perceptual and Motor Skills*, **36**, 551–60.

Gallup, G. (1977) 'Self-recognition in primates', *American Psychologist*, **32**, 329–38.

Ganesan, V. (1979) 'Organisational climate, family climate and self-concept in relation to occupational interests', *Psychological Report*, April, 636–8.

Ganzer, V. J. (1968) 'Effects of audience pressure and test anxiety on learning and retention', *Journal of Personality and Social Psychology*, **8**, 194–9.

Garth, C. E. (1963) 'Self-concepts of Negro students who transferred or did not transfer to formerly all white schools', unpublished PhD thesis, University of Kentucky.

Garvey, R. (1970) 'Self-concept and success in student teaching', *Journal of Teacher Education*, **21**, 357–61.

Garwood, G. (1976) 'First name stereotypes as a factor in self-concept and school achievement', *Journal of Educational Psychology*, **68**, 482–7.

Gaskell, P. J. (1977) 'Structured variables in the analysis of student teaching', paper presented at annual conference of Canadian Society for the Study of Education.

Gecas, V. (1971) 'Parental behaviour and dimensions of adolescent self-evaluation', *Sociometry*, **34**, 466–82.

Gecas, V. (1972) 'Parental behaviour and contextual variations in adolescent self-esteem', *Sociometry*, **35**, 332–45.

Gecas, V., Calonico, J. M. and Thomas, D. L. (1974) 'The development of self concept and the child: mirror theory v. model theory', *Journal of Social Psychology*, **92**, 67–76.

Gecas, V., Thomas, D. L. and Velgart, A. J. (1970) 'Perceived parent child interaction and boys' self-esteem in two cultures', *Journal of Comparative Sociology*, **11**, 317–24.

Gellert, E. (1975) 'Children's construction of their self images', *Perceptual and Motor Skills*, **40**, 307–24.

Gergen, K. J. (1965) 'The effects of interaction goals and personalistic feedback on the presentation of self', *Journal of Personality and Social Psychology*, **1**, 413–24.

Gershman, H. (1967) 'The evolution of gender identity', *Bulletin of New York Academy of Medicine*, **43**, 1000–18.

Gibb, J. R. (1971) 'The effects of human relations training', in Bergin, A. and Garfield, S. (eds.) *Handbook of Psychotherapy and Behavior Change*, New York: Wiley.

Gibby, R. G. and Gabler, R. (1967) 'The self-concept of Negro and white children', *Journal of Clinical Psychology*, **23**, 144–8.

Gilbert, D. and Finell, L. (1978) 'Young child's awareness of self', *Psychological Report, pt 1*, 911–14.

Gill, P. and D'Oyley, V. (1970) Research Note: 'The construction of an objective measure of self concept', *Interchange*, **1**, 110–13.

Ginott, H. G. (1972) *Teacher and Child*, New York: Macmillan.

Glasser, W. (1969) *Schools Without Failure*, New York: Harper and Row.

Glock, M. D. (1972) 'Is there a Pygmalion in the classroom?', *The Reading Teacher*, **25**, 405–8.

Glueck, S. and Glueck, E. (1950) *Unraveling Juvenile Delinquency*, New York: Harper and Row.

Goffman, E. (1955) 'On face-work', *Psychiatry*, **18**, 213–31.

Goffman, E. (1959) *The Presentation of Self in Everyday Life*, New York: Doubleday.

Goffman, E. (1961) *Asylums*, Harmondsworth: Penguin.

Goffman, E. (1963) *Stigma: Notes on the Management of a Spoiled Identity*, New York: Prentice Hall.

Gold, M. (1973) 'Status forces in delinquent boys', Institute of Social Research, University of Michigan.

Goldfarb, W. (1945) 'Effects of psychological deprivation in infancy', *American Journal of Psychiatry*, **102**, 18–33.

Good, T. L., Biddle, B. J. and Brophy, J. E. (1975) *Teachers Make a Difference*, New York: Holt, Rinehart and Winston.

Good, T. L. and Brophy, J. E. (1972) 'Behavioural expression of teacher attitudes', *Journal of Educational Psychology*, **63**, 617–24.

Good, T. L. and Brophy, J. E. (1973) *Looking In Classrooms*, New York: Harper and Row.

Goodenough, F. W. (1957) 'Interest in persons and aspects of sex differences in early years', *Psychology Monograph*, **55**, 287–323.

Goodlad, J. T. (1965) 'An analysis of professional laboratory experience in the education of teachers', *Journal of Teacher Education*, **16**, 263–70.

Goodman, M. E. (1962) *Race Awareness in Young Children*, London: Addison Wesley.

Gordon, C. (1968) 'Self conceptions: configurations of content', in Gordon, C. and Gergen, K. (eds.) *The Self in Social Interaction*, vol. 1, New York: Wiley.

Gordon, I. (1966) *Studying the Child in School*, New York: Wiley.

Gordon, T. (1970) *Parent Effectiveness Training*, New York: Wyden.

Gose, A., Wooden, S. and Muller, D. (1980) 'The relative potential of self-concept and intelligence as predictors of achievement', *Journal of Psychology*, **104**, 279–88.

Gough, H. G. (1950) 'Children's ethnic attitudes: relations to parental beliefs concerning child training', *Child Development*, **21**, 169–81.

Gough, H. G. and Heilbron, A. B. (1965) *Adjective Check List Manual*, Palo Alto, California: Consulting Psychologists Press.

Grabe, M. (1976) 'Big school, small school; impact of the high school environment', *Contemporary Educational Psychology*, **1**, 20–5.

Grand, S. (1972) 'Reactions to unfavourable evaluations as a function of acceptance of disability', *Journal of Counseling Psychology*, **19**, 87–92.

Grater, M. (1959) 'Changes in self and other attitudes in a leadership training group', *Personnel and Guidance Journal*, **37**, 493–6.

Gray, D. and Pepitone, A. (1964) 'Effect of self-esteem on drawings of the human figure', *Journal of Consulting and Clinical Psychology*, **28**, 452–5.

Graybill, D. (1978) 'Relationships of maternal child rearing behaviour to children's self-esteem', *Journal of Psychology*, **100**, 45–8.

Gray-Little, B. (1979) 'Instrumentality effects in the assessment of racial differences in self-esteem', *Journal of Personality and Social Psychology*, **37**, 1221–9.

Greenberg, J. W. (1970) 'Comments on self perceptives of disadvantaged children', *American Educational Research Journal*, **7**, 627–9.

Greenman, G. W. (1963) 'Visual behaviour of newborn infants', in Solnit, A. and Provence, S. (eds.) *Modern Perspectives in Child Development*, New York: Hallmark.

Greenstein, J. (1973) 'Belief system changes in student teachers', *ATE Research Bulletin*, **12**, Washington, D.C.: Association of Teacher Education.

Gregor, A. and Armstrong, C. (1964) 'Integrated schools and Negro character development', *Psychiatry*, **27**, 69–72.

Gregory, A. and Allen, D. I. (1978) 'Some effects of the practicum on the professional self concept of student teachers', *Canadian Journal of Education*, **3**, 53–65.

Griest, J. H. (1978) 'Running as treatment for depression', unpublished paper, University of Wisconsin.

Griffin, J. L. (1969) 'The effects of integration on aptitude, achievement, self-concept, and attitudes to school environment', unpublished PhD thesis, University of Tulsa.

Groobman, D. E., Forward, J. R. and Peterson, C. (1976) 'Attitudes, self-esteem and learning in formal and informal schools', *Journal of Educational Psychology*, **68**, 32–5.

Growe, G. (1980) 'Parental behaviour and self-esteem in children', *Psychological Reports*, **47**, 499–502.

Guildford, J. P. (1954) *Psychometric Methods*, New York: McGraw-Hill.

Gunderson, E. K. (1956) 'Body size, self evaluation and military effectiveness', *Journal of Personality and Social Psychology*, **2**, 902–6.

Guthrie, E. R. (1938) *Psychology of Human Conflict*, New York: Harper and Row.

Guy, R., Rankin, B. and Norvell, M. (1980) 'Relation of sex role stereotyping to body image', *Journal of Psychology*, **105**, 167–73.

Haas, H. I. and Maehr, M. L. (1965) 'Two experiments on the concept of self and the reaction of others', *Journal of Personality and Social Psychology*, **1**, 100–5.

Haith, M. (1966) 'The response of the neonate to visual movement', *Journal of Experimental Child Psychology*, **3**, 235–43.

Haith, M., Bergman, T. and Moore, M. J. (1979) 'Eye contact and face scanning in early infancy', in Hetherington, E. and Parke, E. (eds.) *Child Psychology,* New York: McGraw-Hill.

Hall, P. M. (1963) *The Self Concept of Juvenile Delinquents,* University of Minnesota.

Hall, P. M. (1966) 'Identification with the delinquent sub-culture and level of self-evaluation', *Sociometry,* **29,** 146–58.

Hall, W. S., Cross, W. and Freedle, R. (1972) 'Stages in the development of black awareness', in Jones, R. (ed.) *Black Psychology,* New York: Harper and Row.

Hamachek, D. (1968) 'Characteristics of low achieving, low self-concept junior high school students and the impact of small group and individual counselling on self concept enhancement', ERIC ED 017 549.

Hamid, P. (1969) 'Word meaning and self-description', *Journal of Social Psychology,* **79,** 51–4.

Hamilton, D. (1971) 'A comparative study of five methods of assessing self-esteem, dominance and dogmatism', *Educational and Psychological Measurement,* **31,** 441–82.

Hannum, J. (1974) 'Changing the evaluative self-thoughts of two elementary teachers', Research and Development Memo 122, California: Stanford Centre for Research and Development in Teaching.

Hansen, J. and Maynard, P. (1973) *Youth, Self Concept and Behavior,* Ohio: Merrill.

Harari, H. and McDavid, J. W. (1973) 'Name stereotypes and teachers' expectations', *Journal of Educational Psychology,* **65,** 86–98.

Hardstaffe (1973) 'Some social conceptions of secondary modern school pupils', unpublished MSc dissertation, School of Research in Education, University of Bradford.

Hargreaves, D. H. (1967) *Social Relations in a Secondary School,* London: Routledge and Kegan Paul.

Hargreaves, D. H. (1972) *Interpersonal Relations and Education,* London: Routledge and Kegan Paul.

Harlow, H. C. and Harlow, M. K. (1962) 'Social deprivation in monkeys', *Scientific American,* **207,** 136–46.

Harrop, L. A. (1977) 'The methodology and applications of contingency management in schools', unpublished PhD thesis, University of Liverpool.

Hart, W. F. (1934) *Teachers and Teaching,* New York: Macmillan.

Hartup, W. W. and Moore, S. G. (1963) 'Avoidance of inappropriate sex typing by young children', *Journal of Consulting and Clinical Psychology,* **27,** 467–73.

Harvey, O. J. and Clapp, W. F. (1965) 'Hope, expectancy and reactions to the unexpected', *Journal of Personality and Social Psychology,* **2,** 45–52.

Havighurst, R. J., Robinson, M. and Door, M. (1946) 'Development of the ideal self through childhood and adolescence', *Journal of Educational Research,* **40,** 241–57.

Hawkins, K. (1972) 'West Indian boys in school', unpublished MSc thesis, University of Bradford.

Haworth, M. R. and Normington, C. J. (1961) 'A sexual differential scale for the DAP test', *Journal of Projective Techniques,* **25,** 441–50.

Healey, W. and Bronner, A. (1936) *New Light on Delinquency and its Treatment,* New Haven: Yale University Press.

Hebb, D. O. (1955) 'Drives and the CNS', *Psychological Review,* **62,** 243–54.

Hebron, M. and Ridley, B. (1965) 'Characteristics associated with prejudice in adolescent boys', *British Journal of Social and Clinical Psychology,* **1,** 357–84.

Heider, F. (1958) *Psychology of Interpersonal Relations,* New York: Wiley.

Heil, L. M., Powell, M. and Fiefer, I. (1960) 'Characteristics of teacher behaviour related to the achievement of different kinds of children', Cooperative Research Project 352, New York: US Office of Education.

Heilizer, J. A. (1962) 'A comparison of the doll play of non-handicapped hard of hearing and orthopaedically handicapped child', in Trapp, E. and Himelstein, P. (eds.) *Readings on the Exceptional Child,* New York: Appleton-Century-Crofts.

Heiss, J. and Owens, S. (1972) 'Self evaluations of blacks and whites', *American Journal of Sociology,* **78,** 360–9.

Henderson, E. H., Long, B. H. and Ziller, R. C. (1965) 'Self social constructs of achieving and non-achieving readers', *Reading Teacher,* **19,** 114–18.

Hendrix, B. L. (1980) 'The effects of loss of control on the self esteem of black and white youth', *Journal of Social Psychology,* **112,** 301–2.

Hensley, W. E. (1977) 'Differences between males and females', *Psychological Reports,* **41,** 829–30.

Hensley, W. E. and Roberts, M. K. (1976) 'Dimensions of Rosenberg's self-esteem scale', *Psychological Reports,* **38,** 583–4.

Herskovitz, F. S. (1969) 'The effects of a vocational-educational rehabilitation programme on the self concepts of disadvantaged youth', *Dissertation Abstracts,* **30,** 2801 A.

Hetherington, E. M. (1967) 'The effects of family variables on sex typing and imitation in children', in Hill, J. (ed.) *Minnesota Symposium on Child Psychology,* vol. 1, Minneapolis: University of Minnesota Press.

Hetherington, E. M. (1972) 'Effects of father absence on personality development of adolescent daughters', *Developmental Psychology*, **7**, 313–26.

Hewitt, J. (1970) *Social Stratification and Deviant Behavior*, New York: Random House.

Hewitt, J. and Kraft, M. (1973) 'Effects of encounter group experience on self perception and interpersonal relations', *Journal of Consulting and Clinical Psychology*, **40**, 162.

Hickman, C. and Kuhn, M. H. (1956) *Individuals, Groups and Economic Behavior*, New York: Dryden.

Higgins, L. C. (1962) 'Self concepts of mentally retarded adolescents', unpublished B.Litt thesis, University of New England.

Hilden, A. H. (1954) *Manual of Q Sorts*, Washington University.

Hilgard, E. R. (1949) 'Human motives and the concept of the self', *American Psychologist*, **4**, 374–82.

Hill, D. (1970) 'The attitudes of West Indian and English adolescents in Britain', *Race*, **11**, 313–21.

Hill, D. (1975) 'Personality factors among adolescents in minority ethnic groups', *Educational Studies*, **1**, 43–54.

Hilyer, J. C. and Mitchell, W. (1979) 'Effect of systematic physical fitness training combined with counselling on the self concept of college students', *Counselling Psychology*, **26**, 427–36.

Hodgkins, B. J. and Stakenas, R. G. (1969) 'A study of self concepts of Negro and white youth in segregated environments', *Journal of Negro Education*, **47**, 120–5.

Hoffman, L. W. (1972) 'Early childhood experiences and women's achievement motive', *Journal of Social Issues*, **23**, 129–55.

Holter, H. (1970) *Sex Roles and Social Structure*, Oslo: University Press.

Horney, K. (1937) *Neurotic Personality of Our Times*, New York: Norton.

Horney, K. (1950) *Neurosis and Human Growth*, New York: Norton.

House, P. and More, A. (1974) 'The learning environment as a predictor of the academic self concepts of ninth grade mathematics students', unpublished paper, American Educational Research Association, Chicago.

Hovland, C. I. and Janis, I. L. (1959) *Personality and Persuasibility*, New Haven: Yale University Press.

Hovland, C. I., Lumsdaine, A. A. and Sheffield, F. D. (1949) *Experiments on Mass Communication*, Princetown: Princetown University Press.

Howard, E. Z. (1965) 'To feel like a teacher', *Journal of Teacher Education*, **16**, 453–5.

Hubel, D. H. and Wiesel, T. N. (1962) 'Receptive fields, binocular interaction and functional architecture in the cat's visual cortex', *Journal of Physiology*, **160**, 106–54.

Hughes, C. A. (1974) 'A comparison of the effects of four teaching techniques of body conditioning', *Dissertation Abstracts*, **34**, 3957A.

Hunt, D. and Hardt, R. (1969) 'The effect of upward bound programmes on the attitudes, motivation and academic achievement of Negro students', *Journal of Social Issues*, **25**, 117–29.

Hunt, J. McV. (1961) *Intelligence and Experience*, New York: Ronald Press.

Hunt, J. McV. (1971) 'Using intrinsic motivation to teach young children', *Educational Technology*, **2**, 78–80.

Hutt, C. (1970) 'Curiosity in young children', *Science Journal*, **6**, 68–72.

Hutt, C. (1972b) 'Neuroendocrinological, behavioural and intellectual aspects of sexual differentiation in human development', in Ounsted, C. and Taylor, D. C. (eds.) *Gender Differences—Their Ontogeny and Significance*, London: Churchill.

Hutt, C. (1974) 'Sex: what's the difference?', *New Scientist*, **62**, 898, 405–7.

Hutt, C. (1978) 'Biological bases of psychological sex differences', *American Journal of Diseases of Children*, **132**, 170–7.

Ickes, W., Wicklund, R. A. and Ferris, C. B. (1973) 'Objective self-awareness and self-esteem', *Journal of Experimental Social Psychology*, **9**, 202–19.

Inhelder, B. and Piaget, J. (1958) *The Growth of Logical Thinking from Childhood to Adolescence*, New York: Basic Books.

Insel, P. and Jacobson, L. (1975) *What do you Expect?* Menlo Park, California: Cummings.

Jackson, D. N. and Messick, S. J. (1957) 'A note on ethnocentrism and the acquiescent response set', *Journal of Abnormal and Social Psychology*, **54**, 132–4.

Jackson, P. W. (1968) *Life in Classrooms*, New York: Holt, Rinehart and Winston.

Jackson, P. W. and Lahaderne, H. M. (1967) 'Inequalities of teacher pupil contacts', *Psychology in the Schools*, **4**, 204–8.

Jacobs, A. (1974) 'Use of feedback in groups', in Jacobs, A. and Spradlin, W. (eds.) *Group as an Agent of Change*, New York: Behavioral Publications.

Jacobs, L., Bergscheld, E. and Walster, E. (1971) 'Self-esteem and attraction', *Journal of Personality and Social Psychology*, **17**, 84–91.

Jahoda, M. (1975) 'The roots of prejudice', *New Community*, **4**, 179–87.

James, W. (1890) *Principles of Psychology*, New York: Holt, Rinehart and Winston.

Janis, I. L. et al. (1959) *Personality and Persuasability*, New Haven: Yale University Press.

Jersild, A. T. (1951) 'Self understanding in childhood and adolescence', *American Psychologist*, **6**, 122–6.

Jersild, A. T. (1952) *In Search of Self*, New York: Teachers' College, Columbia University.

Jersild, A. T. (1955) *When Teachers Face Themselves*, New York: Teachers' College, Columbia University.

Johnson, W. R., Fretz, B. and Johnson, J. A. (1968) 'Changes in self-concept during a physical development programme', *Research Quarterly*, **39**, 560–5.

Joiner, L. M., Erickson, E. L., Crittenden, J. B. and Stevenson, V. M. (1969) 'Predicting the academic achievement of the acoustically impaired using intelligence and self-concept of ability', *Journal of Special Education*, **3**, 425–31.

Jones, E. E. (1964) *Ingratiation*, New York: Appleton-Century-Crofts.

Jones, J. G. and Grieneeks, L. (1970) 'Measures of self perception as predictors of scholastic achievement', *Journal of Educational Research*, **63**, 201–3.

Jones, M. C. (1957) 'The later career of boys who were early or late maturing', *Child Development*, **28**, 113–28.

Jones, M. C. (1958) 'A study of socialisation at the high school level', *Journal of Genetic Psychology*, **93**, 87–111.

Jones, M. C. and Baxley, N. (1950) 'Physical maturing among boys as related to behavior', *Journal of Educational Psychology*, **41**, 129–48.

Jones, M. C. and Mussen, P. H. (1958) 'Self conceptions, motivations and interpersonal attitudes of early and late maturing girls', *Child Development*, **29**, 491–501.

Jones, P. (1977) 'Sport and self-esteem in English and West Indian children', unpublished PhD thesis, Guildford: Surrey University.

Jordan, J. (1980) 'Self-concept of primary school children', unpublished PhD thesis, University of Lancaster.

Jorgensen, E. C. and Howell, R. J. (1969) 'Changes in self, ideal self correlations from ages 8 through 18', *Journal of Social Psychology*, **79**, 63–7.

Jourard, S. M. (1958) *Personal Adjustment*, New York: Macmillan.

Jourard, S. (1971) *Self Disclosure*, New York: Wiley.

Jourard, S. M. and Secord, P. F. (1954) 'Body size and body cathexis', *Journal of Consulting Psychology*, **18**, 184.

Jourard, S. M. and Secord, P. F. (1955a) 'Body cathexis and personality', *British Journal of Psychology*, **46**, 130–8.

Jourard, S. M. and Secord, P. F. (1955b) 'Body cathexis and the ideal female figure', *Journal of Abnormal and Social Psychology*, **50**, 243–6.

Kagan, J. (1958) 'The concept of identification', *Psychology Review*, **65**, 296–305.

Kagan, J. (1964) 'The acquisition and significance of sex typing and sex role identity', in Hoffman, M. and Hoffman, L. (eds.) *Review of Child Development Research*, vol. 1, New York: Russell Sage.

Kagan, J. and Moss, H. A. (1962) *Birth to Maturity*, New York: Wiley.

Kahle, L., Kukla, R. and Klingel, D. (1980) 'Low adolescent self-esteem leads to multiple interpersonal problems', *Journal of Personality and Social Psychology*, **39**, 496–502.

Kaltsounis, T. and Nelson, J. L. (1968) 'The mythology of student teaching', *Journal of Teacher Education*, **19**, 277–81.

Kanfer, F. (1971) 'The maintenance of behavior of self generated stimulus and reinforcement', in Jacobs, A. and Sachs, L. (eds.) *The Psychology of Private Events*, New York: Academic Press.

Kaplan, H. (1975) *Self Attitudes and Delinquent Behavior*, Pacific Palisades, California: Goodyear.

Kaplan, J. and Pokorny, D. (1969) 'Self derogation and psycho-social adjustment', *Journal of Nervous and Mental Diseases*, **149**, 421–34.

Kardiner, A. and Ovesey, L. (1951) *The Mark of Oppression*, New York: Norton.

Kates, S. and Diab, D. (1955) 'Authoritarian ideology and attitudes on parent–child relationships', *Journal of Abnormal and Social Psychology*, **51**, 13–16.

Katz, I. (1964) 'Review of evidence relating to effects of desegregation on the intellectual performance of Negroes', *American Psychologist*, **19**, 381–9.

Katz, I. (1969) 'A catalogue of personality approaches to Negro performances', *Journal of Social Issues*, **30**, 13–28.

Katz, P. and Zigler, E. (1967) 'Self-image disparity: a developmental approach', *Journal of Personality and Social Psychology*, **5**, 186–95.

Katz, P., Zigler, E. and Zelk, S. R. (1975) 'Children's self-image disparity', *Developmental Psychology*, **11**, 546–50.

Katzenmeyer, W. and Stenner, A. J. (1977) 'Estimation of the invariance of factor structure across sex and race', *Educational and Psychological Measurement*, **37**, 111–19.

Kay, R. S. (1972) 'Self-concept and level of aspiration in 3rd and 4th grade children', unpublished PhD thesis, Purdue University.

Keeve, P. J. (1967) 'Perpetuating phantom handicaps in schoolchildren', *Exceptional Children*, **33**, 539–44.

Keller, A., Ford, L. H. and Meacham, J. (1978) 'Dimensions of self-concept in pre-school children', *Developmental Psychology*, **14**, 483–9.

Kellogg, R. L. (1969) 'A direct approach to sex role identification of school related objects', *Psychological Reports*, **24**, 839–41.

Kelly, G. A. (1955) *The Psychology of Personal Constructs*, New York: Norton.

Kenny, D. T. (1956) 'The influence of social desirability on discrepancy measures between real self and ideal self', *Journal of Consulting and Clinical Psychology*, **20**, 315–19.

Kesey, K. (1962) *One Flew Over the Cuckoo's Nest*, New York: Viking Press.

Kestenberg, J. S. (1961) 'Menarche', in Lorand, S. and Sehneer, H. (eds.) *Adolescents*, New York: Hoeber Press.

Khanna, J. L. (1971) 'Training for educators for hard core areas', unpublished paper, 17th Congress International Association of Applied Psychology, Liège.

Kifer, E. (1973) 'The effects of school achievement on the affective traits of the learner', unpublished PhD thesis, University of Chicago.

Kilpatrick, F. P. and Cantril, H. (1965) 'Self-anchoring scaling. A measure of individual unique reality worlds', in Hartley, R. E. and Hartley, E. L. (eds.) *Readings in Psychology*, New York: Crowell.

Kim, Y. K. (1967) 'Comparison of self concept of delinquent and nondelinquent boys', unpublished MA thesis, Seoul University.

Kimano, D. (1960) 'An investigation on the meaning of human figure drawing', *Journal of Clinical Psychology*, **16**, 429–30.

Kinch, J. W. (1963) 'A formalised theory of the self concept', *American Journal of Sociology*, **68**, 481–6.

King, M. (1976) 'Changes in self-acceptance of college students associated with the encounter model class', *Small Group Behavior*, **7**, 379–84.

King, M. and Payne, D. (1973) 'The impact of marathon and prolonged sensitivity training on self acceptance', *Small Group Behavior*, **4**, 414–23.

Kirchner, P. and Vondraek, S. (1975) 'Perceived sources of esteem in early childhood', *Journal of Genetic Psychology*, **126**, 169–76.

Kirkpatrick, S. W. and Sanders, D. M. (1978) 'Body image stereotypes: A developmental comparison', *Journal of Genetic Psychology*, **132**, 87–96.

Klaus, W. H. and Hodge, S. E. (1978) 'Self esteem in open and traditional classrooms', *Journal of Educational Psychology*, **70**, 701–5.

Knight, O. (1969) 'Self concept of Negro and white educable mentally retarded boys', *Journal of Negro Education*, **38**, 143–6.

Koff, E., Rierdan, J. and Silverstone, E. (1978) 'Changes in representation of body image as a function of menarcheal status', *Developmental Psychology*, **14**, 635–42.

Kohn, M. L. and Schooler, C. (1969) 'Class, occupation and orientation', *American Sociology Review*, **34**, 659–78.

Korman, A. K. (1966) 'The self esteem variable in vocational choice', *Journal of Applied Psychology*, **50**, 479–86.

Korman, A. K. (1969) 'Self esteem as a moderator in vocational choice: replications and extensions', *Journal of Applied Psychology*, **53**, 188–92.

Kostrubala, T. (1977) *The Joy of Running*, New York: Pocket Books.

Krasno, R. M. (1971) 'A survey of student teaching practices', Report for New England Program in Teacher Education, ERIC ED 067369.

Kretschmer, E. (1925) *Physique and Character*, London: Routledge and Kegan Paul.

Krop, H., Calhoun, B. and Verrier, R. (1971) 'Modification of the self concept of emotionally disturbed children by covert reinforcement', *Behavior Therapy*, **2**, 201–4.

Krug, S. and Henry, T. (1974) 'Personality, motivation and adolescent drug use patterns', *Journal of Counseling Psychology*, **21**, 440–5.

Kuhn, M. H. (1960) 'Self attitudes by age, sex and professional training', *Sociology Quarterly*, **1**, 39–55.

Kuhn, M. H. and McPartland, T. S. (1954) 'An empirical investigation of self attitudes', *American Sociology Review*, **19**, 68–76.

Kuiper, N. (1978) 'Depression and causal attribution for success and failure', *Journal of Personality and Social Psychology*, **36**, 236–46.

Kutner, B. (1958) 'Patterns of mental functioning associated with prejudice in children', *Psychology Monographs*, **72**, 7.

La Benne, W. D. (1965) 'Pupil teacher interaction in a senior ungraded school', unpublished PhD thesis, University of Michigan.

La Benne, W. and Green, B. (1969) *Educational Implications of Self-Concept Theory*, Pacific Palisades, California: Goodyear.

Lacey, C. (1970) *Hightown Grammar*, Manchester: Manchester University Press.

Lamarche, L. (1968) 'Validation of the TSCS', unpublished PhD, University of Montreal.

Lambert, M., Segger, J., Staley, J. and Spenser, B. (1978) 'Reported self-concept and self-actualising value changes as a function of academic classes with wilderness experience', *Perceptual and Motor Skills*, **46**, 1035–40.

Lampl, M. (1968) 'Defensiveness, dogmatism and self-esteem', *Dissertation Abstracts*, **29**, 2194B.

Lane, J. and Muller, D. (1977) 'The effect of altering self descriptive behavior on self-concept and classroom behaviour', *Journal of Psychology*, **97**, 115–25.

Lang, R. J. and Vernon, P. E. (1977) 'Dimensionality of the perceived self', *British Journal of Social and Clinical Psychology*, **16**, 363–72.

La Pierre, R. T. (1934) 'Attitudes versus actions', *Social Forces*, **13**, 230–7.

Larned, D. T. and Muller, D. (1979) 'Development

of self-concept in grades one thru nine',
Journal of Psychology, **102**, 143–8.

Larson, J. L. (1972) 'The effects of a human
relations workshop on personal and interpersonal perceptions', *Dissertation Abstracts*,
33A, 2716.

Lawrence, D. (1971) 'The effects of counselling on
retarded readers', *Educational Research*, **13**,
119–24.

Lawrence, D. (1972) 'Counselling of retarded
readers by non-professionals', *Educational
Research*, **15**, 48–51.

Lawrence, D. (1973) *Improved Reading Through
Counselling*, London: Ward Lock.

Lawrence, E. A. and Winschell, J. F. (1973) 'Self-
concept and the retarded: research and issues',
Exceptional Children, **39**, 310–19.

Lawson, M. (1980) 'Development of body build
stereotypes, peer ratings and self-esteem in
Australian children', *Journal of Psychology*,
104, 111–18.

Lazowick, L. M. (1955) 'On the nature of identification', *Journal of Abnormal and Social
Psychology*, **51**, 175–83.

Leahy, R. L. and Huard, C. (1976) 'Role taking and
self image disparity in children', *Developmental Psychology*, **12**, 509–64.

Lecky, P. (1945) *Self Consistency*, New York:
Island Press.

Lembo, J. M. (1971) *Why Teachers Fail*, New
York: Merrill.

Lepper, M. and Greene, D. (1975) 'Turning play
into work', *Journal of Personality and Social
Psychology*, **31**, 479–86.

Lerner, R. M., Karabenick, S. A. and Meisels, M.
(1975) 'Effects of age and sex on the development of personal space schemata towards body
build', *Journal of Genetic Psychology*, **127**,
91–101.

Lerner, R. M., Karabenick, S. A. and Stuart, J.
(1973) 'Relations between physical attractiveness, body attitudes and self-concept among
college students', *Journal of Psychology*, **85**,
119–29.

Lerner, R. M. and Korn, S. J. (1972) 'Development
of body build stereotypes in males', *Child
Development*, **43**, 908–20.

Lerner, R. M., Orlos, J. and Knapp, J. (1976)
'Physical attractiveness and self-concept in
late adolescence', *Adolescence*, **11**, 317–26.

Levine, E. (1973) 'Affective education', *Psychology
in the Schools*, **10**, 147–50.

Levi-Ran, A. (1974) 'Gender role differentiation in
hermaphrodites', *Archives of Sexual Behavior*,
3, 391–424.

Levitin, T. and Chananie, J. (1972) 'Responses of
female primary teachers to sex typed behaviours in male and female children', *Child
Development*, **43**, 1309–16.

Lewin, K. (1936) *Principles of Topological
Psychology*, New York: McGraw-Hill.

Lewis, A. R. J. (1971) 'Self-concepts of adolescent
ESN boys', *British Journal of Educational
Psychology*, **41**, 222–3.

Lewis, H. G. and Purkey, W. W. (1978) 'Factories
or families', unpublished paper, University of
Florida.

Lewis, J. and Adank, R. (1975) 'Intercorrelations
among measures of IQ, achievement, self
esteem and anxiety in two groups of elementary school pupils exposed to two different
models of instruction', *Educational and
Psychology Measurement*, **35**, 499–501.

Lewis, M. (1977) 'The social nexus', unpublished
paper to the International Society for
Behavioural Development Conference, Pavia.

Lewis, M. and Brooks, J. (1974) 'Self, other and
fear', in Lewis, M. and Rosenblum, L. (eds.)
The Origins of Fear, New York: Wiley.

Liebeman, M. A. (1973) *Encounter Groups*, New
York: Basic Books.

Lifshitz, M. (1975) 'Social differentiation and
organisation of the Ronchach in fatherless and
two parental children', *Journal of Clinical
Psychology*, **31**, 126–30.

Lin, N. (1973) *The Study of Human Communication*, Indianapolis: Bobbs Merrill.

Linton, H. and Graham, E. (1959) 'Personality
Correlates of Persuasability', in Hooland, G.
and Janis, J. (eds.) *Personality and Persuasability*, New Haven: Yale University Press.

Lipsitt, L. P. (1958) 'A self concept scale for
children and its relationship to the children's
form of the MAS', *Child Development*, **29**,
463–9.

Little, J. and Ramrez, A. (1976) 'Ethnicity of
subject and test administrator: their effect on
self esteem', *Journal of Social Psychology*, **99**,
149–50.

Livesley, W. J. and Bromley, D. B. (1973) *Person
Perception in Childhood and Adolescence*,
Wiley: London.

Lockwood, G., Salyberg, H. and Heckel, R. V.
(1978) 'The effects of videotape feedback of
self concept', *Journal of Clinical Psychology*,
34, 718–21.

Loeb, J. and Price, J. R. (1966) 'Mother and child
personality characteristics related to parental
marital status in child guidance cases', *Journal
of Consulting and Clinical Psychology*, **XX**,
115–17.

Lomax, P. M. (1977) 'Self concepts of girls in a
context of disadvantaging environment',
Educational Review, **29**, 107–19.

Long, B. H. (1969) 'Critique of Soares and Soares'
self perceptions of culturally disadvantaged
children', *American Educational Research
Journal*, **6**, 710–11.

Long, B. H. and Henderson, E. H. (1968) 'Self-
social concepts of disadvantaged school
beginners', *Journal of Genetic Psychology*,
113, 41–51.

Long, B. H., Henderson, E. H. and Ziller, R. C. (1967) 'Developmental changes in the self-concept during middle childhood', *Merrill-Palmer Quarterly*, **13**, 201–19.

Long, B. H., Ziller, R. C. and Henderson, E. H. (1968) 'Developmental changes in the self-concept during adolescence', *School Review*, **76**, 210–30.

Loosemore, J. and Carlton, R. A. (1977) 'The student teacher', in Carlton, R. A. et al. (eds.) *Education Change and Society*, Toronto: Gage.

Lortie, D. C. (1975) *School Teacher*, Chicago: University Chicago Press.

Louden, D. M. (1977) 'Conflict and change among West Indian parents and adolescents in Britain', *Educational Research*, **20**, 44–53.

Ludwig, D. J. (1969) 'Self perception and draw a person test', *Journal of Projective Testing and Personality Assessment*, **33**, 257–61.

Lundgren, D. and Schwab, M. (1974) 'Sex differences in the social bases of self esteem', *Personality and Social Psychology Bulletin*, **1**, 316–18.

Lundgren, D. and Schwab, M. (1977) 'Perceived appraisals by others, self-esteem and anxiety', *Journal of Psychology*, **97**, 205–14.

Lynch, S. (1968) 'Intense human experience', unpublished PhD thesis, University of Florida.

Lynn, D. B. (1972) 'Determinants of intellectual growth in women', *School Review*, **80**, 241–60.

McCandless, B. (1967) *Children, Behavior and Development*, New York: Holt, Rinehart and Winston.

McCandless, B. (1970) *Adolescents*, Hinsdale, Illinois: Dryden Press.

McCarthey, J. and Yancey, W. L. (1971) 'Uncle Tom and Mr Charlie', *American Journal of Sociology*, **76**, 648–72.

McClain, A. D. (1971) 'The effect of group counselling on the self-concepts of disabled readers', *Dissertation Abstracts*, **31**, (11A) 5770.

McClain, E. W. (1970) 'Personal growth for teachers in training through self-study', *Journal of Teacher Education*, **21**, 372–7.

McCroskey, J. C., Larson, P. and Knapp, T. (1971) *An Introduction to Interpersonal Communication*, New York: Prentice Hall.

McDonald, R. L. and Gynther, M. D. (1965) 'Relationships of self and ideal self descriptions with sex, race and class in southern adolescents', *Journal of Personality and Social Psychology*, **1**, 85–8.

McFarland, G. N. (1971) 'The effects of sensitivity training utilised as in service training', *Dissertation Abstracts*, **31A**, 4013.

McGinley, P. and McGinley, H. (1970) 'Reading groups as psychological groups', *Journal of Experimental Education*, **39**, 36–42.

McGuinness, D. (1975) 'Away from a unisex psychology', *Perception*, **6**, 22–32.

McGuire, W. J. et al. (1978) 'Salience of ethnicity in the spontaneous self concept as a function of one's ethnic distinctiveness in the social environment', *Journal of Personality and Social Psychology*, **36**, 511–20.

McIntire, W. G. (1973) 'The impact of T group experience on level of self actualisation', *Small Group Behavior*, **4**, 459–65.

McIntosh, N. and Smith, D. (1974) 'The extent of racial discrimination', London: Political and Economic Planning, **XL**, Broadsheet 547.

McMichael, P. (1977) 'Self esteem, behaviour and reading skills in infant school children', in Reid, J. and Donaldson, H. (eds.) *Reading: Problems and Practices*, London: Ward Lock.

McNeil, J. D. (1964) 'Programmed instruction versus usual classroom procedures in teaching boys to read', *American Educational Research Journal*, **1**, 113–20.

Maccoby, E. E. and Jacklin, C. N. (1974) *The Psychology of Sex Differences*, Stanford: Stanford University Press.

Maehr, M. L. (1974) *Socio-cultural origins of Achievement*, Monterey, California: Brooks/Cole.

Machover, K. (1949) *Personality Projection in the Drawing of the Human Figure*, Springfield: Thomas Press.

Mahoney, E. and Finch, M. (1976) 'The dimensionability of body cathexis', *Journal of Psychology*, **92**, 277–9.

Mahoney, E. and Finch, M. (1976) 'Body cathexis and self esteem', *Journal of Social Psychology*, **99**, 251–8.

Mahoney, M. J. (1974) *Cognition and Behavior Modification*, Cambridge: Ballinger.

Mannarino, A. P. (1978) 'Friendship patterns and self-concept development in pre-adolescent males', *Journal of Genetic Psychology*, **133**, 105–10.

Mannheim, B. (1966) 'Reference groups, membership groups and the self image', *Sociometry*, **29**, 263–79.

Many, M. A. and Many, W. A. (1975) 'The relationship between self-esteem and anxiety in grades 4 through 8', *Educational and Psychology Measurement*, **35**, 1017–21.

Maracek, J. and Mettee, D. (1972) 'Avoidance of continued success as a function of self-esteem, level of esteem certainty and responsibility for success', *Journal of Personality and Social Psychology*, **22**, 98–107.

Marcia, J. E. (1966) 'Development and validation of ego identity status', *Journal of Personality and Social Psychology*, **3**, 551–8.

Marcia, J. E. (1967) 'Ego identity status: relationships to change in self-esteem, general adjustment, and authoritarianism', *Journal of Personality*, **35**, 118–33.

Marten, J. and Fitzpatrick, J. (1968) *Delinquent*

Behavior, New York: Random House.

Maslow, A. H. (1954) *Motivation and Personality*, New York: Harper and Row.

Maslow, A. H. (1968) *Towards Psychology of Being*, Princetown, Mass.: Van Nostrand.

Mason, E. P. (1954) 'Some factors in self judgement', *Journal of Clinical Psychology*, **10**, 336–40.

Mason, J. and Blumberg, A. (1969) 'Perceived educational value of the classroom and teacher-pupil interpersonal relationship', *Journal of Secondary Education*, **44**, 135–9.

Masters, J. E. (1971) 'Social comparison by young children', *Young Children*, **27**, 37–60.

Masters, J. and Stanrock, J. (1976) 'Studies in the self regulation of behavior', *Developmental Psychology*, **12**, 334–48.

Mathes, E. W. and Kahn, A. (1975) 'Physical attractiveness, happiness, neuroticism and self-esteem', *Journal of Psychology*, **90**, 27–30.

Matteson, D. R. (1977) 'Exploration and commitment', *Journal of Youth and Adolescence*, **6**, 353–74.

Mazer, G. E. (1971) 'The effects of social class stereotyping on teacher expectation', *Psychology in the Schools*, **8**, 373–8.

Mead, G. H. (1934) *Mind, Self and Society*, Chicago: University of Chicago Press.

Meador, B. D. and Rogers, C. R. (1979) 'Person centred therapy', in Corsini, R. (ed.) *Current Psychotherapies*, Ithaca: Peacock.

Medinnus, G. R. and Curtis, E. J. (1963) 'The relation between maternal self-acceptance and child acceptance', *Journal of Consulting Psychology*, **27**, 542–4.

Mednick, S. A. (1960) 'Body image, personality and chi square', *Contemporary Psychology*, **5**, 316–17.

Messer, S. and Lewis, M. (1972) 'Social class and sex differences in the attachment and play behaviour of the year-old infant', *Merrill-Palmer Quarterly*, **18**, 295–306.

Mettee, D. R. (1971) 'Rejection of unexpected success as a function of the negative consequences of accepting success', *Journal of Personality and Social Psychology*, **71**, 332–41.

Meyer, W. J. and Thompson, G. (1956) 'Teacher interaction with boys as contrasted with girls', *Journal of Educational Psychology*, **47**, 385–97.

Meyerowitz, J. H. (1962) 'Self derogations in young retardates and special case placements', *Child Development*, **33**, 443–51.

Michael, J., Plass, A. and Leey, Y. (1973) 'A comparison of the self report and the observed report in the measurement of the self-concept', *Educational and Psychology Measurement*, **33**, 433–9.

Michael, W., Smith, R. and Michael, L. (1975) 'The factorial validity of the Piers–Harris

children's self-concept scale', *Educational and Psychological Measurement*, **35**, 405–14.

Michael, W. B., Smith, R. A. and Michael, L. (1978) 'Further development and validation of a self-concept measure involving school related activities', *Educational and Psychological Measurement*, **38**, 527–36.

Milgram, R. M. and Milgram, N. A. (1976) 'Self concept differences in student teachers in primary, elementary, secondary and special education', *Psychology in the Schools*, **13**, 439–41.

Miller, D. R. (1963) 'The study of social relationships', in Koch, S. (ed.) *Psychology: a Study of a Science*, vol. 5, New York: McGraw-Hill.

Miller, D. and Ross, M. (1975) 'Self serving bases in the attribution of causality', *Psychology Bulletin*, **82**, 581–96.

Miller, H. and Woock, R. (1970) *Social Foundations of Urban Education*, Hinsdale, Illinois: Dryden Press.

Miller, K. and Coleman, J. C. 'Attitudes to the future as a function of age, sex and school leaving age' (paper in preparation, 1981).

Milner, D. (1973) 'Racial identification and preference in "black" British children', *European Journal of Social Psychology*, **3**, 281–95.

Milner, D. (1975) *Children and Race*, London: Pelican.

Mintz, R. and Muller, D. (1977) 'Academic achievement as a function of specific and global measures of self concept', *Journal of Psychology*, **97**, 53–8.

Minuchin, P. (1964) 'Sex role concepts and sex typing in childhood as a function of school and home environments', *Child Development*, 1033–48.

Mischel, W., Ebbesen, E. and Zeiss, A. R. (1976) 'Determinants of selective memory about the self', *Journal of Consulting and Clinical Psychology*, **44**, 92–103.

Mitchell, J. V. (1959) 'Goal setting behaviour as a function of self acceptance, over and under achievement and related personality variables', *Journal of Educational Psychology*, **50**, 93–104.

Miyamoto, S. and Dornbusch, S. M. (1956) 'A test of interactionist hypothesis of self-conception', *American Journal of Sociology*, **61**, 399–403.

Moffett, L. A. (1975) 'Sex differences on self-concept', *Psychological Reports*, **37**, 74.

Monge, R. H. (1973) 'Developmental trends in factors of adolescent self-concept', *Developmental Psychology*, **8**, 3, 382–93.

Montemayer, M. and Eisen, M. (1977) 'The development of self conceptions from childhood to adolescence', *Developmental Psychology*, **13**, 314–19.

Moran, M., Michael, W. B. and Dembo, M. (1978) 'The factorial validity of three frequently employed self report measures of self-concept',

Educational and Psychology Measurement, **38**, 547–63.

Moreland, J. et al. (1979) 'Sex role self concept and career decision making', *Journal of Counseling Psychology*, **26**, 329–36.

Morland, J. K. (1958) 'Racial recognition by nursery school children', *Social Forces*, **37**, 132–7.

Morgan, J. B. (1944) 'Effect of non-rational factors on inductive reasoning', *Journal of Experimental Psychology*, **34**, 159–68.

Morran, D. and Stockton, R. (1980) 'Effect of self-concept on group member reception of positive and negative feedback', *Journal of Counseling Psychology*, **27**, 260–7.

Morrison, T. L. and Thomas, D. (1975) 'Self-esteem and classroom participation', *Journal of Educational Research*, **68**, 374–7.

Morrison, T. L., Thomas, D. and Weaver, S. J. (1973) 'Self-esteem and self-estimates of academic performances', *Journal of Consulting and Clinical Psychology*, **41**, 412–15.

Morse, S. and Gergen, K. J. (1970) 'Social comparison, self consistency and the concept of self', *Journal of Personality and Social Psychology*, **16**, 148–56.

Morse, W. C. (1964) 'Self-concept in a school setting', *Childhood Education*, December, 195–8.

Moss, H. (1967) 'Sex, age and state as determinants of mother–infant interaction', *Merrill-Palmer Quarterly*, **13**, 19–36.

Mossman, B. and Ziller, R. (1968) 'Self-esteem and consistency of social behavior', *Journal of Abnormal and Social Psychology*, **73**, 363–7.

Motoori, T. (1963) 'A study of juvenile delinquents by the self-concept', *Family Court Probation*, **2**, 44–9.

Mullener, N. and Laird, J. D. (1971) 'Some developmental changes in the organisation of self-evaluations', *Developmental Psychology*, **5**, 237–43.

Muller, D. G. and Leonetti, R. (1972) 'Primary self-concept scale', National Consortia for Bilingual Education, Washington D.C.: Office of Education (DHEW).

Muller, D. G. and Spuhler, R. (1976) 'The effects of experimentally induced changes in self concept on associative learning', *Journal of Psychology*, **92**, 89–95.

Murphy, G. (1947) *Personality, A Bio-Social Approach*, New York: Harper and Row.

Murray, E. (1972) 'Students' perceptions of self-actualising and non self-actualising teachers', *Journal of Teacher Education*, **23**, 383–7.

Murray, H. A. (1953) 'Outline of a conception of personality', in Murray, H. A. and Kluckhohn (eds.) *Personality in Nature, Society and Culture*, New York: Knopf.

Musa, K. and Roach, M. (1973) 'Adolescent appearance and self-concept', *Adolescence*, **8**, 387–94.

Mussen, P. G. and Jones, M. (1957) 'Self conceptions, motivations and interpersonal attitudes of late and early maturing boys', *Child Development*, **28**, 243–56.

Mussen, P. H. and Jones, M. C. (1958) 'The behaviour inferred motivations of late and early maturing boys', *Child Development*, **29**, 61–7.

Mussen, P. H. and Kagan, J. (1958) 'Group conformity and perception of parents', *Child Development*, **29**, 57–60.

Mussen, P., Young, H., Gaddini, R. and Morrante, L. (1963) 'The influence of father–son relationships on adolescent personality and attitudes', *Journal of Child Psychology and Psychiatry*, **4**, 3–16.

Myers, G., Myers, M., Goldberg, A. and Welch, C. (1969) 'Effects of feedback on interpersonal sensitivity in training groups', *Journal of Applied Behavioral Science*, **5**, 175–85.

Myrdal, G. (1944) *The American Dilemma*, New York: Harper and Row.

Nash, R. (1973) *Classrooms Observed*, London: Routledge and Kegan Paul.

Newcomb, T. M. (1956) 'Prediction of interpersonal attraction', *American Psychologist*, **11**, 575–86.

Newcomb, T. M. (1961) *The Acquaintance Process*, New York: Holt, Rinehart and Winston.

Nicholls, J. (1975) 'Causal attributions and other achievement related conditions', *Journal of Personality and Social Psychology*, **31**, 379–89.

Nicholls, J. G. (1979) 'The development of perception of own attainment and causal attribution for success and failure in reading', *Journal of Educational Psychology*, **71**, 94–9.

Nichols, W. J. (1968) 'A study on the effects of tutoring on the self concept', unpublished PhD thesis, Ball State University.

Nisbett, R. and Gordon, A. (1967) 'Self-esteem and susceptibility to social influence', *Journal of Personality and Social Psychology*, **22**, 268–76.

Nobles, W. W. (1973) 'Psychological research and the black self-concept: a critical review', *Journal of Social Issues*, **29**, 11–31.

Northway, M. L. and Detweiler, J. I. (1956) 'Sociometry in education', *Sociometry and the Science of Man*, **18**, 271–5.

Nystul, M. S. (1976) 'The effect of birth order and family size on self concept', *Australian Psychologist*, **11**, 199–201.

Offer, D. (1974) *The Psychological World of the Teenager* (revd ed.), New York: Basic Books.

Ohlsson, M. (1975) 'Effects of physical fitness on mental performance', Report No. 62, Institute of Applied Psychology, University of Stockholm.

Olsen, C. (1969) 'The effects of enrichment tutor-ing on self-concept achievement and measured intelligence on male underachievers in an inner-city primary school', unpublished PhD, Michigan State University.

O'Malley, P. and Bachman, J. (1979) 'Self esteem and education', *Journal of Personality and Social Psychology*, **37**, 1153–9.

Omwake, K. (1954) 'The relation between accept-ance of self and acceptance of others shown by three personality inventories', *Journal of Con-sulting and Clinical Psychology*, **18**, 6, 443–6.

Osgood, C. E., Suci, G. J. and Tannenbaum, P. H. (1957) *The Measurement of Meaning*, Urbana: University of Illinois.

Palardy, M. J. (1969) 'What teachers believe, what children achieve', *Elementary School Journal*, **69**, 370–4.

Palfrey, C. F. (1973) 'Headteachers' expectations and their pupils' self-concepts', *Educational Research*, **15**, 123–7.

Parish, T. and Copeland, T. (1979) 'Relationship between self-concept and evaluation of parents and stepfathers', *Journal of Psychology*, **101**, 135–8.

Parish, T. and Dostal, J. (1980) 'Relationship between evaluation of self and parents by children from intact and divorced families', *Journal of Psychology*, **104**, 35–8.

Parish, T. and Eads, G. (1977) 'The personal attribute inventory as a self-concept measure', *Educational and Psychological Measurement*, **37**, 1063–7.

Parish, T. S., Eads, G. M. and Adams, D. E. (1977) 'The personal attribute inventory as a self-concept scale', *Psychological Reports*, Dec. pt 2, 1141–2.

Parish, T. S. and Taylor, J. C. (1978) 'The personal attribute inventory: a report on its validity and reliability as a self-concept scale', *Educational and Psychological Measurement*, **38**, 565–70.

Parker, C. and Huff, V. (1975) 'The effects of group counselling on rigidity', *Small Group Behavior*, **6**, 402–13.

Parker, J. (1966) 'Relationship of self report to inferred self-concept', *Educational and Psychological Measurement*, **26**, 691–700.

Parrish, L. H. and Kok, M. R. (1980) 'Misinter-pretation hinders mainstreaming', *Yearbook of Special Education*, **6**, No. 24.

Parsons, T. (1955) 'Family structure and the socialisation of the child', in Parsons and Bales (eds.) *Family, Socialisation and Interaction Process*, New York: Glencoe Free Press.

Payne, B. and Dunn, C. J. (1972) 'An analysis of the change in self-concept by racial descent', *Journal of Negro Education*, **41**, 156–63.

Payne, D. E. and Mussen, P. H. (1956) 'Parent–child relations and further identification among adolescent boys', *Journal of Abnormal and Social Psychology*, **52**, 358–62.

Payne, J., Drummond, A. W. and Lunghi, M. (1970) 'Changes in the self concept of school-leavers who participated in an arctic ex-pedition', *British Journal of Educational Psychology*, **40**, 211–16.

Peck, R. F. and Tucker, J. A. (1973) 'Research on teacher education', in Travers, R. (ed.) *Second Handbook on Research in Teaching*, Chicago: Rand McNally.

Percell, L. P., Berwick, P. T. and Beigal, A. (1974) 'The effects of assertive training on self-concept and anxiety', *Archives of General Psychology*, **31**, 502–4.

Perkins, H. V. (1958) 'Factors influencing change in children's self-concepts', *Child Develop-ment*, **29**, 203–20.

Peterson, F. (1972) 'Marijuana smokers and non-smokers—a self-concept study', *Dissertation Abstracts*, **32**, 10A, 5619.

Pettigrew, T. F. (1978) 'Placing Adam's argument in a broader perspective', *Social Psychology*, **41**, 58–61.

Phillips, E. L. (1951) 'Attitudes towards self and others', *Journal of Consulting and Clinical Psychology*, **15**, 1, 79–81.

Phillips, E. L. and Wolf, M. M. (1973) 'Behavior shaping works for delinquents', *Psychology Today*, **7**, 74–9.

Piaget, J. (1932) *The Moral Judgement of the Child*, London: Routledge and Kegan Paul.

Piaget, J. (1952) *The Origins of Intelligence in Children*, New York: International Univer-sities Press.

Piaget, J. (1954) *The Construction of Reality in the Child*, New York: Basic Books.

Piaget, J. and Inhelder, B. (1958) *The Growth of Logical Thinking*, London: Routledge and Kegan Paul.

Piers, E. V. (1969) *Manual of Piers–Harris Children's Self Concept Scale*, Nashville: Counsellor Recordings and Tests.

Piers, E. V. and Harris, D. (1964) 'Age and other correlates of self concept in children', *Journal of Educational Psychology*, **55**, 91–5.

Pigge, F. L. (1970) 'Children and their self concepts', *Childhood Education*, **47**, 107–8.

Pintler, M. H., Sears, P. S. and Sears, R. R. (1946) 'Effects of father separation on pre-school children's doll play aggression', *Child Development*, **17**, 219–43.

Portugues, S. and Feshback, N. D. (1972) 'Influence of sex and socioethnic factors upon imitation of teachers by elementary school children', *Child Development*, **43**, 981–9.

Powell, G. J. (1973) 'Self-concept in white and black children', in Willie, C., Kramer, B. M. and Brown, B. (eds.) *Racism and Mental Health*, Pittsburgh, Penn.: Pittsburgh Univer-sity Press.

Powell, G. J. and Fuller, M. (1973) 'Self-concept and school desegregation', *Journal of Ortho-*

psychiatry, **40**, 303–4.

Prescott, P. A. (1978) 'Sex differences on a measure of self-esteem: theoretical implications', *Journal of Genetic Psychology*, **132**, 67–86.

Primavera, L. H., Simon, W. E. and Primavera, A. M. (1974) 'The relationship between self-esteem, and academic achievement: an investigation of sex differences', *Psychology in the Schools*, **11**, 213–16.

Proshansky, H. and Newton, P. (1968) 'The nature and meaning of Negro self-identity', in Deutsh, M., Katz, I. and Jenson, A. (eds.) *Social Class, Race and Psychological Development*, New York: Holt, Rinehart and Winston.

Purkey, W. W. (1970) *Self-Concept and School Achievement*, New York: Prentice Hall.

Purkey, W. W. (1978) *Inviting School Success*, Belmont: Wadsworth.

Purkey, W. W., Graves, W. and Zelner, M. (1970) 'Self perceptions of pupils in an experimental elementary school', *Elementary School Journal*, **71**, 166–71.

Putnam, B., House, T. and Hansen, J. (1979) 'Sex differences in self-concept variables and vocational attitude maturity in adolescents', *Journal of Experimental Education*, 23–7.

Quarantelli, E. and Cooper, J. (1966) 'Self-conceptions and others', *Sociology Quarterly*, **7**, 281–97.

Rabban, M. (1950) 'Sex-role identification in young children in two diverse social groups', *Genetic Psychology Monographs*, **42**, 81–158.

Radke, M., Yarrow, M., Trager, H. G. and Davis, H. (1949) 'Social perceptions and attitudes of children', *Genetic Psychology Monographs*, **40**, 327–47.

Raimy, V. C. (1943) 'The self-concept as a factor in counseling and personality organisation', unpublished PhD thesis, Ohio State University.

Raimy, V. C. (1948) 'Self reference in counseling interviews', *Journal of Consulting and Clinical Psychology*, **12**, No. 3, 153–63.

Rainwater, L. (1966) 'Crucible of identity: the Negro lower class family', *Daedalus*, **95**, 172–217.

Randall, L. H. (1970) 'A comparison of the self-concept and personality of deaf high school students', unpublished MA thesis, University of Tennessee.

Rapaport, G. M. (1958) 'Ideal self instructions, MMPI profile changes and production of clinical improvement', *Journal of Consulting and Clinical Psychology*, **22**, 459–63.

Reed, H. B. (1962) 'Implications for science education of a teacher competence research', *Science Education*, December, 473–86.

Regan, J. W. (1975) 'Do people have inflated views of their own ability?', *Journal of Personality and Social Psychology*, **31**, 295–301.

Reich, S. and Geller, A. (1976a) 'Self-image of nurses', *Psychological Reports*, October, 401–2.

Reich, S. and Geller, A. (1976b) 'Self-image of social workers', *Psychological Reports*, October, 657–8.

Renbarger, R. N. (1969) 'An experimental investigation of the relationship between self esteem and academic achievement in a population of disadvantaged students', unpublished PhD, Michigan State University.

Rheingold, H. L. (1969) 'The social and socialising infant', in Goslin, D. A. (ed.) *Handbook of Socialization Theory and Research*, Chicago: Rand McNally.

Richardson, S. A., Hastorf, A. H. and Dornbusch, S. M. (1964) 'The effect of physical disability on the child's description of himself', *Child Development*, **35**, 893–907.

Richer, R. L. (1968) 'Schooling and the self-concept', *New Era*, **49**, 177–200.

Rimm, D. and Masters, J. (1979) *Behavior Therapy*, New York: Academic Press.

Rist, R. G. (1970) 'Student social class and teacher expectations', *Harvard Educational Review*, **40**, 411–51.

Roberts, J. (1972) *Self-Image and Delinquency*, Research Series No. 3, Department of Justice, New Zealand.

Robinson, J. and Shaver, P. (1969) *Measures of Social Psychological Attitudes*, Ann Arbor, Michigan: Institute for Social Research.

Robinson, M. and Jacobs, A. (1970) 'Focused videotape feedback and behaviour change in group psychotherapy', *Psychotherapy, Theory, Research and Practice*, **7**, 169–72.

Rogers, C. R. (1951) *Client-Centered Therapy*, Boston: Houghton Mifflin.

Rogers, C. R. (1956) 'Intellectualized psychotherapy', *Contemporary Psychology*, **1**, 357–8.

Rogers, C. R. (1959) 'A theory of therapy, personality and interpersonal relationships as developed in the client-centered framework', in Koch, S. (ed.) *Psychology: a study of a science*, vol. 3, 184–256.

Rogers, C. R. (1961) *On Becoming a Person*, Boston: Houghton Mifflin.

Rogers, C. R. (1969) *Freedom to Learn*, Columbus, Ohio: Merrill.

Rogers, C. R. (1970) *Encounter Groups*, New York: Harper and Row.

Rogers, C. R. (1974) 'In retrospect', *American Psychology*, **29**, 115.

Rogers, C. R. and Dymond, R. F. (1954) *Psychotherapy and Personality Change*, Chicago: University Press.

Rosen, B. (1978) 'Self-concept disturbance among mothers who abuse their children', *Psychological Reports*, **43**, 323–6.

Rosen, E. (1956) 'Self-appraisal and perceived desirability of MMPI personality traits',

Journal of Counseling Psychology, **3**, 44–51.

Rosen, G. and Ross, A. (1968) 'Relationship of body image to self-concept', *Journal of Consulting and Clinical Psychology*, **32**, 100.

Rosenberg, F. and Simmons, R. G. (1975) 'Sex differences in self-concept in adolescence', *Sex Roles*, **1**, 147–59.

Rosenberg, M. (1955) 'Factors influencing change in occupational choice', in Layerfield and Rosenberg (eds.) *The Language of Social Research*, 250–9, New York: Glencoe Free Press.

Rosenberg, M. (1965) *Society and the Adolescent Self-Image*, Princeton: Princeton University Press.

Rosenberg, M. (1968) 'When dissonance fails', *Journal of Personality and Social Psychology*, **4**, 28–42.

Rosenberg, M. (1973) 'Which significant others?', *American Behavioral Scientist*, **16**, 829–60.

Rosenberg, M. and Simmons, R. (1972) *Black and White Self-Esteem: the Urban School Child*, Washington, D.C.: Rosie Monograph Series, American Sociological Association.

Rosenthal, J. H. (1973) 'Self-esteem in dyslexic children', *Academic Therapy*, **9**, 27–39.

Rosenthal, R. and Jacobson, L. (1968) *Pygmalion in the Classroom*, New York: Holt, Rinehart and Winston.

Rosner, J. (1954) 'When white children are in the minority', *Journal of Educational Sociology*, **28**, 69–72.

Rotter, J. B., Rafferty, J. and Schachtitz, E. (1949) 'Validation of the Rotter incomplete sentences blank for college screening', *Journal of Consulting and Clinical Psychology*, **13**, 348–56.

Rotter, J. B. and Willerman, B. (1947) 'The incomplete sentences test as a method of studying personality', *Journal of Consulting and Clinical Psychology*, **11**, 43–8.

Rowe, M. B. (1974) 'Wait time and rewards as instructional variables', *Journal of Research in Science Teaching*, **2**, 81–94.

Rubin, J., Provenzano, F. and Luria, Z. (1974) 'The eye of the beholder', *American Journal of Orthopsychiatry*, **44**, 512–19.

Ruble, D. and Boggiano, A. (1980) 'Development analysis of the role of social comparison in self evaluation', *Developmental Psychology*, **16**, 105–15.

Rubovits, P. C. and Maehr, M. L. (1973) 'Pygmalion black and white', *Journal of Personality, Sociology and Psychology*, **25**, 210–18.

Ruedi, J. and West, C. K. (1973) 'Pupil self-concept in an "open" school and in a "traditional" school', *Psychology in the Schools*, **10**, 48–53.

Rutter, M. (1976) 'Adolescent turmoil: fact or fiction?', *Journal of Child Psychology and Psychiatry*, **17**, 35–56.

Ryans, D. G. (1961) 'Some relationships between pupil behaviour and certain teacher characteristics', *Journal of Educational Psychology*, **52**, 82–90.

Ryden, M. (1978) 'An adult version of the Coopersmith SEI', *Psychological Reports*, **43**, 1189–90.

Samuels, D. and Griffore, R. (1979) 'Ethnic and sex difference in self esteem in pre-school children', *Journal of Genetic Psychology*, **135**, 33–6.

Santrack, J. W. (1970) 'Parental absence sex typing and identification', *Developmental Psychology*, **2**, 264–72.

Schaeffer, J. (1976) 'Correlations between two measures of self-esteem and drug use', *Psychological Reports*, **39**, 915–19.

Schalon, C. (1968) 'The effect of self-esteem upon performance following failure stress', *Journal of Consulting and Clinical Psychology*, **32**, 497.

Schell, R. and Silber, J. W. (1968) 'Sex role discrimination among young children', *Perceptual Motor Skills*, **27**, 379–89.

Scherer, C. (1979) 'Effects of early field experience on student teachers' self-concepts and performance', *Journal of Experimental Education*, **48**, 208–13.

Schilder, P. (1935) *The Image and the Appearance of the Human Body*, London: Routledge and Kegan Paul.

Schmuck, R. A. (1968) 'Helping teachers improve classroom processes', *Journal of Applied Behavioral Science*, **4**, 401–35.

Schneider, D. J. (1969) 'Tactual self-presentation after success and failure', *Journal of Personality and Social Psychology*, **13**, 262–8.

Schneider, D. J. and Turkat, D. (1975) 'Self-presentation following success or failure', *Journal of Personality*, **43**, 127–35.

Schonfield, W. A. (1963) 'Body image in adolescents', *Pediatrics*, **31**, 845–54.

Schooler, C. (1972) 'Birth order effects', *Psychological Bulletin*, **78**, 161–75.

Schuer, A. L. (1971) 'The relationship between personality attributes and effectiveness in teachers of the emotionally disturbed', *Exceptional Children*, **21**, 723–31.

Schuh, A. J. (1966) 'Use of the semantic differential technique in a test of Super's vocational adjustment theory', *Journal of Applied Psychology*, **50**, 103–20.

Schuldermann, S. and Schuldermann, E. (1969) 'A note on the use of discrepancy scores in a self-concept inventory', *Journal of Psychology*, **72**, 33–4.

Schulman, L. S. (1968) 'Negro–white differences in self-concept and related measures in mentally handicapped adolescents', *Journal of Negro Education*, **37**, 227–40.

Schultz, E. W. (1972) 'The influence of teacher

behaviour on clinical gains in arithmetic tutoring', *Journal of Research in Mathematics Education*, **3**, 33–41.

Schurr, K., Towne, R. and Joiner, L. M. (1972) 'Trends in self-concept of ability over two years of special class placement', *Journal of Special Education*, **6**, 161–6.

Sears, R. R. (1970) 'Relation of early socialisation experiences to self-concepts and gender role in middle childhood', *Child Development*, **41**, 267–89.

Sears, R. R., Maccoby, E. and Levin, H. (1957) *Patterns of Child Rearing*, Evanston, Illinois: Row Peterson.

Sears, R. R., Rau, L. and Alpert, R. (1965) *Identification and Child Rearing*, Stanford: Stanford University Press.

Secord, R. F. (1968) 'Consistency theory and self-referent behavior', in Abelson, R. et al. (eds.) *Theories of Cognitive Consistency*, Chicago: Rand McNally.

Secord, R. F. and Backman, C. W. (1964) 'Interpersonal congruency', *Sociometry*, **27**, 115–27.

Secord, R. F. and Backman, C. W. (1974) *Social Psychology*, New York: McGraw-Hill.

Secord, R. F. and Jourard, S. M. (1953) 'The appraisal of body cathexis: body cathexis and the self', *Journal of Consulting and Clinical Psychology*, **17**, 343–7.

Shaplin, J. T. (1961) 'Practice in teaching', *Harvard Educational Review*, **31**, 35–59.

Sharp, G. L. and Muller, D. (1978) 'The effects of lowering self-concept on associative learning', *Journal of Psychology*, **100**, 233–42.

Sharpe, S. (1974) *Just Like a Girl*, Harmondsworth: Penguin.

Shavelson, R., Hubner, J. and Stanton, G. (1976) 'Self-concept—validation of construct interpretations', *Review of Educational Research*, **46**, 407–41.

Shaw, H. E. and Wright, J. M. (1968) *Scales for the Measurement of Attitudes*, New York: McGraw-Hill.

Shaw, M. C. and Alves, G. (1962) 'The self-concept of bright academic under-achievers', *Personnel and Guidance Journal*, **42**, 401–3.

Shaw, M. C., Edson, K. and Bell, H. (1960) 'The self-concept of bright under-achieving high school students as revealed by an adjective check list', *Personnel and Guidance Journal*, **39**, 193–6.

Sheerer, E. T. (1949) 'An analysis of the relationships between acceptance of and respect for self and acceptance of and respect for others', *Journal of Consulting and Clinical Psychology*, **13**, 176–80.

Sheldon, W. H. and Stevens, S. S. (1942) *The Varieties of Temperament*, New York: Harper and Row.

Sherif, M. (1935) 'A study of some social factors in perception', *Archives of Psychology*, whole of No. 187.

Sherif, M. and Cantril, C. W. (1947) *The Psychology of Ego Involvements*, New York: Wiley.

Sherif, M. and Sherif, C. W. (1956) *An Outline of Social Psychology*, New York: Harper and Row.

Sherriffs, A. C. and McKee, J. P. (1957) 'Differential valuation of males and females', *Journal of Personality*, **25**, 326–71.

Shore, M., Masimo, J. and Reids, D. F. (1965) 'A factor analytic study of psychotherapeutic change in delinquent boys', *Journal of Clinical Psychology*, **21**, 208–12.

Short, J. and Strodtbeck, F. (1965) *Group Processes and Gang Delinquency*, Chicago: University of Chicago Press.

Shrauger, J. (1972) 'Self-esteem and reactions to being observed by others', *Journal of Personality and Social Psychology*, **23**, 192–200.

Shrauger, J. S. (1975) 'Responses to evaluation as a function of initial self perception', *Psychological Bulletin*, **82**, 213–25.

Shrauger, J. S. and Lund, A. K. (1975) 'Self-evaluation and reactions to evaluations from others', *Journal of Personality*, **43**, no. 1, 94–108.

Shrauger, S. and Schoeneman, T. (1979) 'Symbolic interactionist view of self-concept', *Psychological Bulletin*, **86**, 549–73.

Silber, E. and Tippett, J. S. (1965) 'Self-esteem: clinical assessment and measurement validation', *Psychological Reports*, **16**, 1017–71.

Silverman, I. (1964) 'Differential effects of ego threat upon persuasability for high and low self-esteem subjects', *Journal of Abnormal and Social Psychology*, **69**, 567–72.

Simmons, R. G. (1978) 'Blacks and high self-esteem', *Social Psychology*, **41**, 54–7.

Simmons, R. and Rosenberg, F. (1975) 'Sex, sex roles and self-image', *Journal of Youth and Adolescence*, **4**, 229–58.

Simmons, R., Rosenberg, F. and Rosenberg, M. (1973) 'Disturbance in the self-image at adolescence', *American Sociology Review*, **38**, 553–68.

Simon, J. (1974) 'A comparison of marijuana users and non-users', *Journal of Counseling and Clinical Psychology*, **42**, 917–18.

Simon, W. E. and Simon, M. G. (1975) 'Self-esteem, intelligence, and standardised academic achievement', *Psychology in the Schools*, **12**, 97–9.

Skinner, B. F. (1953) *Science and Human Behaviour*, New York: Macmillan.

Skolnick, P. (1971) 'Reactions to personal evaluation', *Journal of Personality and Social Psychology*, **18**, 62–7.

Smith, F. and Adams, S. (1972) 'Changes in self-concept during student teaching experience',

Research Report, vol. 2, no. 5 Bureau of Educational Matrimals and Research, Louisiana State University.

Smith, G. M. (1969) 'Personality correlates of academic performance in three dissimilar populations', 77th annual convention American Psychology Association, Washington, D.C.

Smith, I. D. (1975) 'Sex differences in self-concepts of primary school children', *American Psychologist*, **10**, 59–63.

Smith, M. D. et al. (1977) 'School related factors influencing the self-concept of children with learning problems', *Peabody Journal of Education*, **54**, 185–95.

Smith, P. K. and Daglish, L. (1977) 'Sex differences in parent and infant behaviour in the home', *Child Development*, **48**, 1250–4.

Snow, R. (1969) 'Review of Pygmalion in the classroom', *Contemporary Psychology*, **14**, 197–9.

Snygg, D. and Combs, A. W. (1949) *Individual Behavior, A New Frame of Reference for Psychology*, New York: Harper and Row.

Snygg, D. and Combs, A. W. (1950) 'The phenomenological approach', *Journal of Abnormal and Social Psychology*, **45**, 523–8.

Soares, A. T. and Soares, L. M. (1966) 'Self-description and adjustment correlates of occupational choice', *Journal of Educational Research*, **60**, 27–31.

Soares, A. T. and Soares, L. M. (1969) 'Self-perceptions of culturally disadvantaged children', *American Education Research Journal*, **6**, 31–45.

Soares, A. T. and Soares, L. M. (1971) 'Comparative differences in the self-perceptions of disadvantaged students', *Journal of School Psychology*, **9**, 424–9.

Soares, A. T. and Soares, L. M. (1974) 'Self-perceptions as affective dimensions of student teaching', ERIC ED 088 885.

Spaulding, R. (1963) 'Achievement, creativity, and self-concept correlates of teacher–pupil transactions in elementary schools', US Office of Education Cooperative Research Project 1352.

Sperry, R. W. (1956) 'The eye and the brain', *Scientific American*, **19**, 286–322.

Spitzer, S. (1969) 'Test equivalence of instructured self-evaluation instruments', *Sociology Quarterly*, **10**, 204–15.

Spitzer, S., Stratton, J., Fitzgerald, J. and Mach, B. (1966) 'The self-concept: test equivalence and perceived validity', *Sociology Quarterly*, **7**, 265–80.

Staffieri, J. (1957) 'A study of social stereotypes of body image in children', *Journal of Personality and Social Psychology*, **7**, 101–4.

Staines, J. W. (1954) 'A psychological and sociological investigation of the self as a significant factor in education', unpublished PhD thesis, University of London.

Staines, J. W. (1958) 'The self picture as a factor in the classroom', *British Journal of Educational Psychology*, **28**, 2, 97–11.

Stanton, H. E. (1977) 'Self-concept and the SEG', *Australian Journal of Adult Education*, **17**, 2–7.

Stanton, H. E. (1979a) 'The evaluation of a group SE experience', *Australian Journal of Adult Education*, **19**, 57–61.

Stanton, H. E. (1979b) *The Plus Factor: a Guide to a Positive Life*, Sydney: Collins/Fontana.

Stenner, A. J. and Katzenmeyer, W. (1976) 'Self-concept, ability and achievement in a sample of 6th grade students', *Journal of Educational Research*, **69**, 270–3.

Stephan, W. G. and Rosenfield, D. (1978) 'Effects of desegregation on race relations and self esteem', *Journal of Educational Psychology*, **70**, 670–9.

Stephan, W. G. and Rosenfield, D. (1979) 'Black self-rejection', *Journal of Educational Psychology*, **71**, 708–16.

Stephens, N. and Day, H. D. (1979) 'Sex role identity, parental identity and self concept of adolescent daughters from mother absent, father absent and intact families', *Journal of Psychology*, **103**, 193–202.

Stern, G. C. (1942) 'Measuring non-cognitive variables in research on teaching', in Gage, C. L. (ed.) *Handbook of Research on Teaching*, Chicago, Illinois: Rand McNally.

Stevens, D. O. (1971) 'Reading difficulty and classroom acceptance', *The Reading Teacher*, **25**, 197–9.

Stevenson, W. (1953) *The Study of Behavior: A Technique and its Methodology*, Chicago: University Press.

Stewart, R. (1971) 'Multiple regression analysis', unpublished paper, Washington, D.C.: George Peabody College.

St. John, N. (1970) 'Desegregation and minority group performance', *Review of Educational Research*, **40**, 111–13.

St. John, N. (1971) 'The elementary classroom as a frog pond: self-concept, sense of control and social context', *Social Forces*, **49**, 581–95.

St. John, N. (1975) *School Desegregation Outcomes for Children*, New York: Wiley.

Stock, D. (1949) 'An investigation into the interrelations between the self-concept and feelings directed toward other persons and groups', *Journal of Consulting and Clinical Psychology*, **13**, 176–80.

Stock, D. (1964) *A Survey of Research on T Groups*, New York: Wiley.

Stoffer, D. L. (1970) 'Investigation of positive behavioural changes as a function of genuine warmth and empathic understanding', *Journal of Educational Research*, **63**, 225–8.

Stoller, F. H. (1968) 'Focused feedback with videotape', in Gazda, G. (ed.) *Innovations to Group Psychotherapy*, Springfield: Thomas.

Stonequist, E. V. (1961) *Marginal Man*, New York: Russell Sage.

Stoner, S. and Kaiser, L. (1978) 'Sex differences in self-concepts of adolescents', *Psychological Reports*, August 305–6.

Storey, A. G. (1967) 'Acceleration, deceleration and self-concepts', *Alberta Journal of Educational Research*, **13**, 135–43.

Storms, M. and McCaul, K. (1976) 'Attribution processes and emotional exacerbation of dysfunctional behavior', in Harvey, J. (ed.) *New Directions in Attribution Research*, New York: Erlbaum Press.

Stotland, E. and Dunn, R. (1962) 'Identification, opposition, authority, self-esteem and birth order', *Psychology Monographs*, **76**, whole of number 609.

Stotland, E., Thorley, S., Thomas, E., Cohen, A. R. and Zander, A. (1957) 'The effects of group expectation and self-esteem upon self-evaluation', *Journal of Abnormal and Social Psychology*, **54**, 55–63.

Stott, L. H. (1939) 'Some family life patterns and their relation to personality development in children', *Journal of Experimental Education*, **8**, 148–60.

Strang, R. (1957) *The Adolescent Views Himself*, New York: McGraw-Hill.

Sullivan, H. S. (1953) *Interpersonal Theory of Psychiatry*, New York: Norton.

Super, D. E. (1953) 'A theory of vocational development', *American Psychologist*, **8**, 185–90.

Super, D. E. (1957) *Vocational Development: A Framework for Research*, New York: Teachers College Press.

Super, D. E. and Bachrach, P. (1954) *Scientific Careers and Vocational Development Theory*, New York: Columbia University Press.

Super, D. E., Stariskevsky, R., Matlin, N. and Jordaan, J. P. (1963) *Career Development: Self-Concept Theory*, New York: College Entrances Examinations Board.

Tageson, C. F. (1960) *Relationship of Self Perception of Realism of Vocational Preference*, Washington, D.C.: Catholic University of America Press.

Tagiuri, R., Bruner, J. S. and Blake, R. R. (1958) 'On the relation between feelings and perception of feelings among members of small groups', in Maccoby, E. E. (ed.) *Readings in Social Psychology*, New York: Holt, Rinehart and Winston.

Talley, P. (1967) 'The relation of group counseling to changes in the self-concept of Negro eighth grade students', unpublished PhD thesis, University of Miami.

Tattershall, W. R. (1979) 'Patterns of change in teaching anxiety, professional self-concept and self-concept during an extended practicum', unpublished MA thesis, Vancouver: Simon Fraser University.

Tavris, C. and Offir, C. (1977) *The Longest War*, New York: Harcourt Brace.

Taylor, C. and Combs, A. W. (1952) 'Self acceptance and adjustment', *Journal of Consulting and Clinical Psychology*, **16**, 89–91.

Taylor, D. M. (1955) 'Changes on the self-concept without psychotherapy', *Journal of Consulting and Clinical Psychology*, **19**, 205–9.

Taylor, J. and Reitz, W. (1968) 'The three faces of self-esteem', *Research Bulletin*, 80, Department of Psychology, University of Western Ontario.

Taylor, M. and Walsh, E. (1979) 'Explanations of black self-esteem', *Social Psychology Quarterly*, **42**, 242–53.

Terborg, J., Richardson, P. and Pritchard, R. (1980) 'Person–situation effects in the prediction of performance: an investigation of ability, self-esteem and reward', *Journal of Applied Psychology*, **65**, 574–83.

Thomas, J. B. (1974) 'The self-pictures of children in primary schools: some qualitative data', *Froebel Journal*, **30**, 31–6.

Thomas, J. B. (1974) 'School organisation and self-concept', *Durham Research Review*, **33**, 929–37.

Thompson, B. L. (1974) 'Self-concepts among secondary school pupils', *Educational Research*, **17**, 41–7.

Thompson, B. (1975) 'Nursery teachers perceptions of their pupils', in Whitehead, J. M. (ed.) *Personality and Learning*, vol. 1, London: Hodder and Stoughton.

Thompson, S. K. (1975) 'Gender labels and early sex role development', *Child Development*, **46**, 339–47.

Thorndike, R. L. (1968) 'Review of Pygmalion in the classroom', *American Educational Research Journal*, **5**, 708–11.

Toder, N. L. and Marcia, J. E. (1973) 'Ego identity status and response to conformity pressure in college women', *Journal of Personality and Social Psychology*, **26**, 287–94.

Tolor, A., Kelly, B. and Stebbins, C. (1976) 'Assertiveness, sex-role stereotyping and self-concept', *Journal of Psychology*, **93**, 157–68.

Tome, H. R. (1972) *Le Moi et l'autre dans la conscience de l'adolescence*, Paris: Delachaux and Niestle.

Torrance, E. P. (1962) *Guiding Creative Talent*, New York: Prentice Hall.

Torshen, K. (1969) 'The relation of classroom evaluation of students' self-concept and mental health', unpublished PhD thesis, University of Chicago.

Travers, R. M. W. (1973) *The Handbook of Research on Teaching*, Chicago: Rand

McNally.

Trent, R. D. (1957) 'The relationship between expressed self-acceptance and expressed attitudes to Negroes and whites among Negro children', *Journal of Genetic Psychology*, **91**, 25–31.

Trowbridge, N. (1970) 'Effects of socio-economic class on self-concepts of children', *Psychology in the Schools*, **7**, 304–6.

Trowbridge, N. (1972a) 'Self-concept and socio-economic status in elementary school children', *American Educational Research Journal*, **9**, 525–37.

Trowbridge, N. (1972b) 'Socio-economic status and self-concept of children', *Journal of Teacher Education*, **23**, 63–5.

Trowbridge, N. (1973) 'Teacher self-concept and teaching style', in Chanan, G. (ed.) *Towards a Science of Teaching*, Slough: NFER.

Tryon, C. M. (1939) 'Evaluation of adolescent personality by adolescents', *Monographs of Social Research and Child Development*, **4**, No. 4.

Tuinen, M. and Ramanaiah, N. (1979) 'A multimethod analysis of selected self-esteem measures', *Journal of Research in Personality*, **13**, 16–24.

Twenter, C. J. (1977) 'Self-concept—the missing link in perceptual motor development', *Psychology of Education*, **34**, 8–11.

Tyler, L. E. (1965) *Psychology of Human Differences*, New York: Appleton-Century-Crofts.

Vacchiano, R. and Strauss, P. (1968) 'The construct validity of the Tennessee self-concept scale', *Journal of Clinical Psychology*, **24**, 323–6.

Vener, A. M. and Snyder, C. A. (1966) 'The preschool child's awareness of adult sex roles', *Sociometry*, **29**, 159–68.

Veness, T. (1962) *School Leavers: Their Aspiration and Expectations*, London: Methuen.

Videbeck, R. (1960) 'Self conceptions and the reaction of others', *Sociometry*, **23**, 351–62.

Waetjen, W. B. (1963) 'Self-concept as a learner scale', in Argyle, M. and Lee, V. (eds.) *Social Relationships*, Bletchley: Open University Press.

Walberg, H. J. (1966) 'Changes in self-concept during teacher training', *Psychology in the Schools*, **4**, 14–21.

Walberg, H. J. (1967) 'The development of teacher personality', *School Review*, **75**, 187–96.

Walberg, H. J. (1968) 'Personality role conflict and self-conception in urban practice teachers', *School Review*, **76**, 41–9.

Walker, R. N. (1962) 'Body build and behaviour in young children', *Monograph of Social Research in Child Development*, **27**, No. 3.

Walsh, A. M. (1956) *Self-Concepts of Bright Boys with Learning Difficulties*, New York: Teachers College, Columbia University.

Walter, A. G. and Miles, R. E. (1974) 'Changing self-acceptance', *Small Group Behavior*, **5**, 356–64.

Ward, W. (1973) 'Patterns of culturally defined sex role performances and parental imitation', *Journal of Genetic Psychology*, **122**, 337–43.

Warr, P. and Knapper, C. (1968) *Perception of People and Events*, London: Wiley.

Waterman, A. S., Geary, P. S. and Waterman, C. K. (1974) 'Longitudinal study in changes in ego identity status from freshman to senior year at college', *Developmental Psychology*, **10**, 387–92.

Waterman, A. S. and Waterman, C. (1971) 'A longitudinal study of changes in ego identity status in freshman year at college', *Developmental Psychology*, **5**, 167–73.

Watkins, D. (1975) 'Self-esteem as a moderator in vocational choice', *Australian Psychology*, **10**, 75–80.

Watkins, D. (1976) 'The antecedents of self-esteem in Australian university students', *Australian Psychology*, **2**, 169–72.

Wattenberg, W. W. and Clifford, C. (1964) 'Relation of self-concept to beginning achievement in reading', *Child Development*, **35**, 461–7.

Webster, S. and Kroger, M. (1966) 'A comparative study of perceptions and feelings of Negro adolescents in integrated urban high schools', *Journal of Negro Education*, **35**, 55.

Weinberg, J. R. (1960) 'A further investigation of body cathexis and the self', *Journal of Consulting and Clinical Psychology*, **24**, 277.

Weiner, B. (1970) *Perceiving the Causes of Success and Failure*, Morristown, New Jersey: General Learning Press.

Weiner, N. (1974) *Achievement Motivation and Attribution Theory*, Morristown, New Jersey: General Learning Press.

Weiner, B. et al. (1971) *Perceiving the Causes of Success and Failure*, Morristown, New Jersey: General Learning Press.

Weinraub, M. and Frankel, J. (1978) 'Sex differences in parent–infant interaction during free-play, departure and separation', *Child Development*, **49**, 620–34.

Weinreich, P. (1979) 'Ethnicity and adolescent identity crises', in Khan, S. (ed.) *Minority Families in Britain*, London: Macmillan.

Weinreich, P. (1979) 'The locus of identification conflict in immigrant and indigenous adolescents', in Verma, G. and Bagley, C. (eds.) *Race, Education and Identity*, London: Macmillan.

Weitzman, L. J., Eifler, D., Hokada, E. and Ross, C. (1972) 'Sex role socialisation in picture books for pre-school children', *American Journal of Sociology*, **77**, 1125–50.

Wendland, M. (1968) 'Self-concept in southern Negro and white adolescents related to rural and urban residence', unpublished PhD thesis, University of North Carolina.

Werner, H. (1961) *Comparative Psychology of Mental Development*, New York: Science Editions.

Wertham, F. (1952) 'Psychological effects of school segregation', *American Journal of Psychotherapy*, **6**, 94–103.

White, A. J. (1973) 'Interrelationships between measures of physical fitness and measures of self-concept', unpublished PhD thesis, Mississippi State University.

Wickland, R. A. and Duval, S. (1971) 'Opinion change and performance facilitation as a result of objective self-awareness', *Journal of Experimental Social Psychology*, **7**, 319–42.

Williams, D. (1968) 'Self-concept and verbal mental ability in Negro pre-school children', unpublished PhD thesis, St. John's University, Newfoundland.

Williams, F. (1976) 'Rediscovering the 4th grade slump in a study of children's self-concept', *Journal of Creative Behavior*, **10**, 15–28.

Williams, R. and Byars, H. (1968) 'Negro self-esteem in a transitional society', *Personnel and Guidance Journal*, **47**, 120–5.

Williams, R. L. and Cole, S. (1968) 'Self-concept and school adjustment', *Personnel and Guidance Journal*, **46**, 478–81.

Wilson, D. T. (1965) 'Ability evaluation, post decision dissonance and co-worker attractiveness', *Journal of Personality and Social Psychology*, **1**, 486–9.

Wilson, G. (1973) 'Development and evaluation of The *C* scale', in Wilson, G. (ed.) *The Psychology of Conservatism,* London: Academic Press.

Wilson, J. and Wilson, S. (1976) 'Sources of self-esteem', *Psychological Reports*, **38**, 355–8.

Winchell, R., Fenner, D. and Shaver, P. (1974) 'Impact of co-education on fear of success', *Journal of Educational Psychology*, **66**, 726–30.

Wiseman, S. (1973) 'The educational obstacle race: factors that hinder pupil progress', *Educational Research*, **15**, 87–93.

Withycombe, J. S. (1970) 'An analysis by sex and grade level of self-concept and social status of Paiute Indian and white elementary school children', unpublished PhD thesis, University of Connecticut.

Wittrock, M. C. and Husek, T. R. (1962) 'Effect of anxiety upon retention of verbal learning', *Psychological Reports*, **10**, 78.

Witty, P. (1947) 'An analysis of the personality traits of the effective teacher', *Journal of Educational Research*, **40**, 662–71.

Wolf, J. G. (1971) 'Teacher quality of interpersonal relationships and aspects of pupil functioning', unpublished PhD thesis, State University, Buffalo.

Wolfenstein, M. (1968) 'Children's humour, sex names and double meaning', in Talbot, T. (ed.) *The World of the Child*, New York: Anchor Books.

Wolfgang, J. and Wolfgang, A. (1968) 'Personal space', paper presented at annual conference of the American Psychological Association, San Francisco.

Woolner, R. B. (1966) *Pre-School Self-Concept Picture Test*, Memphis: RKA.

Wooster, A. and Harris, G. (1973) 'Concepts of self in highly mobile service boys', *Educational Research*, **14**, 195–9.

Worchel, P. (1957) 'Screening of flying personnel: development of a self-concept inventory for predicting maladjustment', *School of Aviation Medicine*, USAF Report, No. 56–61.

Wright, B. and Tuska, S. A. (1966) 'Student and first year teachers' attitudes towards self and others', Education Report, University of Chicago Press.

Wright, R. J. (1975) 'The affective and cognitive consequences of an open education elementary school', *American Educational Research Journal*, **12**, 449–68.

Wylie, R. (1961) *The Self Concept*, Lincoln: University of Nebraska Press.

Wylie, R. (1963) 'Children's estimates of their schoolwork ability as a function of sex, race and economic level', *Journal of Personality*, **31**, 203–24.

Wylie, R. (1968) 'The present status of the self theory', in Borgatta and Lambert (eds.) *Handbook on Personality*, Chicago: Rand McNally.

Wylie, R. (1974) *The Self Concept*, vol. 1, *A Review of Methodological Considerations and Measuring Instruments* (rev. edn), Lincoln: University of Nebraska Press.

Wylie, R. (1979) *The Self Concept*, vol. 2, Lincoln: University of Nebraska Press.

Wylie, R. and Hutchins, B. (1967) 'Schoolwork, ability estimates and aspirations as a function of socio-economic level, race and sex', *Psychological Reports*, **21**, 781–808.

Yeatts, P. P. (1967) 'An analysis of developmental changes in the self report of Negro and white children', unpublished PhD thesis, University of Florida.

Young, L. and Bagley, C. (1979) 'Identity, self-esteem and evaluation of colour and ethnicity in young children in Jamaica and London', *New Community*, **7**, 154–69.

Zigler, E. and Muenchow, S. (1979) 'Mainstreaming: the proof is in the implementation', *American Psychologist*, **34**, 993–6.

Ziller, R. C. (1973) *The Social Self*, New York: Pergamon Press.

Ziller, R. C., Hagey, J., Smith, M. D. and Long, B. H. (1969) 'Self-esteem: a self–social construct', *Journal of Consulting and Clinical Psychology*, **33**, 84–95.

Ziller, R. C. and Long, B. H. (1964b) 'Self–social constructs and geographic mobility', unpublished paper, University of Delaware.

Ziller, R. C., Long, B. H., Remama, K. and Reddy, V. (1968) 'Self–other orientators of Indian and American adolescents', *Journal of Personality*, **36**, 315–30.

Ziller, R. C., Megas, J. and DeCenio, D. (1964) 'Self–social constructs of normals and acute neuropsychiatric patients', *Journal of Consultative Psychology*, **20**, 50–63.

Zimmer, H. (1954) 'Self-acceptance and its relation to conflict', *Journal of Consulting and Clinical Psychology*, **18**, 447–9.

Zimmerman, I. L. and Allegrand, G. N. (1965) 'Personality characteristics and attitudes toward achievement of good and poor readers', *Journal of Educational Research*, **59**, 28–30.

Zirkel, P. A. (1972) 'Enhancing the self-concept of disadvantaged students', *Californian Journal of Educational Research*, **23**, 125–37.

Zirkel, P. A. and Greene, J. F. (1971) 'The measurement of the self-concept of disadvantaged students', New York: unpublished paper presented at National Council on Measurement in Education.

Zirkel, P. and Moses, E. (1971) 'Self-concept and ethnic group membership among public school students', *American Educational Research Journal*, **8**, 253–65.

Zullo, J. R. (1972) '*T*-group laboratory learning and adolescent ego-development', *Dissertation Abstracts*, **33B**, 2799.

Zuriel, D. and Shakad, A. (1970) 'Self-concept of adolescent female delinquents', unpublished paper, Bar-Ilan, University of Israel.

Name Index

Name Index

Subject Index